C0-CCE-678

UNDERSTANDING PROFITS

THE LIBRARY OF AMERICAN CAPITALISM

CLAUDE ROBINSON

Editor

CHAMBERLAIN, JOHN—*The Roots of Capitalism*

ROBINSON, CLAUDE—*Understanding Profits*

Additional titles will be listed and announced as published.

CLAUDE ROBINSON

UNDERSTANDING PROFITS

D. VAN NOSTRAND COMPANY, INC.
PRINCETON, NEW JERSEY
TORONTO LONDON
NEW YORK

D. VAN NOSTRAND COMPANY, INC.
120 Alexander St., Princeton, New Jersey (*Principal office*)
24 West 40 Street, New York 18, New York

D. VAN NOSTRAND COMPANY, LTD.
358, Kensington High Street, London, W.14, England

D. VAN NOSTRAND COMPANY (Canada), LTD.
25 Hollinger Road, Toronto 16, Canada

Published simultaneously in Canada by
D. VAN NOSTRAND COMPANY (Canada), LTD.

PRINTED IN THE UNITED STATES OF AMERICA

PREFACE

For twenty years as a student of public opinion I have been intrigued by the widespread misunderstanding of profits. While people generally agree to the necessity and desirability of profits, they have fantastic ideas about the size of profits and little knowledge of the relation of profits to human welfare.

In the public debates on economic and social policy, profit is frequently cast in the role of the villain. Profit making is pictured as an exercise in greed and avarice. The word "profit" becomes synonymous with "exploitation," and profit is made to appear as a wicked institution that grinds down the poor and the sick. The worker, it is said, suffers grave economic injustice because the profit maker expropriates the fruits of his labor and denies him the good things of life.

Curiously enough, most of the talk about profits is critical. Profits are too big, monopolistic, unfair, or antisocial. To be sure, some material in defense of profits, mostly from industry, is available, but it seldom makes the headlines. Most economic textbooks devote a few pages to the concept of profit, but so far as I have been able to discover, no study is available that deals systematically with the subject in terms of the current debate. This is a matter of some wonderment, for profit is one of the key institutions of a capitalistic order, and has become a social action word with explosive characteristics.

Three years ago I decided to dig into the subject of profits and try to arrive at a point of view that maintained a decent respect for the facts, and judged the institution of profit by the criterion of service to the community. This book gives the results of my inquiry.

In organizing the material I have elected to follow the lines of the ideological debate on profits. I have done this for two reasons: first, the material is more interesting and timely when presented this way. Secondly, I believe that democracy has a better chance to survive in a hostile world if more people undertake to school themselves in the ideologies on which our free institutions are founded.

A good example of an ideology is the conviction held by the Founding Fathers that a system of checks and balances is necessary for the preservation of individual liberty. So far, the American people have held fast to this belief, but there are strong ideological voices today advancing the idea that an increasingly powerful state is consistent both with individual liberty and welfare.

I believe that the secular goals of the American people are the preservation and practice of individual freedom and control over our standard of living. I am completely convinced that the framers of the American Constitution were inspired in their theory that liberty requires a system of checks and balances; and I feel sure that, unless we maintain some degree of atomization of power, liberty will disappear. I believe that the capitalistic organization of our economy is basic to the American dream, not only for its release of prodigious productive energies, but also because it provides strong checks and balances that help guarantee liberty.

The key institutions of a capitalistic economy, as I see them, are private property, free markets, competition, and profit incentives. One role of government is to provide a political environment in which these institutions can function for the welfare of the community. The free market, it appears to me, is a more democratic economic system in that all buyers and sellers who have a coin can vote their individual preferences without coercion. Government should facilitate the plebiscite of the consumers. As voters we should be reluctant to overturn the market decisions that we make democratically as consumers.

I have no Olympian judgment to offer on the rightness or wrongness of specific reforms over the past thirty years that have increasingly invoked the power of the state. Like many other sober minded people, however, I am concerned about the direction of the trend. We seem to have lost much of our faith in the power of the voluntary (and the local) way of solving social problems. More and more we are looking to the Federal Government, with its coercive sanctions, to educate us, renew our cities, build our houses, guarantee us a job, provide us with medical and old age security and otherwise attend to our wants.

I suspect that we may be disappointed in a Federal Utopia, both on material grounds and on matters of the spirit. Professor Hayek has called this trail *The Road to Serfdom*. I do not believe we are anywhere near the borders of serfdom; but if we continue to concentrate power in the hands of the state, individual liberties will be progressively curtailed and must eventually disappear.

One clear index of this trend is the percentage of net national product taken by the local, state, and federal taxing authorities. In 1929 the tax take was 10.7 per cent; by 1959 it had risen to 28.4 per cent, and the curve shows no signs of leveling off. In return for these tax monies the community has received national defense, roads, schools, welfare payments, research, and other governmental services. There are some who believe that an affluent society should invest an even greater proportion of its income in the public sector, and it is quite possible that the community will elect to do this. But in making up our minds on this question we ought to look at the other side of the coin too, for it is a matter of elementary logic that as public spending claims an increasing proportion of the net national product, the area of free choice on how each person shall spend his income recedes. The issue, therefore, is not limited to whether we provide more social facilities, but increasingly involves the profound question of personal freedom.

In Western history the capitalists have been the great revolutionaries and now, more than ever, they need to take the initiative, invent new capitalistic methods for solving economic problems in a changing world, and explain to the public why this is a better way than funneling an ever increasing proportion of our income through the coercive tax structure. We need to organize the private sector to take on more of the load, not continually enlarge the public sector, if we wish to safeguard our cherished individual freedoms.

This book, I hope, will fortify faith in the voluntary way by giving readers a better understanding of the capitalistic institution of profit and loss and by stimulating more sense of pride in the service this institution renders to the community.

In recent years the capitalistic system has been under such heavy fire that many people have favored abandoning the term "capitalism." They speak of the system as "free," "individual," or "competitive enterprise" or of "the market system." George Romney, President of American Motors, wants to call the system "consumerism" on the ground that it is the consumer who is its chief beneficiary. I am conscious of the negative semantics that cling to the word "capitalism" and am also aware of its serious limitations in describing a privately owned economy. Capital is a necessary factor in a capitalistic order, but so are private ownership of property, incentives, market competition, and individual freedom. If we could coin an entirely new term we would certainly want it to express the idea of freedom as well as the concept of economic production.

Karl Marx gave the capitalistic system its name, and since his day, scholars have referred to it as "capitalism." The term at least has the advantage of usage; and, in this age when the monolithic state is shouting its superiority from every house top, it may even have shock value.

Criticism of profits comes from many sources—economists, political leaders, labor leaders, clergymen, writers, and others—but in recent years the most outspoken critics have been the leaders of labor unions. I have reported labor views in some detail and have undertaken to appraise the merit of union arguments in the light of the data at hand. As the reader will see, I am able to make a great deal of political sense out of the union's arguments, but am at a loss to reconcile many of their views on profits with the economic facts. This will surely subject me to the charge of being anti-union. It is my view that unions came about because workers wanted and needed organization power to counterbalance that of management, and that responsible unionism is here to stay. But I also feel strongly that employee living standards should rise as rapidly as possible; and the evidence is crystal clear that this desired end will come about only through increased productivity, not by any campaign for the redistribution of profits.

I have tried to bring the profits data presented in this book as nearly up-to-date as possible, but the reader should know that some series such as those of the U.S. Treasury and the Department of Commerce involve a time lag of one to two years.

Profits is a complex subject and I have been shameless in calling on my friends for factual data and interpretive views. I, of course, take full responsibility for the use of the material, but wish to express my thanks here for assistance, to the following: Herbert Abelson, Phelps Adams, Armen Alchian, Arthur S. Armstrong, Jean Affleck Asch, Theresa Auletta, Robert Best, Edgar S. Bowerfind, Harold Brayman, Willard W. Brown, Yale Brozen, Mary Burman, G. Rowland Collins, John T. Connor, J. W. Cook, Conrad Cooper, Arthur O. Dahlberg, Virgil Day, Horace J. DePodwin, Michael DeSanna, C. R. Deyo, Edward J. Doherty, Robert G. Dunlop, The Right Reverend Richard S. Emrich, Lawrence Fertig, Wendell Forbes, Milton Friedman, George Freyermuth, Joseph Goeke, P. F. Goodrich, Bert C. Goss, Harry W. Greene, George Hagedorn, Arthur P. Hall, Cameron P. Hall, F. A. Harper, Friedrich A. Hayek, O. L. Hayes, Henry Hazlitt, H. B. Higgins, David G. Hill, John Hill, T. V. Houser, Max D. Howell, B. E. Hutchinson, James W. Irwin, General Robert W. Johnson, Mark Jones, R. W. Kilbon, George Koether, John C. Long, Hugh Macaulay, Alexander Magoun, Edward Maher, Stanley V. Malcuit, Russell W. Morrison, James L. Myers, Edmund A. Opitz, Norma Pace, Lovett C. Peters, William H. Peterson, L. E. Pettit, J. Howard Pew, Thomas W. Phelps, Raymond Pitcairn, Paul Poirot, Frank O. Prior, John G. Pew, Leonard E. Read, Thomas Robertson, B. A. Rogge, A. W. Rucker, Alvin Schwartz, G. A. Sass, Emerson P. Schmidt, Gerald J. Skibbins, Austin Smith,

Bradford B. Smith, J. Stanford Smith, Alfred Sloan Jr., Leonard Spacek, John P. Syme, Leo Teplow, W. H. Turner, John W. Vance, Victor von Szeliski, Edwin Vennard, W. Allen Wallis, Franklyn Waltman, Arthur R. Wengel, Charles M. White, Irving W. Wilson, K. P. Wood, D. Richard Young.

I should particularly like to express my obligation to Gordon Tullock for research assistance; to John Chamberlain for editorial suggestions; to Richard Cornuelle and Ivan Bierly for help on many phases of the project; to A. D. H. Kaplan of the Brookings Institution for taking time out of his busy and fruitful life to talk with me about the problems of a profit and loss economy; to Murray Rothbard for his economic insight and his extraordinary competence in guiding me through the literature; to my colleague, LeBaron Foster for his invaluable commentary on the social process and his incisive chapter by chapter criticism; and to Rosamond Affleck who has been patient beyond the call of duty in typing and retyping the manuscript.

Also I should like to extend my thanks to the Princeton University Library for use of their very fine facilities; and to J. Frank Gaston and the National Industrial Conference Board for winnowing U.S. Treasury data and supplying the long term profit trends appearing in Appendix C-1.

Finally, I wish to record here my very great appreciation to The Princeton Panel and its supporters for underwriting the research assistance required for this project.

CLAUDE ROBINSON

Princeton, N. J.
August, 1961

CONTENTS

CHARTS

TABLES

Tables

ILLUSTRATIONS

CHAPTER ONE

THE GREAT PROFITS DEBATE

On August 16, 1957, Walter Reuther wrote a letter to the presidents of Chrysler, Ford, and General Motors. The United Automobile Workers, he said, was deeply concerned about the growing problem of inflation. Spiraling prices were causing widespread hardship and suffering. Unless this uptrend were checked, the stability of the American economy would be undermined, and with it, the ability of the free world to fight Communist tyranny.

Mr. Reuther said he wished to offer "a positive, practical, and socially responsible program" for averting this catastrophe.

"Specifically," wrote the UAW president, "we propose:

1. That your corporation and leading auto producers reduce prices on 1958 models to levels averaging at least $100 below the prices for comparable 1957 models.

2. That if you do put such price reductions into effect, we for our part will give full consideration to the effect of such reduction on your corporation's financial position in the drafting of our 1958 demands and in our negotiations."

Present profit margins, said Mr. Reuther, provide ample room for substantial price reductions, and put the automobile industry in a singularly advantageous position to assume leadership in reversing the inflationary trend. Even with a one hundred dollar reduction, the union leader said, Chrysler would be making seventeen and three-tenths per cent on its capital; Ford twelve and eight-tenths per cent; and General Motors seventeen per cent. And these projections, it was believed, would probably turn out to be low, for they did not allow for the increased sales that would result from reduced car prices.

Should there be disagreement between the union and the company on the effect of union demands on car prices, the UAW, Mr. Reuther indicated, would be willing to submit the question to review by a three man panel composed of union and company appointees and an impartial chairman. The panel would conduct public hearings, receive testimony, and render an opinion to guide subsequent negotiations.

Needless to say, the automobile company presidents rejected Mr. Reuther's proposal.

In his reply, Mr. Colbert of the Chrysler Corporation said that he too was concerned about rising prices and suggested that one way to reduce inflationary pressures was for the union to stop wildcat strikes, featherbedding, and restrictive work practices. "Would it not be just as logical," wrote Mr. Colbert, "for the automobile industry to ask members of the UAW to take an immediate and sizable wage cut, which the companies would then take into consideration in pricing their 1958 automobiles?"

Mr. Ford pointed out that over a ten-year period wages had risen seventy per cent in his company, car prices thirty per cent, and profits not at all. "Prices and profits," said Mr. Ford, "are not subject to negotiation with your union or any other union. To turn pricing responsibility over to Government, to a union, or to an outside panel of any sort, would be to strike at the very foundation of our free enterprise system."

Mr. Curtice of General Motors, recalling previous exchanges with Mr. Reuther, concluded that "Your proposal is another publicity maneuver, designed to divert attention from the inflationary implications of your announced 1958 bargaining objectives." The way to deal with the problem of inflation, said Mr. Curtice, is to adhere to sound economic policy. One mark of a sound economic policy is to take into account the interests of all groups—cutomers, employees, and investors—not employees alone. Another is to recognize that continuing improvement in the standard of living of employees basically depends on technological progress, better tools, methods, processes, equipment, and a cooperative attitude on the part of all.[1]

Mr. Reuther made his rejoinder in a public statement. He called the company replies "an irresponsible and arbitrary rejection that bespoke anger and emotion rather than calm rational consideration." He said that the automobile companies and others were charging extortionate prices and that the UAW was determined to combat this inflationary practice, not only in the interests of UAW members but in the interest of all American consumers.

Five months later, Mr. Reuther was in the headlines again with another proposal. In the 1958 bargaining talks with the automobile companies, he declared the UAW would not only demand higher wages and increased benefits but also profit sharing.

A fair plan, said Mr. Reuther, would allow the company to make ten per cent (before taxes) on its capital and long-term debt. Any amount in excess of ten per cent would be distributed one-half to company stockholders and executives, one-quarter to wage and salary workers, and one-quarter to car purchasers through a year-end rebate. The workers' share of the profits would be paid out to individuals in the form of a bonus or (more probably) to a union fund for pensions, unemployment benefits, medical care, and other purposes to be administered by the union. The union's profit sharing plan, declared Mr. Reuther, is "economically sound, morally right, and socially responsible."

This time the replies from the auto companies were short and pointed. Mr. Colbert said, "Mr. Reuther appears again to insist that part of management's job be turned over to him, so that he can increase still further the already dangerous degree of monopoly power he possesses."

Mr. Curtice said the UAW plan was "foreign to the concepts of the American free enterprise system."

Mr. Breech, Chairman of the Ford Motor Company, characterized the proposal, "a kill-the-profits plan." The union's proposal, said the Ford executive, would invite increasing demand for union veto power over day-to-day management decisions. Budgets for advertising, research and engineering, new model tooling, capital expansion plans, decisions about whether to make or buy parts—all would be viewed by the union as affecting profits. The union would have no responsibility for increasing earnings, yet it would question all actions of management as tending to limit the hourly employees' share of profits. "We have enough trouble as it is in dealing with the union in our manufacturing operations alone," concluded Mr. Breech.[2]

As the Spring of 1958 wore on, the automobile industry fell into a deep slump. New car sales turned down sharply, dealer inventories rose to dangerous heights, thousands of automobile workers were laid off, and those who remained went on a short work week. In no mood to strike, UAW members took the unorthodox course of working four months without a contract. In September, the dispute was settled for wage and benefit gains considerably short of the union's original demands and widely hailed by commentators as "moderate" and "non-inflationary."

The 1958 automobile bargaining will, no doubt, be consigned to the history books as "just another labor dispute," but to the discerning observer, it is much more than that; it is, in fact, a debate on the fundamental soundness of the primary institutions of capitalism.

In a world where national economies have become increasingly dominated by the state, America still clings to its capitalist mentality, believing basically that the best way to organize the nation's economy is through the institutions of private property, free markets, competition, and profit incentives, working in a legal framework supplied by representative government.

But the institutions of capitalism are no longer taken for granted. In the past thirty years, capitalism as an economic philosophy has lost ground to statism, and the reexamination is still going on. The assumptions of capitalism are under challenge, new patterns for economic organization are being proposed, and enormous pressure is being exerted to substitute political for market control of the economy. The forensics of Reuther vs. the automobile companies are a part of this ferment, and, as such, have important implications not only for the participants but for every thoughtful citizen as well.

One implication is that business is becoming more and more an exercise in politics as well as economics. Business cannot be conducted in a social vacuum; it is an integral part of the community process; it involves community values and responsibilities and is judged on political as well as economic grounds.

Businessmen are not very good politicians. They understand the law of supply and demand and are responsive to the pressures of the market place. But politics is a different art. It is conducted in a goldfish bowl of publicity. It calls for leadership that can mold mass opinion and energize large bodies of people actively to support a cause. Politics depends on slogans, oratory, and the coining of phrases that articulate and crystallize mass feeling. It places a high premium on maneuver and counter-maneuver and the ability to dramatize issues. In the interests of "electioneering," it sometimes take liberties with the truth, and focuses public attention on the trivia rather than on the basic issues.

Businessmen are ill at ease in the world of politics and tend to deplore the necessity of mixing in it. Henry Ford II voiced this distaste when he described his union adversaries as "masters of the righteous slogan, the thinly veiled appeal to selfish interest, the glib response to the serious and complex problem."

Whether businessmen like it or not, there is no escape from operating in a political environment and being subjected to social evaluation. If they wish to be successful they must compete in the game of politics and be sensitive to political realities. One indication that companies are adjusting to the new order of things is found in the increasing tendency to appoint a vice president to deal with industrial and public relations problems and with public affairs.

A more important implication of the debate is the need for a better understanding of how the profit system helps the community achieve its economic and social goals. The American people have great aspirations. They want higher pay, more job security, improved medical care, better homes, more education, and increased leisure; and they want these things without the loss of freedom.

But good things do not come merely from wishing. To manage our environment successfully it is necessary to know and make use of the economic principles that govern the production of wealth. Moreover, if we are to preserve freedom it is supremely necessary to understand the sociological principle that liberty is a function of the dispersion and balancing of power.

The secret of the American standard of living is more efficient production brought about primarily through increased investment in power driven machinery. Profit motivates and energizes the capitalistic system, provides rewards to people who serve the community by taking risks, and functions as the prime instrument of control, enabling the community to do the "economic calculation," as Professor von Mises puts it, to allocate men, money, and resources to those projects closest to the people's desires.

Under communism, people seek material betterment at the sacrifice of individual liberty. Under capitalism, the community can have a rising standard of living and freedom too, for the profit system not only produces more wealth for the people than socialist regimes, but it also articulates to the full the idea of liberty. If the community does not understand how the profit mechanism works and is careless of its maintenance and functioning, liberty will be curtailed and the economy will slow down and operate inefficiently like an automobile with a broken timer or a crankcase without oil. When people see profits as "excessive" and "exorbitant," and a manifestation of "insatiable greed" and other immoralities, they are tempted to wield the sledge hammer of restrictive regulation and confiscatory taxes. The result is the dislocation of incentives, bad economic decisions made for tax purposes, government enterprise that substitutes "social (i.e., pressure group) judgment" for the test of profitability, regulation that slows adaptation to change, and rate making that induces capital starvation for industries and companies. Capital is the primary tool of the entrepreneur. When he has been free to work with capital competitively, earning a profit and plowing it back within the community's rule of law and decency, and without political harassment, the people have prospered. America has proved this to the world, and underdeveloped countries struggling to rise from their poverty may once again be required to make its discovery.

A third and long term implication of the debate over profit has to do with the future direction of the American pattern of social organization. When Premier Khrushchev addressed the National Press Club in Washington he was asked to explain his famous boast, "We will bury you." He answered with the usual party dogma. Communism, said Khrushchev, is the wave of the future; it is historically necessary and therefore inevitable. Capitalism displaced feudalism, said Khrushchev, because capitalism was the superior system. For hundreds of years under capitalism, the Russian leader declared, the minority has appropriated the wealth created by the majority. Communism has resolved this contradiction, he said, by having the working people take over political power and the ownership of the means of production, thereby making it impossible for one man to acquire wealth at the expense of another.

Watching the Khrushchev spectacle on their television sets, the American people were impressed with the hardness of the man, his energy, his fanatical devotion to the communist cause, and his obvious brilliance. Here indeed was the personification of a great world force that is throwing down a crucial challenge to the United States. How will the American people meet this historic test? Will our society move more and more away from individual decision in the market place toward collective political decision of government? Will it tend more toward voluntary or toward coercive systems of organization? Will it abandon the traditional American principle of checks and balances for a form of increased centralization of power? Will it depend for its motive power on private incentive or on state control? Will it emphasize opportunity or security? Will social values spring from the people or be imposed from above by governmental authority?

American capitalism articulates the voluntary way of life with property ownership widely dispersed, with capitalist suppliers competing for public favor, and with consumers controlling the process by exercising free choice in the market place. If the institution of profits is discredited and prevented from functioning properly, the productive powers of the economy will be weakened. Consumer control of the economic machinery will increasingly give way to state control. Should the state eventually become the sole proprietor, the American system of checks and balances will collapse and with it, many believe, the idea of individual freedom. The profits debate, therefore, is much more than a wrangle between capital and labor on the division of economic wealth; it deals with our material well-being, and it reaches into the social system that guarantees our freedom.

Many commentators—scholars, editors, clergymen, judges, economists, political leaders, businessmen, labor leaders—are in the public forums presenting their views on profits. Throughout this book we will be dealing with the arguments of all of them, but a good point of departure is an exposition of labor's position, since labor pivots much of its case on the issue of profits and presents its views colorfully and with considerable spirit.

There is no one union position on the subject of profits, for there are doctrinal differences among union leaders as well as among businessmen and others. But it is correct to say that there is a consensus of union views on profits. In searching for this consensus, it is not always possible to distinguish "electioneering" statements from what union leaders really believe, but one simple way to gain an appreciation of the union point of view is to read systematically a publication like *Economic Trends and Outlook*, the official organ of the AFL-CIO Committee on Economic Policy. The summary that follows is based on positions expounded in this publication since 1940. Reference to "the union" will, therefore, mean the AFL-CIO, and before the amalgamation of these two unions in December 1955, the CIO.

The AFL-CIO says it is not against profits as such, that it believes in profits and the profit system, but wants profits to be "reasonable," "equitable," and "fair." Thus, in his 1957 Labor Day address, George Meany, President of the AFL-CIO said:

> We recognize the right of private capital and private management to receive a fair share of the rewards of production. It is only when profits soar way out of line that we become critical of the profit system.

Economic Trends and Outlook for July 1950, sets forth the union position in this manner:

> Let it be stated clearly that no one can quarrel with any business that is making a legitimate profit. In the enterprise system as it operates in America, legitimate profits are necessary to reward risks, provide incentive for expansion, and lower the cost of production. The need for legitimate reward should not be confused, however, with profiteering and gouging.

Union leaders seldom define in quantitative terms what they mean by "fair" and "legitimate" profits, usually contenting themselves with colorful adjectives implying that profits are too high.

In its April 1944 issue, *Economic Trends and Outlook* indicated that an eight to ten per cent return on capital might qualify as "reasonable." In February 1957 the union publication felt that steel profit rates were excessive because they "far exceed the six per cent return one generally accepted as a fair and reasonable rate." There is no excuse, said the magazine, for industry to insist on earning ten to fifteen per cent on capital.

David J. McDonald, President of the United Steelworkers of America, hewed to this line in defending his union's wage demands before the National Press Club in June 1959. The United States Steel Corporation, said Mr. McDonald, could cut its prices eighteen dollars per ton and still earn six per cent to eight per cent on net worth. "I believe that most everyone would deem that a satisfactory return on almost any sort of investment short of outright usury."

Union leaders, then, would allow the classic six per cent interest rate for profit, but anything much over that is subject to the charge of being "excessive" or even "usurious."

Profit margins, of course, vary widely among companies depending on management skill, position with respect to raw materials, financial setup, technological developments, competition, and many other factors. This variation, as a matter of fact, is one of the most important features of the profit and loss system, for it makes possible the "economic calculation" necessary to organize a free economic society. In their discussion of profits, union leaders do not grapple with the question of what is a "fair profit" when in the same industry one competitor loses money, a second makes eight per cent on its capital, and a third fifteen per cent.

Some sense of what the AFL-CIO thinks of profits can be gained from a sampling of the headlines from numerous articles in *Economic Trends and Outlook:*

"The War Made Profitable"—June 1943
"Profits Soaring to Highest in U. S. History"—November 1946
"The Rich Get Richer"—January 1949
"Profiteers Must Be Stopped"—October 1950
"Oil Profits Can Soak Up Wage Increases"—January 1956
"Gravy Train Still Rolls for Industry"—May 1956
"Big Business Profits Mania Hits Workers"—June 1956
"Boom in Corporate Profits"—August 1959

The stories under these headlines deal with many themes, but the dominant one by all odds is the size of profits. Profits are described as swollen, bloated, large, substantial, big, brilliant, high, record, huge, dizzy, tremendous, breath-taking, phenomenal, fabulous, super, soaring, skyrocketing, zooming, runaway, and fantastic. The list continues with adjectives carrying a strong sense of disapproval: unmatched, unparalleled, unwarranted, unreasonable, unconscionable, excessive, exorbitant, extortionate, and outrageous. Finally, the list winds up with the hard words "gouger" and "profiteer."

As the union spokesmen see it, profits are not only lush, but easy to come by. Practically every company makes a big profit, much of it unearned. Profit is not altogether a reward for constructive entrepreneurial effort on behalf of the community; it has more the appearance of a "windfall," "luck," or even "a swindle." In union cartoons the overfed capitalist sometimes appears as a highwayman, poking a gun into the ribs of the worker, and carrying a swag on his back labelled "profits."

To make its point that profits are too big, union leaders use two kinds of argument: argument by magnitude and argument by comparison. In argument by magnitude profits are described in huge dollar amounts calculated to stagger the imagination of the average man accustomed to struggling along on a wage of one hundred dollars a week. Thus the March 1944 issue of *Economic Trends and Outlook* said: "Corporate profits before taxes in 1943 totaled twenty-three billion, of which ten billion was left after taxes." The November 1947 issue carried a chart showing the trend of profits since 1929—"It can be clearly seen (from the chart) that profits before taxes rose from a level of 9.8 billion in 1929 to 29 billion in 1947."

Because of their interest in large dollar figures, union leaders are not averse to carrying on the debate in terms of profits before taxes. Indeed, taxes are at times regarded as irrelevant to the argument. "In determining whether a corporation has the ability to pay certain wages," said *Economic Trends and Outlook* (July 1942), "it is submitted that the only criterion is one of net profits before taxes."

Argument by magnitude is an effective device to persuade people that profits are unfair, for the average man has difficulty visualizing large dollar sums and supplying the necessary comparative data for their interpretation. The bigger the dollar profit, therefore, the more people are inclined to regard it as unfair.

In argument by comparison, union leaders choose a base

Shame on U. S. Steel for trying to deny its workers a raise

Today, at the stockholders meeting in Hoboken, N.J., the United States Steel Corporation is scheduled to reveal tremendous quarterly profits. Thanks to our country's laws, to a certain extent they must count their profits in public.

These vast profits, these great riches, have been amassed for the most part by the labors of over 100,000 Steelworkers.

What is to become of these new riches? The Steelworkers are told they should not have even the tiniest share of the fruits of their labor. "A wage increase," the Steel Industry advises, "would be inflationary, hurt our national economy." "Be patriotic," they say, "forego a wage increase."

Paying huge sums of money to Stockholders and Management however, is not inflationary, the Corporation must conclude... is not unpatriotic... does not hurt our national economy.

It's a story very old, but a story ever new. More money for the few and less money for the many.

Let us warn you now. The Corporation may try to explain away its riches. Management will try to "excuse" profits for many reasons including *scare buying* by their customers.

Mr. and Mrs. America, when they do this—please keep these thoughts in mind:

1. That the Steel Industry operated at only 84% of capacity in the 1st Quarter, far short of what they have done before and will do again.
2. That in 1958 the Industry operated at only 60% of capacity and realized profits of 8% in a recession year!
3. For every $1.00 in wage increases the Steelworkers have received, the Corporation consistently has raised its prices $3.00.
4. Fewer Steelworkers are producing more steel than ever before.

Now you know how such record-smashing profits can be set.

DAVID J. MCDONALD, *President*

See the United Steelworkers' "TV meeting of the Month." Sunday, Channel 11 at 12:15 P. M.

United Steelworkers Of America

I. W. Abel, *Secretary-Treasurer* David J. McDonald, *President* Howard R. Hague, *Vice-President*

DISTRICT DIRECTORS of the United Steelworkers of America

District 1
Martin J. Walsh
110 Tremont Street
Boston 8, Mass.

District 4
Joseph P. Molony
155 Franklin Street
Buffalo 2, New York

District 7
Hugh P. Carcella
1617 Pennsylvania Blvd.
Philadelphia 3, Pa.

District 8
Albert Atallah
3600 Eastern Avenue
Baltimore 24, Maryland

District 9
Carmon B. Newell
1330 Center Street
Bethlehem, Pa.

District 11
George Medrick
112 Market Street
Harrisburg, Pa.

District 13
Eugene Maurice
36—1st National Bank Bldg.
Charleroi, Pa.

District 15
Paul M. Hilbert
419 Huey Street
McKeesport, Pa.

District 16
John F. Murray
511 S. Main Street
Pittsburgh 20, Pa.

District 19
William J. Hart
400 Lock Street
Tarentum, Pa.

District 20
Bert Hough
1008 Merchant Street
Ambridge, Pa.

District 21
John W. Grajciar
Room 4, Boyle Bldg.
Sharon, Pa.

District 23
Paul Rusen
1329 Market Street
Wheeling, W. Va.

District 25
Al Whitehouse
525 Walnut Street
Cincinnati 2, Ohio

District 26
James P. Griffin
2400 Market Street
Youngstown, Ohio

District 27
John S. Johns
529 Walnut Avenue, N.E.
Canton, Ohio

District 28
Paul E. Schremp
803 Chester-Ninth Bldg.
Cleveland 14, Ohio

District 29
Thomas Shane
2211 Woodward Avenue
Detroit 1, Michigan

District 30
James Robb
911-922 Lemcke Building
Indianapolis 4, Indiana

District 31
Joseph Germano
720 West Chicago Avenue
East Chicago, Indiana

District 32
Walter J. Burke
714 West Wisconsin Avenue
Milwaukee 3, Wisconsin

District 33
Earl T. Bester
332 W. Superior Street
Duluth 2, Minnesota

District 34
A. F. Kojetinsky
721 Olive Street
St. Louis 1, Missouri

District 35
Lorne H. Nelles
95 Merritts Avenue, N.E.
Atlanta 8, Georgia

District 36
R. E. Farr
320-326 Stallings Bldg.
Birmingham 3, Alabama

District 36-G
Philip J. Clowes
4302 Henderson Blvd.
Tampa, Florida

District 37
Martin Burne
1101 Continental Bank Bldg.
Houston 2, Texas

District 38
Charles J. Smith
117 W. 9th Street
Los Angeles 15, California

The union pictures profits as a fantastic hoard of riches, amassed for the most part by the workers, but denied them by the greedy employers.

Steel Labor, Nov. 1959

The Profit Picture as the Union Sees It

period or point of reference, then show that profits have risen sharply, and that wage increases have lagged far behind profit gains.

Thus in March 1944, *Economic Trends and Outlook* reported that "Profits after taxes in 1943 were more than double the 1939 figures, while wages and salaries have increased only thirty-eight per cent."

During the decade of the forties, the union's standard base year for argument by comparison was 1939.[4] Although business was emerging from the 1932 depression, 1939 was still a poor year. Total unemployment was nine and one-half million. In the steel industry, the operating rate was sixty-four and one-half per

Economic Outlook, January 1949

Re-investment of profits is pictured as exploitive—made possible by lower wages and higher prices.

cent. Company profits were low and only seven out of twenty-one steel companies were paying dividends.

With 1939 as the base year, some startling comparisons resulted. In March 1942, *Economic Trends and Outlook* showed that earnings for the Aviation Corporation were up from $88,000 to $2,000,004, a gain of 2173 per cent.

The September 1943 issue of the magazine showed that American Car & Foundry's earnings averaged seventy-two thousand dollars during the period 1936-1939, but in 1942 the company earned $7,056,000 for an increase of 9700 per cent!

The inescapable conclusion from all this, says the AFL-CIO, is that wages can be raised without raising prices; in fact, profits are so huge that wages can be increased and prices lowered at the same time. In recent years, when prices have been rising,

Economic Outlook, March 1946

Profits are stigmatized as burglary.

the union has pressed this theme more than any other. The reader can gain some sense of the union's insistence on this point by the following quotations from *Economic Trends and Outlook:*

November 1946: "Industries could have paid the 1946 wage increase without increasing the prices of their products and still have been left with profits at least equal to those made during the war years 1942-45."

February 1948: "The CIO demands will lead to higher prices only if corporate greed is not satisfied with profits far above previous peak levels. In many circumstances these wage increases could be granted along with sizable price reduction and still leave sufficient profit for stockholders."

September 1952: ". . . wage and salary boosts generally can arise out of the economy's increasing productivity and business profits without the need to raise the price level."

Marxist influence on labor thought: the worker produces the wealth; the overfed capitalist expropriates it.

In his testimony before the Congressional Joint Economic Committee on January 31, 1957, Otis Brubaker, Research Director for The United Steelworkers of America, laid the union view squarely on the line in these words:

> Wage increases in steel have not caused even a single steel price increase since the formation of the steelworkers union twenty years ago. The rise in steel prices has arisen because the industry has been determined to widen its already excessive profit margins.[5]

Increase in Profits after Taxes of 50 Companies, 1945-46

NAME OF COMPANY	1st Nine Months 1946	1st Nine Months 1945	Percentage Increase in Profits Above 1945
Atlantic Refining Co.	$4,922,000	$572,000	760.5%
Long-Bell Lumber Co.	1,562,904	266,211	487.6%
Powdrell & Alexander	2,185,370	509,574	328.4%
Maytag Company	2,067,609	488,546	322.9%
Sunshine Biscuits	4,023,529	1,021,200	294.1%
Food Fair Stores	2,937,535	747,343	293.3%
Pacific Mills	4,648,000	1,256,000	270.1%
American Woolen Co.	16,259,000	4,540,000	258.1%
International Silver Co.	1,014,998*	284,664*	256.1%
National Container Corp.	3,330,140	952,946	246.3%
Park & Tilford	3,588,641	1,092,160	228.7%
Republic Steel Corp.	5,039,071*	1,617,676*	211.4%
United Biscuit Co.	3,004,388	985,243	204.9%
Youngstown Sheet & Tube	4,871,852	1,627,080	199.4%
Electrolux Corporation	2,184,329	730,996	198.8%
United States Steel	33,329,353*	11,624,420*	196.9%
National Tea Co.	1,877,556†	636,400†	195.3%
Mathieson Alkali Works	1,431,804	488,249	193.4%
Marshall Field & Co.	10,132,053	3,594,763	181.8%
Ward Baking Company	2,681,884‡	959,220‡	179.6%
Continental Baking Co.	5,078,293	1,883,904	169.5%
Heyden Chemical Corp.	2,218,391	834,353	165.9%
Union Bag and Paper Corp.	3,643,599	1,472,957	147.4%
Gillette Safety Razor Co.	7,513,640	3,051,360	146.3%
American Viscose Corp.	8,179,612	3,475,321	135.9%
Johns-Manville Corp.	2,310,466	1,038,867	122.3%
Remington Rand, Inc.	5,770,505	2,630,842	119.3%
Parmelee Transportation Co.	1,804,620	922,222	95.8%
Staley Manufacturing Co.	3,339,547	1,785,625	87. %
Commonwealth & Southern	27,289,233§	14,618,827§	86.7%
Allegheny Ludlum Steel	4,559,139	2,500,866	82.3%
Distillers Corp.-Seagrams	24,530,122§	13,803,800§	77.7%
Federated Dept. Stores	9,645,587§	5,581,755§	72.8%
Int. Business Machines	13,115,986	7,776,539	68.7%
Commercial Solvents Corp.	3,008,669	1,789,838	68.1%
Creameries of America, Inc.	1,612,036	963,463	67.4%
National Steel Corp.	13,941,320	8,910,673	56.4%
St. Regis Paper Co.	3,914,052	2,545,448	53.8%
DuPont de Nemours & Co.	82,179,876	53,975,625	52.3%
Harbison-Walker Re'tories	1,823,300	1,236,700	47.8%
General Foods Corporation	4,683,529	3,228,939	45. %
Hercules Powder Co.	5,631,636	4,096,183	37.5%
Inland Steel Co.	9,900,773	7,228,617	37. %
Owens-Illinois Glass Co.	11,211,455§	8,291,777§	35.2%
Pittsburgh Plate Glass Co.	13,168,435	9,961,357	32.2%
Texas Company	50,360,115	39,028,476	29. %
Mid-Continent Petroleum Co.	7,662,872	5,966,581	28.4%
National Biscuit Co.	13,513,255	10,663,335	26.7%
Hinde & Dauch Paper Co.	1,101,426	879,288	25.2%
Standard Brands, Inc.	8,821,486	7,190,037	22.7%

* 3rd Quarter Only. † 40 Weeks. ‡ 42 Weeks. § 12-month period.

Economic Outlook, July 1946

Profits, says the union, always increase faster than wages.

Economic Outlook, November 1946

A full tank of "purchasing power," the union believes, is what makes the economic machine run.

At times the argument that wages can be raised without affecting prices takes on a novel logic. Corporate profits in 1944, says *Economic Trends and Outlook* (March 1948), were twenty-five billion dollars before taxes. This was "almost twice that spent by the Federal government during the World War I years 1917 and 1918 (which shows) only too well that large wage increases can easily be absorbed by business."

It is a lie and a canard, says the union, to claim that wage increases cause higher prices. "What accounts for the inflationary trend?" asks the August 1943 issue. "Is labor responsible for the price increases that have occurred since 1939?" "No," says the union publication. "The answer is increased profits."

In an article entitled "Why Do Prices Go Up—It's Simple—More Profit," Nat Goldfinger, CIO economist, explains it this way:

> There is little, if any, price competition in most manufacturing industries. Why do prices rise? Usually because the giant firms see a chance to increase their unit profit margins. Profits are the major reason for most price boosts.[6]

As union leaders see it, consumer purchasing power is the primary key to prosperity and the economic well-being of the masses. Business has failed to share the benefits of industrial progress with wage and salary earners. Through administered prices and monopolistic practices, prices and profit margins have been kept unduly high. As the profit hoard increases, the rich grow richer and the poor grow poorer. The workers are unable to buy back the goods they produce, and sooner or later this lack of purchasing power brings on depression.

Sustained and rising purchasing power, say union spokesmen, is the answer. In good times substantial wage increases are needed to increase purchasing power to ward off depression. In bad times, substantial wage increases are needed to overcome depression.

Thus, in January 1949, *Economic Trends and Outlook* declared that:

Understanding Profits

Profits are too high for the nation's welfare. For three years inflated prices and corporate earnings have enriched the few at the top by siphoning off the purchasing power base which is essential to maintain prosperity and full employment.

Again, in September 1953, the publication warned that an economic imbalance was building up because of "increasingly high business profits that are saved rather than spent for new and improved plant and equipment." Rising consumer expenditures, said the union publication, are required to fill the gap. Business can help solve the problem by increasing purchasing power through "reduction of exorbitant prices" and "by accepting narrowed profit margins."

In judging the merits of the purchasing power theory, the question immediately arises: Where do the dollars come from to raise wages and increase purchasing power?

Businessmen see purchasing power coming from the cycle of production. Over a period of time, say industry leaders, production finances its own consumption because companies automatically return their gross receipts to the income stream through spending for wages, raw materials, taxes, dividends, replacement, and expansion. Living standards rise, businessmen think, because industry becomes more productive. Investors in search of a profit furnish companies with capital to buy tools and equipment. As tools become more efficient, wages rise, unit costs decline, and people are able to buy more and better products with fewer man-hours of work. The businessman's attention is focused on productivity and production, as well as on distribution. As productivity rises, the businessman thinks it should be shared broadly, with consumers in lower prices, with stockholders in large dividends, and with employees in the form of increased wages.

Union thinking is geared more to dollar wages than to real wages, more to sharing and redistributing income than to producing it. In two decades of publication, *Economic Trends and Outlook* has discussed productivity with its readers in only two lead articles. To the economically sophisticated this would appear to be a considerable understatement of this subject's importance to the well-being of the worker.

Increased output of goods and services, says *Economic Trends and Outlook* (November 1950), is partly the result of high levels of business investment in new and improved plants and equipment, but increased skill in the labor force has also played a major role. Continued trade union pressure for wage increases and improved working conditions has prodded management into technological improvements that increase efficiency and reduce unit production costs.

American workers, the union agrees, have shared "to some extent" in the benefits of increased production efficiency, but this sharing is by no means "adequate." Workers can expect little or no sharing through lower prices because "in our economy most prices are administered by business to a large degree rather than arrived at by supply and demand." Industry, say union spokesmen, tries to hold most of the benefits of rising productivity for itself in the form of profits, and only through union pressure can it be made to disgorge and pass on to the wage earner the benefits of technological progress.

"From the viewpoint of justice and economic reality," *Economic Trends and Outlook* editorializes, "the fruits of rising output per man-hour should be shared by workers, industry, and consumer through wage increases for workers, reduced prices for consumers, and business profits that raise from an increasing volume of sales at lower unit profit margins." Businessmen agree that productivity should be shared with workers, consumers, and stockholders; but they ask: Why doesn't the union set its policies to achieve this end? Why do unions featherbed, set low work quotas, and insist on "make work" rules that raise cost and decrease productivity? Why do unions demand wage increases that outrun productivity and force price increases?

Manufacturing companies are currently reinvesting about three-fifths of their yearly earnings in new plants and equipment and in working capital. This is bad social policy, union leaders contend. "The problem in America today," says *Economic Trends and Outlook* (May 1948) "is certainly not that

of finding capital. It is rather the problem of finding outlets for tremendous amounts of capital which corporations and high income individuals accumulated."

Reinvestment of earnings in a business, says *Economic Trends and Outlook* (May 1955), is a diversion of funds that might otherwise go to workers in wage increases or to customers in reduced prices:

> Retained earnings are a kind of inequity capital . . . in that they are drawn out of the hides of workers and consumers who are cast in the role of underwriting vast new facilities without receiving any share in running these new operations and without any share in deciding where they should be started. The huge corporate resources that make larger scale internal financing possible arise from high unit profit margins, from wages that are too low and prices that are too high.

Mr. Reuther followed this line in his 1957 debate with the automobile companies. "The consumer," said the UAW president, "has not only been denied his equity in the fruits of advancing technology and increased productivity, but in addition has been charged unnecessarily high prices to pay for virtually all expansion of these corporations. Through extortionate prices, the American consumers have made compulsory investments to finance the expansion of these three giant corporations without receiving any equity in them, or any return on their involuntary investment."[7]

Moral as well as economic issues come strongly to the fore in the debate over profits. Businessmen think that the institution of profits serves the community well in providing incentives for progress, in creating productive jobs, in supplying men with modern tools, in raising the standard of living, and in providing a system of accountancy whereby the economic machine can be made responsive to the public's desires and needs. In a competitive market, say businessmen, profits provide a very real measure of the social service rendered by companies.

Union spokesmen describe the institution of profits in less glowing terms. In their eyes, profits are exploitative; they represent wealth that was really created by the worker but which is taken from him unfairly by the bosses. Profits are made with callous disregard for social values and the integrity of men's souls. Property rights are placed above human rights; efficiency is preferred over social justice; profit is given priority over the welfare of the masses. Profit makers are morally sick; they are cunning, heartless, unconscionable, unethical, coarse, sordid, oppressive, cut-throat, barbarian; they are usurers motivated by overweening money lust and insatiable greed, even to the point of starting wars to make a profit.

In 1906 Upton Sinclair set the classic tone for disparagement of the profit and loss system in his famous novel *The Jungle,* in these words:

> . . . the odor of a fertilizer man would scare any ordinary visitor at a hundred yards, and as for the other men who worked in tank rooms full of steam and in some of which there were open vats near the level of the floor, their peculiar trouble was they fell into the vats; and when they were fished out, there was never enough of them to be worth exhibiting . . . sometimes they would be overlooked for days, till all the bones of them had gone to the world as Durham's Pure Leaf Lard.

Union leaders do not see the industrial picture today in the extreme terms of Upton Sinclair, but they contend that the profit makers thrive on human misery. "Profiteering at Peak as Unemployment Grows," reads the headline of an article in the *U. E. News* for April 28, 1959. "For the corporations," says the article, "this is the most profitable depression in history. For the worker, it is the highest priced."

In the debate over profits, union leaders go to considerable pains to make common cause with the general public.

> "It isn't only labor which should be interested in seeing wage rates raised," says *Economic Trends and Outlook* (October 1944). "The entire country for the sake of its future should be concerned in maintaining and increasing the purchasing power of the millions."

David J. McDonald, President of the United Steelworkers Union of America, used this theme in a major advertising campaign to generate public support for his 1959 wage demands. Addressing garden supply dealers as one of the many groups to whom the appeal was made, he asked "How many lawn mowers could you sell for an extra billion dollars?" "Garden tool manufacturers," said the copy, "must realize that sales and profits come only from people. Soon over a million steelworkers will begin negotiating a new contract. Their success will be directly reflected in your sales and profits." [8]

Mr. Reuther, who unquestionably is one of the most skillful and imaginative labor leaders of modern times, appears to be particularly sensitive to the possibilities of a conflict of interest between union members and the rest of the community. Time and time again, in his 1957-1958 skirmish with the automobile manufacturers, he returned to the theme of "social responsibility." Said Mr. Reuther:

> Neither stockholders nor workers have a right to insist on levels of income through inflationary prices that deny to other citizens their full and proper equity in national product.[9]
>
> Labor must make progress with the community and not at the expense of the community.[10]

No doubt Mr. Reuther's antenna are good, for with the continued rise in the cost of living and the revelations of the McClellan Committee on corruption in the labor movement, the issue of social responsibility on both the labor and business side has increasingly come into public consciousnsss.

It would be easy to dismiss union arguments as "electioneering" in the campaign for higher wages or as idle theory of little practical consequence. Certainly with the widespread ownership of homes, automobiles, electrical appliances, insurance, and with the mass enjoyment of the amenities of life—all on a declining work week—it is odd to read a statement in *Economic Trends and Outlook* (May 1940) that, "In most industries the products of increased efficiency have not been passed on either to workers or consumers in any substantial measure." Or more recently, to hear Mr. Reuther declare that "The consumer has . . . been denied his equity in the fruits of advancing technology and increased productivity."

It would be an error, however, to dismiss the union pronouncements as meaningless political utterances. In the union world, profit is a social action word. It is the pivot around which the economic rationale of the union is built. It is the battle cry which, more than any other, sets the legions of labor on the march. Fighting against the inequity of profits is a good and just and righteous cause. There is honor as well as material gain in winning, and great sacrifices can be called for in the name of this crusade. Examination of all major labor disturbances following World War II shows that almost without exception, strikes led off with the charge that companies were making enormous profits and that the wage demands of the unions could easily be met.

Research evidence clearly shows that union members' attitudes toward the vital problem of productivity *are* importantly influenced by the union view on profits. In 1955, *The Public Opinion Index for Industry* asked a nationwide cross section which was the best way to improve the workers' standard of living, to produce more or to get more of the money companies were already making. As indicated in Table 1, forty-three per cent of union members voted that the road to a higher standard of living is to re-divide company profits; only twenty-six per cent said that the answer was to produce more. Twenty-seven per cent of the general public voted for redistribution of profits, but only eight per cent of business executives favored this view. Thus a sizable proportion of the community is committed to the idea that redistribution of profits offers the best way to a higher standard of living.

TABLE 1.

	General Public	*Union Members*	*Business Executives*
Produce more	42%	26%	72%
Get more of the company money	27	43	8
Both	23	26	18
No opinion	8	5	2

(Source: *The Public Opinion Index*)

Understanding Profits

Sermons calling for fairer distribution between wages and profits are regularly preached. Students in economics and social studies are taught that wage increases come primarily from collective bargaining. Debates in Congress and state legislatures ring with declarations that the profits of industry are too high and that taxes on business should be raised. Government boards and bureaus hold hearings and emerge with the findings that profits are big enough to permit wage advances without price increases.

President Truman's seizure of the steel industry in 1952 provides the classic illustration of the influence of debate over profits on governmental policy. In November of the preceding year the United Steel Workers demanded a wage increase and a union shop. Because of the Korean War, the government was operating under emergency rules, with the Wage Stabilization Board passing on wage increases and the Office of Price Stabilization controlling prices. The price administrator, Roger L. Putnam, told the steel companies that industry profits were too high to permit price increases to offset a wage gain. The Wage Stabilization Board, with labor union and government members in the majority, recommended the union shop and a wage advance of seventeen and a half cents an hour, with an additional five cents for fringe benefits. Negotiations between the union and the steel companies promptly broke down, and President Truman ordered the Secretary of Commerce, Charles Sawyer, to take over the industry.

On the evening of the seizure, Mr. Truman made a telecast to the nation which historians are likely to regard as a most remarkable bit of Americana. The companies, said Mr. Truman, "are raising all this hullabaloo in an attempt to force the government to give them a big big boost in prices." It is not true, said Mr. Truman, that the companies need a big increase in prices in order to raise wages:

> The plain fact is, though most people don't realize it, the steel industry has never been so profitable as it is today, at least, not since the profiteering days of World War I. . . . The steel com-

> panies are now making a profit of $19.50 on every ton of steel they produce. . . . The companies could absorb this wage increase entirely out of profits, and still be making much higher profits than they made in the three prosperous years before Korea.[11]

Shaking with anger, Clarance Randall, President of the Inland Steel Company, appeared on television the following night and denounced Mr. Truman's carelessness with the facts. The President, said Mr. Randall, had told his audience that the steel companies were making a profit of $19.50 per ton, but had neglected to tell them that this was profit before taxes, and that of this sum, two-thirds was taken by government levies. "Steel companies," Mr. Randall observed wryly, "cannot pay wages and taxes with the same dollar." [12]

The steel companies promptly took their case to the courts, and on April 29, 1952, United States Judge David A. Pine ruled that the President's seizure of the steel industry was "illegal and without authority of the law." Four weeks later the United States Supreme Court upheld Judge Pine's decision by a vote of six to three, and the steelworkers immediately walked out.

For 53 days the strike continued, with union leaders and the price stabilizers and other administration officials insisting that wage increases could be absorbed out of profits and with steel industry leaders adamant that they could not. Finally, when steel inventories were exhausted and vital defense plants began closing, President Truman, in a grim mood, summoned Benjamin Fairless, President of the United States Steel Corporation, Philip Murray, President of the United Steel Workers of America, and Dr. John Steelman, Acting Director of Defense Mobilization, and instructed them to work out a settlement. The strike ended on a compromise with steelworkers getting the union shop and a 21.4c per hour increase, and the steel companies a price boost of $5.20 a ton.

A recent philosophical work by Richard M. Weaver carries the provocative title, Ideas Have Consequences. Ideas about profits have social consequences of vast importance. The community seeks a progressively higher standard of living with more and better products and more leisure. The people want their economic institutions to serve moral as well as material purposes, to be just and to fit into the pattern of freedom that from the beginning has characterized American life.

The practical problem is deciding which means are best for reaching these ends? There is no escape from the hard choice of means, and in a democracy these choices must have wide understanding and public approval. What is the realistic path to a higher standard of living under a system of freedom? Is it through redistribution of profits, as the union contends, or through increased productivity?

How much do companies actually make?

How do companies earn profits—by exploiting workers, customers, and other publics with whom they deal, or by serving them?

What do companies do with their profits?

Is there a vast profit hoard that can be redistributed?

Is it sound social policy for companies to reinvest profits in the business?

Does the institution of profits serve a socially useful function and, if so, how?

What mechanisms does the community have for controlling profits, and are new devices needed?

Is it true that the profit and loss system fails to share?

Would it be better if every company had a formal profit sharing plan?

Is profit-making ethical?

What are companies doing to interpret profits, and what needs to be done to get the facts about profits before the American people?

In broad outline, these are the matters to be discussed in the chapters that follow.

CHAPTER TWO

WHAT THE PUBLIC THINKS OF PROFITS

The debate over profits has been going on for a long time, but the controversy has become an increasingly heated one with the rise of labor unions in the past twenty years.

What is the public's reaction to this debate?
Do people approve or disapprove of the idea of profits?
Do they think companies are making too much profit?
Does the public agree with union leaders that wages can be raised without increasing prices?
Do people believe the profit system shares fairly?
Where do people get their ideas about profits?

Fortunately, we have a considerably body of research evidence to answer these questions. For twenty years, the Opinion Research Corporation, through its *Public Opinion Index for Industry*, has sampled public attitudes on issues having to do with business policy. These surveys have all been made by personal interview, using carefully worked out questionnaires, and scientific sampling procedures.[1] Many of these studies have dealt with company earnings, and, taken together, they furnish a comprehensive picture of what the public thinks about profits. Since much of the research was done with "closed end" questions where the respondent was asked to choose one of two or more possible answers, the analysis that follows is cast largely in simple quantitative terms.

The data show first that those who say the profits system is basically wrong have not made a believable case with the public. The samples report that:

> Ninety-eight per cent of the public at large says profits are a necessary part of our business system.
>
> Eighty-seven per cent agree with the statement that "most industrial progress in the United States has come about because companies have been able to make a profit."

Among clergymen, ninety-three per cent reject the proposition "that making a profit inherently and of its very nature is a violation of Christian (ethical) ideals and principles."

Operating a business without thought of making a profit seems silly and unrealistic to most people. "You couldn't run a business without profit," says the man in the street; "You can't work for nothing. You have to make money to keep going."

People back up their belief in profit making by telling where they like to work and buy:

> Seventy-eight per cent of the general public says that a company that makes a good profit is likely to pay higher wages than a company that just breaks even.
>
> Seventy-seven per cent say that a company that makes a good profit is most likely to make and sell products of better value than a company that just breaks even.

When times are prosperous, people say, companies make larger profits, employ workers, pay good wages, give job benefits, do research, make better products. Profit making, the public believes, is basic to the American concept of living.

The question in the public's mind is not whether profit making as such is valid, but whether profits of a given amount are "fair."

The debaters for the negative have concentrated their oratorical fire mostly on the size of profits, describing them with such colorful adjectives as: "fabulous," "fantastic," "unreasonable," and "exorbitant." This line of attack, Index studies show, has made a strong impression on the public mind.

The market economy is correctly described as a "profit-and-loss-system"—profits for businesses that serve the customers well; losses for those that don't. But the public tend to see only the profit side of the ledger. Business, it believes, is inherently profitable; losses do not frequently occur.

Thus *The Public Opinion Index* reports that eighty-seven per cent of the general public thinks that "in an average year, nearly every corporation makes a profit." The Bureau of Internal Revenue reports that in the past forty-two years, forty-five per cent of companies, on the average, have shown losses. *The Index* put this fact before high school teachers, clergymen, and foremen in companies by asking:

> Which of these statements is correct:
>
> In an average year, more than four out of ten companies make no profit, or
>
> Few companies operate at a loss.

Among high school teachers and foremen in companies, sixty-seven per cent said "Few companies operate at a loss"; seventy-seven per cent of clergymen subscribed to this point of view.

"Too much," has been the constant theme of the critics of the profit system. In July 1951, *The Public Opinion Index* asked a nationwide cross section this question:

> Do you think business as a whole is making too much profit, a reasonable profit, or not enough profit?

As Table 2 below indicates, forty per cent of the general public said, "Too much profit." This feeling was particularly pronounced among union members, farmers, semi- and unskilled workers, and professional people—teachers, doctors, lawyers, and clergymen. Even one-fourth of the proprietor and manager classification, which is made up mostly of small businessmen, subscribed to the "too much profit" point of view.

TABLE 2. IS BUSINESS MAKING TOO MUCH PROFIT?

	Per Cent Saying Too Much Profit
Proprietors and managers (mostly small businessmen)	24
White-collar workers	36
General public	40
Skilled workers	41
Professional	42
Semi- and unskilled workers	43
Farmers	49
Union members	50

(Source: *The Public Opinion Index*)

In an effort to get the public to put a quantitative measure on company profits, *The Public Opinion Index* has, in a number of studies, asked people to guess the size of profits. The July 1951 study asked the general public: "Just as a rough guess, what per cent profit on sales do you think the average manufacturer makes —after paying taxes and all expenses?"

The median average guess was twenty-one per cent. Actually, as will be shown in Chapter Four, profit on sales from manufacturing has averaged 3.8 per cent for the past ten years; for the past thirty-three years it has averaged 4.3 per cent. Only six per cent of respondents guessed profit on sales at less than five per cent. The actual distribution of the guesses is shown in Table 3.

TABLE 3. PUBLIC'S ESTIMATE OF PER CENT PROFIT ON SALES

Less than 5%	6%
5 but less than 10	12
10 but less than 20	19
20 but less than 30	16
30 but less than 40	8
40 but less than 50	5
50% or more	10
No opinion	24

(Source: *The Public Opinion Index*)

Curiously enough, in offering their guesses, people make little distinction between profit on sales and profit on investment. In one test, *The Public Opinion Index* asked respondents whether they thought a percentage profit figure meant profit on sales or on investment. Half said it meant profit on sales; half said profit on investment. The distribution of estimates is remarkably similar whether the question specifies the profits base or not.

The public's idea of "too much profit" comes sharply into focus when people are asked to estimate how many cents the meat packer makes on one dollar's worth of beef. The median guess is twenty-three cents. Swift & Company's annual reports show that its average profit per dollar of sale for the past fifty years has been one and four-tenths cent, and for the past ten years, nine-tenths of one cent. On invested capital, Swift's fifty-year-profit record is six and one-tenth per cent; its record for the past ten years, six and seven-tenths per cent.

People think that profits vary widely by different types of companies. Seventy-three per cent think big companies make more than small companies. Twelve per cent think the reverse. Forty-four per cent of the public thinks that manufacturers make more than retailers; twenty-seven per cent disagree. Fifty-three, as opposed to fifteen, per cent, think war contractors make more than do the manufacturers of civilian products. In 1945, at the close of World War II, sixty-nine per cent of the general public said they favored a Congressional investigation of war profits.

The charge of profiteering was made freely in both World War II and in the Korean War. To prevent undue profits, Congress provided for renegotiation of war contracts, and passed an "excess profits" tax that took up to ninety-five per cent of profits that exceeded those earned during the period 1936-1939. Prior to this legislation, General Motors had voluntarily adopted the policy of limiting profit on war contracts to a rate equalling one-half of its profit on sales for the previous peacetime year of 1941. Other large companies made similar policy declarations. These company and governmental curbs on wartime profits appear to have been very effective.

Believing that company profits are large, the public agrees, up to a point, that prices can be reduced and wages raised if companies are willing to accept smaller earnings. In 1951, *The Public Opinion Index* reported that seventy-five per cent of the general public agreed with the statement that "Profits should be reduced to keep prices from rising." Only eighteen per cent disagreed. In 1955, *The Index* found fifty-seven per cent of the general public agreeing with the statement that, "Most companies in the United States make enough profit so they could afford to raise wages ten cents per hour without raising prices." [2] Among union members, seventy-two per cent agreed.

But the public overwhelmingly rejects the idea that wage costs can be dissociated from prices. After World War II, each round of wage increases was followed by price increases, and people became painfully aware of the fact that big wage boosts are always followed by higher price tags. In 1959, eighty-nine per cent of the general public and eighty-eight per cent of union members told *The Public Opinion Index* that a big wage increase that year would increase the prices of things they bought.

At its 1958 mid-winter meeting of the Executive Council, the AFL-CIO urged its member unions to press for "substantial wage increases." When asked whether the steel workers should demand a big or a modest wage boost, *The Index,* in a nationwide sample, found union members voting sixty-six to eleven for moderation. Not only were union members aware that big wage increases would raise their cost of living, but fifty-eight per cent of them said there was danger that rising wage costs would make it more difficult to compete with foreign producers.

One of the most insistent criticisms of the profit-and-loss system is that it produces great wealth, but fails to share. Thus, in 1955, *The Index* reported that fifty per cent of the general public agreed that: "One of the faults of the business system in this country is that owners get too much of the money companies make compared to what employees get."

Actually, the average factory worker receives eighty-four per cent of the money paid either to employees or credited to stockholders as profits, but employees have little knowledge of this fact. In 1958 workers in one large industry were asked to guess what part of the dollar going either to employers or owners goes to employees. As indicated in Table 4, only one in four knew that workers got the lion's share.

TABLE 4. EMPLOYEE ESTIMATES OF DIVISION OF EMPLOYEE-PROFIT DOLLAR

	Per Cent Guessing Each Category
Worker 80% - owner 20%	28
Worker 60% - owner 40%	23
Worker 40% - owner 60%	25
Worker 20% - owner 80%	14
No opinion	10

Source: *Opinion Research Corporation*

The history of the United States has been one of rising productivity and a dramatic increase in the standard of living. Or, saying it another way, the profit-and-loss system has produced an ever-increasing abundance and shared it widely with the buying public. But so effective has been the forensic barrage against profits that the public's views of this process have become enormously distorted. In its 1955 study, *The Public Opinion Index* asked a nationwide sample of respondents to agree or disagree with this statement:

> Money invested in new machinery and equipment has increased output. The workers have got some of the increase, but the larger share has gone to the owners.

Table 5 shows that sixty-three per cent of the general public subscribes to this statement. Agreement appears to be correlated with education and economic interest. Thus, respondents with an eighth grade education (seventy-two per cent) are more in agreement than college graduates (forty-six per cent), and college graduates are more in agreement than college teachers (thirty-six per cent). Seventy-nine per cent of the union members and twenty-two per cent of the business executives, and fifty-eight per cent of the foremen in manufacturing agree that the largest share of productivity increase has gone to owners. This is a remarkable commentary on the failure of companies to educate their supervisors on how the profit-and-loss system works. If the managers themselves have so little understanding, it is unrealistic to expect others in the community to have more.

TABLE 5. PER CENT AGREEING THAT LARGER SHARE OF PRODUCTIVITY INCREASE HAS GONE TO OWNERS

	Per Cent in Agreement
Union members	79
8th grade or less	72
High school graduate	65
Farmers	64
General public	63
Government employees	62
White-collar workers	59
Foremen in manufacturing	58
College graduates	46
Clergymen	46
Professional	45
Stockholders	45
High school teachers	42
Small businessmen	41
College teachers	36
Business executives	22

(Source: *The Public Opinion Index*)

The belief that workers create the wealth but do not share it fairly has, without question, been one of the primary forces to push government toward intervention in the economic life of the nation. A dramatic demonstration of this fact was made by the 1955 *Public Opinion Index* study which included a series of questions about government intervention in the economy. One question was:

> Would you say it is better to regulate business pretty closely, or would you say the less regulation of business the better?

The data show that a feeling of nonsharing and desire for government intervention are closely related. Thus eighty-eight per cent of those who thought intervention was necessary also thought that the business system was at fault because the owners got too much of the money companies make. Only eight per cent of noninterventionists agreed with this statement. Again, ninety per cent of interventionists agreed that the larger share of productivity increase has gone to owners; twenty-three per cent of noninterventionists said they believed this to be true.

From this and other survey evidence the conclusion can be safely drawn that much of the driving power for increased government regulation and control of the market process has come from the public's desire to redress what is believed to be an unfair distribution of the wealth. Much of the argument about profits has revolved around the moral concept of a "fair profit." In an economic sense, there is no such thing as a fair profit. The capitalist believes that a profit is earned fairly provided it is gained under competitive conditions in times other than war or national emergency, and provided further that the law and the rules of decency are respected.

Clergymen disagree with this conception. *The Public Opinion Index* put the issue to them in these words:

> Some economists say that as long as a company competes fairly, there is no such thing as too big a profit in the moral sense. How do you feel about this?

Sixty-two per cent of the clergymen disagreed with these economists; fifteen per cent agreed; and twenty-three per cent gave qualified answers.

Typical of clergy thinking were these responses:

> "Big profit is like usury."
> "It's too much like monopoly."
> "I am against big profits."
> "When the profits get big they should share more with the workers."

This moral concern of the clergy is echoed by the general public, as indicated in Table 6.

Table 6. What Do Companies Do to Deserve Their Profit?	*Leading Mentions*
Turn out good honest products at reasonable prices	42%
Treat employees fairly—pay decent wages	28
Help the community	14
Treat the public fairly	12

(Source: *The Public Opinion Index*)

When people are requested to name a profit figure they think is fair, their replies range widely, but average out at ten per cent. This figure, however, is not too meaningful because no distinction is made between profit on sales and profit on investment. Moreover, the idea of a fair profit is equated more to "treating employees fairly" and "turning out honest products" than to any specific profit statistic.

Where do people get their ideas about the size and fairness of profits? In some cases it is imputed from the general conduct of a company. A very revealing experiment that illustrates this process was conducted at the Walter Baker Chocolate plant of General Foods Corporation. Housewives were brought to the factory for a plant tour. They were welcomed by the personnel officer, briefed on what they were to see, and given information on why the plant is a good place to work, how it contributes to the welfare of the community, and how modern machine technology lowers prices of manufactured products and furnishes good jobs. No information on profits was given to the visitors.

A week later, the housewives who had been on the plant tour were interviewed and questioned on their retention of economic information. For control purposes, a sample of housewives who had not visited the plant was taken. Although nothing had been said to the visitors about fair profits, seventy per cent of them thought the company's profits were "reasonable"; only forty per cent of the nonvisitors agreed. In other words, the visitors saw a clean factory and clean rest rooms for employees, heard the personnel officer expound on the contributions of the company to the community, and the advantages of modern machine technology, and drew the conclusion that profits were fair.

So the idea of "reasonable," "legitimate," or "fair" profits is rooted in more than profit statistics. The man who is satisfied with his work and with the way his company treats him is more likely to be convinced that profits are fair than the man who is dissatisfied with his job. When people think that a company makes an honest product, deals sympathetically with labor, takes part in community activities, and otherwise conducts itself as a "good corporate citizen" they tend to label its profit as "fair."

A second source of ideas about profits is obviously the debate waged in the mass media. In a test conducted by *The Public Opinion Index* in 1951, thirty-five per cent of the people interviewed said they had read something in the newspaper or heard something about profits over the radio or TV. When asked what they had read or heard, the key idea was "too much profit." They said:

"Defense plants are making big profits"
"Profits are greatest in history"
"Labor thinks profits are too high"
"The OPA is trying to hold the line"
"The government is putting a tax on excess profits"

Perhaps an even more illuminating indication of the source of people's ideas about profits is the public response to the question:

> What things do you yourself go by in deciding how much money companies are making?

One answer has to do with the price people pay for things they buy:

"I pay more for everything."
"I judge by what I have to pay."
"At those prices they must be making a lot."

Another answer is the public's estimate of cost in relation to price. A factory worker says:

"I make valves. It costs 98c to make a valve. You know what they get for it? Four dollars. You can't tell me they aren't making plenty."

A housewife says:

"Look at the price of steak—$1.25 a pound. What do they pay the farmer? The newspaper says cattle are selling for $30 per hundred pounds. That's a big difference."

This folk system of accounting, however unrealistic, is quite understandable, for what is out of sight is out of mind. A person is aware of one phase of cost, but items such as overhead, research, and distribution expense are not within his purview. Moreover, it is easy to misinterpret scraps of information. The farmer may indeed be getting thirty cents a pound for cattle, but this includes hooves, hide, hair, entrails and shoulder as well as rump meat. Only a small part of the carcass is sold as steak. Moreover, the retail price of meat must allow for the economic value added by killing, dressing, storing, transportation and retail distribution. Hence the difference between the average man's knowledge of selling price and his estimate of cost may be very large indeed.

A third source of the public's impressions about the size of profits is simple observation of industrial activity. Almost every company makes a profit, the public thinks, hence where there is activity there is profit. In the testimony on how people judge the size of profits appear many statements like these:

"The company is expanding."
"The mills are running full time."
"Production is up."
"There is plenty of money in circulation."
"They are building a new factory."

A fourth source of ideas about profits is news stories emanating from industry. Since managements wish to impress stockholders with their stewardship, their news releases tend to "emphasize the positive." "Sales and profits reach all time high," says a company news release, and this is promptly translated by some members of the public as "too much profit."

The very mechanics of numbers have an important bearing on the public's thinking about profits. In handling their household budgets, people deal in terms of hundreds of dollars, or at best in terms of a few thousand dollars. Profits of large scale enterprise run to millions and hundreds of millions, and these are staggering sums for the man in the street to comprehend. The influence on public attitudes of describing profits in dollar amounts is clearly demonstrated by an experiment conducted by *The Public Opinion Index.* Interviewers went to a nationwide cross section of people and asked:

> I would like to get your opinions on profits made by some typical companies last year. One company made eighteen million dollars net profit after taxes were paid. Would you say this is too much profit or not?
>
> Another company had sales of 300 million dollars and made six per cent on its sales after taxes were paid. Would you say this is too much profit or not?

In both examples the company obviously made $18,000,000 (six per cent of $300,000,000 equals $18,000,000), but the questions required people to react first to profit in terms of dollars, then in terms of per cent of sales.

Table 7 shows that only fourteen per cent thought an eighteen million dollar profit was reasonable, but sixty-nine per cent said it was reasonable that a company should make a six per cent profit on $300 million of sales.

TABLE 7. PUBLIC'S VIEWS ON FAIRNESS OF DOLLAR AND RELATIVE PROFITS

	Eighteen Million Dollars Profit	*Six Per Cent on $300 Million Sales*
Too much	38%	19%
Reasonable	14	69
No opinion	48	12

(Source: *The Public Opinion Index*)

Understanding Profits

When, in other questions, profits were expressed as a percentage of sales or investment there was little difference in the public's judgment of fairness. Sixty-one per cent said a ten per cent profit on $185 million of investment was reasonable. Fifty-nine per cent said a ten per cent profit on $310 million of sales was reasonable.

Thus large dollar amounts lead many people to think profits are too high. Profits expressed as a rate on sales or investment appear much more reasonable to the public.

One indication of the skill of participants in the profits debate is their knowledge of this fact. By this test, union leaders must be scored as the better persuaders for they consistently use large profit sums, or "proof by magnitude," to carry their point that profits are too large. If companies were equally skilled in their communications on profits, they would invariably supply an interpretive figure expressing profits as a per cent of sales or investment, or some other relevant base, as well as the dollar amount. Moreover, they would report the size of profit in relation to employment costs and taxes to show who is the principal beneficiary of the production process.

In tracing the source of ideas about profits it would appear that indoctrination begins at a very early age. *The Public Opinion Index,* in collaboration with the Youngstown Industrial Information Institute, studied the economic views of children from the seventh to the twelfth grades in the Youngstown schools. Among other things, the children were asked to complete a sentence starting out with "Business profits are . . ." Half the pupils completed the sentence with ideas having to do with the size of profits. Fourteen per cent of the pupils wrote about the function of profits; ten per cent discussed the fairness and importance of earnings; and six per cent referred to the recipients of profits. Thus profit size is an idea that is afloat in the community, and one that is absorbed by the children at the knee of the parent and teacher.

The children, like adults, did not express hostility toward the concept of profit. Their views tended to be neutral and uninvolved. Children in the United States today are raised in a society with great affluence, and quite understandably their views are oriented more in the direction of consumption than production. They and their elders seem to take the production of goods more or less for granted. This may be one of the greatest hazards of affluence. People become soft and neglectful of the principles on which their prosperity is built; only when the good things disappear do they awaken to a new appreciation of economic truths.

Capitalists believe that under the rules of a competitive market economy, it is socially useful to allow companies to make as much as they can; but many critics of the capitalistic system believe that government should limit profits. Where does the public stand on this issue? For almost a decade, *The Public Opinion Index for Industry* has maintained a trend series on this issue, using the following question:

> In industry where there is competition, do you think companies should be allowed to make all they can or should the government put a limit on the profits companies can make?

In Chart 1 below, the reader will note that the vote for "make all they can" under competitive conditions is about two to one, except for the period 1946 to 1948 when steeply rising prices stimulated a sharp increase in sentiment for government regulation.

The institution of profit performs the important social functions of energizing the economy and serves as an instrument of control. The fact that approximately one third of the American people have favored government limitation of profits during the past decade should give the thoughtful capitalist considerable pause. If the capitalist wants public support for a free market economy, he quite obviously must make a greater effort to tell people how the profit system works for the common good.

What then does the public think of profits? The answer can be summarized in six points, as follows:

1. The public believes basically in the idea of profit.
2. People think that profits are very large—their guess on profits on sales is four times the reality.
3. The public thinks profits are so large that some price reduc-

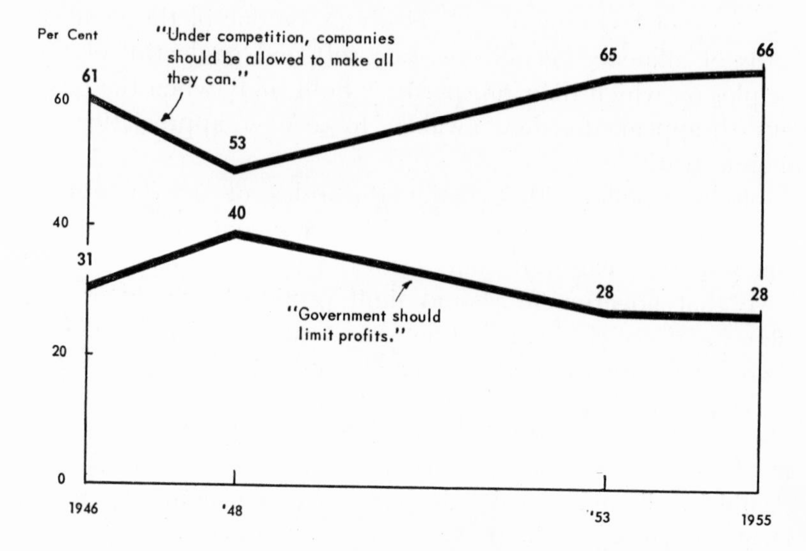

tions and wage increases can be made out of profits, but they overwhelmingly reject the union's contention that union demands for big wage increases can be met without raising prices.

4. The public criticizes the profit system for not sharing, but are grossly ignorant of how it does share. Much of the public's support for government regulation and control springs from the belief that wealth is distributed unfairly.
5. "Fair profits" is a moral issue. People formulate their ideas about fairness not only from profit data, but from many diverse and irrelevant impressions, including job satisfaction.
6. About one-third of the people believe government should put a top limit on the profits a corporation can make.

CHAPTER THREE

THE MEASUREMENT OF PROFITS

To the man in the street, the idea of profit is simple: It is what is left over after the bills are paid. The accountant agrees in the main—he defines it as "the excess of revenues over applicable expenses,"—but he would not agree that the measurement of profit is a simple process. The computation of profit presents many complex and even baffling problems.

The nature of the accountant's dilemma can be illustrated by problem situations.

A storekeeper has ten thousand dollars left after he has paid his bills and after allowing for inventory change during the fiscal year. What is his profit? If he pays himself a salary of five thousand dollars he has a profit of five thousand dollars. If he pays himself a salary of ten thousand dollars he has no profit.

An airline introduces a new airplane and spends $2,000,000 training pilots and ground crew. Should all this expense be charged to this year's cost of operation, thereby reducing current profits, or should this cost be spread over two or more years?

A company produces defense goods under a contract that permits renegotiation of the price after the goods have been delivered. The renegotiated price will be known a year hence. How much profit has the company earned on its defense business this fiscal year?

It would be nice if companies could feed data on sales, wages, raw material costs, rent, taxes, and other items, into an electric computer and ask it to produce an unimpeachable answer on profit. But this is not likely to happen in the foreseeable future. The computer would do its arithmetic with miraculous speed and accuracy, but it would surely blow a transistor if it were asked to set up the bookkeeping rules and make the judgments that an accountant is required to make every day. In the sense of physics or chemistry, accounting is not an exact science. It is a set of rules, customs, conventions, postulates, usages and practices that guide accountants in the handling of business data.

Over the past fifty years, as the accounting profession has grown and taken on status, certain standards of procedure have crystallized into what is called "generally accepted accounting principles." In the old days, for example, bookkeepers charged depreciation when there was a profit and skipped this cost item when there was a loss. Today, no self-respecting accountant would keep his books that way; but, as we shall see presently, the accounting profession is currently engaged in a monumental argument on how to handle depreciation charges. As Paton and Littleton have pointed out, current accounting practice is in conflict at "a hundred points." [1] Accountants, like other professional men, adhere to different schools of thought; they have prolonged discussions on the proper handling of accounting problems, and considerable difference of opinion may develop among them on the way a company should keep its books.

In measuring profits, the accountant is immediately forced to make assumptions. Actually no one can know for sure what a business earns over its lifetime until it is liquidated. But profits must be measured currently, so the accountant adopts "the going concern" principle; he assumes that the business will continue from year to year. Only by making this assumption can he break down the stream of business events by time periods and make quarterly or annual reports. Also, this concept enables him to report a rate of earnings, more or less comparable over a period of time. This then enables management to analyze its stewardship in terms of trends, and permits stockholders to judge the worth of their property as a producer of income.

A major decision for the accountant as he undertakes to measure profits is where in the business stream he should place his meters to gauge the flow. If the books are set up on a cash basis, he records financial transactions at the time monetary units change hands. Under the cash system of accounting it is possible, out of revenues, to build up inventories, accounts receivable and plant and equipment, yet show no "profit" until liquidation, or a downturn, forces conversion of assets into cash. With certain qualifications, measurement of profits on a cash basis is acceptable to the Internal Revenue Service, but it is of little value for purposes of measuring results of operations or for business control, and few corporations use it.

The more common basis for profit accounting is the accrual system where the accountant records the stream of revenue for a given accounting period, then undertakes to determine the costs that are applicable to these revenues. The difference between revenue and applicable cost represents the net profit for the period.

In matching revenues and costs, the accountant recognizes two kinds of costs—product and period. Product costs are those that can be pretty definitely attached to goods or services. These are raw materials, cost of labor, and various kinds of manufacturing expense that clearly and directly are assignable to the product. Ideally, the accountant would like to assign all costs to products or services, but it is difficult to link certain administrative and sales costs like executive salaries, office costs, advertising, etc., to specific products; so he is forced to fall back upon a time period as the unit for associating these costs with revenues. These "period costs" he matches against the revenue stream as the costs are incurred. Cost for a product that has not been sold is charged to inventory. Inventory is product cost "in suspense"—costs deferred to future periods where they presumably can be matched against appropriate revenues.

When the accountant has measured the profits of a company for a given time period, he reports the results in a financial statement usually referred to as a "Statement of Income" or "Statement of Earnings." The earnings statement used to be called "Statement of Profit and Loss," which is probably more accurate since companies lose money as well as make it, but usage of this term has decreased considerably in the past few years.

Every company sets up its earnings statement in its own way, but the 1959 statement of General Motors, as reproduced on page 50, may be taken as typical.

General Motors issues a consolidated report, i.e., it includes the earnings of certain wholly owned subsidiaries in the same line of business as the parent. Because of the complexities of trade, however, some companies prefer to consolidate only the earnings of domestic subsidiaries, or subsidiaries in a certain part of the world like the Western Hemisphere, rather than all subsidiaries foreign and domestic.

The first caption in the General Motors' income statement, is "Net Sales." These sales were recorded during the year when title passed to the buyers and at the amount charged the buyer. The word "net" indicates that deduction had been made for returns, allowances, discounts, freight, warranties, and other similar items.

The second caption in the statement, "Equity in earnings of subsidiary companies not consolidated," records the company's share of the 1959 earnings of subsidiaries whose operations are not included in the consolidated figures. Some companies report this type of income only when interest or dividends have been received by the parent from unconsolidated subsidiaries. General Motors, however, chooses to record its equity in the earnings of subsidiary companies during the period in which the earnings occur. From the General Motors' income statement it is evident that the equity in earnings exceeded dividends and interest received from nonconsolidated subsidiaries by some $16,358,091.

"Other income less sundry income deductions" is the next caption in the income statement. A note in the report reveals that this income consisted mainly of dividends received and interest earned from sources other than investments in unconsolidated subsidiaries.

On the cost side of the income statement the biggest item is "Cost of Sales." This is what was referred to above as "product cost"—raw materials, labor, and various manufacturing costs that could be clearly charged to product

The second cost item is "Selling, General, and Administrative Expense." This is basically selling and advertising expense, salaries of executives and office personnel, and other costs that are not assigned directly to products. It is therefore regarded as a period cost to be deducted from revenues for the 1959 accounting period.

The earnings statement then itemizes other types of cost, including interest and amortization of discount on borrowed funds, depreciation, bonuses paid to employees, and taxes. The final result is "Net Income for the Year."

In addition to the Statement of Income, companies report their assets and liabilities in their "Statement of Financial Position" or "Balance Sheet." Also, they normally provide a "Statement of Earned Surplus" or of "Retained Earnings." Earned surplus and retained earnings are the accounting terms for profits re-invested in the business. Capital Surplus and Paid-In Surplus are the terms for monies invested in the business through sale of stock or in certain other ways such as the capitalization of earned surplus through stock dividends, in excess of the amounts assigned to capital stock.

While each company can and does set up its books in its own way for purposes of financial reporting and control, the Internal Revenue Service requires all corporations to report on a common form under accounting definitions suitable for tax purposes. As a general rule profits reported for tax purposes vary from those used for the control of the business and reported to the stockholders. There is nothing sinister in this; it merely represents organization of the accounting data for two different purposes.

General Motors Corporation and Consolidates Subsidiaries
Statement of Consolidated Income for the year ended December 31, 1959.

NET SALES	11,233,057,200
Equity in earnings of subsidiary companies not consolidated (dividends and interest received amounted to $34,835,979)	51,194,070
Other income less sundry income deductions	69,446,743
TOTAL	11,353,698,013
LESS:	
Cost of sales and other operating charges, exclusive of items listed below	8,468,713,900
Selling, general, and administrative expenses	589,239,985
Interest and amortization of discount on three and a quarter per cent debentures	6,229,780
Provision for:	
Depreciation and obsolescence of real estate, plants, and equipment	413,703,473
Employee bonus and stock option plan	83,610,726
United States and foreign income taxes	919,100,000
Total	10,480,597,864
NET INCOME for the year	873,100,149
Dividends on preferred stock	12,928,296
AMOUNT EARNED ON COMMON STOCK	860,171,853
Average number of shares of common stock outstanding during the year	280,909,414
AMOUNT EARNED PER SHARE OF COMMON STOCK	$ 3.06

Under the Internal Revenue Code certain items will be taxable or deductible in one time period, but will be applied to company accounts in a different accounting period. Again special allowances such as percentage depletion are taken in the tax return but are not registered on the company books.

Union spokesmen point to this variation in tax and control accounting as a proof of dishonest bookkeeping. "Then corporation profits are higher than is reported?" asked *Economic Trends and Outlook* (May, 1948). "Yes, much higher," is the answer, "but we will never know the correct figure. Many corporations even go so far as to have two sets of books, one for the United States Government and one for the public."

Writing on the difference between tax and control accounting, Carmen Blough, Research Director of the American Institute of Accounting, comments:

> Time was when the keeping of two sets of books was viewed with alarm as a breech of business morality, but the ever increasing divergence between tax accounting as required by our income tax laws and generally accepted accounting principles as required for the presentation of financial data to investors and creditors has made multiple records a necessity.[2]

Economic Trends and Outlook reproduced this quotation for its readers, and observed that now even industry admits that it is telling one story about profits to the government and another to the public.

When prices are stable over extended periods of time, accountants are able to render a reasonably accurate report on the condition of a business; but during periods of price instability the gremlins of accounting create great confusion, and it becomes extremely difficult to know in an economic sense what companies earn. The difficulty springs from the "historical cost" basis of accounting where the assumption is made that after the cost of acquiring goods is entered on the books subsequent changes in the value of money may properly be ignored.

Since World War II the change in the value of money has been marked. Costs have risen sharply and the purchasing power of the dollar has declined. The Construction Index of the *Engineering News Record,* which leading companies say has accurately reflected their cost experience in building new plants, rose from seventy-seven in 1946 to one hundred eighty-three in September of 1960, an increase of one hundred thirty-eight per cent. In other words, it took two dollars and thirty-eight cents in 1960 to do the work that one dollar did in 1946.

The distortion in profits measurement that results from the changing value of money has to do with the variations in purchasing power of a company's net monetary assets and with inventory valuation and charges for depreciation. A searching discussion is now going on in the accounting profession on the proper way to handle inventory and depreciation. Happily we can leave this discussion to the experts, but the reader needs to know the main outlines of the problem in order to understand the limitations of profit accounting.

Let us first describe the problem of inventory valuation and its effect on profits. In accrual accounting, it is necessary to arrive at a figure for the cost of sales. The formula for computing the cost of sales is:

> Inventory at beginning of year; plus merchandise bought for manufacture, inventory, or sale; plus salaries, wages, and other costs applicable to the product; less inventory at the end of the year.

The crucial question is, what value should be placed on inventory? The oldest and most used accounting procedure for this purpose is called "First in—First out," or "FIFO" for short. If one thinks in terms of running a store, he knows that older merchandise should be disposed of before newer goods are sold. Under FIFO, the goods that are received in first are deemed to be the first goods sold, and cost at the time of acquisition is used to compute "cost of sales" for matching against revenues.

The reader can easily follow this accounting procedure on Chart 2. The firm using FIFO has bought nine hundred units at generally rising prices and sold six hundred units, leaving a closing inventory of three hundred units. Revenue from sales totaled $11,400. Cost of sales computed on the "First in—First out" basis, amounted to $7500 leaving a gross profit of $3900.

The units sold on November 15, 1961 for $2100 are entered at the 6/4/61 cost of $1500, notwithstanding the fact that the last units coming into inventory on August 15, 1961, the date of the last purchase, cost $1700. Thus FIFO inflates profits in periods of rising price, because the current sales dollar is charged with goods bought or manufactured at lower cost. This lag in costing produces what is known as "inventory profit." Inventory profit would be real if the company were going out of business, otherwise it is a bookkeeping fiction. In the example used above, the company must replace inventory at $1700 per unit that it costed out at $1500. Not only that, the company must pay taxes up to fifty-two per cent on the spurious gain, thereby consuming capital.

Chart 2

THE ACCOUNTANCY OF FIFO AND LIFO

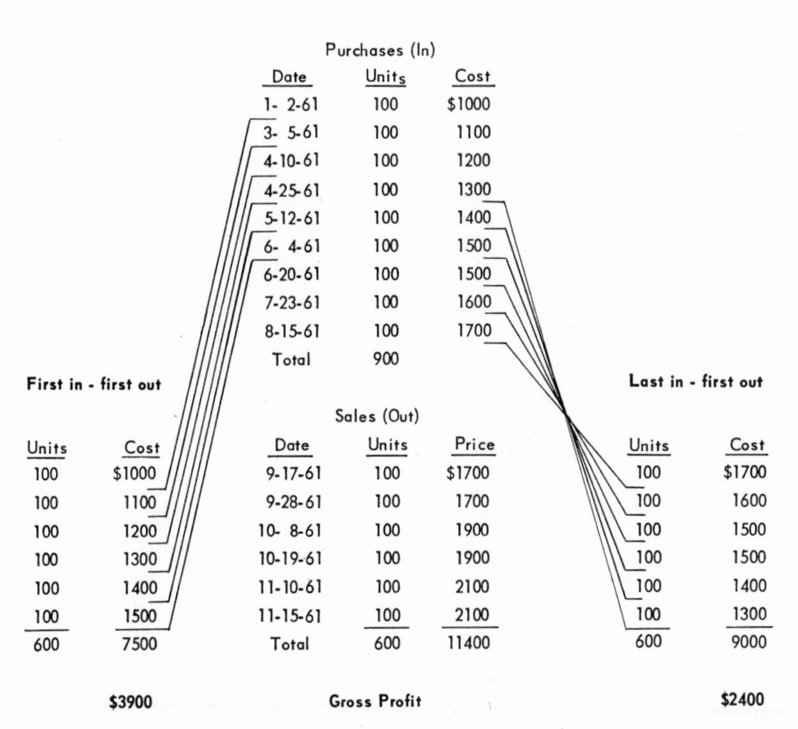

Purchases (In)

Date	Units	Cost
1- 2-61	100	$1000
3- 5-61	100	1100
4-10-61	100	1200
4-25-61	100	1300
5-12-61	100	1400
6- 4-61	100	1500
6-20-61	100	1500
7-23-61	100	1600
8-15-61	100	1700
Total	900	

Sales (Out)

Date	Units	Price
9-17-61	100	$1700
9-28-61	100	1700
10- 8-61	100	1900
10-19-61	100	1900
11-10-61	100	2100
11-15-61	100	2100
Total	600	11400

First in - first out

Units	Cost
100	$1000
100	1100
100	1200
100	1300
100	1400
100	1500
600	7500

Last in - first out

Units	Cost
100	$1700
100	1600
100	1500
100	1500
100	1400
100	1300
600	9000

Gross Profit: First in - first out **$3900**; Last in - first out **$2400**

Under the FIFO method, the same mechanics of accounting that magnify profits on a rising price trend understate profits and magnify losses on a declining curve. Historically the trend has been for prices to rise and the purchasing power of money to decline, hence the general tendency of FIFO has been to overstate profits.

In companies where the turnover of goods is rapid and the time lag between acquisition and sales is short, FIFO causes little profit distortion. But for companies with slower turnover and greater time lag, the problem of profit distortion as a result of FIFO accounting methods may become quite acute. To overcome the problems of First in—First out, accountants developed the procedure of Last in—First out, and this system, called "LIFO" for short, was accepted for tax purposes by the Internal Revenue Service in 1938.

In costing sales under the LIFO method, the accountant starts with the goods last purchased or manufactured, and works back. Chart 2 shows that the LIFO method minimizes the lag between cost of goods and current revenues. Revenue from high sales prices is charged with the costs that cause these prices; or putting it another way, revenues tend to be charged with the cost of replacing the goods sold, not with the historical cost of acquiring the goods.

In the illustration in Chart 2, the firm reports total sales of $11,400. FIFO reports cost at $7500, leaving a gross profit of $3900; LIFO reports cost at $9000, leaving a gross profit of $2400. Thus LIFO tends to reduce the profit distortion caused by rising prices.

In rising price trends LIFO is best suited for companies with relatively low turnover and longer time lag between acquisition of goods and their sale and for companies that have any appreciable inventories among their assets. LIFO accounting is being used more both because it permits a better matching of current costs and current sales, and because it offers the advantage of income tax deferral resulting from lower profit showings in periods of rising prices. Some appreciation of the significance of inventory valuation in the measurement of profit can be gained from estimates by the Department of Commerce which show that eight per cent of reported profits for manufacturing corporations for the ten year period ending in 1959 represented an overstatement due to distortion in inventory accounting.

An even bigger headache for accountants than inventory valuation is the handling of depreciation. Depreciation is a charge levied against current revenues for the cost of machines, buildings, equipment, or other assets wearing out or becoming obsolete. The accountant estimates the useful life of a piece of equipment, then recovers its original cost by setting up a depreciation formula and charging a specified amount to production cost each year.

Depreciation accounting is heavily influenced by the rulings of the Internal Revenue Service. In the eyes of the tax authorities, the useful life of a pretzel machine is ten years. A small air conditioner is given a five-year longevity, a large one twenty years. Faucets are expected to last fifteen years and bathtubs twenty-five years. An office safe is scheduled for fifty years, but a typewriter is "extinguished" in five years.

The taxpayer may elect one of several procedures to report depreciation charges of which the following are the most common:

The Straight Line Method charges off equal amounts for depreciation over the life of the asset. More companies employ this method than any other.

The Unit Cost Method estimates the number of units a machine can turn out over its lifetime, then charges depreciation at a given amount per unit produced.

The Declining Balance Method charges off a constant percentage of the net depreciated balance each year, thus speeding up depreciation charges in the early years and slowing them down as the balance left to be depreciated declines.

The Sum of the Digits Method is a little more complicated. If a property has a useful life of five years, the Sum of the Digits is $1 + 2 + 3 + 4 + 5$ for a total of 15. For the first year, 5/15 of the original cost is charged for depreciation; 4/15 for the second year, and so on. This formula, like the Declining Balance Method, enables companies to make the heaviest depreciation charge early in the life cycle of the asset.

Whatever the procedure for charging depreciation, the assumption of historical cost is made—namely, that the taxpayer is entitled to recover only the cost of acquiring the asset, without regard to the cost of its replacement.

As in the case of inventory valuation, the historical cost is satisfactory in periods of price stability, but in times of sharply rising prices, such as have occurred since World War II, this accounting procedure leads companies to overstate their profits and consume their capital. The dilemma can be illustrated simply by taking the case of Joe, the taxi driver. Joe buys a taxi for $2000. The life expectancy of his cab is three years, and its resale value at the end of that period is two hundred dollars. Joe and his brother-in-law drive the taxi six days a week, hence over a three year period he must put away about two dollars a day for depreciation against the purchase of a new cab. But when Joe comes to buy a new automobile he finds that the price has gone up to three thousand dollars. His "depreciation reserve" has accumulated an amount equal to the original cost of his cab, but he is short one thousand dollars for the purchase of a new car. So Joe has to borrow or dig down in his pocket for this extra money in order to stay in business. One thousand dollars of what he thought was wages or profits, and on which he paid income tax, was actually business expense for the replacement of his worn out cab. Joe was not charging enough depreciation to keep his capital equipment intact. Had he been unable to find the additional capital required to buy a new vehicle, he would have been forced out of business.

The problem is the same with corporations. The case of the turret lathe at Thompson Products Company (now Thompson Ramo Wooldridge) provides a good illustration. In 1942, Thompson Products bought a Warner-Swasey 3A saddle-type turret lathe for one of its divisions engaged in aircraft work. The lathe cost twelve thousand dollars. The useful life of the lathe was fixed at fourteen years, and over that period the company charged off twelve thousand dollars for depreciation. By 1956 the lathe had become obsolete and had to be replaced. Machine technology, of course, had greatly improved between 1942 and 1956, and Thompson Products bought a new lathe with hydraulic tracing attachments and other advances at a cost of sixty-seven thousand dollars. But short of these technical advances the company could have bought a new lathe that would do the same work as the old one for thirty-five thousand dollars, the price having risen two hundred ninety per cent in fourteen years.

To make this purchase the company had twelve thousand dollars of depreciation money, plus one thousand from the resale of the old lathe, less two hundred fifty in capital gains tax on the resale transaction, a total of $12,750. Due to the increase in the cost of turret lathes, and the historical basis of depreciation accounting, Thompson Products, at replacement time, was short $22,250 of the funds necessary to keep its equipment intact. These funds had to be made up from other capital sources, in this case from earnings. Since the corporate income tax rate is fifty-two per cent, the company had to earn $46,350 to make up the difference in the cost of the new lathe, and in order to earn this amount, it had to sell about five hundred thousand dollars' worth of its product to customers. In short, the underdepreciation of its lathe led Thompson Products to undercost its output and report as earnings what actually was capital erosion.

The extent of profit distortion resulting from the use of the historical cost assumption for inventory and/or depreciation accounting has been the subject of a number of studies.

In a speech before the Chicago Control of the Controllers Institute of America, Leonard Spacek, Managing Partner of the big accounting firm Arthur Andersen & Company, reported profit distortion from unrealistic depreciation accounting for six manu-

TABLE 8. INCOME OVERSTATEMENT OF SIX COMPANIES

Type of Manufacture	*1955 Reported Income*	*1955 Income Adjusted for Realistic Depreciation*	*Reported Income Overstatement*
Building supply	$23,500,000	$16,000,000	32%
Chemical	52,000,000	33,000,000	36
Paper	36,000,000	24,500,000	32
Rubber	47,000,000	38,000,000	19
Photographic	86,000,000	69,000,000	20
Food	11,000,000	9,000,000	18

(Source: *Arthur Andersen & Company*)

facturing companies. As indicated in Table 8, income overstatement for these companies ran from eighteen to thirty-six per cent.

To illustrate the possibilities for investor confusion resulting from what he called "misrepresentation of earnings," Mr. Spacek computed the price earning ratios (price of common stock divided by per share earnings) for the six companies on the basis of reported earnings, then applied these ratios to the adjusted or "real" earnings to arrive at a common stock price that was more in line with the facts. On the basis of this test he found the common stock of the six companies overpriced from twenty to sixty per cent. There is, of course, no way of telling how much the buyers and sellers of the common stock of the six companies had already taken into account the overstatement of profits disclosed in Mr. Spacek's analysis; but, as a general proposition, investors can make wiser decisions in placing their capital when they have sound accounting information.

A second noteworthy study is that of the Indiana Telephone Corporation. This small "independent" furnishes its stockholders an orthodox income statement (column A) and an adjusted statement (column B) designed to tell stockholders the true state of the company's affairs. As indicated in Table 9, orthodox accounting showed net income of $103,557; but, when depreciation was computed in terms of current cost, the company showed a deficit of $5,718.

TABLE 9. INDIANA TELEPHONE CORPORATION
ANNUAL REPORT TO STOCKHOLDERS - 1956

	Column A *Orthodox Income Statement*	*Column B* *Adjusted Income Statement*
Total Revenue	$2,241,783	$2,241,783
Less		
Operating expenses	1,440,285	1,440,285
Depreciation	301,514	410,790
Taxes	282,849	282,849
Interest and fixed charges	113,578	113,578
Net Income Loss)	103,557	(5,718)

(Source: *Indiana Telephone Corporation*)

A third study comes from testimony by officials of United States Steel Corporation before the Subcommittee on Anti-trust and Monopoly of The Senate Committee on the Judiciary. At this hearing, Mr. Robert C. Tyson, Chief Finance Officer of the Corporation, testified that during the period 1940-1956, wear and exhaustion of equipment in terms of current prices amounted to $3,706,000,000. Only $2,802,000,000, he said, had been provided for by regular and accelerated depreciation and by amortization. This left a depreciation deficiency of $904,000,000. United States Steel reported a total profit of $2,661,300,000 for the period 1940-1956, hence its $904,000,000 deficiency means that thirty-four per cent of its reported profit was an overstatement due to historical cost accounting for depreciation. The Federal income tax on this overstatement of profit, Mr. Tyson pointed out, was $608,000,000. This sum, he said, was a measure of the erosion of his company's capital due to unrealistic tax rules on depreciation.

In a recent study, "Corporate Profits in the Decade 1947-1956," Dr. George Terborgh, Director of Research for the Machinery and Allied Products Institute, showed that for the decade 1947 to 1956, reported corporate profits exceeded the correct figure by thirty-one per cent. One result of this overstatement, says Terborgh, has been to raise the effective corporate tax rate from fifty-two per cent to fifty-seven and one-tenth per cent for the five year period 1952-1956 and to fifty-seven and nine-tenths per cent for the year 1956.

Probably the most exhaustive studies of profit overstatement as a result of inflationary price trends have been made by Professor Ralph Coughenour Jones of Yale University. Professor Jones' analytic technique is to convert company earnings and financial statements into constant dollars by relating them to the 1935-1939 average for the Consumers' Price Index of the U. S. Bureau of Labor Statistics.

Under this analytic procedure, three types of profit distortion are revealed: inventory, depreciation, and what Professor Jones calls "purchasing power gains and losses from monetary assets and losses." Monetary assets consist primarily of cash and claims to cash, such as accounts receivable and notes. Monetary liabilities are payable in cash.

Professor Jones agrees that his adjustment of income statements for purchasing power gains or losses of monetary assets or liabilities is "highly controversial," but insists that these adjustments must be made if the economic truth is to be known. To demonstrate the point Professor Jones says: "If a cash balance of ten thousand dollars is maintained from the beginning to the end of a year, and if the price level rises ten per cent during the year, a ten per cent or one thousand dollar loss has occurred in the sense that it takes $11,000 at the end of the year to buy as much as ten thousand dollars would have bought at the beginning of the year. This is a purchasing power loss. Conversely, on a ten thousand dollar loan outstanding during a year (i.e., borrowing) there is a purchasing power gain of one thousand dollars if the price level rises ten per cent during the year. Hence, during a period of rising prices a purchasing power loss from the holding of cash may be offset by a purchasing power gain from the carrying of liabilities of the same amount. Just the reverse would occur during a period of falling prices." [3] Under the Jones system of analysis, reported and adjusted income figures paint vastly different pictures of company earning power. In the case of four companies studied, the adjusted average rate of return was approximately half the reported rate, as shown on Table 10.[4]

TABLE 10. REPORTED AND ADJUSTED PROFITS FOR FOUR COMPANIES

	Average Rate of Return	
	Reported	*Adjusted*
Armstrong Cork Company		
1946-1948	10.4%	5.0%
1949-1951	10.1	5.8
The Reece Corporation		
1946-1948	9.6	4.7
1949-1951	7.3	4.3
Sargent & Company		
1946-1948	9.5	3.3
1949-1951	6.7	3.4
New York Telephone Company		
1946-1948	6.3	3.3
1949-1951	5.5	2.8

In a second study, Professor Jones analyzed the distortions in the earnings and financial statements of nine steel companies accounting for eighty-one per cent of the ingot capacity of the industry for the seven-year period 1941 to 1947, with the results shown in Table 11.[5]

TABLE 11. DISTORTIONS IN FINANCIAL STATEMENTS OF NINE STEEL COMPANIES

	Nine Company Totals
Reported income	$1,638,000,000
Actual income	556,000,000
Overstatement of Income	1,082,000,000
Explained by	
Higher cost of inventory replacement	248,000,000
Higher cost of plant replacement	395,000,000
Purchasing power losses on net monetary assets	439,000,000

The figures in the table above show that reported income is three times actual income. Higher cost of inventory replacement accounts for fifteen per cent of the overstatement of income and underdepreciation or higher cost of plant replacement, another twenty-four per cent. In other words, if the adjustment had to be confined to inventory and depreciation alone, the reported earnings of the nine steel companies would have decreased thirty-nine per cent.

On many counts, the true condition of the nine steel companies, Professor Jones points out, was far different from what was reported by conventional accounting. The companies reported dividends earned by a substantial margin each year; actually dividends were not earned in any year. The companies reported that working capital during the seven-year period had increased fifty-one per cent. Actually working capital increased two per cent. The companies reported five to nine per cent earnings on investors' equity; actually there was loss or a greatly reduced gain, as shown in Table 12.

Professor Jones says, with some cynicism, that in view of these facts the President of The (mythical) Big Nine Steel Company would have reported for 1946, "The net income of your company for the year 1946 as certified by accountants

TABLE 12. REPORTED AND ACTUAL EARNINGS ON INVESTMENT, NINE STEEL COMPANIES

	Average 1941-1945	*1946*	*1947*
Reported	5.25%	6.21%	8.7%
Actual	3.38	—3.23	1.63

elected at the last Annual Meeting was $244,000,000, or six and two-tenths per cent of the total book equity of all permanent investors. The increase over last year was better than twenty-five per cent. But confidentially, we didn't make a dime. We really lost $155,000,000."

One final study that sums up the situation for manufacturing corporations comes from the Department of Commerce. Since, in making its estimate of national income, the Commerce Department seeks to reflect the flow of actual goods and services, it undertakes to correct corporation profits for distortions due to inventory valuation and understatement of depreciation. To eliminate inventory profit from national income, the government statisticians, with the use of data on inventory turnover and monthly commodity price changes, convert beginning and ending inventory into constant dollars. This gives them a measure of the real change in the value of inventory. The difference between the real and reported change provides a measure of profit distortion due to inventory valuation.

To compute depreciation costs, the Commerce Department estimates corporate expenditures for buildings and equipment, then fixes the period of useful life, and depreciates on a straight line basis in terms of current dollars. The difference between this replacement type of depreciation and that reported by corporations under the rules of the Internal Revenue Service is a measure of the distortion in the costing of the consumption of capital goods.

The profit adjustments of the Department of Commerce from 1929 to 1956 are shown in Chart 3. In the depression years of 1929 to 1932 and again in 1938, when prices were falling, corporate profits were understated. In all other years for the period shown, profits were overstated. In 1946, this overstatement reached a high of fifty-seven per cent. The cumulated overstatement of profits for the decade ending in 1959, according to the Department of Commerce, was eight per cent on account of an inventory valuation and twenty per cent for underdepreciation for a total of twenty-eight per cent.

Chart 3

PROFITS AFTER TAXES

REPORTED VS. ADJUSTED FOR INVENTORY VALUATION AND DEPRECIATION

MANUFACTURING CORPORATIONS -- 1929 - 1959

U. S. Department of Commerce

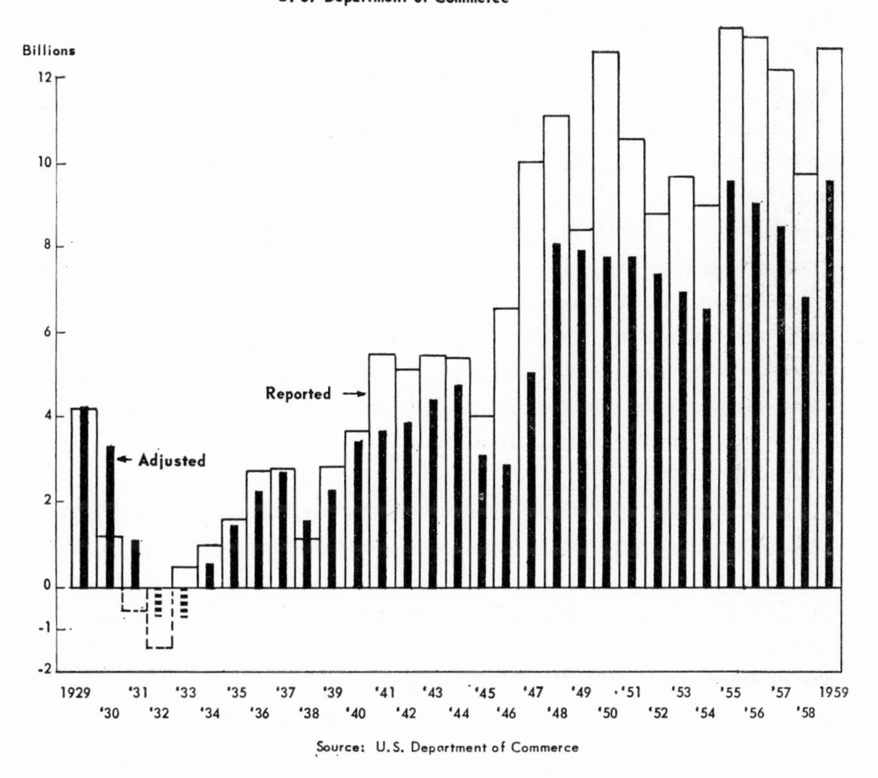

Statisticians will properly point out that the Commerce Department adjustments are based on generalized price indexes and, at best, are only estimates. But if the absolute facts were known, it is quite probable that the Department of Commerce figures would be closer to the truth than those appearing in the annual reports of corporations.[6]

It is clear from the foregoing that the mechanics of accounting cause companies to overstate their profits in periods of rising prices and understate them when prices are on the decline. The amount of overstatement varies by company and by industry. Likewise, it varies by the analytic technique employed in measuring the overstatement. When Professor Jones adds losses of purchasing power of net monetary assets to underdepreciation and failure to recover current inventory cost, profit distortions of one-half to two-thirds are reported. When the Department of Commerce makes its inventory and depreciation adjustments for the past ten years, the distortion is reported at twenty-eight per cent.

If an accountant went to the Board of Directors of Company X and reported a profit of $1,000,000, but next day confessed that he had made an error in his arithmetic and that the profit was actually $700,000 instead of $1,000,000, he would be disgraced and quickly read out of the profession as an incompetent. Yet misrepresentation of this magnitude is currently being made by corporations in their earnings statements. How can we explain this curious situation where accountants slave to balance their books to the last penny, but, because of inadequate measuring devices, come up with accounting errors that run into the billions?

There appear to be two main reasons for the current dilemma of business accounting. One is the enormous complexity of the problem presented by the inflationary price trend; the other is the inertia of the system. Accountants must work with simple and verifiable, conceptual vehicles lest they be swamped in a sea of confusion. A bill of sale is a verifiable conceptual vehicle; so too is money in the bank. Money in the bank can be counted, transferred, and held in one's hands if necessary. "When we start keeping our bank accounts in terms of purchasing power of the balances," writes William S. Bell in a symposium on 'Depreciation and the Price Level,' "we shall need more than accountants to do the job." [7]

The bookkeeping problems presented by inflation are extremely complex. If it were agreed that companies should charge for wear and tear on machinery on the basis of current replacement cost, what system should be used for translating depreciation in terms of current purchasing power? How much of the added cost of the replacement is due to technological change, and therefore a legitimate charge on capital, and how much due to the declining value of money? Again, if companies depart from the historical cost basis for depreciation accounting, shouldn't they adjust the value of all their assets and liabilities for the changing value of money? Accountants have the difficult job of measuring profits with a rubber dollar. If scientists generally had to use elastic foot rules and variable weights and measures, the resulting intellectual confusion would be indescribable.

The inertia of the system also works against adaptation to change. The economy is a vast network of contractual relations and legal decisions that enforce these agreements. No one is gifted with the omniscience to foretell what would happen if the basic postulates of accounting were suddenly altered. The social web can adjust to change only by the process of gradualness. It takes time to spin new ideas and rewrite the laws and the textbooks.

It is probable, too, that businessmen have lacked courage, or conviction, or both, in telling their stockholders what inflation is doing to their properties, and how the present accounting system is concealing from them the hard facts of economic life. The mark of success of management is earnings. The "system," hallowed by tradition and approved by the Internal Revenue Service, says that profits should be measured on the basis of charging off facilities at historical cost. It is easier for managements to report ten per cent earnings on net worth than eight per cent, which might be closer to the fact if adequate depreciation charges were made. This is particularly true when competitors in the capital markets report their earnings on an unadjusted basis.

Some companies have undertaken to inform their stockholders about depreciation deficiencies by making special deductions from earnings for this purpose, but this effort has not usually lasted long. In 1947, a study by the National Industrial Conference Board revealed only twelve per cent of the companies making special provision. The American Institute of Certified Accountants lists twenty-one companies that disclosed reserves for higher plant costs in 1951. By 1955 this number had dwindled to ten. To depart from orthodox accounting practices a management must have strong conviction and be willing to stand alone from the crowd.

But the issue of proper accountancy to cope with the problems of inflation will not down. In 1947, the Committee on Accounting Procedure of the American Institute of Accountants advised against "radical changes in accounting procedure—at least until a stable price level would make it practical for business as a whole to make the change at the same time." Meanwhile, prices have risen steadily and many competent observers believe that through deficit spending, social security, and collective bargaining the nation has built inflation into its institutions.

Since corporate bookkeeping practices are heavily influenced and controlled by the rules of the Internal Revenue Service, little change is likely to occur until the accounting profession invents new procedures to cope with the inflation spiral, achieves professional consensus on what should be done, and marshalls public opinion to bring pressure on the government to amend the rules.

One proposal for dealing with underdepreciation was made to The House Ways and Means Committee in 1957 by the New York accountant, Maurice E. Peloubet and others. Under this formula—called "The Re-investment Allowance Formula"—a company would calculate the total original cost of items being scrapped in a particular year, and would apply to that cost a special government cost index figure. The excess of this new cost over the original cost would be available to the company that year as a special "re-investment allowance" provided the company bought new buildings, machinery, equipment, etc., whose cost exceeded the original cost of the scrapped items.

The firm of Arthur Andersen & Company feels that the Peloubet proposal does not go far enough and that full allowance for price level depreciation should be made for income tax purposes. They say, "The current provision for depreciation should be an amount equivalent in current purchasing power to that which the depreciation computed on historical cost had at the time the property was acquired. An investment in property represents a commitment of purchasing power, and no real profit in an economic sense can result until the equivalent purchasing power consumed in operations is recovered." The computation of price level depreciation involves no insurmountable accounting problems. It involves only the selection of a generally accepted price index such as the Bureau of Labor Statistics Consumer Price Index or the Commerce Department's composite construction cost index, and the adjustment up or down of historical cost depreciation to take account of changing price levels.

Profits are a barometer of the economic weather and when they are understated in periods of falling prices, or overstated when prices are rising, people make bad economic decisions that are inimical to the general welfare. On the rising price trend, which has been the predominant condition, businessmen pay out too much dividend or optimistically overexpand; stockholders are misguided in placing their capital; labor leaders make demands for higher wages that are unearned through greater productivity, and government levies taxes that consume capital and impair the workings of the economic machine.

Since the beginning of civilization, folk wisdom has placed great store on taking care of one's tools. The hunter cleans and oils his gun; the fisherman protects his boats from the storm; the carpenter sees to it that his saw does not rust; the farmer is careful not to eat his seed corn. So, too, in the highest tradition of his craft, the businessman abhors the impairment of capital. If business is to be healthy and perform its duties in the community, capital must be conserved and expanded, for it is only through the use of better tools and equipment that the standard of living of a people can be raised.

The concepts of depletion and accelerated amortization are often said to be devices for hiding profits from the public view.

Depletion is a charge added to production cost to pay for the consumption or exhausting of natural resources. In depreciation accounting annual charges are made over the lifetime of the property to recover the original cost. In periods of price stability a business can compute replacement cost with a good deal of certainty, "save" depreciation funds, and replace the property at the end of its useful life.

Companies producing raw materials, however, cannot replace their mines and wells at will; they can only attempt to do it through exploration, which is a very chancy business. Eight out of ten oil holes drilled are dry. The recent odds have been one in forty-nine that a wildcatter on any given well will bring in a field of 1,000,000 barrels, and one in 1149 that he will strike a field with 50,000,000 barrels. Unlike the manufacturer who can forecast replacement cost with some degree of accuracy, raw material producers such as oil companies have no control over how much oil they will find for any given expenditure, or how much the oil will be worth.

In the Revenue Act of 1916 depletion for oil was limited to the cost of discovering and developing the well. This depletion system allowed enough incentive for risk capital to search for oil because corporate taxes at that time did not exceed two per cent. With the entry of the United States into World War I, however, tax rates rose sharply, and it soon became evident that cost depletion would no longer provide the incentive needed. In 1918, Congress adopted the principle of "discovery depletion" for tax purposes. Under this system, when a new well was brought in, an engineering survey was made to determine the fair market value of the oil discovered, and depletion allowance was based on this evaluation. Although this system worked, it proved to be difficult to administer, and Congress sought a simpler method to deal with the problem. During the period 1918 to 1925 it was found that the Internal Revenue Service was typically allowing twenty-five to forty per cent of the gross income of oil operators for depletion, so the idea of "percentage depletion" was advanced as the simplest administrative system. After a good deal of jockeying between the House and Senate as to whether the depletion rate should be thirty or twenty-five per cent, a compromise was reached setting the rate at twenty-seven and one-half per cent.

Under the present law, an oil producer may deduct twenty-seven and one-half per cent of the gross income from the production of a given oil well for depletion, except he is not allowed to take more than fifty per cent of the net income of the producing property for this purpose. In addition, he is allowed to deduct certain drilling costs. Depletion is applicable only to producing properties; it has nothing to do with the refining, transportation, or marketing of oil.

Since the Revenue Act of 1926 was passed there have been many efforts in Congress to lower the oil depletion allowance, but so far, none have succeeded. The debate however goes on.

Senator William Proxmire of Wisconsin denounces the twenty-seven and one-half per cent depletion allowance as "a notorious and unconscionable give-away," and proposes legislation to reduce depletion on oil production to fifteen per cent.[8]

Fortune Magazine says that in 1957 thirty-three major oil companies paid an average of only twenty-four per cent in Federal and state income taxes on their pre-tax and pre-depletion income, whereas other industries pay close to fifty per cent. This, says *Fortune,* is too large a subsidy for the industry. Instead of percentage depletion on production, say the editors, the oil industry should be allowed depletion only on original cost of a new well plus the expenses of drilling and intangible costs for unsuccessful ventures. This reform, the magazine says, would give approximately the same tax treatment to petroleum as to manufacturing industries generally and would about double the government's tax take from oil.[9]

The petroleum industry replies that depletion allowances are a payment for the consumption of a capital asset, i.e., oil in the ground, and that the twenty-seven and one-half per cent rate is not too far out of line with economic realities.

One indication, says the industry is this: the "discovery value" of oil in the ground was recently computed at ninety cents a barrel. At the same time oil brought to the surface sold at $3.03

per barrel, including nineteen cents for the gas by-product. On this basis, a twenty-nine and seven-tenths per cent depletion allowance would be needed to recover the ninety cents per barrel discovery value ($90 \div 3.03 \times 100 = 29.7\%$). As depletion actually works out in practice, the oil industry recovers not twenty-seven and one-half per cent but twenty-three per cent, which is considerably below the twenty-nine and seven-tenths per cent that would be required to match the discovery value of the oil.

The problem, say oil people, may be looked at yet another way: the discoverer of an oil field has the choice of working the field or selling it. With discovery value at ninety cents per barrel he can sell, pay his capital gains tax of twenty-five per cent and put sixty-eight cents per barrel in his pocket. With oil above ground selling at $3.03 a barrel and with an effective depletion rate of twenty-three per cent, he can work the field and still keep seventy cents (23% of $3.03 equals 70c). If the depletion allowance were reduced, the discoverer would have an incentive to sell, and possibly retire from the business of wildcatting, which would diminish the search for oil.

The First National City Bank of New York reports oil profits at fourteen and three-tenths per cent on investment for the decade ending in 1959 versus twelve and six-tenths per cent for all manufacturing. If the current depletion allowances for income tax purposes were a profit bonanza, say oil men, the industry should be markedly out in front as a profit leader, which it is not.

Oil, the industry points out, is crucial to the welfare of the nation; it has increasingly powered the industrial machine and has been a prime factor in national defense. Even with the twenty-seven and one-half per cent depletion allowance for tax purposes, drilling in the United States has not quite kept pace with annual demand. In 1936-1940, proved reserves of crude oil and natural gas were twelve and one-half times the annual demand; by 1959 the ratio of proved reserves to annual demand had dropped slightly to ten and nine-tenths.

If depletion allowances are reduced, oil leaders warn, the nation must be prepared to accept the economic consequences.

Exploration will be decreased, because fewer people and less money will take the risks of wildcatting; some currently proved reserves will be lost because continued production will become uneconomic; dependence on foreign oil will be increased with the possibility that the nation's supply may be shut off in the event of another war.

These are the main outlines of the debate on depletion. Depletion is not a nefarious practice as so often charged; it is a tax allowance to compensate producers of minerals for the consumption of their assets and to stimulate the search for new sources of supply. Some seventy or more minerals are given percentage depletion allowances running from five per cent for brine wells and sand and gravel pits, to twenty-seven and one-half per cent for oil. In no case may the percentage depletion deduction exceed fifty per cent of the taxable income from the property. With changing economic conditions and shifts in national policy emphasis, the amounts allowed for depletion on any one resource will no doubt continue in dispute. Depletion allowances, particularly in the oil industry, have a very important influence on profits, and any marked change in the rates will obviously have pronounced repercussions on the industry affected.

Accelerated amortization, like depletion, has also been assailed as a profiteering device and a way of deceiving the public about profits. Accelerated amortization is a technique used by government to speed up the production of defense materials. If the government wants more steel, or ships, or missiles to fight or prepare for a war, it can build and operate plants to produce these goods or it can procure them from private suppliers. In the past the government has built some war plants, had them managed by companies, and after the war has sold them for salvage value at great loss. To induce a company to take the risks of building and owning a factory for the production of war goods, the government gives a "certificate of necessity" which permits the company to write off the investment in the plant, in whole or part, as a cost of production over a short period of time, usually five years or the duration of the emergency.

Under this procedure, monies that would otherwise go to taxes are temporarily diverted to the building of production facilities. Accelerated amortization does not increase the total tax free allowance for the consumption of capital; it merely makes the tax allowance available to the company earlier in the life of the facility. The company pays less tax during the period of accelerated amortization, but more after the allowance is exhausted. If the company stays in business after the emergency and the tax rates remain the same, it has, at best, received an interest-free loan of monies that would otherwise have been paid out in taxes. If the company stays in business and the tax goes down, it gets a windfall; if the tax goes up after the emergency, the company may lose.

Whatever else happens, accelerated amortization has introduced certain distortions in the measurement of profit. A good many railroads, for example, purchased rolling stock, which is usually depreciated over twenty-five or thirty years, and took advantage of five-year amortization for tax purposes without providing the deferred taxes to take care of the added income tax that are payable when their depreciation allowances are used up. Thus they overstated their profits in the years they were taking high depreciation and, by the same token, they will understate their profits when these depreciation allowances are no longer available.[10]

There are cases in which companies have taken their five-year amortization both for book and tax purposes. In these instances profits may have been understated if the property depreciated has a lasting value beyond the five year period. In still other cases companies took the five-year deduction for tax purposes, but properly depreciated the property over its estimated life for book purposes. Where this was done there was no distortion of profit measurement. The same problem of profit distortion, of course, arises when a company takes accelerated depreciation for tax purposes, usually by the declining-balance method or the sum-of-the-digits method, but for book purposes deducts depreciation on a straight line basis and fails to provide for deferred taxes.

In World War II, the Federal government spent seventeen billion dollars for emergency war facilities, and industry spent six billion dollars, of which five and seven-tenths billion dollars were covered by accelerated amortization.[11] For the Korean War and its aftermath through 1963, Maurice E. Peloubet estimates the five-year amortization total at eighteen billion dollars.[12] Thus, for some companies profit distortion from rapid amortization is substantial, but for the economy as a whole its influence is minor.

Profits are commonly stated two ways—as a percentage of sales and as a percentage of capital invested. Capital invested, usually termed "net worth," represents all the money secured from stockholders ("capital stock" plus "paid-in capital") and earnings retained for use in the business. In addition to invested capital, business also uses capital that it borrows from the general public or from lending institutions through the sale of bonds, debentures, notes, and other forms of indebtedness.[13] These borrowed dollars perform much the same economic function as invested capital, and if we were relating earnings to all the capital employed in a business, we would need to add interest payments to profits and include borrowed as well as invested funds in the capital base. If this were done, profit on all capital employed would be lower for most companies, since earnings usually exceed the interest rate on funds loaned to the enterprise. Borrowed capital is secured by the assets of the borrower, and undertakes the least risk. Under accounting conventions, interest on borrowed capital is regarded as a cost and profits are computed after this cost has been deducted. When we speak of profits on capital invested, therefore, we are referring, not to all capital used in a business, but only to that capital owned by the shareholders.

As profit indicators, both profit on sales and profit on investment have advantages and limitations. Profit on sales provides a control figure that quickly tells management and investors what slice of the sales dollar, in terms of current money values, is left for earnings after all costs. In relating earnings to the amount of business transacted, profit on sales is an important gauge of the efficiency with which a firm handles its operations. Profit on sales also informs the consumer what part of his purchase dollar went for profit.

Profits on sales reveal nothing about return on investment. In 1959 leading food chains made one and four-tenths cents per dollar of sale, but because of their rapid turnover of inventory, earned thirteen and nine-tenths cents for each dollar invested. The relation between profit on sales and profit on investment becomes clear when one knows how much investment is required to produce a dollar of sale. In the apparel industry twenty-one cents is invested for every dollar of sale; capital turnover is four and eight-tenths times per year ($100 \div 21c = 4.8$). Since it takes very little capital to produce a dollar of sale, profit per dollar of sale is low, only nine-tenths of a cent on the average over the past decade. Capital turnover times profit per dollar of sale gives profit per dollar of investment, which, in the case of the apparel industry, adds up to four and three-tenths cents.

In the electric and gas industry, on the other hand, it requires $1.61 of capital to produce a dollar of sale. Over the past ten years profits on sales have been nine and four-tenths cents, capital turnover sixty-two hundredths per year and profit on investment five and eight-tenths cents. When capital turns over once a year, profit on sales and profit on investment are the same. When capital turns over less than once a year, profit on sales is greater than profit on investment. When capital turns over more than once a year, which is true of most companies, profit on sales is less than profit on investment.

Of the two measures, profit on investment is the more volatile. Profit on sales can remain relatively constant, but because of variation in the rate of turnover, profit on investment can rise or fall precipitately. Because profit on sales is relatively small, management likes to use this measure in public discussions of earnings. Labor leaders, on the other hand, prefer the higher numbers and almost always talk about company earnings in terms of profit on investment.

Managers and investors are basically interested in return on capital, hence profit on investment—its current or potential amount and its degree of risk—is the controlling consideration when companies are allocating capital for various projects or when investors are making up their minds to buy or sell securities. Profit on investment, however, needs to be interpreted with care, for in periods of broad price change this measure can be considerably distorted.

A company invests its money in plant and equipment at a given price level. Then prices rise and the "hard" dollar of investment produces more inflated dollars of revenue. Under these conditions profit as a percentage of investment goes up, and the company appears to be more prosperous. But the catch is that profits on investment are reflecting the earnings of old dollars put into plant and equipment at lower prices; they are not reflecting the earning power of dollars invested currently. This point is so important to the interpretation of profit on investment trends that a simple illustration is in order.

Assume that a company invests one hundred dollars in the first year but none thereafter (Table 13). Assume it sells 100 units each year at ten per cent profit on sales. Assume that it sells each unit at one dollar the first year but thereafter prices go up twenty per cent annually. Under these circumstances, the dollar profit on sales rises, but the rate holds constant. Per cent profit on investment, however, rises sharply, not because the capital is actually earning more in an economic sense but because it is producing a greater number of dollars with low grade purchasing power.

TABLE 13. PROFIT ON SALES AND INVESTMENT WITH CONSTANT CAPITAL

Year	*1*	*2*	*3*	*4*	*5*
Total capital invested	$100	—	—	—	—
Sales	100	120	144	173	208
Dollar profit on sales	10	12	14	17	21
Per cent profit on sales	10	10	10	10	10
Per cent profit on investment	10	12	14	17	21

Now assume that the company liquidates and starts fresh each year, thus having to install its capital equipment at inflated dollar prices (Table 14). Continue to assume that capital is equal to first year sales, and that one hundred units are sold each year at ten per cent profit on sales. Profit on investment does not rise as in the example above, but remains constant at ten per cent. The reason, of course, is that profit is related to investment dollars that reflect current prices.

TABLE 14. PROFIT ON SALES AND INVESTMENT WITH INCREASING CAPITAL

Year	*1*	*2*	*3*	*4*	*5*
Capital invested	$100	120	144	173	208
Sales	100	120	144	173	208
Dollar profit on sales	10	12	14	17	21
Per cent profit on sales	10	10	10	10	10
Per cent profit on investment	10	10	10	10	10

Thus, in periods of rising prices, profit on investment is inflated, and what appears to be a rising trend of profit may be partly a bookkeeping fiction. In periods of falling prices, the same mechanics of accounting produce an understatement and magnify a declining profit trend.

Frequently companies are accused of dishonesty in their bookkeeping. They are said to hide their profits, keep two sets of books, one for their own guidance and one for public consumption, and otherwise manipulate their accounts to deceive the public. Without doubt, in their earnings statements, managements do put their best or worst accounting foot forward depending on what impression they wish to create. But on the test of calculated distortion and the bearing of false witness, managements are simon pure compared to their opponents in the profits debate.

Should management's desire to tell the truth about earnings grow slack, they can never forget the fact that they live in a goldfish bowl of accountancy. Certified Public Accountants with high standards of probity are normally retained to examine the company's books. Security analysts for investment trusts and brokerage houses are constantly assaying company figures and writing reports. Thousands of individual stock holders pore over financial statements to decide whether to buy or sell. When a company seeks new capital, The Securities Exchange Commission requires it to disclose all relevant facts under severe compliance penalties. Above all, the tax collector is inquisitive about company earnings. With corporate income taxes at fifty-two per cent, Uncle Sam feels he has a vital interest in corporate accountancy, so he lays down a massive book of rules, and conducts searching audits to make sure he collects all the tax that is due him. Evidently, the tax collector picks the bones pretty clean, for in the decade ending in 1957, tax auditors were able to increase declared profits an average of only two and two-tenths per cent per year.

There can be little question, therefore, about the basic honesty of company earnings statements. The problem of measuring profits is not a matter of good intent or of arithmetic; it is what accounting assumptions should be made and what bookkeeping practices should be adopted to furnish a realistic report on the workings of the economic machine. Despite all the difficulties of measurement, profit figures are arrived at periodically, and people do base judgments on them.

CHAPTER FOUR

PROFIT FACTS AS THE ACCOUNTANTS REPORT THEM

The competitive enterprise system is a profit-and-loss system. Companies make profits when they produce superior products, price them attractively, give satisfactory service, keep their finances in order, and generally manage their affairs well. Companies sustain losses when their products get out-of-date, when they fail to keep cost under control, get over-extended on debt, or commit other management errors that make them vulnerable to competition. In broad economic tides such as the 1932 depression or the great boom after World War II, well-managed companies may lose money and poorly directed enterprises may make money; but even in these circumstances the well-managed property usually enjoys a favorable profit differential.

The public appears to have no trouble visualizing profits on the earnings statement; but it has considerable difficulty seeing losses. This may be due to the fact that companies talk more about their successes than their failures; it may result from union electioneering on the big profits issue; or it may simply reflect people's inclination to look on the bright side of life.

In any event, nine out of ten people believe that in normal times nearly every company makes a profit. Since loss is a very real and painful economic experience, let us first look at the deficits recorded on company ledgers.

The facts about profit and loss, insofar as they are reflected by orthodox tax accounting, are regularly reported by the United States Treasury in its publication, "The Statistics of Income." The Treasury's picture of the loss experience of American corporations over the forty year period 1916 to 1958 is summarized in Chart 4.[1] Line A shows the per cent of all active corporations, year by year, that reported losses to the Collector of Internal Revenue. From 1916 to 1929, an average of forty-one out of one hundred companies sustained losses. By 1932 this figure had risen to eighty-two per cent. From 1933 to 1946 the percentage of earnings statements with losses declined to twenty-seven per cent. Then with entrepreneurs becoming more venturesome in the boom following World War II, the loss curve began a slow rise. For the whole period 1916 to 1958, an average of forty-five per cent of companies reported losses annually. As a general rule, small companies suffered losses more frequently than did the large companies.

Line B in Chart 4 shows the total dollars annually lost by companies for every one hundred dollars gained before taxes. As would be expected, loss peaks in depression years are very high. In the 1921 depression, ninety dollars was lost for every one hundred dollars gained. From 1931 to 1934, conditions were so bad that total losses ran two to three times the total gains. The 1938 recession was considerably milder, with forty-three dollars lost for every one hundred dollars gained.

Chart 4 shows that between 1920 and 1940 there was a plateau of losses ranging from twenty to thirty dollars for one hundred dollars of gain, except during depression periods when the ratios of loss to gain peak markedly. A loss configuration of eleven dollars or under is shown for the periods between 1916 and 1920 and between 1940 and today. Both of these low-loss periods were boom times when even marginal companies were able to make profits. In both periods, prices rose sharply, with the likelihood

Chart 4

CORPORATION LOSSES
(1916 - 1958)

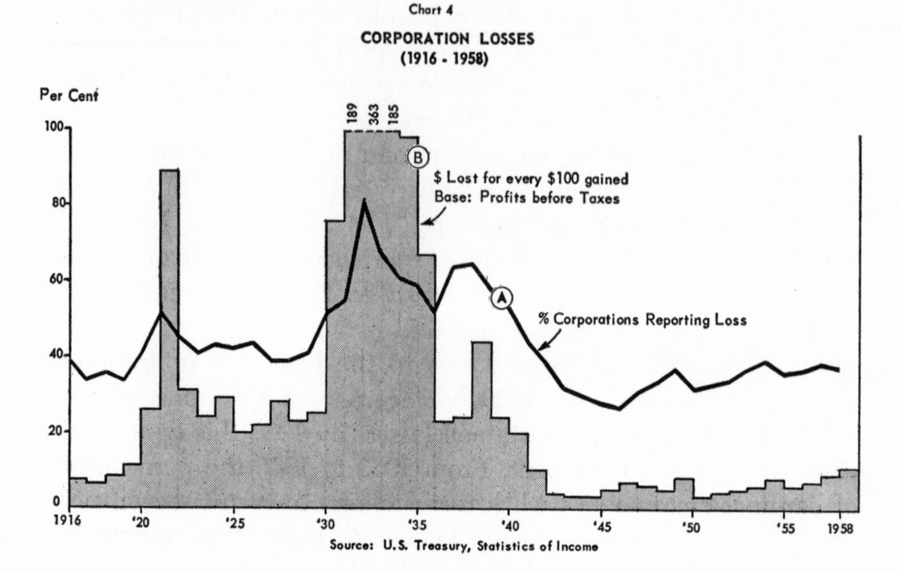

Source: U.S. Treasury, Statistics of Income

that profits were overstated. If inventory profits had been eliminated from company earnings statements in these years, and depreciation costs charged at replacement prices, the loss ratio for the 1940-1958 period would probably be much closer to the plateau charted for earlier years.

Losses, then, even though they are not registered strongly on the public mind, are quite substantial. In the years 1920 to 1939, forty-five dollars was lost for every one hundred dollars gained by corporations reporting to the Collector of Internal Revenue. During World War II and the years following, the reported loss was seven dollars and eighty-five cents for every one hundred dollars gained. Companies must earn more than they lose or they could not long remain in business, hence the next question is: How much profit do companies make?

In answering this question, we must keep in mind not only the limitations of accounting as described in Chapter Three, but also the first law of profit making—namely, "Profits vary." Profits vary between industries, between companies in the same industry, between companies of different sizes and between time periods. Any shorthand summary, therefore, can at best be only a summary of variations. Moreover, profit expressed as a percentage of sales is a different figure from profit expressed as a percentage of investment. To complicate the descriptive task still further, the compilers of profit data do not all use the same classifications, nor for that matter even hold their classifications constant over a period of time.

Extensive profit figures for separate industries, and companies going as far back as 1925 in some instances, are given in Appendix C. Here we will summarize the data as simply as possible to give the reader a basic grasp of the facts as the accountants report them and without adjustment for inventory and depreciation distortions.

Table 15 shows the ten-year aggregate for profits on sales and profits on invested capital for all active corporations with balance sheets in thirty-six business classifications for the years 1949 to 1958, ranked by the size of profits on sales. (See Appendix C-1 for detailed tabulations.) The profit on sales ranges all the way from nine-tenths per cent for apparel manufacturing to nine and four-tenths per cent for electric and gas utilities. Profit on investment varies from three and one-tenth per cent for bituminous coal mining to fourteen and two-tenths per cent for motor vehicles. In the translation of profit on sales to profit on investment, the controlling factor is the rapidity of capital turnover. For the reader's convenience in making these translations, Table 15 shows both the amount of invested capital per dollar of sale and the number of times this capital turns over annually for each industry.

The most profitable industries for the ten year period, on the basis of return on investment, were motor vehicles, chemicals, paper, glass, rubber goods, lumber, instruments, and machinery. The least profitable industries include transportation, textiles, coal mining, leather, hotels, motion pictures, personal service, and public utilities. The average profit for all manufacturing companies for the period was 3.9c on sales and 8.6c on investment.

The United States Treasury is the most authoritative source of information on profits because its statistics are official and all inclusive, reflecting the earnings experience of big and little

TABLE 15. PROFITS ON SALE AND INVESTMENT AGGREGATE 1949-1958

	Per Cent Profit on Sales	*Investment per Sale Dollar*	*Capital Turn-over*	*Per Cent Profit on Investment*
Apparel	0.9	.21	4.8	4.3
Wholesale trade	1.2	.16	6.3	7.5
Retail trade	1.5	.22	4.5	6.7
Construction	1.6	.19	5.3	8.5
Food	1.8	.23	4.3	7.5
Leather	1.8	.30	3.3	5.8
Personal services	2.1	.33	3.0	6.4
Bituminous coal	2.2	.72	1.4	3.1
Textile mill products	2.4	.49	2.0	4.8
Hotels—lodging places	2.4	.58	1.7	4.1
Motion pictures	2.5	.63	1.6	4.0
Furniture and fixtures	2.6	.32	3.1	8.0
Transportation equipment	2.9	.27	3.7	11.1
Beverages	3.0	.38	2.6	7.8
Transportation	3.5	1.05	1.0	3.5
Fabricated metal products	3.7	.41	2.4	9.0
Rubber goods	3.8	.36	2.8	10.3
All manufacturing	3.9	.48	2.1	8.6
Printing and publishing	4.0	.43	2.3	9.0
Electrical machinery	4.0	.38	2.6	10.7
Petroleum and coal	4.0	.74	1.4	5.3
Lumber	4.0	.51	2.0	8.0
Tobacco	4.6	.42	2.4	10.7
Non-electrical machinery	4.6	.49	2.0	9.2
Primary metals	4.7	.54	1.9	8.7
Instruments	4.9	.46	2.2	10.5
Paper	5.6	.59	1.7	9.5
Motor vehicles	5.6	.40	2.5	14.2
Crude petroleum	5.9	.95	1.1	6.2
Stone, clay, and glass	6.1	.59	1.7	11.0
Chemicals	6.6	.59	1.7	11.3
Metal mining	8.2	1.30	7.8	6.5
Communications	8.5	1.22	8.8	7.0
Electric and gas utilities	9.4	1.61	6.6	5.8
Banks and trust companies	—	—	—	6.7
Finance, insurance, real estate	—	—	—	9.7

Source: *The United States Treasury—Statistics of Income.*

corporations, successful and unsuccessful ones, and those that publicize their affairs as well as those that don't. A second widely used compilation of profits data is that furnished by The First National City Bank of New York. The Bank began collecting earnings figures from published sources in 1925. In that year its tabulations included 232 companies. By 1928, this number had grown to nine hundred. With the increasing tendency of corporations to make their reports public, the Bank currently includes the earnings of 3433 companies in its compilation.

The system of classification followed by the Bank is similar to that of the United States Treasury, except that the industry categories used by the Bank are somewhat more detailed. The Treasury, for example, lumps iron, steel, and nonferrous metals companies under the heading of "Primary Metals;" the Bank, following the thinking of the business community, furnishes separate reports for these two industries. Again, the Treasury includes many diverse companies under the general heading of "Machinery;" the Bank provides breakdowns for groups like agricultural implements, building, household appliances and office equipment.

Table 16 shows the average profit on sales and on investment for sixty-two industry classifications for the period 1949 to 1958. (The complete profit tabulations of The First National City Bank of New York are given in Appendix C2.) The range of profit on sales for the most successful companies for the ten year period was six-tenths cents for meat packing to fourteen and seven-tenths cents for cement. Profit on investment ranged from four and one-tenth per cent for traction and bus lines to twenty and eight-tenths per cent for automobiles and trucks.

Except for amount, the industry profit pattern reported by the Bank parallels that indicated by the United States Treasury. For the period 1926 to 1958, the Bank's median average profit on investment for all manufacturing was ten and eight-tenths per cent; the Treasury's figure was eight and one-tenth per cent, a difference of two and seven-tenths per cent. For the last decade (1949-1958) the Bank reports profit on investment for all manu-

TABLE 16. PROFIT ON SALES AND INVESTMENT FOR LEADING COMPANIES—MEDIANS 1949-1958
As compiled by First National City Bank of New York

	Per Cent Sales	*Per Cent Investment*		*Per Cent Sales*	*Per Cent Investment*
Meat packing	0.6	5.0	Agricultural implements	5.4	10.0
Chain stores—food	1.3	14.4	Hardware—tools	5.6	10.6
Wholesale trade	2.2	10.2	Soaps—cosmetics	5.7	15.8
Dairy products	2.5	12.3	Machinery	5.8	12.9
Traction—bus lines	2.6	4.1	Paint—varnish	5.9	14.0
All trade	2.7	11.4	All manufacturing	6.1	13.4
Department and specialty stores	2.8	10.8	Automobiles—trucks	6.2	20.8
Clothing—apparel	3.0	7.2	Iron & steel	6.6	11.7
Aircraft	3.1	17.8	Instruments—photo goods	6.6	15.2
Shoes—leather	3.3	10.2	Office equipment	7.2	16.2
Construction	3.4	13.9	Shipping	7.2	8.9
Chain stores—variety	3.5	10.2	Class 1 railroads	7.4	4.8
Restaurant—hotel	3.6	9.1	Paper—allied products	7.8	13.0
Baking	3.7	13.0	Lumber	8.1	12.0
Amusements	3.8	6.7	Glass products	8.3	16.8
Textile products	3.8	7.6	Non-ferrous metals	8.3	12.0
Misc. food products	4.0	12.0	Soft drinks	8.4	13.7
Distilling	4.1	9.5	Stone-clay products	8.5	14.2
Sugar	4.1	7.6	Chemicals	9.0	15.4
Tires, rubber goods	4.2	13.1	Drugs	9.2	19.0
Mail order stores	4.3	12.6	Metal mining	9.9	11.1
Brewing	4.3	9.5	Petroleum prods. & refining	10.3	14.0
Railway equipment	4.3	8.5	Telephone—telegraph	11.3	8.9
Air transport	4.4	11.6	Electricity—gas	13.7	9.6
Printing and publishing	4.5	12.3	Cement	14.7	17.0
Household appliances	4.7	12.3	Investment trusts	—	6.1
Tobacco	4.7	11.8	Fire & casualty insur.	—	6.3
Furniture—wood products	4.8	11.5	Commercial banks	—	9.1
Coal mining	4.8	6.9	Real estate companies	—	10.4
Automobile parts	4.9	14.2	Sales—finance companies	—	16.1
Electrical equipment	4.9	15.2			
Building materials	4.9	11.6			

facturing at thirteen and four-tenths per cent; the Treasury's figure was eight and six-tenths per cent, a difference of four and eight-tenths per cent.

There are several reasons for this variation. The Treasury figures reflect tax accounting, whereas the Bank data are drawn from book accounting organized for purposes of business control. For example, tax laws permit certain deductions for depletion or accelerated depreciation which may be handled differently in company accounting. Again, a company may report earnings from foreign subsidiaries to its shareholders; but, since the earnings are not returned to the United States, exclude them in its tax declaration. Most of the differences, however, are a reflection of the way companies are sampled by the Bank. The Treasury statistics represent all corporate experience; the Bank data reveal only the profit margins of enterprises that make their earnings public, which is to say the largest and most successful companies.

This point is of key importance in interpreting the Bank's figures. Through the courtesy of The First National City Bank of New York, a special tabulation for key years was undertaken to determine the percentage of companies in the Bank's sample that reported losses, and the number of dollars lost for every one hundred dollars gained. The comparative figures for the Bank and the United States Treasury are shown in Table 17. In most years the percentage of companies showing losses runs five times greater in the Treasury tabulations than in those of the Bank. On the amount of loss reported, the Treasury figures run consistently higher than those indicated by the Bank. Thus, it is clear that the profit figures reported by the Bank represent the earnings of the strongest and most profitable companies.

The market is a great testing ground where the buyers examine competing merchandise and make their judgments. In boom times, the tests are less severe than in times of depression, but it is characteristic of the market place that the weighing and judging and choosing goes on ceaselessly and inexorably. Every company comes to the testing ground with a unique combination of assets and liabilities. Like the gladiators of old, some

TABLE 17. PER CENT OF CORPORATIONS REPORTING LOSSES AND RATIO OF LOSSES TO GAINS.
COMPARISONS FOR SELECTED YEARS
U. S. TREASURY AND FIRST NATIONAL CITY BANK OF NEW YORK

	Per Cent of Companies Reporting Losses		*Dollars Lost for Every $100 Gained*	
	Treasury	*Bank*	*Treasury*	*Bank*
1928	40	8	$ 22.00	$ 3.90
1932	82	67	360.00	92.60
1936	62	14	23.00	1.90
1945	28	6	4.60	2.40
1955	36	4	6.80	.60

are strong of heart and bold of limb and some are wanting. The list of company attributes that determine the competitive outcome are legion. They include such factors as raw material position, capital structure, diversification, strength of dealerships, brand name position, manufacturing efficiency, product mix, geographical location, patent position, research facilities, experience and imagination of leadership, labor relations, and many others.

Profits provide the scoring system for the market test. Like a giant computer, the market, with almost miraculous facility, puts a value on every variable, adds it all up, and announces the results with stern finality. A dramatic picture of this process is given in Appendix C-3 where recent profits on sales and investment are tabulated for six hundred companies in fifty-two industry classifications. Here the American economy—alive and pulsating, competitive, changing, progressive in some sectors, retrogressive in others, and infinitely complex—is spread out on one great instrument panel for all to see. The reader can observe these profit indicators and draw his own conclusions.

In every industry classification some companies do well; others poorly. Pabst Beer shows deficits, but Falstaff Brewing earns twelve to sixteen per cent on its capital. Admiral barely breaks even, but Zenith makes up to twenty-one per cent profit on investment. Even over a short period of four years, the time span shown in Appendix C-3, profits for many companies show marked changes. Profits of aluminum companies were cut in half between 1956 and 1959. In tobacco, Lorillard's profit on investment rose from five and six-tenths to twenty and two-tenths per cent in four years. Thus there is nothing automatic about profits; they vary with changing markets and management skills.

The indicators strongly suggest that profit making is a struggle. In 1959 over half the companies listed fell short of a ten per cent profit on investment. Only one out of eight earned over fifteen per cent on capital invested. Most companies earn enough to pay dividends and reinvest a small amount in the business, but not enough for much in the way of arbitrary wage increases or price reductions. It is a common complaint that the farmer suffers because the meat packers make too much profit. The evidence shows that most packing companies earn less than one cent per dollar of sale, and appear to have great difficulty earning even six per cent on their risk capital.

Some industries—like textiles, liquor, agricultural implements, and railroads—have fallen on hard times; others—like office equipment, instruments and drugs—are doing well.

The best profit makers are the innovators. Included among these are companies like: International Business Machines with its sorters and computers; Minnesota Mining & Manufacturing with its Scotch Tape and other adhesives; Smith, Kline, and French with its tranquilizers; Tecumseh Products with its efficient compressors for refrigeration; Briggs and Stratton with its small gasoline motors for lawn mowers and other uses; Otis Elevator with its escalators and automatic elevators; Gerber Products with a fine line of baby food during a baby boom; Polaroid with its quick picture; The Brunswick Corporation with its automatic pin setting machine for bowling.

The profit figures for companies reported in Appendix C-3 are a reflection of success and failure in risk taking. Technology and markets are forever in a state of flux. So long as the economy is organized competitively under private ownership, the profit indicator will spin back and forth continuously, revealing the winners and the losers in the struggle for customer favor.

In summarizing the profits experience of American companies and industries, we have, up to this point, relied mainly on ten year averages (1949-1958) for various industries and three and four year arrays of profits for leading companies. Let us now look more closely at the size of profits as they are revealed in time series over the past three decades. Chart 5 shows profits on sales and on investment as reported by the United States Treasury for all manufacturing concerns for the years 1926 to 1958. Except for the depression years 1931 to 1933, profit on sales has fluctuated in a flat band roughly between three and six per cent. Profit on investment declined from eight and six-tenths per cent in 1929 to a deficit position in 1931 and 1932, then rose in a long band-like formation to a high of thirteen and four-tenths per cent in 1950. Contrary to popular belief, the war years were marked with declining profits. With the return of peace, the economy continued to work at capacity for five years to supply pent-up civilian demand. During this period of peak activity (1946 to 1950), profit on sales hugged the top side of the earnings band in the five to six per cent range, while profits on investment moved to the thirteen per cent level. Since 1950 profits have been in a declining phase, reaching a low of two and eight-tenths per cent on sales and five and eight-tenths on investment by 1958.

This is the picture of the earnings trend for all manufacturing as reported by the United States Treasury, without correction for inventory and depreciation distortion. In Chart 6 the profit trend picture is shown in other perspectives. Profit on investment for the most successful manufacturing companies as reported by the First National City Bank is indicated by Line A. The earnings trend line was below the ten per cent mark in thirteen of thirty-five years; it fluctuated in the ten to fifteen per cent range in nineteen years; and rose above the fifteen per cent level in three years. The highest reported profit on investment was eighteen

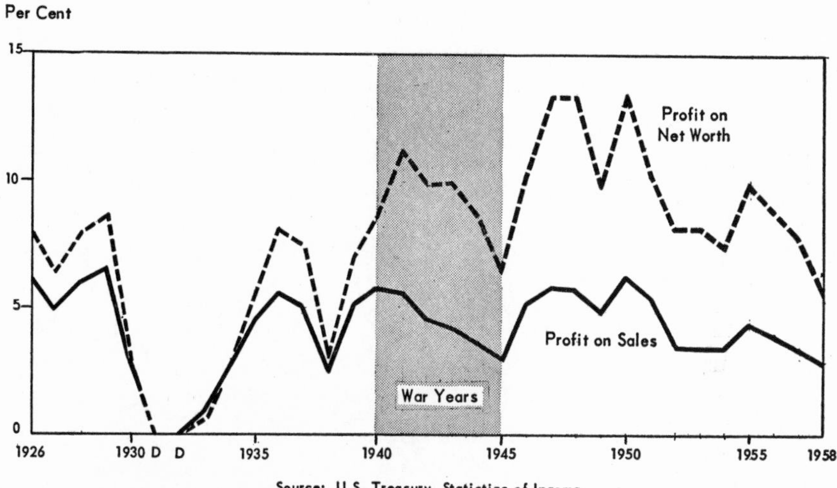

and nine-tenths per cent, recorded in 1948, when companies were working at full capacity to overcome shortages in consumer products induced by the war.

For comparative purposes, profit on investment for all active manufacturing corporations as reported by the Treasury is shown in Line B. This trend line shows profits at or below the ten per cent line in twenty-seven out of thirty-three years. The configurations of the Bank and Treasury profit lines are similar, except for amount. Profit on investment for the larger and stronger manufacturing companies has consistently run ahead of the Treasury's figure, with the spread narrowing in times of depression and widening in times of boom.

In Chapter Three it was pointed out that in a sharply rising price trend profits on investment tend to be inflated because current earnings, consisting of cheap dollars, are expressed as a percentage of invested capital which is in good part made up of

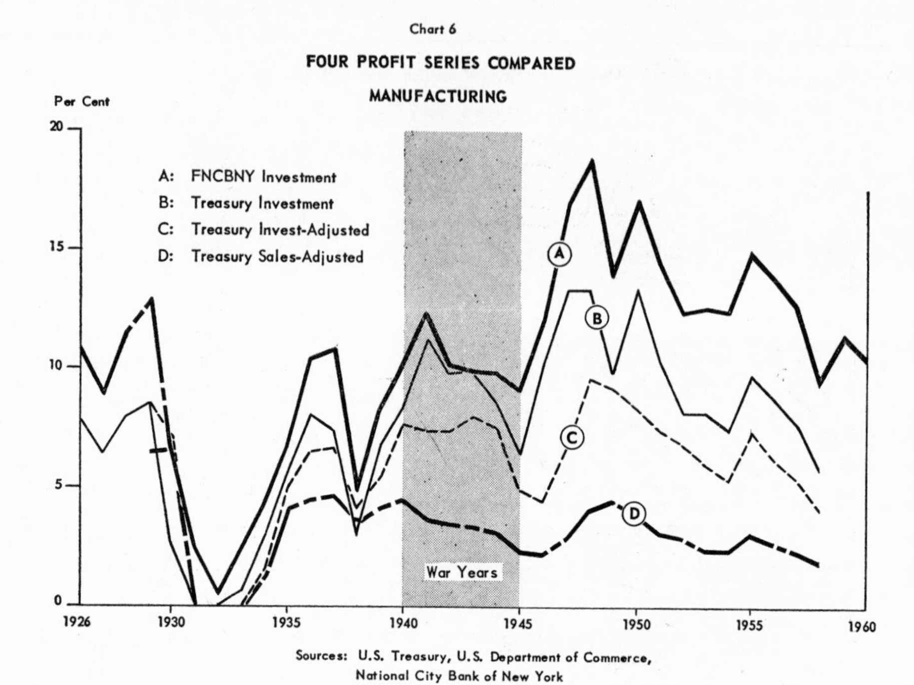

hard or dear dollars. When the Department of Commerce corrections are applied to the Treasury's series of profit on investment for all manufacturing, the earnings picture that emerges is indicated by Line C.

The spread between reported profits (Line B) and corrected profits (Line C) became quite marked in the boom following World War II. As prices continued to rise, profits were increasingly overstated because depreciation was understated. In 1952 and 1954, for example, the Department of Commerce deflated reported profits twenty-five per cent on the score of underdepreciation alone. Thus, profits in the boom years after 1945 look considerably different when allowance is made for accounting distortions. In twenty-six of the thirty years for which this corrected series is available, profit on investment for all manufacturing companies is at the level of eight per cent or below. Line

D shows corrected profits on sales for all manufacturing in the Treasury series. For most years this figure fluctuates between two and four per cent.

We have now examined the size of company profits in several perspectives and are in a position to compare the public's views with what the facts appear to show. The public thinks that manufacturers earn more than retailers. The evidence does not appear to sustain this view. In the Treasury series from 1938 to 1956, profit on investment for manufacturing averaged nine and one-tenth per cent and for retail trade eight and six-tenths per cent. This slight edge for manufacturing is more apparent than real because many small companies are engaged in retailing, and in these companies some confusion always exists on what should be called profit and what should be charged as wages for the owners. If, for the comparison between manufacturing and retail trade, officers' wages and profits could have been lumped together, the small difference indicated above would probably have disappeared.

In The First National City Bank tabulations for the period 1928 to 1959, profit on investment for manufacturing averages ten and one-half per cent compared with eleven and four-tenths per cent for all trade. Thus, in the larger and more successful firms where wages and profit accounting is more precise, earnings for trade appears to be a little above that for manufacturing.

The public believes that war contractors make more than manufacturers of civilian products. It is possible that this was true before World War II, but the evidence from the last conflict does not support it. Chart 5 shows that on an uncorrected basis, profit on both sales and investment declined steadily during the war years. Chart 6, giving a corrected version of profits, shows a declining curve for profits on sales, and a flat to declining curve for profit on investment. Voluntary profit restriction by companies, together with heavy taxation and price restriction and renegotiation, evidently kept company profits within market bounds in World War II.

The public has a strong penchant for believing that company

profits are not only large but are earned almost automatically. Eighty-seven per cent believe that in an average year, nearly every corporation makes a profit. Actually, in the boom leading up to 1929, forty to forty-five per cent of the corporations reporting to the Treasury lost money. In the boom following World War II, the number of companies reporting losses has again climbed back to approximately the forty per cent level. For every dollar gained in the period, 1920-1940, forty-five cents were lost. Since 1946, this loss ratio has been running at an average of 7.85 cents for every dollar gained, but would undoubtedly be higher if allowance were made for profit overstatement due to inventory and depreciation accounting.

In July 1951, *The Public Opinion Index* reported the public's average profit "guesstimate" at twenty-one cents per dollar of sale. Actually, for the ten year period 1949-1958, the Treasury reports profit at three and nine-tenths cents per dollar of sale and eight and six-tenths cents per dollar of investment for all manufacturing companies. The First National City Bank reports profits at six and one-tenth cents on sales and thirteen and four-tenths cents on investment. If these profit measures allowed for inventory and depreciation distortion, as calculated by the Department of Commerce, they would be reduced approximately twenty-eight per cent. Thus the public's idea of the size of company profit is fantastically inflated.

Whether or not the arithmetic of the public's views on profits agrees with the facts, large segments of the American people believe that companies make too much money, and that if they were content to earn less, the average man would be better off. In many minds, these views are buttressed by strong emotional conviction that the amount of profit is unfair and morally wrong. This belief generates support for militant unionism and for government regulation and control of the economy.

The facts are that industry operates on a very modest profit margin which must be preserved if the economy is to remain healthy and to grow. The dynamic of the American system is the use of capital to increase productivity. Savers and owners provide workmen with modern tools that bring about a continuous increase in output which is almost completely distributed in the form of higher wages and goods of better quality at lower prices. If the shareholder is denied an adequate reward for his contribution to this productive process, the collaboration between owner and employees that has been so fruitful in the past, will deteriorate and everyone will suffer.

CHAPTER FIVE

HOW COMPANIES EARN A PROFIT

How do companies earn a profit? The critics of profit-making say it is by a process of exploitation. Profits take something away from people. When one man makes a profit, it is always at the expense of his neighbor. Profit-making is said to be an expression of man's baser instincts. It is motivated by "money lust" and "insatiable greed." The capitalist grinds the faces of the poor, expropriates what really belongs to the worker (surplus value), cheats the customer by charging a "monopoly" or "administered price," misleads him by false advertising, despoils natural resources with no thought of conservation—in short, is an exploiter who operates on the theory of all take and no give.

Central to the thinking of critics of the profit-and-loss system is the idea that profits are practically an automatic accompaniment of doing business. They are regarded as a fixed part of the process. The enterpriser, sitting at an advantageous spot ("the economic narrows"), scoops off all the cream as the milk of trade flows past him. He is taking something that really belongs to the "people." His activities are basically predatory. Under capitalism, say the critics, production is for profit. If economic activity is to serve a social purpose, it should be operated on the principle of "production for use." The controlling idea ought to be, not how much money can be made by manufacturing and distributing goods, but what can be produced that will be useful to people and serve a good social end.

The finger of shame is often pointed at the profit maker. "Shame on United States Steel," says the United Steel Workers, for making "fantastic" profits and refusing to share them with its workers. Evidently the idea that profit making contributes to human betterment is not strongly imbedded in community thinking, for many organizations dedicated to the welfare of their fellow men prominently display the qualifying phrase, "A non-profit organization." No company, it seems, has deemed it advisable to announce itself to the public as "The XYZ Corporation, a Profit Making Company."

Modern psychology has demonstrated that two people may view the same phenomena but perceive them differently, because what they see "out there" is heavily influenced by their own conditioning. Certainly the description of the profit-making process supplied by the critics is not what the businessman experiences or sees. The businessman, like everyone else, views the world through his own preconceptions, but his testimony has some claim to validity because he moves and has his being in the hard world of profit reality. If his perceptions of the profit-making process are too imaginary, he not only suffers the pain and anguish of an operator with his world out of control, but he loses his cash.

The idea, for example, that there is a conflict between production for profit and production for use appears to the businessman to be downright naive. In order to make a profit, a company must be able to sell its goods to purchasers who presumably voluntarily buy in order to use. If a firm is able to make a profit in a competitive market, this is a sure indication that the consumers think the use value of the product justifies its cost; if there is a loss, it is a signal that many people think the product is not worth what it costs. Production for profit, in other words, is production for use, with the consumers themselves having the power to decide what is useful. It is probably of some significance that many of the writers who have urged the concept of production for use as an alternative to profit-making are of the view that the state is better able to judge the utility of goods than the consumers themselves.

In every occupation there are chiselers and cheats, and business is no exception. If one looks in the files of the Better Business Bureau and law enforcement agencies, he will find sordid cases of profits that have been made through fraud and misrepresentation, adulteration, short weight, and other shady practices. But most of the country's business is done by men who are sure that profits are not made through exploitation, but through service. "The customer must be satisfied." "The customer is always right." "Satisfaction or your money back." These are almost truisms in the business world. This the surest way to make a profit, and it provides the satisfactions of craftsmanship without which no job is worthwhile.

Every businessman must keep his eye on the profit indicator to know whether he is in tune with his publics, but actually he spends very little time counting his cash. On the contrary, in order to stay in business, most of his time and imagination must be spent in the search for better ways of serving his customers. How can he cut costs and lower prices? Can he make his product more dependable by changing the design or the technique of manufacture? How can he make his packaging more sanitary and attractive? What can he do to improve his service and distribution system? Is he spending enough money on research to develop new and better products for his customers? Above all, what does the customer want? What are his needs? What are his preferences in style, design, flavor, price? All progressive companies today lean heavily on market research to guide their manufacturing and marketing decisions. This, of course, is another way of saying that the controlling principle of profit-making is "Let the customer be served."

Harry Bullis, Chairman of General Mills, voiced a realistic point of view when he analyzed for the Northwest Mutual Life Underwriters Association the key to sales success. "When I go out in the morning," said Mr. Bullis, "I never ask, 'How many commissions can I make today?' I ask, 'How many people can I help today.' In this frame of mind, I can, with confidence, ask people for their time and attention, and by devoting my thought to their problems, I am able to earn larger commissions."

All sales experience bears out the Bullis theme. The secret of salesmanship—and profit making—is to produce a good product that meets a customer need, and sell it by demonstrating that this product will better satisfy the prospect than the product of the competition. Quite obviously, showmanship plays a part in selling, as it does in every other human activity, but the secret of selling is not razzle-dazzle, but consumer benefit.

The advertising studies of Gallup & Robinson provide a unique demonstration of the power of the service theme in selling. These studies show conclusively that the public rejects brag and boast advertising, but eagerly pursues advertising that reports news about products, demonstrates product features, indicates price, and tells what the product will do for the buyer. Madison Avenue speaks of this as the "you" element in advertising.

Two magazine ads that tested in the top bracket of effectiveness are shown. The one for Carnation Milk pictures a dish of strawberry shortcake with a generous helping of what in Grandma's day used to be called "whipped cream." The test evidence indicated that this rendition had high "appetite appeal," with many respondents commenting "Um, it looked delicious." The headline and copy talk pure consumer benefit: "Imagine! A milk that whips. This creamy looking shortcake topping is whipped Carnation Milk. Whips easily, quickly—yet the large serving above costs less than two cents."

The housewife who would like to serve her family strawberry shortcake with whipped cream, but who cannot afford it, finds a solution to her problem in the Carnation ad. So, too, the housewife who overeats, but is worried about calories. The ad provides an additional service for the reader by furnishing a recipe and a picture of the Carnation can to help the buyer identify it in the store.

The second ad is for the Westinghouse Steam Iron. The headline reads: "New Westinghouse Steam or Dry Iron Presses with

Wider Steam Path." The illustration shows fifteen steam vents arranged in the sole-plate to put more steam over a wider area, and thus enable the user to iron garments with less expenditure of time and energy. The small cut shows the open handle design which is said to ban wrist strain. The palm, it is explained,

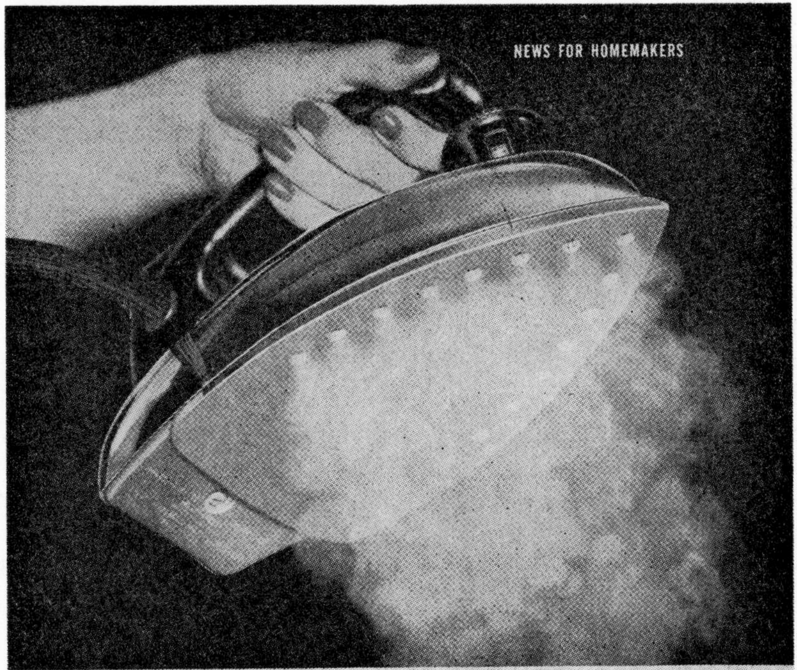

SECRET OF WESTINGHOUSE'S WIDER STEAM PATH is 15 steam vents scientifically placed in the wide soleplate of the new Westinghouse Steam or Dry Iron. These extra vents—more than used in any other iron—put more steam over a wider area for faster, more efficient ironing. Dramatic photograph, above, shows how the new Westinghouse Steam or Dry Iron turns one drop of water at a time into a mist-fine pressureless vapor that steams gently, continuously out of each of the 15 vents. New Iron retails for only $19.95.

NEW WESTINGHOUSE STEAM or DRY IRON PRESSES WITH WIDER STEAM PATH

OPEN HANDLE DESIGN bans wrist strain. Wrist stays relaxed and at ease. Palm spreads out over handle to take the weight.

New Iron Presses Skirt in 90 Seconds—Irons Slip in Half the Time!

More steam placed over a wider area, for perfect dampening and faster ironing, is the outstanding feature of a new Westinghouse lightweight steam or dry iron demonstrated on two network TV shows this week—Westinghouse Studio One and Professional Football.

Better dampening is assured, says Westinghouse, through the use of a wider soleplate with 15 scientifically spaced steam vents—more vents than currently used in other steam irons.

The extra vents, explains Westinghouse, can be compared to the openings in a sprinkler top. A housewife can dampen clothes faster and more evenly, over a greater area, with a sprinkler having a great many openings than she can with a sprinkler having only a few openings.

The new iron, which irons either steam or dry at the turn of a dial, bans wrist strain by way of an exclusive open handle design. Weight of the iron is 3½ lbs. empty; under 4 lbs. filled. The Westinghouse Iron uses ordinary tap water in all but exceptionally hard water areas. At only $19.95*, the new iron soon pays for itself in pressing bills alone.

spreads out over the handle to take the weight and the wrist stays relaxed and at ease. This, of course, is sales argument directed straight to consumer benefit.

The housewife's profession is her home and family. She is constantly on the lookout for foods that are nutritious, tasty, and easy to prepare. She likes color and beauty in her home, hence she is interested in product news about rugs, curtains, paint, colored towels, and other household accessories. Dishwashing, cleaning, bed making, laundering, and other homemaking chores become monotonous, so the housewife is constantly on the hunt for products that lessen drudgery and give her more leisure for social and cultural activities.

Vance Packard's book, *The Hidden Persuaders,* pictures advertising as sneaky, underhanded and menacing, playing on human weaknesses and frailties. The puppet masters it seems, use the awesome tools of psychiatry, to find out about the daydreams, misty human yearnings, and guilt complexes of the consuming public, then they pull the strings of symbol manipulation, and the great American public madly switch from Moggs to Boggs soap on a treadmill of frustration.

There is much that is objectionable about advertising. It frequently exaggerates its claims and is sometimes misleading and fraudulent. Too often it is silly, boring, and in bad taste. No advertiser has yet gone to the extremes of sending a peanut vendor down the aisles of a church during a religious ceremony crying "Peanuts, popcorn and candy bars," but they have occasionally intruded blatant commercialism where it does not belong.

Having said this, the evidence is clear that people like advertising and depend on it for news about products. In a test of housewives conducted by Gallup & Robinson, homemakers denounced fraudulent and boring advertising, but—ninety-nine per cent agreed that advertising is often helpful in giving people information about new products; eighty-six per cent agreed that some advertising is dishonest, but for the most part it is truthful; seventy-six per cent agreed that "advertising makes newspapers and magazines more interesting." The Gallup & Robinson tests on why people buy, show clearly that consumers are constantly looking for new and better ways to satisfy their needs, and that advertising is their primary source for news about a world of products that is both fascinating and wonderful.

The controlling concept of profit making, then, is not exploitation, but service in exchange for a price that presumably is mutually agreeable to both buyer and seller. So long as suppliers are competing in the market for public favor, service will continue to govern profit making, for any company that fails to please its customers will soon find its trade falling off, and its costs exceeding its income.

The businessman and the critic of the profit system are also in disagreement on the ease with which profits are made. In the businessman's experience, profits are seldom lush and there is certainly nothing automatic about them. Profits are the result of old-fashioned hard work, the willingness to take risks, a never-ending attention to detail, with perhaps a bit of luck thrown in. Consider what a business manager must do to earn a profit. First, he must have an idea for a product or a service that will meet a customer's need. Howard Johnson's restaurant chain, where a traveler can be sure of high quality food, was such an idea. So was George Romney's concept of the compact car or William Rentschler's idea for the "Candy-gram," which permits people to "wire" a box of chocolates along with a message of sentiment to a relative or a friend.

The American Machine and Foundry Company, which developed the automatic pinsetter for bowling alleys, and which is riding a great wave of prosperity as a result, has recently been surveying the sweeping changes that have occurred in its fortunes and making an effort to define what kind of company it is and wants to be. It has arrived at the answer that it must grow or die, hence it wishes to be "a growth company." The operating pattern for a growth company, says Chairman Morehead Patterson, is:

a. Find the need—have "a perception of requirement"
b. Develop a device that will fill the need
c. Have a man who knows the industry you plan to enter [1]

Good ideas do not come a dime a dozen; they are in short supply. Too often what seemed like a wonderful idea at the time turns out to be a resounding flop with loss instead of profit, and a humiliating deflation of management ego.

Having dreamed up what appears to be a good idea, it is necessary to spend time, money and effort to develop it. This requires capital and the willingness to take a chance. According to statistics of the Department of Commerce, the odds are one in two that a newly established or acquired firm will last two years under the same management. The odds decline to one in five that the firm will last ten years under the same management.[2] When a man takes his life's savings to open a little machine shop or gives up a good paying job to go into business for himself, he is likely to experience a moment of visceral tension that calls for inner conviction and steadfastness of purpose to control. Some of the same feeling, no doubt, grips the directors of a large corporation when they vote to commit twenty or fifty million dollars to a new and uncertain venture.

In addition to finding capital, it is necessary to hire and train people to put a new project into being. Fitting the round pegs into the round holes and square pegs into square holes on the personnel roster is a never-ending puzzle. Aptitude tests are of help in some instances, but a great deal of trial and error invariably takes place before a competent industrial team can be welded together. Dealing with this human equation calls for leadership of the highest order.

After the people are hired, it is necessary to produce and inventory the product. Every new product is cursed with "bugs." No matter how expert the designers, or how experienced the production men, something invariably goes wrong. A part is made of the wrong alloy; the packaging isn't quite right; the flavor is a bit too sweet. Testing may be elaborate and thorough, yet the "bugs" slip through. As Stanley C. Allyn, Chairman of National Cash Register says, "No laboratory test can ever take the place of a human finger pressing down on the key of a cash register." When trouble appears, products have to be called back or adjustments made, to the chagrin of the manufacturer and loss to his pocketbook.

While the product is being manufactured, the businessman must organize his dealerships, run test marketing programs in selected cities, retain an advertising agency, find a sales theme that will interest his audience, buy media time and space, and finally conduct his sales campaign. Then he must collect his bills, pay his taxes, and hope there is something left over for profit. Manufacturing companies crossed the finish line with an aggregate profit of 3.9c per dollar of sales and 8.6c per dollar of investment for the decade ending in 1958. The idea that profits are lush and automatic, then, is more a figment of imagination than a fact.

The profit maker asks no indulgence for his struggle to make a profit. It is the businessman's job to create ideas, take risks, employ people, produce and distribute goods—to manage the private sector of the nation's economy with all the headaches and harassments that this responsibility involves. Since managerial talent is long on demand and short on supply, the businessman is well paid for the work he does. Whenever he tires of his assignment he is quite free to quit and take a job more to his liking. Similarly, the opportunity is presented to anyone who thinks profit making is simple and easy to try his hand at reaping the golden harvest. The market is quite impartial. The only test it imposes is the test of consumer acceptance. To succeed, the consumer must be served. It is about as simple as that.

Not all companies are equally successful in running the profits race. In every industry there are low cost producers, high cost and marginal producers, and some in between. Economists describe this situation as "the entrepreneurial cost differential," which is a learned way of saying that some companies can produce goods cheaper than other companies. This is a key idea in explaining how companies make profits, and one which is of great significance to every consumer.

Entrepreneurial differential costs are illustrated in Chart 7. In a hypothetical industry it is assumed that there are eleven producers, each with different costs. All of these companies are assumed to be making a nearly identical product, selling competitively at a fairly uniform price.[3] The demand is such that people are willing to buy the product at one dollar a unit. The diagram shows that the marginal producer, whose costs are equal to the selling price, is just breaking even. A few companies, the sub-marginal ones, are incurring losses. Some companies are making medium profits, while others are making very large profits.

Chart 7

ENTREPRENEURIAL DIFFERENTIAL COSTS

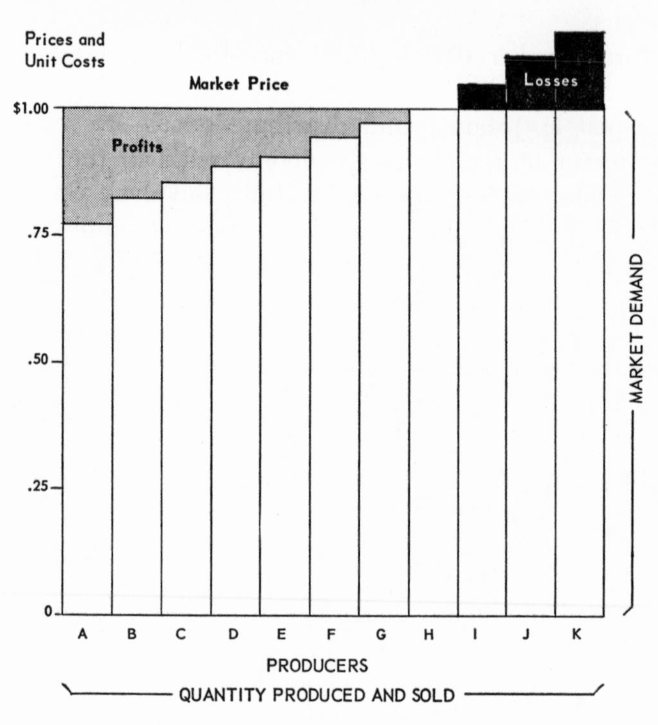

Diagram from ECONOMIC INTELLIGENCE, Chamber of Commerce of the Chamber of Commerce of the United States, September 1959.

What does this mean to the consumer? It means that the profitable companies have found ways to produce and distribute goods cheaper than their competition. They are using human and other resources with greater skill—their personnel is superior, their location is better, their manufacturing techniques are more advanced, and their buying and distributing methods are more efficient. It is likely, too, that the profit makers are spending larger sums of money than their competitors to find and develop new and better products and to engineer low cost methods for their manufacture. The dealers of the profitable companies are likely to be more substantial and equipped to give good service. The employees of the profit makers probably have good job benefits and a high degree of job security.

Sooner or later the high cost and marginal producers must mend their ways, get new blood and new ideas, up-date their manufacturing and distributing methods, and make products closer to the customer's needs and desires. When that happens, price, quality, and service competition is likely to intensify, with each company trying to out-do the other in satisfying the consumer. The result is a consumer bonanza with more and better things for less.

The entrepreneurial differential cost curve works for the consumer in another way. Almost every company is on the lookout for new and profitable fields to enter. When a low-cost producer in any given field makes substantial profits, he inevitably attracts competition. Price tends to go down, quality and service improve, and profits decline to the point at which it is no longer attractive for new firms to enter. Over and over again, elements in this cycle have been repeated—in penicillin, television, the compact car, and thousands of other cases.

So it makes no economic sense to say, "Shame on the high profit maker." In a competitive market, the high profit maker is truly the buyer's best friend, for it is he who pioneers the way toward better products at lower cost. So long as buyers can shop around in a market with more than one supplier and choose between independent offerings, large profits are a very real measure, not of exploitation, but of service rendered.

The notion that profits are lush and a more-or-less automatic feature of the capitalistic system leads to grave errors in the formulation of social policy. Profits are thought of as a huge and ill-begotten hoard which is cached in the strong boxes of the rich, but which really belong to the people. Therefore, tax away the profit or expropriate the property so that all the people can have a share of the profits.

The fallacy in this proposition is that profit making is an economic process, not something that can be expropriated. Profits are not a hoard; they are a measure of the success or failure of the production and distribution process. In a capitalistic society, profit making is based on certain institutions—private property, incentive, free markets, competition, and a legal framework that enforces law and order and sets the rules of the competitive game. The process is changed when the conditions under which it operates are altered. When graduated taxes limit gains, entrepreneurs are less inclined to take risks. When the price mechanism is thrown out of gear by government imposition of ceilings and floors, the profit system is no longer able to speed up the production machinery or slow it down as the consumer directs.

When properties are expropriated and operated by the government, the profit-making process disappears and the political process takes over, with different organizational and administrative techniques and different values for measuring the failure or success of the operation.

One fact seems clear: When the political process takes over, profits have a bad habit of disappearing. The lush hoard that belongs to all the people somehow dissolves into thin air. Prices rise to defray increased costs, and service deteriorates. Income falls short of outgo, and deficits are made up out of taxes.

One case study that illustrates the problems involved in capturing profits for the people by substituting the political for the profit-making process is Mexico's expropriation of the British and American oil companies in 1938. Under Porfirio Diaz, the Mexican government sought to hasten industrialization by granting attractive mineral concessions to foreign capital. Diaz increased the material prosperity of Mexico, but his regime was marked by repression and discontent, particularly over the concentration of land ownership. At one time it was said that one-fifth of the land mass of Mexico was owned by seventeen persons.[4]

In 1936, the Syndicate of Petroleum Workers made what the oil companies thought were extravagant demands for increased wages and benefits. The companies refused to agree to the union contract, and in May 1937 the workers struck. Under Mexican law the dispute quickly went to compulsory arbitration, and the workers resumed their posts. A year later, the arbitration commission made a report that roundly condemned the principal oil companies. The companies, said the Commission, had displayed alien and sometimes opposing interests to those of the country; they were failing to cooperate in the social progress of Mexico and were interfering with the nation's political life; they were exploiting the country's rich subsoil, leaving only wages and taxes in Mexico; they were making enormous profits, estimated at sixteen and eighty-one one hundredths per cent on invested capital for the years 1934-1936.[5] The Commission concluded that the past earnings and future prospects of the oil companies warranted granting the employees' demands. The companies demurred, whereupon the government, under President Cardenas, nationalized the oil properties, setting up Petroleos Mexicano, or Pemex, as it is called, to run the industry for the government.

The statistics of the Mexican oil industry tell an interesting story of what happened. In 1920 oil production in Mexico reached a high of 193,398,000 barrels. By 1938, because of world economic conditions and a hostile political environment, production sank to 38,506,000 barrels. For eight years after expropriation, national production remained below 50,000,000 barrels, then a belated rise started, reaching 99,000,000 barrels in 1958. The drilling of exploratory wells described a similar curve. From 1938 to 1946, exploratory wells averaged six per year. During the next six years, the average number rose to 37; by 1953-1957, the average number had reached 112.

Set against world trends in the oil industry, Mexico, under Pemex management, has declined from seventh to eleventh place as an oil producer. It has failed to keep pace with domestic demand, and has dropped from its former position of exporter to one of net importer of oil. The development of the spectacular field of petro-chemicals, which has characterized North American and European oil companies, has in Mexico almost gone by default.

All this caused Mexico's energetic President, Adolfo Lopez Mateos, to attempt a reform of the industry. Until recently, Pemex has held a special position in the eyes of Mexicans. It was at once a source of national pride and a symbol of better things to come. Every filling station in Mexico carries the motto: "In the Nation's Service." Until now, criticism of Pemex has seemed almost unpatriotic.

The veil was torn from Pemex in a series of newspaper articles by Antonio Vargas MacDonald, noted Mexican scholar and long-time technical adviser to the President.[6] As the newly appointed press secretary or public relations official of the company, Senor Vargas MacDonald undertook to tell the story of Pemex's accomplishments and its bad management in order to force the issue of Pemex's reform. Even though Pemex has obviously resolved to purge itself of bad practices, the facts seem to endorse the suspicion that politics and efficient management somehow do not mix.

According to Antonio Vargas MacDonald, Pemex's image of itself has been that of patron of all good causes, some of them not remotely connected with running an efficient oil industry. As a patron of "labor," the company has entered into labor contracts that have been unfavorable to it. It has seldom resisted the demand for higher wages and more and greater fringe benefits. It has indirectly subsidized popular transportation and small farming, and it has directly subsidized the production of fertilizers. It has contributed to the black fly campaign—and, as Vargas MacDonald puts it, "One cannot fail but be surprised that it is not made to contribute to some society for the prevention of cruelty to shrimp." "When the cow belonged to someone else," says Public Relations Adviser Vargas MacDonald, "we were content with whatever milk it would give us. . . . Now, we bleed it to death. After all, it is ours."

The basic trouble with Pemex is that, to the Mexican governing classes, it represents a conquest, not a business. The workers took part in the conquest, successfully vanquishing the English and American "outsiders" who had invested considerable capital in the development of the Mexican oil fields. "After the conquest," says Vargas MacDonald, "comes the booty."

Some of the booty has been taken in the form of corruption. Where employment in the Mexican oil fields used to be contracted for, it is now frequently sold as a favor. An aspiring oil worker has had to pay from six thousand to fifteen thousand pesos to get a job. It has been worth it to him, for he has been able to recoup his original outlay—and them some!—by collecting for overtime hours that were not worked, and by taking extra paid vacations in the form of fictitious illnesses. Meanwhile, proletarian leaders who have intervened to get their followers accredited to the Pemex payroll have retired on their "pay-offs." In the Mexico of 1959, the cynical word is that "the old ideologists are either dead or have made fortunes."

Some of the Pemex bosses have used their economic power to establish themselves as political tyrants. In the Poza Rica de Hidalgo district in the State of Vera Cruz, a company superintendent used his position to build up a strong labor machine. Company money has been spent to support whatever political maneuvers or candidates the superintendent favored.

In Tampico, corrupt employees permitted valuable equipment to rust in the tropical rains. Then they sold it as scrap to friends on the outside, splitting the proceeds with their chosen conspirators. On the inside, Pemex has been flagrantly overstaffed and riddled with featherbedding practices. Two men have frequently been assigned to work which one man could easily handle. According to Antonio Vargas MacDonald, Pemex could cut its payrolls by some two hundred million pesos—or sixteen million dollars—without endangering either its production of oil or the quality of its services.

Not being subject to market competition, Pemex has aimed at a deliberate give-away of its products on the theory that the business of a nationalized industry is to make things easy for other industries. It has sold Diesel oil at twenty-one per cent less than production cost. Mexican industrialists have fallen into the habit of using Diesel oil in place of ordinary fuel oil to fire vats and bread ovens, and ordinary folks have even fed it into their stoves. Since Diesel oil represents an upgraded product especially designed for use in complicated internal combustion motors, this represents a sheer waste of labor. It is as if Pemex's customers had been handed banknotes at a discount that would make them cheaper than matches in lighting their cigars.

Because of the scandals in Pemex, President, Lopez Mateos, has decreed a change. But the sanctified malpractices of many years will make it difficult to effect a cure as long as Pemex is sheltered, by its position as a favored government monopoly, from having to earn a profit or shut up shop. On the one hand, there are its high labor costs; on the other, there is the fact that it has not been permitted to accumulate a surplus to provide for long-range planning and for new investment. As for reforming its price policy, that must prove difficult in a nation where farmers and taxi drivers—to say nothing of the nationalized railroads—have become accustomed to special cut rates.

It might, of course, be argued that Pemex is a special case, reflecting local conditions, and that no basic deductions can be drawn from it. But the experience of England with its nationalized industries roughly parallels that of Mexico with its governmental oil monopoly. The nationalized British gas companies have been losing customers; the nationalized coal mines have discovered that a sizable portion of their product—the "small" coal—is unsaleable. As for the nationalized transport industry, it incurred a deficit of eleven and nine tenths million pounds in 1954; by 1959 the annual deficit had risen to eighty-four million pounds, which had to be absorbed by the Treasury and paid for out of taxes.[7]

In the British iron and steel industry, which was nominally nationalized for a short period during the last days of Labour Party majority power, government ownership did not last long enough to change things. The Labour Party could not figure out a quick way of regrouping the extremely complicated constituent elements of an industry which makes everything from girders to nails, and from high-grade alloys to plain tin plate. As a reluctant tribute to the accomplishments of the private citizens who had built a most efficient industry, the Labour government left all managements intact for the time being. "Ownership" was vested in a public holding company which took over all private stock issues, and when the Conservatives returned to power, it was a comparatively easy matter to resell the stock to private investors. Thus the high tide of nationalization in England was reached and turned just short of doing irreparable damage to an industry which had always had a progressive record under private management.

Operation of the economy by the political process may, as its advocates insist, lift the national spirit and produce a different kind of "economic justice," but the record shows that it does not make for productive efficiency. The difficulty, as Ludwig von Mises has pointed out, stems from the organizational character of the process: socialism has no satisfactory method of economic calculation.[8]

In a competitive economy, buyers and sellers mutually agree on the price at which exchange can take place. If the prices that add up to income exceed the prices that add up to cost, the supplier makes a profit. By watching the profit indicator, the supplier can always know whether he is in tune with his market. In a Socialist economy there is no market to guide decision making. Public policy has value, but it is difficult to measure. The will of the people, which is transmitted almost instantaneously in a profit-making society, is slowed down and frequently lost in the bureaucratic maze.

When authority and responsibility are delegated in the political process, the assignment must be accompanied by elaborate instructions. Codes, directives, and statutes are at hand to tell the government official what to do if a problem arises. On-the-spot discretion is limited. The first duty of the political functionary is to comply with the regulations. The premium is not in finding the most appropriate solution, but in following the rule book. There is little opportunity and no reward for taking a big gamble on new and untried ideas that might bring real benefits to the community. Responsibility is diffused and decision making is slowed down. Payrolls are frequently loaded with employees who have political pull but little qualification for the work. Under Civil Service, once an employee has tenure, it is almost impossible to disconnect him from the payroll even though he is a misfit or is no longer able to perform his duties efficiently.

Some government bureaus, because of the dedication and experience of their personnel, manage the public's affairs efficiently and well. In national defense, great forward strides have been made by giving scientists liberal budgets and latitude with which to work. But, because of its administrative characteristics, the political process can never organize an economy as efficiently or be as responsive to the public will as the profit-making process.

Bureaucracy, however, is not the sole prerogative of government. It is incipient in every organization, and sometimes flowers profusely in large corporations. But in a competitive economy, bureaucratic inefficiencies never last long. The high-cost producer loses sales to the low-cost producer, profit margins decline and corrective action is taken or the company goes bankrupt.

Perhaps the best way to learn how a company makes a profit, whether by exploitation or service, is to examine one company in some detail. The National Homes Corporation of Lafayette, Indiana, a relatively young company, may be taken for this purpose. It was established in 1940 by James and George Price. James Price left Indiana University in his junior year because of the depression. He drifted into real estate and soon found his big idea—low cost housing. In 1939, he set up the firm of Price and Price to become a dealer-builder for Gunnison Homes, which was then the principal producer of prefabricated units. In short order, Price became Gunnison's biggest dealer, but his passion from the beginning was for efficient, low cost, mass produced homes. The Gunnison product, he felt, was aimed at the carriage trade, too high on the economic scale.

So Jim Price scraped up a few thousand dollars from his own savings and from local investors, and in July 1940, with his brother George, set up National Homes in a 50 x 100-foot plant in Lafayette. The war came, and the company went heavily into the building of emergency housing, scoring the impressive record of 4,500 homes by the end of 1945. The Prices had hired some young engineers to run their small plant in Lafayette, but they became ensnarled in production difficulties. In January 1944, the brothers took over the complete management of the operation. A month later, just as the company was getting its tangled affairs straightened out, an explosion occurred in the lacquer department, killing three men and burning down the plant. With great determination, Jim and George collected additional capital and credit to build a new plant and resumed production in the short space of five months.

Looking forward to a post-war building boom, the Prices sold their first issue of unlisted stock, enlarged their plant and began building a dealer organization. But the enterprise soon encountered strong headwinds and rough business waters. The customer was willing to buy a prefabricated house if the price was right. Archaic building codes and hostility from the labor unions were bothersome, but could be overcome. The difficulties came from two unexpected sources. Builders, accustomed to on-site construction, looked on prefabs with a jaundiced eye. "We were as popular as the measles," says Jim Price. "No legitimate builder wanted our houses."

The conservative attitude of the bankers and other lenders threw up a second roadblock. Housing is sold largely on installment terms; and, without a satisfactory flow of credit, a builder cannot operate. To solve this problem, the Prices set up National Homes Acceptance Corporation to finance mortgages and got a line of credit of $1,800,000. This, of course, was but a drop in the bucket, and the Prices turned to a New York bank for further credit. When this was refused, they went to the Reconstruction Finance Corporation and got a loan of $6,500,000. Thereafter a group of banks got together and furnished the young company with loans at an interest rate below that of the R.F.C. By 1960 National Home Acceptance Corporation had a credit line of $45,000,000.

In 1948, National Homes introduced the Thrift House to sell at $6,000 and by 1950, production was running at nearly 10,000 per year. The recession of 1951 caused a sharp decline in housing starts, but National's sales rose slightly over the preceding year.

Then near disaster engulfed the company. Coming home from a hunting trip, the Company plane crashed short of the Lafayette airfield. Three men were killed, George was badly burned, and Jim's injuries sent him to the hospital for four months. But the Prices were not easily defeated, and Jim hobbled back to the job, bought another company airplane, and started planning the company's most ambitious house, The Ranger.

To design this house, Jim secured the services of Charles M. Goodman, one of the country's outstanding specialists in contemporary architecture. The Ranger was introduced in 1953. It was an attractive house of functional style, but did not break any sales records. Price modified the design to make it more conservative. National's sales continued to climb slowly, but prices were rising (the average price rose from $12,300 in 1954 to $13,700 in 1955) and low income buyers were being forced out of the market.

Price decided to redesign his houses toward more conservative lines and in 1957 came out with a new line of Cape Cod and

Crowd standing in line to see the new National Viking low cost aluminum house. If profit making is exploitation, as the critics declare, this caption might ironically read: Crowd standing in line to be exploited by the National Homes Corporation.

National Viking aluminum home in $8,000 price class—land additional —for owners with income as low as $87 per week.

National Viking aluminum home, $13,000 price class.

Colonial designs to sell in the twelve to fifteen thousand dollar range. Sales continued to be sticky and Price drastically overhauled the line. He lopped off the frills of his cheapest houses to cut the price to the bone, and redesigned the units to reduce on-site labor costs. The new Fairlane line, as it was called, was offered at ten to twelve thousand dollars, a price which could be managed by a person making seventy-five dollars a week. At first, sales continued to be slow but when, early in 1958, Congress made more mortgage money available, sales rose sharply and reached a record 23,826 for the year.

In the pursuit of low-cost housing, National Homes has worked with all materials—wood, gypsum board, plastics, and metals. In 1958 it put its first aluminum house, the Viking, on the market. Made up of aluminum sheathing side walls and roofs, the Viking comes with its finish baked on at the plant, which means freedom from outside maintenance for the natural life span of the house. There is no corrosion, no paint flaking, and no high original painting cost at the site. The Viking caught on immediately and in 1959 three out of four single unit buyers from National Homes chose an aluminum house.

In 1958, National Homes expanded into a new area by organizing the Kahler Craft Homes Corporation to produce the "you finish it" type of home. National supplies the shell, the builder-dealer erects it, and the purchaser finishes the interior. Considerable savings in home building can be obtained this way by families who have the skills and are willing to spend their leisure time on home construction.

With sales momentum gaining, Jim and George Price decided the time had come to spread National Homes over the United States. In 1959 they engineered a merger with five other leading prefabricators. Through this merger, National's annual sales increased over night from $65,000,000 to $94,000,000, and lifted its share of the prefabricated market from one-third to one-half.

These acquisitions were challenged almost immediately with a civil antitrust suit brought by the Department of Justice. The government contends that within the line of commerce represented by prefabricated housing, the mergers substantially lessen competition and tend to create a monopoly. The company's answer is that National Homes must compete not only with suppliers of prefabricated houses, but with every contractor and developer in the home building industry, and that the company's three and four-tenths per cent share of the market could hardly be called a monopoly.

How can we account for the growth of prefabrication and

National Homes? What does the company have that interests customers and causes them to buy its product? The answers to these questions are not hard to find. The Price brothers sensed a consumer need and figured out a way to satisfy it. The consumer need was quality low-cost housing. The need was for both beauty and value. The original Price houses were not triumphs of aesthetic beauty. They were boxy and utilitarian. National houses retain their high utility value, but they now come in many combinations and are well designed. It would take an alert and ingenious inspector to distinguish a National Homes prefabricated product from a custom-built house down the street.

The Prices built value into their houses in many ways. They are probably the largest buyers of building materials in the United States, hence can purchase quality products at the lowest price. Prefabrication, before the Price brothers came along, had been largely a matter of precutting materials in the factory. The practice at the time was to dump precut beams and siding on the building site for local carpenters to nail up. With the Prices, precutting and assembling in the factory have undergone a fantastic evolution; huge multiple saws perform ten operations in one, nailing machines do in a minute what scores of carpenters used to do in an hour. And now with aluminum taking the place of wood, highly efficient metal working machines continue to keep hand labor cost at the minimum. When orders for homes come in, the fabrication and assembly of some six hundred to nine hundred pieces is begun. The complex flow of pieces is controlled by an electronic computer so that the right pieces in the right numbers will arrive at the shipping dock at the same time.

The package is loaded on tractor trailers and hauled to the building site. The exterior walls of a National house arrive with insulation and windows already installed; plumbing comes precut. The shell is up by quitting time on the first day on location, thereby eliminating possible weather damage. Three weeks later the interiors are done, the house is painted, the utility lines are connected, and the owner can move in.

But prefabricated housing, as the Prices quickly learned, is more than manufacturing; its success is heavily dependent on the solution of land development, finance, and sales techniques. To all these aspects of the business as well as manufacturing, the Price brothers brought great persistence and ingenuity. As the system now works, a builder-dealer secures a piece of undeveloped land at a favorable location in or adjacent to a city. The site experts of National Homes help him lay out the ground and engineer the roads and sewers. The financial subsidiaries of the company lend the builder-dealer fifty per cent of the land cost and seventy-five per cent of the cost of utilities. For every house and lot the builder-dealer sells, National advances the money to develop two more lots. The builder-dealer is content with a small mark-up because he is selling houses in volume.

When the site is completed and the first houses are up, a gala opening with local advertising, flags, and a general carnival atmosphere is staged. People come from miles around to inspect the new homes, and in one development over a weekend as many as 192 houses have been sold. In order to smooth out the production curve, National started holding gala openings in January and, in the first month of 1959, 8,500 units were sold ahead. This maneuver helped cut overhead, made jobs at the factory more regular and increased profits.

The saving in the purchase of a home from National varies by geographical area, depending on labor costs, the keenness of competition, and other factors. In Chicago, to take one example, a National Fairlane house with three bedrooms and a bath, totaling about nine hundred square feet of living space, costs $10,809. The price tag for a comparable house built by conventional methods is $12,754. Thus the buyer saves almost two thousand dollars or sixteen per cent on his home purchase. He gets a guarantee of one year and, dealing with a substantial builder, he knows that any defects will be made good without argument.[9]

National Homes has sold approximately two hundred thousand homes in its nineteen years of existence, which adds up to about one-half billion dollars worth of housing. What profit did it make from this gigantic effort? In the past ten years profits have averaged five cents per dollar of sale and eighteen cents per dollar of investment. This is about at the norm for profit on sales for all manufacturing and considerably above the norm for profit on investment. To earn these profits in this fiercely competitive industry, it had to invent superior techniques of manufacture, develop new methods of financing, and organize a highly efficient sales and distribution system.

The magic of competitive profit making in a capitalistic society is that it benefits everyone—stockholders, employees, buyers, the community. National Homes has plowed most of its earnings back into the business and has paid practically no dividends. The stockholders who numbered almost 7,246 by the end of 1959, are not complaining because the book value of their property has risen five hundred fifty per cent over the past ten years.

The Price family owns approximately twenty per cent of the company's shares. At recent market prices, these shares were worth approximately $10,000,000. So, for their foresight and hard work, the Price brothers have been well paid. Starting with nothing, they have arrived at affluence in the short span of nineteen years. If money were their only goal, they could quit now and live luxuriously for the rest of their days. But they show no signs of quitting; on the contrary, says Jim Price, they are nowhere near the end of their expansion plans for National. Just as artists take satisfaction in their painting or their music, the Prices evidently experience great recompense in watching an institution like National Homes grow, prosper, and serve its publics.

The Prices have been strongly motivated by the dream of profits, but they certainly do not present the stereotyped picture of exploiters whose lives are ruled by "money lust" and "insatiable greed."

The National Homes enterprise has been good for the worker. It has created approximately three thousand jobs at its factories and many more in supplier and related industries. Its factory operatives, mostly unskilled, earn an average of sixteen dollars a day. Employees receive paid vacations in relation to length of service and fringe benefits such as life, accident, and hospital insurance for which the company pays half. After service of one year, employees may purchase a National house at ten per cent discount and company stock at one-third discount up to ten per cent of the preceding year's wages. After five years of service, the employee may purchase stock at fifty per cent of its declared value. National's factory employees belong to the United Brotherhood of Carpenters and Joiners, American Federation of Labor. Since its founding the company has never had a strike.

The National Homes buyer has been well served because he has been able to purchase an expertly designed and well built home at a very attractive price. One good measure of the standard of living of a people is the number of minutes' work they are required to trade for bread, shoes, clothing, automobiles, and other products they buy. In Chicago, a buyer earning $75 a week, could acquire a National home in exchange for 144 weeks of work.

The community also has been served in many ways by National Homes. Nearly two hundred thousand families have found shelter under a National Homes roof. Good architecture and trim design, together with variations in components, have brought beauty in housing and have helped to alleviate the awful sameness that characterizes some low-cost housing developments. With land improvement, tax revenues have been created that help to pay for schools, roads, and other city conveniences. In the ten year period ending in 1959, the company paid $26,600,000 in Federal income taxes, a sum amounting to fifty-two per cent of its gross earnings before taxes.

National Homes is only a small factor in the building industry. A thousand other home building companies could have been used as examples of how profit making is linked with human welfare. By the nature of the process, companies must serve the consumer and meet his needs or there can be no profits. It is possible that profits have been disassociated from welfare in many minds because the activities of companies are reported in cold, emotionless dollar figures. In the annual reports of companies appear entries for sales, costs, earnings, cash, receivables, liabilities, long term debt, book value of shares, etc. Since business is essentially relations between people, there are human stories in back of each of these entries.

In the past fifteen years a radical change has occurred in stockholder journalism. From the stiff, formal, brief and unattractive reports of a few years ago have evolved reports that are highly readable and informative. Accounting data are presented in simplified terms, interpretation of business trends is being supplied, product lines are discussed, graphs and pictures now accompany the text, and the reader is informed about the problems of the business and how they are being solved.

Possibly the annual reports of companies need to give more emphasis to "the social balance sheet." How does all this economic activity benefit people as people? What did last year's sales mean in the lives of consumers? How was living made better, more comfortable and cheaper? How were services improved? What is on the drawing boards for the future? What will these new products do for people?

How many persons were employed and what were their conditions of employment? What is the company doing to provide opportunity? How is the company helping its employees to improve their job status and earnings?

What is the company contributing to community life? How do its wage payments and material procurements flow through the economic pipelines of the community? How have its tax monies helped to pay for schools, roads, and community services?

A company is not an eleemosynary institution. It is an economic organization set up to seek a profit by serving its publics. It must, by the nature of its being, devote its energies to income producing activities. Its revenue must be greater than its costs or it fails. Profit is its chief guide, although it is obviously not its only guide. Profit must be made in a social value system that penalizes adulteration and fraud and frowns on the maltreatment of persons. Companies will serve their publics best if, within the rules, they strive to improve their profit record, for higher profits most likely mean lower costs, new inventions, or better customer service.

There is a crying need, however, for better interpretation of the profit-making process. It is ironic in the extreme that capitalism, which has made the American standard of living the envy of peoples all over the world, is so widely misunderstood and so roundly denounced. Companies can accept a great deal of the blame for this for they have failed to interpret their activities adequately. One of the keys to better interpretation is to show how the profit-making process performs the jobs that the consumers want done, and how it can help people achieve their economic aspirations for the future.

CHAPTER SIX

WHAT CORPORATIONS DO WITH PROFITS

Almost everyone knows that corporations use profits for two purposes: first, to compensate stockholders for the use of their money, i.e., pay dividends; and second, to strengthen the business by building or modernizing the plant, buying new machinery, or increasing working capital.

In 1958, eighty per cent of the earnings of manufacturing companies were paid out in dividends. Chart 8 shows the record for dividend payments for all manufacturing companies from 1922 to 1958. In the boom years leading up to 1929, the payout averaged seventy per cent, with the trend rising sharply. Throughout the depression years 1930-1935, manufacturing companies made dividend payments greatly in excess of their earnings. In 1933, for example, approximately four dollars was paid out for every dollar earned. For the six year depression period, 1930-1935, manufacturing companies paid out $11,580,000,000 in dividends, but earned only $2,974,000,000. This "dis-saving" of $8,705,000,000 consumed all of the net earnings that manufacturing companies had accumulated in the previous eight years.

During World War II, the curve of dividend payments fell precipitously, reaching a low of forty-one per cent of earnings in 1947-1948. In adopting this tight-fisted dividend policy, boards of directors were actuated by a number of reasons. Capital had been depleted during the depression years. Price inflation required more dollars to finance new purchases and carry inventories. Companies needed capital to replace worn-out machinery and expand plants to meet the post-war demand. The legislation creating the Securities Exchange Commission made external financing more laborious and costly. Corporate taxes had risen from fifteen per cent in 1937 to forty per cent in 1942, thus increasing the penalty of double taxation. When earnings took the dividend route, the government exacted a corporate tax plus a normal and a graduated surtax on the investors income. When earnings took the route of reinvestment, the corporate tax still had to be paid, but the investor could realize his gains through increase in the value of his stock which, when sold, carried a capital gains tax of only twenty-five per cent.

Since 1948, as Chart 8 shows, the curve of dividend payments has been rising, with the payout averaging fifty-nine per cent for the ten-year period ending in 1958.

Dividend policies vary greatly by industry, by company, and by the changing circumstances of the times. In the ten-year period, 1948-1957, the electric and gas industry paid out all of its taxable earnings. Rate-making commissions normally try to restrict public utility profits to a level somewhat above interest rates, hence most of the profit in this industry must be used to pay dividends. To keep up with a growing, and more demanding, population, public utilities are constantly in the money markets for new capital, and a liberal dividend policy is one way to attract the needed funds.

Tobacco, with relatively stable earnings, has paid out sixty-three per cent of profits over the past decade. The chemical industry has prospered and grown on a sixty-six per cent payout. Industries with the lowest percentage of dividend payout include construction (twenty-seven per cent), furniture and fixtures

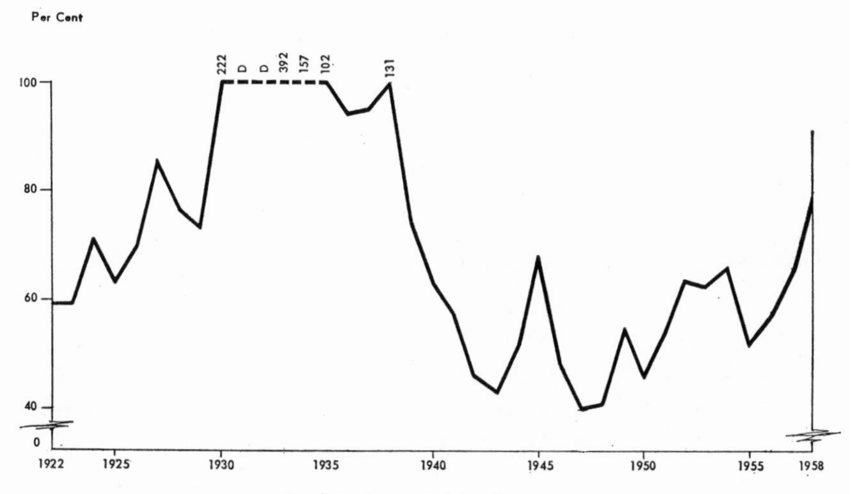

(thirty-nine per cent), and wholesale trade (thirty-five per cent).[1]

The circumstances that dictate the dividend policies of companies are as complex as the economy itself. A company that has suffered losses stops payments and, on the resumption of earnings, restores dividends with great caution. A growing company reinvests its earnings and pays no dividends for years in the expectation of stockholder rewards in the future. A company heavily owned by a single interest pays a token cash dividend but declares liberal stock dividends, thus permitting the company to retain its earnings and the stockholder to minimize the penalties of double taxation.

The primary key to dividend policy, however, should and must always be stockholder interest. Investors entrust their money to managements, not for fun, but for monetary gain. They perform an important economic service in saving capital and putting it at risk to increase the nation's productivity. They demand, and are entitled to, adequate compensation for their contribution; their reward comes in dividends and growth in the value of their investment.

Investors, like other people, develop certain spending habits, and gear their lives to dividend expectancies. As a consequence, boards of directors put great stress on the continuity of dividend payments, setting the rate at a level which can likely be maintained over the longest period of time. It is for this reason that dividend payments markedly lag the ups and downs of earnings. In his study, "Corporate Income Retention—1915-1943," Sergei Dobrovolsky found that, on the average, each dollar of increased earnings was allocated twenty-eight to thirty cents to dividends and seventy to eighty cents to reinvestment. By the same token, when earnings were contracting, dividend payments were cut twenty to thirty cents on the average and reinvestment was decreased seventy to eighty cents.

Because of the depression, manufacturing corporations made no net capital gains during the period 1922 to 1935. Now they are plowing back a little more than half (fifty-nine per cent in the decade ending in 1958) of their profits for use in the business.

In the profits debate, the union contends that reinvestment of earnings is bad. Profits that are plowed back, they say, are taken out of the hides of the workers in decreased wages and out of the pockets of consumers in increased prices. The union calls reinvested earnings "inequity capital." The worker and consumer, says the union, are involuntarily investors who have nothing to say about the way their "investments" are managed. In his recent debate with the automobile companies, Walter Reuther put it this way: "Through extortionate prices, the American consumers have made compulsory investments to finance the expansion of these three giant (automobile) corporations without receiving any equity in them, or any return on their involuntary investment." [2]

In union literature, capital is pictured as an exploiter and oppressor. The workers make the wealth but capital, as symbolized by the repulsive character in the cartoon in Chapter One, takes it away from them unjustly. Capital is not a friend of the workingman; it is his foe who must be overcome through the class struggle. This is an exceedingly perverse view of capital and capitalists and needs examination.

We live in a comfortable world in modern homes, equipped with running hot and cold water and almost miraculous electrical instruments that sweep our rugs, preserve and cook our food, wash our clothes and dishes and, at the twist of a dial bring us worldwide information and entertainment. If we wish to travel, we step into a luxurious car, bus, train, boat, or airplane and journey to our destination. If we are in need of food, we drive to an elegant supermarket with shelves bulging with thousands of different kinds and brands of food. If we are ill, we go to a hospital with modern X-ray and surgical equipment. If we want education, we attend schools or universities elaborately equipped with classrooms, teachers, and books. We Americans get so accustomed to this bountiful world that we take it for granted and forget what has made, and does make, it possible.

Imagine taking an ocean voyage and having the misfortune of a shipwreck. You and a few others reach the shore of an unpopulated island with nothing more than your life vest and the clothes on your back. In this situation you would be confronted with the problem of maintaining life without the benefit of capital.

The first thing you would do, depending on the climate, would be to seek shelter. It might be a cave or a crevice in a rock, or a rude hut made of boughs or fronds of palm trees. Shortly, you would be looking for food—berries or nuts or fish perhaps. To carry your harvest of berries, you might weave a rude basket of twigs. Soon you would find it highly advantageous to tie a stone to a stick and use it as a crude axe. It would be difficult to catch fish with your hands, so you would weave a net of vines, and later, with great labor, hollow out a log and make a boat to take you to better fishing grounds. Instead of making a trip to the spring each time you wanted a drink, you would hollow out a gourd and use it as a bucket. And if you really began adding luxury to your housekeeping, you might spend time shaping logs in the form of pipes to bring water from the spring to your front door.

What you would be doing is what men have done since the beginning of time—engaging in "capital formation." Unlike other vertebrates, man is a tool-making animal. He early learned that if he invested some of his time in toolmaking, he could catch more fish and game with less effort, have better clothing and shelter, and otherwise better his lot.

In the British Museum there is a splendid collection of stone-age tools, some of which may date back as much as five hundred thousand years. The visitor can see stones fashioned into scrapers, knives, hand axes, sickles, choppers, daggers, arrowheads, and other useful shapes. From these crude beginnings to the modern age of atomic reactors and space flight, man has painstakingly developed his technology and, pretty consistently, has saved a portion of his current production for use as capital to increase his future output.

The simplest form of capital formation is the allocation of part of one's working time to toolmaking. As society evolves, with labor divided into many specializations, and with money as a medium of exchange, financial organizations such as banks, brokerage houses, insurance companies, mortgage loan associations and investment trusts take over the function of gathering individual savings and channeling them into productive use. In every society where men have consumed less than they produced—investing their savings in factories, machinery, roads, transportation vehicles, research laboratories and other forms of capital equipment—they have improved the conditions of their existence.

No one knows how much capital formation a modern society should undertake in order to achieve economic progress. In Russia this question is decided for the nation by the Kremlin. The people are required to put up with crowded quarters, coarse food, shoddy clothing, and fewer hours of leisure while they build dams, blast furnaces, factories, and intercontinental missiles. The average Russian might wish to make progress at a slower pace and enjoy himself a little more along the way, and certainly he would like to rid himself of the burden of armaments. But in the Dictatorship of the Proletariat, it is the dictator, not the proletarian, who has the say.

In the United States and other free countries, capital formation is a matter of voluntary choice. When a family elects to save for a house, buys a life insurance policy, establishes a bank account, or buys bonds, stocks, or mortgages, it is engaging in capital formation. When a board of directors reinvests in the business a part of company annual earnings, they are increasing the nation's capital stock, thereby enabling the people to live better with less effort. When a community builds a bridge, a road, a water system or makes other productive installations, it, too, is increasing the nation's capital store. In a free society, the spirit of the people, their sense of industry and thrift, their productivity, their possession of natural resources, the belligerence of their neighbors—hence the necessity to spend wealth wastefully in preparation for war—all help to determine the amount of saving or capital formation.

In the United States, except during the 1932 depression and World War II, about fifteen per cent of our gross national product [3] has been saved for production purposes. The record is portrayed in Chart 9. The chart is divided into two sections. The scale on the left measures capital formation as a per cent of gross national product for overlapping decades from 1869 to 1918, as estimated by the National Bureau of Economic Research.[4] Included in these estimates are four types of capital:

1. Producers durable goods, i.e., tools, machinery, equipment.
2. Construction of all types—residential and nonresidential, both public and private. It is an accounting convention to include residences as a capital good. It could be argued that a house is "consumed" just as much as a suit of clothes or an automobile, but since it is a large item of capital expenditure and since many homes are built to rent, the category of housing is put in the producers goods column.
3. Net changes in inventory. Inventory, of course, is a necessary part of the equipment for carrying on production, and the net physical change in inventory from year to year must be

taken into account in order to measure the growth of the nation's capital stock.

4. Net changes in claims against foreign countries or, in other words, the net excess of exports over imports. The balance of foreign trade must be put into the estimates in order to determine the actual capital formation to be attributed to our own efforts.

Under the accounting system of the National Bureau of Economic Research, the United States steadily channeled about twenty per cent of its gross national product into capital formation from 1869 to 1918.

Chart 9

CAPITOL FORMATION IN THE UNITED STATES AS A PER CENT OF GROSS NATIONAL PRODUCT 1869 - 1959

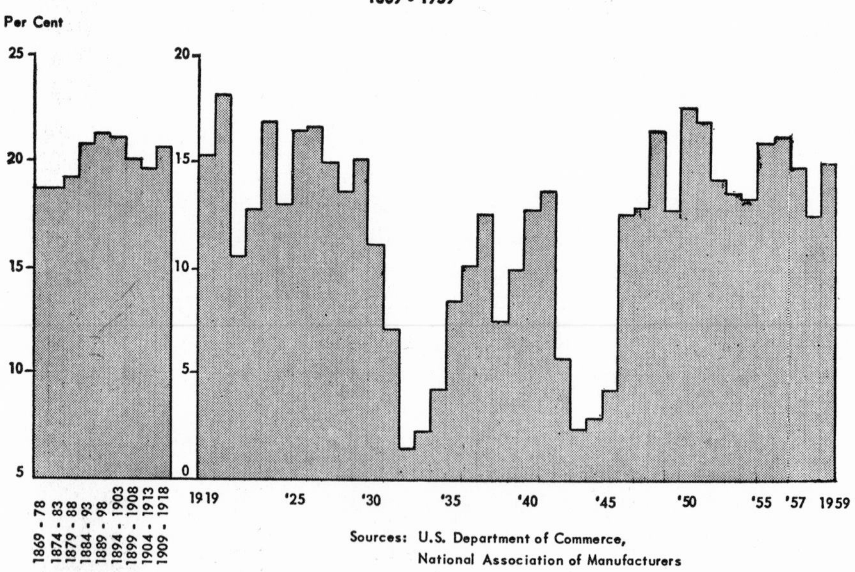

Sources: U.S. Department of Commerce, National Association of Manufacturers

For the period before 1918, we have only the decade estimates of the National Bureau of Economic Research to reflect the nation's capital formation. From 1919 on, two annual series for capital formation are available. The National Bureau has made yearly estimates for the period 1919 to 1943. The Department of Commerce has made yearly estimates of capital formation since 1929. The Commerce Department's trend series has been carried back to 1919 by means of data presented to the House Committee on Ways and Means of the 80th Congress.

The accounting practice of the Department of Commerce differs from that of the National Bureau of Economic Research. The National Bureau includes government expenditures for producers goods and construction. The Commerce Department treats all government capital expenditures separately from the private sector. In the private sector are included producers' durables, new construction, change in business inventories, and net change in private claims on foreign countries.

Since annual estimates of capital formation are available for the period 1919 to 1943 from both the National Bureau and the Department of Commerce, the difference in the estimates can readily be ascertained. It comes to approximately five percentage points, with the National Bureau's estimate consistently above that of the Department of Commerce by about this amount. We can therefore change the scale on the left side of Chart 9, making twenty per cent on the National Bureau's estimates equivalent to fifteen per cent for the estimates of the Department of Commerce, and thereby plot a trend line from 1869 to 1918 on a decade basis and from 1920 to 1959 on an annual basis.

With this statistical correction, and using the Department of Commerce's definition of capital formation, we can see that saving for future production in the private sector of the economy has averaged fifteen per cent of the gross national product for most of the last ninety years. During the 1932 depression, capital formation in the private sector of the economy fell off to one and one-half per cent, then rose steadily toward the fifteen per cent line. In World War II, capital formation fell to two and four-tenths per cent in 1943, but after the end of hostilities rose again to the traditional fifteen per cent level. It has fluctuated around this level for the past decade. If there is a norm for capital formation in a healthy growing society on the American model then, history sets it at approximately fifteen per cent. The efficiency with which capital has been employed has varied a good deal in the past, hence there is nothing absolute or inevitable about a fifteen per cent norm. For one thing, we have no sure way of knowing what kind of saving will be necessary to maintain desired standards in the future under a rapidly changing technology. For another, we do not know how much of the capital structure will be controlled by government and how much it will be responsive to market influences. Nevertheless, the remarkable fact is that a fifteen per cent annual saving from national output has resulted in a golden age of material betterment for the American people.

What capital formation and the use of better tools means to the average man can be seen dramatically by looking at the working time required to buy food and other items of the household budget. Table 18 shows the working time required in 1950 in twenty countries to buy a basket of food containing one dozen eggs and one pound each of wheat flour, bread, butter, cheese, potatoes, sugar, and lard. The American workman traded only ninety-eight minutes of labor time for this basket of food, whereas the Soviet workman gave 852 minutes of labor. In Great Britain the food cost in terms of working time was 168 minutes, and in France 560 minutes.

Chart 15 shows the increase in capital stock per member of the labor force, the increase in man-hour output, and the rise in the real wage in the United States from 1890 to 1955-1957. Table 19 translates the real wage gain between 1914 and 1948 in terms of hours of working time required to buy typical items on the household buying list. The rise in the worker's purchasing power, as indicated by the decline in working hours necessary to buy goods, is spectacular in the extreme. In 1948, milk, eggs, sugar, suits, autmobiles and washing machines cost about one-third as much working time as they did in 1914. Meat, cotton shirts, sheets, haircuts, and newspapers were down one-third to one-half. Toothpaste and cleaning powder cost one-seventh as much working time in 1948 as it did in 1914!

TABLE 18. WORKING TIME REQUIRED TO BUY A MARKET BASKET * OF FOOD IN 1950

	Number of Working Minutes
United States	98
Australia	123
Canada	133
Israel	147
Great Britain	168
Sweden	171
Norway	180
Denmark	219
Germany	285
Ireland	291
Switzerland	310
Czechoslovakia	346
Finland	349
Hungary	471
Netherlands	515
Chile	522
France	560
Austria	561
Italy	567
USSR	852

* The basket of food included one pound each of wheat, flour, bread, butter, cheese, potatoes, candy, sugar, and one dozen eggs.
Source: *America's Needs and Resources*

The idea that capital is "a foe of the workingman," then, is clearly not consistent with the facts. From the stone ages to the present, the economic experience of mankind has been that capital is crucial to survival, that without it man would be little better than animals, and that it holds one of the principal keys to the advancement of well-being. Putting it in personal terms, capital is a great and good friend of the workingman and a prodigious helper to all who have the sense to save it and use it wisely.

It may be objected that no one says that capital per se is a foe of the workingman; the issue is the ownership of capital. Socialist societies engage in capital formation just as capitalistic

TABLE 19. HOURS OF WORKING TIME REQUIRED IN THE UNITED STATES IN 1914 AND 1948 TO BUY VARIOUS PRODUCTS

			Decline	
	1914	*1948*	*Hours*	*1948 as Per Cent 1914*
Food				
Rib roast, lb.	.8	.47	.34	58
Butter, lb.	1.4	.62	.80	44
Milk, qt.	.36	.14	.22	39
Eggs, doz.	1.3	.45	.74	35
Bread, lb.	.25	.09	.16	64
Sugar, lb.	.21	.06	.15	31
Clothing				
Man's suit	67.8	23.6	44.2	35
Cotton shirt	3.5	2.4	1.1	68
Man's felt hat	16.2	3.2	12.9	20
Woman's wool suit	37.1	11.4	25.7	30
Cotton dress	4.2	3.0	1.2	71
Silk hose	2.3	.9	1.4	38
Household items				
Carpet	80.4	33.7	46.6	42
Livingroom suite, 2 pc.	154.4	116.2	38.2	75
Mattress	26.2	11.5	14.7	44
Sheets	3.2	1.7	1.5	53
Vacuum cleaner	79.5	44.1	35.5	55
Washing machine	220.0	63.7	156.3	29
Transportation				
Automobile	2763.2	953.5	1809.7	35
Gasoline	.7	.2	.5	28
Tires	96.0	10.8	95.2	11
Miscellaneous				
Aspirin tablets	3.2	.4	2.8	44
Cleaning powder	.7	.1	.6	14
Man's haircut	1.2	.6	.6	50
Newspaper yearly	21.9	9.9	12.0	45
Toothpaste	.7	.1	.6	14

Source: *America's Needs and Resources.*

societies do, but under socialism the people own the community's capital equally through the state, not individually and in unequal amounts as under capitalism. The question, then, is: which system of capital ownership and use best serves community needs and values? In the United States capital is widely owned; capitalists compete with each other to serve the customer and make a profit; social control of capital is achieved quickly and continuously through the "plebiscite of the consumers"; men and resources are allocated by the choices of the people; and the workingman can earn a basket of food, an automobile, a home, and other goods and services with the expenditure of less working time than anywhere else in the world.

In socialist societies the governors set up master plans which they think are good for the people; coerce the citizenry into observance of the plans; curtail freedom of choice; substitute the judgments of boards and committees for the judgment of the market; decrease the economic efficiency of the community with endless red tape and generally dampen the creative energies of the people. When in 1948 Ludwig Erhard, the Bizonal Economic Adviser to the British and American occupation authorities, issued his famous decree ending rationing and price controls, Germany started an economic recovery that has astonished the world. "Turn the people and money loose," said Erhard, "and they will make the country strong."

On his visit to the United States, Premier Khrushchev undertook to substantiate the myth of collective ownership by pointing to his comrade, Nikolai Tikhonov and remarking, "He does not possess anything but the pants he wears." What Khrushchev did not say is that the rulers of a Socialist society, in effect, "own" the wealth and use it as they see fit. In Russia the ruling class enjoys its luxuries—dachas, fine automobiles, private airplanes, caviar, and vacations on the Black Sea—at government expense. In capitalistic countries the well-to-do are required to pay for their own indulgences.

The great Italian scholar, Gaetano Mosca, hit the nail squarely on the head in his brilliant treatise, *The Ruling Class,* when he wrote, "If all the instruments of production pass into the hands of the government, the officials who control and apportion production become the arbiters of the fortunes and welfare of all, and we get a more powerful oligarchy, a more embracing 'racket' than has ever been seen in a society of advanced civilization."

Of the nation's private domestic capital formation, about three-fourths is funneled through corporations. Let us therefore examine the sources of company capital to see what part profits play in the saving process. Chart 10, prepared by Dr. Arthur O. Dahlberg, President of the U.S. Economics Corporation, provides a simple road map through the forest of corporate finance.[6] The data displayed on the diagram are for non-financial business firms as reported by the Federal Reserve Board's *Flow of Funds in the United States*. The time unit is the average year for the ten year period 1950-1959.

During this decade, income for non-financial corporations averaged 599.7 billion dollars per year. For each dollar of income, ninety-one cents was paid out for raw materials, wages, taxes (other than Federal income levies) and other expenses, leaving nine cents for profits, depreciation and Federal income taxes. Of this nine cents, depreciation and depletion claimed three cents, leaving six cents for profit before Federal income taxes. Of the six cents profit before taxes, the government took three cents, leaving three cents for profit after tax.

As we have seen previously, companies have been using approximately half of their earnings to pay dividends, hence Chart 10 shows one and one-half cents for dividends and one and one-half cents for reinvestment in the business.

For the average year, as indicated in Chart 10 and Table 20, non-financial corporations gathered thirty-eight and four-tenths billions for capital use. Of this fund, sixteen and seven-tenths billions came from charges to depreciation, eight and seven-tenths billions from profits and thirteen billions from external sources, such as the sale of stocks and bonds, borrowings of various kinds, and increase in trade payables.

Theoretically, monies from depreciation charges are supposed to pay for worn out buildings, machinery, and equipment; growth and expansion comes from reinvested earnings and new

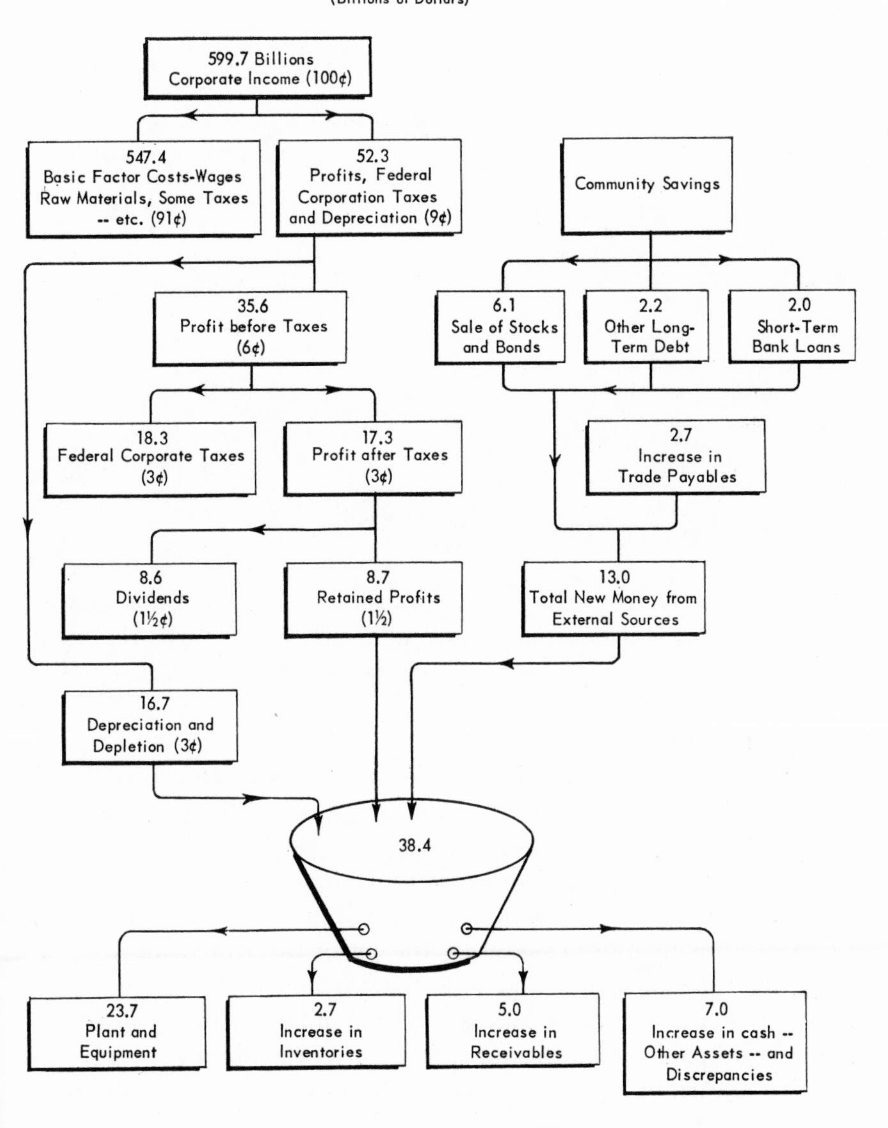

Source: Federal Reserve Board, Flow of Funds in the United States

TABLE 20. SOURCES AND USES OF CORPORATE FUNDS
FOR NON-FINANCIAL BUSINESS FIRMS
FOR THE AVERAGE YEAR 1947-1956

Source of Funds	*Billions*	*Per Cent*
Total funds	38.4	
Less depreciation	16.7	
Retained profit and funds from external sources	21.7	100
Retained profits	8.7	40
Sale of stocks and bonds	6.1	28
Other long term debt	2.2	10
Short term bank loans	2.0	9
Increase in trade payables	2.7	12
Use of Funds		
Plant and equipment	23.7	62
Increase in inventories	2.7	7
Increase in receivables	5.0	13
Increase in cash and other assets and adjustment for statistical discrepancies	7.0	18
Total source of funds	38.4	100

Source: *Federal Reserve Board, Flow of Funds.*

money, mostly from the sale of stocks and bonds. Among non-financial corporations for the decade ending in 1959, retained earnings averaged forty per cent of the total coming from profits and from external sources.

The secret of rising productivity is the use of capital to equip workingmen with better tools. As power and advanced technology have been applied to production, output has increased, cost and price in relation to wages have declined, and the real wage has risen an average of two and four-tenths per cent per year for three generations. Reinvested profits, therefore, have played a major role in bettering the lot of the American people.

Critics of the profit and loss system, including some economists who believe in capitalism, argue that all corporate earnings should be paid out to the stockholders.[7] Ownership, it is argued, means the right to receive the fruits emanating from property. Stockholders, not boards of directors, it is held, should decide how much profit is to be plowed back. If all corporate earnings were paid out in dividends, the stockholder could decide for himself how much he wishes to reinvest, and the market, not the managers, would allocate capital funds.

Stockholders are probably pretty well satisfied with the system of retaining some part of earnings for growth and expansion, for it increases the value of their equities and reduces taxes. Dividend income is taxed twice, once as corporate earnings and once as personal income; hence many stockholders, particularly those in the higher tax brackets, place their funds in growing companies that reinvest a large part of their earnings in the business. The shares of most companies have some degree of liquidity, and stockholders who become too disgruntled with their managements usually have an opportunity to sell and invest their funds in situations more to their liking.

Security underwriters are usually sensitive to what investors will and will not buy. If there were a strong market demand for securities with a complete payout feature, there would probably be more offerings of this type. Some security prospectuses do say that "Company X has long followed a liberal dividend policy" to stress the attractiveness of dividend payments, but the writer has never seen one that says, "It is Company Y's policy to pay out all earnings in dividends and go to the money markets for new capital." When companies find that they can do better for their stockholders by adopting a complete payout policy, we can be pretty sure, competition for funds being what it is, that many boards of directors will elect to follow this course.

To see how capital flows in a company and what it means to the community, we may take the Johns-Manville Corporation as a case study. In 1956 and 1957, Johns-Manville engaged in a large expansion program, building eight new plants and facilities to enlarge its manufacture of products from asbestos, wood, and mineral fibres. During the two year period, the company spent seventy-one and eight-tenths million dollars on its capital program. Table 21 shows the sources of this money.

TABLE 21. JOHNS-MANVILLE CORPORATION
SOURCES OF CAPITAL—1956-1957

	1956	1957	Two-Year Total
	(Millions)		
Earnings after taxes	$25.0	$17.8	$42.8
Less dividends at $2 per share	15.0	14.3	29.3
Retained earnings	10.0	3.5	13.5
Sale of common stock	29.9	0.5	30.4
Total new money	39.9	4.0	43.9
Depreciation and depletion	13.6	14.5	28.1
Total capital available	53.5	18.5	72.0
Capital expenditures	26.1	45.7	71.8

Of the seventy-two million dollars in capital available, twenty-eight and one-tenth million came from depreciation and depletion charged to current costs. Sales of common stock accounted for thirty and four-tenths million or sixty-nine per cent of the new money obtained by the company and retained earnings thirteen and a half million, or thirty-one per cent. Over a period of the last thirty years, reinvested earnings amounted to forty per cent of Johns-Manville's capital expenditures, hence a substantial part of its present facilities have been paid for out of earnings.

One of the eight plants erected by Johns-Manville in its expansion program was a facility for the manufacture of transite pipe in Dennison, Texas. Transite pipe is a tube formed on steel mandrels under tremendous pressure, using a mix of asbestos fiber, silica, and Portland cement. After being formed, the pipe is cured in a steam chamber to fix its chemical and physical properties. The asbestos fibres reinforce and tie together the silica and cement mix and give the pipe a tough homogeneous structure of unusual strength and density.

Transite pipe is used for water mains, irrigation systems, sewers, and for various installations in home building. The pipe is said to have a number of advantages. It is easy to install; it will not rust or corrode; it has a high flow coefficient which reduces pumping costs to the minimum; it is durable and strong; it has a long life; and it is virtually maintenance free.

To build and equip the Dennison, Texas, Transite Pipe Plant cost Johns-Manville approximately $10,000,000, equivalent to the reinvested earnings for the year 1956. The Dennison factory employs two hundred and fifty people in diversified jobs at an average yearly income of $5500 for a total payroll of $1,375,000. The plant spends $700,000 per year for raw materials and supplies, $200,000 for electric power and $320,000 per year for freight. The plant, of course, pays local taxes to help meet the cost of community schools, roads, and municipal administration. When running to capacity, Johns-Manville's Dennison facility can produce 2500 miles of water and sewer lines annually.

The outstanding characteristic of capitalistic enterprise is that it normally benefits all the publics with whom it deals. In Dennison, Texas, the $10,000,000 of reinvested Johns-Manville profits gives good paying jobs to two hundred and fifty people, who use their wages to buy homes, food, automobiles, insurance, education and other accouterments of good living. The pipe turned out by the plant furnishes users a solution to water main and sewer problems at an advantageous cost. The community benefits by having payrolls, taxes, and procurement expenditures channeled its way. And the Johns-Manville stockholders gain by adding a modern new property in a growing territory to help the company continue earning its traditional profit of twelve to fifteen per cent on invested capital.

The Johns-Manville pattern of earning a dollar, paying out part of it in dividends, and plowing the remainder back in the business has become so commonplace that most people take it for granted. It is important, however, that we understand the social significance of the process, for the principles of wealth creation are inexorable. If we want higher standards of living and desire to remain strong in a hostile world, we must become more productive. In order to become more productive, we must save capital and equip ourselves with better tools.

CHAPTER SEVEN

REDIVIDING THE PIE

Some participants in the debate over profits think of them as a huge hoard that is unfairly deflected away from the workers into the pockets of the owners. With purchasing power denied them, they say, workers are unable to buy back the fruits of their labor, and sooner or later depression ensues, bringing joblessness, hunger, and other miseries to the worker. The remedy for this situation, it is held, is to redivide the pie—raise wages, cut prices, lower profits, give the workers more, give the owner less. The number one goal of unionism, declare union leaders, is "to secure a larger portion of the proceeds of production." [1]

Is this sound doctrine for social action? How well has this plan worked in the past? What chance does the worker have of improving his standard of living by forcing companies to increase wages at the expense of profits? The idea that profits represent a huge pie that can be redivided among workers and customers is a beautifully simple one, and politically attractive; but it quickly runs head-on into some hard economic facts.

The first hard fact is that profits represent a very small part of the corporate dollar. Profits for all manufacturing corporations for the decade, 1949-1958, averaged only three and nine-tenths cents per dollar of sale; this does not constitute a very big hoard for redistribution. Moreover, if we are to believe the Department of Commerce, even this figure is an overstatement; for if allowances were made for inventory and depreciation distortion, the profit reported by manufacturing concerns to the Bureau of Internal Revenue would be reduced by twenty-eight per cent to two and eight-tenths cents per dollar of sale.[2]

The second hard economic fact is that employees of corporations already get the lion's share of corporate payments that are made either to employees or accounted for as profit. Take General Electric as an example. From its simplified income statement for 1959, as shown in Table 22, it can be seen that out of every dollar the company took in it spent forty-three cents for raw materials, supplies, and various manufacturing costs. Depreciation took two and seven-tenths cents, interest and finance three-tenths of a cent, and taxes seven and one-tenths cents, leaving forty-six and nine-tenths cents for distribution to employees in the form of wages and salaries and for profit. Of this forty-six and nine-tenths cents, employees received forty and one-half cents, stockholders were paid four cents in dividends and two and four-tenths cents was reinvested in the business.

If we think of the forty-six and nine-tenths cents remaining for employees and stockholders as the employee-profit dollar, then employees received eighty-six per cent of this sum. No one, of course, would argue that stockholders should get nothing from the business; but, had the stockholders' interest been eliminated and all of General Electric's profit distributed to employees, their pay would have increased only sixteen per cent. This would not move the wage earner very far toward his millenium; moreover, this kind of wage increase obviously wouldn't last long, for General Electric's earning power, as that of all corporations, depends on successful collaboration between stockholders, who supply capital to buy tools and equipment, and employees, who use this equipment. If the stockholder is not adequately com-

TABLE 22. SIMPLIFIED GENERAL ELECTRIC INCOME STATEMENT—1949

	In Dollars	*Per Cent*				
In 1959 General Electric sold goods and received miscellaneous revenue amounting to	4,400,600,000	100				
For materials, supplies, and all other items (net) not shown separately, its costs were	1,893,100,000	43.0				
For obsolescence, wear and tear on tools, i.e., depreciation, its costs were	119,900,000	2.7				
Interest and other financial charges were	10,600,000	.3				
Taxes amounted to	313,100,000	7.1				
Leaving for distribution to employees and for profit i.e., "the employee profit dollar"	2,063,900,000	46.9				
Employee compensation, including benefits, amounted to			1,783,700,000	40.5		
Leaving profits of			280,200,000	6.4		
In the disposition of profits:						
Stockholders received dividends of					174,300,000	4.0
Leaving for reinvestment in the business					105,900,000	2.4

pensated for the use of his funds, he will lose interest in replacing and maintaining production equipment and will refuse to provide new capital for modernization or for additional ventures.

The four cents dividend pay-out in 1959 gave each General Electric stockholder two dollars per share for the use of his capital. Since the company's shares sold at an average price of eighty dollars during that year, the yield for an investor committing his funds at the eighty dollar price was two and one-half per cent. This return on capital would hardly classify as an investor's bonanza. The reason investors were willing to entrust their money to the General Electric management at this low rate of return was the hope that the company would grow and become more prosperous, pay a bigger dividend, increase the yield and enhance the value of the stock. Early in 1961 the stock fell to sixty-one and one-quarter. Only the future will reveal whether an investment in General Electric at a price yielding two and one-half per cent will prove to be sound. Investing money is a risky business, and even the most astute investors take losses as well as gains.

General Electric's management reinvested two and four-tenth cents of its revenue dollar in the business for modernization, new facilities, and other capital requirements. If this money had been paid out in wages and salaries, employee income would have increased approximately six per cent. This, in all likelihood, would have been a bad decision for the employees, for General Electric people can be productive and earn high wages only if they have good tools to work with. Throughout its history, the company has plowed back part of its profits for expansion and new equipment. The intricacies of corporate finance are such that it is difficult to say how much of the company's present facilities have been paid for out of earnings, but it probably is as much as two-thirds. Thus profits have helped to build a great industrial complex that provides good paying jobs to thousands of employees, gives stockholders an opportunity to invest their savings and get a reasonable return, and furnishes customers with a torrent of products that enable them to enjoy the comforts and amenities of the electrical age.

Understanding Profits

The General Electric experience in the distribution of monies between employees and owners is widely duplicated in American industry. Not all companies publish data on employment costs in their annual reports, but many of them do, and it is possible to compare the amounts paid to employees with that accounted for as profit. Table 23 shows employment costs as a percentage of the total of profit and employment cost for one hundred leading corporations in fifteen industry classifications for the year 1956. Also shown is the amount of company equity capital employed per job holder, as listed in the company statements.

TABLE 23. EMPLOYMENT COST AS A PERCENTAGE OF TOTAL PROFIT AND EMPLOYMENT COST. EQUITY CAPITAL PER EMPLOYEE FOR ONE HUNDRED LEADING COMPANIES—1956

Number and Type of Company	*Employment Per Cent*	*Equity Capital per Employee*
9 Airplane	93	2,400
7 Electrical	90	5,200
5 Auto Parts	89	6,300
5 Agricultural Machinery	89	10,000
11 Food	87	7,500
2 Can	87	10,000
5 Rubber	84	6,500
3 Building	82	10,000
4 Auto	82	7,600
4 Glass	81	10,500
13 Steel	81	14,000
7 Paper	78	15,500
2 Aluminum	78	18,000
10 Chemical	70	17,500
13 Oils	61	42,500

Table 23 shows that payments to employees run from ninety-three per cent of total employment cost and profit for airplane companies to sixty-one per cent for the oil industry. The evidence shows that employees receive a larger per cent of the total when capital per job holder is small and a smaller per cent when the capital is large. In other words, when capital performs more work with less manpower, the proportion of the reward going to capital rises. In the case of the nine airplane companies, the capital listed is company capital. Airplane companies working on national defense employ more capital per worker than is here indicated, but much of their equipment is government owned. Since we are interested in company wage and profit experience, it is correct to show employment cost in relation to the use of company capital.

The idea that the profits pie can be redivided among workers, customers, and owners runs up against a third hard economic fact; namely, that having already claimed and received the lion's share of the rewards going to employees and owners, the worker in recent decades has made no apparent progress in his drive "to secure a larger portion of the proceeds of production."

This conclusion flies in the face of widely held beliefs, hence careful consideration of the evidence is necessary.

Chart 11 provides two trend lines that measure the employee share of the employee-profit dollar. The data for Line A are drawn from the national income accounts furnished by the Department of Commerce.[3] In its reports the Commerce Department presents profits for incorporated and unincorporated manufacturing firms separately, but lumps together wages paid by incorporated and unincorporated businesses. Line A shows the employee percentage of the employee profit dollar for incorporated and unincorporated business combined as follows:

$$\text{Line A} = \frac{\text{Employment Cost for All Manufacturing Firms}}{\begin{array}{c}\text{Employment Cost for All Manufacturing Firms}\\ \text{Plus Profits for Incorporated Firms}\\ \text{Plus Profits for Unincorporated Firms}\end{array}} \times 100$$

In small corporations the owner-managers seek to minimize double taxation by taking as much of their income as possible in the form of salaries rather than dividends. To the extent that small owner-managed corporate "profits" appear as employment cost in the government tabulations, the employees' share of the employee-profit dollar is inflated.

To overcome this difficulty, a second version of the employee share of the employee-profit dollar is presented in Line B, Chart 11. This line is based on data drawn from the annual reports of thirty leading corporations. An increasing number of corporations are routinely disclosing employment cost, but it required the sifting of hundreds of annual reports to find thirty companies that made public their employment costs as far back as 1938. Lines A and B tell the same story despite the fact that the data were gathered from two separate and distinct sources.

Chart 11

EMPLOYEE PER CENT OF EMPLOYEE-- PROFIT DOLLAR

1938 - 1959

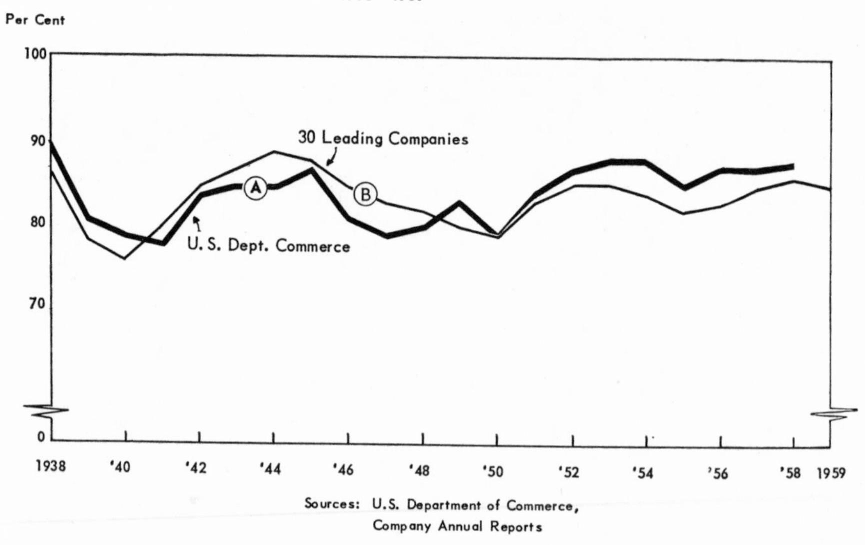

Sources: U.S. Department of Commerce, Company Annual Reports

Since 1938 employment costs have consistently absorbed from seventy-six to ninety per cent of the total dollars available for employees and profits. When profits were relatively poor (1938, 1942-1945 and 1952-1956) employment costs took eighty-five to ninety per cent of the employee-profit dollar. When profits were relatively good (1939-1940, 1946-1950) employment costs absorbed roughly seventy-eight to eighty-two per cent of this dollar.

For the twenty-two year period, 1938-1959, employees received eighty-four per cent of the total paid to employees or accounted for as profit on company books. The employee share undulates within the limits of a flat band, giving no suggestion that employees today are receiving a larger share of this money than they did twenty years ago.

These data tell the story of the distribution of monies between employees and owners simply, and with a minimum of statistical complication; it is regrettable that they are not available for a longer period of time. However, the same conclusion emerges from the statistics of "value added by manufacture," which go back to the turn of the century.

As defined in the Census of Manufacturers, value added by manufacture is the amount of the sales dollar left after purchases from others—such as raw materials, fuel, electricity, rent, etc. The accountancy of value added can be visualized in a simplified statement, prepared by Allen Rucker,[4] for all manufacturing combined for census years from 1914 to 1947 (Table 24).

TABLE 24.
THE ACCOUNTANCY OF "VALUE ADDED"

	Billion	*Per Cent*
A. Received from customers	785.9	
B. Deduct amounts paid to others for raw materials, supplies, power and like items	455.2	
C. Value added by manufacturers	330.7	100.0
Disbursed for:		
1. Factory hourly rated labor costs	130.3	39.4
2. Management costs		
a. Other operating expenses—all salary compensation, depreciation, real estate taxes, insurance, research, sales travel, advertising and all expense other than hourly wages b. Ownership obligations—interest on borrowed monies, Federal and State income taxes, Dividends to stockholders, Earnings reinvested	200.4	60.6

Chart 12 shows labor's share of value added for all United States manufacturing from 1899 to 1958. The trend, it will be noted, is quite flat, holding close to the forty per cent line except in years of recession.[5] Evidently the market has, and does, put a certain price tag on labor and other factors of production, and the relation between these factors for manufacturing as a whole does not appear to have been appreciably altered by the rise of collective bargaining.

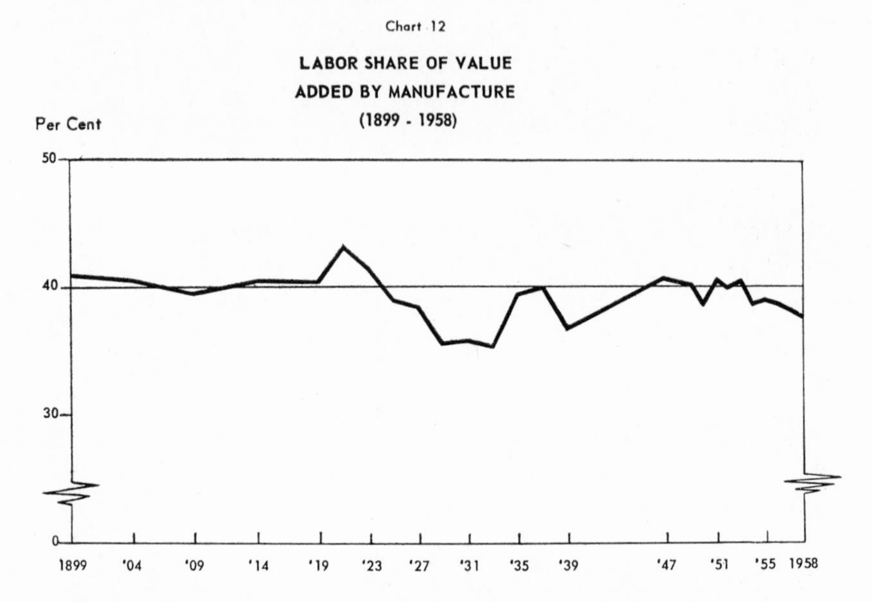

In dealing with the relative shares of workers and owners, many writers and public speakers turn to the national income accounts of the Department of Commerce for data on trends. There, for example, it is found that the employee share of the national income rose from sixty-two per cent in 1941 to seventy per cent in 1959, and this fact is taken as proof that the workers are gaining in their struggle for a larger share of the wealth. But national income accounting is extremely complex, and figures drawn from this source may or may not mean what they appear to say on the surface.

Actually the rise in the employee share of the national income between 1941 and 1959 is probably a result of structural changes in the economy such as the movement of farmers to the cities (i.e., from an entrepreneurial to an employee classification) and the increase in the number of government employees. The salaries of people who work for government appear in the employee column of the national income accounts, but there is no companion entry on the property side of the ledger. Thus, as the government payroll increases, the share of the national income going to employees tends to rise.

A number of writers have tried to analyze trends in the division of national income between property (rent, interest, and profits) and labor. All of them have been forced to deal with the inadequacies of census data and the complexities of accounting definitions. Should "transfer payments" such as interest on government bonds and social security payments be included or excluded from the computations? Should the property account be credited with profits before or after taxes? Should capital gains be regarded as property income? Is income from proprietorships (farmers, doctors, lawyers, retail business, etc.) employee income or partly property income? Jesse Burkhead says it is impossible to separate the labor and property elements and classifies income from proprietorships as labor.[6] D. Gale Johnson, on the other hand, finds evidence to justify the distribution of proprietor's income in the ratio of approximately sixty-five per cent to labor and thirty-five per cent to property.[7] Since the experts disagree on the correct answers, many versions of distributive shares reflecting different accounting concepts are to be found in the literature.

Looking at the long term trend, Jesse Burkhead thinks labor shares of the national income were on a higher plateau in the thirties and forties than in the twenties; but the curves he displays for labor's share for the period 1929 to 1950 are remarkably flat.

D. Gale Johnson, after examining the available national income data, writes: "There is a fairly widespread view that labor's share of the national income has increased. The present analysis does not indicate that there has been a significant secular change in the share of the national income received by labor." [8]

Johnson's conclusion is supported by our previous analysis of labor's share of value added by manufacture and the employee's share of the employee profit dollar.

It was in 1937 that labor unions began their militant organization of industrial workers with the now famous maneuver of the sit-down strike. Since that time, unions have grown spectacularly from four to eighteen million members. It has been the avowed purpose of unions to "secure a larger portion of the proceeds of production." Through strikes and other forms of mass pressure, an all-out effort has been made to force the owner to take less in order that the worker could have more.

Evidently unions have not succeeded in their drive to redivide the pie between owners and workers, for all during the golden era of union growth, labor's share of value added by manufacture has held close to the forty per cent level, and the employee's share of the employee-profit dollar has continued to fluctuate around the eighty-four per cent mark. The explanation of this lies in the fact that profits relative to wages and salaries are so small that wages could not be raised appreciably even if stockholders were liquidated and all profits were handed over to the employees. The division of the employee-profit pie, as the diagram below demonstrates, is now so one-sided in favor of the employee that little is left to be redivided.

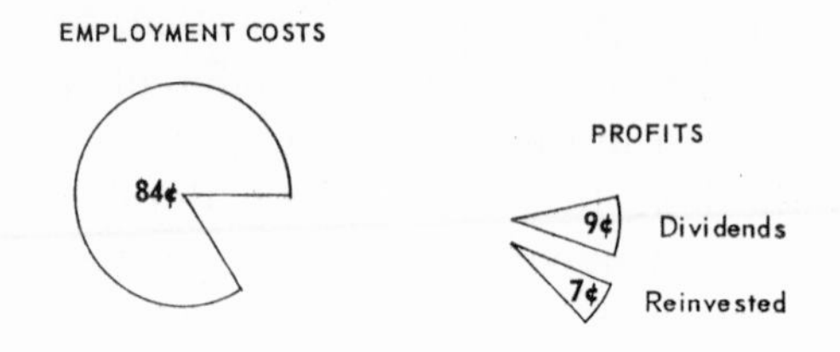

There is, therefore, no opportunity for the worker to increase wages through a redistribution of profits. Employees have prospered greatly through their collaboration with share owners. Should the private owner be eliminated, it would still be necessary to employ capital, and the successor to the individual investor would most likely be the state. That day would mark the end of voluntary cooperation between capital and labor, for states have the power of coercion, and all experience shows that the state does not hesitate to use this power to accumulate capital through forced savings, and to fix the conditions of employment by decree.

People who seek a higher standard of living through the redivision of profits are doomed to disappointment. The idea that companies have a huge profit hoard that can be tapped to raise wages, increase benefits, and lower prices is a myth. It is a powerful and oft repeated myth, but as a blueprint for social action to raise the workers' standard of living, it has about as much promise as trying to increase the food supply by planting potatoes by the moon.

This is a strong statement that seems to deny common observation and experience. Everyone knows that unions make demands on employers, and that, after a period of bargaining, sometimes involving a strike, a settlement is effected that usually raises the wages and fringe benefits of the union members. How do these wage increases come about? There are only four sources from which they can come. These are:

1. Redistribution of profits.
2. Inflation of the price and wage structure through increase in the money supply or through union pressure.
3. Redistribution of the wealth of other workers through the price mechanism or through unemployment.
4. Raising productivity through better organization of men and processes and through application of capital resources.

We have already seen that wage increases, by and large, have not come out of profits. Let us now discuss briefly the other three sources from which they may be derived. Inflation is known to all through the painful experience of skyrocketing prices. Clothing and food costs more; the landlord wants to raise the rent; it becomes increasingly difficult to make ends meet. Or, if boom psychology fills the air, the common attitude is likely to be: "Yes, everyone is making more money, but the cost of living has gone up too." Inflationary price movements have occurred in the United States in every war except the Spanish

American War in 1898. Previous to World War II, as Chart 13 shows, price inflation has always been followed by severe deflation, but this did not happen after World War II and the Korean War. The Index of Wholesale prices, standing at 51 in 1940, climbed to 120 by 1960 and continues to point upward.

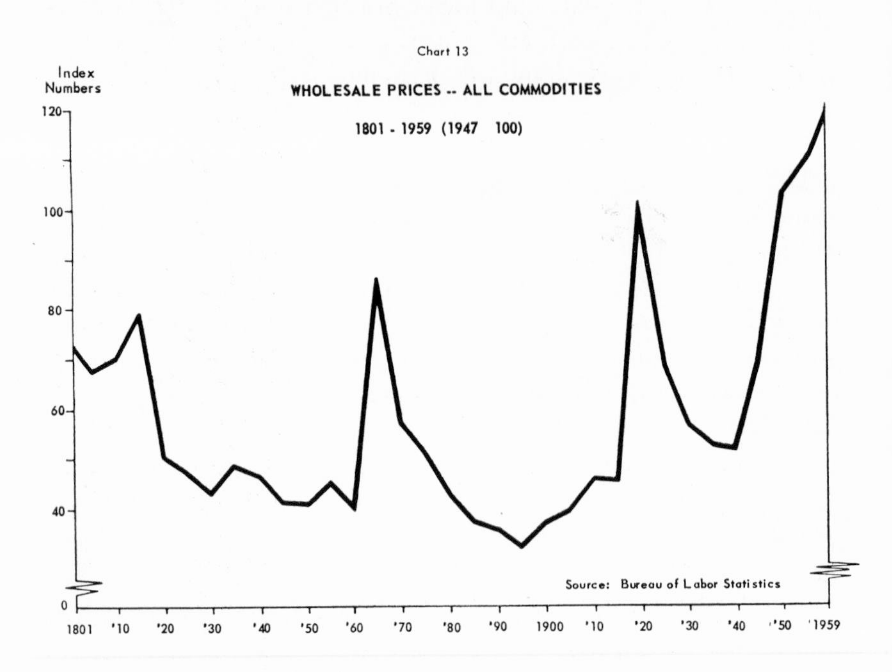

The great inflationary movements of the past have been caused by war finance and the shifting of economic resources from consumer goods to war production. With growing welfare costs, full employment schemes, cost of living provisions in wage contracts, strong unions pressing for "more," and the propensity of politicians for deficit spending, inflation may have become an institutionalized part of American life. Indeed the late Sumner Slichter, noted Harvard economist, argued that "creeping inflation" was necessary to maximum economic growth. He suggested that the community should adapt to the new order through escalator clauses in pension agreements, bond yields that are high enough to compensate for the expected erosion of capital, and other arrangements to get in line with the inevitable trend.[9]

Many economists see inflation in terms of "demand pull" and "cost push" forces. In "demand-pull" inflation the volume of spending increases faster than the supply of goods. Increased spending can come as a result of private expansion of the economy or from government orders for goods, but mostly inflationary spending pressures result from the government's increasing the money supply.

Discussing the inflation that occurred between 1940 and 1950, Yale Brozen, Professor of Economics at the University of Chicago, points out that during this period the federal government ran huge deficits. In order to finance these deficits, the government sold large quantities of bonds to the commercial banks, which the banks largely paid for by setting up "demand deposits" to the credit of the government. Banks operate by taking in the money of depositors, maintaining a reserve to meet the day-to-day demands of the depositors, and lending out the remainder at interest.[10] Government placement of bonds with commercial banks increased their deposits and their lending power. As the government drew on its bank credit from the sale of bonds, the new money circulated through the economy and was redeposited in the banks, thereby creating new lending power. In short, government sales of bonds to commercial banks became a new type of "printing-press money."

With more money in their pockets, people sought to buy goods. Since the supply of money increased faster than the supply of goods, eager buyers raised their bids, and prices went up. Between 1940 and 1950, says Professor Brozen, the quantity of money rose 180 per cent, from thirty-nine dollars to one hundred ten billion dollars. The volume of goods offered for sale increased fifty-five per cent and the price level advanced eighty-four per cent. Inflation, Professor Brozen flatly declares, is a result of increasing the money supply in order to enable the federal government to spend more than it takes in. "The only way we are going to avoid inflation in the future," says Professor Brozen, "is by avoiding deficits in government budgets." [11]

"Cost-push" inflation is said to result primarily from massive wage increases won by labor unions. There is a great deal of controversy about "cost-push" factors as a cause of inflation. Businessmen are generally convinced that excessive labor union demands have forced up the general price level. Labor leaders hotly deny this. Such authorities as the late Sumner Slichter, Allan Sproul, and Raymond J. Saulnier, say that labor wage demands are one of the primary causes of inflation; other savants, such as Milton Friedman, Yale Brozen, and Henry Hazlitt, say that the influence of unions as an inflationary force has been greatly exaggerated; that consumers, not producers, control the price level; and that the money supply, not labor unions, is the principal cause of inflation.

From the housewife's point of view, the cost of living goes up whether inflation is caused by demand-pull or cost-push forces. Big money wage increases that come during a period of inflation look good on the face of it, and are often exhilarating, but, as everyone comes to realize, they are a poor measure of betterment, for wages are worth only what they will buy.

If everyone belonged to one big union, and the union demanded and won a one hundred per cent wage increase, the members would not be much better off, for most production expense is ultimately employment cost. If productivity remained stable, prices would about double.

The key indicator of well-being is the real wage, i.e., money wages measured in terms of the price of goods. In the period 1940 to 1959, the average annual wage in manufacturing rose 260 per cent, but much of this gain was illusory, for retail prices rose eighty-five per cent during this period, leaving a real wage increase of only ninety-one per cent.

Thus, much of the money wage gains since 1940 have come as a result of inflation. Unions made demands on employers for increases. Goods were in short supply and buyers with money in their pockets stood ready to absorb new production at higher prices. The employer could afford to raise wages, because he could pass increased costs on to the consumer. Even in non-union shops, employers bid wages up in order to get enough help to produce goods to sell at advancing prices. This process could go on so long as government continued to increase the money supply. If the money stock were not expanded, consumers would stop raising their bids for goods, producers who allowed labor costs to rise above production would find themselves priced out of the market, and unemployment would result.

Inflation as a source of wage increases is a cruel process filled with rank injustice. Inflation dissipates the purchasing power of savings, consumes capital, disrupts the bond of confidence between borrower and lender, squeezes the pensioner, and cuts down the little man who cannot keep his income abreast of advancing prices. An insidious force, inflation sneaks up on people without their being aware and robs them of their savings in ways that are difficult to comprehend. Actually, monetary inflation is a dishonest method of taxation, forcing the creditor, the pensioner and the man of stable income to reduce his purchases in order to pay for government deficits. Price stability, as Treasury Secretary Robert B. Anderson has pointed out, has been more characteristic of the nation's growth than price instability, and it is hard to believe that continual cheapening of the value of money can do anything but impair the nation's economic health.[12]

A third source of wage increase is redistribution of the wealth of other workers through the price mechanism. The process is said to work this way:

> A strong union demands a large wage increase that reaches beyond gains in productivity. The employer cannot, or will not, absorb the increase out of profits, so he undertakes to pass cost on to the consumer by increasing prices. The consumer can either pay the increased price and carry the burden of higher wages or he can withhold his purchases by getting along without the product for a while longer, or by purchasing a substitute. If the buyer cannot postpone his purchase and if his income lags behind the wage price spiral, union members have succeeded in exchanging their labor with others on a more favorable ratio or, in other words, they have redivided the wealth of pensioners and other workers.

If the potenial purchaser refuses to buy at the increased price, demand falls off with the result that some members of the union are thrown out of work. Thus the unemployed man is forced to pay part of the social cost of the wage increase. It might be argued that labor-saving machinery likewise throws men out of work and puts the social cost on the unemployed. Certainly, advancing technology has required re-shuffling of labor assignments with temporary hardship in some cases, but history has demonstrated that better technology has continually created new employment opportunities and raised the standard of living. Monopoly pricing above the market, however, can only result in permanent unemployment.

Wages, like other prices, are in the long run determined by supply and demand working through the institutional framework that exists at any one time. But militant unionism, it would appear, can win advantages for one group of workers at the expense of other groups. This is demonstrated in Chart 14, which shows median hourly wage trends for four industrial classifications grouped by their history of unionization.[13]

> Group 1 includes occupations such as rubber, steel and automobiles that were almost wholly unorganized in 1934-1936, but through militant organization are now approximately one hundred per cent unionized.
>
> Group 2 lists occupations that had few or no unions in 1934-1936, but are heavily, though not completely, unionized now.
>
> Group 3 includes occupations with old line unions such as printing, apparel, railroads and construction that were almost wholly organized in 1934-1936, and still are.
>
> Group 4 lists nonunion occupations such as wholesale and retail trade, hotels, and crude petroleum and natural gas where organization either has not been attempted or has made little headway.

Wages in all four groups have risen substantially in the past twenty years, but the militant groups have made the largest wage gains. Group 1, now totally unionized, has increased its hourly wage 342 per cent since 1934-1936. Group 2, partially unionized, has scored a 306 per cent gain. The nonunion Group 4 gained 234 per cent, considerably less than the highly unionized occupations. Interestingly enough, Group 3, consisting of old line unions, gained only 240 per cent, which was only a little better than the nonunion group.

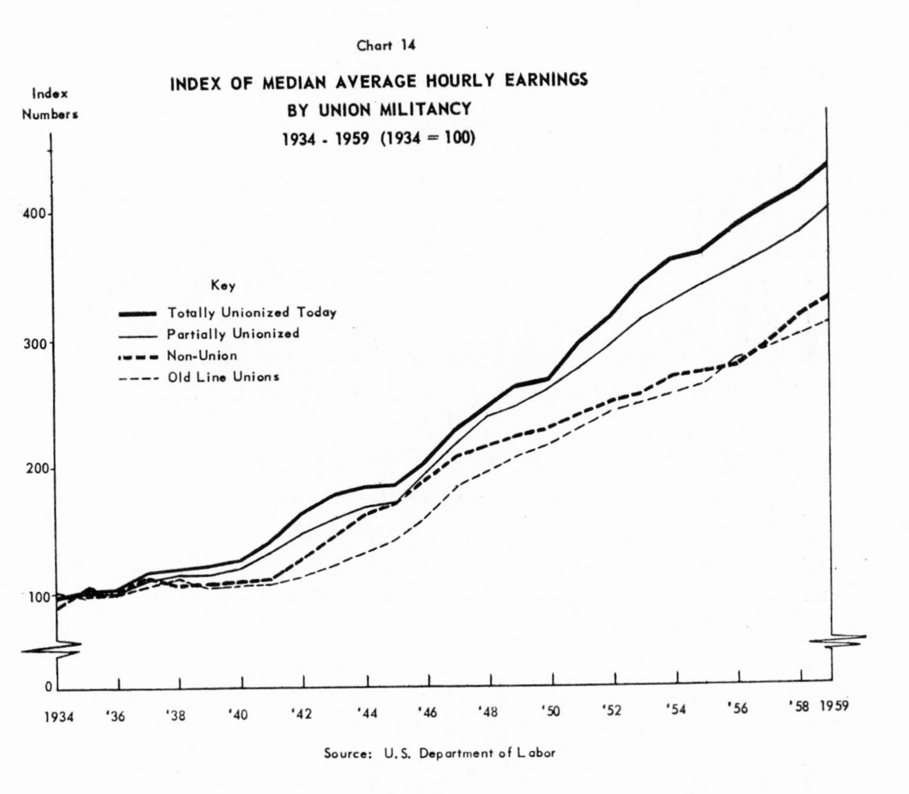

During the war years, hourly wages in all four groups rose at about the same rate, but after the war Groups 1 and 2, with their new-found union militancy, pulled ahead of the nonunion occupations and those with old line unions.

The economic and organizational factors that controlled the wage experience of these four groups are obviously complex. Productivity in the four groups, for example, may have varied somewhat; but each group represents a broad sampling of industry, and it is probably fair to conclude from Chart 14 that militant unionism can, for a time at least, win wage advantages over other worker groups. The total real wage of any country, except for temporary variation resulting from the balance of foreign trade, is what it can produce. If one group gets more, someone else must get correspondingly less. There is no evidence to indicate that militant union groups have secured their pre-eminent wage position through redistribution of company profits. The more probable explanation for their advantage is that they have redistributed the incomes of other workers through the price mechanism.

When wage increases outrun productivity, prices go up and some customers are unable, or refuse, to buy. The result is unemployment. A striking demonstration of how this process works was recently made by Professor Yale Brozen. He broke the period 1920 to 1958 into eight time segments when real hourly earnings of employees in manufacturing were rising and computed the percentage of increase for each segment (see Table 25). He then made the same calculation for average productivity in the private non-farm section of the economy. By comparing changes in real hourly earnings and average productivity, he arrived at a figure showing the crude percentage change in productivity relative to the real wage rate. In 1920-1921, for example, the real wage rose four per cent, but productivity fell one and one-tenth per cent, which added up to a five and one-tenth per cent decline in productivity relative to the wage rate. In these two years unemployment rose from 1,700,000 to 5,000,000.

In every time segment studied, unemployment rose as real hourly earnings outran productivity. To put it another way, when employees in manufacturing were paid more than the increase in production justified, supply of product declined, prices went up, buyers made fewer purchases, and men were thrown out of work. Brozen's study further shows that when productivity rose faster than real wages, unemployment declined.

Thus, says Professor Brozen, "wage rates are shown to have direct impact on the number of jobs available. If wage rates are

TABLE 25. MOVEMENT OF PRODUCTIVITY, WAGE RATES, AND UNEMPLOYMENT
(In periods of rising unemployment)

Year	Real Hourly Earnings (manuf.) (1958 dollars)	Per Cent Change	Average Productivity (Private non-farm sector)	Per Cent Change	Crude Per Cent Change in Productivity Relative to Wage Rate	Unemployment (Millions)
1920	$0.80		$1.55			1.7
21	0.83	+4.0	1.53	−1.1	−5.1	5.0
1923	0.88		1.71			1.4
24	0.92	4.5	1.77	+3.5	−1.0	2.4
1926	0.90		1.87			0.9
28	0.95	5.8	1.86	−0.4	−6.2	2.1
1929	0.96		1.88			1.6
33	0.99	3.6	1.81	−3.4	−7.0	12.8
1937	1.24		2.21			7.7
38	1.28	3.3	2.25	+2.0	−1.3	10.4
1948	1.62		2.67			2.1
49	1.70	4.8	2.75	+3.0	−1.8	3.4
1952	1.82		3.10			1.7
54	1.95	7.1	3.27	+5.4	−1.7	3.2
1956	2.10		3.43			2.6
58	2.13	1.5	3.45	+0.7	−0.8	4.3

too high, there will be a shortage of jobs and men will be unemployed. If wage rates are too low, there will be a surplus of jobs or a shortage of labor. Other things being equal, the number of jobs available is inversely related to the wage rate. Wage rates can be raised without causing unemployment only if productivity is raised at the same time." [14]

In the September 1953 issue of *Economic Trends and Outlook*, the AFL-CIO declared, "The buying power of wages and salaries must not only catch up with productivity, it must forge ahead." Professor Brozen's data indicate that forging ahead actually means "creating unemployment."

The accusing finger is continually pointed at excessive profits as the cause of depression and joblessness. Owners, it is said, expropriate too much of the product of labor, the masses are unable to purchase the fruits of their toil, and men are thrown out of work. But profits have tended to go down since the postwar highs of 1947-1948, hence in recent years other causes for unemployment must have been operating. Brozen's analysis suggests that one cause is union policies that force wage increases above productivity. Economic law will not be put off. When management bids too enthusiastically for labor, or when unions force wages above the point the consumer thinks labor service is worth, costs go up, demand drops off, and joblessness results. Management and unions have it within their power to reduce unemployment. The key is to keep wage demands and costs within realistic bounds as indicated by the market so that goods can be offered to consumers at such attractive prices that they will be motivated to buy.

We have now analyzed three sources of wage increases—redistribution of profits, inflation, and redistribution of the wealth of other workers. Productivity, the fourth source of wage increases, has already entered the discussion, but we can now deal with this crucial factor in the greater detail it deserves.

Rising productivity means turning out more or better goods at the same or less cost; or, in the modern jargon, achieving greater output with less input. Since most production cost is ultimately payment for work supplied by people, one simple way to measure productivity is to relate the total physical output of a plant, an industry, or a nation to the total man-hours involved in that production. Thus, in the bituminous coal industry, production in 1929 was .57 short tons per man-hour; in 1956 it was 1.11 short tons, representing a productivity gain of ninety-five per cent. During this period average hourly earnings rose 313 per cent from 68c per hour in 1929 to $2.81 in 1956. Since wages went up approximately three times as fast as productivity, the unit labor cost per ton doubled from $1.20 per ton in 1929 to $2.54 per ton in 1956.

Another illustration of productivity measurement is Dewhurst's analysis of national productivity for the century ending in 1950.[15] Dewhurst computed the total man-hour input by multiplying the number of employed workers by the annual man hours worked, then dividing national income by total man hours to arrive at the dollar value of output per man-hour. Expressed in terms of 1950 prices, productivity per man-hour was 33.7 cents in 1850 and $1.93 in 1950. Thus, over the century, man-hour output increased six times.

Measuring productivity in terms of man-hour costs has many technical flaws. It fails to make allowance for the changing quality of goods produced. It doesn't take account of change in the composition, the education, or the skill of labor. It focuses only on labor input, although, as everyone knows, capital input makes the difference between handicraft and mass production. Productivity in a factory or an industry may rise or fall because of changes in product mix, degree of capacity operation, and a myriad of other causes that have nothing to do with the skill or the willingness of men to work.

With measurement techniques varying with different writers, a certain amount of confusion is inevitable in the discussion of productivity. One conclusion, however, is clear: it is that real wages are closely and intimately bound up with productivity. When more and better goods are turned out at less cost, the wage dollar of the workingman "goes further" and his standard of living rises. This is the great secret of American capitalism, and is the reason why our system of economic organization has virtually eliminated poverty and brought the amenities of life to the masses.

Chart 15 shows the relation between real hourly earnings (Line A) and productivity (Line B) in the private domestic economy of the United States from 1889 to 1957, as reported in the authoritative studies by John Kendrick of The National Bureau of Economic Research.[16] From 1889 to 1919 the average annual productivity gain per man-hour was two per cent. After World War I, productivity gains quickened, to an average of two and six-tenths per cent per annum between the years 1919 to 1957. For the whole period 1889 to 1957, productivity in the private domestic sector of the economy rose at the rate of two and four-tenths per cent per annum.

Real hourly earnings for all workers in the private domestic economy were closely geared to productivity. As more goods were turned out at less unit cost, the purchasing power of the wage dollar went steadily upward. From 1930 on, the data appear to show that real hourly earnings gained slightly more than productivity. The probable reason for this, says Solomon Fabricant, the National Bureau's Director of Research, is increasing scarcity of labor relative to capital and improved quality of labor.

Whatever the system of measurement, real hourly earnings for the population as a whole must continue to be intimately geared to productivity, because a community must produce before it can consume.

Productivity is a result of the availability of natural resources, the education and training of employees, the efficiency of work flow, the utilization of plant capacity, the competence of supervision, and the morale of the work force, etc. But the main causes of increased productivity are the advances in technology, the greater application of power, and the increased use of capital.

The advance in technology in recent years, has been spectacular in the extreme. Everywhere one looks there are new machines, new processes, new ways of doing things that are bringing about astonishing increases in yield.[17] Through the use of

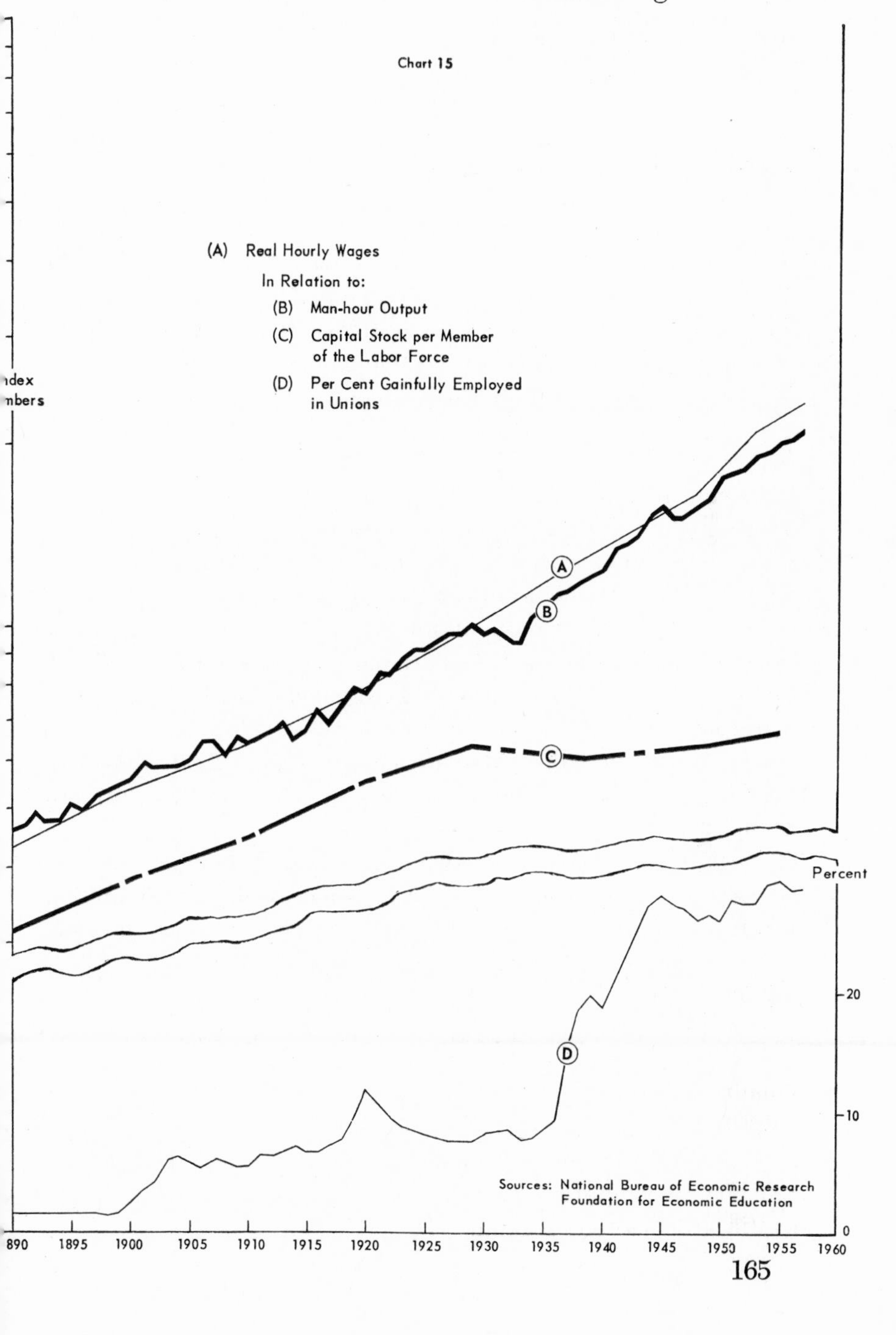

Chart 15
(A) Real Hourly Wages
In Relation to:
(B) Man-hour Output
(C) Capital Stock per Member of the Labor Force
(D) Per Cent Gainfully Employed in Unions
ndex
mbers
A
B
C
D
Percent
20
10
0
890
1895
1900
1905
1910
1915
1920
1925
1930
1935
1940
1945
1950
1955
1960
Sources: National Bureau of Economic Research
Foundation for Economic Education

tractors, mechanical harvesting devices, fertilizer, insecticides, new seed strains and more advanced soil conservation practices, farm productivity increased 110 per cent between 1935 and 1955. In transportation, the horse and buggy has given way to the automobile, bus, and truck; the steam locomotive has yielded to the diesel; and now people are taking to jet flight to travel farther, faster, and at less cost. Metallurgists have worked miracles in alloying metals, and production efficiency has reached the point where steel strip can be rolled at a speed of eighty miles per hour. In communication, the swift couriers of today are coaxial cables, microwaves, dial telephones, teletype, radio, television, telephoto, photoelectric type setting and high speed printing presses that bring the world to our door, visually and by word of mouth, almost instantaneously.

Chemical plants and oil refineries no longer mix and stir by the batch; they run rivers of fluids through their stills by the continuous flow process. In factories, ingenious machines, directed by electronic brains, conduct elaborate machining and assembly operations without the touch of a human hand. The great earth-moving machines dramatically summarize the story of advancing technology and its significance for mankind. A Caterpillar DW 21 wheel tractor and No. 470 scraper with a nineteen-and-one-half-cubic-yard capacity, on a 2,000-foot haul, can move the same amount of dirt in one day that formerly required six men with hand shovels and a horse-drawn wagon 53 days to move. At current wages the cost of moving one yard of earth one hundred feet by the man and wheelbarrow method is one dollar. The huge Caterpillar D 9 Bulldozer does the same job for four cents.

If we want to add a Jules Verne touch to the story of how modern technology extends man's productive powers, it can be found in the electronic computer. A mathematical problem which took seven months for one man to solve with a desk calculator can now be solved in less than one minute with an International Business Machines 704 computer. IBM's new STRETCH computer can do even better; it can solve the problem in less than one second!

Advancing technology is one reason why man's productive powers are rising; another is the greater use of power. In the United States the substitution of mechanical for muscle power over the past century has been one of the most dramatic and meaningful aspects of our national life. As Table 26 below indicates, two-thirds of the power used in the United States in 1850 was supplied by men and animals. Fifty years later seventy-three and two tenths per cent of the energy used in the country came from coal, oil, or water power. By 1950 practically all of the power used in the country (ninety-eight and one-half per cent) was derived from inanimate sources.

TABLE 26. SOURCE OF POWER IN U.S. [18]

(In Per Cents)

	1850	*1900*	*1950*
Human	13.0	5.3	0.9
Animal	52.4	21.5	0.6
Inanimate	34.6	73.2	98.5

Source: *America's Needs and Resources*

The toiler, bending his back to the task, and sweating at his work, has increasingly given way to the technician who commands his mechanical slaves in air-conditioned comfort by simply moving levers or pushing buttons. The dignity of work, long venerated in our religious tradition, has been given new meaning. Modern technology calls for brain rather than brawn, and has achieved the astonishing result of making work easier while making it vastly more productive.

As a "high-energy civilization," America has succeeded in creating more wealth for its people than any nation in the world. In Burma, where the population largely subsists on agriculture, the per capita consumption of power in 1949 was 570 pounds of "coal equivalent," yielding an average income of thirty-six dollars per head. In the United States, by contrast, energy use per head in 1949 was nearly eight tons of coal equivalent, and the per capita income was $1453.[19]

Energy use and the creation of wealth go hand in hand. In

Chart 16, energy consumption (Line A) is compared with national income (Line B).[20] In general, increases in national income have been nearly proportional to increases in the use of power.

The third factor that explains the rise in productivity is capital. To apply power to production through advanced technology requires the construction of costly machines. Society is able to pay for these machines by consuming less than it produces, or, in other words, by saving capital and plowing it back into the productive process. The supply of capital, therefore, is a crucial factor in raising wages and advancing the standard of living. In Chart 15, Line C shows the capital stock of the United States per member of the labor force. In 1889 the nation was using capital stock valued at $3060 for each worker; by 1955 this sum had grown to $6740 per worker.[21]

The capital stock per worker grew steadily until 1929, then leveled off; but productivity and real hourly wages continued to rise. Observing the parallel growth of capital per member of the labor force and productivity up to 1929, one might have concluded that there is more or less a fixed relationship between output and the amount of capital employed. But this overlooks the factor of the efficiency with which capital is applied. Daniel Creamer [22] has shown that from 1880 to 1919-1929 an increasing amount of capital per man-hour was being applied, but the curve of efficiency in capital use was falling. Since that time the amount of capital per man-hour has been more or less constant but the efficiency of capital use has increased. Thus productivity and real hourly earnings have risen in recent years, not because more capital has been applied, but because it has been used more efficiently.

No one, of course, knows how much capital will be necessary to maintain and increase the standard of living in the future—there are too many unknown technological and economic variables to make such a calculation. But if past experience is any guide, the community can feel better about its prospects if the curve of capital stock per worker is rising or moving horizontally, as it has over the past three decades.

The importance of capital to the wage earner is demonstrated

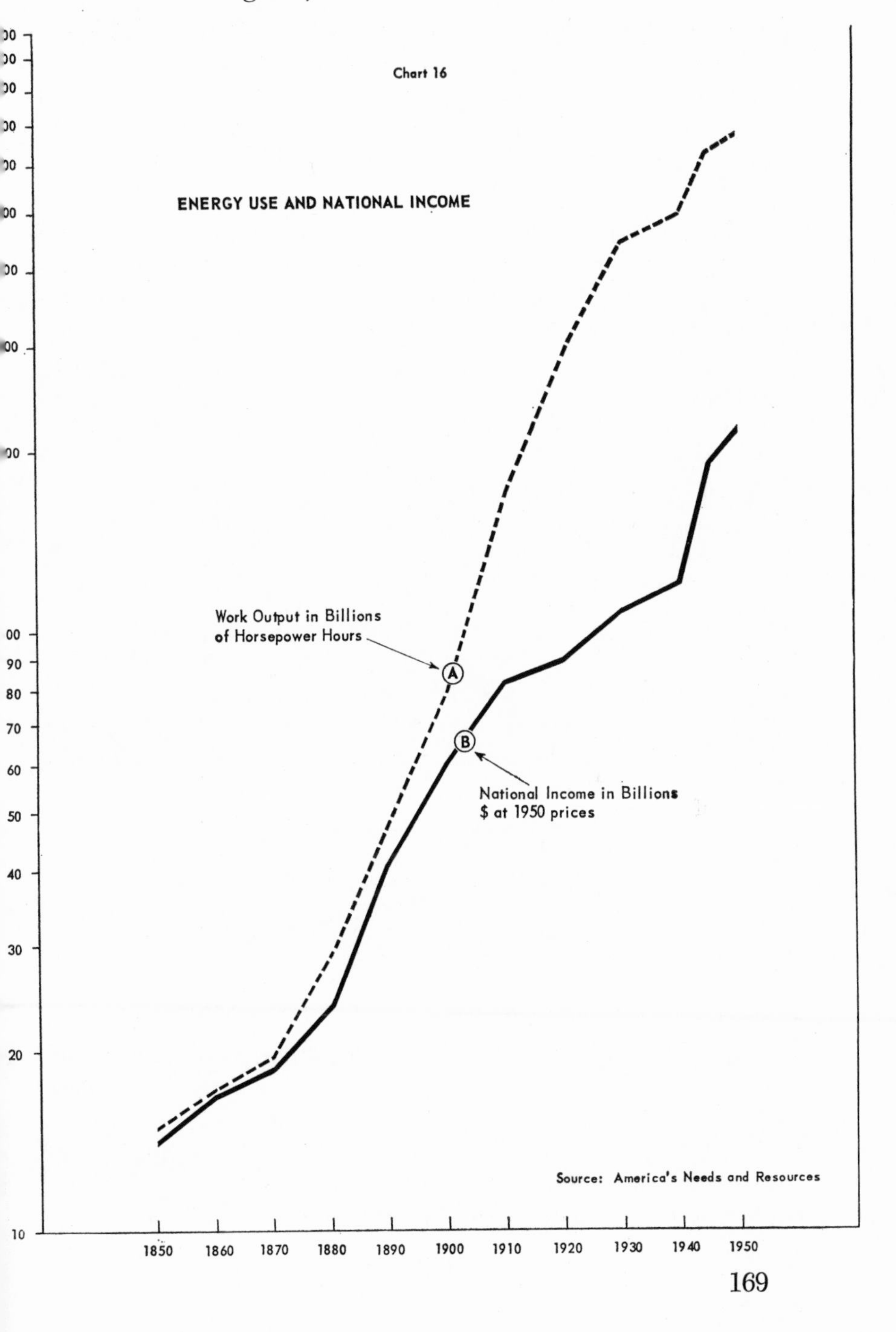

Chart 16
ENERGY USE AND NATIONAL INCOME
Work Output in Billions of Horsepower Hours
National Income in Billions $ at 1950 prices
Source: America's Needs and Resources
100
90
80
70
60
50
40
30
20
10
1850
1860
1870
1880
1890
1900
1910
1920
1930
1940
1950

even more forcefully in Table 27 which shows the average annual wage paid to employees, capital per jobholder, and the return on capital investment for twenty manufacturing classifications.[23] Table 27 shows that wages tend to be highest in those industries where capital per jobholder is high and where return on capital is good. Wages tend to be lowest in those industries where capital per jobholder and return on capital is low. Capital is another name for tools. The better the tools, the more productive is the worker and the higher the wages for both capital and labor.

TABLE 27. ANNUAL WAGES, CAPITAL PER JOB HOLDER AND RETURN ON INVESTMENT FOR TWENTY MANUFACTURING CLASSIFICATIONS—1956

	Annual Wage	*Capital Per Jobholder*	*Return on Investment*
Transportation equipment	$ 5,456	$ 11,672	13.1%
Motor vehicles	5,450	18,936	11.9
Primary metals	5,448	16,793	10.2
Chemicals	5,297	28,570	11.6
Nonelectrical machinery	5,265	14,237	13.1
Instruments	4,985	14,250	11.1
Printing and publishing	4,918	10,959	10.6
Fabricated metal products	4,911	9,681	9.0
Rubber	4,818	15,526	10.6
Paper	4,764	15,841	10.7
Electrical machinery	4,728	11,401	9.3
All manufacturing	4,584	15,006	8.8
Stone, clay, glass	4,560	12,496	11.0
Food and kindred	4,192	16,182	7.7
Furniture and fixtures	3,935	6,492	9.6
Lumber and wood	3,377	8,025	6.6
Textile mill products	3,282	8,831	4.4
Leather	3,249	4,420	6.0
Tobacco	3,186	32,630	11.2
Apparel	3,011	3,564	5.1

Source: *The Economic Almanac, Statistics of Income, US Income and Output*

In the normal course of events, the fruits of productivity are distributed three ways: higher wages to the employee, reduced prices or better quality to the consumer, and increased profits to the stockholder. Let us see how the distributive process works by considering two hypothetical situations.

In situation 1, we will assume that the unit cost of materials is four dollars, labor three dollars and other manufacturing cost two dollars for a total of nine dollars. Assume we sell each unit at ten dollars for a profit of one dollar.

In situation 2, our material and other costs are the same, but the productivity of labor has doubled so that labor cost per unit is one dollar and a half and total cost of seven dollars and a half. We now have two dollars and a half to distribute against one dollar in situation 1. (Table 28)

TABLE 28. HYPOTHETICAL SITUATIONS ILLUSTRATING DISTRIBUTION OF INCREASED PRODUCTIVITY

	Situation 1	*Situation 2*
Unit selling price	$10.00	?
Cost of materials	4.00	4.00
Labor cost	3.00	1.50 (at old wage rate)
Other costs	2.00	2.00
Total cost	$9.00	$ 7.50
Profit	1.00	2.50 to distribute

If labor claims all of the one dollar and a half in productivity increase and if wages paid at our hypothetical plant were previously equal to those paid for similar work in other firms in the same locality, the wage rates for our plant will be substantially higher than elsewhere in the area. All or part of the initial productivity gain may be retained by labor, but subsequent gains are not likely to be appropriated for wages. The operators of the business will object to paying substantially more than a competitive wage for the same kind of work. Moreover, competition will, in all likelihood, limit the extent to which our firm has freedom of action to pay wage premiums.

If profits claim all of the productivity increase, it may mean that our firm is more profitable than other firms. Competing firms will sense a new product opportunity, change their technology to compete with us on quality, price and service, and force our profits down to levels that cease to attract newcomers into the business.

What is more likely to happen is that productivity gains will be used in part to establish favorable wage and profit differentials for our hypothetical firm, but thereafter competition will force the distribution of gain to the customer in the form of lower prices, better quality, or improved service. From society's point of view, this is the way distribution should be effected, for everyone is a consumer, and the fruits of the economy can be most widely and justly distributed to the general public as consumers rather than to specialized publics as producers.

To recapitulate this phase of the argument, then, wage increases throughout the economy have not come out of profits, because profit margins are relatively modest. Employment costs take the lion's share of the wage-profit dollar, and there is little opportunity for redistribution in this direction. Inflation has increased money wages, but it has also lifted prices. This type of wage increase has yielded no general benefit because wages are worth only what they will buy. Moreover, inflation has vicious side effects such as erosion of pensions and savings and the dislocation of relation between borrower and lender that are inimical to a healthy economy. Wage increases that exceed productivity tend to redistribute the income of other workers through creating unfavorable ratios of labor exchange. They bring on unemployment by pricing goods out of the market. No one can condone wage increases of this type.

The true explanation for the steady advance in real wages is increased productivity. This is the key to material betterment. By producing more for less cost, everyone—employees, stockholders and consumers—have gained. There is no other known way; or if there is, the economic experience of mankind has so far failed to reveal it.

We are now in a position to weigh the arguments made for the redistribution of profits. Union debaters insist that large wage increases can be given without raising prices. This is true only if productivity gains in the general economy are large enough to permit wage advances; otherwise, the argument is false. In manufacturing, wage payments now take eighty-four cents out of employee-profit dollar leaving only sixteen cents for the shareholder. If the shareholder is further squeezed, the wage earner will, in all probability, be hurt. Unless the share owner is properly rewarded, he will not provide the tools that enable the worker to raise his productivity and increase his standard of living.

The National Industrial Conference Board has recently set this matter in proper perspective by showing the labor, property, and tax content of the selling price of eight basic commodities.[24] When a man buys an automobile, the study finds that he pays thirty-six and nine-tenths cents out of each dollar for taxes, fifty and one-half cents for labor, and twelve and six-tenths cents for property services. After taxes, his automobile dollar is spent eighty and one-tenth cents for labor and nineteen and nine-tenths cents for property services.

The breakdown for the eight commodities is shown in Table 29. Taxes take sixty-two and three-tenths cents of the cigarette dollar and forty-five and six-tenths cents of the gasoline dollar. For all eight commodities, labor claims, after taxes, absorb from seventy-one to eighty-seven cents of the consumer's dollar.

TABLE 29. LABOR, PROPERTY, AND TAX CLAIMS OF THE FINAL SELLING PRICES OF EIGHT BASIC COMMODITIES
(In Per Cent)

				After Tax	
	Labor	*Property*	*Tax*	*Labor*	*Property*
Automobile	50.5	12.6	36.9	80.1	19.9
Beef	56.4	22.6	21.0	71.4	28.6
Bus Ride	58.5	8.6	33.0	87.2	12.8
Cigarettes	29.7	8.1	62.3	78.6	21.4
Gasoline	43.3	11.1	45.6	79.6	20.4
Man's Shirt	60.6	14.8	24.7	80.4	19.6
Man's Work Shoes	56.8	19.2	24.1	74.8	25.3
Steel Plate	61.2	12.7	26.1	82.8	17.2

When the National Industrial Conference Board distributed the Gross National Product, representing the nation's total expenditures for 1954, it found that labor received sixty-three and one-tenths per cent of the total; property (i.e., rent, interest and profits) received sixteen and eight-tenths per cent; and government got twenty-four and two-tenths per cent. After taxes, labor's share of the total was eighty-three and two-tenths per cent. Thus when the consumer purchases a product, he is, for the most part, buying labor. If the unit price of labor increases, the selling price must go up, for no one is willing for long to produce goods unless he can earn an adequate profit.

This is all pretty obvious, yet there are stout men who continue to insist that labor cost has little to do with price. If any further demonstration is needed that labor costs and price cannot be separated, it can be found in Chart 17 which shows the behavior of the Bureau of Labor Statistics index of Unit Labor Cost (Line A) in relation to the Bureau's index of prices for manufactured goods (Line B).[25]

The price of manufactured goods is closely related to unit labor cost. From 1920 to 1933 unit labor cost fell, as did prices. From 1933 to 1940, unit labor costs and prices rose gradually, then took off on a sharp rise to 1950. A wide variation between unit labor cost and the price of manufactured goods occurred during the war years, 1943-1945. It is quite likely that the price line during this period is artificially low because of OPA price regulation, and that if allowances were made for black-market pricing, the divergence between the two series would be smaller. It makes no economic sense, then, to talk as if prices can be dissociated from wages. Prices and wages are two sides of the same coin, forever bound together, and no dialectic, however skillful, can dispose of this elementary fact of life.

Union leaders put major emphasis on purchasing power as the key to a healthy economy. They call for public support for wage increases in order that workers can buy more and thus stimulate prosperity. This argument has surface plausibility—everyone is in favor of increased purchasing power—but it runs into difficulty when one asks the simple question: Where does the money come from to provide increased purchasing power?

The economic bloodstream, like that of the human body, is

Chart 17

RELATIONSHIP BETWEEN UNIT LABOR COST AND PRICE OF MANUFACTURED GOODS 1914 - 1959 (1947 - 49 = 100)

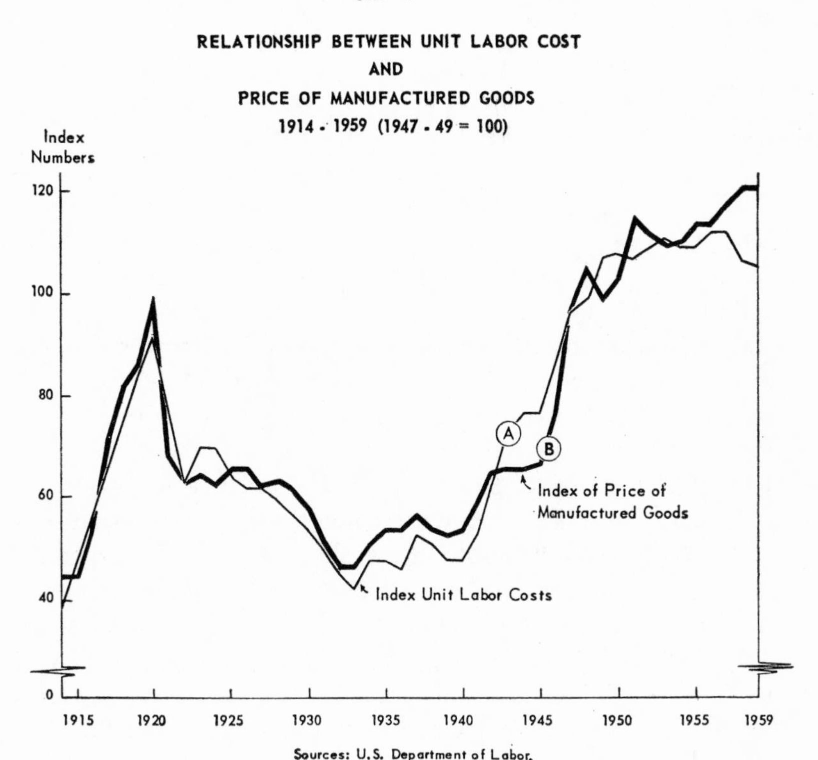

Sources: U.S. Department of Labor, Federal Reserve Board

circulatory. One man's purchasing power is another man's cost. Customers get their purchasing power from wages and salaries and from ownership of property through rent, interest, and profits. Business gets its purchasing power from the sale of goods and services to customers and from the sale of stocks and bonds to investors. Government get its purchasing power mostly from taxes. All three spending groups can enlarge their purchasing power through borrowing from lenders. As the purchasing power of the government rises, the buying power of the taxpayer falls by the amount of the tax, and that of the bond buyer by the amount of his purchase less interest. When government gains purchasing power by inflating the money supply, it takes buying power away from bondholders and people on fixed incomes through increased prices. Government cannot conjure up purchasing power; it can never give anything to the people but what it must first take away.

It is true that strong unions can force wages and prices up to a certain extent and thereby increase the purchasing power of the union members at the expense of other consumers. If the consumers refuse to buy at the increased price, unemployment results. No one, of course, is in favor of increasing purchasing power either for companies or for union members at the price of chronic unemployment.

The only way to increased real purchasing power for the community as a whole is through rising productivity. If the union demand for more buying power for the mass of workers is to have any economic reality, unions and companies must find ways to collaborate to produce more and better things at a cheaper cost. Purchasing power is not the battle cry that will win the victory; the call to arms should be for lower costs through greater productivity so that the worker can buy more of the necessities and comforts of life with his wage dollar.

The great and compelling union argument is, of course, that collective bargaining has won increased wages for the workers. In 1935 the average hourly wage in manufacturing was fifty-five cents; by 1959 it had reached $2.22. The annual income per full-time employee in manufacturing rose from $1216 in 1938; to $5214 in 1959. "These gains," says *Economic Trends and Outlook* (December 1955—referring both to wage and non-wage gains) "have not been handed to the workers on silver platters; they have been the product of organized strength of the local unions in the factories, shops, mines, offices, and other places of work. They have been the result of strong national unions equipped with field, research, legal, educational, and publicity staffs. They are preceded in most instances by tough negotiations, and all too frequently by the necessity of strikes."

Wages, the union thinks, rise largely because of union pressure. Companies hold down wages and jack up prices to increase their profits. But the unions, through tough negotiations and strikes, force the employer to give the worker a larger share of production in the form of higher pay.

This mental picture of why wages rise is widely held, not only among union members, but among the general public as well. *The Public Opinion Index* reports that sixty-seven per cent of the general public believes that wages are higher today than they would have been without union presure. The majority (fifty-six per cent) believe that companies hold back on wage increases and give reluctantly only when forced. When manufacturing workers are asked who has done most to raise wages, sixty-three per cent give credit to labor unions, twenty-four per cent name management and thirteen per cent cite government.

Chart 14, shows how a few aggressive unions that have achieved monopoly status in their industries since World War II, succeeded in pushing their wages ahead of other union and nonunion wage-earner groups. They have thus obtained an increase in real wages for their members and can be said to have "caused" wages to rise for the favored few. But this victory is largely at the expense of other workers, for in good part it represents a redistribution of the wealth of consumers through raising the price of goods produced by the favored unions. It also probably creates some unemployment through pricing the product out of the reach of consumers.

Has collective bargaining brought about a general increase in real wages in the community? The evidence appears to suggest not. The widespread belief that unions have raised the general level of real wages apparently is the result of a curious economic optical illusion.

There seems to be little relation between union activity and the rise in real wages. The story of rising real hourly wages and productivity has been told in Chart 15. Line D on this chart indicates the percentage of those gainfully employed who are members of labor unions. While there is close affinity between productivity and real hourly wages, there is no discernible relation between real hourly earnings and the activity of labor unions, as gauged by the percentage of the gainfully employed who belonged to unions.

Between 1890 and 1899 real hourly earnings rose twelve per cent and the percentage of gainfully employed workers who were members of unions increased by a like amount. From 1899 to 1903 union membership rose from one and nine-tenths to six per cent, a 215 per cent increase, but real hourly earnings gained only six per cent. From 1903 to 1936 real hourly wages doubled, with union membership gaining fifty-seven per cent. Between 1936 and 1945, union membership gained two hundred per cent, but real hourly earnings increased only twenty-six per cent. From 1945 to 1957, union membership showed no gain, but real hourly earnings climbed fifty-three per cent. The reason for this lack of correlation between the increase in real hourly earnings and the percentage of union members among the gainfully employed, of course, is that productivity, not collective bargaining, is the primary cause of the rise in the real wage.

If unionization is to be credited with a subsidiary causal role in raising real wages, it must be shown how collective bargaining has contributed to increased productivity. The union deals with the point by contending that collective bargaining has brought order into mass production and has given the worker a sense of dignity and security so he can produce at his best. Moreover, says the union, through pressure for higher wages, unions have "prodded" managements to invest in technological advance, and, like the United Mine Workers, have accepted mechanization in exchange for a good share of the gains.

Management has a different view of the influence of unionization on productivity. Most industry heads believe unions have raised costs and slowed down the advance toward more efficient production. As evidence they point to strikes and work stoppages, featherbedding and make-work rules, the breakdown of authority and discipline, and the increasing rigidity of employer-employee relation in a technological age that is putting an ever greater premium on flexibility. There is, unfortunately, little objective scholarship on the subject of restrictive work practices. The few available books and articles appear to agree that featherbedding occurs in almost every industry, but is particularly prevalent in such skilled trades as construction, printing, amusements, railroading, and trucking.[26] The scholars agree that make-work practice occurs in nonunion as well as union shops, but that it is easier to organize in union shops because leadership is available, and the men are habituated to thinking in terms of group action.

According to Sumner Slichter, union policies on restrictive work practices vary widely.[27] In 1926 the Typographical Union established maximum output rates for linotypists. In Chicago the standard was 3,000 to 3,500 ems per hour, while in Memphis (a weaker union town) it was 8,000 ems per hour. In each issue of its paper, *The Hot Slug*, the union printed a "Speedometer," indicating what the standard output should be, and added exhortation such as the following:

> Mr. Operator
>
> When you sit down to the linotype to begin your day's work, do you remember that you are a union man?
>
> Do you remember that the union has established a deadline—the amount of type that is a fair day's work?
>
> Do you realize that when you produce a much larger amount than the deadline you are forcing some brother member to walk the streets who should be receiving pay for doing that work that you are doing for nothing?

The Amalgamated Clothing Workers, says Slichter, dealt with the competitive problem in the 1920's in quite another way. It made wage concessions to get in line with economic realities and got rid of restrictive rules and work practices that were raising the cost of production in union shops.

In a remarkable interview with the editors of *U.S. News & World Report*,[28] John L. Lewis, President of the United Mine Workers, said that not only did his union cooperate with the operators in modernizing the mines, but, he declared, "we invented the policy." Employment in the mines has fallen from four hundred thousand in 1948 to under two hundred thousand today, but, said Mr. Lewis, wages have risen to twenty-six dollars per day; and, while the change has been hard on some miners, most of them have found jobs in other industries where they can work in "God's sunshine."

Featherbedding is an economically wasteful practice, but an understandable one because it represents the worker's effort to protect his dignity, his pay rate, or his job. Some argue that society should not require the worker to bear the major cost of technological and market change but should help him adjust. This, of course, poses one of the primary issues of our time—Should the state try to forestall change, as in the case of farm aid, or recognize it and help people adjust? In the adjustment should the interests of the producer or consumer take precedence? The featherbedder himself furnishes an answer to this problem for, as a producer, he wants other people to pay for his inefficiency; but, as a consumer, he resists paying premium prices to subsidize the inefficiencies of others. In competitive markets, featherbedding disappears in a hurry because people generally buy from the suppliers who offer the best values.

One of the greatest challenges to modern management is conducting business in such manner as to enlist the cooperation of employees in maintaining reasonable work standards and, at the same time, achieving maximum productivity. The solution for this problem is not simple, but neither does it involve any great mystery. In the experience of successful managements, the answer is found when (1) employees are treated as people rather than as economic units; (2) the work is so arranged that employees are not penalized unduly by change; and (3) employee creativity is called on to help solve the problems of the business.

The reader can strike his own balance on the contributions of collective bargaining to productivity. If he thinks that unions have added more to the efficiency of production than they have taken away, he is justified in believing that unionization has helped to raise the general level of real wages. If, on the other hand, he believes that unions have reduced productive efficiency, he must conclude that real wages are lower, not higher, as a result of unionization.

The widespread belief that unions have "caused" wages to rise is understandable. Unions are rowing with the productivity stream, and at the finish line they take the bow and receive the public's applause. Professor Milton Friedman of the University of Chicago has described the situation this way:

> In a dynamic world, economic forces are always arising that tend to change relative wage rates. Shift in demand for final products, changes in techniques, discovery of new resources—all produce changes in the demand for and supply of labor of various grades, and hence changes in wage rates. In the absence of unions, these forces will operate more or less directly on wage rates. Given unions, the same forces will be present but they will operate indirectly on wage rates through the mediation of the union. For example, a change in demand that would have led to an increased wage rate in the absence of the union is likely to do so in the presence of the union. Strikes may be required to produce wage rises that would have occurred in the absence of the union. This change in the process whereby the underlying forces work themselves out leads to unions being regarded as causes of changes rather than as intermediaries.

Moreover, says Friedman, "Collective bargaining is regarded as causal in wage increases because union maneuvers become newsworthy. Since union-management dealings can only take place at discreet intervals of time and with respect to matters of some moment, forces that would work themselves out slowly, gradually and unnoticeably accumulate until they come to a head. They must then be dealt with at one point in time and at a stage when consequences are dramatic and obvious. On the other hand, the forces that bring about wage changes in non-unionized areas operate subtly, impersonally, and continuously and so tend to go unnoticed." [29]

In accounting for the public's confusion on the cause of wage increases, it should be observed that people find it easier to think in terms of money wages than in real wages. Since 1940 money wages in manufacturing have risen 260 per cent on the average, but real wages have risen only ninety-one per cent. Because of the inflationary policies of the federal government and the consequent cheapening of the dollar, large and frequent wage increases have been relatively easy to get, enabling unions to point to "substantial" money gains as a measure of their success. It is only later that the employee finds that the cost of living has risen and that his money wage increase is less of a boon than he had anticipated.

If it is difficult to make out a case for unions as a primary cause for a general increase in real wages, it is easy to demonstrate that in non-wage areas collective bargaining has indeed been a dynamic force. Unions have, for example, greatly influenced the form of wage payments. Instead of taking his wage in one lump sum, the worker now takes his share partly in money wages and partly in pensions and supplementary benefits, paid vacations, severance pay, daily and weekly wage guarantees, and other institutionalized forms of wage payments. Moreover, with union pressure directed at a shorter work week, the employee takes more leisure and less work. In some industries, such as rubber, where the work week has been reduced to thirty-six hours, many unionists have reasserted their desire for more work and less leisure by "moonlighting" or taking a second job to supplement their incomes.

Through negotiation with employers, unions have set up an elaborate system of work rules governing the relation between the worker and his supervisor, setting up grievance machinery, giving seniority or job security for older workers, and regulating other aspects of the job.[30]

On the psychological front unions have given the worker the feeling that someone is looking out for his interests, and that the boss can no longer push him around with impunity. The union has provided shop stewards and other officers status and career opportunities, and it has lifted the spirit of many workers by instilling in them a sense of mission and a belief that right is on their side. The depth of worker feeling for their unions is expressed by the sacrifice they are willing to make for their cause. Arthur Fox, for example, was a picket captain for five years in the Kohler strike. "What I am doing I can't measure in money,"

Fox told a *Chicago Daily News* reporter. "It's something greater than that." Fox was a bathtub enameler at the Kohler factory in 1954, earning ninety-eight dollars per week. To take his place on the picket line, he got up every morning at 3:30 A.M., and for this duty he drew fifty-two dollars per week from the union benefit fund. To make ends meet, Mrs. Fox took in washing and sewing. "If the wife wasn't such a good manager," said Fox, "we'd never make it." [31]

On the political front, too, unions have exercised considerable influence. They have thrown their weight behind welfare plans, supported government spending and easy-money policies; and, as a general rule, have expressed more confidence in government regulation and control than in market determination of the nation's economic affairs.

All good things, it is said, come at a price, and collective bargaining is no exception. In unionizing, the worker has exchanged individual for group choice; he has narrowed employment opportunities by various forms of the closed and union shop; he has lost income through unwanted strikes; he has gotten the company boss off his neck, but his pyramid of union power has become a great prize for gangsters and thugs, who view it as a golden opportunity to feather their own nests.

Senator John L. McClellan, Chairman of the Senate Select Committee on Improper Activities in the Labor or Management Field, after hearing hundreds of witnesses, rose in the Senate and declared that he and other members of the Committee were "shocked and nauseated by the disclosures of impositions and abuses which have been perpetrated upon the working people of many of our states by the thugs who have muscled into positions of power in labor unions and who masquerade as labor leaders and friends of the working people." [32] Making it clear that he believed the great majority of union leaders were honest, Senator McClellan declared that in errant unions the members have been denied their right to vote or voice opinions on union affairs; they have become victims of coercion and brutal physical violence; union treasuries have been looted and welfare funds stolen; public officials have been corrupted; and money has been extorted from small businessmen who were vulnerable to union shakedown tactics.

Many employers believe that union members do not wish to pay a price for unionization, and that workers are organized against their will. The evidence does not support this point of view. In the ten-year period from 1936 to 1945, when the movement for collective bargaining enjoyed its greatest period of growth, unions won seventy-five to ninety-four per cent of the elections conducted by the National Labor Relations Board. By 1958, when the movement had shaken down and more disaffection was beginning to appear, unions were still winning sixty-one per cent of the NRLB elections.

In January 1960, the Gallup Poll asked the national public: "In general, do you approve or disapprove of labor unions?" Seventy per cent of the general public said they approved. Among union members, ninety-one per cent voted approval; only four per cent said they disapproved.

This is not to say that union members have liked the price they were required to pay for collective bargaining. Tens of thousands of letters protesting union terrorism and corruption came to the McClellan Committee from union families. So great was the demand for reform that in June 1959 *The Public Opinion Index* reported eighty-five per cent of union men and members of their families voting for reforms such as publicity for union finances, secret strike votes, and the guarantee of the secret ballot in electing union officers.

Broad wage gains have not, and cannot, come out of profits. Wages constitute the principal cost element in price to the consumer. If wage costs are pushed up faster than productivity, prices must rise, creating unemployment in many instances. Militant unions can, by pressure tactics, improve their wage position in relation to other worker groups. But the true cause of rising real wages for the labor force as a whole is not mass pressure through collective bargaining, nor arbitrary increases in purchasing power; the only road to worker betterment is increased productivity, brought about mainly by more and better applications of capital.

If the union arguments in the profits debate fail to square with economic facts, they make good sense when viewed as an exercise in politics. Consider the problem of the union leader. He sits precariously on top of a power pyramid with his job continuously in jeopardy. Other unions may out-perform him in getting wage increases for their members. Strong factions grow within the union, constantly on the lookout for an opportunity to depose the present leadership and take over the direction of union affairs.

Union leaders employ various tactics to hold on to their jobs. One way is to keep the opposing factions off balance. Another is to control the opposition by giving or withholding union jobs. In some instances, as were brought out in the testimony before the McCellan Committee, the blackjack has been found to be an effective instrument of persuasion. But the surest way to maintain power is to win higher wages and benefits for the union constituents. It is for this reason that the primary battle cry of the union leader has been, and probably always will be, the one impressive word: "More."

Chart 15 shows the average rise in productivity from 1889 to 1957 was two and four tenths per cent. In the last decade the increase has averaged three and six tenths per cent. The rate of productivity gain has varied, of course, by industry as well as by time period, but it is probable that a two to four per cent average annual gain can be achieved in the foreseeable future. This gain can be distributed to stockholders in the form of larger profits and dividends, to consumers in the form of lower prices or better quality, or to wage earners in the form of higher wages. The whole or any part of a two to four per cent yearly gain is quite unspectacular from the union's point of view. In terms of the current mood, it hardly provides the platform on which a labor leader feels he can whip up the enthusiasm of his followers. As a consequence, he is under political pressure to "go for the big one."

In the campaign for the big wage increase, the profit issue is a highly useful political vehicle. It is a simple concept, easily visualized by the rank-and-file union member and capable of provoking moral indignation and other forms of emotion. All leaders of mass movements, it seems, feel the need for a devil against whom they can rally their forces and vent their wrath. Hitler chose the Jew for this role; Khrushchev uses "the capitalist war mongers" as his target; and Castro inveighs against "Yankee imperialism." Struggling for "fair wages" against "the avarice and greed" of the employer is well calculated to lift men's spirits and create a state of mind that willingly submits to discipline and makes the economic sacrifice necessary to further the cause. No one can feel too sorry for Mr. Moneybags when the union sets out to get a wage increase. "The steel industry fights for money," says a United Steelworkers advertisement. "Our union fights for people."

The idea of exorbitant profits is important for union electioneering, but it is crucial to the union's economic rationale. Real wages for the whole community can rise only through an increase in productivity. When the union wins a greater-than-productivity wage increase, prices are forced up and some workers are priced out of their jobs. This, of course, is an impossible public relations position for the union, hence the imperative need for the theory of the profit hoard. Profits are super, colossal, swollen, unconscionable, etc.; therefore, goes the argument, redivide the hoard. Wages can be increased without upping prices simply by drawing on the hoard. People obviously must have money to exchange for goods and services, therefore increase mass purchasing power by diverting funds to workers from the profit hoard. Without the rationale of the profit hoard, unions would have to seek a source from which increased wage and benefit payments could be made. The only sources, other than profits, are increased productivity, higher prices, or in the case of money wages, inflation. Productivity is too slow, responsibility for price increase is out of the question, and inflation is bad. The only practical political answer is the big profit idea. Companies are making fantastic profits, says the union; they can grant union wage and benefit demands and lower prices at the same time. If companies raise prices after giving a big wage increase, it only goes to prove once more that corporate greed is insatiable.

There is no denying that the big profit issue is good politics. Using this issue as the spearhead of their campaign, unions have raised their membership from four to eighteen million, and have succeeded in convincing two-thirds of the American people that wages are generally higher as a result of collective bargaining.

But politics cannot feed people, nor clothe them, nor pay for their life insurance. In order to enjoy wealth, the community must first produce it, and the laws of wealth creation, like the laws of gravity, are inexorable. Irresponsible unionism is already under heavy fire, both from the general public and union members themselves. The argument that wages in the United States can be raised by redistributing profits is an irresponsible idea that has not worked in the past, and will not work in the future. There is no promise in trying to redivide the economic pie. The only way the American people can better their lot is to work together to bake a bigger one.

CHAPTER EIGHT

THE SOCIAL FUNCTION OF PROFITS

In a capitalistic society profits have three functions to perform. They:

(1) Motivate men to undertake economic activity that is useful to the community
(2) Reward the risk-takers for saving capital and putting it to work in productive enterprise
(3) Provide a mechanism for social control, both for management and the consuming public, in allocating labor and resources to the jobs society wants done.

While monetary gain is the principal motivation for economic activity, it is by no means the only one. The idea of economic man, however useful as an analytic abstraction, is far removed from the total psychological reality. Every morale study dealing with employee motivations, of which the writer is aware, shows that "man does not live by bread alone." The adage of the old-time bosses that all you have to do to get along with the men is to "put it in the pay envelope" is no longer valid, if it ever was. Men want good pay, but today they demand more than that. They want congenial and healthful work surroundings, reasonable hours and work quotas, and job continuity. Particularly, the modern employee wants to be treated as a person, not as a number on the payroll. He has a strong desire for recognition and a sense of belonging on the team. He wants to feel that management takes account of human values as well as dollars. He respects a boss who knows his job and requires performance, but is fair-minded about it. He is flattered and pleased when management keeps him informed and invites his help, where appropriate, in the solution of company problems.

If money were the only motivation of employees, the greatest worker satisfaction would be found in companies paying the highest wages. Yet it is commonplace in employee attitude research to find marked worker dissatisfaction where the primary differentiating factor is high wages. The companies that get along best with their employees are the ones that pay good wages and provide the non-material job satisfactions as well.

Similarly, profits are obviously but one factor motivating the enterprisers. Power and influence, prestige, social approval, independence, creative desire, and the simple love of the game influence the behavior of the profit makers.

Probably the realistic way to look at economic motivation is to see that it, like all human behavior, is a result of an infinitely complex pattern of drives, but that in economic situations this pattern is organized primarily around monetary gain. Even the minister, as Reinhold Niebuhr points out, is economically motivated "when he moves to a new charge because the old one did not give him a big enough parsonage or a salary adequate for his growing family." [1]

The Socialists have tried to do away with competition and the profit motive. Human nature, they say, is essentially good; it is capitalistic organization of the economy that brings out the worst in man. In a capitalistic society excessive individualism takes over; one man tries to profit at the expense of the other; and the tooth and claw of jungle competition take the place of love and cooperation in men's affairs. Robert Owen, the British woolen manufacturer who established the utopian community, New Harmony, in Indiana in 1825, thought that in a perfect social order incentives were unnecessary, and that man's natural goodness would lead him to undertake the economic tasks required for community well-being.

The great French socialist, Charles Fourier, depended on love or "The Law of Attraction" for his economic incentive. In his "phalansteries" or communes, each family (four hundred to a phalanstery) would be assured the necessities and comforts of life. Milk and honey would flow because labor was naturally attractive and agreeable. People would enjoy work as children relish play. Even the children, organized into "Little Hordes," would be about their tasks at three in the morning cleaning stables, tending the cattle and horses, and toiling in the slaughter houses. So stirred were Americans by Fourier's dream of a utopian social order that some fifty phalansteries were organized in the United States between 1843 and 1845. Horace Greeley, the noted editor of the New York *Herald Tribune,* became a convert for a time, and joined with Albert Brisbane in publishing the Fourierist journal, *Future*.

In his great novel, *Looking Backward,* published in 1888, Edward Bellamy expounded, entertainingly and in some detail, on how a socialist society would get its work done without the spur of the profit incentive. In Bellamy's utopia the community guaranteed "the nurture, education, and comfortable maintenance of every citizen from the cradle to the grave." All men received the same wage and had equal claim on the community's goods. The "coarser motive" of profits was eliminated. Honor, patriotism, the hope of men's gratitude, the inspiration of duty, and the satisfaction of social rank were the things that moved men.

Interestingly enough, in liberating his utopians Bellamy also regimented them. Production was conducted by "the industrial army," whose discipline was so strict that "a man able to do his duty and persistently refusing is cut off from all human society." A young man entered the industrial army as an unclassified laborer and for three years was required to do menial work. Then he became an apprentice, and if he showed ability, became a "full worker" and eventually an "officer." Every year each man was graded on his "diligence in the national service" and his standing in the community depended on these grades.

While non-profit factors took precedence in motivating men, even Bellamy had a hard time getting rid of incentives altogether. His utopians volunteered for jobs, but in order to balance supply and demand for any one job, the administration had to equalize the perquisites of the trades, so that all would be equally attractive. It did this by regulating hours. "The lighter trades," explained Dr. Leete to his visitor from Boston, "prosecuted under the most agreeable conditions, have in the way the longest hours, while an arduous trade, such as mining, has very short hours." From time to time, too, prizes and other emoluments were given to spur people to work.

The only trouble with the Socialist theories of eliminating wage differentials and profits as economic incentives is that no one outside of strictly disciplined religious communities has been able to make them work. The Pilgrims tried communism but within three years were forced to give it up or starve. The agreement among the Pilgrim Fathers signed July 1, 1620, specified that each person was to contribute certain shares to the common venture and in turn become a joint partner for seven years, "during which time all profits and benefits that are got by trade, traffic, trucking, working, fishing or any other means of any person or persons remain still in the common stock," until the "division" at the end of seven years. The agreement also provided that each person would be assigned to productive tasks "as shall be most useful to the colony." While individual families lived in separate houses, the lands, houses, and other chattels were communally owned. Food and apparel were to be drawn from the common store—"all such persons as are of this colony are to have their meat and drink, apparel and all provisions out of the common stock and goods of the said colony." [2]

The Pilgrims landed at Plymouth Rock on December 21, 1620. So hard were the conditions of existence that fifty of the one hundred settlers had perished within three months. The simple economy fared badly. Knowing that economic communism was practiced, outsiders were drawn to the colony to sponge on the Pilgrim's store of food. Christian brotherhood was beset by thievery. Said Governor Bradford in his quaint account of the problems of the colony, "Much was stolen both by night and day before it became scarce eatable, and much more afterward. And though many were well whipped, when they were taken for a few ears of corn; yet hunger made others whom conscience did not restrain, to venture."

The communistic system of the Pilgrims was not productive. In 1623 Governor Bradford, after much discussion, felt compelled to end it. The explanation of his course was brief and eloquent:

> All this while no supply (of food) was heard of, neither knew they when they might expect any. So they began to think how they might raise as much corn (wheat) as they could, and obtain a better crop than they had done, that they might not still thus languish in misery. At length, after much debate of things, the Governor (with the advice of the chiefest amongst them) gave way that they should set corn every man for his own particular, and in that regard trust to themselves; in all other things to go on in the general way as before. And so assigned to every family a parcel of land, according to the proportion of their number, for that end, only for present use (but made no division for inheritance). . . . This had very good success, for it made all hands very industrious, so as much more corn was planted than otherwise would have been by any means the Governor or any other could use, and saved him a great deal of trouble, and gave far better content. The women now went willingly into the field . . . which before would allege weakness and inability; whom to have compelled would have been thought great tyranny and oppression.[3]

The utopian colonies of Robert Owen and Charles Fourier likewise had unfortunate experiences with the socialist dream. Owen's *New Harmony*, which he hoped would spread "from community to community, from state to state, from continent to continent, finally over-shadowing the whole earth, shedding light, fragrance and abundance, intelligence and happiness upon the sons of man," closed its doors after only three years, taking four-fifths of Owen's fortune.

Josiah Warren, one of the founders of *New Harmony*, whose experience with the communal colony was later to lead him to extreme individualistic doctrines, blamed the colony's demise on "the submergence of the individual within the confines of the community. Not only was individual initiative stifled by failure to provide a place . . . for personal rights and interests beyond the sphere of religious matters, but the elimination of individual property rights resulted in almost total dissipation of responsibility for the occurrence of individual incapacity, failure, and short comings of other kinds." [4]

None of the fifty or so Fourier phalanxes lasted very long, most of them disappearing within two years or less. Only the Wisconsin phalanx ended with a profit, and this after six years time. The Central Phalanstery at *Brook Farm* burned at the end of 1846, and the colony quickly collapsed.

Russia, of course, provides the most dramatic modern demonstration that a civilized economy cannot be made to work without the incentive of private gain. At the beginning of the Bolshevik Revolution, the Soviets tried to put into effect two cardinal Communist tenets: absolute equality of income for all, with engineers and technicians receiving the same pay as laborers and night watchmen, and "worker control" of production. Both policies were soon abandoned as unworkable. In 1921 under the N.E.P. (New Economic Policy) managers were installed to direct the plants, and the former workers' "plant committees," which had been running industry, were transformed into regular trade unions with, however, no right to strike. As Lenin explained it, the N.E.P. in 1922 was "urgently necessary to increase labor productivity, to abolish deficits and to assure profitability in every factory." [5] In 1921, wage differentials were set with ratios as follows:

	Range
Manual and lower clerical workers	1-2.7
Other clerical workers	1.2-3.5
Technical personnel	1.6-5.0
Leading administrative personnel	4-5

In 1929, N.E.P. was abandoned and the full collectivization of the Stalinist period was launched. The quasi-independent trade union movement was broken up and its leaders were replaced by staunch Communist Party members. From then on the unions were not supposed to represent the workers, but had as their main task the improvement of labor discipline and labor productivity. The plant managers were the new bosses of production and labor productivity was stimulated by "socialist competition." It was in this atmosphere of emphasis on productivity that the Stakhanovite Movement was launched in 1935. The purpose of the movement was to raise production norms by setting them according to the ability of the fastest and most efficient workers, "the Stakhanovites."

The movement fostered great outbursts of "production miracles," which could hardly be sustained permanently but which dramatized incentives and set production goals. In the late 1930's the rate of production of a certain automobile valve in the United States was one hundred per hour; the Stakhanovite, Busigin, produced 127 per hour. In the United States a weaver usually tended fifty to eighty automatic looms; the Stakhanovite, Vinogradova, attended 208 looms.

If we can believe the reports, the most prodigious feats occurred in the coal mines. In Germany the average number of tons of coal broken per hammer was sixteen to eighteen. The original Stakhanov set a new record by breaking 102 tons per hammer. From then on, one Stakhanovite hero after another strained to exceed the record. When Izatov reached 240 tons he was "strewn with flowers," but he was soon surpassed by the incredible Pavlov who achieved the fantastic mark of 981 tons per hammer.

The Stakhanovites were merely the window dressing in the

great Communist show. What was happening was that, in order to get their work done, the Soviets were compelled to adopt the capitalistic institution of economic reward. As the government put it, "The toilers can exceed their present tempo and for the additional production above the existing scale they will receive a progressively higher remuneration." Many Soviet toilers took advantage of the offer. An auto worker, Kulakov, managed to produce in three hours what took other workers sixty-three hours, so Kulakov received 150 rubles for three hours of work, which was twice the monthly minimum wage of his fellow workers. In another factory, Khudoleev produced 1462 per cent of the norm one night and received 266 rubles or one month's pay for his efforts. In the ore mines the Stakhanovites, Sheirstnev, and Druzhmin, produced three thousand per cent of the norm and received 541 rubles each for six hours of work, twice the average monthly pay. By the late 1930's the average wage for workers was 250 rubles per month. Stakhanovites were averaging 1300 to 1600 per month with some getting as high as 2300 per month.

Today most Russian workers are paid on a piece-rate basis. In medium sized factories the ratio of management income to that of workers, says Harrison Salisbury, *New York Times* specialist in Russian affairs, is about seven to one. In the United States, after income taxes, the pay ratio between plant managers and workers is about four or five to one. Thus Premier Khrushchev had a point then when he twitted President Eisenhower on the American penchant for stifling initiative. Russia, he said, is making more use of incentives to spur production than is the United States.

It is surely one of the great ironies of history that after becoming strong under an incentive system, the United States has embraced the philosophy of leveling through steeply graduated income taxes, subsidies, work quotas and other devices. Meanwhile Communist Russia, in order to become economically strong, has abandoned leveling in favor of pay differentials and wealth consumption in accordance with what one can earn.

In his final telecast in the United States, Premier Khrushchev undertook to explain this anomaly by saying that "under socialism a working man's remuneration is determined by the quantity and quality of his work for society." But, said Khrushchev, "when we in our country expand our production still more and accumulate more wealth, we will go over to the Communist principle of distributing wealth (where) each will work according to his ability and receive according to his needs." [6] Such is the obtuseness of Communist dogma! Russia has been forced to adopt the capitalistic idea of wage incentives in order to create wealth, but later will revert to the equalitarian principle that never worked in the first place. Should history bear out Khrushchev's boast that communism will succeed capitalism, the reason will likely be that Russia embraced capitalistic techniques while we, turning our backs on the lessons of experience, abandoned them.

Russia, of course, is not the only country to feel the economic power of incentives. Before World War II, practically no one wanted uranium. It was found in small quantities, along with vanadium, in carnotite ore. In 1939, six thousand tons of carnotite ore were shipped of which twenty-nine and one-half tons were sold as uranium bearing ore. During World War II uranium was mined and processed under the strictest secrecy by the Atomic Energy Commission. At the close of the war, the Commission decided that "new reserves of scarce materials can best be developed by competitive private industry under the stimulus of profits." Under the Atomic Energy Act of 1946 private individuals were permitted to mine uranium ore, but were required to sell it to the government or its agents. The last free price for uranium ore was posted at thirty-five cents per pound for two-tenths-per-cent ore by the Vanadium Corporation of America in 1948. The ore assays out with varying percentages of uranium content and prices are usually quoted from one-tenth-per-cent ore up.

In the spring of 1947 the Atomic Energy Commission offered thirty cents per pound for one-tenth-per-cent ore, together with haulage allowances and special premiums for new ore and richness of ore. Production lagged expectancies, and in 1949 the Atomic Energy Commission raised its bid to fifty cents. Production continued to fall behind requirements so in February 1951 the Commission boosted the price of one-tenth-per-cent ore to one and one-half dollars per pound, increased the premium for high quality ores, and guaranteed the price until 1958.

These incentives broke the dam. Almost everybody and his brother bought a Geiger counter and started combing the countryside for the telltale click that spelled uranium. Hordes of prospectors descended on the Colorado Plateau and performed great feats of derring-do looking for the magic metal. The Atomic Energy Commission estimates that between 1952 and 1956 more man hours were devoted to the search for uranium than had been spent for all the metals in human history.

The results of the search exceeded even the wildest dreams of government officials. In 1948 known uranium ore reserves in the United States were one million tons. By 1953 the reserve jumped to five million tons and continued steadily up to seventy-six million tons in 1957. In this year 727 mining companies were operating 1300 mines and sixteen mills processed 8600 tons of ore.

Elsewhere in the world a similar story was told. In Canada enormous ore bodies were found in the Blind River Area and, by 1957, 320 million tons had been proved. Large bodies of uranium bearing ore were also found in South Africa, Rhodesia, Argentina, and Australia. In 1957 free world reserves of ore were estimated at over one and one half billion tons with an expected yield of one million tons of uranium oxide.

So prolific was the discovery of uranium that in October 1957 the Atomic Energy Commission announced it was no longer interested in expanding the supply and henceforth would make no new commitments. Thus the profit motive solved a great national problem in a hurry. Since uranium mining is of recent origin, producer interests were not able to build enough political strength to oppose the Commission's decision to shut off the supply.

The incentives provided under the government's farm program have likewise provided a superabundance, but the production process has run wild because of the breakdown of controls. As a result of mechanization and the use of fertilizers, insecticides, and hybrid seed stocks, farm productivity has soared at a spectacular rate. The productivity of an acre of corn has risen from thirty-one bushels in 1939-1943 to fifty-one bushels today. Test programs with nitrogen fertilization have produced yields of one hundred bushels per acre and the prospect is for one hundred fifty bushels per acre in the future. In 1940 one farmer could feed only twelve people; today he can produce enough to feed twenty people.

Under competition the rising productivity of an industry is shared with consumers in the form of lower prices. In a market free of government restrictions this sharing would have taken place in agriculture, but government's response to the technological advance in farming has been to withhold its fruits from the people and deny the necessity for social readjustment. The mechanism of intervention has been to hold the price of farm products above the level that would be set by the law of supply and demand. The farmer puts his wheat, corn, or cotton in storage and receives a "loan" from the Commodity Credit Corporation. When the money is due, the farmer cancels his loan by letting the government keep his produce or repays the loan, withdraws the produce and sells it on the open market. Since, by design, the government's fixed price is higher than the market price, the farmer is glad to pocket the money from his loan and permit the Commodity Credit Corporation to take ownership of his produce.

As a result of the government's price maintenance policy, profit margins on protected crops have been sufficiently attractive to induce farmers to produce mountainous quantities. In 1958 the Commodity Credit Corporation owned outright or had liens on one and three-tenths billion bushels of wheat and one and one-half billion bushels of corn, many times the "normal" inventory carry-over for these crops.

To stem this torrent of agricultural production, the government has tried production controls, but to no avail. When acreage restrictions were imposed, farmers merely planted the rows closer together and poured on the fertilizer. In 1956 a Soil Bank program was inaugurated which paid farmers for taking land out of production. Under this program 28,400,000 acres were made idle by 1957, but usually these acres were the poorer crop land. Meanwhile government reclamation activities were bringing new high-cost land into production to replace less costly land put into the Soil Bank!

In order to get rid of the surplus the government has tried to give it away through relief and school lunch programs and to dump it abroad at prices below cost. Foreign dumping has tended to disorganize world markets and has brought sharp protests from Canada and other agricultural countries.

If control of agriculture had been left to the market process, a working balance between supply and demand would have been quickly established and maintained. With advancing technology and mounting supply, prices would have gone down, profit margins would have been narrowed and marginal producers would have shifted to occupations of greater value to the consumers. This readjustment would have been painful to the producers and, for many of them, would have involved loss. But in trying to protect producers from the judgment of the market place, governments probably do more harm than good. Intervention results in inefficiency and waste, and produces a new kind of economic disorder and social injustice.

The marginal farmer has not been saved by government price maintenance. On a few acres the small operator cannot support the capital investment required by modern farm technology, nor can he achieve the specialization needed for advanced farming methods. As competition has become more severe, millions of farm families have given up and relocated in occupations with greater opportunity. In 1940, farmers represented twenty-three per cent of the population in the United States; by 1956 this figure had dropped to thirteen per cent, and preliminary estimates for 1959 put it at eleven per cent. For many farm families government intervention has succeeded only in prolonging their occupational insecurity and retarding the adjustments which technological progress has made inevitable.

The principal beneficiaries of farm price maintenance, in any case, have been the well-to-do, efficient growers, not the marginal ones. Like companies, certain farmers manage their affairs well and produce crops at the lowest cost. The larger the margin between cost and maintained price, the greater the profit. In California in 1953 the five biggest crop "loans" averaged $649,000. In Mississippi the same year the five biggest cotton loans averaged $480,000; in the state of Washington, the five largest wheat loans averaged $220,000; in Iowa the top five loans on corn averaged $99,000. In 1957 the Soil Bank paid the farm interests of the John W. Baughman family of Colorado and Kansas $1,114,152 for not growing wheat and corn. As the cynics say, these people do extremely well "farming the government." If the market were in control of agriculture, the efficient farmer would still be in business earning an acceptable profit, but his efficiencies would be shared with the consumers in the form of lower prices for foodstuffs.

One result of government price maintenance has been the loss of world markets. In 1928, for example, the United States shipped seven million bales of cotton abroad; by 1955 our export trade in cotton had declined to two million bales. Meanwhile, foreign production has risen from eleven million bales in 1928 to twenty-five million bales in 1955. Mexico, selling mostly to world markets, has increased its cotton production ten-fold in the past twenty years.

Another result of intervention has been to dislocate the farm balance between producers. Of some 260 farm commodities commercially grown in the United States, a few basic crops such as wheat, corn, cotton, tobacco, rice, and peanuts, which represent but twenty-four per cent of the total cash receipts from agriculture, have received the major share of monies allocated for price maintenance. Farmers in protected crops have switched to unrestricted crops, thereby creating new surpluses and depressing prices. Poultry raisers are required to buy feed at protected prices, but sell their stock competitively at prices fixed by auction.

The cost of government intervention in agriculture has been staggering. In 1954, two and one half billion dollars were spent for price maintenance. By 1959 this cost had grown to seven billion dollars, or approximately $140 per family. By 1963, under present laws, the cost is expected to climb to twelve billion dollars! The public is required to pay this enormous bill out of taxes, and is further compelled to pay higher prices for foodstuffs than they would if the market were in control. To thoughtful people this must appear as a strange kind of social justice.

The farmer, of course, has a point when he says that tariffs and labor monopolies raise the prices of the things he buys and that his dependence on government is no different than that of other producers. The solution, however, is less, not more, government intervention in the market process.[7] The profit motive is an enormously powerful force which produces abundance when allowed to function. But a crucial part of the profit mechanism is some form of social control. When control is exercised by the market, rising profits signal the need for expanded production, while falling profits call for curtailment of supply. The profit signal has the necessary sanction for compliance, because producers obey the commands of their pocketbooks. But when control is taken from the market process and handed over to the political process, the producers see to it that the controls are set in their favor, and the consumer suffers injury.

As members of the community, individual profit-makers have ethical and religious values and most of them operate honorably and with good conscience. On the simple test of honesty, the soulless corporations also stand high. In his interesting book, *The Promises Men Live By,* Harry Scherman points out that insurance companies, brokerage houses, manufacturing establishments, and other business firms that buy from and sell to each other have a record of ninety-nine to one hundred per cent fulfilling their commitments. Government, on the other hand, has a long history of breaking its promises. For 2500 years, from the time powerful rulers learned how to clip the coins until today's sale of Federal bonds to commercial banks, governments have welshed on their debts by debasing their currencies. The losses of investors in the 1929-1932 depression were extremely painful, yet these losses were but a drop in the bucket compared with the purchasing power losses sustained by savers in recent years as a result of inflation. Today's dollar is worth forty-eight cents in terms of the purchasing power of the 1940 dollar; this is another way of saying that people who put a dollar in bonds, insurance, mortgages, or other fixed instruments in 1940, and who still hold them, have been defrauded of fifty-two cents by their Federal government through currency manipulation. We can vent our wrath on the dishonest corporation because we can define the crime, but inflation is so subtle, elusive and complex in its manifestations that government can be a thief in the night and escape moral opprobrium.

Expected and actual profits are likely to be distinctly different quantities. To accomplish anything an entrepreneur must be able to dream—to escape from the world of today and visualize the world of tomorrow. And, in dreaming, he must have the confidence of his convictions—a certain fanaticism that enables him to brush aside the views of people who know that what he is about to do cannot be done.

If the entrepreneur has no conviction he cannot do his job. But his need to believe produces blind spots. He may be too sour on the world and, like Sewell Avery, hang onto his cash too long; or he may be too hopeful about his dreams. He overestimates income and underestimates cost; he thinks a new product has more interest for the public than it does; he fails properly to evaluate a circumstance that hindsight reveals was directly under his nose. Under capitalism the opportunity for profit is always accompanied by the possibility of loss. That is why it is called "the profit and loss system."

The profit motive is compounded in good part of hope as well as of actual dollars earned. Profits constitute a prize that men strive for. In dangling this prize before the entrepreneurially minded, society gets a great deal of its work done "on speculation." Many thoughtful observers are concerned lest the assault on profits and incentives undermine American economic strength. Professor Nutter of the University of Virginia, who is currently conducting a broad study on Russian economic growth for the National Bureau of Economic Research, is one of these. Testifying before the Joint Economic Committee for Congress Dr.

Nutter said: "The driving force within the American economy has been private initiative mobilized by the incentives inherent in a free society. The trend of the day is in the direction of choking off incentives. One foreboding economic symptom is the slackening speed at which resource production (i.e., capital formation) has been growing in American industry. Incentives are being strangled and nothing is being put in their place to drive the machinery of growth."[8]

Profits are the primary, though not the only, motivating force for economic activity. Socialist experimenters have tried to substitute love, patriotism, public acclaim, and other inducements for the profit motive; but these have never worked. Because profits are tangible, measurable, and greatly desired by individuals, they are a powerful energizer for the economy. This is the first social function of profits.

The second social function of profits is to reward the risk-takers for saving capital and putting it to work in productive enterprise. Karl Marx thought that labor created all value. He saw no contribution to the productive process by the entrepreneur. What was taken by the capitalist was stolen from the worker. Actually the capitalist earns his wage just as every other participant in production earns his. He supplies the capital that pays wages to workers who are engaged in making things that require extended periods for production. It may take two or three years to build a complicated chemical plant or a complex machine tool. During this period, the capitalist foots the bill. He restricts his own consumption out of previous production and transfers his savings to workers and landowners to make them more efficient producers. Ordinarily the longer the period required for fabricating production goods the greater is their productivity.

The capitalist also takes most of the risks that are required in a dynamic economy. In order to visualize the risk-taking function of the entrepreneur, the economist imagines an "evenly rotating economy" where there is no risk. In this economic dream world prices are perfectly stabilized; every person knows in advance exactly what future income and costs will be; like an automaton, everyone does the same thing over and over again with no variation; there is never any change and no future uncertainty. In this kind of an imaginary society, say the economists, there would be no profit, only interest payment for the loan of capital that involves no risk.[9]

But the actual world is not like this. It is a changing world in a constant state of flux. Technologies are advancing, styles and tastes are changing, population is growing and shifting geographically, variations in weather are raising or lowering crop yields, new companies are being founded and old ones are going into bankruptcy. The economic process never holds still, even for a minute. The only certainty in an uncertain world is that tomorrow will be different from today.

In a capitalistic society, the entrepreneur is the man who takes charge of the community's privately owned economic resources and organizes them through continual change to satisfy consumer wants. It is his job to determine the course of production. Just as a man has only twenty-four hours a day and must allocate his time to those things he wants most, so too the community has a finite amount of manpower and resources with which to produce wealth. The entrepreneur is charged with the responsibility of using men, raw materials, and capital to provide the most wanted goods and services at the most economical price. He must know his customers and be responsive to their wishes. He must have intimate knowledge not only of what buyers want today but what they will want tomorrow. He must know production techniques and how to select the technology that will produce the best quality of article at the lowest cost. He must know how to finance his inventories and collect capital for building new factories and equipping them with modern machinery. He must understand the psychology of the employee so that he can develop a loyal and efficient work force. He must understand the processes of government and adjust his operations to the political requirements of the community.

Above all, the entrepreneur must have adaptability and foresight. In a changing world he is in a very real sense an agent of progress. It is his job to conduct research and innovate. In economic matters he must never be content with the status quo. His professional posture must be that of reaching for and anticipating change. Since change means risk and uncertainty, he must be willing to speculate and gamble on what lies beyond the turn of the road.

This fixing of responsibility with corresponding penalties and rewards is good organization technique, for what is everybody's business is nobody's business. To get anything done it is necessary to give someone the proper authority and exact the commensurate responsibility. The community sets up a web of custom and law in which the entrepreneur can operate. If he does his work satisfactorily—produces and distributes goods and services at attractive prices—he is rewarded with profit. If he fails in his job—produces the wrong thing at the wrong time, makes errors in committing capital, finds himself unable to adjust to change—he is penalized with loss.

As the economist sees it, then profit is composed of two elements: interest for the use of capital and "pure profit" for entrepreneurial risk-taking. The worker, of course, also takes economic risk—injury, unemployment, technological displacement—and in this sense he might be said to perform an entrepreneurial function, but the worker is paid wages whether the firm makes money or not. The entrepeneur is usually regarded as the one who accepts financial responsibility for the business. We speak of "the entrepreneur," but economic function and men do not necessarily coincide. The owner-manager is probably the purest form of entrepreneur, yet functionally he may be said to receive three kinds of income—managerial wages, interest, and profit. The managements of large corporations receive wages for performing an entrepreneurial type of work, but the share-owners are looked upon as the entrepreneurs because they are the ones who take the profit or loss.

All enterprisers in manufacturing, the more successful and the less successful, have over the past decade earned an average profit of eight and six-tenths cents per dollar of investment. If the going interest rate is five per cent, then it could be said that the community paid the enterprisers in manufacturing five per cent for the use of their capital and three and six tenths per cent for taking entreprenurial risks.

In a progressive society the entrepreneur pays his own way and then some, for he creates much more wealth than he puts into his own pocket, sharing the increase with wage earners in the form of higher wages and with the customers in the form of lower prices. It is as if an enterpriser came to one's home and made this kind of proposition: "I will show you how to save X per cent on your household expenses if you give me Y per cent of the savings as my fee." Essentially this is the way successful salesmen operate except that their fee is normally computed as a percentage of the sales price. The fact that Americans are extremely well fed, well housed, well automobiled, and well everything else is dramatic, though unsung, proof that the entrepreneurship of the capitalists has been a good bargain for the consuming public.

In practice, of course, profit cannot be divided into its theoretical components of interest and entrepreneurial wages or fees, hence in reply to the question "What are profits paid for?" the businessman answers, "Profits are the aggregate monetary reward for the enterpriser who accepts the final responsibility for the employment of risk capital."

The third social function of profits is to furnish a mechanism for control; for the managers, control in running their firms; for society, control in directing the managers. So complex is the ordinary business that no human mind can hope to encompass the myriad of detail without some system for guidance. As with an airplane pilot or sea captain, the businessman must have instruments like the artificial horizon and the compass by which to check his course. A business, by its very nature, must take in more than it pays out or go bankrupt. The principal compass by which the businessman steers is the margin between income and outgo, or profit.

Each company sets up its profit control system in accordance with its lights and needs. The E. I. duPont de Nemours and Company, which is widely recognized as one of the best managed firms in the United States, set up a profit control system in 1919 with a special chart room where the executive committee of the company meets once a month to review the progress of the business. For control purposes, the operation is broken down into product groups, with data plotted for the ten preceding years and a forecast for the ensuing twelve months. The key chart for each product group is profit on investment. The purpose of the company is to serve its customers well and make an optimum profit in competition with other suppliers within the standards of law and decency set by the community. Profit on investment is the master gauge of the process, indicating whether the business is going poorly or well.

After looking at the end-result, profit on investment, the executive committee examines the gauges that show why profits are rising or falling. The first two gauges reveal profit on sales and turnover. If profit on sales is rising it means that unit costs are declining. Turnover indicates how hard capital is working. Profit on sales multiplied by turnover equals profit on investment. The committee then examines total sales and the cost of these sales, broken down by the mill cost of producing the product, selling expense, costs of freight and delivery, and administrative costs in order to determine whether expense is in or out of line. The executive committee next analyzes working capital. It looks first at inventories of raw materials, semifinished products and finished products. It then examines the totals for accounts receivable and cash and studies the depreciation reserve against the total of funds invested.

With this kind of control system, showing the condition of the various factors that add up to profit and loss, corrective action can be taken early in the production sequence. Profit as the guidance mechanism for enterprise permits the manager to achieve control over many facets of the business. It enables him, for example, to make efficient delegation of authority. It is usual for a company to organize by profit centers and keep accounts on the activities of each center. The profit-making center may be a department, a division, or a subsidiary company.

Through profit control, a great deal of latitude can be given the manager of a profit-making center. If a man makes money over a reasonable period of time, the presumption is that he knows his business and his judgment can be trusted. Companies, in fact, recruit their officer personnel in good part by means of the profit test. A man who can run a department at a profit may be able to run a plant; a profit-minded plant manager may make a good division head; a good division head may become an officer at headquarters and eventually become president or chief executive officer of the corporation.

While profits provide the key test, no company can delegate power with the simple instruction, "Make profit," for there are other factors involved. Profit making must be conducted within the lines of company policy. Ideally, each profit center has a charter that states the rules under which it must operate, the product field for which it is responsible, the amount of capital it can commit without higher authorization, and other basic policy specifications.

When the profit center is evaluated, its ability to earn a profit is the most important test; but other tests of responsibility are also required. Is the division gaining or losing its share of the market? Is it maintaining product leadership through research, development, and manufacturing efficiency? Is it training competent young leaders to take the place of those who retire? Does it have good employee and community relations? Is it planning thoughtfully and realistically for the future? Unless there are good answers for questions such as these, what looks like a good profit today can turn into a staggering loss tomorrow.

Profit control also helps management to drive ceaselessly toward efficiency. Profit margins are normally small and are constantly under a two-way squeeze. Since the consumer is continually shopping for better goods at lower prices and competitors are striving to satisfy this demand, there is always a downward pressure on sales prices. As a result of advancing technology, the unit cost of the product tends to fall but seldom as fast as anyone would like. Employees want wage increases that exceed their productivity; upgrading of precision raises manufacturing cost; competition requires an increase in selling effort.

To protect profit margins, therefore, management must always seek ways to cut cost. Many companies maintain engineering and research departments to make continual studies of cost cutting. The market for production equipment is searched for machines or processes that will produce more for less. Employees are given money prizes for ideas on how to produce more efficiently. Companies that are integrated vertically give their divisions the right to procure raw materials and components outside the firm if competitors can supply the items cheaper. Naturally not much of this type of outside buying is done because the supplying division inside the firm is forced to become as efficient as its outside competitor. Nevertheless, freedom to buy outside is a strong stimulant to efficiency.

All organizations, public and private, tend to become bureaucratic. One function grows on another. A man needs a secretary, then a filing clerk, then an office boy; and the volume of paper shuffling grows. Each function acquires what appears to be a reasonable rationale and, after a time, the function is thought of as a normal part of cost. It takes a hard-fisted and determined management to cope with these encrustations of bureaucracy. Should management's zeal flag in this respect, however, a shrinking profit margin usually provides the needed stimulus for housecleaning.

Profit control helps management decide what to produce, when and where to produce it, when to expand or contract, where to locate plants, when to increase or decrease inventories, when and how to refinance, and all other major operating problems in the conduct of the business. In a capitalistic society the social function of a business is to provide the goods and services people want. If the economy is competitive and people have an opportunity to choose between suppliers, the size of a company's profit is a reasonable measure of the fulfillment of its mission. Profit making must always be conducted within the value system of the community; but when a company competes for public favor in accordance with the law and the rules of custom its profits are, in fact, a measure of public acclaim for services rendered.

In the interest of their firms and that of the consumers, managements must seek maximum long-term profits with due regard to public decency and the factors of risk.[10] This requires them to offer goods at competitive prices and, at the same time, drive down unit cost in order to earn the most satisfactory profit. With this compass as their guide, managements can organize their men and resources to serve the consumer as the consumer wishes to be served.

It is difficult for people to visualize the profit mechanism this way. Big profits are often interpreted as "exploitation," but the fact is that when a large profit is earned in competition it usually means that the successful company is getting greater output with fewer men, materials, and capital; it is freeing these scarce factors of production for the manufacture of other articles people want. This means that the efficiencies of the big-profit company will sooner or later become standard in the industry and will be passed on to workers in higher wages, to customers in lower prices, and to stockholders in larger dividends.

Profit control is exercised largely through the allocation of capital, a prime resource in the production process. Every competent businessman knows that it is his duty to conserve and expand the capital supply. Not only is this to his personal advantage but it is to the consumer's interest as well. Capital is both scarce and hard to come by; to dissipate it or handle it badly is a distinct disservice to the community. So important to a company is the handling of capital that decisions respecting its use in any appreciable amounts are usually lodged with the board of directors. In the delegation of authority a president or a division head may be given discretion on the commitment of capital up to a limited amount; above this it is a matter for board decision.

In managing capital for profit, many factors are taken into consideration. An alert board must weigh possible gains against the risk of losing the principal; it must think about the constancy of return and also the need for diversification in making commitments.

When a management takes a project for capital expenditure to its board, its case is normally carefully documented. It includes answers to these questions: What are the prospects for market demand? What is the nature of the competition? How does this capital expenditure fit in with the total profit-making plan of the company? What is the expected return in relation to the risk?

In budgeting for profits, companies usually set norms of profit expectancy before new capital will be committed. At Johns Manville Corporation, for example, in the present stage of the market a seven per cent return is required for capital used to finance expansion of inventory. Before authorization is granted for the purchase of equipment to replace a machine producing a market-tested product, a fifteen per cent return must be in prospect. Before capital is committed to a completely new product, a twenty per cent return must be attainable. Actually, of course, an average of twenty per cent return for a whole line of new products is seldom achieved, for some ventures succeed and others fail. But unless the goal for new products is put this high, management may not have enough profit from its successes to make up for losses on its failures. Balancing the profit and loss for all of its divisions over the past thirty years, Johns Manville has earned an average of twelve to fifteen per cent profit on investment.

The decision of the duPont Company to seek competition in the manufacture of nylon and cellophane illustrates the complexity of the problem of capital allocation in American business. Nylon was brought to the market after the expenditure of twenty-five million dollars in research and development; cellophane cost a like amount. Both products caught the public's fancy and sales rose rapidly. For many years duPont was the sole producer of these products. Profits from their sale were evidently satisfactory, for they bulked large in the company's sales volume, and duPont has customarily earned ten per cent on its operating investment.

When demand continued to rise, the company was faced with the necessity of committing more capital to plant expansion or encouraging other firms to come into the business. It chose the latter course, licensing The Chemstrand Corporation to produce nylon and Olin Mathieson Chemical Corporation to manufacture cellophane. Both licensees were given engineering assistance in the construction of their new plants with the result that the competitors now have modern plants that in some respects are more efficient than those of duPont.

In making the decision to license other companies to manufacture nylon and cellophane, duPont achieved what it thought were several advantages. With competitors in the field, it could measure its own production efficiency against that of outsiders. Moreover, government would not be bringing monopoly suits that cost time and money to defend. The additional capital that duPont might have put into the expansion of nylon and cellophane production was released for employment in other promising chemical ventures such as Orlon, Mylar, and Delrin. Finally, by directing its funds away from old products to new ones, duPont avoided putting too many of its capital eggs in one basket, thus hedging the future continuity of its earnings.

No two companies are alike. Their resources, managements, market position, operating problems, and everything else about them differ. But this welter of complexity is reduced to the common denominator of consumer service by the profit motive. The necessity to make profit and avoid loss, guides management in its business decisions and furnishes the social mechanism whereby the consumer can exercise control over his suppliers.

It is a remarkable commentary on modern discourse that so many commentators see the profit-and-loss system darkly in terms of selfishness, greed, and man's inhumanity to man, and are blinded to the fact that it stands for economic democracy and freedom of choice. In a socialistic economy, the state (i.e., the ruling class) owns the property, defines the social goals, tells people where to work, and denies or restricts freedom of choice. In a capitalistic society, as we know it in America, the people are the bosses. They own the property; they are free to move from one job to another; they decide what they will save and what they will spend; and very importantly, they rule on which entrepreneurs and entrepreneurial groups shall occupy the offices that organize the production and distribution of economic goods.

The competitive market, in fact, is a great polling booth where everyone with a penny votes. The market is a purer form of popular rule even than political democracy, for the consumer votes every time he spends a coin. Moreover, he votes specifically and in detail for the things he personally wants. In the market, minorities can readily be heard, for if only a few people want an off-beat product or service, some supplier in search of a profit will surely make it available. If anyone has any doubt on this score, he will be enlightened by the Yellow Pages of the Telephone Directory where he will discover firms specializing in everything from abdominal supporters to zippers.

In a political democracy, the voter can exercise his preference only every two, four, or six years; he must choose between a few candidates standing for generalized points of view on the conduct of government; and he must abide by majority rule whether that suits him or not. It is true, of course, that in a market democracy the preferences of the person who is well-to-do weigh more than the vote of the man of average means, but, as consumers, the rich are very few in number and their vote is outweighed by that of the mass. In the market democracy, the well-to-do hold entrepreneurial office because control of capital is a prerequisite to economic service, but under a competitive system they remain in power only so long as they please their constituents. The entrepreneurs propose, but the consumers dispose. Whenever the Samsons of industry forget this elementary fact of life, new entrepreneurs who are willing to abide by the wishes of the consumers come into office.

The apparatus of control in a market democracy is competition and the price system. There is considerable difference among economists as to how competition should be defined and how much competition actually exists. For purposes of discussion of consumer control, competition can be defined as rivalry between buyers and sellers for the consummation of exchange. By the price system, we mean simply the expression of exchange activity in terms of money. The prices which enable the community to do most of its economic calculation are cost price, selling price, interest, wages, and profit.

Any attempt to describe the operation of the price system must of necessity involve oversimplification, but basically it works this way: When consumer demand is strong and more production is needed, prices tend to be firm or rising and profits go up. When consumer demand is falling or when there is more supply than the consumers want, prices become "soft" and tend to decline. Suppliers, seeking optimum earnings, expand the production of goods in markets where prices are firm and the profit possibilities look good, and contract them in the soft markets where the selling price is barely sufficient to cover costs.

Thus the consumers telegraph their wishes by the prices they will pay for any given quality and volume of goods. The supplier executes these instructions by drawing workers from the less wanted industries or releasing them to the more wanted lines. Similarly, he channels capital, machinery and raw materials to the manufacture of the things the consumer wants and away from the things he doesn't want. It is imperative that he follow the consumers' wishes, for in order to survive he must take in more than he pays out, and the only way to secure income is to offer goods and services that people desire at prices they are willing to pay. Whenever this market system is unduly obstructed or interfered with it compromises democratic control. Business and labor monopoly substitute producer for consumer control; price fixing and government restrictions on exchange replace market judgment with political judgment.

The market is much closer to the people than the state. Pressure groups heavily influence the decisions of government, and these groups are usually unrepresentative of the interests of the mass of voters. When people buy and sell of their own volition, they are more likely to articulate their personal values than when the state intervenes. The case for government intervention in the market is always proclaimed in terms of the public good, but there is no escaping the fact that when exchange is hampered, the regulator assumes that he knows better than the regulated what is good for them.

When exchange is free and the consumer can communicate his wishes to the supplier by means of the price system, the economy tends to progress. Any innovator is at liberty to try his hand at enticing the consumer with new products or new ways of doing things. He doesn't have to convince a commissar or a congress; all he has to do is to produce a new article that catches the fancy of the buyers and he is, as the saying goes, "in business." For most articles he is required to interest only a few buyers. If he can sell to a few and they like what they have bought, the word will soon spread and the innovator will grow in importance as a supplier. In the 1920's even Henry Ford was not strong enough to resist the demand for a gear-shift car; nor could General Motors overlook the compact car after American Motors and foreign producers had demonstrated that there was a sizable market for this form of transportation in the United States.

The status quo is a tough opponent. Someone is always discomfited by change; it means loss of profit or market position; it makes reorganization necessary; it makes skills obsolete, and means that people have to unlearn much of their previous knowledge. Resistance to change is a natural and understandable form of ego defense. When matters are so organized that decision rests with a few people, the Horatios of the status quo can defend their bridges; but when the innovators can infiltrate freely and offer their leadership for consumer judgment, the status quo disintegrates and progress takes place.

It is the unhampered economy that achieves the highest degree of efficiency in the satisfaction of consumer wants. The inefficient producer soon finds his costs above his selling prices and is forced either to improve his handling of men and resources or give way to some entrepreneur who can. The business graveyard is filled with entrepreneurs who were complacent about cost and who woke up too late to do anything about the diversion of patronage to the competition.

When the economy is free, it is acutely sensitive to the shifting needs and desires of the consumers and adjusts to the new demands with extraordinary speed. All companies have some form of intelligence to know what is going on in the trade. Most large companies reconnoiter the future through market research and undertake pre-tests of products to determine what articles people will buy, what prices they will pay, and to ascertain the right time to introduce innovations.

In the democratic control of an economy, the test of profit is particularly important to lenders and investors in the allocation of their capital. We have already seen how suppliers seek to commit their capital in firm markets and withdraw it from markets that are soft. Lenders and investors react much the same way. Banks and insurance companies expand credit to companies with good earnings records and contract it with companies that have narrow margins of profit. Professionals in brokerage houses, investment trusts and other fiduciary institutions, as well as individual investors operating for their own account, are constantly analyzing the earnings statements of companies to decide whether to withdraw funds or commit new ones.

The stock markets, where company securities are bought and sold daily at auction, provides a continuous indicator for the guidance of investors. When company earnings are rising and the prospects for increased dividends are enhanced, buyers bid prices up. When earnings are falling and dividends are likely to be cut, the concessions of sellers cause prices to fall. Securities, like commodities, are subject to the law of supply and demand. When people are extremely bullish they buy stocks at thirty to thirty-five times the dividend; when they are gloomy and pessimistic they will pay only ten to fifteen times the dividend. Throughout the present century security purchasers have normally been willing to pay from twenty-five to fifteen times the dividend for yields of from four to seven per cent.

Companies with high price-dividend ratios and low yields frequently have great appeal for investors, because this market circumstance is often an indication of vitality and growth. Investors are willing to accept low yields temporarily in the hope of higher future yields with an appreciation in the market value of the stock.

The stock market is pitiless in its evaluation of company managements; in bull markets the shares of well-managed companies rise faster than the industry average, and in bear markets they fall less than the average. No management can long hide its light under a bushel, for the market is continuously revealing which companies have the most appeal for security owners.

When an investor buys a company's shares on the stock market, this does not, of course, make new money available to the company; it merely transfers holdings from one investor to another. But the existence of auction markets, where securities can be liquidated, increases their attractiveness to investors. The continuous establishment of market price also helps the investor decide on the desirability of subscribing to new underwritings.

The market is stern and unyielding in its insistence on control. Consumers are interested in their own satisfactions and expect the producers to cater to them. When women decided they no longer wished to wear hair nets, all the advertising and public relations pressure was of no avail. In a market economy the consumers insist on having their way. The market is as impersonal as it is unyielding. It turns a deaf ear to the cries of distress of entrepreneurs or workmen who fall out of its favor. It is like the mountain in the assignment of personal responsibility; people climb at their own risk. If they fail or fall they have only themselves to blame.

The fact that the market is impersonal is one reason why it has the power of control. When the community puts its confidence in the market, buyers and sellers have no recourse but to abide by the decisions of the market place. When control is taken from the market process and lodged in the political process, the impersonal character of decision is lost. Government is people, and vested interests are extremely adept at finding ways to influence the decisions of government officials. The personalization of decision results in favoritism, waste, and many forms of social injustice. Above all, it tends to make economic activity insensitive to the wishes of the people. The community must have government and government officials must make decisions, but the consumer should think long and hard before he turns over his individual power of decision in the market to an elected official.

Under the profit-and-loss system the workers as well as the entrepreneurs are under consumer control. If workers featherbed and indulge in other inefficient production practices, costs rise and profit margins narrow. The consumers, including the workers as consumers, will tend to buy from the low cost producers because they offer the best values. In other words, the consumers will eliminate the jobs of the inefficient workmen and give them to the men who are willing to produce the values the consumer wants. The entrepreneur cannot shield his employees from this evaluation. The market talks sternly to the entrepreneur in terms of profit and loss and if he is looking out for the interests of his employees, he must communicate to them the directives he has received from the consumers.

In a capitalistic society the consumer rules; in a socialist society consumer control is eliminated. Direction for the economy and, for that matter, the whole society is furnished by a political party, a commissariat or a dictator. Two consequences appear to be inevitable: economic inefficiency and loss of freedom.

A socialist society, as Professor von Mises has pointed out, has no satisfactory method for economic calculation. In a capitalistic society the entrepreneur is guided in his management of manpower and resources by profit and loss. The socialist functionary has no such mechanism. If he wants more electricity he cannot know whether the greatest social efficiency can be achieved by building a steam plant or an hydroelectric dam. If he wants to increase steel mill capacity he has no way of computing the relative economic cost of bricks over concrete blocks, nor how large the mill should be, nor whether it should be located in Minsk or Pinsk. He makes these decisions, to be sure, but compared with a market economy he makes them like the blindfolded child trying to pin the tail on the donkey.

Moreover, the decisions of the directors of the socialist apparatus have a poor degree of coordination. The lumber for the house arrives in time, but the nails are missing; and when the paint comes there are no paintbrushes. As the division of labor proliferates, coordination in planning increasingly defies solution unless there is some simple method of economic calculation such as that supplied by profit and loss.

In a capitalistic society economic calculation is automatically geared to consumers' wishes. Socialist economies receive their orders from above with the result that consumers take what they can get instead of getting what they want. In Russia the

Kremlin assigns quotas to each factory and fixes prices. Most consumer goods quotas are stated in terms of ruble value. Under this system a shoe factory can fulfill its quota and apply for its bonuses by turning out any old shoe instead of shoes the customers want. It is easier for a furniture factory to reach its ruble quota by manufacturing massive veneered tables rather than serviceable kitchen stools, or heavy clumsy beds rather than lightweight cots that the consumers might prefer.

Fringed lampshades that hark back to the Victorian era are part of the furnishings of practically every Russian household. But by modern standards they are ugly; they collect dirt, and they absorb up to ninety per cent of the light. Recently a husband and wife team came out of retirement to open a highly successful lampshade shop in Moscow. They supplied attractively designed plastic lampshades to hotels and soon had hundreds of orders from stores who were besieged by prospective customers. The couple produced lampshades to meet their demand and stored them in a warehouse until the government could set the retail price. But the bureaucracy, after many months of delay, was unable to arrive at a price, with the result that the couple ran out of funds, shut up shop and returned to their pension!

The director of Moscow's big department store, GUM, says Max Frankel in the *New York Times,* has mercilessly denounced factories for continuing to produce outdated merchandise, arbitrarily stopping the production of useful and popular items and disdainfully ignoring the supplying of spare parts which count little in fulfilling ruble quotas. It has been suggested that stores be permitted to "buy" from factories in accordance with consumer wishes and needs; but, if this were permitted, centrally directed plans would be compelled to stand the profits test which would upset the whole machinery of central planning.[11]

The inability of the planners to calculate economically is why socialist economies have low productivity and why the great promises of abundance by the leaders have actually been fulfilled with austerity. Professor Hayek has pointed out that the possibilities for central planning diminish as society becomes more complex. The only conceivable way an advanced society can efficiently organize the myriad of interests, talents, and resources of its citizens, says Hayek, is through the competitive profit system which leaves each separate agency free to go about its business, but through price quotations conveys to each agent the information he needs to adjust his behavior to that of others.[12]

In a socialist society freedom cannot be tolerated. The commissar has a grand plan for the good of his people, and since the plan articulates the higher good, he can brook no opposition. The people may prefer opera or jazz, but they are supplied music with a moral; they may desire pots and pans, but they receive guns; they may want to worship God, but they are given the state in the person of the dictator as their deity.

As the Chinese Communes have recently demonstrated in horrible detail, George Orwell's picture of the society of Big Brother was not far wide of the mark.[13] In a monolithic state, control builds on control; power over jobs and the necessities and comforts of life fall into the hands of petty bureaucrats; and the individual becomes the victim of a system of tyranny that wounds his pride and destroys his dignity.

The American constitutional system of democracy was founded on the principle of the limitation of governmental power. The word "no," used as a direct restraint on government, occurs twenty-six times in the original seven articles of the Constitution and five times more in the first ten amendments which comprise the Bill of Rights. To guard against concentration of power, the governmental structure was set up on the basis of checks and balances with separate legislative, executive, and judicial functions. The legislative branch was further divided into two houses with different terms of office and different systems of representation. Moreover, the sovereignty of the people was spread between state and national governments.

The profit-and-loss system is part and parcel of the American form of constitutional democracy, for it extends the principle of free choice to the nation's economic life and guards consumer liberties with an elaborate system of competitive checks and balances. When the profit-and-loss system is under attack, it is usually by someone who wishes to circumscribe consumer choice and substitute his own preferences through the power of the state. The defense of the profit-and-loss system, therefore, is in a very real sense a defense of personal freedom. Most of the changes in the political rules affecting the market that are currently being urged by reform groups would further hamper exchange and constrict free choice. If we believe in and value the democratic process, we should insist on reform that would require suppliers to compete in the market place and stand or fall on their ability to serve the consumer.

To summarize, then, the social function of profits is to energize the economy, reward the entrepreneur for his services and provide a mechanism for social control. When the profit mechanism operates in a competitive market, the consumer not only earns the greatest amount of goods and services with the least effort, but, more importantly, he preserves his most precious asset, the freedom of choice.

CHAPTER NINE

THE SOCIAL CONTROL OF PROFITS —COMPETITION

It is unthinkable that society would permit profit making without social control. None of us would open his purse to the profit maker and invite him to help himself. Nor would we be content to allow entrepreneurs to organize larger complexes of property and economic power without some form of social control to insure their use for the community's good.

Basically the community exercises two kinds of control over profits: market control and government control. Under market control profits are regulated by competition. Consumers can exercise choice. In giving their patronage to one supplier and withholding it from others, consumers affect profit margins and cause suppliers to conform to the wishes of the buying public. Under a system of market control government provides a political environment in which the market can function. It keeps public order, sets up laws of property and contract, coins money, fixes standards for weights and measures, enforces regulations for sanitation and public health, and formulates the basic rules under which competition can operate. Government undertakes to facilitate market decision, not to influence it. When buyers and sellers, operating within the rules, come to their decisions, government allows these decisions to stand. The state does not try to overrule the plebiscite of the consumers.

Government control of profits takes many forms. Every law or administrative regulation affects the profits of some industries or some companies to a greater or less degree. In wartime, government controls profits by fixing prices and levying special taxes on what is defined as "excess" profits. Ordinarily when businesses are given exclusive franchises to supply public services like transportation, communication, or gas and electric power, their rates and profits are usually subjected to governmental control through regulatory commissions.

In recent years the public's faith in market control of the economy has declined, and the community has turned more and more to government for the organization and regulation of economic activity. One reason for this trend, of course, was the Great Depression of the 1930's. Another reason is the revelation of conspiracies by business firms, as in the electrical case, to avoid competition through price fixing and market allocation. Still another important influence has been the growth of a school of economic thought that has raised serious questions about the adequacy of market control through competition. This school agrees that when competition is vigorous, market controls are satisfactory; but strong monopoly elements, it is said, have entered the economy and compromised the regulatory function of competition. Suppliers earn "monopoly profits" by means of "administered prices" and "contrived scarcities." Since social control of profits through competition has broken down, says this school, the community must regain mastery by turning more to government.

Within the value system that society sets up, the problem of the social control of profits pivots for the most part around the efficacy of competition. Let us examine this situation by asking two questions: What competitive conditions are necessary for the consumer to have control over his suppliers? and, having established these criteria, How well does the American economy measure up?

The classical economists were not very precise in their definition of competition. Adam Smith thought of competition as the independent rivalry of two or more persons. He defined monopoly as a grant of exclusive privilege by the state.[1] Little was done toward refinement of the classical idea of competition until the advent of the mathematical economists in the middle of the nineteenth century. Mathematicians must have precise definitions in order to make their models work. Augustin Cournot, for example, writing in 1838, laid down the proposition that:

$$\text{Profit} = \text{Revenue} - \text{Cost.}$$

and reasoned that the difference between revenue and cost (i.e. profit) approaches zero as the number of rivals approach infinity. Hence the greater the number of rivals the more perfect the competition.

With all the refinements, the textbook conception of competition remained basically that of the classical economists until the 1920's. With many buyers and sellers competing in the market, supply and demand were said to be brought into balance at a price that stimulated maximum economic activity; production would be increased or decreased to meet consumer needs; men and resources would be shifted to those industries where demand was greatest and away from those where demand was least; savings for capital formation would rise or fall as dictated by the interest rate and the possibilities for profit; people would find gainful employment at market wages; and under market control this vast economic complex would operate more or less automatically in the public interest.

The classical model, like all economic models, was obviously an idealization, not a true picture of what actually takes place in a market. It assumed that differences in the product were negligible; that all buyers and sellers were of equal status; and that capital, labor, and goods possessed a high degree of mobility. It further assumed that marginal suppliers automatically held back supply as prices fell below costs.

In the 1920's a new burst of theoretical model building occurred to explain the workings of the exchange economy, and new definitions of competition were advanced. By what he called "a process of heroic abstraction," Frank H. Knight, visualized an imaginary society with perfect competition as one where buyers and sellers act rationally, have perfect knowledge of the market, act with complete independence of one another, exchange only products that have infinite divisibility, and consummate this exchange instantaneously.[2]

In 1933 two books appeared that radically changed economic thought on the subject of competition and monopoly. These were: *The Theory of Monopolistic Competition* by Professor Edward H. Chamberlin of Harvard, and *Economics of Imperfect Competition* by the English economist, Mrs. Joan Robinson of Cambridge. The theories of these two writers quickly became the focus of economic discourse, rapidly saturated the textbooks, and began exercising profound influence on public policy.

The theory of monopolistic or imperfect competition, as expounded by its leading proponents, visualizes economic exchange as running the gamut from perfect competition to absolute monopoly. An imaginary market with perfect competition would meet five conditions, as follows:

1. The commodity dealt in must be "homogeneous," i.e., it must be supplied in quantity, and each unit must be so like every other unit that buyers can shift quickly from one seller to another in order to obtain the advantage of a lower price.
2. Buyers and sellers must have "knowledge," i.e., the market in which the commodity is bought and sold must be well organized, trading must be continuous, and traders must be so well informed that every unit sold at the same time will sell at the same price.
3. Buyers and sellers must be small enough so that their transactions will have no appreciable influence on the market price.
4. Buyers and sellers must act independently and without

collusion or fear of reprisal. Each person must be free to act in his own interest without regard to the interests of others.

5. Market price must be flexible—constantly rising and falling in response to changing conditions of supply and demand. This means that there shall be no "friction" to impede the movement of capital between individuals, firms or products, and no barriers to entry of new firms into an industry nor exit of old firms from an industry.

At one end of the scale is perfect competition; at the other end monopoly. While there are varying degrees of monopoly, the term always means some measure of control over supply and price of a commodity in a specific market. Monopoly power implies that the seller has relative freedom from pressure to reduce costs, develop new products, and diffuse the benefits of innovation among the consumers. A monopoly would be absolute when it controlled a product which was necessary for the life of the consumer and for which there was no substitute. An absolute monopoly could only be visualized if the state were part of the monopoly, for it alone possesses the all-embracing coercive power to enforce the dictates of the supplier.[3] Short of absolute monopoly, the theorists describe monopolies in which a single seller may control the entire supply or a number of sellers, acting in unison, may exercise such control.

By and large, anything less than "perfect" competition is termed "imperfect" competition. Under the latter condition, sellers are few in number and large enough to influence price; manpower, capital, and goods are not homogeneous and lack mobility; sellers "differentiate" (i.e., find ways to individualize) their product to mitigate price competition; some buyers and sellers do not possess the vital information necessary to be perfect competitors.

In real life the nearest thing to perfect competition is a commodity auction market where the product is more or less homogeneous and where, ordinarily no one buyer or seller is large enough to have much influence on price. Professor Chamberlin calls this "pure competition," and reserves the term "monopolistic competition" for markets with few sellers who offer differentiated products.

Under the new economics most markets are said to be "oligopolistic," i.e., supplied by few sellers. Oligopolists, according to the theory, are not competitors in the classical sense; they are hybrids, part monopolists and part competitors who engage in "imperfect" or "monopolistic" competition. The oligopolist is said to exercise a large measure of control over his price. Unlike the wheat farmer, who engages in "pure" competition, he does not throw his goods on the market and take what the auction will bring. He "administers" his price. If the buyer won't take goods at the price he sets, he cuts production and thereby "contrives scarcities" in order to hold up the price. In order to reduce price competition he differentiates his product—raises quality, makes the package more attractive, increases availability, gives easier credit, advertises to create brand loyalty, or makes other maneuvers that help him monopolize consumer loyalties and deter them from switching to a competitor.

Oligopolists also are said to work in collusion with one another at times. In pricing its product, the single firm takes into account the likely response of other firms. If a leading oligopolist cuts price, he knows that others will follow and his profit margins will probably decline. So oligopolists make agreements, or at least come to chummy understandings on prices to be charged. John K. Galbraith, a leading exponent of the theory of monopolistic competition, calls this understanding "a convention" and says quite flatly that "a convention against price competition is inevitable under oligopoly." [4]

The leading economics textbook, by Paul A. Samuelson, is also quite explicit on the collusive behavior of the oligopolists. As Samuelson describes it to his student readers, the system works this way:

> in industries characterized by heavy overhead costs and identical products, there usually grows up the realization that competition is ruinous. Formal or informal meetings are held, whose

> theme song is 'We're all in it together.' Each firm is taught the lesson that other firms will not stand idly by while it cuts its prices; rather they too will cut their prices, so that everyone will end up worse off. Therefore, tacitly or explicitly, the firms try to agree on a price that maximizes profits for all.[5]

This account of how oligopolistic markets operate is given high plausibility by the recent electrical conspiracy where representatives of leading firms got together and attempted to hold up prices for certain types of equipment by agreeing to share the market and rotate bids on major jobs between companies. But before this conclusion would be valid, it would be necessary to show that the behavior of the electrical firms is typical of most industries with few sellers.

Perhaps of even greater significance than the revelation that some firms conspire to fix prices is the testimony in the electrical case that indicates how difficult it is to substitute a private government for market control. The representatives of the electrical companies were quickly confronted with the problem of writing the rules for monopoly conduct, adjudicating differences between the principals, and adjusting their agreements to changing industry conditions. How do you price a new product? How do you police the pricing scheme and prevent competitive concessions? How do you handle the entry of a newcomer into the industry? Because of the difficulty of finding answers to questions such as these, the electrical conspiracy turned out to be a very unstable arrangement, proving once again that in the profit-and-loss system the innate tendency to compete is not easily restrained.

Because of the opportunities for collusion between oligopolists, some leading exponents of the monopolistic-competition school of thought believe that competition is no longer providing adequate control over the profit-making process. The economy is not as efficient as it should be because the oligopolists hold a price umbrella over the heads of all members of the trade, preventing the elimination of the least efficient. Progress is held back because a handful of producers may prefer "profitable and comfortable stagnation" over the hazards of innovation.

Price no longer is the signal of the consumer's wishes, because the oligopolists exercise "jurisdiction" over price. Firms exact from the consumers "monopoly profits" which are always higher than they would be under competition. The self-regulating character of the economy, which was the predominant feature of the classical model, has been lost. Social control must be reestablished by regulation or government ownership or by "countervailing power" where large aggregations like corporations and unions deal with each other under the supervision of the state.

The theory of imperfect or monopolistic competition took hold quickly, both because it had attractive theoretical features and because it offered a scholarly rationale for intervention by the state when people were calling for government to "do something" about the depression. The theory served to focus attention on the fact that modern competition is unlike that of an auction market, that rivalry between firms supplying differentiated products is different than price competition between firms supplying homogeneous products, and that new economic models, indeed, were needed to describe what actually takes place today in exchange.

For those who believed in more government control over the economy the new theory was a great boon; for, if monopoly were in fact supplanting competition, social control would need to be restored through intervention by the state. One historic maneuver in this direction was the launching of the Temporary National Economic Committee in 1938 to investigate the concentration of economic power. After the demise of NRA, with its government sponsored cartelization of industry, the Roosevelt Administration advanced the view that recovery was being held up because of the inflexibilities of big business. Oligopolies were restricting output and insisting on price rigidities, with the result that purchasing power remained low and unemployment high. Since the system was incapable of self-adjustment, government, it was held, would need to underwrite high production and employment and break up concentrations of business in order to restore democratic control.

Leon Henderson, wartime head of OPA and one of the New

Deal's most influential braintrusters, who was instrumental in getting the TNEC corps of investigators organized, was known to have been vastly impressed by Mrs. Robinson's theories of imperfect competition. The new economics evidently furnished President Roosevelt his cue, for in requesting legislative authorization for the TNEC investigation, he laid the blame for the country's plight at the door of monopoly. "Once it is realized that business monopoly in America paralyzes the system of free enterprise on which it is grafted, and is as fatal to those who manipulate it as the people who suffer its impositions," said the President, "action by government to eliminate these artificial restraints will be welcomed by industry throughout the nation." [6]

After twenty thousand pages of testimony from 552 leaders in industry and the preparation of forty-three monographs on important economic problems, the TNEC fell considerably short of the Administration's expectations, for it could reach full agreement only on the broad statement that—"this Committee recommends the maintenance of free competitive enterprise by the effective suppression of the restrictive practices which have always been recognized as evil." [7]

Today political leaders such as Senator Estes Kefauver of Tennessee and Congressman Emanuel Celler cf New York pivot a good deal of their economic thinking around the concepts of "administered prices," "contrived scarcities," and "monopoly profits" and press for legislation to regulate business practices. The faithfulness of Mr. Celler to the monopolistic competition line can be seen in his remarks to the Management Club of the Whirlpool-Seeger Corporation in St. Joseph, Michigan, on February 22, 1957, where he said:

> One result of corporate growth during the last sixty years, is that American private free enterprise no longer resembles the classic system where numerous sellers competed on equal terms in a free market composed of equally numerous buyers. The picture presented by an economic system now is one where the American community depends upon the operations of a relatively few very large corporations . . .

> Significant changes in the nature of competition have accompanied the development of the 'concentrate' structure of American industry. First, competition no longer takes the form of vigorous price rivalry . . . there appears to be a 'follow the leader' policy in pricing. . . . Price movements of the leader are followed almost automatically. . . . In all probability the absence of price competition often results from recognition of the mutual hazards of a price war among the members rather than from an 'agreement' to adhere to the pricing system that exists. . . . A result of the development of the 'concentrate' has been to reduce competiton to a struggle for power, to balance supply against demand rather than to secure additional customers by price competition.

Some political leaders were even finding it possible to explain inflation in terms of monopolistic competition. Thus, in an address to the District 31 Conference of the United Steel Workers of America, Joseph D. Lohman, Treasurer of the State of Illinois, said of the current price trend:

> It is not an inflation which reflects the cost of labor. It is not an inflation which reflects a fair share on the part of the farmer in the prices for his goods and services. It is an inflation which stems from one thing and one thing alone: the monopolistic position which has permitted the great corporations and combines of this country to establish an administered price policy which permits them to fix prices and syphon off profits at the expense of the consuming public—the ordinary men.[8]

Labor leaders find the theory of monopolistic competition congenial, because it furnishes scholarly backing for their argument that companies fix prices where they please and thereby divert purchasing power from the masses into company treasuries that are already overflowing with enormous profits. In the experience of businessmen it is quite clear that they can quote an asking price, but it is equally clear that it is the buyer who decides whether the asking price is reasonable enough to consummate a sale. Yet so pervasive is the "administered price" idea that fifty per cent of the people in the United States agree with the statement that "Consumers do not have much influence on price, since companies set the price and the customers have to pay it." [9] As shown in Table 30, only a minority of the better-educated and higher-income people believe this idea, but a majority of the less well-educated and lower-income people feel that it squares with their experience. Thus it appears that the concept of "administered price" has been more effectively distributed by labor unions to working men than by textbook authors to students and teachers.

TABLE No. 30.

"Consumers do not have much influence on price since some companies set the price, and the customers have to pay it."

Ranking by Per Cent of Those Who Agree:

Group	Per Cent	Group	Per Cent
Business executives	9%	Government employees	47%
High school teachers	23	General public	50
Professional men	25	High school graduates	50
College graduates	25	Farmers	53
College teachers	28	Union members	56
Factory foremen	28	Skilled workers	59
Small businessmen	32	Unskilled workers	61
Clergymen	34	Eighth grade or less	66
White collar workers	44		

Source: *The Public Opinion Index*

Certainly the semantic choices of the monopolistic-imperfect competition theorists has helped to make their ideas influential on matters of public policy. The terms "imperfect competition," "monopolistic competition," "administered prices," "collusion" and "contrived scarcities," have a sinister quality that provides exquisite devils for political orators to denounce.

Professor Chamberlin and other theorists insist that they have no interest whatsoever in public agitation and that they chose language vehicles for their ideas that would permit them to speak clearly with their professional peers. But the key words of the monopolistic-imperfect competition theorists are so heavily loaded with negative semantics that it is doubtful whether any but a few highly specialized scholars can interpret them neutrally. The dictionary says that collusion means "underhanded scheming; deceit; fraud; trickery." In using the word "collusion," the textbooks usually make the routine disclaimers that no ethical connotation is intended—it is just a form of cooperation; it is all legal, etc.—but words like this are so prejudicial that a student's conception of the market system cannot help but be colored. All experts in communication know that words are vehicles for emotion as well as reason, and there can be little doubt that the purple nomenclature of the monopolistic-imperfect competition theorists has stimulated a great deal of popular distrust for the profit and loss system.

Like all new economic theories, those of Chamberlin and Robinson have been undergoing revision under heavy critical fire. Three of the principal criticisms leveled at the new economics would appear to be pertinent to our discussion here.

The Chamberlin-Robinson models of perfect competition are purely imaginary. No society ever has or ever will conform to the conditions called for by the theory. This is not to say that model building is an idle practice. Unlike the physical scientist, the economist is unable to put his subjects in a test tube or set up controlled experiments to test his hypotheses. In the absence of laboratory procedures he finds it useful to construct economies in his imagination, give them certain characteristics, hold some factors constant and vary others, and deduce the principles by which these fictional economies work. In this way he can simplify economic relationships enough to make them mentally manageable.

The danger in the use of imaginary constructions is in their application to real life. The model may illuminate economic tendencies, but it never constitutes a blueprint of the actual structure. The temptation of writers on economics is to confuse the model with the real thing. With the "good guy" vs. the "bad guy" nomenclature, this temptation is almost irresistible. Perfect competition is visualized as the desired condition toward which public policy should point. Anything short of perfect competition is "imperfect," "monopolistic," "collusive"—in short, bad.

The report of the Attorney General's National Committee to

Study the Anti-Trust Laws recognized the theoretical character of the monopolistic competition models when it said, "We do not regard these models as offering any basis for anti-trust policy. Indeed, departures from conditions of price or perfect competition are inevitable, pervasive, and many of them useful to competition as a dynamic process." [10]

In the popularization of the monopolistic-imperfect competition theory, much confusion would have been avoided if "perfect" had been translated as "theoretical" competition and "imperfect" or "monopolistic" as "workable" competition. Professor Chamberlin has taken some pains to point out that monopolistic competition may add up to public welfare, and that, so far as public policy is concerned, workable competition is good enough for him.[11]

The second criticism of the new economics is directed at its theory of price jurisdiction. According to the theory, oligopolists cry "We're all in it together," and set prices high enough to make fat "monopoly profits." But as A. D. H. Kaplan points out in his extremely competent study, *Big Enterprise in a Competitive System*, this model of oligopolists' behavior makes some extraordinary assumptions.[12] Before the oligopolists could make their collusion pay, some or all of the following conditions would have to be met:

> The market judgment of the oligopolists on price would have to coincide, or, lacking unanimity, each member of the oligopoly would have to act as though his judgment were the same as others.
>
> Each would have to be satisfied with his market share. No member must be tempted to get more business by offering special terms.
>
> Each oligopolist would need to be reasonably certain that each seller would go along with the agreed price change, and not undercut through hidden price or quality discounts.
>
> The products of the oligopolists would need to be uniform. Any quality improvement by one must immediately be matched by all the others if they are to maintain their respective shares of the market.

Each member of the oligopoly must have a constant flow of accurate information to know at all times what the other members are doing.

Among the customers of the oligopoly, none must be so powerful that he can play off one seller against another to force competitive price concessions.

As we have seen in the case of the electrical conspiracy, it is probably easier to suffer the problems of market competition than to try to operate an association of monopolists.

To the businessman the idea that he has effective jurisdiction over prices does not square with his experience. It is certainly true that the pricing of manufactured goods is different from that of a commodity auction market. On the floor of a highly organized exchange, a steady flow of bids and offers can set the price for more or less homogeneous goods. But few manufactured goods are sold through auction markets. In setting (or finding) his offering price, the manufacturer takes many elements into consideration. He estimates probable sales volume, figures costs and the break even point, scouts his competitors to find out what kind of offers they are likely to make, considers the possibilities of consumer price resistance, sets a budget for optimum profits, then offers his product at a price. But short of conspiracy, his offer is just that—an offer. The consumers may buy his merchandise at that price or allow it to remain on the shelves. Certainly the fierce trading in the automobile markets, the rise of the discount house, and the failure of fair trade laws, strongly indicate that the consumers are still insisting on having the last word. And this insistence is by no means directed to the retailer alone, for if a supplier tries to peg his wholesale price unrealistically above the market, his dealers will shift to another supplier, go bankrupt or quit, and the manufacturer will find himself in the embarrassing position of having a plant on his hands with no outlets.

As companies grow larger and raise their stakes, pricing policy looks more to the long term and becomes less interested in charging what the traffic will bear. Large-scale manufacture, with its long-range research programs, lead-time engineering, large capital investment, complex dealer and distribution setup, and extensive division of labor among its personnel must, as a matter of necessity, take the long view on pricing in order to foster continuity and sustain growth of production and earnings.

In order to have price competition not every supplier needs to be driven to the brink of bankruptcy. Unless an entrepreneur has an opportunity to make a satisfactory profit he presumably will quit the old trade and not enter a new one. An attractive profit, earned in competition, is an indication that the entrepreneur is doing his job well, and that the consumers are willing to pay him for his services.

Identical bids from suppliers on identical or relatively uniform prices in retail markets, as for example with food or gasoline, is taken as an indication that suppliers get together to fix prices. When bids are identical on projects with non-standard specifications, collusion can fairly be implied. But otherwise price similarity may be just as much an evidence of competition as of monopoly, for if two products are similar in quality, Competitor A dare not ask a higher price than Competitor B in the same market or he will lose his patronage. Actually, as will be pointed out presently, price rivalry is but one form of competition. Quality rivalry may be intensive even though prices are more or less uniform, thus offering the consumer a wide range of choice.

Much of the belief that oligopolists administer price is based on the observation that throughout the course of a business cycle the price of agricultural commodities, which are bought and sold under conditions of "pure" competition, fluctuate more than manufactured commodities which, by definition, are traded under conditions of "imperfect" or "monopolistic" competition.

Thus, in 1935, Gardner Means of Columbia University compared price movements in industries made up of small firms with those of industries dominated by a few large companies and concluded that prices in the few seller industries were inflexible because they were administered.[13]

A similar finding was reported by the National Resources Committee in its study on "The Structure of the American Economy." "The main conclusion to be reached from this analysis," said the Committee, "is that the dominant factor in making for depression insensitivity of prices is the administrative control over prices which results from the relatively small number of concerns dominating particular markets." [14]

Subsequent studies of price trends, however, cast grave doubt on the validity of these conclusions. Thorp and Crowder, in their report to the TNEC, made an exhaustive examination of the behavior of prices and production of 407 manufactured products for the period 1929-1937 and found no demonstrable difference between the amplitude of price fluctuation and concentration of output. "Concentration of control of production of manufactured products," Thorp and Crowder concluded, "was not associated with any consistent or predictable patterns of price and behavior." [15]

Big business, says A. D. H. Kaplan, has not significantly changed the long-term price characteristics of established commodities. For the past fifty years, and for traceable commodities much longer, the prices of finished goods have fluctuated less than the prices of raw materials. The major determinants of price, says Kaplan, are to be found in the nature of the product, the type of customer, and the pattern of costs. In agriculture, supply cannot be shut off short of a growing season and must be sold on the market for what price it will bring. Labor cost is what a farmer and his family can earn. Durable goods purchases, however, are postponable, and it would take extreme price cutting to change the resolve of consumers not to buy. Moreover, industrial wage costs and overhead are generally sticky and set a price floor beyond which a company cannot go and remain solvent.

If "price jurisdiction" is a dominant force in the market, as the new economics contends, efficient oligopolists ought to be able, not only to make high profits, but keep them high without much fluctuation. If the reader examines the profits data in Appendix C, he will observe that not only are profits less than what a good oligopolist might desire but they also fluctuate, and describe adverse trends, which no good oligopolist would want.

It should also be said that, in the interest of fostering continuity and growth in earnings, leading oligopolists have a history of innovating new production methods and effecting major price reductions over a period of years. Thus it would appear that these oligopolists are "administering" prices downward, a behavior which appears to have much in common with competition.

The third criticism leveled at the new economics has to do with quality as a factor in competition. Whenever a shopper contemplates a purchase, he considers what he gets for the price he is asked to pay. Price is meaningless without the specification of quality. As every buyer knows, the highest priced article may be the cheapest in the long run; the lowest priced article may be the dearest. Price and quality are invariably two sides of the same purchasing coin; no one can buy intelligently unless he weighs one in relation to the other.

This situation poses a hard dilemma for the monopolistic-imperfect competition theorists. They are interested in building a price theory of exchange. Price is easy to compute, but it is very difficult to measure quality. So the theorists solve their problem by making quality constant in order that they can look at price as a variable. By definition, "perfect" competition requires an homogeneous product or product units that are uniform and identical. The nearest thing in actual life to homogeneous product is wheat or some other uniform commodity, hence wheat markets become the prototype for "pure" competition.

But the world of commerce doesn't exhibit the characteristics of the wheat market. As technology and industrialization have advanced, products have become more heterogeneous and less uniform. Flour is transformed into bread, pastry, or muffins; wool is fabricated into dresses or sweaters of many hues; sand and cement is converted into pre-stressed beams and cement blocks. A steel mill processing what might appear to be a uniform commodity is required to meet hundreds of customer specifications; so too with oil refineries where runs must be broken down into an almost endless variety of petroleum fractions.

The theorists of the new economics react to this diversity of product in a curious way; they contend that differentiation of product is monopolistic. In order to escape price competition a company varies color, style, features, credit, availability, or any one of a number of factors. It seeks to establish a reputation, handles its customers courteously, finds good locations for its outlets, advertises and promotes in order to establish brand awareness and loyalty. But the more the firm succeeds in individualizing its product, the more monopolistic it becomes, for it has a monopoly over the production and sale of a unique product. As Dennison and Galbraith express it, "we may regard the producer of a branded product as having a monopoly of the particular brand which he sells. The perfection of the monopoly depends on the degree to which the branded product differs from competing brands or the degree to which buyers think it differs. The seller of the brand has the jurisdiction over the price of his product that is the same in kind if different in degree as that which has long been associated with monopoly." [16] Hence the use of the term "monopolistic competition" to describe sellers who are both monopolistic and competitive.

This position leads to some strange conclusions. "Perfect" competition requires that products have uniform quality or be "homogeneous." But in nature no two things are ever alike. Even wheat, which lends itself to "pure" competition differs in mineral, vitamin, and protein content. In mass production, manufacturers are eternally struggling to maintain uniformity of quality but never quite succeeding. Since every product has some degree of uniqueness, every supplier is a monopolist hence the term becomes meaningless.

One factor of differentiation is location. A barber is an oligopolist when there are only a few shops in town. If he has a good location for his barber shop, he is a "monopolistic" competitor because location gives him a unique advantage. But since no two people can occupy the same space at the same time, it is spatially impossible to have "perfect" competition.

Under the model of "perfect" competition, it is assumed that there is no selling problem. Buyers and sellers are perfectly informed and their exchange relationship is controlled by price.

Thus advertising or sales promotion has no place in an imaginary society where competition is "perfect." Advertising is an adjunct of "imperfect" or "monopolistic" competition. It establishes images of product difference in the minds of consumers and helps the supplier to fix his price and make a "monopoly profit." To many theorists, advertising looks like economic waste. Yet one important criterion of "perfect" competition is that buyers and sellers be well informed. Since advertising informs consumers about products and at the same time creates a sense of product difference, advertising, under the new economics, is at once an agent of both monopoly and competition!

One of the best critiques of the monopolistic-imperfect competition theory has been furnished by Professor Lawrence Abbott of Union College in his scholarly and highly readable book, *Quality and Competition.* Professor Abbott points out that, in its insistence on product homogeneity as a criterion of perfect competition, the new economics is describing the conditions of primitive societies more than modern ones. As societies progress they become heterogeneous; people develop more individuality and discrimination in taste; their needs become more complex; and only products with endless permutations and combinations of quality features can satisfy consumer demands. In other words, if we follow the new theory, society must become more monopolistic in order to progress! The great flaw in monopolistic-imperfect competition theory, says Abbott, is that it allows no room for quality competition. Far from being monopolistic, quality variations increase competition because they widen the area of choice and give the competitive struggle an added dimension. If economic theory is to be adequate for the modern age, Professor Abbott holds, it must talk, not about "perfect" competition, but about "complete" competition which includes both the variables of quality and price.

John Chamberlain believes that the monopolistic-imperfect competition theorists ran into difficulty primarily because they undertook to abstract the characteristics of one form of competition and make them do duty for the whole. He says:

> If they had started with the idea that 'perfection' should be based on a competitor's ability to change and improve his product every year or so to get an edge over his fellows in appealing to the public taste, they might well have made the coach making industry, not the wheat market, their idea of the 'norm.' In which case, present day competition among Chevrolets, Plymouths, Fords, Ramblers—yes, and Volkswagens—would seem perfect—and the market for wheat and cabbages would loom up as a departure from the rule.[17]

However much the concepts of "monopolistic" and "imperfect" competition have contributed to economic theorizing, they offer little guidance for the formulation of public policy. In a democratic society, the consumer must have control over the supplier. Control is achieved when competitors are offering the consumer enough choices so that, by the allocation of his patronage, the buyer can affect the supplier's profit margin enough to cause him to do what the consumer wants done. A. D. H. Kaplan has set forth seven criteria for workable competition as follows: [18]

1. The number of sellers or buyers should be sufficient to provide a real choice among alternative sources.
2. The position of any one company must not be so powerful that it can dictate the conduct of its competitors.
3. The position of any member of the industry must not be so secure that there is no further incentive to increase profits by reducing costs and prices or improving product and service.
4. There must be opportunity for the members of the industry to make their decisions independently without coercive pressure to join in trade agreements to narrow competition.
5. Business entry or access to markets must not be hindered by deliberate restrictions or collusive measures as distinguished from the natural advantages of know-how and experience of established enterprise.
6. The opportunity of buyers or suppliers to shop around must not be hampered by arbitrary private agreements.
7. There must be no arbitrary discrimination among buyers and sellers similarly situated.

How well does the American economy meet the test of alternate choice? The best answer based on data available up to 1952, is given by A. D. H. Kaplan in his Brookings Institution study, "Big Enterprise in a Competitive Society."

In visualizing the American economy it is necessary to keep in mind the fact that the economy is made up of both little and big business enterprises. Of the almost four million firms operating, only thirty-one hundred employed more than one thousand people. Firms with ten thousand or more employees numbered only 260. Eight million people worked for companies with ten thousand employees or more; 14,700,000 people worked for firms employing less than one hundred people.

In terms of asset size, as indicated in Table 31, 361 companies with fifty million dollars or over in 1948 had a total of seventy-two billion dollars of assets as compared with eighty-two billion dollars for medium sized companies and seventy-six billion for small corporations and unincorporated firms. One reason big companies are big is that they are required to gather large amounts of capital to purchase the machinery for mass production.

TABLE 31. FINANCIAL CONCENTRATION BY ASSET SIZE

	Number of Firms	*Total Assets (Billions)*	
Small unincorporated	3,265,200	46	76
Corporations under $500,000	330,706	30	
Intermediate corporations (500,000 to 50,000,000 and over)	33,564	82	
Big corporations (50,000,000 and over)	361	72	

Source: *Big Enterprise in a Competitive Society,* A.D.H. Kaplan, p. 117.

In the American economy, big and little firms both compete and work together to get the nation's housekeeping done. A big company like General Motors buys raw materials and finished parts from big and little companies and retails its cars through thousands of small firms. Sears, Roebuck, also a big company, buys from thousands of small suppliers, but concentrates the advantages of its size on distribution.

Even when one company completely dominates an industry, there is competition, as we shall see presently, but the requirement of choice is, of course, more fully met when there are several or many suppliers. Certainly anyone examining American markets today must be impressed with the diversity of source from which goods and services can be procured.

It is frequently charged that industry is growing more monopolistic in the United States, with big companies gobbling up the little ones or squeezing them out. Kaplan's data do not bear out this conclusion.

As one test of the competitive trend, Kaplan analyzed the percentage of total wage earners in small and large manufacturing establishments from 1914 to 1947. The findings reproduced in Table 32 show that the distribution of employees by the size of business has not changed radically over a period of four decades. The smallest seventy-five per cent of establishments accounted for thirteen and two-tenths per cent of the total employment in manufacturing in 1914 and eleven and three-tenths per cent in 1947. The largest five per cent of companies in manufacturing employed fifty-five and three-tenths per cent of the total in 1914 and sixty-two and three-tenths per cent in 1947.

TABLE 32. PERCENTAGE OF TOTAL WAGE EARNERS IN SMALL AND LARGE MANUFACTURING ESTABLISHMENTS

	Smallest 75%	*Next* 20%	*Largest* 5%
1914	13.2%	31.6%	55.3%
1929	10.5	29.7	59.8
1939	11.5	30.7	57.0
1947	11.3	26.4	62.3

Source: Kaplan, p. 70.

A third test of the competitive trend is furnished by the relative position in assets and profit for the one hundred largest industrial corporations between 1909 and 1948. Table 33 shows that the one hundred largest companies accounted for one-fourth of the total assets for all industrial corporations in 1909 and were at approximately the same level in 1948. In 1909 the one hundred largest industries accounted for thirty-one and one-tenth per cent of the profit before taxes for all industrial corporations; in 1929 this figure rose to forty-three and four-tenths per cent, but dropped back to thirty and one-tenth per cent in 1948.

TABLE 33. TREND OF ASSET AND PROFIT SHARE OF ONE HUNDRED LARGEST INDUSTRIAL CORPORATIONS 1909-1948

	1909	*1929*	*1948*
Total Assets		*(Billions of dollars)*	
All industrial corporations	33.4	114.9	184.2
One hundred largest	8.2	29.3	49.1
Per cent one hundred largest	24.6	25.5	26.7
Profits Before Taxes		*(Millions of dollars)*	
All corporations	1,686	6,552	27,788
One hundred largest	525	2,841	8,357
Per cent of one hundred largest	31.1	43.1	30.1

Source: Kaplan, pp. 126-7.

The record shows that company leadership of an industry is never secure. Success, it would seem, is a heady wine. Under its influence some tycoons of business tend to forget the need for humility; they begin thinking they have infallible judgment and, like Henry Ford, lose touch with their constituents, only to be cast down by an aggressive competitor who is closer to the people. A. D. H. Kaplan's study of the fortunes of one hundred leading companies over the past fifty years tells this story in dramatic detail. Starting with the top one hundred companies by asset size in 1909, Kaplan finds that only thirty-six were still in the top group by 1948. Companies like United States Steel, Standard Oil of New Jersey, International Harvester, Swift, and American Tobacco remained in the top one hundred over the four decades, but how many readers of this book today could fill in the details on International Mercantile Marine, New England Navigation, Consolidation Coal, International Steam Pump, and

Greenwater Copper Mines and Smelter that were among the top one hundred in 1909?

Companies like Westinghouse and duPont, that have been in the top one hundred list since 1909, are hardly recognizable as the same companies today, so extensive has been the change in their product lines. The majority of companies in the top one hundred list—firms like General Foods, International Business Machines, Dow Chemical, Western Electric, and Sun Oil—have achieved this distinction in the past two decades, which is further evidence of the rapid pace of change.

Says A. D. H. Kaplan: "There is no reason to believe that those now on top can remain there any more than did their predecessors, short of alert participation in continuous product and market development." [19]

Some observers hold that the competitive character of the American market has been substantially weakened in the past decade, but the data offered in support of this view, mostly dealing with "concentration ratios," are very inconclusive. Professor Kaplan is continuing his studies as later census data become available, and he informs this writer that up to now he has no data that would require him to change his basic conclusions about the competitiveness of business.

Examination of the American economy shows that competitive drives are built into almost every phase of it. Companies have large fixed investments and large employee rosters to maintain. "Share of market," therefore, becomes a matter of very grave concern. One measure of successful management is profit increase with a rising share of market. In a growing industry a stable share of market is tolerable, but no management nor board of directors can view a declining share with equanimity, for it may signal managerial weakness and a decline in profit.

Within the corporate structure of large-scale enterprise there are also strong competitive drives. In almost every big corporation, the sales, production, and research departments make strong demands on each other. Production asks sales why it doesn't do a better job of selling to keep the plants busy and the overhead low. Sales calls on research for new products and on production for better products at lower prices. New and better products permit salesmen to call back on prospective buyers who previously have said "no." Moreover, product leadership inflates morale and gives the company representatives the elan and conviction which are necessary to storm the strongholds of the competition.

The need for product leadership is particularly evident among the dealers. Dealers put constant pressure on their suppliers to come up with good designs at prices satisfactory to the consumers. It is extremely difficult to build an effective dealer organization, and no company can long maintain a strong network of outlets unless it is intensely competitive in every phase of manufacture and distribution.

Many corporations—like those in the auto, food, and soap industries—lay down the policy of divisional competition. Market studies show clearly that General Motors' Chevrolet takes some business away from Pontiac and Oldsmobile, and Procter and Gamble's Fluffo draws customers from Crisco.

Internal operating and profit comparisons also produce strong competitive drives. In the periodic company roundup, where division heads get together to review results and plan for the future, the inefficient manager stands out like the proverbial sore thumb. He either gains control of his problems, or the company finds a new manager. Stockholders put pressure on their managements to stay competitive; otherwise profits go down, dividends are cut, and the market value of the shares falls.

But the real pressure for competition comes from the consumer. The public expects new products, new features on old lines, and better values. The consumer is forever shopping around looking for different solutions to his problems, trying new products, comparing price and quality of competitive offerings. He favors brand names in his shopping because a brand name gives him assurance of quality. But his brand loyalty is very tenuous, for other brands with quality and price claims are constantly urging him to see, try, or buy their merchandise. In a recent study of the purchasing habits of housewives, Gallup & Robinson found that twenty-five per cent of the purchasers of food, soap, and drugs had bought a different brand last time. These data strongly suggest that the monopolistic-imperfect competition theorists overestimate the monopoly power of brand names.

Probably the greatest spur to competition in the American economy is innovation. Straight price competition, as the textile industry has discovered, yields low profits. If any supplier can perform the job, his reward for entrepreneurship must be correspondingly low. The way to achieve a good profit is to make the old obsolete, develop products to meet new needs, add attractive features, offer greater values, provide better methods of financing, and work out more economical techniques of distribution.

Today, more than ever before, research and development has become a competitive spur. Total expenditures for research from industry sources rose from less than $100,000,000 in 1920 to $4,149,000,000 in 1959. In addition, the Federal government has appropriated increasing amounts of money for defense and other forms of research. In 1959 the total amounted to $6,130,000,000 of which approximately $4,250,000,000 was contracted to industry. Thus in 1959 American industry spent over eight billion dollars for research and development. In 1962, according to the National Science Foundation, industry will be spending about twelve billion dollars for research with about fifty per cent of the money coming from government contracts. By the end of the decade, the Foundation estimates total industry spending for research at approximately twenty billion dollars.

As a result of this furious innovative race, the product mix of leading companies has been in a constant state of ferment. At Radio Corporation of America, the product mix has changed so rapidly that eighty per cent of its more than billion dollar business in 1959 was in products that did not exist at the end of World War II.

So swift has been the pace of change that many companies have found they have outgrown their corporate names. Thus National Cylinder Gas Company became The Chemetron Corporation, and Electric Boat Company evolved into General Dynamics Corporation. The Radio Corporation of America was formed in 1919 in the early days of radio. Today, only forty years later, the company would have a more descriptive name if it were called The Electronics Corporation of America. The Armstrong Cork Company currently uses very little cork in its products, and the National Cash Register Company is gradually becoming a manufacturer of data processing equipment. Under these conditions of innovation, the idea advanced by writers like John K. Galbraith that oligopolists may choose "profitable and comfortable stagnation" appears fanciful, to say the least.

Aluminum provides a good case study of competition through innovation. The first commercial aluminum was made in the United States in 1888 by the Pittsburgh Reduction Company, later to become the Aluminum Company of America. Because it had unique characteristics of light weight, heat and electrical conductivity, strength in alloys, ease of machining, appearance and resistance to corrosion, aluminum was able to compete with other metals from the beginning. In 1900, five million pounds of aluminum were produced; by 1959 production had risen 780 times to a total of thirty-nine hundred million pounds.

Aluminum got its commercial start by invading the household utensil market which had previously been dominated by iron, copper and glass. In 1909, thirty-five per cent of aluminum production was used in the manufacture of utensils. In the same year, only eighteeen per cent of aluminum output was used by the transportation industry. With the rise of auto production, transportation took half of the aluminum output in 1920; but thereafter, even though the air age arrived on aluminum wings, the percentage of the light metal going into transportation products declined. In 1939, four per cent of aluminum production went into building; by 1958 this percentage had risen to twenty-seven per cent with the metal going into door and window frames, roofs and sidings, and other uses. One of the most popular models in the National Homes lines has been the new Viking all-aluminum house which has the special sales appeal of low cost maintenance.

In the expansion of the electric power industry, aluminum has had a long running battle with copper. In the early years of the century, copper supplied more than seventy per cent of the total miles of electrical transmission and primary distribution lines in the United States. Today the tables are reversed with aluminum-type cable installed in about seventy-five per cent of such lines.

Until the end of World War II, the principal producer of the light metal was the Aluminum Company of America. Under the Surplus Property Act, government-owned aluminum plants were sold to other companies, and the basic producing industry now consists of six firms, with Alcoa, Reynolds and Kaiser the principal factors. The number of aluminum fabricators, of course, is legion.

Under Alcoa management the price of primary aluminum pig in 1909 was thirty-three cents a pound. By 1942 the price had dropped to fourteen cents, and remained there until 1948. Today the price of aluminum pig stands at twenty-six cents per pound. The market for aluminum, says A. D. H. Kaplan, has been largely determined by the success of the metal in its struggle for preference over established materials and in withstanding competition from new ones. No one, of course, knows whether this market would have developed faster or slower if there had been more than one supplier. The historical price series for primary aluminum shows that over the short term the price of the metal was "administered" by its chief producer. But, says Kaplan, because of the availability of substitute materials, "the continuous record leaves no doubt that in the final analysis the price has been determined competitively in the market place." [20] In this competition by substitution the Aluminum Company of America has an average lifetime earnings of approximately ten per cent on invested capital.

The effect of product innovation is everywhere in evidence. City streetcars have given way to buses and autos; railroad passenger travel has moved to airplanes and other forms of transportation; diesel propulsion has taken over from steam; local movie theatres have succumbed to television; nylon has replaced cotton in stockings, and the percentage of synthetic fiber used in fabrics is rising; chain stores have taken over from the old "mom and pop" store; paper milk containers have substituted for glass bottles; and a whole new line of plastics has revolutionized the packaging industry and set in motion a strong rivalry between various kinds of materials for small part fabrication.

The opportunity for alternate choice is a part of everyone's daily experience. So numerous, in fact, are the offerings in the

Competition by Substitution. Only two companies manufacture cellophane but they must compete with fourteen other wrapping materials.

Radio Corporation of America's David Sarnoff Research Center at Princeton typifies competition by innovation. Out of this laboratory came the image orthicon scanner—the eye of television—and color television. In various stages of development is dream stuff like mural television, the phonetic typewriter and electronic refrigeration.

great American bazaar that the consumer is almost bewildered in making his choice.

Do you want an automobile? There are two dozen domestic makes and an untold number of foreign brands with scores of models featuring different styles at varying prices. In addition, there is the vast second-hand car market where a used car that cost three or four thousand dollars new can be bought for a few hundred dollars.

Do you want food? You can go to any one of a number of super-markets and there shop among eight to nine thousand separate items to find victuals that fit your taste and pocketbook. Do you want wearing apparel? The number of stores and styles within the stores are almost too numerous to mention.

Aluminum competes with steel for the automobile materials business.

Do you want television, household appliances, dishes, sheets, carpets, drugs, insurance or anything else? You can find them in profusion at close by shopping centers, with a wide variety of makes, styles, features, colors and price. If you live in a remote place, the mail order catalogs will bring an assortment of one hundred thousand items to your very door. But even remoteness is a receding factor in the competitive scene, for fifty-eight per cent of the population now lives in a metropolitan area where stores abound, and very few people in the United States are

Seventy-two brands of cleaning products compete for the housewife's dollar. In the modern supermarket shoppers have the choice of approximately 9,000 items.

Discount houses and "Bargain City" type of stores, displaying thousands of articles in a warehouse setting, have revolutionized retailing.

Main Street in every American city is lined with dress shops catering to shoppers with diverse interests—stouts, employed women, brides, expectant mothers, luxury buyers, women looking for bargains.

Mail order catalogs of Wards and Sears contain approximately 100,000 items, bringing the great American bazaar into the homes of housebound and remote shoppers.

further removed than two hundred miles from a big city, which is no more than an easy morning's drive.

Public policy requires consumer control of suppliers and their profits. The effectiveness of consumer control is not measured by how closely the economy conforms to an imaginary society with

The Social Control of Profits—Competition

0 Accounting—Acoustical MANHATTAN NY City Area Code 212

Accounting Supplies

A&M Stationery Co
105JohnsonAv HackensackNJ-201 HU 7-6117
ACCOUNTANTS SUPPLY HOUSE
518RockawayAv ValleyStream-LOcust 1-7700
CYPRESS CO
64W23 ---------------WAtkns 4-5730
(SEE ADVERTISEMENT THIS PAGE)
Oestler Acctg Supls 799Bway ----- SPrng 7-6640
Elbe File&Binder Co Inc 411 4Av-MUryhil 3-8620
Excelsior Statnry Co 43PkPl ------BEekmn 3-3037
Filing Equip Bur Inc 117Lbrty -------WO 4-3626
GOLDMAN M L & SON
90WBway ---------------COrtlnd 7-4635
Index Cards Inc 28Howrd ----------CAnl 6-6575
Ryan Jas A Co 101Beekmn ------BEekmn 3-9193
Systomatic Business Forms Inc
480Canal ---------------CAnl 6-4003

TRANSFACE PRODUCTS
TRANSLUCENT 2 SIDED PRINTED MASTERS
TRANSFACE
TRANSFACE Tax Forms
TRANSFACE Analysis
TRANSFACE Schedules
TRANSFACE Custom Printed Masters
"WHERE TO BUY IT"
TRANSFACE PROCESS CO
170Varick -------------WA 4-5985
Underwood Corp 1PkAv ---------LExngtn 2-7000

THE CYPRESS CO.
PUBLISHERS & PRINTERS OF ACCOUNTING & TAX FORMS
TRANSLUCENT } • TAX FORMS • COLUMNAR PADS • SCHEDULES
FOR BRUNING COPYFLEX • OZALID
TWO SIDED PRINTING OUR SPECIALTY
FOR STOCK FORMS OR OTHER PRINTING
Call . . . WAtkins 4-5730
64 W. 23rd ST., N.Y.C.

COLOR TELEPHONES
Beautiful, decorator-style telephones . . . to match or contrast your home or office color scheme. Choice of a wide variety of colors.
NEW YORK TELEPHONE COMPANY

Kitchen, bedroom, living room—these are only a few of the rooms where Extension Telephones will save you steps all day long. Each additional telephone costs only pennies a day. We can install as many as you need right away. Just call our Business Office.

▶ Accounts Receivable Financed
See "Financing"; also "Factors"

▶ Accumulators
Aircraft Internatl Co 3W29 ---------LE 2-6944
GREER HYDRAULICS INC
NewYorkInternationalAirport
Jamaica OLmpia 9-9700
Parker Hannifin Corp
Piston Type Accumulators
6PennPl Pelham ---------------PE 8-3000

▶ Acetate Fabrics
See "Rayon Fabrics"

▶ Acetylene
Acme Oxygen Co
111 S 4 HarrisonNJ--BArcly 7-7685
AIR PRODUCTS OF NY INC
13-11 44Av LICity---------ST 4-6561
Air Reduction Sales Co Div of Air Reduction
Co Inc 181PacificAv JerseyCityNJ-REctr 2-0520
AMERICAN MESSER CORP
Acetylene Producing Plant Manufacturers
405LexingtonAv ------------OXfrd 7-6550
Amer Oxygen Svce Corp
111 S 4 HarrisonNJ-REctr 2-2920
CARBIDE REDUCTION INC
604JohnsonAv Bklyn -------------GL 6-1335
95Brook Statnls ----------------GI 2-5740
EVANS AIR PRODUCTS INC
604JohnsonAv Bklyn -------------EV 6-6883
95Brook Statnls ----------------GI 7-1037
LINDE ACETYLENE SALES AND SERVICE—
SALES OFFICE
LINDE CO DIV OF UNION CARBIDE CORP
2065USHwyNo22 UnionNJ -MU 6-5100
Order Department
2365LindenAv LindenNJ --WO 4-7987
GASES & EQUIPMENT
SMITH T W WELDING SUPPLY CORP
446 W 54---------------CI 7-6322
McKINNEY WELDING SUPPLY CO
535W52 ----------------CIrcl 6-4390
PREST-O-LITE GAS & APPLIANCES—
IGNITION & MAGNETO SERVICE
75Kenmare ------- CAnal 6-5531
SMITH T W WELDING SUPPLY
CORP 446W54 ------------CIrcl 7-6322
SMITH T W WELDING SUPPLY CORP
446W54 -------------------CI 7-6322
SUPERIOR INDUSTRIAL GAS CORP
24-54 47 LICity---------AStora 8-1008
Watkins Air Prods Co 81Divsn -------WA 5-3277
Weldox Equip Co Inc 543E75 -----TRaflgr 9-3970

▶ Acetylene Welding
See "Welding"

▶ Acetylene Welding Equipment
See "Welding Equipment & Supplies"

▶ Acid-Proofing Materials
ATLAS ACID-ALKALI PROOF CEMENTS—
ATLAS MINERAL PRODUCTS CO THE
475 5Av ------------MUryhil 3-1868
Atlas Mineral Prods Co The
475 5Av-MUryhil 3-1868
BALLARD SPRAGUE & THOMAS INC
Engineers, Contractors, Sales & Installation 25E26 -------------MU 3-6464
Ceilcote Co Inc
134Nassau PrincetonNJ--609 WA 1-6969

▶ Acids
AMERICAN CYANAMID CO
30RockefellerPlz ----------CIrcl 7-0100
Bios Laboratories Inc 17W60 -----PLaza 7-8171
COLUMBIA-SOUTHERN—
COLUMBIA-SOUTHERN CHEMICAL
CORP 579 5Av -------------MU 8-8350
HARSTAN CHEMICAL CORP
1247 38 Bklyn-----------GEdny 5-8225
PETROLEUM BY-PRODUCTS & CHEMICAL CO
Acids–Naphthenic; Carloads, Tankcars, Export 19BBway ----------------WO 2-3975
Publicker Alcohol&Chemcl Sales Corp
350 5Av-OXfrd 5-4160
Tar Residuals Inc 420LexAv ------LExngtn 2-9164

▶ Acids–Fatty
See "Fatty Acids"

▶ Acoustic Instruments
See "Hearing Aids"

▶ Acoustical Contractors
ABBINGDON CEILING CO
OFFICES, PLANTS, SHOWROOMS MADE ACOUSTICALLY EFFICIENT
421E5 -----------------GRmrcy 7-6505
ACE METAL CEILING CO
Established 1920; Acousticals, All Types 416W46 ---------------PL 7-6288
ACOUSTI CELOTEX SOUND CONDITIONING—
JACOBSON & CO INC 227E44----MU 7-7450

Acoustical Contractors (Cont'd)

Acoustic Engrng Co 71W47 ----------CI 7-7077
ACOUSTONE
Incombustible mineral acoustical tile. AUDITONE* - Woodfibre acoustical tile - beautiful CORRUTONE - Perforated metal acoustical panels. *T.M. Reg. U.S. Pat. Off. Prod. of U.S. Gypsum Co. SOUND CONTROL is a job for experts.
"WHERE TO BUY IT"
WALDVOGEL BROS INC
219E44 ---------------MU 2-0680
ADAMS LEONARD C CO INC
224E41 -------------MU 7-2145
Adams Leonard C Co Inc 224E41 ------MU 7-2145
ALLIED BUILDING & CONSTRUCTION CO
SPECIALISTS IN MODERN SOUND CONDITIONING FOR CEILINGS & WALLS
• SHOWROOMS • OFFICES
• FACTORIES • RESIDENTIAL
FREE CONSULTATION
28W31 St(off5thAv) ------CHikrng 4-5737
Arcade Carpet Co 8 Styvsnt----------GR 5-7044
ARMSTRONG ACOUSTICAL CEILINGS
Commercial and Residential Sound Conditioning
Armstrong ACOUSTICAL CEILINGS
Armstrong Cushiontone® • Travertone* • Crestone* Arrestone® • Minatone® • Corkoustic® Perforated Asbestos Board *T.M.
"WHERE TO BUY THEM"
DISTRICT OFFICE
Armstrong Cork Co Inc
295 5Av -----------MUryhil 4-6900
CONTRACTORS
HANNAM & SCHEDE INC
318E45 -------------ORegn 9-8440
PHILLIPS JAS A INC
1776ParkAv ------------LE 4-4535
SCULLY WM J ACOUSTICS CORP
425LexingtonAv -----MUryhil 2-5991

CELOTEX Sound Conditioning
Complete Line of Materials including incombustible Mineral & Metal Tiles
For information call Mr. Herbert
JACOBSON & CO., INC.
Contractors Since 1889
227 E. 44th St., N.Y.
MU rray Hill 7-7450

WILLIAM J. SCULLY ACOUSTICS CORP.
SINCE 1920
• ARMSTRONG
• CURON
• FIBERGLAS
• HANSSON
• KILNOISE
• SIMPLEX
Acoustical Contractors & Engineers
OFFICE
41 E. 42nd ST., N.Y.C.
MUrray Hill 2-5991

Acoustical Contractors (Cont'd)

ASBESTO SPRAY—
NY ARTCRAFTS INC
280MadisonAv ----------MUryhil 5-0919
ASBESTOSPRAY APPLICATORS INC
SPRAYED-ON
Acoustical & Thermal Insulation
Fireproofing & Condensation Control
300ThomasSt NewarkNJ -----BArcly 7-3539
Ceiling Contractors Inc 552W52 --JUdson 6-1844
Davimor Const Co Inc 243W34 ---WIscnsn 7-2019
East Side Metal Ceiling Co 421E5-GRmrcy 7-6505
FIBERGLAS NOISE CONTROL PRODUCTS
Textured, Perforated, Stria and Sonofaced* Acoustical Tile, Textured and Sonofaced Ceiling Board and Noise-Stop* Baffles. Quiet-Lasting Beauty—Firesafety at Low Cost. Efficient—Light Weight. *T.M.O.C.F. Corp.
OWENS-CORNING FIBERGLAS TM
"WHERE TO BUY IT"
CONTRACTORS
NATIONAL ACOUSTICS
514W36 ---------OXfrd 5-1252
PHILLIPS JAMES A INC
1776ParkAv ---- LEhl 4-4535
SCULLY WM J ACOUSTICS CORP
425LexingtonAv --MUryhil 2-5991
WALDVOGEL BROS INC
219E44 -------------MU 2-0680
FLUSHING METAL CEILING CORP INC
670FlushingAv Bklyn -EVrgrn 8-3635
HARDER ROBT J INC
34ForestAv Lynbrook -----LYnbrk 9-4640
HENENFELD ACOUSTIC CEILINGS
Sound Conditioning
OFFICES & SHOWROOMS
CELOTEX CEILINGS
CYpress 3-6363
3527 3Av --------------CYpress 3-6363
INDUSTRIAL ACOUSTICS PRODUCTS
To Silence Noise from Industrial Machinery, Air Conditioning & Ventilating Systems, Cooling Towers, Jet Engines, Etc. America's Largest Mfr. of Sound-Proof Rooms, Quiet Rooms, Audiometric Test Rooms.
"FOR INFORMATION CALL"
INDUSTRIAL ACOUSTICS COMPANY
INC 341JacksonAv ------ CYprss 2-0180
Isherwood Wm Inc 6E46 --------MUryhil 7-4782
JACOBSON & CO INC
227E44 --------MUryhil 7-7450
(SEE ADVERTISEMENT THIS PAGE)
JOHNS-MANVILLE
ACOUSTICAL MATERIALS
Highly efficient sound-absorbing materials for every acoustical need . . . new buildings or modernization. Installed direct by Johns-Manville, "Pioneers in Sound Control."
JM PRODUCTS
"WHERE TO BUY THEM"
JOHNS-MANVILLE CORP
270MadisonAv --------LE 2-7600

EST. 1930
Robert M. Cathcart, Pres.
Only Local Based Applicator in Greater N.Y. Area for
ASBESTOSPRAY
• Sprayed-On Fibre Insulation
• Thermal&Acoustical
• Fireproofing
• Condensation Control
• Decorative or Industrial Finish
NEW YORK ARTCRAFTS Inc.
MU rray Hill 5-0919
280 MADISON AVE. N.Y. 16

Competitors in all lines of goods and services may be identified in the Yellow Pages of the telephone directory and contacted by telephone at the turn of a dial.

Re-sale market places old products in competition with new. Every car owner is a potential supplier of a used car.

New "Rent—Don't Buy" services have become big business.

"perfect" competition, but whether or not consumers have enough alternate choice so that by directing their patronage they can influence supplier profit margins and thereby motivate entrepreneurial groups to conform to consumer wishes. Under the test of alternate choice, despite occasional business conspiracies and efforts by government to thwart competition, the American economy would appear to be highly responsive to consumer control.

Consumer control requires competition, and competition assumes a set of rules by which the game is played. From the community's point of view, the competition must be hard enough to test the mettle of the competitors, but not so hard as to reach the condition of conflict. In a progressive economy there must be order, but not so much order as to stifle initiative and prevent adaptation and change. Implicit in the idea of competition is that some contestants will outscore their opponents, hence, if the market is to control, both competitors and members of the community must be willing to abide by the verdict of the consumers. In a competitive economy, the community never ignores the interests of the producer, for he is usually well organized and motivated to press his views. But the consumer's interests must be paramount, because the consumer is everybody.

CHAPTER TEN

THE SOCIAL CONTROL OF PROFITS —LEGISLATION

The principle of consumer control of suppliers through competition and choice is a very simple one, but American experience shows that writing and enforcing the legal rules to preserve competition poses many difficult problems. Markets and market structures are infinitely complex and are always changing. In their interpretation of the law, courts shift their ground as the political mood changes and new judicial personnel mounts the bench. Strong pressure groups seek and obtain exemption from the laws against monopoly, and the competitive principle is compromised through the tax laws, tariffs, building codes, licensing procedures, conservation, and other legislation. At times, particularly in the depression years of the 1930's, public faith in the idea of competition as an organizing principle has wavered.

A good rule book states the rules clearly enough so that the contestants can, with reasonable assurance, anticipate when the referee will blow his whistle and when he will permit play. The antitrust laws are not a rule book in the ordinary sense of the word. They are a set of broad prohibitions that attempt to define the standards of conduct the community wishes to have businessmen observe.

The cornerstone of the antitrust laws in the United States is the Sherman Act, passed in 1890. Previous to the passage of the Sherman Act, seventeen western states had legislated against trusts, and the common law held contracts in restraint of trade unenforceable. But the accumulation of wealth in the hands of individuals and corporations, the multiplication of trusts, and the fear that this power would be used to oppress individuals and injure the public led Congress to legislate sterner controls.

Section 1 of the Sherman Act makes illegal "Every contract, combination in the form of trust or otherwise, or conspiracy in restraint of trade." Section 2 prohibits a person from monopolizing or attempting to monopolize or combine or conspire with other persons to monopolize any part of the trade or commerce among the several states or with foreign nations. Thus, the law is designed to maintain competition by insuring that competition will not be eliminated or drastically reduced.

In 1914 Congress added the Clayton Act which forebade predatory price cutting, price discrimination and tying contracts, and proscribed mergers and interlocking directorates where these would "substantially lessen competition."

In the same year, Congress authorized the creation of the Federal Trade Commission and charged it with the duty of enforcing the provisions of the Clayton Act and policing "unfair methods of competition." The Commission was given broad powers to issue complaints, subpoena papers, hold hearings and issue cease and desist orders. The Department of Justice and the Federal Trade Commission are the principal agencies for the enforcement of the antitrust laws.

The modern trend of judicial interpretation of the Sherman Act began in 1911 with the Supreme Court decision ordering the dissolution of the Standard Oil Company of New Jersey. In this case the court laid down the famous "Rule of Reason" as the guide for future determinations of the meaning of the Act. Under the Rule of Reason the courts undertake to judge violations by taking into account all the factors and circumstances bearing on the case. Unlike *per se* rulings, where the existence of certain types of conduct are in and of themselves declared unlawful, the Rule of Reason permits great flexibility and gives the courts wide latitude for "judicial legislation." This introduces uncertainties as successive judges expound their differing social and legal philosophies, but it also avoids mechanistic interpretation of the law and makes possible the formulation of a body of rules that reach for principle yet adapt to changing market conditions.

In their interpretation of the antitrust law, the courts have had little difficulty in deciding that agreements between competitors to limit production or apportion markets,[1] or fix or substantially affect prices,[2] or boycott other traders or otherwise exclude competitors from the market[3] are conclusively presumed to be unreasonable and in violation of the law.

But the definition of what constitutes a monopoly or attempts to monopolize, forbidden in Section 2 of the Sherman Act, has been more difficult. Monopoly and monopolizing has been defined as the possession of or attempt to acquire power to control a market, coupled with the intention to exercise that power.[4] The power to control has been generally stated to be the power to control market prices or exclude competition. But this raises the question of what products comprise the competitive market, and what are the geographic boundaries of the market for this product. By jockeying product classifications and their geographical market areas, the government and other parties to the action can make out a case best suited to their purposes.

The appropriate market, the courts have said, is the "area of effective competition."[5] But the interpretation of this doctrine has varied widely in different cases. In *Fargo Glass and Paint Co.* v. *Globe American et al.*[6] the court found that Globe American and the Maytag Company had monopolized interstate commerce in the field of gas ranges, even though Globe American manufactured less than two per cent of the total and its production at no time ranked higher than eighteenth in the nation. The court achieved this surprising result by defining the line of commerce as the "distribution of the automatic-shut-off, heat-retained gas ranges manufactured by the defendant, Globe American Corporation." Happily, this decision was reversed by the Seventh Circuit Court of Appeals which held that Globe's ranges were competitive with other types.

In *United States* v. *Columbia Steel Company*,[7] where the government was contesting a merger between two steel companies, the court found the relevant market was different for each product affected by the merger.

In the Farmer's Guide Publishing Company case,[8] the lower court saw a national market for farm journal advertising, but the Supreme Court found the appropriate market in the eight states where the litigant's newspapers principally circulated. In the Paramount Pictures case [9] the Court narrowed the market from the exhibition of films in theatres generally to exhibition in first-run theatres.

Of great importance as a guide to what products are involved in the relevant market is the Cellophane Case [10] in which, even though duPont was the sole producer, the court found no monopoly because cellophane and other packaging materials are interchangeable and therefore competitive. This decision gives judicial recognition to the fact that in today's markets consumers have wide latitude for choice through the opportunity to purchase substitute goods.

The courts have encountered further difficulties in deciding when a defendent possesses the power to monopolize and what constitutes intent to use that power. If actual control of prices or actual exclusion of competition from the market is shown, the courts have found *per se* violation of the statutes. But there is divergence of opinion when the charge is the existence of unexercised monopoly power.

In 1920 the court refused to dissolve the United States Steel Corporation on the charge that it had the power to restrain trade. Justice McKenna, who wrote the decision, conceded that in 1901 the original promoters of U. S. Steel had intended to monopolize the industry, but observed that they had long since given this up, and that in any event, the Corporation's share of the market was declining. "The government," said Justice McKenna, "is reduced to the assertion that the size of the corporation, the power it may have, not the exertion of the power, is an abhorrence in the law." But, he declared, "The law does not make mere size an offense or the existence of unexerted power an offense." [11]

But in the Alcoa case [12] in 1945, the court took a different point of view. Alcoa's sales of aluminum represented thirty-three per cent of the total national market when virgin and secondary (reclaimed) aluminum were lumped; sixty-four per cent when fabricated, virgin, and secondary aluminum were classified as one, and ninety per cent when only virgin aluminum was considered. Taking virgin aluminum as the relevant market, Judge Learned Hand said that a one-third share of the market could not be adjudged a monopoly; that it was doubtful if two-thirds were enough, but that ninety per cent definitely constituted a monopoly. Conceding that Alcoa had not earned exorbitant profits (ten per cent on investment, historically) and that it was not guilty of collusion or predatory practices, Judge Hand ruled that monopoly power need not be abused to be unlawful; it need only exist. "It (Congress) did not condone 'good trusts' and condemn 'bad' ones; it forbade all," said the Judge. Size alone, agreed Judge Hand, does not determine guilt. There must be exclusion of competitors, coercive behavior, and wrongful intent. Alcoa, it is true, stimulated demand and opened up new uses for aluminum, but it doubled and redoubled its capacity to meet the demand, and this behavior, said Judge Hand, constituted an attempt to monopolize.

The courts have found no single test by which the existence of a monopoly or unexercised monopoly power can be determined. In the Columbia Steel Case, three years after the Alcoa decision, the Court summarized its criteria in terms of the Rule of Reason, as follows:

> In determining what constitutes unreasonable restraint of trade—we look rather to the percentage of business controlled, the strength of the remaining competition, whether the action springs from business requirements or purpose to monopolize, the probable development in the industry, consumer demands and other characteristics of the market.[13]

The courts have been faced with further interpretive problems in determining what constitutes a conspiracy to restrain trade. A conspiracy involves a meeting of the minds of two or more persons on a common course of action. In antitrust cases agreement is seldom established by direct testimony. The courts listen to evidence on what the parties have said or done and then infer intent from patterns of behavior. In a number of cases, the courts have gone far toward inferring conspiracy from uniformity of conduct in which the parties, with knowledge that a plan involved concerted action, have given adherence to and participated in it.[14] In the Triangle Conduit case the Court of Appeals for the Seventh Circuit went to the extreme of holding that conspiracy was established merely by a showing of identical conduct by competitors, each knowing what the other was doing. The Federal Trade Commission thereupon declared that "the economic effect of identical prices, achieved through conscious parallel action, is the same as that of similar prices achieved through overt collusion,"[15] and ruled that conscious parallelism is a violation of the Federal Trade Commission Act.

The Supreme Court was not long in striking down this doctrine, when, in the Paramount case, it said "—this court has never held that proof of parallel business behavior conclusively establishes agreement or . . . that such behavior itself establishes a Sherman Act offense."[16] Vigorous competition tends to force uniformity of price and terms of sale. If the test of conspiracy were market uniformity instead of proof that two or more parties did, in fact, tacitly or expressly agree to restrain trade, the business world would be thrown into chaos.

It has long been held to be a *per se* violation of the antitrust laws when companies agree to fix prices, apportion markets, or limit production. But if these companies are merged they may be able to do legally what they are not permitted to do as separate entities. Thus the problem of the double standard has been raised in the enforcement of the anti-trust laws.

Section 7 of the Clayton Act of 1914 forbade the acquisition by a corporation of stock in another corporation "where the effect of such acquisition may be to substantially lessen competition" between the acquiring and acquired companies. Up to 1914 mergers had been effected largely through stock purchase. After 1914 mergers were consummated mainly through the acquisition of the physical assets of one corporation by another. In its decision on the Thatcher case in 1925, the court held that the Federal Trade Commission's power to prevent mergers under Section 7 of the Clayton Act extended only to acquisitions of stock and not to assets.[17] For all practical purposes this decision eliminated the anti-merger provisions of the Clayton Act.

After World War II, the problem of merger was again brought to the fore by the case of Columbia Steel.[18] The government tried to enjoin Columbia Steel Company, a subsidiary of U. S. Steel, from purchasing the assets of Consolidated Steel Corporation, a West Coast fabricator which had a three per cent share of the market for rolled steel and a thirteen per cent share of plates and shapes in its eleven state marketing area. Applying the Rule of Reason, and taking into account such factors even as the probable development of the West Coast steel industry, the court ruled that merging this share of the market would not constitute an unreasonable restraint of trade.

The Columbia Steel case led to agitation for strengthening anti-trust laws governing merger, and in 1950 Congress passed the Celler Anti-Merger Amendment to Section 7 of the Clayton Act. The new legislation now covers vertical as well as horizontal mergers; it widens the test of the adverse effect of merger on competition by dropping the qualifying phrase "between the acquiring and acquired corporation"; and it prohibits the acquisition of assets as well as stock, "where in any line of commerce in any section of the country the effect of such acquisition may be substantially to lessen competition."

The new law is currently undergoing judicial clarification. The key issues are how narrowly the courts will interpret the phrases "in any line of commerce" and "any section of the country," and under what conditions and how much of the market must be affected before it can be said that competition is substantially lessened. The early decisions point to a tougher antitrust policy on mergers.

In the Pillsbury case, decided by tthe Federal Trade Commission in 1953, Pillsbury Mills had purchased the assets of Ballard and Ballard Company and Duff's Baking Mix Division of American Home Products Company, thereby increasing its share of the mix market in the Southeast from twenty-two and seven-tenths per cent to approximately forty-five per cent. This increase in market share, said the Commission, is sufficient to condemn the merger as one that might substantially lessen competition. In coming to this decision, the Commission stated that, "There is nothing in the record to indicate that the mergers will at present convert the industry in the Southeast from a competitive to a non-competitive pattern. The inference, in fact, must be to the contrary inasmuch as large national distributors such as General Mills and Quaker Oats and large regional distributors remain to furnish effective competition to Pillsbury Mills." However, the Commission thought it advisable to take steps to head off the trend to "what is sometimes called oligopolistic or monopolistic competition" for, "If (the) respondent should continue to acquire competitors at the rate it has since 1940, and other large competitors should do the same, the urban markets in the Southeast may come to be dominated by a few large milling companies." [19] This is a noteworthy statement, not only for its speculation about the future of the economy but also because it appears to equate "monopolistic competition" with monopoly.

In his decision enjoining a proposed merger between Bethlehem Steel Corporation and The Youngstown Sheet & Tube

Company, Judge Edward Weinfeld followed a somewhat similar course of reasoning. Bethlehem, with twenty per cent of the national market largely concentrated in the East and on the Pacific Coast, wanted to merge with Youngstown, with five per cent of the national market concentrated in the Middle West. The companies contended that, through merger, competition with U. S. Steel, Republic, and others in the Mid-Continent Area would be intensified. After the usual skirmishing on what constitutes a line of products and what constitutes the relevant market, the judge found that Bethlehem shipped into the Mid-Continent Area 2,034,783 tons of common finished steel products, or four and nine-tenths per cent of total industry shipments in 1955, and Youngstown shipped 2,823,992 tons or six and seven-tenths per cent of the industry in the same year. This traffic, he said, was enough to show that these two companies were "effective competitors" in the Mid-Continent Area, and that merger would substantially lessen competition there. In the national market, the judge held, competition would be substantially lessened by the addition of Youngstown's five per cent share with Bethlehem's twenty per cent share.

Looking to the future, Judge Weinfeld said, "The merger offers an incipient threat of setting into motion a chain reaction of further mergers by the other but less powerful companies in the steel industry." In writing the Clayton Act, the Judge said, the Congress was trying "to arrest the creation of trusts, conspiracies, and monopolies in their incipiency and before consummation" and that to permit Bethlehem to merge with Youngstown would render sterile the policy Congress adopted in Section 7 of the amended Clayton Act.[20]

Interestingly enough, well-placed people in firms competing with Bethlehem and Youngstown privately disagreed with Judge Weinfeld that Bethlehem's entry into the Mid-Continent Area through merger would lessen competition. In the trade, Bethlehem is known as an extremely aggressive competitor, and the men on the firing line, thinking not about public policy but about the problem of selling steel, foresaw an era of harder competition, had the merger been allowed.

The District Court decision against the merger of Brown Shoe Company and G. R. Kinney Co. in 1959, if it stands, puts an even greater roadblock in the way of company growth through acquisition. In 1955 the Brown Company manufactured three and ninety-seven hundredths per cent of the shoes made for the national market. Kinney produced only one-half of one per cent of the nation's output, but operated a chain of retail stores that had a one and two-tenths per cent share of the national market. Judge Weber ruled that the relevant market for men's, women's and children's shoes was cities of ten thousand and over. In 141 of these cities Kinney had a retail store and Brown also had some type of outlet. Kinney distributed seven million pairs of shoes through its outlets in these cities and Brown sold twelve million pairs. The merging of this volume, said the court, would substantially lessen competition.

The Judge dealt specifically with the small market shares of retail sales involved in the merger. The Brown and Kinney stores, said Judge Weber, now have a certain percentage of the market and a combination of their businesses would increase that percentage. "Such increase, *regardless of percentage amount* gives them power. Such power not only tends to create a monopoly, but substantially lessens competition by eliminating the effectiveness of the independent retailer and the small manufacturer." [21] If this ruling stands, merger between companies with any market overlap will be at an end.

That business is beginning to feel the impact of the new crackdown is indicated by current newspaper headlines. "California Packing, Van Camp Abandon All Merger Plans" says a Wall Street Journal headline. And again, "Texaco Calls Off Merger With Superior Oil Co." In commenting on the Texaco case, Robert A. Bicks, acting head of the Antitrust Division, said, "We felt the proposed merger would immeasurably restrain competition in the oil industry in violation of the Clayton Act." Whereupon the *Wall Street Journal* commented editorially, "Superior Oil claims it produces but one-half of one percent of U.S. oil—hardly enough to affect U.S. competition seriously."

The decision in the Brown Shoe case points up the dilemma of writing the rule book for competition. Mergers may tend to create a monopoly with all its drawbacks, as Judge Weber points out, or they may increase competition and be an agent of progress. Integration frequently brings gains in efficiency through joint utilization of plants, natural resources, by-products, and managerial and technological skills. Integrated companies may be able to attract capital more easily and maintain research that produces better and cheaper products for consumers. Also integration may eliminate some of the profit required by supplier firms in the chain of production, and lead to lower prices.

Judge Weber agreed that company-owned retail stores have definite advantages in buying, in obtaining credit, and in advertising and inventory control, and that these advantages might result in lower prices or higher quality for the same price. But, he said, the independents have difficulty competing under these conditions, and noted that Congress has steadfastly voted to tighten the screws on mergers which may eliminate the smaller operators and possibly lead to monopoly. Quite obviously Judge Weber was struggling here with the confusion on the purpose of the antitrust laws.

The antitrust laws are based on belief in competition. Their premise is that if unfair trade tactics and excessive merging are prevented, consumer control of suppliers can be maintained, and that, in the long run, the competitive system, under market regulation, will be the most effective means for promoting economic progress, economic justice, and the general welfare. But this belief in competition as an organizing principle was seriously shaken in the Great Depression of the nineteen thirties. With prices falling and the misery of twelve million unemployed vividly present in the national consciousness, many people began to believe that competition was "cut-throat" and "anti-social," and that some new form of cooperation was needed to operate the nation's economy. In the desperate search for remedies, the thinking of leaders went back to the war mobilization experience of World War I, where, under the aegis of government, the economic forces of the country were organized to meet the emergency of war.

Out of this crisis came the National Recovery Act to cartelize American industry. So great was the popular demand for dramatic action to end the depression that the House passed the revolutionary National Recovery Act in one week. The Senate took longer; it passed the bill in eight weeks. Businessmen wanted the legislation to protect prices and profits; labor wanted it to gain better wage and hour standards and to establish the principle of collective bargaining; liberal reformers, flushed with new-found governmental power, wanted it to provide a political vehicle for national planning.

The National Recovery Act permitted the setting up of industry codes of fair competition and provided for exemption of these codes from the anti-trust laws. In Section 7A, the Act pledged collective bargaining, maximum hours, and minimum wages. The Act also provided for Federal licensing of corporations, but in its administration, this provision was not pressed.

To get action quickly, General Hugh Johnson, the NRA Administrator, started a mass movement to pledge all employers to a blanket agreement to uphold the NRA standards of a forty-hour week and a minimum wage of thirteen to fourteen dollars per week. A poster was designed around a symbolic thunderbird, with the slogan "We do our Part." Employers who signed the agreement were permitted to display the NRA "blue eagle" as a public notice of compliance. Mass meetings and parades with floats and brass bands were employed to whip up enthusiasm. In New York City in September 1933, two hundred fifty thousand people paraded up Fifth Avenue to celebrate the coming of N.R.A.

Representatives of business, labor and government held non-stop meetings to hammer out industry codes, and by August 1933, 546 codes were approved with only oil, coal, steel, autos, and lumber remaining as holdouts. Under pressure from the White House and the N.R.A., these industries were brought into the code structure by September.

In exempting industry codes from the anti-trust laws, the National Recovery Act piously declared that the codes shall not permit monopolies or monopolistic practices, but the industry agreements were clearly in violation of what up to that point had been regarded as restraint of trade. In the name of fair competition most codes provided for some form of price control, usually through minimum price regulations. More than half of the first two hundred fifty codes prohibited selling an article below its cost of production, and most codes undertook to police this agreement by adopting rules for uniform accounting and open price systems. Under the typical open price system companies were required to file prices, discounts and terms of sale, and thereafter abide by these conditions until a new schedule had been filed and the prescribed waiting period had expired. The open price system enabled members of an industry to identify price cutters and exert pressure on them to hold the line.

In addition to attempting to fix prices, some industry codes undertook to curb output by setting production quotas, limiting machine time, and requiring a company to get the consent of the code administration before installing new capacity.[22]

The NRA quickly proved to be an administrative monstrosity, for no sooner had a code been signed than its administrators found themselves deeply embroiled in enforcement difficulties. Labor and government were pressing to raise wages and increase purchasing power; business was pressing to raise prices to cover costs and make a profit. Evidently President Roosevelt was confused on the relation between labor cost, prices, and profit; for, upon the enactment of NRA, he called for an increase in wages and a hold-the-line policy on prices. "The aim of this whole effort," he said, "is to restore our rich domestic market by raising its vast consuming capacity. If we now inflate prices as fast and as far as we increase wages, the whole project will be set to naught."[23] In 1932 the loss on sales for all manufacturing companies was a billion and one-half dollars; in 1933 profits were $295,000,000 or a little less than nine-tenths of one cent per dollar of sales. The chances of raising wages out of profits and holding prices steady, therefore, were nil.

Discontent with NRA was soon manifest. Labor was dissatisfied with wages; consumers protested price increases; businessmen, particularly little businessmen, violated, evaded, or ignored the stipulations of the codes. In March 1934 the National Recovery Review Board was set up to investigate monopolistic tendencies in the codes and Clarence Darrow, the noted criminal lawyer, was made chairman. In May the Board declared that "All competition is savage, wolfish and relentless;" nevertheless, the Board said, "A return to the antitrust laws for the purpose of restoring competition, we believe to be one of the great needs of our time.[24]

Mercifully, on May 27, 1935, the Supreme Court, in the Schechter Poultry Corporation case, handed down a unanimous decision that the National Recovery Act was unconstitutional on the ground that Congress had exceeded its powers under the Interstate Commerce clause by giving the codes power to make industry agreements on wages and hours.

Legally, the Supreme Court decision killed the NRA, but its influence lingered on in the antitrust laws. During the depression independent wholesalers and retailers had fared badly, not only because of the general decline in trade, but because of the rising competition from the mail order houses and chain stores. The chains purchased goods in large quantities, turned their inventory over rapidly and used other cost-saving techniques to cut retail prices to the bone. The independents fought back by inducing various states to levy discriminatory taxes on chains, and in 1936 they prevailed on Congress to pass the Robinson-Patman Act to strengthen the price discrimination prohibitions of Section 2 of the 1914 Clayton Act.

The Robinson-Patman Act makes it unlawful for any person engaged in commerce to discriminate in price between purchasers of commodities of like grade or quality where the effect of such discrimination may be substantially to lessen competition or tend to create a monopoly. Price discrimination, however, is permitted under the Act when the discriminatory lower price is made to meet changing conditions of the market; or is made in good faith to meet an equally low price of a competitor; or makes due allowance for differences in the cost of manufacture, delivery, or sale that results from quantity transactions or different business methods.

The Act undertakes to prevent the camouflaging of price discrimination by forbidding sellers to pay brokerage fees in any guise to buyers or their agents, and by requiring that any services or advertising allowances offered by sellers must be made on "proportionally equal" terms to all customers.

The Robinson-Patman Act has proved to be one of the most controversial of the antitrust laws. Proponents say that small business must have protection against price discrimination. Critics agree that price discrimination for the purpose of monopolization should be curbed, but, they say, the Robinson-Patman Act is so ambiguous and poorly drafted that it is "a legislative monstrosity" with "a law suit in every word of it." In an article in the *Journal of Marketing,* David Robbins, Dean of the School of Business, University of Richmond, observed that: "Twenty-three years of enforcement have produced crystal-clear confusion regarding some of its provisions." [25] Judge Lindley in the Great Atlantic and Pacific Tea case, declared, "I doubt if any judge would assert that he knows exactly what does or does not amount to a violation of the Robinson-Patman Act in any or all instances." [26]

One complication is that the law draws the courts away from decision on general principle into judgment of a myriad of business details. The law, for example, forbids sellers to pay brokerage fees to anyone connected with a seller. But what is a broker? What is a proper discount when the services of brokers vary? What is legal pricing when a firm is part wholesaler and part retailer? Again, the law requires that any services or advertising allowances given by the seller to the buyer be made "proportionally equal" to all customers. But does this mean "proportionally equal" on last year's sales, current sales, anticipated sales or what? How does a supplier stay within the law when he has one thousand manufacturers as customers and wishes to run an ad in a national magazine illustrating end-product use for his commodity?

But a more serious criticism of the Robinson-Patman Act is that it is anti-competitive and basically in conflict with the Sherman Act. The Sherman Act calls for "hard competition"; but the

Robinson-Patman Act fosters "soft competition." Companies may run afoul of the Sherman Act on charges of monopolizing if they raise prices or charge "identical prices"; but if they lower prices they may be confronted with a charge of price discrimination and unfair competition under the Robinson-Patman Act. The special virtue of the price system is that in infinitely complex markets it can set a price on any combination of variables governing exchange between buyers and sellers. Competition requires price and quality differences (i.e., discrimination) in order to function effectively. As Professor Adelman observes; when price discrimination is sporadic or unsystematic, it becomes a powerful competitive force. It is only when price discrimination is systematic and precisely ordered for the purpose of destroying competition that its effects can be condemned.[27] The Robinson-Patman Act encourages price uniformity and rigidity. Suppliers must have intimate knowledge of the prices and terms of sale of competitors, and be cautious of departing from the norm lest they be charged with unfair competition.

One reason that courts have undertaken to outlaw price discrimination is the belief that it is desirable to stop monopolistic tendencies in their incipiency. But, says, Edward A. Levi, Dean of the University of Chicago School of Law, "It is this 'incipiency theory' which makes easier the transition from a price freedom to a price control measure, and under the rubric of outlawing specific practices, legislation to preserve competition can be converted into an act to destroy it." [28]

Since 1936, says W. David Robbins, there have been three Robinson-Patman Acts. Up to 1945 there was limited enforcement of the Act because of the country's preoccupation with the war. In the late 1940's the Federal Trade Commission, with the approval of the Supreme Court, came dangerously close to outlawing price differentials. In the late 1940's both the Commission and the courts have been more temperate and reasonable in their interpretation of the Act.[29]

The statutory language of the Robinson-Patman Act would seem to make proof of substantial injury to competition, actual or probable, the core of any price discrimination charge. But in the 1940's, in three pivotal cases, it was held that a minute price difference was automatic proof of illegality without regard to the degree and nature of the adverse effects on competition. In the Moss case, the Second Circuit Court of Appeals read the Act as "shifting the burden of proof to anyone who sets two prices, and who probably knows why he has done so, and what has been the result." The Court held that the proof of a price differential in itself constituted price discrimination where the competitive injury in question was between sellers.[30] In the Corn Products case, the Supreme Court found that, "The statute does not require that the discrimination must in fact have harmed competition, but only that there is a reasonable possibility that they may have had such an effect." [31] In the Morton Salt case, the Supreme Court concluded that, "In a case involving competitive injury between a seller's customers, the Commission need only prove that a seller has charged one purchaser a higher price for the goods than he had charged one or more of the purchaser's competitors." [32]

Legal humorists used the initials of these three cases—MMSCP—to remember the rule of law that "Manufacturers must stop competitive pricing" and adopt uniform pricing practices. To many observers it seemed that the law was bent on protecting competitors, not the practice of competition.

The first indication of change in the Federal Trade Commission's attitude was in the three Spark Plug cases in 1953, when the Commission dismissed the complaints of price discrimination on the ground that neither injury to competition nor an "undue loss of business" was found among competing manufacturers.[33]

A year later, in the General Foods case, the Commission declared that "the substantiality of effects reasonably probable" is the key idea in judging price discrimination cases, and that complainants have the burden of proving injury to competition.[34] In the Doubleday Incorporated case the Commission found that "Any price differential remain(s) lawful under the Robinson-Patman Act unless endangering adverse effects on competition.[35]

In 1956 Yale and Town Manufacturing Company successfully

defended substantial preferential discounts before the Commission on the basis of performance, engineering specifications, and adaptability to customer's individual requirements. The trial examiner found that, along with preferential discounts, there was evidence of healthy competition, with consumers enjoying choice of alternative products and a vigorous technological race for product improvement.[36]

In recent years, the Courts as well as the Federal Trade Commission have moved toward a more realistic interpretation of price discrimination, although they have still displayed a tendency to infer injury when price discrepancies have been substantial. Thus, in the Whitaker Cable Corporation case, the Court sustained the Federal Trade Commission finding that price differentials as high as thirty per cent were in fact price discriminations, but went on to say that Congress has not outlawed price differentials per se. . . . "The Act was not intended to reach every remote, adverse effect in competition—We construe the Act to require substantial, not trivial or sporadic interference with competition to establish a violation of its mandate—Any other construction would turn the Act into a price control law contrary to its manifest purpose." [37]

How well have the antitrust laws worked? There is a big difference of opinion on the correct answer. One school of thought believes that, by the nature of the problem, the antitrust laws can never be made to work. What we should do is get rid of them and let entrepreneurs scramble in the market for such place and position as they can win and hold under a legal code that governs contracts and outlaws fraud.

A second school of thought believes that the antitrust laws should be made much tougher. Big business should be broken up and competition between many smaller firms should be required.[38]

A third point of view is that competition is not an adequate organizing principle for a complex economy. Competition in a free market, this school believes, leads to economic chaos and disaster. Therefore the whole concept of competition under antitrust laws should be superseded by a mixed system where private enterprise operates under production practices and pricing policies laid down by government.[39]

A fourth point of view, and the one to which most businessmen subscribe, is that competition is vital to a dynamic economy, and that the antitrust laws, by and large, have served a wise and useful purpose. Businessmen would like to resolve some of the contradictions and uncertainties of the present laws and bring them more into harmony with economic realities, but there are no serious advocates of abolition.

Over the past twenty years the antitrust thinking of the Congress, the administrative agencies, and the courts have been greatly influenced by the theory of imperfect or monopolistic competition. This theory holds that the nation's economy is shot through with monopolistic elements. Companies "differentiate" their products in order to escape competition; oligopolists have a "convention" against price competition; they work in "collusion"; and, because they have "price jurisdiction," they are able to milk the public and make "monopoly profits." The ideal state of affairs is "perfect competition," and, even though this concept is an abstraction that can have no counterpart in reality, it is thought of as a standard toward which the community should strive.

Looking at the world through this frame of reference, some legislators, administrators, commissioners, and judges have taken a dim view of the competitiveness of the American economy. In their minds, oligopoly and size tends to be equated with monopoly; uniformity in pricing is interpreted as overt collusion; the existence of market power, whether exercised or not, is thought of as a violation of the law against monopolization; any increase in market share through merger is viewed as a step toward monopoly; competition is thought to revolve almost wholly around price, and little dependence is placed on quality competition and substitution as regulatory forces.

In recent years a new theory, that of workable competition, has been gaining ground among the economists; and it is likely that in the years to come, this point of view will exercise more influence in the writing and the interpretation of the antitrust laws.

The term "workable competition" was first used by John M. Clark in a paper read before the American Economic Association in 1940.[40] Professor Clark argued that perfect competition is not necessary for social control. Rivalry among oligopolists, he said, would insure a variety of goods and services, and substitution and the threat of potential competition would protect the consumer from oligopolistic exploitation. Since 1940 many economists have joined the debate on workable competition, and Professor Clark himself has developed his views in an important new theoretical work entitled *Competitive Forces in a Dynamic Economy*, under the auspices of The Brookings Institution.

Like other theorists, the proponents of workable competition believe that competition provides the only alternative to authoritarian control by the state. But, they say, competition is not an end in itself. What the community is seeking is economic progress and human betterment under a system of free choice. This has been brought about by large-scale or "oligopolic" enterprise, with its mass production technique and emphasis on research and innovation.

The key to social control, say the proponents of workable competition, is enough choice so that the consumer can influence supplier profit margins through the allocation of patronage. The problem is: What criteria should be used to decide when there is enough choice? Agreeing that at this stage the answer is nebulous at best, the workable competition theorists seek the criteria in three areas: market structure, conduct, and performance.

Under the heading of market structure the proponents of workable competition would examine such factors as the number of sellers, their relative importance, and the ease of entry. It is believed that competition is generally more dependable as a control mechanism when there are many suppliers than when there are few. But they also agree with Clare E. Griffen that the existence and virility of competition depends more on the competitive spirit of suppliers and their desire to make their decisions independently than on their number and size.[41]

The theorists of workable competition think that business conduct must remain an important criterion for judging the competitiveness of the economy. Firms must behave like competitors, and be willing to test themselves in the market. They must eschew conspiracy, coercion of rivals, and trade practices that interfere with the consumer's plebiscite. This, of course, is the prime focus of the Sherman Act. But in seeking to prevent monopolization, the courts, say the proponents of workable competition, have paid too little attention to economic performance. If an industry is efficient and is passing its technological gains on to the public, if its profits are within reason for successful enterprise, and if it is offering the consumers a real range of choice, then the courts, the workable competition theorists believe, should require strong evidence of monopolization on other grounds before judgment of violation of the anti-trust law is made.

Jesse W. Markham has given this point of view definite expression when he suggests that:

> An industry may be judged to be workably competitive, when after the structural characteristics of its market and the depressive forces that shaped them have been thoroughly examined, there is no clearly indicated change that can be effected through public policy measures that would result in greater social gains than social losses. (i.e. better performance)[42]

A. D. H. Kaplan's criteria, as set forth in Chapter Nine, represent another attempt to define workable competition.

The applications of any set of criteria are, of course, complex matters in which economists, as well as judges, may disagree. In antitrust law, the need is for more precise and objective standards, yet ones that avoid the injustice of mechanistic *per se* interpretation. In this paradoxical situation, there would appear to be no recourse except to the Rule of Reason, and a continued search for competitive standards that are both economically realistic and geared to community values.

Businessmen have given great fortunes to foundations whose

trustees struggle with the problem of how to spend the money wisely in the best interests of the community. One or more of these foundations could make an important contribution to the nation's welfare by underwriting a continuous series of studies by separate scholars or groups of scholars on competition as an organizing principle for a free society. These studies should examine the economic and sociological aspects of the problem as well as the legal side. Does competition negate human cooperation or provide one of the best vehicles for its expression? How much and what kind of competition is needed for orderly and dynamic progress? How should the community handle those defeated in the competitive race? When should we make economic decisions through the consumer's plebiscite and when through the polling booths or the voters?

According to Fritz Machlup, peoples and their governments have long had difficulty making up their minds whether they disliked competition or monopoly more. Governments intervene to restrain monopoly and aid competition, then they restrain competition to aid monopoly.[43] Ludwig von Mises says: "The great monopoly problem mankind has to face today is not an outgrowth of the operation of the market economy. It is a product of purposive action on the part of governments."[44]

Certainly the United States is displaying certain schizophrenic tendencies on the issue of competition and monopoly. On the one hand, we have the anti-trust laws to preserve competition but, on the other, we have laws to curtail competition or prevent it. In agriculture, government has undertaken to shield suppliers from competition through price supports, acreage control, marketing restrictions, and international price and import programs. Labor unions, except for collusive agreements between workers and employers, have been exempted from laws against monopoly. Tariffs shield domestic producers from foreign competition; and resale maintenance laws, although they are becoming increasingly unworkable, seek to protect retailers from price competition. Inheritance taxes stimulate the growth of large companies by forcing individual entrepreneurs to merge to pay the tax collector. State licensing laws set professional standards that curtail freedom of entry; and local building codes, in the name of sanitation and public safety, discriminate against new products and more efficient building procedures.

One of the most interesting and philosophically challenging cases of the mitigation of competition through government intervention is in the conservation of natural resources, particularly in the oil and gas industry. Oil and gas are found trapped in sections of porous rocks such as sandstone and limestone, usually under considerable pressure. A property owner can claim possession of the oil underneath his land only if he can bring it to the surface before his neighbors do; hence whenever oil is discovered there is a wild scramble to drill and produce as fast as possible. If oil and gas are to be conserved and a newly discovered pool is to be exploited with the greatest possible efficiency, it should be operated as a unit with particular attention to maintaining the right underground pressures.

In 1919 the state of Texas gave the Railroad Commission of Texas considerable regulatory power over the oil industry to prevent waste. Since that year the powers of the Commission have grown and other oil-producing states have set up similar regulatory bodies. Under an Interstate Oil Compact authorized by Congress in 1935, the several states undertake to coordinate their activities.

As the production system now works, the United States Bureau of Mines makes monthly estimates of consumption demand. Each state commission sets a production figure for "reasonable market demand" and pro-rates the total among the various producers in terms of the number of days of allowable production. In early 1960, the Texas rate had been reduced to eight days per month. The Federal government assists the states in enforcing pro-rationing by prohibiting the movement in interstate commerce of "hot oil" or oil in excess of the allotted quota.

Without doubt oil pro-rationing has helped to ensure the nation's supply of oil and gas, but it has also served as a vehicle for price stabilization. The oil industry is intensely competitive in manufacturing and marketing, but production pro-rationing quite obviously represents a partial retreat from the principle of competitive control. It does not follow that competition in oil production is unworkable. What is required, say students of the oil industry, is a change in the property laws to require oil pools to be operated as single units. If this were done, oil would be properly conserved, and production would be controlled by the competitive price of crude.

If we are to have a coherent national policy on competition as a regulatory force, Congress, sooner or later, should undertake to state what that policy is. What are our economic and social goals? Are we seeking to mass produce and distribute goods and services at the lowest cost, or are we desirous of protecting the way of life of the small producer or tradesman even at the cost of economic inefficiency? Should we abandon the judicial practice of trying to anticipate monopoly and allow the economy to make its own adjustments, subject to the condition that consumers are provided with a satisfactory range of choice? Can we depend on competition between a few sellers to protect the consumer, and what are the conditions required for such competition? These are hard questions for which there probably are no tidy answers. Perhaps the best we can hope for on a problem so complex as social control through competition is to "muddle through." But in a free society we will surely "muddle" better if we see to it that the rules of competition are continually brought up-to-date and are written wisely, both with respect to economic reality and social values.

So much for competition as the primary mechanism for the control of profits. Let us now look briefly at government control through price fixing and taxation and through rate making for public utilities. In the United States these types of control have been reserved for war emergencies during which the market process has been compromised, and for "natural monopoly" industries where the needs of the consumers are thought to be best served by one supplier.

Wars are always marked by economic dislocations. In wartime it is necessary to shift men and resources quickly from civilian to military production, and to curtail the consumption of peacetime goods. This could be done through the market by raising wages to attract workers to war industries, and by allowing price increases on civilian goods to curtail demand. But this course would violate the principle of "equality of sacrifice" and would be politically untenable. The price of food might go beyond the means of a minister or a teacher. Some entrepreneurs would surely have the foresight to accumulate inventories of goods that promised to be short in supply, and thereby make "a profit killing."

Governments normally fight wars, therefore, with heavily controlled economies, including price fixing, subsidies, materials allocation, and consumer rationing. In the process, government usually develops a bad case of economic schizophrenia, for wars are normally financed in good part by inflation, which puts the controllers in the paradoxical position of pushing up prices with one hand and trying to hold them down with the other.

In World War I price controls were placed on metals and other items needed for the war effort and were extended to food and fuels in the consumer field. Various departments of government quickly found themselves working at cross purposes, but the war was over before the situation got out of hand.

Following the First World War, considerable attention was given to the problem of war mobilization and profit control in Congress and out of it. In 1926, Bernard M. Baruch published an article in the *Atlantic Monthly* entitled "Take the Profits Out of War," in which he proposed a universal price freeze at the outbreak of hostilities. Congress created a War Policies Commission in 1930 to develop methods to control wartime profits. The Attorney General advised the Commission that universal price controls for the purpose of prosecuting a war would be unconstitutional, but price control for the purpose of preventing profiteering would not be. In its final report, the War Policies Commission recommended a constitutional amendment to empower Congress to institute price control to prevent war profiteering.

In the hearings leading up to the passage of The Price Control Act of 1942, the testimony dealt mostly with wartime inflation and the necessity of price control to keep it in check; but one of the purposes of the Act as stated in its preamble, was "to eliminate and prevent profiteering." The law set up the Office of Price Administration and instructed it to set prices in such manner that they are generally "fair and reasonable."

In the last three wars, three methods of price control have been employed. The first is the selective method. Under this procedure prices are set for basic commodities on the theory that this will hold the price structure of the whole economy in check. This approach quickly breaks down because the favorable price for controlled items increases demand at the same time supply is being decreased as a result of rising costs and declining profits. Selective controls, therefore, inevitably give way to universal control.

The second method is the general price freeze. This method does not work very long because it does not allow for the changing demands on the economy. Also, it is almost impossible to enforce. Suppliers adjust to unfavorable prices by cheapening the quality of the goods or by concentrating on high priced items which have adequate profit margins. The customer is forced to take what he is offered or go without.

The third method employed to control prices is formula pricing, based either on cost of production or on profits for a given period preceding the emergency. In World War II, 1936-1939, were used as the base years. Formula pricing, like all other methods of price control, incurs monumental difficulties. How are costs to be defined? How much should be allowed for overhead? Should advertising be allowed as cost? How can regional variations in costs be coped with? How can the prices of low and high cost producers be fixed? How can there be an allowance for companies that suffered low profit margins in the base period?

The problem of controlling prices in a complex economy almost defies description. Price control assumes rules and rules require that economic goods, processes, and producing firms be classified and defined. In World War II a volume of several hundred pages was needed merely to list the commodities subject to control. The reader can get some flavor of the labyrinthine struggle by the following instructions on hot water bottles issued by the Office of Price Administration:

> There are three grades of hot-water bottles, Grade I, Grade II, and hospital grade. Most manufacturers of Grade I also make Grade II, but many do not make the hospital grade. Except for the molds used, Grade I and II bottles are similar in specifications and manufacturing processes, while materials used in the hospital grade are substantially different. Except for the difference in materials, the impact of cost increases is about the same for the Grade I and II bottles and quite similar for the hospital grade. There is an historical price relationship between Grade I and II bottles (Grade I bottle has always been sold at a high price differential), whereas the prices of the hospital grade vary independently. The hospital grade is distributed mainly through hospital supply houses, while Grade I and II are distributed through wholesale drug houses, retail drug stores, department stores, and mail order houses. The fact that hospital grade bottles are made by only a few of the people who make Grades I and II is also important (it is not appropriate to meet the standard for the entire group on the basis of revenue from a commodity not sold by many of the manufacturers). Accordingly Grade I and II hot water bottles have been treated as a product distinct from hospital grade bottles.[45]

In Princeton, New Jersey, the dilemma of definition of the firm got the OPA into a hair pulling match with local housewives. For thirty-nine years, hundreds of local residents had purchased their food supplies from F. H. Bamman, Inc., an independent wholesale and retail grocer. Bamman's was one of those old-fashioned stores that women loved. It stocked exotic food, took telephoned orders, delivered a package of cigarettes five miles away, extended liberal credit, and no doubt would have minded the baby if a customer had asked. With this amiable service it built up a large volume of business which, under OPA rulings, put it in Group 4, along with the chain stores. Bamman's obviously could not render its kind of service at chain store prices, and announced that it had no alternative but to close its doors.

The announcement stirred up a hornet's nest. Housewives, under the energetic leadership of Mrs. A. M. Crossley, circulated petitions, wrote letters to OPA, filled out affidavits, and sent a formidable delegation to Washington, including a Princeton University professor, a wife of a United States Senator, and the Chairman of the local rationing board, to argue that the closing of Bamman's would cause a "community hardship." In the face of this onslaught, the chief of OPA's price section decided to fall back and regroup, and gave Bamman's a three month reprieve from compliance, subject to a hearing to be held in Washington. Having turned aside the first wave of protest, OPA decided to stand its ground and again ordered Bamman's to behave like a super market, adding helpfully that the store could comply if it would go over to cash and carry, or at least add a charge for deliveries. Happily for all concerned, the war ended and Bamman's was saved for a few years until the local residents voted it out of business by transferring their patronage to the more efficiently operated chain stores.

If the problem of classification presents the controllers with a giant sized dilemma, the enigma of price relatedness poses an even greater one. In a specialized economy the price of peanuts is geared delicately to the price of coal and the price of coal has something to do with the price of women's hats. Change the price of one item and, willy-nilly, the price of every other item is affected. The market can and does solve this infinite tangle, but no human mind or group of minds can hope to order the gearing of prices without the most grotesque forms of distortion.

Even batteries of the latest electronic computers would be of no help, for the controller has no measure of the value that buyers and sellers place on goods and services. The only way this can be known is through competitive bidding and offering in the market place. When the price is set by the arbitrary rulings of the controllers, it quickly gets out of phase with the values of the buyers and sellers and a black market inevitably appears. The coming of a black market is certain proof that the controllers have failed to solve the problems of value and price relatedness, for a black market, even though it is proscribed by law, is nothing more nor less than the natural functioning of the price system in equating supply and demand.

Seymour Harris says that price control in World War II was successful because the rise in the cost of living was held to twenty-five and nine-tenths per cent as against sixty-four and six-tenths per cent increase in World War I.[46] This assessment, in all likelihood, is on the optimistic side, because it makes no allowance for black market prices.

Summing up the experience with OPA in World War II, A. D. H. Kaplan says:

> Any of us who had to administer price control know that it can work if at all, only as an intensive short term program. We could mobilize patriotism in the realization of a national emergency. But, in World War II, it didn't take more than about a year after price control was instituted before the problem of enforcement became almost insoluble.[47]

The anomalies of price control became abundantly evident to the nation in 1946, when a severe meat shortage developed. Black market operators had taken over a substantial part of the industry, and few butcher shops could be found that were selling meat at controlled prices. President Truman said the government had given consideration to seizing cattle that were being withheld on the farms, but decided that this would be impractical. Controls on meat were lifted on October 16, 1946, and the meat shortage quickly disappeared. Three weeks later, on November 9, all price controls were abolished, and the country breathed an audible sigh of relief.

In January 1951, during the Korean War, a general price-wage freeze was imposed under a new Office of Price Stabilization, but the control program had little real effect on the economy and was completely scrapped in 1953, when Dwight D. Eisenhower took over the presidency.

The Public Opinion Index reports that approximately one-third of the public still looks with favor on some form of price control. But this sentiment would appear to be more an expression of annoyance with the cost of living than a considered judgment on national policy. The country has recently had direct experience with price control, and this experience shows that this form of regulation inevitably leads to economic inefficiency, shortages, black markets, and the breakdown of law and order. Apart from industries where one supplier is given an exclusive franchise, competition offers the only feasible peacetime method for the social control of prices and profits. When competition is allowed to function, the evidence shows that price clings closely to cost, and profits rarely get very far out of hand.

Price control is one method employed by government to limit profits in wartime. Another method is to levy a so called "excess profits" tax. In all three of the last wars in which the country has been engaged, government has attempted "to take the profits out of war" by this form of tax.

The basic problem in levying an excess profits tax is to define what is excess. One solution is to set a norm for return on capital, and tax everything over that as excess. A second approach is to assume that company profits for some period before the emergency are "normal," and regard anything over that amount as excess.

In World War I, both systems were used. Normal return on investment was fixed at seven to nine per cent, or that amount earned in the 1911-1913 base period, and excess profits taxes were levied on whichever method of computation yielded the highest tax. Companies making less than twenty per cent on invested capital paid up to thirty per cent excess profits tax; those making over twenty per cent paid up to sixty-five per cent excess profits tax.

In World War II, base years were set for 1936-1939, and the tax took up to ninety-five per cent of the excess. In the Korean War the base years were 1946-1949 with the tax on the excess running up to eighty-two per cent.

After every war strong arguments have been made for continuance of excess profits taxes. The tax, it is said, would eliminate "monopoly profits," bring about a fairer distribution of income, prevent inflation, check inventory speculation and provide other benefits. But the proponents of excess profits taxes have always been beaten because this form of taxation is extremely disruptive to the functioning of a peacetime economy. Excess profits taxes reduce the incentive to produce efficiently, and encourage waste and a careless attitude toward cost. They assume a static economy and place heavy tax penalties on growing companies that pioneer technological advance. They place a low ceiling on profits and thereby deter companies from taking the risks that are vital to economic progress and industrial health.

Government succeeded in restricting profits in World War II, for company earnings rates trended downward during the war years. No one can argue seriously with heavy taxes on profits in wartime. Wars are costly and must be paid for, hence excess profits taxes, consumption taxes, income taxes, and other levies are appropriate. But in peacetime the concept of an excess profits tax contradicts the basic principles of a capitalistic order. In a competitive market there is no such thing as an excess profit. Profit is an indicator on the economic machine which tells the operators when to speed up the mechanism and when to slow it down. A high profit is as valid and necessary a signal as a low profit. Actually, the profit indicator never stays very long on the high side, for too many operators are eager to make the economic adjustments that cause the needle to fall. Unless the American people are prepared to turn their backs on the capitalistic organization of the economy, therefore an excess profit tax has no place in our affairs.

A second area where government control of profits is held necessary is in the public utility field involving transportation, communication, and the supply of electricity and gas. These industries pose different problems than other lines of business. In telephone communication, for example, the value of the service is greatly enhanced when every subscriber is linked into the same system. In the electric power business it would be a nuisance if the streets were continually torn up or cluttered with competing lines. Also plant and equipment costs are high. Today it requires an investment of four and a half dollars for every dollar of gross annual sale of electricity, compared with forty-seven cents investment per dollar of sale for manufacturing. If several companies were to compete for the electric power business, the capital cost would substantially increase the cost of the service to the consumer. For these and other reasons, it is generally held to be good social policy to have one supplier for each public utility service. No public utility is completely without competition, and, in some fields like transportation, intense competition exists. Nevertheless the restriction of consumer opportunities for alternate choice has led communities to regulate public utility services by law. Public control of railroads in interstate commerce was taken over by the Federal Government in 1887 when the Interstate Commerce Commission was established. State regulation of electric utility companies dates back to 1907 when New York created, and Wisconsin extended an existing body to form a public service commission. Today forty-five states have commissions to regulate the electric power industry. Four states operate through local regulation and one state, Nebraska, has state ownership of power. In 1920 the Federal Power Commission was established to create public policy for water resource use, and in 1945 this Commission was given authority to regulate electric power sold across state lines.

The Federal Radio Commission was created in 1927 to regulate radio and subsequently television. In 1934 this Commission was given authority to control interstate telegraphy.

Since 1938 airlines have been under the regulatory control of the Civil Aeronautics Board which issues route permits, sets rates, supervises mergers, authorizes subsidies, and investigates accidents.

We are here interested only in the general principles of profit control by government in the public utility field, and for this purpose our brief discussion will be restricted to the electric power and railroad fields. Public service commissions are usually independent bodies of government. In the electric power field they have jurisdiction over accounting practices of companies, finance, service policies, reorganization, and rates. They are legislator, administrator, and judge. They may initiate inquiries and hold formal hearings to decide rates or negotiate informally with company managements. Their decisions are subject to review by the courts, and a great deal of "judicial law" has accumulated through the years to guide public utilities commissions.

As a part of their exclusive franchise, electric power companies are required to serve all consumers at prescribed rates without discrimination, and to make provision for anticipated future needs. In the interest of encouraging good electric power service, the public utility is permitted to earn what is thought to be a reasonable return on a fair value of the property. Fair return is not a guarantee; it is conceived more as a "zone of reasonableness" that will give the company a rate sufficient to attract capital in the competitive money markets, yet provide electricity to the consumer at a fair price.

Rate making is a highly technical operation and, as might be expected, there is usually a difference of opinion between the companies and the regulatory authorities on what constitutes a fair return. The reasoning of public utility commissions tends to go this way: Given the present or near term anticipated volume of sales, a fair rate is that which covers out of pocket costs plus a reasonable return on a fair value of the property. But immediately the question arises: What is the fair value of the property in use? Is it original cost less depreciation charged to reserve, or the cost at which prudent investors would value the property, or reproduction cost? And how is depreciation to be charged; is it measured by decline in the operating efficiency of a plant or by writing off each year a part of the original cost of the plant and equipment? The tendency of commissions has been to think in terms of original cost less depreciation charged to reserve as the basis for a fair valuation of utility property.

So far, this system of regulation appears to have worked well. As indicated in Appendix C1, the average return on investment for all electric and gas utilities under tax accounting methods has been approximately six per cent. Appendix C2 shows that the return for leading gas and electric utilities under book accounting methods runs between six and nine per cent. This return has enabled electric power companies to attract enough capital to finance steady growth. In 1912 privately owned electric systems generated eleven billion kilowatt hours of electricity. By 1959 this output had increased approximately fifteen times to a total of 544 billion kilowatt hours. With only six per cent of the world's population, the United States now generates forty-one per cent of the world's electric power output. Tremendous technical strides in productivity have been made by the industry, with consequent savings to the consumer. Between 1913 and 1955 the cost of living went up nearly three times, but in 1955 the average price of residential electricity was only thirty per cent of what it was in 1913.

The story of public regulation of the railroads is much less satisfactory. When the Interstate Commerce Commission was created in 1887, the railroads enjoyed a virtual monopoly in inter-city transportation. Their rates were frequently excessive on certain types of goods and there was discrimination against persons and localities. The objective of the original Act to Regulate Commerce was to curb the excesses of rail monopoly power.

The Transportation Act of 1920 gave the Interstate Commerce Commission power to set minimum rates for railroads, and the Motor Carrier Act of 1935 and the Transportation Act of 1940 authorized the Commission to "foster sound economic conditions in transportation and among several carriers" and "to encourage . . . reasonable charges . . . without unfair or destructive competitive charges." With this legislative authorization, the Commission began setting rates that in effect allocated traffic among the several carriers. The complaint of the railroads was that when they sought to capitalize on their economic advantages and petitioned for a rate reduction on certain types of freight, the Interstate Commerce Commission would deliberate on what effect the change would have in diverting traffic, and set the rate at that point which would give each carrier the share of traffic the Commission thought advisable. The railroads themselves had argued for equal regulatory burdens for all competing carriers, but they were not prepared for Commission rulings against rate decreases. In 1946, sixty per cent of the protests filed with the Commission were against rate increases; in 1957, ninety-two per cent of the protests were against rate decreases.

In 1946, thirty-three per cent of the protests achieved suspension by the Interstate Commerce Commission, but in 1957, when the protests were predominantly against rate decreases, forty-eight per cent received suspension.[48]

Over the past three decades and with government aid, a great technological revolution has taken place in the field of transportation. Oil pipelines and tanker fleets have taken over the movement of petroleum. A vast network of roads and super highways has been constructed to carry automobiles and fast inter-city freight trucks; inland waterways have been improved for the passage of water borne commerce; and scores of airfields and depots have been built and airway beacons and traffic control systems set up to stimulate air travel. While the railroads have been required to maintain their own rights-of-way and depots and pay taxes on them, competing carriers have received the benefit of tax free facilities supplied by government.

The regulatory response to this change has not been to return social control of transportation to competition, but to guard against the past excess of monopoly, and to allocate traffic between rival carriers. To make matters worse, all interstate railroad rates are under the jurisdiction of the Interstate Commerce Commission, but only one-third of inter-city freight trucking and about one-seventh of waterborne commerce are under Commission regulation.

The effect on the railroads, of course, has been disastrous. In terms of revenue miles, the rail share of inter-city freight movement declined from seventy-six per cent in 1926 to forty-four per cent in 1960. Between 1946 and 1960 the airline share of the passenger business rose from six to forty-four per cent, while the railroad share of this business dropped from sixty-six to twenty-eight per cent.[49] In the face of this poor revenue situation, costs for equipment and labor rose sharply. While railroad productivity has increased impressively—product per locomotive, for example, has increased three and a half times since 1921—it has not been enough to cope with the adverse forces that have beset the industry. Railroad profits as a consequence have declined to the level of three to four per cent profit on investment. (See Appendices C1 and C2.) This has meant insufficient dividends to attract new capital and has seriously limited the ability of management to modernize rail equipment to compete with the technological advances of the other carriers.

Some of the decline of the once great railroad industry has, of course, been due to poor management; but no management, however intelligent and energetic, is likely to have overcome the tide of governmental subsidy for competing carriers, the delay of the regulatory authorities in granting general rate increases,[50] and the extreme frustration of being unable to make management decisions on rates and services required to meet the competition.

In 1954 President Eisenhower appointed The President's Cabinet Committee on Transport Policy and Organization and this Committee found that for all practical purposes a changing technology had eliminated the monopoly element in transportation. Regulatory policy, the Committee said, had not kept pace with change and should be altered to permit competitive forces, within limits, to allocate traffic and determine the reasonableness of rates. Specifically, the Committee proposed that the Interstate Commerce Commission set maximum rates to prevent exploitation of the shipper and minimum rates (i.e. cost of the service to the carrier), and allow management wide discretion to set differential rates within these limits. All carriers have cost and service advantages and disadvantages. If the Committee's suggestion is adopted, it should permit more competitive pricing and greater market determination of how economic resources are to be used in meeting the nation's transportation needs. Probably too, in order to become fully competitive, the railroads will require some equalization of tax burdens and perhaps the right to own coordinate non-rail facilities.

In industries where one supplier is given an exclusive franchise, the community undertakes to achieve social control of service and profit through public utility regulations. This policy, like all social arrangements, has its advantages and disadvantages. The advantage is that reasonable standards of service are required, and consumers are protected against discrimination and exhorbitant rates. The disadvantages stem from the organizational anomaly that divides authority and responsibility. The managers and owners are responsible for costs, but the regulatory bodies have large authority over income. Management and ownership must answer to economic forces; and, while public utility commissioners must likewise heed them, political pressures often delay their response.

In the nature of things the inertia factor is much greater in regulated than in competitive industry. Under the stress of competition management is required to make prompt and oftentimes far reaching decisions for change when cost, sales, or profit trends dictate. In regulated industry the decision making process is greatly slowed down. Management must clear basic policy matters with the regulatory authorities, present data in public hearings and answer protests. The result is that response to change usually involves a considerable time lag. In the case of the railroads this lag has been so extended that most railroads are suffering from financial anemia and some are likely to expire.

In competitive industry the hope and prospect of profit acts as a great spur to progress. By intelligent control of costs, or by risking money on research, or the purchase of modern equipment, or the re-organization of a distribution system, companies can create profit through what we have previously discussed as the "entrepreneural cost differential." Through cost reduction a competitor can frequently meet or lower the price asked by his rivals and still increase profit. In regulated industries there continues to be a premium for efficient management, but the driving force of the prospect for large profit is in large part lost, for when the return on investment rises much above the interest rate the regulatory bodies order a reduction in rates.

There is possibly no answer to this dilemma except public enlightenment on how the profit and loss system works for the benefit of the community. In its study "Profit, Performance and Progress," the American Telephone and Telegraph Company compared significant operating data for twenty-five of the most profitable and twenty-five of the least profitable companies. On every criterion of social usefulness, such as increase in capital equipment, rise in sales, and enlargement of job opportunities, the most profitable companies outscored the least profitable ones. It is an error to assume that the low profit company is the best servant of the community. Certainly in competitive industry the company that makes the best profit is likely to be the one that is doing the best job for the community, and in regulated industry this principle is operative too. In the American Telephone and Telegraph study a comparison of thirty-eight most profitable electric power companies with thirty-eight least profitable ones showed that the best earners had the lowest operating and plant cost and sold electricity at the lowest rates.

Human motivation is much broader than monetary incentive, but dollar incentives vastly influence the patterns of economic effort. It would be a boon to the community if some ingenious social engineer invented new techniques whereby regulated industries could be allowed to make outstanding profit for outstanding service.

To summarize the discussion of the social control of profits: the community requires that profits be subjected to some form of control, and the apparatus best suited for this purpose, it would appear, is competition. The essence of competition is rivalry between suppliers and the offering of choice to the consumer. The factors of alternate choice are never restricted to price alone, but always involve quality as well. There is price competition where quality is the same and quality competition where price is the same. Competition permits impartial and individualized judgment by consumers and makes suppliers quickly responsive to consumer needs. It allocates men and economic resources in conformity with consumer wishes, and coordinates the infinite complexity of economic relations with great efficiency. Moreover, the hope and prospect of competitive profit provides a strong driving force for progress.

The effort to substitute conscious control for competition, as indicated by the experience with the N.R.A. and O.P.A., and the attempt to take away "excess" profits by taxation, has produced economic dislocation, inefficiency, and the breakdown of law and order. Public service regulation appears to have worked reasonably well except for transportation where regulatory policies have lagged technological change and brought disaster to the railroads.

The maintenance of competition for purposes of social control requires a set of rules provided by government and trade custom and supported by business. The complexities of economic activity pose difficult problems for the rule makers, but the Sherman Act and other legislation, with judicial interpretations by the Rule of Reason, have provided a legal framework for competitive practice. With the 1932 depression, the country's confidence in competition as an organizing principle, however, has been shaken, and today we have something of a national schizophrenia on the subject, with business required to compete under the Sherman Act, but under the Robinson-Patman Act not compete too much, and with the government undertaking to shield certain agricultural and other groups from the effects of competition. Despite these aberrations and the occasional disclosures of price rigging by business, the American economy is still highly competitive and offers the consuming public a wide range of choice.

The competitive principle is part of the pattern of freedom, and the American people should be reluctant to compromise it. Businessmen particularly should have a deep conviction about the necessity to compete, for unless they are willing to operate by the test of the market, the community will certainly impose other forms of control which will limit their freedom. So great is the community's stake in a workable system of competition that strong efforts need to be made by scholars and men of affairs to clarify the public mind on the purpose of competition and to formulate a coherent body of competitive rules by which the community can live. Businessmen are often critical of government. They could make a constructive contribution if they would dedicate some of their resources, their competent personnel and their knowledge of living economics to the job of re-thinking and re-vitalizing a national point of view on competition.

CHAPTER ELEVEN

PROFIT SHARING

One of the great paradoxes of our times is the seeming inability of Americans to visualize the profit-and-loss economy as a sharing system. Whether we rely on personal experience or on statistical demonstration the evidence of sharing is on every hand. The multiplicity of schools and colleges shows that people have enough wealth to educate their children; the widespread incidence of corpulence shows that the average man has more than enough to eat; the daily traffic jam, however annoying, furnishes unique proof that automobile production is shared with millions of car buyers.

Chart 18 makes the sharing of the profit-and-loss system obvious. The graphs indicate that real wages have risen steadily, and, by the same token, that labor time required to buy food and other items has declined. Wherever one looks—education, insurance in force, per capita savings, growth of newsprint used for communication, consumption of meat, ownership and electrification of homes, and ownership of automobiles and telephones—the data reflect human betterment. These are the facts.

Nor is it difficult to ascertain why the system shares so bountifully. The reason is that suppliers in search of profit compete to serve the consumer. To succeed in this competition they must produce goods and services with features, styles, taste, and other attributes that satisfy the buyer. Moreover, they must continually find ways to produce these goods and services at less cost. Should a company become laggard in this respect, there is every likelihood that competition will take away its trade. Innovation is one way to stay ahead of the competition, but even the innovator is not safe; for when a company introduces a new product and makes an above average profit, it is soon confronted with competition from other suppliers who are attracted by the possibilities of good earnings. Costs and selling prices are driven down, with the result that the consumer gets more for his income dollar.

Thus, in the American economy, we have capital working, for an average fee of three to six per cent profit per dollar of sales and five to ten per cent profit per dollar of investment. For this modest fee, which tends to remain remarkably constant over a long period of time, the owners of capital have managed an increasingly productive economy and handed the fruits over to the people.

This conclusion flies in the face of the popular stereotype, but Chart 19 offers simple proof of its accuracy. Line A plots the Index of Real Hourly Wages in manufacturing, as compiled by John W. Kendrick under the auspices of the National Bureau of Economic Research.[1] Line B shows profit on investment for all manufacturing as reported by the United States Treasury. Line C traces profit on investment as corrected by the Department of Commerce for distortions of inventory valuation and depreciation. Line D shows profit on sales for all manufacturing as reported by the United States Treasury.

Real wages in manufacturing (Line A) have risen steadily, the average yearly increase from 1926 to date being two and six-tenths per cent. In the same period, profits on manufacturing have moved sidewise in a horizontal band. Profit per dollar of sales (Line D) has, in most years, ranged from three to six cents. Profit on investment (Line B) appears to have described an uptrend from 1933 to 1947, but much of this is illusory, for, when the data are corrected for the distortions of inventory valuation

Chart 18 (a)

Sharing Under the American Profit and Loss System

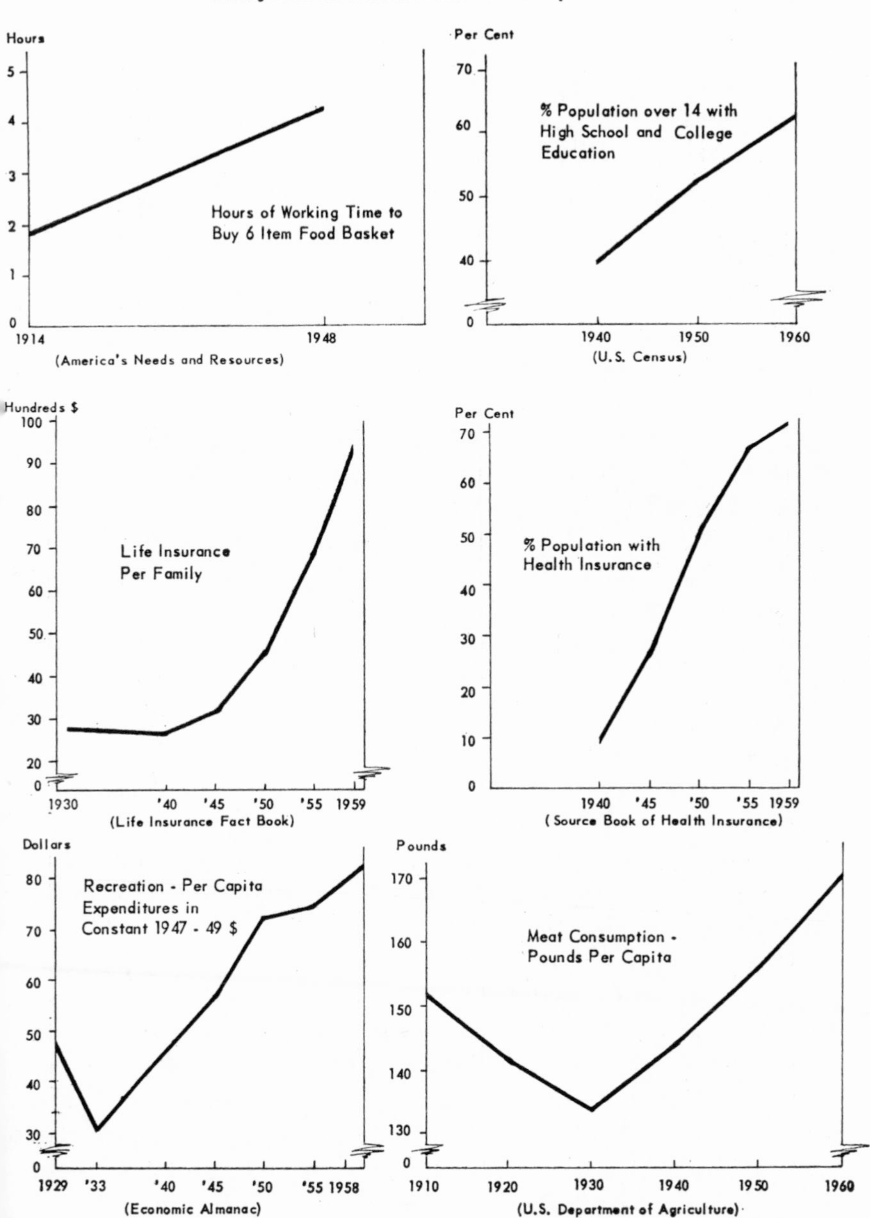

Chart 18 (b)

Sharing Under the American Profit and Loss System

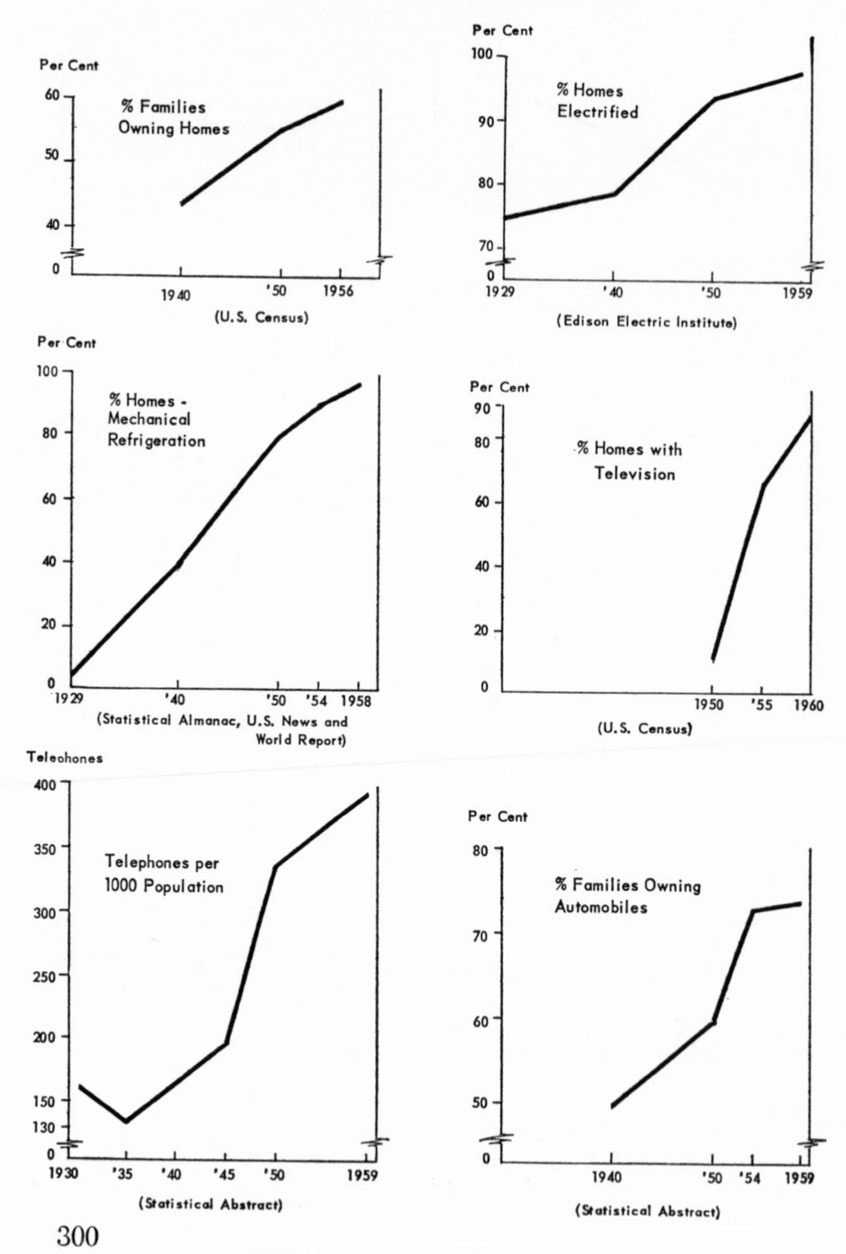

and depreciation that resulted from changing price levels (Line C), the curve flattens out, ranging in most years between five and ten cents per dollar of investment.[2]

The facts, then, show that owners of capital have supplied funds for a moderate profit and, because competition requires it, have distributed the fruits of increasing productivity to the people.[3] The public, however, holds a different view. Through the years the cry has been that profits are exorbitant, that owners get too much of the wealth produced, and that, if justice is to prevail, the workers should receive a greater share. Out of this psychology arose the labor movement to force companies to give the workers more; and out of it, too, has grown the idea of voluntary sharing of profits.[4]

For many people the concept of profit sharing evokes a missionary zeal. It provides the matrix for human cooperation in industry, they believe, and holds the key to industrial peace. It puts into practice the ideal of industrial democracy and provides a grand design for the living expression of Christianity. Louis Affleck, banker and economist, declared that, profit sharing "follows the teachings of the greatest of all economists, Jesus Christ."[5]

In 1938, a Senate committee, after a series of hearings, put its stamp of approval on profit sharing by declaring that profit sharing is "essential to the ultimate maintenance of the capitalistic system." "The safest way to protect the system in a democracy," says the Committee's report, "is to make the largest number of our people conscious of what a 'profit' means, how it is produced, upon what it depends, its interrelations and our mass dependence upon it. When that is accomplished, the capitalistic system with its profit motive . . . and our democracy as well . . . will call more dependable and intelligent defenders to its support."[6]

Businessmen who operate under profit sharing give many reasons for adopting their plans. They want to underscore the mutuality of interest between the employee and the company and give employees a sense of partnership in the enterprise. They seek to raise worker morale, avoid strikes, reduce turnover,

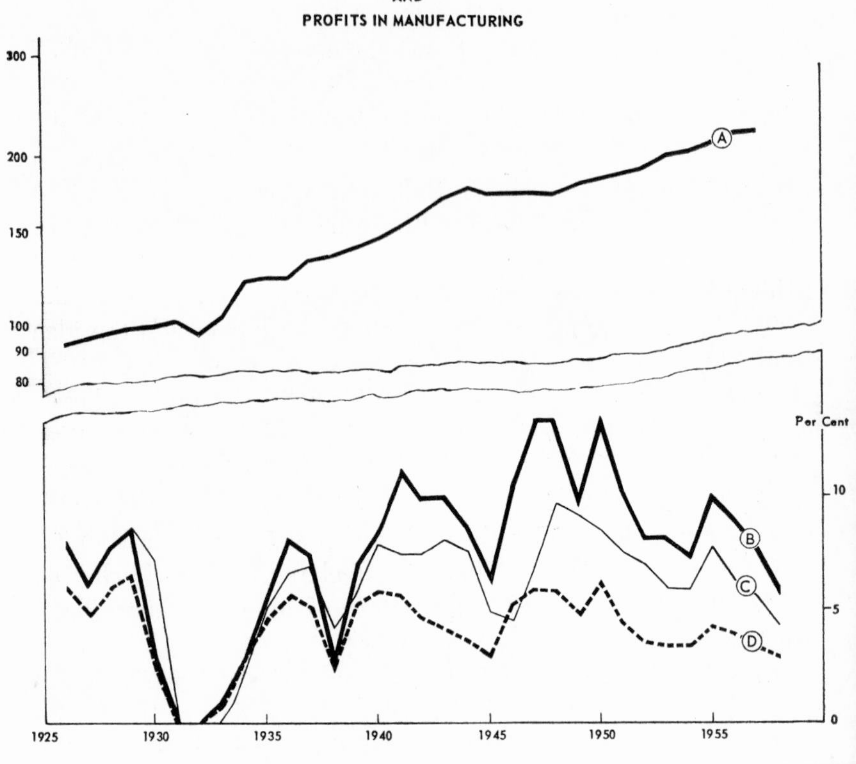

Sources: U.S. Treasury Statistics of Income
National Bureau of Economic Research

decrease absenteeism, gain greater cooperation and loyalty. They wish to increase efficiency, cut costs, reduce waste, get employees to join up in the competitive battle. They want greater flexibility in their wage payments. They believe that employees help earn profits and want them to share. They desire to encourage thrift and help employees save for old age or provide for sickness or other emergencies. They think profit sharing improves their public relations. They would like to give employees a stake in the capitalistic system, stimulate a better understanding of the way the system works, and increase employee defenses against the blandishments of socialism. In some instances, it must be said, the principal motive for installing a profit sharing plan has been to forestall union organization.

Profit sharing, of course, is not a new idea. Albert Gallatin, Secretary of the Treasury under Presidents Jefferson and Madison, installed profit sharing in his glass works at New Geneva, Pennsylvania, in 1794. Horace Greeley had a profit sharing plan for certain employees at the *New York Tribune*, and was a strong advocate. In 1886, Colonel Procter introduced a profit sharing and general employee relations program at Procter and Gamble. Eastman Kodak joined the ranks of the profit sharers in 1912, and Sears, Roebuck and Company in 1916. In 1920 the National Industrial Conference Board surveyed the field and found fifty-four companies with profit sharing plans; in 1940, its survey uncovered 158 plans.

The statistical record of the growth of profit sharing is sketchy, not only because of the variations in sampling methods employed in successive surveys, but also because of differing views of what constitutes profit sharing. To classify as profit sharing under the most commonly accepted definition, payments over and above regular wages must be made on a current or deferred basis according to some defined plan, and these payments must be contingent upon company earnings for a given time period. In the 1938 Senate hearings on profit sharing, 728 plans were reported. This list, however, was an exaggeration because it included pension and bonus programs that had no relationship to profits.

World War II gave a strong impetus to the profit-sharing movement. Under the Economic Stabilization Act of 1942, which laid down the government's wartime policy for the control of wages and salaries, companies with established profit sharing plans were allowed to continue their payments, but new plans were approved only if they deferred payments for a minimum of ten years. A company was permitted to appropriate fifteen per cent of its wage and salary payments to profit sharing, and include this as a cost for tax purposes. The monies were to be paid over to an irrevocable trust to be invested under certain statutory regulations. The principal and interest were not taxable to the employee until the money was withdrawn. If taken in one lump sum, the employee would pay the long-term tax on capital gains; if taken as a pension, the regular payments would be taxed as ordinary income.

This arrangement was attractive for several reasons. In a period of great labor shortage, it enabled companies to provide extra job advantages that held good employees and attracted new ones; and these advantages could be bought for a small cost since the excess profits tax took up to ninety-five per cent of profit.[7] Before World War II, profit sharing was looked upon mainly as a supplement for wages, and the majority of plans provided for current (i.e., cash) distribution of benefits. With the war labor shortage, together with the increased interest of an aging population in pensions, and the stimulus of tax advantages, the number of deferred profit sharing plans began a sharp climb.

Since 1942, the Internal Revenue Service has approved approximately twenty thousand new deferred profit sharing plans.[8] A liberal estimate of the number of cash and deferred plans in existence today would put the figure in the neighborhood of twenty-five thousand. The total number of business units operating in the country in 1959 was approximately four and a half million, of which one million were corporations. Profit sharing, therefore, has not yet become a widespread practice.

While profit sharing is found in both large and small companies, all surveys have indicated that it has the most attraction for small firms. In 1956, the New York State Banking Department made a study of all pension, profit sharing, and other employee welfare plans under trusteeship of state and national banks in the State of New York. The Department found that for pension trusts the average number of employees was 2512 per firm; for profit sharing plans the average number of employees per firm was 290.[9] P. A. Knowlton's study of three hundred companies in 1954 likewise showed profit sharing concentrated in small firms, two-thirds of which were closely held.[10]

Deferred profit sharing plans are attractve to small firms because they enable these companies to compete in the labor market with a retirement benefit plan, but one that does not require regular payments into a pension fund. Payments into the profit-sharing fund are made if profits are earned, and at the discretion of management. For the employee this type of benefit is less certain than a pension trust, but it allows many small firms to offer a retirement plan which it would be reluctant to take on a fixed obligation.

Profit sharing plans are as diverse in their characteristics as companies. They may be of the current or deferred type, or a combination of the two. In the current type, the company pays profit shares in cash, usually on an annual basis, but in some instances semi-annually or quarterly. In the deferred type, profit shares are cumulated until retirement, death, or withdrawal from the company, when the monies are paid in one lump or in the form of a pension. Many plans provide for sickness and disability. According to the findings of *The Public Opinion Index,* employees tend to favor whatever type of plan they have, but exhibit the strongest preference for a plan that combines cash distribution and deferred benefits.

In some deferred types of profit-sharing plans, in addition to company contributions, the employee is required to pay from two to five per cent of his salary. This practice is thought to encourage savings, avoid paternalism, and remind the employee that the good things of life come at a price. It is quite common for such plans to set a top limit on the amount employees can contribute in order to prevent the higher paid employees from gaining too large a share.

Virtually all plans give the employee a vested right to recover his own contribution plus interest earned, and most plans vest the employee's right to the company contribution as well. In some cases, when an employee leaves the company his share of the company contribution is re-distributed to the remaining members of the plan.

Employee shares in profit sharing plans are usually linked with the annual wage or salary of the employee, but some companies also use length of service as an additional criterion, and a few introduce merit ratings and other considerations. Most plans are open to all regular full-time employees, but many require a service period of from one to five years.

Understanding Profits

The percentage of net profit paid out by profit sharing companies varies, of course, with the business cycle and the liberality of the plan. In a study of profit sharing plans in 1954, Edwin Flippo found two-thirds of the companies paying out from seven to twenty-five per cent of net profits, as indicated in Table 34.

TABLE 34. PER CENT OF COMPANY NET PROFIT ALLOCATED TO PROFIT SHARING

Per Cent	*No. Companies*	*Per Cent Companies*
1 - 6	24	8
7 - 10	67	24
11 - 15	47	17
16 - 25	77	27
26 - 40	39	14
Over 40	30	10
Total	284	100

Source: *Profit Sharing in American Business,* Edwin Flippo, p. 39.

Company payout expressed as a percentage of dividends, of course, is even more impressive. In a study of 145 profit sharing companies in 1957, the National Industrial Conference Board placed the modal per cent of dividends shared at twenty-five to fifty per cent. In thirty-one out of the 145 companies, as shown in Table 35 below, profit sharing payments equalled or exceeded dividend payments.

TABLE 35. PROFIT SHARING AS PER CENT OF DIVIDENDS

Per Cent	*No. Companies*	*Per Cent Companies*
Under 10	13	9
10 under 15	10	7
15 under 25	15	10
25 under 50	30	21
50 under 100	26	18
100 under 300	19	13
300 and over	12	8
No dividends	14	10
No profit distribution	6	4
Total	145	100

Source: *Sharing Profits with Employees,* F. Beatrice Brower, National Industrial Conference Board, Studies in Personnel Policy No. 162, 1957.

According to the National Industrial Conference Board, one-third of the employees included in the 1957 study received five hundred dollars or more in cash or benefits, half the employees received from one hundred to five hundred dollars, and ten per cent received less than one hundred dollars.

In companies with successful profit sharing plans, employee reaction as reported by *The Public Opinion Index* is quite favorable. Analyzing the views of 2153 employees in thirty-three small, medium and large profit-sharing companies, the Index reported that their respondents most often rated steady employment (eighty-seven per cent) as the primary factor that made their company a good place to work, but they named profit sharing (eighty-four per cent) as the second most important advantage.

In successful profit sharing companies, employee confidence in management appears to be higher than in the average company. For the thirty-three firms in the Index sample, sixty-six per cent of the production employees rated their managements "outstanding." The average rating for nonprofit-sharing companies of comparable size and industrial character was thirty-five per cent, "outstanding."

Among successful profit-sharing companies, eighty-three per cent of the production employees testified that management takes a personal interest in them; seventy-nine per cent said that management gives employees the proper share of credit for the progress of the company. Attitude research has shown over and over again that employees place high value on recognition for good work, and the evidence would appear to indicate that profit sharing helps to satisfy this need. Among nonprofit-sharing companies, the Index reported forty-three per cent of the production employees said that their managements gave them the proper credit for company progress.

Attitudes toward productivity also appear to be better in successful profit sharing companies. Productivity is a complex phenomenon and the attitudes of employees toward increased efficiency may or may not be borne out by their behavior. The Index, however, found sixty per cent of the workers in profit sharing companies agreeing with the statement: "In our company when employees find ways to cut costs and save money they gain in wages and benefits." In nonprofit-sharing companies, forty per cent of the workers subscribed to this view.

The size of the payout, the Index study shows, influences employee attitudes, but this influence appears to be subsidiary to the spirit of sharing. Table 36 shows profit-sharing companies have succeeded much better than nonprofit-sharing companies in identifying cost-cutting with the interest of employees, and in convincing employees that they have shared in the company's success; but it is evident from the data that employees whose pay has been increased only from one to four per cent by profit sharing think not too differently from those whose pay has gone up by a greater amount. The simple idea of sharing, as well as the amount, appears to influence employee thinking.

TABLE 36. PRODUCTION WORKER ATTITUDES IN RELATION TO SIZE OF PROFIT SHARING

	Per Cent Who Agree				
	Non-Profit Sharing Companies	*Profit Sharing Companies Per Cent Added to Pay*			
	All	*1-4%*	*5-9%*	*10-19%*	*20% and over*
"In our company when employees find ways to cut costs and save money, they gain in wages and benefits."	40	55	65	68	78
"As my company has grown and prospered, employees have gotten their share."	47	77	79	87	96

Source: *The Public Opinion Index.*

One finding from the Index study that gives advocates of profit sharing something of a jolt is that employees who share profits appear to be about as critical of the business system as those who do not. In Table 37, it can be seen that half of profit-sharing employees think that owners in general get too much of company income and almost two-thirds think that the largest share of increased output has gone to owners. Among nonprofit sharing employees, the proportions agreeing with these points of view is only ten and twelve percentage points higher. Curiously enough, the vote for close regulation of business is higher among profit sharers (fifty-five per cent) than among those who do not share profits (forty-five per cent). Thus profit sharing can set a favorable climate for economic education, but the simple experience of sharing profits, without interpretation of its meaning, does not appear to be very satisfactory as an educational process.

TABLE 37. EMPLOYEE ATTITUDES ON THE BUSINESS SYSTEM IN PROFIT SHARING AND NON-PROFIT SHARING COMPANIES

	Per Cent Who Agree		
	Non-Profit Sharing Cos.	*Profit Sharing Companies*	*Difference*
"One fault of the business system is that owners get too much compared to employees."	62	50	−12
"Machinery increased output but the largest share has gone to the owners."	75	65	−10
"Government should regulate business to the owners."	45	55	+10
"Government should put a limit on company profits."	31	31	0

Source: *The Public Opinion Index*

Experience with profit sharing is now quite extensive, and certain conclusions about the factors that make for success and failure can be drawn. The first conclusion is the obvious one that profit sharing requires sustained profits. The adoption and discontinuance of profit sharing plans appear to bear some relationship to the business cycle. Previous to World War II, according to the National Industrial Conference Board, the mortality rate of profit sharing plans was fifty to sixty per cent. In Great Britain the abandonment rate, reported by the British Ministry of Labor, prior to 1936 was sixty-two per cent. Since 1940, with the prosperity of the war and post-war periods, discontinuance in the United States has dropped sharply. For the decade 1937 to 1946, the National Industrial Conference Board reported a mortality rate of seventeen and three-tenths per cent and for the ten years ending in 1956, discontinuance at the rate of fifteen and seven-tenths per cent.

Experience with profit sharing plans indicates that, not only must there be profits to make the plans succeed, but profits must be substantial or the amounts shared may be so small as to be almost meaningless to employees. Also profits must have a high degree of continuity or employees tend to lose interest. Many profit sharing companies have had poor years when there was nothing to be shared, and they have coped with these difficulties without too much damage to their plans. Edwin Flippo, in his 1954 study, found ninety-three firms that had undergone profitless periods. In three-fourths of the cases, management reported that employees accepted the situation willingly.[11]

An occasional lapse of profit may very well add spice to the venture, for it provides fresh opportunity for management and employees to remind themselves that it is first necessary to earn a profit before it can be shared. Testifying to this point in the 1938 Senate hearings on profit sharing, Marion B. Folsom, Vice President and Treasurer of Eastman Kodak Company, said:

> The employees understand their share in the business is dependent upon the company's operations. For instance, in 1934, the one year we had no wage dividends, the employees realized why it was so. We think that because of that suspension and low payments during two or three years, the employees really appreciate and understand the plan more than they did before.[12]

The second conclusion from the experience with profit sharing is that this practice is no cure-all for personnel problems. Good industrial relations depend on many factors, and, unless employees are basically satisfied with their jobs, profit sharing is likely to fail. The pay must be at the going market rate; the benefits must be reasonably good; the working conditions must be acceptable; above all, the employees must have confidence in management, not only for its ability to give competent direction in running the business, but also for its concern about employees as people and its sense of fair play in the handling of human relationships. Where these conditions are not present, where the job atmosphere is surcharged with conflict and mutual distrust, profit sharing will not work. As a matter of fact, it may only add to the confusion, for in these situations profit sharing may be interpreted as an attempt to buy men's souls, which is the supreme affront to human dignity.

The third conclusion underscored by profit-sharing companies is that success requires continuous two-way communication between management and the employees. Profits are not an immediate part of the individual employee's experience; they are influenced by many complex factors that even management at times has trouble understanding; the individual employee has difficulty seeing how his own work performance makes much difference in the total profit result; a long waiting period is ordinarily necessary before profit sharing pays off; and, in the case of deferred plans, the benefits involved may seem remote, particularly to the younger people in the work force. A constant flow of information and interpretation, therefore, is necessary to the success of profit sharing plans.

The crucial influence of communication on employee attitudes toward profit sharing is demonstrated clearly in the study conducted by *The Public Opinion Index*. Employees in the thirty-three profit-sharing companies were asked how good a job their company had done in keeping them informed about their profit sharing plan. Table 38 shows that employees who feel their company does "very well" on keeping them informed reveal decidedly better attitudes than those who rate their company as doing "not very well."

TABLE 38. EMPLOYEE ATTITUDE IN RELATION TO INFORMATION ON PROFIT SHARING

	Rate Profit Sharing Information		
	Not Very Well	*Very Well*	*Gain*
Testify that profit sharing creates a feeling of partnership	49%	70%	+21
Say company takes personal interest in employees	68	91	+23
Agree as company has grown employees have gotten their share	63	89	+26
Say company gives employee proper share of credit	63	89	+26
Rate top management pretty outstanding	48	78	+30

Source: *The Public Opinion Index.*

In view of these findings, it would seem that all profit sharing companies would place great emphasis on channeling information to their employees on the state of the business. Flippo found that two-thirds of his companies made an effort to explain profit sharing, but one-third did not. Among the two-thirds that operated a communications program, most dependence was placed on reports to the employee on his share of profits, on group meetings and on presidents' letters to employees. Somewhat less dependence was placed on articles in employee publications and interpretation through supervisors.[13]

One of the objectives of profit sharing is to create a sense of partnership between the employee and the company. To some students of the subject, joint administration of profit sharing plans is needed as tangible evidence of the philosophy of employee partnership. Evidently this concept is not very acceptable to management, for Flippo's study found only seventy-one out of 252 companies with jointly administered plans.[14] Rightly or wrongly, management fears that employee participation in the administration of profit sharing plans will dissipate management authority and will lead to unsound fiscal management.

The influence of unions on the success of profit sharing appears to vary a great deal with companies. According to the 1954 studies of Edwin Flippo and the 1957 survey of the National Industrial Conference Board, somewhat less than half of the profit-sharing companies are unionized. However, two-thirds of the unionized companies reported to the National Industrial Conference Board that the heads of their locals looked favorably upon their profit sharing plans.

The traditional attitude of organized labor toward profit sharing has been one of hostility, or at least one of great skepticism. Union leaders have viewed sharing as paternalistic and a device to combat or undermine the union. Samuel Gompers, the first President of the American Federation of Labor, declared that unions were more interested in a fair wage, reasonable hours and fair conditions of employment than in profit sharing.[15]

Testifying before the Senate Subcommittee on Profit Sharing in 1938, John L. Lewis, head of the United Mine Workers, said that too frequently profit sharing has been put forward as a substitute for collecting bargaining. "Labor's disillusioned experience in regard to profit sharing," said the mine union chief, "has been that they have been used as a device to avoid the payment of an immediate decent wage and made labor dependent upon haphazard industrial and financial policies of management.[16]

Appearing before the same Committee, William Green, President of the American Federation of Labor, declared that labor is not opposed to the principle of profit sharing but, he said, "Labor believes all plans affecting labor must rest on collective bargaining . . . All the terms and conditions of payment for work should be determined through joint conference of representatives of management and workers concerned." Should union and management consider profit sharing, said Mr. Green, production and cost records must be equally available, sales policies must be considered by both parties, and be mutually acceptable, and financial policies and proposals must be subjected to the same review and decisions.[17] In other words, the AFL would accept profit sharing if there were co-determination of management policies.

Apparently unions have retreated somewhat from this position, for in 1951 the International Union of Electrical Workers made a formal demand for profit sharing on Westinghouse and General Electric, and in 1957 Walter Reuther asked for profit sharing (probably for a union controlled welfare fund) from the automobile companies.

Under the Wagner Labor Act, the National Labor Relations Board has made pensions bargainable, but no ruling has been undertaken for profit-sharing plans. Should the Board rule that contemplated plans or those already in existence are bargainable, profit sharing as a pattern of industrial relations would likely disappear, for owners historically, and by what they think is their moral and legal right, have viewed profits after taxes as belonging to them, to be dispersed at their own discretion.

In 1957 the National Industrial Conference Board asked 198 companies to sum up their experience with profit sharing. Fifty-eight per cent said that they had received "important benefits"; thirty-five per cent reported "some general benefits" and six per cent indicated "no very noticeable benefits." The advantages named included improved employee morale, increased interest in the company's welfare, better teamwork and greater cooperation, improved production and decrease in labor turnover. The company managements were overwhelmingly of the opinion that profit sharing had improved morale and created employee interest; but the evaluation was considerably less enthusiastic about the effectiveness of their plans in increasing efficiency and reducing turnover.[18]

What then is the significance of profit sharing? Does it provide the key to economic cooperation and industrial peace? Is it likely to grow in the future and become a standard practice in American industry? Certainly many companies have been able to make profit sharing work. The practice has become part and parcel of their industrial relations policies; their plans have survived downtrends in the business cycle, and they have given management and rank-and-file employees an added bond of common interest.

In other companies, however, including large ones like General Electric and Westinghouse, profit sharing has failed. The reasons are many. Workers tend to lose interest when profit shares are modest and when there is a prolonged break in their continuity; employees have difficulty visualizing how their individual efforts fit into the total profit picture; workers need assured income and find it unsettling to adjust to the ups and downs of profit shares; employees tend to take profit sharing for granted unless continually reminded of the way profits are earned; management becomes lax in providing interpretive information and the profit sharing ideal succumbs to apathy and distrust.

On balance, it is probably correct to say that the experience of companies with profit sharing has been more favorable than unfavorable, and companies are likely to continue to experiment with it in the future, particularly if tax advantages continue. But there are very basic reasons for believing that the field for profit sharing is a limited one. The first and compelling reason is that industry doesn't have much profit to share. Since 1916, forty-five per cent of the companies, on the average, have reported no profit. Companies that lose money frequently or intermittently are obviously poor candidates for profit sharing. Again, the division of the employee-profit dollar in manufacturing averages eighty-four cents to employees in wages and sixteen cents to owners in profits. The simple arithmetic of this situation is that, even if owners were disposed to share profits liberally with employees, they have very little to share.

The same conclusion is evident when the arithmetic is cast in terms of profit on investment. The average annual earnings for all manufacturing companies for the past ten years was eight and six-tenths cents per dollar of investment. If we allow five cents as a form of interest, the remaining three and six-tenths cents is left for entrepreneurial risk taking. Should the three and six-tenths cents entrepreneurial fee be shared, it could at best mean an insignificant wage increase, and would surely decrease the willingness of owners to take the investment risks involved in providing better tools for workers. Sharing the entrepreneurial fee, therefore, would likely do the wage-earner more harm than good.

The limited possibilities for profit sharing can be illustrated in yet another way: In 1956, which was a typical profit year, all manufacturing companies made twelve and three-tenths billion dollars after taxes, a return of eight and eight-tenths per cent on a net worth of 139 billion dollars. If we assume that government must have its tax cut of profits and that stockholders are to receive dividends equaling five per cent of the net worth of their companies, seven billion dollars would be allocated for dividends, leaving five and three-tenths billion dollars for entrepreneurial reward.

In 1956 there were sixteen and nine-tenths million employees in manufacturing. If in this year the owners had elected to split their five and three-tenths billion dollars of entrepreneurial reward, twenty-five per cent to employees and seventy-five per cent to owners, each employee would have received an additional seventy-eight dollars. If the split had been half and half, each employee would have received $156. These sums are so small, relative to the annual pay of employees, that their effect on employee psychology would have been negligible. The effect of such a diversion of profits on investor psychology, however, would have been marked, for it would have reduced company profit from eight and eight-tenths per cent on investment to six and six-tenths and four and four-tenths per cent respectively, thereby decreasing an already low profit margin and narrowing the earnings cushion that protects dividend payouts.

The dramatic increase in productivity in the United States, and the resulting rise in the standard of living is due largely to advancing technology and the increased use of capital. If we are interested in human betterment, the nation's economic experience would counsel us to increase the reward for saving and risk taking, not decrease it. Savers provide better tools for workers. Better tools decrease the cost of goods and services, with the result that the consumer can buy more and better goods for less work time.

It could be argued, of course, that if all companies undertook to share profits with their employees, productivity would rise, and everybody—employees, shareholders, and consumers—would be better off. But in this event, competition would drive prices and profits toward the minimum market rate, and there would be no excess profits to share. Or, saying it another way, sharing of this kind would not be restricted to employees but would be extended to all consumers through lower prices. If profit sharing is adopted by some, but not all, companies, and if productivity of the profit-sharing companies rises as a result, some extra profit may be available for sharing with employees; but, in this event, profit sharing must remain a limited industrial practice.

Fundamental economics argues against a strong growth of profit sharing, and differences of philosophy between union officials and management point the same way. If profit sharing grows, unions will doubtless insist that this type of compensation be made a bargainable issue. Every decision a company makes affects profits. If profit sharing were a bargainable issue, then, as William Green insisted before the Senate Committee in 1938, union officials would wish to review production, sales, finance, and other company policies to protect the workers' interest in profits. No competent manager is likely to undertake managerial responsibility under these conditions; and, even if he did, policy indecision would be such that there would probably be no profit to share.

So, while profit sharing appeals to many as a noble ideal and works in some companies, it appears to hold no magic key to industrial cooperation and rising standards of living. If the American people want more income and more leisure, meanwhile maintaining an adequate defense in a troubled world, the way to achieve it is not by re-dividing profits. It is by stimulating investors to invest and managers to manage so that the tremendous potential of a dawning technology will be harnessed to raise the output of each hour of work. This is the opportunity and the promise of the future.

CHAPTER TWELVE

THE INTERPRETATION OF PROFITS

Of all the key institutions in a capitalistic society, profit is the most widely criticized and the least understood. Economics, of course, is a complex subject, and it is not to be expected that every man can be an expert in this field. But people have strong feelings about profits, and their notions importantly influence their behavior. Union members under the influence of the big profit idea, choose redivision of profits over increased productivity as the best route to a higher standard of living. The people who are most strongly in favor of government intervention in the economy are those who believe that owners get too much of the wealth produced, while workers get too little.

Unless the average citizen comprehends the role of profits, he is ill prepared to pass on public policy or deal with his own interests whether as employee, proprietor, investor, or consumer. Drawing on research studies which reveal the informational gaps, it is possible to outline a twelve-point platform of understanding:

1. The prospect of a good profit is a primary motivation for effort and innovation. If incentive is pinched off then the citizen

must reconcile himself to slower economic growth and limited job opportunities.

2. Profits are not automatic; some companies make a profit, others suffer losses. Anyone who overlooks that hard fact will risk losing his money when he buys stock or ventures into business for himself.

3. People should know the facts on the size of profits. In most years they have run three to five per cent on sales and five to ten per cent on capital invested. When the citizen exaggerates the size, as he usually does, he sees a shortcut to the better life which can only end up in disillusionment.

4. The key to a rising standard of living is increased productivity—more and better goods at less cost. Increasing wages faster than productivity merely pushes up prices. One particularly militant group may wrest advantage for its members, but other workers must accept a smaller share through higher prices or unemployment.

5. The gains from technological advance and improved productivity flow mainly to employees and consumers. The owners provide the capital but in the split of the gains eighty-four cents of the employee-profit dollar goes to the employees and sixteen cents to the owners. This is a very favorable arrangement for the employee and when one is aware of this fact, the partnership of capital and labor takes on real meaning.

6. Companies are able to sell goods, provide jobs and make a profit by serving the consumer, not through exploiting him. For this service consumers reward employees with wages and, if there is anything left over, compensate owners with profits. In earning a living, therefore, it is sound advice to "Take good care of the customers."

7. About three-fifths of company earnings are currently being plowed back into the business to pay for expansion or buy modern equipment. Companies that provide their employees with the best tools are the ones most likely to survive in competition and provide steady jobs at good pay. When a young man is starting out in his career, his promise will be greater if he joins up with a company that makes a good profit and plows back part of it to keep ahead of the competition and grow.

8. The best guarantee that wages, prices and profits will be reasonable is competition. In public utility industries, where

direct competition is not feasible, rate-making bodies set prices and thereby control profits. Competition is frequently hard on people, resulting in decreased profits and even loss of capital to investors, and often requiring employees to find new jobs. But competition is a democratic process, which provides the principal mechanism whereby consumers can control their suppliers. Owners and their employees should be willing to take their chances in competition, and abide by the decisions of the market place. Citizens, in their own interest and that of the community, should support public policy that requires competition.

9. Variation in profits is normal for a market economy and should be expected. In practically every industry some companies make good profits while others barely break even or lose money. This is one sure way consumers have of informing managements that they are doing a good or a poor job. It is also a way of telling inefficient companies that they ought to go out of business, or signalling new and venturesome companies that the rewards are great for undertaking to provide a new source of supply.

10. When there is competition, "fairness" of profit cannot be judged by amount. Ordinarily when companies are earning big profits it means that they have produced new products that people are eager to buy or have found ways to cut cost and give better service. In passing judgment on the size of profits, therefore, consumers need always to ask: What are we getting in return for the profits companies make?

11. This is an age in which people want companies to observe the rules of decency and fair play and conduct themselves with some sense of social responsibility. One of the paramount responsibilities of companies is to satisfy the economic needs of the community by making good use of men and resources with the minimum of waste. When there is competition, the companies that are making the best profit are usually the ones that are most socially responsible in their use of community resources. The company that makes fifteen per cent profit on its investment is likely to provide better jobs, pay higher dividends to stockholders and offer better merchandise values to consumers than the company making five per cent. Actually there is widespread agreement with this principle for most people prefer to invest in, work for, and buy the products of profitable companies.

12. All of us cherish the right to buy where we want to and

> accept or reject the offers that are made to us by competing suppliers. Profit and loss is a key part of this apparatus of freedom, for when companies are required to compete for our business, we can patronize them or not as we choose. If enough of us are of one mind in directing our patronage, we can influence company profit margins by rewarding the companies that do our bidding and penalizing those that don't. This is a very precious freedom that not only protects our pocketbook but also preserves our dignity and self-respect. To the extent that the profit and loss system is compromised, we inevitably lose freedom of choice.

If the public is to have this twelve-point understanding, the schools and industry must assume the primary responsibility for informing the student and adult publics. We have already seen the extent of adult misunderstanding of profits. The situation is even more lamentable among students. After a study of economic literacy among students in twelve midwestern liberal arts colleges, *The Public Opinion Index* reported that "The typical freshman enters college almost totally ignorant of the facts and principles required to understand how our economic system works."

66% of freshmen didn't know that in an average year many companies make no profit.

64% believed that owners, rather than workers have got the lion's share from productivity increases due to mechanization.

61% didn't understand that productivity is the key to rising standards of living.

It would seem that some knowledge of how the community goes about its economic housekeeping is requisite for good citizenship. Moreover, our standard of living and our ability to defend ourselves against hostile nations is based squarely on the strength of our economy. Yet the Brookings Institution reports that less than five per cent of all high school students take the equivalent of a semester course in economics.[1]

Understanding Profits

When Dr. James B. Conant made his thoroughgoing analysis of high school education, he, curiously enough, devoted very little attention to improving economics instruction. In a report studded with specific and detailed commentary, the only mention of economics was a recommendation that "as much material on economics as students can effectively handle" should be included in one required twelfth-grade course on American problems or American government.[2]

That some college educators are aware of the deficiencies in economic instruction is indicated in a statement by the American Economic Association which declared: "We have been too modest in our demands for a share of the student's time—a campaign for more emphasis on the study of economics at the college level is long overdue." [3]

In *The Public Opinion Index* sample of midwest college students, forty-six per cent of seniors had taken at least one course in economics. As will be shown presently, and as one might expect, their grasp of the subject improved materially with the teaching.

Industry is in primary possession of the facts about profit and loss and has first-hand operating experience on how the system produces and distributes goods. It has an obligation to assist teachers in obtaining factual material about the economy and a special responsibility to widen the public's understanding. Companies can make their best contribution to the community only if the people have confidence in their economic institutions, know something of how they work, and give support to public policy that stimulates, instead of retards, healthy economic activity.

How well is industry discharging this responsibility? Certainly, within the limitations of accounting there is a large flow of factual data about profits. For tax purposes, companies report their earnings to the Internal Revenue Service, and these data are compiled and reported in elaborate detail by the various departments of government (See Appendix C-1).

Companies with widespread share ownership regularly provide earnings reports to their stockholders on a quarterly, semi-annual, or annual basis, and, in most instances, issue news releases on earning to the press. In recent years company annual reports have become increasingly informative, with more detail on earning trends and interpretive commentary by management. Every stockholder of record receives a copy of the annual report, and, with most widely held companies, a non-stockholder may secure a copy simply by writing for it. Some companies place ads in daily newspapers and financial journals to distribute information about their earnings. A few companies like General Mills, celebrate an anniversary or some other occasion by taking a special section in a daily newspaper to report on the company's products, progress and financial standing. Many companies make their annual reports available to school libraries, and in 1958 one company, Scott Paper, prepared a special educational edition with interleafing that provided the student with a running commentary on the meaning and significance of each section of the report.

With the growth of popular interest in stock ownership, corporation officers spend much time with the representatives of investment trusts and brokerage houses, and make frequent appearances before analyst societies to discuss their company's earnings and the future outlook.

Companies also make considerable effort to inform their employees about earnings. *The Public Opinion Index* reports that among companies with five million dollars or more of assets:

53% send their annual report to employees or offer to send it on request.

47% excerpt parts of the stockholder report or give some account of earnings in the employee magazine or newspaper.

13% hold meetings with supervisors or with rank and file employees to review the earnings picture.

12% report company earnings through employee letters or post the story on bulletin boards.

11% put out a special annual financial report to employees.

In addition to company and government reporting activity, many trade associations, like the American Iron & Steel Institute, the National Coal Association and the Edison Electric Institute publish yearbooks for their industries, giving earnings data and other operating statistics. The National Industrial Conference Board publishes detailed profit tables annually in "The Economic Almanac." The First National City Bank of New York compiles and annually publishes the earnings on sales and investment for over three thousand leading companies in eighty industry classifications. (Appendix C-2). Since 1955, *Fortune* has published earnings data annually for the five hundred largest industrials and the fifty largest companies in transportation, merchandising, life insurance, public utilities and commercial banking (Appendix C-3). Investment services like *Moody's* and *Standard and Poor's* produce fat volumes annually giving earnings, capitalizations, and operational data on thousands of corporations whose shares are held by the investing public.

Certainly with all this flood of data the facts about profits are freely available to anyone who has the time and inclination to dig them out. But two observations must be made about this information flow; it is of recent origin, and it consists mostly of bare-bone facts, with little commentary on the social significance of the data. It was as late as 1934 when the first comprehensive study of industry profits was produced by Ralph C. Epstein. With monumental energy Epstein gathered earnings data on 3,144 large enterprises and approximately fifteen hundred small companies for the decade 1919-1928. "The person who has not worked in the field of corporate earnings," wrote Epstein feelingly, "does not realize the paucity of published financial data." [4]

In the early 1930's many companies saw no reason to inform their publics about their affairs. Profits were thought to be primarily the concern of management and, while it was agreed that stockholders were entitled to at least some of the details, there appeared to be no call to discuss company affairs with outsiders.

Then came the Great Depression with its New Deal reforms and rising criticism of business leadership. Suddenly management was confronted with a new order of problem that pivoted basically around public opinion. Candidates for public office sought votes on anti-business platforms, labor leaders organized workers to demand higher wages and work-rule changes, and even dealer and stockholder groups became more vocal. The pressure of public opinion required companies to orient their policies closer to humanistic values and to provide more information about company affairs. The problem of "relations" with company publics—employees, the plant community, suppliers, government officials, stockholders—became more urgent, and gradually over the past thirty years most large companies have developed policies and specialized personnel to deal with it.

On the communications side this change in management thinking has been marked by three phases:

> *Phase 1* is characterized by secrecy. Managements in this phase feel that it is desirable to reveal as little information as possible about their companies.
>
> *Phase 2* can properly be called "the era of facts." In this evolutionary phase, companies give out more factual information about their affairs but supply a minimum of interpretation, allowing the facts, more or less, to "speak for themselves."
>
> *Phase 3* is the era of interpretation. In this phase companies not only supply facts, but undertake to interpret them with respect to public policy and the primary concerns of their audience.

In their communications thinking, some companies today are still in Phase 1, but most companies are well advanced into Phase 2. A few far-sighted and progressive companies have moved strongly into Phase 3.

There is, then, no current shortage of facts about profits. The deficiency is in interpretation. The need is to establish the meaning of profits for public policy, and to indicate how profits help the community, and individuals within the community, to reach their objectives. Despite the fact that profit data describe economic and social relationships that are vital to the average man's welfare, the statistics standing alone are cold, impersonal and unrelated to human concerns. The missing link in public understanding is what profits mean to people.

Understanding Profits

It is not difficult to demonstrate the current inadequacies of profit interpretation. One obvious example is the almost universal practice of reporting profits in dollar amounts, without supplying relative interpretation in terms of sales, investment or wage payments. The tendency now is for the company news release to read—

"X Y Z Corporation Reports Eighteen Million Dollar profit," and the local newspaper proclaims this part of the story in bold black headlines.

The average man has difficulty visualizing large dollar sums. Compared to his annual budget of a few thousand dollars, eighteen million dollars looks like a lot of money. In the nationwide test by *The Public Opinion Index,* fourteen per cent said a profit of eighteen million dollars was "reasonable," but when this profit was described as six per cent on sales of three hundred ten million dollars, the proportion saying "reasonable" rose to sixty-nine per cent. The United States is a big country with a huge industrial establishment that can be described only by astronomical statistics. If the public is to comprehend these magnitudes, they must be supplied with meaningful points of reference. In the interest of truth, it ought to be standard practice for companies to report profits, not only in terms of dollar totals but as a percentage of sales, investment, wage payments or other appropriate bases.

Examination of company efforts to communicate profit information to employees likewise shows glaring deficiencies. In a study of one hundred employee publications in companies with assets of five million dollars or more, *The Public Opinion Index* found sixty-one per cent of plant magazines and newspapers devoting three per cent of their space to company financial reports. Only eleven per cent of the plant publications, however, oriented their profit stories to employee interests. Much of the material on earnings presented in these publications was excerpted directly from the company annual report. The articles bristled with financial information showing sales, cost of materials, taxes, net earnings, special credits, current liabilities, working capital, and other important accounting matters. The commentary discussed subjects like LIFO, depreciation, consent decrees, capital expenditures, operations and maintenance, competition, and the cost of doing business.

To make the financial statements easier for the employees to read, many companies presented simplified income statements in terms of "What We Took In and Paid Out," or undertook to explain an item on the income statement by drawing a line from a significant figure to a balloon containing interpretive commentary.

To show the employee "Where the Money Went," the most frequently used device was the pie diagram, indicating the percentage of the income dollar paid out for materials and services, wages and salaries, depreciation, taxes, dividends, and earnings reinvested in the business. Since earnings for manufacturing companies average three to five cents on the dollar of sale, the slices represented by profit, i.e., dividends and retained earnings, were inevitably small.

Some of the articles sounded an optimistic note, while others viewed the situation with alarm. Managerial exhortation that "we must do better" were not uncommon. In a memorable appeal to his employees, one company head declared that the company was caught in a cost-price squeeze, that profit was the foundation for jobs, and that he was confident that the employees would put forth extra effort so the company's profit the next year could be increased several million dollars.

A fair description of the majority of profit stories in plant publications would be: management talking about management problems which might incidentally be of interest to employees. In sharp contrast are the relatively few plant publications that orient their profit stories to employee interests.

In 1956, Continental Oil Company's, *The CONOCOan,* headlined its profit story: "56 Was Successful Due to Your Efforts." "The job you did in 1956," says the article, "was a good one. In every way, Conoco in 1956 had a successful year. Your job and the work of almost ten thousand other employees contributed to Conoco's progress."

Similarly, in 1959, the Cleveland Electric Illuminating Company's *Motor* reported income and outgo with special emphasis on "What did we as employees do in 1959?" Employees, says the article, worked more safely, enrolled in after-hour classes to improve their knowledge, advanced to better jobs, put money aside through the Thrift Plan, and by suggesting how operations could be improved, saved the company $1,537,000.

DuPont's *Better Living* reported earnings of $397,000,000 for 1957, up $13,000,000 from 1956. The accompanying story, under the headline "Decade's Net Gain," told employees how they had fared in the last ten years of employment with the company. The real wage increase for the average duPont employee, the article pointed out, has aggregated $5,044 for the decade. This sum, said *Better Living,* would furnish a six room house. But, instead of leaving the reader to visualize this fact, *Better Living* provided a picture of employee James Bohlen and his family sitting in the middle of an array of household equipment including beds, carpets, electrical appliances, easy chairs, and even a power lawnmower. The article indicated the decline in work hours required to purchase various family items, and explained how investment in research and company expenditures for better tools and equipment had brought this about.

In 1959 Caterpillar Tractor Company's *News and Views* reported "Sales the Largest in History" and "Profits Higher than in 1958." The story indicated that employment had reached an all time peak during the year and that the company's advance steel purchases had prevented a long shutdown as a result of the steel strike. The magazine reviewed the company's growth during the decade of the 1950's, described the diversification of the product line, pointed out that the Caterpillar employee body had nearly doubled and indicated how jobs and opportunity could be increased in the future. "We have tried to keep the personal touch in a growing organization" wrote Louis B. Neumiller, Chairman of the Board. "We have worked to put credit where credit is due, and to keep the avenues of progress open to all. Our abiding hope has been to build a company where the emphasis would be squarely on integrity and quality, and where people might find careers and associations at Caterpillar a satisfying experience."

It is an elementary principle of communication that people attend to and read articles that interest them, and believe in or buy a product, a leadership, or a philosophy that they think will help them realize their goals. The interests and objectives of employees can be variously described as job security, opportunity for promotion, safety on the job, an increased wage, better retirement, medical and job benefits, pride in workmanship, a feeling of accomplishment, status in the work community, knowledge of what is happening in the company, and some conception of what the future is likely to hold. This is the employee world and, unless companies make an effort to relate profit to these interests and goals, employee understanding of this key institution of a free market society is not likely to be significantly increased.

Some observers are pessimistic about the possibilities and worth of company communication to employees. It is held that employees are not interested in company problems, that matters like profits are too far away from their immediate concerns for comprehension and that information and interpretive material from management changes no opinions. Research data do not bear out these conclusions. On the contrary, the findings show that employees are eager for news about their companies on matters that affect their interests, that they read and retain ideas that are properly presented, and that their views are changed when they are exposed to the economic facts of life.

Misunderstanding of the function and worth of communication with employees on profits and other matters pertaining to the business are so widespread that a brief summary of research findings is in order. In a recent study of what kind of information employees want from their companies,[5] *The Public Opinion Index* offered employees a list of nineteen topics, and asked respondents if they get enough information on these topics, want more information, or are not interested. Table 39 shows that the majority of employees say they get enough information on personal news, safety, and recreation, but they want more information on such topics as company plans for the future, the competition the company faces, taxes, how company policies affect employees, and what management is doing to provide job security. About half of the employees in the six-company sample said they would like to have more information on how American business operates, management views on economic issues, and how the company is doing financially.

TABLE 39. WHAT KINDS OF INFORMATION EMPLOYEES WANT

	Six-Company Average		
	Want More Information	*Have Enough Information*	*Not Interested*
Company plans for the future	73%	23%	4%
Work different locations are doing	64	30	6
Company policies, rules, plans affecting employees	59	38	3
Company stand on labor-union relations	58	29	13
Competition the company faces	57	37	6
Reducing waste, cutting production cost	57	36	7
Taxes, government regulation	57	31	12
What management is doing to provide job security	57	38	5
How American business operates	51	33	16
Job transfers—new openings	49	47	4
Management's views on economic issues	47	23	30
Company product line—customer use	47	47	6
How company is doing financially	45	53	2
Experiences and activities of management people	45	47	8
How your work fits into company picture	40	56	4
Employee wages and benefits	43	51	6
Personal news about company employees	31	58	11
Safety at work-play-home	27	67	6
Employee recreation and social news	25	59	16

Source: *The Public Opinion Index*

pany is doing financially. The strong desire among employees for information about company affairs and for the views of company leaders does not mean that employees necessarily agree with what management says or does. "We want to hear what company leaders think," testifies the typical employee. "We will make up our own minds."

Readership and impact studies of plant publications furnishes a second measure of the reaction of employees to company efforts to communicate information. Data gathered by *The Public Opinion Index* show tremendous variation in the communications effectiveness of different articles, but again, the evidence is clear that serious material dealing with employee interests does reach a wide audience. One of the best read articles measured by the Index was "Can You Beat Inflation" by the noted economist, Henry Hazlitt, published in The Sun Oil Company's employee magazine, *Our Sun*. Among hourly employees forty-five per cent could play back one or more ideas from the Hazlitt article, and among foremen sixty-seven per cent could perform this test.

When *Our Sun* ran an article by President Robert G. Dunlop with the headline, "Outlook for the Oil Industry is Generally Optimistic," only thirteen per cent of the company's employees could play back any ideas from it. But when reporters from *Our Sun News*, the company's plant newspaper, set up an interview with their company president on the state of the business and ran the questions and answers under the headline: "Mr. Dunlop, *Our Sun News* Readers Would Like to Learn . . . ," forty-four per cent of the employee readers were able to play back one or more ideas. Both the articles involving Mr. Dunlop dealt with the state of the business, but the question and answer rendition apparently looked more rewarding to readers than the article on the generally optimistic outlook.

A third measure of the reaction of employees to company information comes from studies undertaken to evaluate company courses in economics. The research technique was to give employees a battery of tests before the course to determine their knowledge of economic principles and facts, and their attitudes on matters of public policy affecting the business. After the course, the same tests were given to measure the differences. In every case that has come under the observation of *The Public Opinion Index*, where serious teaching was undertaken, employees increased their knowledge and understanding of economic principles and facts, and registered greater or less change, depending on the materials presented in the course, on attitudes toward economic issues.

Understanding Profits

The data are quite voluminous, but there is space here for one example. A large metals company undertook a series of economic discussions for foremen which dealt with the subjects of profits, competition, productivity, the role of capital, and how the economic system shares. To evaluate the discussions, foremen were tested before and after the seminars. Typical questions on profits used in the test were:

> Any company that makes one hundred million dollars in profits in one year is making too much profit—agree or disagree?
>
> You can't expect stockholders and employees to work together in harmony; their interests are opposed—agree or disagree?
>
> On the average, figuring the good years with the bad, industry makes a profit on sales of less than three per cent; three to six per cent; seven to ten per cent; eleven to fifteen per cent; sixteen to twenty-five per cent; more than twenty-five per cent?

The test included approximately ten statements for each subject area covered, and respondents were scored in terms of "correct" answers, much as a teacher of economics scores his test papers. On matters of fact and economic principle the correct answer was either demonstrable or rested on a concensus of the views of economists. On matters of ideology, the position of management was taken as "correct." The test results as shown in Table 40, indicate that the seminars brought about marked changes in foremen thinking in every subject category.

TABLE 40. CHANGES IN FOREMAN THINKING RESULTING FROM ECONOMICS COURSE IN A LARGE METALS COMPANY

	Average "Correct" Scores		
Subject Area	*Pre-Course*	*Post-Course*	*Change*
Profits	52%	78%	+26%
Competition	64	85	+21
Sharing	67	87	+21
Productivity	56	76	+20
Role of Capital	70	83	+13

Source: *The Public Opinion Index*

When foremen attending the course were asked "Should the company hold regular meetings to discuss economic subjects?" ninety-nine percent answered in the affirmative. In seven other companies where the same question was asked after the completion of a course, the favorable vote ranged from ninety-five per cent to ninety-eight per cent.

Similar demonstrations in economic learning can be drawn from the experience of universities. The Industrial Relations Center of the University of Chicago, collaborating with Republic Steel Corporation, reports that before taking their course in basic economics, foremen scored forty-five per cent correct in all questions dealing with profits. At the conclusion of the course, foremen were able to raise this score to sixty-five per cent.

The Public Opinion Index gave a modified version of its economics test to forty-five hundred students registered in twelve private colleges in one large midwestern state. The results, as given in Table 41, show that students who have had one or more courses in economics uniformly outscore those who have had no economics training. Significantly, students who are majoring in education and who will become the teachers of tomorrow are the least literate in the field of economics. High school graduates, *The Public Opinion Index* has found, are very poorly informed on how a community goes about its economic housekeeping, and the poor scores of education majors may be one reason for this.

TABLE 41. ECONOMIC LITERACY OF COLLEGE SENIORS IN ONE LARGE MIDWESTERN STATE

	Average "Correct" Scores		
Subject Area	*All Seniors Majoring in Education*	*All Seniors with No Economics Course*	*All Seniors with One or More Economics Course*
Profits	46%	50%	62%
Competition	48	52	66
Productivity—Sharing	43	45	58
Role of Capital	44	48	63

Source: *The Public Opinion Index*

The study of economic literacy among college students reveals another significant point: e.g., the more a student studies economics, the closer he draws to the ideological point of view of business executives. Thirteen of the test questions used by *The Public Opinion Index* had ideological content, mostly dealing with some aspect of government intervention in the market process. The scores given in Table 42 show a strong progression toward the business point of view as the student is increasingly exposed to the principles of economics. Economic reality is a harsh task master. Experience in the market place obviously molds the thinking of businessmen, and evidently the views of others are influenced as they become better acquainted with the workings of the economy.

TABLE 42. IDEOLOGICAL SCORES OF COLLEGE STUDENTS, HIGH SCHOOL TEACHERS, AND BUSINESS EXECUTIVES

	"Correct" Answers
High School students	48%
College freshmen	54
Education majors	55
College seniors	61
High School teachers	63
Seniors with economics	66
Business majors	69
Economics majors	72
Business Executives	96

(Source: *The Public Opinion Index*)

The evidence, then, is quite clear that employees are interested in information about their company, read and absorb ideas from presentations that are geared to their interests and draw closer to management's point of view as they are exposed to the economic realities. Does this mean that giving employees economic information is a cure-all for the tensions between employees and their companies? The answer, of course, is "no." The fact that there is marked strain between the managers of American industry and those who are managed is indicated by the rise of unions, the disinterest of many employees in productivity, the elaboration of work rules, and the lack of pride in job craftsmanship. The hostility of workers toward the economic system is further indicated in national elections where skilled and unskilled factory workers normally vote about two to one for the party that promises to throttle business.

Peter Drucker finds the cause of this strain in the fact that profitability takes precedence over individual needs. In computing profits, wages must be classified impersonally as a cost, the same as any commodity. But to the worker wages are a highly personal matter in that they mean food, shelter, job security, status, self-respect and dignity as an individual. The most likely answer to this conflict of interest between the individual and the system, says Drucker, is the creation of new industrial arrangements that provide protection against unemployment, and, short of impairing management's right to manage, give workers more voice in the plant community.[6]

Chris Argyris is another scholar who finds the answer to employee hostility in the conflict between the needs of individuals and the requirements of organizations as these organizations are currently managed.[7] In the development of the self from infancy to adulthood, says Argyris, men move from a state of dependence to relative independence, from shallow to deep and challenging interests, from preoccupation with things of the moment to concern for the longer term future, from a subordinate to an equal or superordinate position and from less to more control of self. Modern organizational practices, says Argyris, are in conflict with the need for self-realization. Organization routinizes jobs through extreme specialization, thereby minimizing instead of maximizing the opportunity for creativity on the job. Organization operates through a chain of command, with leaders controlling, directing, and coordinating, thereby making individuals dependent instead of independent, subordinate instead of equal, and narrowing the individual's control of the present and the future.

This basic conflict between organization and the needs of the self, says Argyris, frustrates the individual and sets his defense mechanisms in motion. He slows down, quits, or absents himself from the job, turns out shoddy work, complains of the light or ventilation, blames the boss for his failure, joins a union, strikes, and generally becomes uncooperative.

The boss reacts by penalizing the employee, by increasing direction and control, by talking about profits or the free enterprise system, or by instituting "human relations" programs. This only makes matters worse, Argyris contends, because it is doing more of the same things that caused the difficulty in the first place. Friction can be reduced to a healthy level, Argyris concludes, only when work and organization are arranged to satisfy the employee's craving for self-realization.

Scholars like Drucker and Argyris are no doubt on the right track when they seek the primary causes of industrial conflict in organizational arrangements and the relationship between the needs of the individual and those of the system and when they begin their search at the work level. After all, most of the employee's experience is at the work level, and his attitudes are importantly conditioned by his work group, his immediate boss and how company policy affects his day to day life.

Profit is inevitably remote from the worker's experience. The social process by which the work group decides how much volume and what quality of product it will turn out is not intimately geared to the income statement. Moreover, under the profit and loss system, wages do not fluctuate in close relationship to profitability. Nevertheless the employee is caught in a web of economic circumstances along with his company, and his fortunes are not unrelated to those of his employer. If the company is indifferent to production cost, or loses business to competitors, or is unprofitable, the employee's job may become insecure. On the other hand, if the business is well-managed, makes a good product, has control of its costs, is profitable and growing, the employee is likely to have more job security, more opportunity, more income and more pride in his job.

Not every employee is interested in, or capable of understanding the economic and social factors that make up the background of his job, but, desire for information about them is surprisingly high. Of perhaps even greater significance, the demand for serious information about company affairs appears to be highest among employees who are the most influential. In its six-company study of employee information needs, *The Public Opinion Index* asked each respondent to rate himself on a battery of questions designed to reveal personal characteristics related to social influence. When the information needs of high and low influence employees were compared, the data revealed that high influence employees are markedly more interested in subjects like profits, government negotiation, production costs and how the business system operates. Ideas about the company, then, can reach the most perceptive employees directly or filter through these influential employees to those who are less perceptive.

A good example of the kind of reporting that goes home to employees is a picture story, "The Battle of New Orleans," which appeared in the November 1960 issue of International Harvester's employee magazine, *Today*. The article points out that, due to lower wage and other costs, foreign competition was underselling International Harvester in the twine market. Profit had disappeared and the company was faced with the alternatives of getting out of the twine business, shifting production to foreign factories, or fighting it out in its New Orleans plant. Choosing to fight it out, the company modernized its mill with high speed equipment, introduced novel manufacturing techniques, and sought enlightened employee cooperation in cutting costs. Through these efforts the company raised productivity three hundred pounds of twine per employee per day, made the operation profitable once more, and saved 180 jobs. The article gives credit to Machinist Crighton Booth for devising a method of crimping packages mechanically in the hand wrapping operation, and shows Mr. and Mrs. Curry Dufour, veteran employees of the twine factory, in the home they were able to maintain by helping the company to stay competitive.

"The Battle of New Orleans" is what we might call "functional reporting." It deals with a real life situation of concern to employees and makes statements that are verifiable in the employee's experience, or if not verifiable, have the ring of truth that commands respect. The article draws economic conclusions—its purpose quite obviously is to persuade—but the conclusions came out of the exigencies of the situation.

It is not necessary to have crisis as the backdrop for functional reporting. The law of life for privately-owned companies is profitability. Under the rules of the game, companies either take in more than they pay out or they go out of business. By requiring companies to balance their books under the competitive test of the market, and to live within the rules of decency and fair play laid down by law and custom, the community assures itself that its economic housekeeping will be conducted efficiently and be responsive to the public will. Everything a company does, therefore, must sooner or later be submitted to the profit test. No employer can long shield his employees from this test, and he only hurts their interests if he tries. Employees know that their company must make a profit. By wide majorities, people say they would rather work for and buy the products of profitable companies. A perennial source of functional news therefore is how the company and its employees are meeting the test of profitability and what they can do to increase their scores. Some managements hold Monday morning meetings with their department heads to review the flow of events, after which each department head holds a meeting with employees in his section to tell them what is happening in the company, go over the work plan, and discuss production problems. Employees have an interest in staying ahead of the competition, in making a quality product at an attractive price, in diversification of the line, in attracting good capital partners, in maintaining a strong research effort and in helping to build a work environment that advances the common cause.

The challenge to management is to gain willing cooperation of employees in achieving profitability. The old idea was to order and forbid; the new idea is to organize responsible people and enlist their creative talents in the solution of company problems. The functional interpretation of company affairs, including profits, in terms of employee interests, has a big role to play in successful company operations. The sharing of information and problems elevates the dignity of the employee and makes him feel that he has the confidence and respect of his leaders. It gives him knowledge that enables him to be a more effective citizen in the company community.

In recent years the profits debate has revolved to some extent around the purpose of business—is the primary purpose of business to make a profit or to serve its various publics? Traditionally, corporations have been visualized solely as profit seekers. In the eyes of the law the Board of Directors is the servant of the property interest, not of anyone else. Orthodox economics says that corporations should do their competitive best to maximize their profits, for, in behaving in this manner, they will express the will of the buyers and sellers and thus bring about the most efficient allocation of men and resources. Business is business, according to this point of view, and managements will achieve the greatest economic progress for the community by sticking strictly with their appointed job, that of making a profit.

With the rising criticism of business and the growth of social consciousness that has occurred in the past three decades, description of the managerial function has changed. Nowadays it is said that the job of the manager is to serve the public; that he and his company have obligations of corporate citizenship and that his function is to balance or mediate the interests of the several publics with which the corporation deals.[8] As Frank Abrams, the retired Board Chairman of the Standard Oil Company of New Jersey put it: "The job of professional management is to conduct the affairs of the enterprise in its charge in such a way as to maintain an equitable and workable balance among the claims of the variously interested groups—stockholders, employees, customers and the public at large."[9]

To articulate good corporate citizenship and manage with social conscience, companies have instituted welfare benefits for employees, conducted community relations programs, subsidized the opera, contributed to local hospital and charity funds and made gifts to colleges and universities. This trend in corporate affairs has aroused some vigorous criticism. Dean Edward S. Mason of Harvard calls it, "The Apologetics of Mangerialism."[10]

Banker Gaylord A. Freeman fears that management is growing slack in living up to the test of profitability. "I have been interested to hear several business leaders declare that the purpose of companies is service to their customers," said Freeman in a speech to the Illinois Bankers Association. But, "I cannot imagine tough minded leaders commencing their annual reports: 'This has been our most successful year; we have served an additional million customers. This additional service resulted in a loss of $20 million, but we consider this our finest year.'"

Market consultant Theodore Levitt says that the danger of the new concept of social responsibility is that the corporation will try to minister to the whole man; that it is bad for society to be shaped by a single functional group; and that corporate welfarism will inevitably lead to a monolithic state.[11] Economist-lawyer, Eugene W. Rostow of Yale University, calls the new corporate morality "bewildering balderdash," for, he says, it squares neither with legal principle nor with good economics. The only meaningful criteria for managerial decision, declares Rostow, are those of the market place. To depend on vague concepts of social responsibility instead of the price system is to sabotage the market and systematically distort the economic allocation of resources.[12]

Under the battering of continuous criticism, some businessmen, it is true, have become a little apologetic for profits, but few would concede that they have taken their eye very far off the profit indicator. The reason is quite elemental. If in the name of welfare they paid too much for wages or engaged in community programs that substantially raised their costs, they would soon be priced out of the market. Or if in a period of shortage they exercised too much price restraint, a gray market would quickly develop and the speculator, not the ultimate consumer, would be the beneficiary. It is of the essence of a free market that entrepreneurs, eager to make a profit, are continually looking for imbalances that they can exploit, hence the market itself polices the extent to which individual companies can go on incurring costs that are not closely related to profits.

Nor would it seem that the threat of the corporation taking

over the whole man is very immediate or menacing. Business is geared to the production and distribution of goods and services. A corporation makes a poor church; it scarcely can substitute for a school; and, although it is said to "govern" its people in the plant, it certainly is not cut out to perform the services of the state. Because employees have wanted to institutionalize social risk, corporations have split the wage check into wage payments and deferred benefits. Because public opinion requires it, corporations contribute to local charities. But this is hardly to say that companies are about to take over the whole man. Every age has its own climate of opinion, and, in responding to the demands of modern times, businessmen are of necessity changing their operational procedures and their description of these procedures, but they are still profit minded, as they must be.

The debate over the purpose of business can be resolved by the recognition of the fact that, under market competition, service to consumers and profits are, for the most part, two sides of the same coin. If one wants to make a profit he must think first of the service he can render a buyer. If he can supply a superior service at a cheaper price than the competition, he will surely make a profit and it might even exceed his wildest expectations. Many of the most hard-headed and successful money makers in American industry have declared that their secret is "What can I give," not "What can I get." George Merck, founder of Merck & Co., drug manufacturers, put it this way: "We try never to forget that medicine is for the people. It is not for profits. The profits follow, and if we have remembered that, they have never failed to appear. The better we have remembered it, the larger they have been." [14]

The statement that best describes the views of modern managers on the objectives of business, then, is that the purpose of companies is to serve the community and, within the rules of decency and fair play, to serve it so well competitively that it will realize the greatest amount of profit over the long term. This position is not only good economics, but it also provides a strong platform on which business can go to its publics and ask for support for what it thinks is sound economic and social policy.

Understanding Profits

The importance of profit interpretation with the general public and the validity of the service theme can be well illustrated by two case studies. The first deals with the experience of the American Telephone and Telegraph Company. The central problem of the Telephone Company is capital. Every new home installation requires an investment of $375. In the past fifteen years, the Telephone Company has plowed back or gathered from the sales of new securities the enormous sum of sixteen billion dollars to finance the expansion of its service to an ever widening body of users. To generate capital requires profit—profits to plow back into the business and profits to pay out as dividends to investors for the use of their money. The Company and its predecessors have paid a continuous dividend for more than eighty years and has become a financial Rock of Gibraltar for widows and orphans, schools and churches, and thrifty people who are struggling to build a modest estate. In 1960 the Company had 1,900,000 stockholders of record, more than any other American corporation.

The Telephone Company is a "natural monopoly" whose rates are fixed, not by competition, but by public authority. The operating dilemma of the management is that they have responsibility for making a profit, but no control over inflationary costs or for rates set by the regulatory commissions. If profit is insufficient to cover dividends and more, the confidence of investors is shaken, capital becomes harder to get, service deteriorates and the technological progress which has made American telephone service far superior to anything in the world, begins to lag.

Management has three ways to protect profit margins: cut costs, seek additional revenue by offering extra services, or apply for and win a rate increase from the public authorities. Rate-making officials, like all political functionaries, are susceptible to public opinion. If people are hostile to the idea of profit, or feel that the Telephone Company makes too much profit, the decisions of the rate-makers are likely to be adverse. If profit declines and financial starvation sets in, service deteriorates, and the consumer gets what he is willing to pay for—no more.

Telephone Company policy, therefore, has long been geared

to the concept that good telephone service and profits are inseparable.[13] The Company has made service its watchword. It has maintained a great scientific laboratory to advance communications technology; it has tried to deal fairly with its employees and draw them into creative cooperation in carrying out the Company's purposes; it has gone to great lengths to give good customer service and maintain cordial relationships with the people who pay the bills. But lest the public lose sight of the key to good service, it has ceaselessly proclaimed the need for adequate profits. In the company annual reports, in pamphlets and speeches, in employee communication, in advertisements, in local plant visits, and in hearings before public bodies, the Telephone Company has repeated the theme that companies that show good profit records are the ones that do the best job for the stockholders, the employees, the customers and the whole community.

Evidently the Telephone Company has achieved a high degree of success in rendering service for a profit and in interpreting this service to the public, for it has largely escaped the agitation for public ownership that has shaken the electric power industry in recent years, and, up to now, has avoided the financial starvation that is gradually paralyzing the publicly regulated railroads. The Telephone Company management, however, is not complacent. It knows full well that everything the Company stands for pivots eventually on popular understanding of profits, and that to create this understanding constitutes one of the primary responsibilities of management.

The second case study that illuminates the importance of profit interpretation and the validity of the service theme comes from the drug industry, which is currently under heavy fire from Senator Estes Kefauver and his Subcommittee on Antitrust and Monopoly. One of the leading political exponents of the theory of monopolistic competition, Senator Kefauver sees oligopolies milking the public through brand name differentiation, excessive advertising, and administered pricing. In the hearings on the drug industry he sought to show that drug manufacturers make unconscionable profits, that prices are so high that needy persons are deprived of medicine, that too much money is spent on advertising and selling and that the trade is less competitive than it should be.

All students of government recognize the Congressional inquiry as a powerful tool for establishing the facts upon which sound legislation can be based. They are also aware that, while some hearings seek the facts in a highly judicial manner, others are stage-managed to produce headlines calculated to arouse public opinion. The drug industry hearings were obviously of the latter type. The plot was the age-old one of "Profits vs. Humanity" with the current episode—"How Greedy Profit Seekers Exploit the Poor and the Sick." The dramatic vehicle was to set a price on the raw materials going into a drug, then compare this figure with the price paid by the druggist or that paid by the consumer and compute the mark-up.

This type of showmanship produced mark-ups that were truly astronomical. In the Schering hearings, for example, the cost of the raw material for Meticortelone was said to be one and fifty-six-hundredths of a cent per tablet, while the price to the druggist was seventeen and nine-tenths cents, a mark-up of 1118 per cent. For ethinyl, a drug for internal female disorders, the cost of the chemicals was reported at twenty-eight cents and the selling price to the druggist at $8., a mark-up of 2757 per cent. The raw material cost for Progynon, another drug for female disorders, was said to be eleven and seven-tenths cents for sixty tablets, the price to the druggist eight dollars and forty cents, or a mark-up of 7079 per cent.

The Chairman of the Committee on Antitrust and Monopoly was equal to the drama of the occasion. Repeatedly he hammered his witness, Francis C. Brown, President of Schering Corporation, with questions designed to make mark-up appear as profit and aimed hard at the newspaper headlines:

> "What is the public going to think about a mark-up from eleven and seven-tenths cents to eight dollars and forty cents which finally costs the customer fourteen dollars? What do you think about it?"

"You mean you admit you are making this mark-up of 7.079 per cent on (Ethinyl) estradiol?"

"Do you think honestly, Mr. Brown, that this is a fair and reasonable mark-up?" [14]

Mr. Brown testified again and again that raw materials represent only a small part of the end cost of drugs; that exacting controls to insure purity and quality added to cost as did education of doctors in use of the drug; that drug research has accounted for much of the recent advance in medicine; and that the successful drugs must command a price that will help pay for the unsuccessful ones. "Men walking who were crippled, and working who were incapacitated, at a cost of between thirty to sixty cents a day (for Meticorten) seems to me to be pretty reasonable," declared Mr. Brown.[15]

As might be expected, the mark-up showmanship produced a rich crop of newspaper headlines that were well calculated to discredit the drug industry. "Firm Accused of Boosting Product Price Seven Thousand Per Cent Above Cost," read the headline in the *Los Angeles Times*. "Find Drug Mark-ups as High as Seven Thousand Per Cent" was the story in the *New York Daily News*.

Readers, of course, were not expected to distinguish between mark-up and profit, or to recognize the fact that value added to the cost of raw materials through processing and distribution accounts for most of the wholesale and retail price of goods. It was inevitable, therefore, that mark-up would be interpreted as profit, even by newspapermen. When the hearings dealt with Progesterone, a female sex hormone produced by the Upjohn Company, the Committee's counsel fixed the cost of the raw materials at fourteen cents per gram and the price to the druggist at fifteen dollars, a mark-up of over ten thousand per cent.[16] The next day the *New York Herald Tribune* headlined its story "10,000 Pct. Drug Mark-up Charged," but in the *New York Mirror* the news was "Made 10,000% on Drug."

When Walter A. Munns, President of Smith, Kline and French, was put on the witness stand, he testified that the use of tranquilizers had for the first time in 185 years reversed the population trend in mental hospitals, and that in 1958 alone this meant twenty thousand fewer persons in confinement than previously projected. No monetary measurement, of course, can begin to describe the relief of a human soul released from a strait jacket, or the joy of leaving a mental hospital and returning to one's family and friends. But Munns pointed out that the government had been saved seventy-five million dollars in 1959 by reduction of the patient load, and that tranquilizers had obviated the necessity for making enormous additional capital outlays for new facilities. A later witness in the hearings estimated savings in hospital construction at $860,000,000 over a three year period.

The press, however, saw little news in this part of the testimony. "Big Profit Found in Tranquilizers," read the *New York Times* headline. Prices of tranquilizers were so high, said the story, that many patients released from mental hospitals were forced to return, because they could not afford to buy the needed drugs on the outside. With this kind of reporting, few readers of the *New York Times* or other newspapers could escape the belief that the company was heartlessly exploiting the sick for private gain.

Students of propaganda recognize the drug hearings as one of the most technically perfect jobs of discrediting an industry in recent times. The dramatic exhibits, the parade of accusing witnesses, the timing of the testimony to gear with newspaper deadlines, the innuendo of wrongdoing in the questioning—all these were skillfully calculated to build a public opinion that would support legislation to regulate the drug industry. There are no published data describing the reaction of the general public, but the show was put on with such consummate skill that no one need question the hypothesis that a large segment of the citizenry got the message that drug manufacturers were profiteering on human misery and that something should be done about it.

The truth about the drug industry is that while it does not even begin to realize the Committee's outrageous raw material mark-up figures as profit, drug companies are among the best profit makers in the American economy. As reported by the First National City Bank of New York (Table 43), profits on sales for the ten year period 1950-1959 averaged ten and nine-tenths per cent and profit on investment averaged twenty and five-tenths per cent. For leading companies in all manufacturing for the same period, profit for sales averaged five and eight-tenths per cent and profit on investment twelve and six-tenths per cent.

TABLE 43. PROFIT FOR LEADING DRUG COMPANIES

	Per Cent Sales	*Per Cent Investment*
1950	11.3	21.9
1951	9.4	19.2
1952	8.4	14.0
1953	8.1	13.7
1954	9.2	15.8
1955	10.5	18.3
1956	11.9	22.4
1957	11.7	24.0
1958	11.4	21.9
1959	11.6	21.9
Average Drug Companies	10.9	20.5
Average leading companies in manufacturing	5.8	12.6

It has been the experience of American industry that the highest profits have come from innovation, and the drug industry provides a prime example of the relationship between profits and industrial creativity. In 1948 the drug industry spent thirty million dollars on research; by 1959 research expenditures had increased five-fold to one hundred and seventy million dollars. This sum represented eight and seven-tenths per cent of total sales of human ethical pharmaceutical products in the United States, a rate more than double that for all manufacturing.[17]

In 1958 the research teams of drug companies screened 114,600 chemical compounds of which 2,865 were promising enough to be clinically tested. From this screening, approximately forty compounds actually reached the market. It has been estimated that over the years the average research and development cost to bring a new drug to market is about six million dollars.

A company that achieves a dramatic break-through in the drug field can earn very large profits. Sales of a new miracle drug expand rapidly and profits soar. Then competition quickly sets in and prices and profits on the new item begin a sharp descent. For antibiotics, for example, the price fell from $860 to $160 per pound between 1948 and 1959. Penicillin was sold at one hundred dollars for one hundred thousand units in 1943 and for twenty-two cents in 1956. Insulin today costs patients one-seventeenth of what it did thirty years ago when the drug was first introduced.

The earnings of individual drug companies are largely a reflection of their product mix. A few companies that have been fortunate enough to have a high percentage of their sales in new break-through drugs have made as much as fifty-five percent profit on their invested capital in a single year. When the product mix has failed to include new drugs, however, profit margins have fallen sharply, seeking levels similar to those for other manufacturing industries.

Cortisone provides a good case study in the profit economics of drug innovation. As early as 1929 it was discovered that an extract from the adrenal cortex could maintain life in animals after the removal of adrenal glands. With this lead, the search was on for chemical synthesis of the crucial therapeutic agent, notably a substance called Compound E. In 1941 a working committee was formed under the National Research Council, but after two years, gave up the search. Two groups, however, persisted in the hunt, one led by Dr. Edward C. Kendall of the Mayo Clinic in Rochester, Minnesota, and the other by Dr. Lewis H. Sarett of Merck & Company of Rahway, New Jersey.

By the end of 1944 Dr. Sarett had synthesized Compound E and by 1948 was able to manufacture enough of the drug to begin clinical testing. On September 21, 1948, Dr. Philip S. Hench, head of the Department of Rheumatic Diseases at the Mayo Clinic, administered the first dose of cortisone for rheumatoid arthritis. The results were almost miraculous. Bedridden cripples were suddenly given hope and made to walk. One young woman who had been crippled for four years went on a shopping spree in less than a week after she began taking cortisone.

Merck & Company moved quickly to get into production with its great new drug. It also decided to take its lumps in competition and made no attempt to maintain an exclusive position in the field. In 1949, Merck & Company put the drug, Cortone, on the market at two hundred dollars per gram, approximately what it cost to manufacture. In the beginning it took the organs of forty steers to supply enough cortisone to treat one person for one day. As might be expected, competitors quickly entered the race to supply the new drug. The research team of one competing firm found that microbes could be used to perform certain complex chemical processes and thereby greatly reduce the cost of manufacturing. With the rising demand and declining costs of production, Merck & Company initiated eight price reductions, dropping the price to twenty dollars per gram by midyear of 1952. By 1957 the price per gram had declined to two dollars.

In 1950 Merck's Cortone had one hundred per cent of the market. By 1952, Cortone's share had dropped to seventy-nine per cent, and the trend continued down to twenty-seven per cent in 1954 and three per cent in 1958. Merck & Company followed Cortone with Hydrocortone, a more powerful drug with fewer undesirable side effects, and with this formulation won twenty-four per cent of the market in 1954. But in 1955 Schering came into the competition with Meticorten and in 1956 took fifty-four per cent of the trade. Late in 1958 Merck & Company introduced its new steroid, Decadron, with thirty-five times the potency of its initial drug, Cortone, and reduced the price. But within a few weeks Schering came out with the same compound, and by the end of the year Ciba had also entered the competition. In 1958 twenty-nine companies were offering steroid products for prescription, and three of them—Squibb, Upjohn and Lederle, whose combined sales represented only a small fraction of the market two years before—were now accounting for half of corticosteroid plain tablet sales. Only a vigorous industry could play this kind of competitive musical chairs.

So great has been the obsolescence rate in the drug industry that seventy per cent of the drugs used in today's prescriptions were non-existent in 1935. Forty per cent of today's prescriptions were unavailable as recently as five years ago.

What has the public gained from the great competition for innovation and profit in the drug industry? The medical team, of course, is composed of doctors, pharmacists, public health authorities, and hospitals as well as drug manufacturers, but it is fair to say that the discovery and mass production and distribution of the wonder drugs has played a key role in the medical progress of the nation. This progress can be described in many ways, as follows:

> Since 1937 the average life span of individuals has increased nearly ten years. If the 1937 death rate had continued, more than three million Americans who are alive today would be dead.
>
> During the period 1930 to 1934, one mother in 157 died in childbirth. In 1958 only one mother in 2222 died in this manner.
>
> Between 1930 and 1958 the death rate for babies was reduced fifty-seven per cent; for children one to four years of age, the death rate fell eighty per cent.
>
> The death rate from influenza and pneumonia fell from 102 per thousand in 1930 to thirty-three per thousand in 1958, a decline of sixty-eight per cent.
>
> Between 1944 and 1957, the death rate from tuberculosis fell eighty per cent; from mastoiditis seventy-eight per cent; from syphilis seventy-four per cent; from whooping cough ninety-three per cent.

The new wonder drugs have not only performed a mission of mercy in relieving pain and suffering, but they have also materially reduced the cost of medical care and loss of wages resulting from sickness. Twenty years ago a case of lobar pneumonia meant five weeks in the hospital, a long convalescence and three hundred to four hundred dollars for doctors, nurses, medicines, oxygen and medical care. Today it means two weeks of illness, generally at home, an immediate return to work and fifteen dollars to thirty dollars for drugs.

Thirty years ago the treatment for mastoiditis cost at least one thousand dollars for hospitalization and surgery and involved the possibility of permanent impairment of hearing. Today fifteen dollars worth of antibiotics clears up most cases.

The cost of medicine, like the cost of bread, is beyond the means of some people, but drug costs are not a major item in the family budget. For every one hundred dollars the average family spends on personal consumption items, drugs and sundries claim approximately ninety cents. The average prescription cost is three dollars. Only one in ten prescriptions cost as much as ten dollars. In 1959 the average adult spent eleven dollars per year on prescription drugs but he spent forty dollars for tobacco and fifty-four dollars for alcoholic beverages.

The cost of drugs in relation to the cost of medical care has not changed appreciably in thirty years. In 1930 drugs represented twenty per cent of the cost of medical care, and in 1958 the figure was nineteen and nine-tenths per cent.

In the decade following 1947-1949, the rise in the retail price of prescription drugs was twenty-one and four-tenths per cent compared with twenty-three and seven-tenths per cent for all items in the Bureau of Labor Consumer Price Index.

If drug company profits were cut in half or eliminated entirely, it would scarcely be felt in the consumer's pocketbook. Merck & Company, for example, breaks down the per-tablet cost for its new steroid, Decadron, as follows:

Cost to Merck	10.7¢
Mark-up for manufacture	3.5
Cost to druggist	14.2
Mark-up for cost of distribution and profit	13.0
Sale price to patient	27.2

Merck & Company's average profit after taxes is one and sixty-eight hundredths cents per tablet. If the manufacturer reduced his profit by half, the consumer at best would save about one cent per tablet. The profit margin, of course, varies for different drugs, but there is no evidence to sustain the charge that drug profits constitute a threat to the family pocketbook. On the contrary, drug profits have helped remove a major threat to the family bank account by preventing and reducing the cost of illness.

Before the discovery of cortisone, rheumatoid arthritis ravaged the human frame and left seven out of ten of its victims so badly crippled that they were unable to lead normal lives. Now under steroid therapy, two out of three sufferers from this disease can regain a satisfactory degree of normalcy in their daily living, and a return to work. The cost of cortisone medication in relation to the restoration of income and saving on hospital and doctor bills is so small that it loses all significance.

The nation's economic gain from the development of cortisone and its derivatives is enormous. It is estimated that the steroids have restored one million patients to near normalcy who otherwise would be invalids. If the saving in the cost of caring for these patients is put at $1,000 a year, the annual economic contribution of the cortisone family of drugs would work out to one billion dollars. If the earnings of patients restored to their jobs were included, it would likely add to another two billion dollars.

The case of the drug industry poses the basic probem of profit interpretation. Here we have an industry that has engaged in a highly competitive race for innovation, in the course of which it has made excellent profits and rendered monumental service to the nation in saving lives, reducing suffering and drastically cutting the cost of illness. In this great achievement profit has played a primary role, for it has provided a strong incentive in the search for new drugs, and has been sufficient in amount to enable drug manufacturers to risk large sums on research and development and production facilities.

In the drug hearings, John T. Connor, President of Merck & Company, put the case this way: "This eleven per cent profit on sales looks like a relatively profitable business. When our research laboratories succeed in finding effective new drugs it is. And I submit, Mr. Chairman, that it ought to be. As long as the result of harnessing the energies of Merck & Company to the hope of a good profit continues to result in a stream of new weapons in the war on disease, the American people, I believe, are getting a reasonable bargain. When our well runs dry, if it does, then no matter what our profits, we will be no bargain at all."[18]

The drug companies have long believed that their relationship was primarily with the doctor and the druggist, and have made little effort to interpret their work or their profits to the general public. With the Kefauver Subcommittee now pointing the accusing finger of profiteering, they, like other managements, must undertake to inform the public about their operations. There should be no mystery about the workings of the drug companies or those in any other industry. Moreover, the community should applaud Congressmen when they conduct judicially fair inquiries of industry to see if competition is operating effectively to protect the public interest.

The profit story is basically the service story, and it is hard to believe that the competitive profit and loss system will lack support if it is properly reported to the public. One of the biggest contributions of the Kefauver hearings may well be the goad they provide management for better interpretation of the role of profits in the service of humanity.

To sum up, the successful interpretation of profits requires not only facts but interpretation of facts. It requires functional reporting on how profits fit into real life situations. Above all, it requires that profit and loss be related to human concerns. "What profits mean to people" is likely to continue to be the most effective theme in widening the public's understanding of this key institution of a capitalistic society.

CHAPTER THIRTEEN

THE ETHICS OF PROFIT MAKING

One of man's principal distinctions is that he possesses a conscience. The sins of the flesh are such that he does not always follow his inner promptings, but the deep satisfaction of doing what is right and avoiding what is wrong has always been a powerful force drawing men toward the paths of rectitude. In static societies the rules of ethical conduct are well crystallized and men know what is expected of them. In dynamic societies, where technological change is rapid and the division of labor is highly proliferated, the rules of ethical behavior become much more difficult to define.

Since men have always been heavily preoccupied with earning a living, the accumulation and administration of wealth has from the beginning of recorded history been a focal point for ethical thought. The Hebrew prophets had much to say about the proper point of view toward wealth; the Greek philosophers speculated on the subject; the Medieval Churchmen discoursed at great length on it; the Puritans wove their views on work and the production of wealth intimately into the fabric of their religion; and the great moral philosophers of the eighteenth century pondered the influence of property in the affairs of men.

Today in classrooms, church forums, labor unions, trade associations, and elsewhere we continue to discuss the subject and grope for ethical norms to guide our economic behavior. The answers are not easily come by, for wrapped up in them are the questions of the nature and purpose of human existence and the supreme goals for which men should strive. We can only outline here some of the key concepts that are involved in the present-day discussion and sketch out some ideas that need to be taken into consideration in formulating a point of view on the ethics of profit making. The simplest way to get into the subject is to consider some of the major points of the ethical indictment of the profit-and-loss system, with particular reference to the history of these criticisms.

The world has always had reservations about rich men. This may be partly due to envy, but more likely it is because the rich often have loved their lucre more than their fellow men. Not all profit makers, of course, are rich, but many are. Wealth is the principal tool of the profit maker. He accumulates wealth and puts it to work to make more wealth for himself and the community. By the nature of his calling, the profit maker must be wealthier than the average citizen.

The Bible has good things to say about the poor but it goes to some pains to castigate the sins of the rich. In the sermon on the Mount, Jesus said: "Blessed be ye poor; for yours is the kingdom of God. Blessed are ye that hunger now; for ye shall be filled. But woe unto you that are rich for ye have received your consolation. Woe unto you that are full for ye shall hunger." (Luke 6:20-25)

Again, when Jesus was preaching in Judea, a young man stepped forward and asked what he must do to have eternal life. The Master answered that he should keep the commandments—do not murder, do not commit adultery, do not steal, do not bear false witness, honor thy mother and father, and love thy neighbor as thyself. The young man said he had done all these things; what did he still lack? Jesus replied that if the young man wished to be perfect, he would sell what he owned, give it to the poor and follow the Master. Whereupon the young man turned away, for he was a man of great possessions. Jesus exclaimed to his disciples: "Verily I say unto you. That a rich man shall hardly enter the kingdom of heaven. And again I say to you. It is easier for a camel to go through the eye of a needle than for a rich man to enter the Kingdom of God" (Matthew 20: 16-24).

These are hard words for they seem to say that a rich man is a lost soul. But the meaning becomes more intelligible when it is noted that Jesus, with the phrase, "If thou wilt be perfect," was offering his young interrogator the counsel of perfection. In mortal life men strive for perfection, but no one ever achieves it.

The point is clarified further in St. Mark's account of the colloquy between Jesus and his rich young interrogator. As the young man strode away, Mark quoted Jesus as saying to his disciples: "How hardly shall they that have riches enter into the kingdom of God!" When Jesus saw that his disciples were astonished by this statement he elaborated: "Children, how hard is it for *them that trust in riches* to enter the Kingdom of God." (Mark 10:23-24) Thus Jesus actually taught that it is not the possession of riches that is sinful, but the trust in them for salvation.

St. Paul made the same point when he was giving fatherly advice to his young assistant Timothy. "And having food and raiment," wrote Paul, "let us therewith be content. But they that will be rich fall into temptation, and a snare and into many foolish and hurtful lusts, which drown men in destruction and perdition. *For the love of money* is the root of all evil; which while some coveted after, all have erred from the faith, and pierced themselves through with many sorrows" (I Timothy 6:8-10.) Thus, the teaching is that the root of all evil is not money itself, but the love of money.

Many of the early church fathers felt called upon to discuss the question of riches, and one in particular, Clement of Alexandria (150-215), wrote a short treatise on the subject entitled "The Rich Man's Salvation." Clement was ministering to a wealthy congregation in Alexandria. He felt he had to say something about a rich man's prospect for salvation, and, in particular, to point out that Christianity is a religion for all regardless of wealth or station in life. "It is no great or enviable thing," wrote Clement, "to be simply without riches." Those who "lie along the roads in abject poverty" are not for that reason alone assured of God's blessedness. Jesus' advice to his rich young interrogator, according to Clement, was that he should banish his morbid excitement and anxious care for his possessions and strive for personal worth in the sight of God. What matters, Clement says, is not wealth, but the way in which wealth is used. "You can use it rightly; it ministers to righteousness. But if one uses it wrongly, it is found to be a minister of wrong." [1] This remains the essence of religious teaching on wealth today.

In the current debate, making profits is continually stigmatized as an exercise in avarice and greed reflecting the baser instincts of man. Avarice, of course, is a deadly sin, and if profit making and avarice are one and the same, it would be difficult indeed to make out an ethical case for earning a profit. Much of the confusion on this point, no doubt, stems from the teachings of the Middle Ages when what we now regard as profit was looked upon as avarice.

The Medieval Schoolmen held that the purpose of life was salvation. Economic conduct is one aspect of personal conduct and the rules of morality here as elsewhere are binding. Material riches are necessary, but secondary. Economic appetites are powerful passions and need to be repressed. No economic activity is justified if not related to a moral end. It is right for a man to seek such wealth as is necessary for his station, but to seek more is to commit the sin of avarice. Said the 14th century Schoolman, Henry of Langenstein, "He who has enough to satisfy his wants, nevertheless ceaselessly labors to acquire riches either in order to obtain a social position, or that subsequently he may have enough to live without labor, or that his sons may become men of wealth and importance—all such men are incited by a damnable avarice, sensuality, or pride." [2]

The dangers of economic interest, the Schoolmen believed, increased in direct proportion to the prominence of the pecuniary motives associated with them. Labor is the common lot of mankind and is necessary and honorable; finance, if not immoral, is at least sordid and disreputable; trade is necessary for the exchange of goods, but, in the words of St. Thomas Aquinas, it has "a certain debasement attached thereto." Said the Schoolman Gratian: "Whosoever buys a thing, not that he may sell it whole and unchanged, but that he may have material for fashioning something, he is no merchant. But the man who buys it in order that he may gain by selling it again unchanged and as he bought it, that man is of the buyers and sellers who are cast from God's temple." [3] This was the extreme view, nevertheless, tradesmen were looked upon with suspicion and their activities were surrounded by many restrictions.

The Medieval conception of usury was considerably different from our definition today. In general the term meant extortion, either through the taking of simple interest or the charging of what was thought to be an unjust price. The word "usurer," however, was so much on the popular tongue that it became a name calling device. If you didn't like someone you called him a usurer. Today the name calling function survives when men are denounced as usurers for making a profit.

In the Middle Ages the taking of interest for the loan of money was thought to be usurious because the lender was asking for a specific return whether the borrower gained or not. Interest taking was contrary to Scripture (Exodus 22:25); it was to live without labor and therefore contrary to nature; it was unjust because the benefit of the money to the borrower cannot be greater than the total of the sum loaned. Manifest usurers were dealt with severely. They were denied confession, absolution, and Christian burial. In the Councils of Lyons (1274) a person who even let his house to an usurer could be excommunicated. In Florence in the middle of the thirteenth century the authorities repeatedly fined bankers for usury, and toward the close of the century prohibited credit transactions altogether.

To repress avarice and control the practice of usury, the Medieval Schoolmen not only forbade the taking of interest but also developed the concept of the just price. A man was entitled to a fair price for his goods, but he must not take advantage of another by charging more. But what was a just price? There were many answers. The dominant one was that advanced by

St. Thomas Aquinas (1225-1274) who believed that the just price depended on "a kind of estimate" which made exchange mutually advantageous to both parties. While this price would vary with circumstances in different markets, it should correspond to the labor and cost of the producer.

Some Schoolmen of the fourteenth century emphasized the subjective element in the common estimate and insisted that the essence of value was utility. They concluded that a fair price was most likely to be reached if men dealt with each other in a market. If exchange took place in a central market where there were other buyers and sellers, and if it took place without coercion, the price was likely to be just. The fact that a bargain had been struck showed that both parties were satisfied. This view, remarkably ahead of its time, is similar to the one widely held today.

In the Middle Ages it was thought that public officials were best able to fix the just price, but it was recognized that the drive of the trader to buy as cheaply and sell as dearly as he could was effectively held in check by competing rivals. The Medieval Churchmen and the public authorities actively supported and encouraged the creation of town markets. Short of direction from the market or from public authority, the individual seller would be guided by "what he must charge in order to maintain his position, and nourish himself suitably in it, and by a reasonable estimate of his expenditure and labor." [4]

In developing their ideas on usury and the just price, the Schoolmen had their eyes on the little man. Popes, feudal lords and large-scale traders borrowed money and paid interest in direct contradiction to the laws against usury. But the gentry could take care of themselves. If the little man fell on hard times and was compelled to borrow money at high interest, he might lose his livelihood. For this reason, no doubt, the ethical teachings of the Schoolmen on usury were translated in secular law that found widespread support.

Two great historical developments changed public thought on usury. One was the Protestant Reformation; the other was the Industrial Revolution. The Reformation, of course, broke religious unity and paved the way for new religious and moral formulations. In the beginning, the Protestant reformers were fanatical in their determination to stamp out usury. Luther denounced the Catholic Church for the sin of avarice and berated the Schoolmen who had made concessions to the material world in their definition of usury. Interest and all forms of profit came under Luther's interdict. Trade only was permissible when the seller's income compensated him for his labor. In the Calvinist theocracy in Geneva, the Consistory, in the seventeenth century, repeatedly fined and punished creditors, usurers, engrossers, "monopolists," and retailers who sold goods above the prices fixed by the authorities. In England, the Puritans of the sixteenth and early seventeenth centuries denounced usury as a "vice most odyous and detestable" and, similarly, in the Massachusetts settlement the Fathers tried to curb usury by fixing prices, interest, wages, and profit.

But these formulations of the Schoolmen and the early Protestant reformers could not contain the newly-established economic life of America and the continent. The admonition to "be content with your lot" or "seek only enough to satisfy an humble want" was no longer satisfactory. With the coming of mass production and widened trade, the people were eager to embrace the possibilities of increased control over their environment and a better material existence. The village gave way to the city, enterprising gildsmen became entrepreneurs, merchants distributed a continually increasing variety of goods, and bankers set up credit mechanisms to finance the swelling stream of manufacture and trade. The times simply outdistanced the old ethical strictures, which were gradually abandoned as archaic and out of date.

Into this breach moved the later Puritanism with its emphasis on individualism and its formulation of life as a Calling. For the Puritan, says Tawney, toil in itself became a kind of sacrament. The Puritans believed that the rational order of the universe is the work of God, and that its plan requires the individual to labor for God's glory. The faith by which one is to be saved, however, is the faith that produces works. "God doth call every man and woman to serve him in some peculiar employment in this world, both for their own and common good," wrote the Puritan divine, Richard Steele. "The Great Governour of the world hath appointed to every man his proper post and province, and let him be never so active out of his sphere, he will be at a great loss if he does not keep his own vineyard and mind his own business." [5]

The Puritans tended to be of the entrepreneurial class and the ethical rules prescribed for them contributed to the successful conduct of business. They were to be diligent, sober, and thrifty in their labors. Their moral duty was to choose the most profitable occupation. Said the Reverend Richard Baxter: "If God show you a way in which you may lawfully get more than in another way (without wrong to your soul or to any other) if you refuse this and choose the less gainful way, you cross one of the ends of your calling, and you refuse to be God's steward." [6] To the Puritan, success in business was a sign that "God has blessed his trade." "Next to the saving of his soul (the tradesman's) care and business," wrote the Reverend Richard Steele, "is to serve God in his calling, and to drive it as far as it will go." [7]

No one can measure the influence of the Puritans on present day concepts of economic ethics, but the verdict of scholarship is that it has been very large.

The present-day tactic of equating profit making with avarice, then, is to play tricks with history. It is to urge the medieval view on the modern world. It can lay no claim to fact or reason; it is simple disparagement through name calling. Some profit makers, no doubt, are avaricious, but so too are some teachers and labor leaders and probably even some clergymen. Avarice is a sin of the flesh in which the poor can indulge as well as the rich. St. Paul's wise observation that the love of money leads men into foolish and hurtful lusts which end in their own destruction is as true today as it was nineteen hundred years ago. The creative and ethical use of money in profit making, however, has resulted in great blessings for humanity. Unless we are prepared to belive that salvation is to be found in asceticism, profit making has an honorable and beneficial role to play in modern society.

In addition to "avarice" and "greed," the words "exploiter" and "exploitation" enter strongly into the ethical indictment of the profit-and-loss system. The concept of exploitation was injected into the main stream of western thought by Karl Marx and no discussion of the ethics of profit making can overlook the implications of the Marxian doctrine. In the Middle Ages most goods were hand produced and little capital was used. It was natural, therefore, that Medieval thought should hold that a fair and just price should pretty much reflect its labor content. The unpardonable sin was that of the speculator or middleman who came by private gain through the exploitation of public necessity. Marx took this idea of the Medieval Schoolmen, mixed it with Hegel's thesis, anti-thesis, and synthesis and Ricardo's iron law of wages and came out with a revolutionary brew from which the world is still reeling. Says Tawney: "The last of the Schoolmen was Karl Marx." [8]

According to Marx, commodities are exclusively the products of labor. The capitalist buys "labor power," but pays only a subsistence price for it. The worker may earn his subsistence in six hours but work twelve. The goods produced in the remaining six hours constitute "surplus value," which goes into the coffers of the capitalist. Marx, following a line of abstraction that no other writer follows, looked upon machinery as constant capital and labor power as variable capital. Machinery, or constant capital, transfers its value to the product and hence creates no surplus value. The measure of exploitation of the worker is the difference between the value he creates and his subsistence wage. In the Marxian lingo the capitalist exploiter is an idle capitalist who lives entirely off the surplus value extracted from workers in his employment. Little capitalists who work part time, and thus steal from the workers less than enough to support themselves in complete idleness, are apparently excluded from the hated class.

Marx prophesied that capitalistic exploitation would continue and that, while the capitalists were growing fewer and richer, the masses would be thrust down into ever increasing misery and degradation. The class war would continue until the grand finale when the dictatorship of the proletariat would take over the state and "expropriate the expropriators." After class distinctions had been eliminated, the state gradually would "wither away."

Marxism is without doubt one of the most extraordinary social phenomena of modern times. Marx's writings were so abstract, vague, and inconsistent that no one is really sure of what he was saying or trying to say. Many scholars have attempted to clarify the Marxian doctrine—a late volume by G.D.H. Cole carries the intriguing title, *What Marx Really Meant*—but the confusion remains. *Das Kapital* was supposed to expound a theory of value, but, according to his scholarly critics, Marx never got around to defining it. In Volume I Marx seems to be talking about value in terms of price, but in Volume 3 the reader is told that commodities are almost always exchanged at prices above or below value.[9]

As a prophet Marx was totally wrong. Far from progressively sinking into misery and degradation, the worker in capitalistic societies has dramatically bettered his material lot.

The Marxian idea that the workers produce the wealth, but the capitalist takes it away from them, has no validity either in theory or in fact. All responsible economic analyses show that wealth is produced by a collaboration of capital and labor, with capital supplying tools and equipment to the workers. The rise in worker productivity is largely accounted for by better machinery and larger capital investment. Yet Chart 19 shows capital has taken very little of the gain, working for a relatively small and risky fee and handing over almost all of the fruits of production to the recipients of wages and salaries. This is surely a strange way for the capitalists to "exploit" the working man!

The Marxian doctrine is so patently in error that it probably would have little influence if it were confined to economics. What gives it power is its ethical appeal. Mankind has long had a penchant for believing that a man has a right to the fruits of his own labor. "Thou shalt not steal" is a commandment indelibly engraved on the conscience of every person raised in the

Judeo-Christian faith. According to Marx, the capitalists steal. They take what does not belong to them; they grind the faces of the poor; they are altogether wicked and unjust. Happily, says Marx, there is the promise of a better day; for it is an historical imperative that the oppressors will be overthrown, after which the downtrodden will inherit a communistic heaven where there is peace and plenty and where universal brotherhood prevails.

This is pretty potent stuff. It rationalizes discontent; it gives revolutionaries a blueprint to guide their fanaticism without requiring them to think; it marshals sympathy and public support for righting supposed wrongs. But living experiments with Marxism demonstrate that the end of the dream is not the promised heaven, but an Orwellian hell where men lose their dignity and freedom, where they are brutally separated from their families and friends, and where they become slaves of the state and often starve. Under Marxist communism, as the Chinese communes have demonstrated, men descend to the level of ants in the communal ant hill.

To a considerable extent the profit makers have let their argument go by default. They have been busy producing and distributing and have neglected to link up their activities with the ethical values of the community. Meanwhile, the Marxists have perpetrated their monumental intellectual fraud on the minds of men. Under their technique of the Big Lie, the worker makes the wealth, but it is stolen from him by the capitalist. So down with the capitalist exploiters! The tragedy is that many unthinking people believe this and give their allegiance to men who would destroy them.

The Marxist doctrine with its charge of exploitation has been one of the primary latter-day sources of criticism of the profit-and-loss system. In the United States another strong source of criticism has been the social gospel. Beginning in the 1870's, as a reaction to the economic turbulence of the Gilded Age, the social gospel movement waxed strong around the turn of the century. In 1908 it gave birth to the mighty Federal Council of Churches of Christ in America, which with mergers of various Protestant agencies has now become the National Council of

Churches. There have been many currents of thought in the social gospel, and some shifts of emphasis at different periods of time, but the basic conceptions of the movement can be sketched with reasonable faithfulness.

The social gospel held that environment is a primary cause of sin and that, if sinful behavior is to be minimized or eliminated, society as well as the individual must be christianized. All social institutions must be put to the test of whether or not they advance Christian ends. The social gospel held that the profit and loss system, when put to this test, is found wanting on several counts.

First, it is said, the profit motive gives selfishness, and not service, top priority. The Christian ethic requires men to sacrifice comfort, property and even their lives for others. It enjoins men to take care of themselves and their families, but primarily to help others. The profit motive, it is contended, flies in the face of this ethic. It enthrones the spirit of self-seeking and makes acquisitiveness the primary goal. Thus profit making and Christian values are in fundamental conflict.

Second, the profit-and-loss system operates through competition which is the antithesis of the cooperation envisaged in a Christian society. Competition is the tooth-and-claw rule of the jungle where the strong triumph over the weak, and the devil takes the hindmost. Competition introduces hostility where there should be mutual trust; it makes men lie, and cheat, and engage in other immoral practices; it is a denial of the principle of mutual service and a negation of the concept of the brotherhood of man.

Third, the profit-and-loss system results in great inequalities of wealth and social status. It gives power to the few to exploit the many. Inequalities of wealth poison human relations and destroy the sense of fellowship. Men crave justice in the division of the fruits of industry, but under the profit-and-loss system this is denied them. Men strongly desire respect and personal dignity, but the system depersonalizes them. It has neither heart of pity nor bowels of compassion.

Fourth, the profit-and-loss system is based on the materialistic creed of Mammon, not on values of the spirit as laid down in the teachings of Jesus. The earlier expositors of the social gospel talked a good deal about the misery and poverty of the oppressed. It was their view that the profit-and-loss system could only result in depression, starvation, and degradation for the masses. But with the increasing productivity of the economy and the rising standard of living for the whole population, the criticism has shifted to the debilitating effects of affluence. Nowadays, it is said, we have the power to produce more things than we know how to use wisely. We are caught up in a kind of materialistic rat race. We go for novelty for its own sake, self-indulgence, emulation of our neighbors, noise and superficiality. What we need is a philosophy of consumption that will direct the use of our surplus to higher and more Christian ends.

The social gospel and present-day Protestantism insist that Christianity should not be identified with any political or economic order. The gospel, it is held, is founded on the Bible and the continuing revelation of God and is morally superior to any political or economic "ism." The idea of a self-regulating market mechanism falls short of moral need and this deficiency must be met by more emphasis on Christian behavior and by controls instituted by government. The state, declared the eminent social gospeler, the Reverend Walter Rauschenbusch, has superior Christian ethics. "The state is like a breakwater pounded by heavy seas. As long as it holds let us thank God." [10]

In the depression years, some Protestant leaders believed that capitalism had reached a dead end and that some form of socialism held the most likely answer. But the godlessness of the commissars and their ruthless disregard for the lives and feelings of individuals have changed this point of view. Spiritual and cultural freedom, says the National Council of Churches, is essential in a Christian society:

> In some situations Christians have had the misconception that one sure road to economic justice is the socialization of all the major means of production. Today we have enough knowledge of what happens under a thorough-going collectivism to realize that

> uncritical recourse to the state to remedy every evil creates its own evils. It may easily become a threat to freedom as well as to efficiency. The weight of evidence shows that some use of government in relation to economic activities is essential to provide the environment in which human freedom can flourish. (But) The union of political and economic power is a dangerous road, whether it leads toward complete state control of economic life or toward control of the state by private centers of economic power. A wide distribution of centers of power and decision is important to the preservation of democratic freedom.[11]

The Catholic position on the problems of a capitalistic society was stated clearly in the encyclical of Pope Leo XIII, "The Condition of Labor" (*Rarum Novarum*—1891) and that of Pope Pius XI, "Reconstructing the Social Order," (*Quadragesimo Anno* 1931). The Holy Fathers were gravely concerned by the poverty of large masses of people, the power of the wealthy class, and the breakdown in Christian fellowship between the classes. They also were concerned by the tendency of some of the faithful to embrace Socialistic solutions. The encyclicals undertook to diagnose the cause of the difficulty and to indicate the rights and duties of the poor and the wealthy and the obligations of state and Church.

The difficulty, said the encyclicals, is that men have strayed from God's teachings. The wealthy have become hard-hearted and callous in their search for temporal possessions, and so despotic in their handling of power that "no one dare breathe against their will" (*Quadragesimo Anno* 106). Moreover, said the Holy Fathers, the one-sided division of wealth violates the rules of common justice.

The encyclicals make it clear that the institution of private property is not at fault. "Every man," says Leo XIII, "has by nature the right to possess property as his own" (*Rarum Novarum*—5). Private ownership is in accord with the natural order of things and is confirmed by the wisdom of the ages. When men own property they are more productive, better able to care for their families, and there is more peace and tranquility in the community.

The problem, say the Holy Fathers, is not private ownership of property, but the use to which it is put. Under Church rule, property is both individual and social. A man should live becomingly and he has the right to use the income from his property to provide for his family and maintain his station in life. But his superfluous income should be used for charity and for acts of beneficence and liberality. As Rarum Novarum puts it, "Whoever has received from the Divine bounty a large share of blessings, whether they be external and corporal, or gifts of the mind, has received them for the purpose of using them for perfecting his own nature, and at the same time, that he may employ them as the minister of God's province, for the benefit of others" (19).

Acts of beneficience and liberality need not be the giving of alms. The wealthy may not hoard their money, but "the investment of superfluous income in searching favorable opportunities for employment, provided the labor employed produces results which are really useful, is to be considered . . . an act of real liberality particularly appropriate to the needs of our time" (*Quadragemiso Anno* 51).

In the distribution of the product of industry, says *Quadragesimo Anno,* both the wealthy and the laborers must receive their "due share" in conformity with the demands of social justice and the common good. The worker should receive a wage that will enable him to support himself and his family in decency. It is better even when the worker, through a good wage and frugal management, can acquire a little land or property of his own. When there is an "immense number of propertyless wage earners on the one hand, and the superabundant riches of the fortunate few on the other, (it) is an unanswerable argument that the earthly goods so abundantly produced in this age of industrialism are far from rightly distributed and equitably shared among the various classes of men" (*Quadragesimo Anno* 60).

The encyclicals reject out of hand the Marxian concept that labor produces the wealth and belongs by right to the workingman. The production of goods is a collaboration between labor and capital. "Capital cannot do without labor," said Leo XIII, "and labor cannot do without capital" (*Rarum Novarum* 15).

In discussing the principles of just distribution, Pius XI says that wealth must be divided so that the common good of all classes be promoted. He then adds, "By these principles of social justice one class is forbidden to exclude the other from a share of the profits" (*Quadragesimo Anno* 57). The word "profits" is not used here in the accounting sense but more in the sense of the fruits of industry, for Pius XI goes on to say that the product of the economic system should be shared and that neither the wealthy nor the laborers should demand all for themselves. Catholic scholars point out that profits belong to the owners, but that under the teachings of the Church the owners are obligated to use them for the common good.

The encyclicals reject the tenets of socialism. The socialist state, say the Holy Fathers, abrogates the right of private property in the name of economic production and subordinates the individual, even to taking away his liberty. The socialist state pervades the family and claims the children from the father. Above all, socialism is godless. Christianity believes that the purpose of temporal existence is to earn eternal life. But socialism says that communal living was instituted merely for the material advantages it brings mankind. "No one," says *Quadragesimo Anno* flatly, "can at the same time be a sincere Catholic and true socialist" (120).

This does not mean that the ordering of economic affairs can be left to free competition without intervention by the state. Free competition, say the Holy Fathers, has resulted in tyrannical power by the few and unjust division of the wealth. The guiding principle of the economy and of all social life must be charity, defined as that "bond of perfection . . . when all sections of society have the intimate conviction that they are members of a single family and children of the same Heavenly Father" (*Quadragesimo Anno* 137). The guiding principle of moral life must come from God through the Church. The state should protect and defend the principle of social charity and "make the whole of human society conform to the common good" (*Quadragesimo Anno* 110). In this effort the state should, among other things, safeguard private property, keep competition, and particularly economic domination, within definite limits, set up a judicial order that promotes prosperity and well-being, and be especially solicitous for the welfare and the comfort of the poor. But the state should not go too far. It is an injustice and a harmful disturbance of the social order, says Quadragesimo Anno, when the wider collectivities arrogate to themselves social functions that can be efficiently performed by smaller bodies (79).

Catholic doctrine says that both the dangers of individualism and collectivism must be avoided. In the view of the American bishops, however, the trend toward collectivism has gone so far that individual responsibility is being seriously compromised. In their pastoral letter of November 25, 1960, the bishops declare that American progress in human welfare is due in large measure to personal initiative and responsibility, that people today are relinquishing their rights and responsibilities and placing greater and greater reliance on collectivism, and that personal freedom is being infringed. "We must seek to enlarge the area of personal responsibility," say the bishops, "to protect human personality from a greater encroachment on its freedom and responsibility." [12]

The great problem of religious teachers and men of affairs, of course, is to bridge the gap between the ideal and the practical world. Religious teachers and ethicists generally tend to be ends minded. They deal with values and set up the guide lines for moral striving. The profit makers, as men of affairs, are necessarily means minded. They are required to organize the realities of the work-a-day world and deal with human nature as it is.

Some of the unpopularity of the profit makers, no doubt, stems from their preoccupation with means. People have a profound need for hope and belief in a better life. To protect their beliefs they become uncritical of means and hostile to anyone who casts doubt on the soundness of a particular means suggested for a desired end. As realists the profit makers are continually pricking idealistic bubbles, dragging soaring imaginations back from the stratosphere, and demanding that men face the unpleasant facts of earthly existence. They seem always to be defending the status quo. They hesitate to talk about the promise of the future, because they see obstacles along the road to its realization. Being means minded, the profit makers frequently appear to be in opposition to the good ends.

There is no escape, however, from the necessity of dealing with means. No community can wish itself into the more perfect life. If we are to proceed soundly toward that goal we must discipline ourselves to distinguish between means and ends and be prepared to examine critically the alternatives proposed for the status quo. Will the proposed reform work as claimed? What has been the history of similar attempts? Does the plan for reform have elements of impracticability? What logic or evidence is there that the new system will work better than the present one? There is always the urge to tinker and to be doing something for the sake of action. But tinkering is not good morality either. As Professor Frank H. Knight has well said: "I wish to insist on the moral obligation to understand before acting . . . and not simply to 'monkey' with complex and sensitive machinery or apply snap judgments drawn from sentimental principles." [13]

Religious leaders are conscious of this problem. They insist on the supremacy of moral law, but they recognize that they are not equipped to write the work-a-day rules nor lay down the operative specifications for economic activities. They agree that the best answers to the problems of economic ethics are likely to be derived from a realistic understanding of how the economy works, together with an ethical sensitivity for the good ends, and a knowledge of how the means adopted affect people.

The problem of economic ethics always boils down to two basic questions: In his economic relationships how should an ethical man behave? And, secondly: How should society be organized to provide an environment which encourages ethical behavior?

In formulating his rules of conduct, the individual quickly discovers that there are no quick-and-easy answers to the ethical problems involved in profit making. Unlike the world of manners where there is an Emily Post to indicate what is proper, ethical questions always involve struggle and soul-searching and the continuous questioning: "Am I doing the right thing under these circumstances?" Guidance in these matters comes principally from one's upbringing and personal character; and these in turn are deeply influenced by religious teaching. No one can escape personal responsibility for his ethical conduct, but when questions arise he can, and does, seek the counsel of others. He may discuss his problems with his minister, or search out a person who is wise in the ways of men and who has character, or talk with his colleagues about what is right and wrong. Every management group is continually called on to make decisions that are both ethical and economic in content.

In the Christian formulation, several key words stand out to give form and structure to what is right conduct. These words include truth-telling, respect for property, justice, personal fulfillment, responsibility, stewardship, service, personal dignity, and fellowship. This list is by no means exhaustive, for everyone can add other concepts to it. But men who conduct themselves with due respect for the precepts suggested in this list can be said to behave ethically.

The Christian derives his ethical sanction from God. It is his view that God created man according to a divine plan, and that man's purpose on earth is to glorify God through communion with Him; and, through this communion, achieve love and fellowship with other men.

Every man, the Christian believes, has infinite worth and stands equal before his Creator. God knows persons as souls, not as man or woman, rich or poor, black or white, worker or boss. It is His will that the dignity of persons be respected, whatever their station in life.

Under Christian tenets, God gives every man certain talents and freedom to exercise these talents. In working out his salvation the individual is expected to fulfill this endowment to the best of his ability. God requires the individual to be responsible in the use of his freedom and the employment of his skills and demands an accounting for his stewardship of them.

The Christian holds that, while men are created equal in dignity, each person is unique and unequal in capacities. He is, therefore, predestined for human fellowship, for he could not achieve his being without association with others, as in the case of marriage, raising children, or earning a living. The key words in this fellowship are love and service. The Christian works toward fulfilling God's purpose by loving and serving his fellow man.[14]

The ethical injunctions that flow from these teachings are clear. Man should seek to fulfill himself by doing good work. He should have pride in craftsmanship and in a job well done. He should try to make the most of his talents and grow. He should help others to fulfill themselves by encouraging them, giving them opportunity for advancement and fitting them into positions where their talents can be best used.

Man should accept responsiblity for his work and his acts, make good on his guarantees, and live up to his contracts. His word should be as good as his bond. He should, insofar as possible, seek understanding before taking action.

In dealing with others, the ethical man should be just and render unto others what is their due. He should be impartial in his judgments, recognize merit, and avoid favoritism. He should give praise where praise is due and be honest in all things. He should not misrepresent his proposition or his product. Since property is a part of God's plan, the ethical man should have a proper regard for it. He should be scrupulous about what is mine and thine. He should not waste or destroy property. He should use his possessions becomingly as befits his station in life, and make his property work for the service of others.

The ethical man should respect the dignity of other persons and not offend it. He should remember that all work is important in the sight of God and to the man who is performing it; and he should have appreciation for a job well done at whatever level. The ethical man should see his work as service to his fellow man, and find his greatest satisfaction in this service. In discharging his community function, the entrepreneur must balance his books and, if possible, make a profit; but his motivation should always involve the service he can render others.

Above all, man should cultivate and strengthen human fellowship and refrain from acts that weaken or destroy it. The essence of Christian teaching is to love one's neighbor as oneself; and the working admonition of neighborliness is "Therefore all things whatsoever ye would that men should do to you, do ye even so to them" (Matthew 7-12). There are some who scoff at the Golden Rule as "Sunday schoolish" and inapplicable in the work-a-day world. But in all human utterance there is probably no advice to match this, for it combines perfectly the ideal of fellowship with eminently practical counsel on how to achieve it. Many of America's best profit makers consciously pivot their efforts around this precept, for they know that it is both profitable and right. When one treats stockholders well they supply funds for new ventures. When employees are highly regarded they cooperate enthusiastically in getting the work done. When the consumers are given an honest product at an attractive price, they buy and continue to buy.

Many companies have written credos to state what they stand for and believe in, and the thesis that constantly runs through these credos is service and the Golden rule. There is no basic conflict between ethical behavior and the making of profit. Some profit, to be sure, is made through unethical practices, but the most by far is earned through conduct that is both ethical and in the service of the community.

The second great ethical question dealing with the organization of society may be phrased this way: Does the profit-and-loss system provide a good social environment for ethical man? In answering this question, it is not enough to measure an operative system against an ideal society, for men always fall short of perfection. If the question is to be meaningful it must be rephrased to: Does the profit-and-loss system provide a better or worse ethical environment than alternative systems?

But how can alternate systems be defined for purposes of comparison? The most decisive element that differentiates social systems in the world today, and the one that is most hotly debated, is how far the state should go in organizing and regulating the life of its people. At one end of the scale is anarchism and at the other end, totalitarianism. In between are various gradations from a society with a minimum of state intervention in the economy, often called laissez-faire capitalism, to a mixed economy where organization is part private and part public, to some form of benevolent socialism, where the state undertakes to run the show through government ownership and control of the productive facilities, but tries at the same time to maintain respect for the individual.

The profit-and-loss system presupposes a political environment maintained by the state. In order to conduct commerce it is necessary to have law and order, a monetary system, standards for weights and measures, and a legal system that defines property rights, lays down the rules for contracts, and sets up a judicial apparatus for settling disputes. In the United States it has been thought necessary to have rules to preserve competition, plus laws to protect the public health and to safeguard the rights and working conditions of employees.

Since the Great Depression and World War II, the Federal government has greatly increased its organizing and controlling activities—regulating the hours, wages, and conditions of labor, providing unemployment benefits, laying down rules for issuance of securities, guaranteeing mortgages on home, fixing the price of some agricultural products and limiting the use of acreage, subsidizing shipping and low rent housing, setting up an elaborate social security system, and undertaking to counterbalance cyclical economic trends through public works and the manipulation of the money supply. More recently, powerful movements have sprung up to draw the Federal government decisively into the fields of education, urban renewal, and medical care. The most direct measure of the increased role of government in our affairs is the percentage of net national product taken in taxes by the local, state, and Federal governments. This figure has risen from ten and seven-tenths per cent in 1929 to twenty-eight and four-tenths per cent in 1959, and the trend continues to point in the upward direction. Much of this increase, to be sure, reflects the requirements of war and national defense, but in practically all categories the trend of governmental expenditure is up. Because of technological advance and increased productivity, disposable income has risen even though the three forms of government have increased their tax bite. But it should be clear that as the percentage of net national product taken by taxes rises, the proportionate area for free choice on how to spend one's income declines.

There is no clear dividing line between a capitalistic and a socialistic form of society. Up to a point the difference is one of degree. As the state increases its ownership of land and industry, as it employs a larger percentage of the work force, as the area of decision for entrepreneurs is narrowed by regulation, as distributive shares are increasingly set by political fiat, as the price system is superseded by government directive, as taxes increase and the proportion of income that is disposable declines, as people look more to the state for their security and less to themselves—in short, as economic decision is transferred from the market to the political process—we have more socialism and less capitalism. Moving along this road we are confronted with both practical and ethical questions. On the practical side, will more dependence on the political process accelerate or slow down the rising standard of living? Will we as a nation be better or worse prepared to defend ourselves and live in a troubled world? On the ethical side, will we find more justice and human fellowship along the road to statism, or will the path lead eventually to tyranny and the destruction of freedom and the dignity of men?

In assessing the possibilities it is appropriate to look down the road and identify the factors that operate under extreme conditions and which come more and more into play as we proceed along the present course. This type of analysis makes it clear that the profit-and-loss system is a superior form of economic organization well adapted for the purposes of ethical man. The argument for this conclusion can be stated in the form of six theses as follows:

The Thesis of Freedom. The profit-and-loss system allows maximum individual freedom and is therefore well suited to moral man. Morality implies a conscience and personal responsibility for the choices that are made. Morality does not mean absolute freedom to do as one chooses, for as the Irishman says: "Where my nose begins, your liberty ends." There must be a stoplight at the busy corner and accepted rules for movement in order that traffic going both ways may be free to pass. But, in a moral community the rules should be basic and minimal, for as the power of individual decision is curtailed man becomes less and less a moral man.

In the profit-and-loss system a man is entitled to the fruits of his labor and he is free, within minimal limits, to dispose of his earnings as he sees fit. He may buy in the market place or sell, and he may choose between the different buying and selling alternatives that are offered. If he wishes to assume the risk, he may quit one job and take another, or go into business for himself. He is not bound in his living by occupational class or by geography. Not all men are equal by heredity or environmental conditioning, but, given these differences, any individual may move up in the hierarchy of accomplishment as far as his talents and industry will carry him.

The profit-and-loss system is the economic expression of voluntarism. No life is free of the compulsions of nature or the pressures of a social system, but the market process affords maximum opportunity for people to do things because they want to, not because they are compelled.

The distinguishing characteristic of the political process is that it is all embracing and coercive. The law is laid down by the rulers or by the representatives of the majorities and all must conform under pain of fine, imprisonment, or even forfeiture of life itself. This characteristic of government has great social advantages. Among other things, it gives the state the power to get things done in the name of the common good. But it is also the point of greatest danger, for in coercive power lies the seed of tyranny. This is why the Founding Fathers were so careful to circumscribe the power of government, setting up a system of checks and balances and going to great pains to indicate what the state was not permitted to do.

One of the great moral flaws of modern liberalism is its penchant for knowing what is good for the other fellow and its willingness to coerce the other man for his own good. When the state becomes monolithic this moral deficiency is elevated to the status of a virtue. The state defines the common goal and the individual must conform. There is little room for individual taste and certainly none for dissent. The state claims the whole man and is jealous of associations like the family, the church, and the lodge, even to the point of making it impossible for them to exist.

It is often said that the control of economic activity can be divorced from other aspects of life. This is a great delusion. As Professor Hayek has pointed out, economic striving is always in the service of other ends.[15] People seek money because this medium opens a wide range of choice. As the state increases its control over economic means, it invariably enlarges its control over ends. It decides what is for the individual and common good and allocates economic means only for these purposes. No one should ever make the mistake of assuming that economic freedom can be divorced from political, religious, and cultural freedoms. As Alexander Hamilton reminded us, "Power over a man's subsistence is power over his will." Even more vivid is the statement by Leon Trotsky, the colleague of Lenin. Said Trotsky:

> In a country where the sole employer is the State, opposition means death by slow starvation. The old principle: who does not work shall not eat, has been replaced by a new one: who does not obey shall not eat.[16]

The Thesis of Service. In an ethical system the virtue of mutual service always is given high rank. In his relationship with others, a man is morally required to help not hurt his fellow man. The profit-and-loss system provides some very effective social apparatus for carrying out this requirement. In a competitive economy, the supplier seeks out the need of the consumer and tries to best his competitors in satisfying these needs, both with respect to price and quality. The consumer is the judge of the service offered. If his judgments favor one supplier over another the favored supplier is rewarded with patronage and presumably profits. The incentives are placed on service and the ethical motivation of the supplier is strongly backed up by material penalties and rewards.

When a company makes a profit, some of it goes into the pockets of the owners as compensation for the use of their savings, but one-third to one-half is normally reinvested in the business to produce more and better goods and services for the consumers. Thus the service function of profit pyramids—the rendering of a service produces a profit and some of the profit is re-cycled to produce more service. This, of course, was what Pope Pius XI was talking about when he wrote in *Quadragesimo Anno* that the investment of superfluous income to create opportunity for employment in useful work was an act of real liberality.

The profit-and-loss system serves the values of the parties involved in exchange. Since men have vices as well as virtues, the law of mutual service operates in socially disapproved areas as well as those that are approved. Profits can be made by selling narcotics to drug addicts as well as to hospitals for the relief of pain or by distributing pornographic literature as well as by selling text books to schools. The values that exist in the community are influenced by the offerings in the market, but mostly they are instilled in the individual in the home, the school, the church, the labor union, the lodge, the corporation, and other groups. Values naturally differ among individuals, religious sects, races, and socio-economic groups, and the market serves them all. Interestingly enough, in a market society everyone is free to be an ethicist, for if one does not like the present standard of values he is free to formulate his own, proselyte them, and go as far as he can find support.

When the power of bargaining between the parties to exchange is one-sided, one party may take advantage or exploit the other party's extreme need. This situation has been and is of concern to ethically minded men, but, in making adjustments in the rules governing the competitive market system, great humility and extraordinary insight is needed lest the changes invoked in the name of justice introduce more injustice than already is involved.

Understanding Profits

The critics of the profit-and-loss system concentrate their observations largely on the acquisitive side of the equation and neglect the service side. In an ethical system people should behave in a given way because it is right, not because in this way lies reward. But it is reassuring that the rightness of ethical behavior is repeatedly validated in terms of tangible reward as well as in matters of the spirit. Successful businessmen know that service and profits are two side of the same coin. They first look at the need or service side of the coin before looking at the profit side. If they can find a need which they can satisfy more advantageously than other suppliers, then and only then are they able to turn their minds realistically to a calculation of what profits can be expected. Without doubt, some profits stem from the worst expressions of avarice, greed, cheating and lawlessness; but most profits are earned in mutual service where both parties to the transaction gain.

In the profit-and-loss system a man must serve in order to gain, but as the economy moves under the control of the state, men organize pressure groups and engage in high politics in order to grab. We can feel most confident about the ethical implications of an economic system if it rewards those who serve their fellow men, with the parties to the exchange judging the merit of the service. In appraising proposed changes in our economic system, we will be well advised if we ask: Does the new system put the premium on service, and who is to have final say about the service, the individual, a private group, or the state?

The Thesis of Democratic Allocation of Power. Power is heady stuff and the allocation and handling of power pose hard ethical questions. Under the market system, where competition is operative, the leaders who gain power are the ones who have provided an economic service that pleases the consumer. They are the entrepreneurial candidates, as it were, who have won the consumer's plebiscite. Since the markets are open every working day, they must continually validate their right to hold economic office. That this is a tenuous right is indicated by the statistics of business failure, by the shifts in company leadership of industry and by the constant replacement of company men who fail to measure up to the demands of the consumers.

Where economic privilege is entrenched and beyond the power of consumer control, it is frequently because of special grants by the state. The test of competition is hard and many businessmen shrink from it, but in a well ordered capitalistic society the privilege of entrepreneurial property should be accompanied by the requirement that suppliers either submit themselves to the vote of the consumers or, as in the case of natural monopolies, to the regulation of public service commissions. It should be the business of the state to lay down the rules that are necessary to preserve and make effective the continual referendum of the consumers.

As social organization moves away from the capitalistic to the political process and as the state becomes more monopolistic in its practices, the allocation of power involves great ethical hazards. Under these circumstances, as Professor Hayek has aptly phrased it, "The worst get on top." This is true for several reasons. As the pyramid of power grows larger the prizes for wielding this power increase, and men are tempted to seize them with little regard for ethical norms. Large corporations sometimes become the target of unscrupulous exploiters and honest labor leaders are called on to fend off the thugs and racketeers who would gain control of the union to feather their own nests.

Again, as society becomes more monolithic, people must be bent increasingly to the common will. This calls for a ruling elite whose moral sense is so dulled that they can accept a dictated hierarchy of values for themselves and force them on others. Since it is easier to get men to agree on negative programs than on positive ones, the rulers usually summon a devil—a Jew, a kulak, a Yanqui imperialist—on whom to spew their hate, and party members find it convenient to dedicate their vices to the service of the state. To act in behalf of the group seems to free people from many of the moral restraints which control their behavior as individuals living within a group. The end begins to justify the means. The good of the whole is the standard of what ought to be done, and there is nothing that the party man must be unprepared to do if it serves the state. As William Shirer indicates in *The Rise and Fall of the Third Reich,* the tragedy of the German people was their obeisance to the fiendish brutality of the Nazi rulers and their tolerance of a social order that violated every standard of human decency.

In a market society people may be motivated by ignoble motives, but no one is ever alloted much power, and when the grant of power is given, it is subject to being taken away when the leader no longer pleases his constituents. Actually the American millionaire has trifling power compared with the power of the local gauleiter in a socialist society.

It is a delusion to think that in the American democracy the Constitution in reality guarantees the right of the people to grant or withhold power from political aspirants. The Constitution expresses the principle of limited government, but the real force is the people's belief in this principle, backed up by an atomization of power in the political, economic, and cultural spheres, making it difficult for anyone to gain a monopoly. The capitalistic system, with its diversification of economic power and its perpetual market test of leadership, is basic to the American proposition. If we want a society where ethical norms can prevail, we must be forever reluctant to yield to monopoly in the economic realm or any other phase of our society.

The Thesis of Market Distributive Justice. In a market society a person acquires the goods and services of others to the extent that he supplies others with goods and services that they desire and value. Exchange is voluntary and each man earns only what others are willing to supply him voluntarily. In simple societies exchange is man to man and personal; in complex societies exchange becomes impersonal and it is impossible to know the effect on people of a chain of transactions.

Since men are of different talent, of different circumstance, and even of different luck, the fruits of production are distributed unevenly, with some receiving more than others. It is difficult to visualize a society of economic equals. If all men started the economic race evenly today, inequality would appear tomorrow because some men were born to run faster or are better trained to run. The division of labor itself requires inequality in skill, for a man who is a good piano player has little time to learn how to carpenter, and a surgeon who can repair a valve in a human heart probably would be helpless to deal with a valve in an automobile engine.

The market system distributes goods with a rough justice, using economic criteria as the guide. Without doubt, some people are shunted to the end of the line and receive less than they need to sustain body and soul. All societies set up systems of charity or special aid to care for these unfortunates, but even here the problem of distributive justice remains for it is still necessary to determine what standard of living they are entitled to.

If the distribution of goods is to be effected by other than a market system, some standard of justice must be set up in its place. One standard is the communist theory of absolute equality—from each according to his abilities, to each according to his needs—but this has never worked. Even the Russians, who give it lip service, have gone hard over to incentive payments.

In the United States the distributive justice of the market place is modified with laws favoring the interests of various pressure groups. Certain goods are protected by tariffs, prices on some agricultural products are fixed, mass housing is subsidized, and labor unions are permitted to monopolize industries and withhold services until wage demands are met. Is it fair to protect the price of peanuts but not of rutabagas? Is it just to raise the tariff on glassware but not on automobiles? Is it right to subsidize rents with tax monies, so that the recipient can buy a better television set? If the control of the economy by the state is to be extended, is there anything in human experience that indicates that the commissar will mete out more distributive justice than the market?

There is, of course, no such thing as a pure market in a social vacuum. Markets are governed by rules and circumstances, and market justice obviously is conditioned by these factors. But as some of the Medieval Schoolmen found in their search for the just price, the market place, with its competitive bids and offers, achieves a rough economic justice that is pretty hard to match by conscious control.

The problem of distributive justice will always be with us. If we solve it tolerably well today, it will be out of balance tomorrow since no social equilibrium ever lasts very long. The market system, where men can freely buy and sell and where service is rewarded through the judgment of the parties to the exchange, has provided one practical answer. This system, supplemented with aid to those who have fallen below the levels of a decent existence have carried us far. To look in the direction of increased political apportionment of goods for more ethical solutions to the problem of distribution is likely to repeat historical errors. The perfection of the market process still holds the best promise for justice in giving each man his share of the community product.

The Thesis of Cooperation Through Competition. Competition has been continually pictured as the tooth and claw rule of the jungle and the negation of human cooperation and fellowship. Actually, competition is a remarkable system for cooperation that can and does bring out the best in men.

When teams organize to compete, they must achieve a high degree of cooperation between the members if they are to succeed. The term "cooperative" usually is applied to economic associations where men pool their buying and selling. A corporation, however, might well be called a cooperative for it is an association where men earn their living by working together to produce goods and services. In a corporation the terms of cooperation are different from those in a buyers' or growers' association, but far more economic activity occurs under the corporate form of cooperation than any other, and therefore the term "cooperative" is fully deserved.

For the wider society, competition provides a social apparatus whereby free men can cooperate without being subjected to the control of a dictator or supreme authority. As a matter of fact, competition is the only method yet devised where the activities of free men in a whole society can be coordinated and adjusted without the use of coercion by a higher sovereignty. In a competitive system men are free to enter a market or not as they choose, free to buy and sell, and to effect exchange at any price agreeable to the parties of interest. The primary information that emerges from a market is price. With this information individuals or economic cooperatives can produce more or less, change styles or features, move goods from one area to another, employ more or fewer people, or make whatever changes are necessary to gear these activities with the whole.

It is said that as the division of labor proliferates and society grows more complex, the need for conscious control by a central direction increases. But no central director can hope to visualize the infinite ramifications of economic activity that take place in a nation, or the values that people want served, or the complex system of interpersonal relations that are built to conduct the community's housekeeping. One practical answer to this question is decentralization, with authority and responsibility being pushed as close to the scene of action as possible. With decentralization must go coordination and this function can be supplied either by central direction or by competition in the marketplace. Coordination through competition has many imperfections, but the experience with coordination through central direction for an economy as a whole is even less reassuring. Economic confusion and inefficiency quickly descends on a country when the Office of Price Administration undertakes to substitute central direction for market control. If central control is insisted on, police methods of enforcement quickly follow, and individual freedom disappears.

Competition, it is true, makes skills obsolete, takes away men's livelihood, renders some property worthless and causes pain and injury to those who lose in the competition. But this is the inevitable price of progress. It is impossible to visualize progress without someone being discomfited or getting hurt. The question is whose interests should take precedence and be served. The only tenable answer, it would seem, is that the consumer's interests should take precedence over those of the producer. Most adult males and some adult females are producers in the economic sense, but everyone in the population is a consumer. The consumers of a company's product almost always outnumber those employed in its production and distribution. Producers continually seek to vest their interests; they limit admission to a trade, ask for tax exemptions, seek official specifications that favor their product—but the community should be extremely reluctant to grant any producing groups a haven from the market test. As a matter of fact, the producer who demands protection for his interests as a consumer usually denies similar protection to his suppliers.

In requiring producers to stand up to the market test it is possible that the community may at times want to extend special aid to the losers in the competitive race to help them readjust. But such aid should be of a temporary nature. In the case of agriculture we have the ironic situation of government countermanding the decision of the market and at great cost trying to sweep back the tide of technological progress. Since the Revolution in 1776 farmers have been leaving their farms to improve their fortunes through work in other industries, and this trend away from an agricultural economy has been marked by a spectacular rise in the national standard of living. If the principle that the consumer's interest should take precedence over the producer's interest were applied, the agricultural problem in the United States would be quickly solved to everyone's advantage.

The fact that competition provides a favorable environment for progress is one more point in its favor. Progress comes from non-conformists who must be free to differ from established norms and who need the opportunity of offering their new formulations to the public for judgment. When economic activity is carried on by many groups in competition with each other, almost every dissenter can find a backer to exploit his unorthodox ideas. If the new idea catches on with the consuming public, the status quo, with all its vestments, is altered or swept aside and change occurs.

An examination of the profit on investment data for individual companies (in Appendix C3), shows that companies with a good record for innovation are the ones that tend to earn the most profit. Increased control over one's environment is not an ethical imperative, but man's quest for knowledge is a very strong force in human affairs, and the results from this quest at least give moral man better instruments to use in seeking his ends, whatever they may be.

In thinking about the ethics of competition, it is not a question of whether a society will or will not have rivalry among individuals and groups. The issue is what form will such rivalry take. In a society dominated by the state, competition tends to take the form of bootlicking for special privileges. In a market society competition takes the form of rivalry to serve the consumer and make a profit. The fellowship of man requires, not the abolition of competition, but the channeling of man's competitive urge so that it serves the interests of himself and others.

The Thesis of Material Abundance. Scarcity of economic goods, with resultant poverty, has long plagued mankind, and beginning with the preachings of Jesus, has been of central concern to the church. Repeatedly through the centuries churchmen have been admonished to open their hearts and pocketbooks to the poor. According to Christian tradition, Jesus fed the multitudes by performing the miracle of the loaves and fishes, but mortal man is denied these powers. Some societies, however, have learned how to increase the production of goods to the point at which almost everyone has enough to eat, clothes to wear, a house to live in and sufficient domestic accessories to make living attractive, with leisure to spare. The secret is a simple one: men put aside a portion of their product for tools and equipment, and use these tools to produce more goods with fewer man-hours of work. When this capitalistic process has been encouraged by respect for private property, freedom to buy and sell, and the incentive of profit, the creative capacities of people have been released and the problem of poverty has been largely solved.

Compassion is a moral virtue and it is assuaged by the giving of alms. But no one would wish to keep some people in poverty in order that others might have the satisfaction of giving alms. As the encyclicals of Pope Leo XIII and Pius XI have pointed out, it is good to raise men from the status of the poor to the status of men with possessions, however small, so that they can care for their families and lift their heads with the dignity of men who have some control over their environment.

Most religious teachers agree that the satisfaction of physical want and enough leisure for contemplation of spiritual things are necessary for a moral life. Most agree, too, that the profit and loss system has produced economic goods and leisure in abundance. But the path of virtue is never smooth, and with abundance comes the temptation to mammonism, which leads men to become so preoccupied with material possessions that they neglect their spiritual life. Mammonism, of course, is as old as Christianity. It was Jesus who in the Sermon on the Mount declared, "Ye cannot serve God and Mammon" (Matthew 6:24). With each step along the way, from the simple agricultural existence of Biblical times to the life of modern suburbia, men have had to pause and ask whether they were keeping their interests in material and spiritual things in balance. Spiritual leaders have been inclined to pass a negative judgment. The Reverend Walter Rauschenbusch, whose eloquent voice preached the social gospel around the turn of the century, felt that women's styles, with their constant novelty and change, were excessively commercialized and mammonistic. To him the dress of the old-fashioned Quaker lady and the Salvation Army lass was a simple and angelic style that "sets off womanly sweetness and individuality wonderfully well." [17]

The problem of defining mammonism is complicated by the fact that yesterday's luxury is today's necessity. Is it mammonistic when the farmer's wife wants a refrigerator or the surburban lady wishes to deck herself out in Easter finery? Probably the advice of Clement given eighteen hundred years ago is still applicable. People should banish their anxious cares and their morbid excitement about their material possessions. Their material goods should be the means to higher ends, and the division of their time should achieve a reasonable balance between material and spiritual interests.

It is probably fair to say that profit makers have given more thought to production than to distribution, both because they are impressed by the obstacles that must be overcome to achieve production and by the belief that goods must be produced before they can be distributed. Religious leaders focus more on distribution. Their interest is distributive justice and succor for the weak. Most people agree that a better accommodation of these two points of view is needed. The idea of sharing poverty is neither attractive nor necessary. What is needed is a social environment that encourages abundance and organizes incentives to stimulate men to produce and distribute the fruits of their labor so that all may have a sufficient share.

Karl Marx advanced the theory that complete organization of society by the state is an imperative of history and this idea has gained wide currency. Many people think that modern problems are so complex and all-embracing that nothing short of central control will be sufficient to cope with them. They have lost faith in the organizational principles of voluntarism, capitalism, and decentralization, and embrace the order and coercive authority of the Federal State.

It would be foolish to deny that technological advance, population shifts, and social change raise problems that call for new solutions. The coming of airplanes that can fly faster than the speed of sound obviously requires central traffic control across state and city boundaries, and the protection of cities from the risk of atomic explosion may call for some form of reinsurance through the medium of the state.

But there is nothing in the evidence that indicates that central direction and control is an imperative of history. There are no deterministic forces in nature that are required to find their sequel in an all-powerful state. It is only thinking that makes it so. Free human beings who are conscious of and responsible for their acts can have any form of society they wish.

One organizational hypothesis is to have central government with its coercive sanctions take over more of the functions of local government, increase the dependence of the individual on the state, channel more of the nation's income through the tax structure, and transfer economic decisions from the market place to the political process. Experience with this hypothesis is not reassuring. It has produced neither material abundance nor an ethical society where free men can live in justice and human brotherhood.

A second hypothesis is to seek solutions to social problems at the local level, emphasize personal initiative and mutual self-help, and encourage capitalistic enterprise to perform the nation's housekeeping. In our national experience this hypothesis, as the Catholic bishops remind us, has produced good results. The American people need to search their souls on which road to follow, for their future greatly depends on the decision they make.

NOTES

Chapter One

1. *U.S. News & World Report,* September 6, 1957.
2. *New York Times,* January 14, 1958; also "Union Monopoly vs. The Public Mind," Ernest R. Breech, *Vital Speeches,* Vol. 24, April 1958, p. 379.
3. *U.S. News & World Report,* June 8, 1959.
4. Management uses the same debating trick to show that profits have lagged. Industry's favorite base years for argument by comparison are 1948 and 1950. In these years profits were at their Post-War peaks, and comparisons with subsequent years naturally show declines.
5. *Hearings*—Congressional Joint Economic Committee, January 31, 1957.
6. *AFL-CIO News,* March 10, 1956.
7. *U.S. News & World Report,* September 6, 1957.
8. *New York Herald Tribune,* April 27, 1959.
9. *U.S. News & World Report,* September 6, 1957.
10. *New York Times,* January 14, 1958.
11. *New York Times,* April 9, 1952.
12. *New York Times,* April 10, 1952.

Chapter Two

1. In the early days of opinion sampling socio-economic quotas were drawn up and interviewers were asked to find and interview respondents with the characteristics indicated. This left the selection of respondents to the interviewer and normally resulted in a sample skewed toward upper income and better educated respondents since these people were easier to interview. Modern sampling techniques now proceed by probability methods where the selection of respondents is removed from the interviewer's discretion and follow selection methods that approach randomness. The number of cases required for an adequate sample varies with the demands of the study. Nationwide samples drawn for the Public Opinion Index are usually in excess of 1,000 cases.
2. The ten-cent-an-hour wage increase would have been approximately six per cent at the average weekly wage in manufacturing.

Chapter Three

1. Paton, William A. and A. C. Littleton, *An Introduction to Corporate Accounting Standards.*
2. *Accounting Review,* July 1947.
3. *Price Level Changes and Financial Statements,* p. 126.
4. As tabulated in "Steel Prices, Profits, Productivity and Wages," by Jules Backman for the U. S. Steel Corporation, p. 70.
5. "Effect of Inflation on Capital and Profits: The Record of 9 Steel Companies," *The Journal of Accounting,* Vol. 87, No. 1, January 1949.
6. Department of Commerce Data for Inventory and Depreciation Distortion are given in Appendix A.
7. *Accounting Review,* Vol. 23, April 1948, pp. 115-136.
8. *Congressional Record,* June 19, 1958.
9. *Fortune,* May 1959.
10. James C. Nelson in "Railroad Transportation and Public Policy" says: "Deferral of income taxes under accelerated amortization has raised the 1951-1955 rates of return on net investment of Class I railroads by almost one-half of one per cent. Had the

entire income tax liability been paid in that period without benefit of tax credits from rapid amortization, the average rate of return would have been 3.45 per cent instead of 3.92 per cent." (Washington: Brookings Institution, 1959).

11. Terborgh, George, *Amortization in World War II* (Chicago: Machinery and Allied Products Institute), p. 29.
12. Committee on Ways and Means, *Tax Revision Hearings,* January 15, 1958.
13. Capital may in effect be "borrowed" in other ways, i.e., through accounts payable, use of machinery and equipment supplied by the purchaser, postponement of taxes through accelerated depreciation, etc.

Chapter Four

1. See Appendix B for tabulation of loss experience.

Chapter Five

1. *Business Week,* September 1, 1959.
2. *Survey of Current Business,* December 1955.
3. For the sake of simplicity it is assumed that total supply is given and that all producers manufacture and sell identical amounts of the same product.
4. Powell, Jack Richard, *The Mexican Petroleum Industry: 1938-1950* (Berkeley: University of California Press, 1956), p. 9.
5. The most successful oil companies in the United States, according to the First National City Bank of New York, earned an average of fourteen and three tenths per cent on their investment for the decade ending in 1959.
6. *Mexico City News,* January 1959.
7. British Nationalized Transport Industry Statistics.
8. Von Mises, Ludwig, *Bureaucracy* (New Haven; Yale University Press, 1944).
9. *Fortune,* September 1959.

Chapter Six

1. See Appendix C-1 for detailed industry statistics on percentage of earnings paid out in dividends.
2. *U.S. News & World Report,* September 6, 1957.
3. Gross national product is defined as the market value of the output of goods and services produced by the nation's economy before deduction of depreciation charges and other allowances for consumption of capital. It is measured by the purchases of goods and services by consumers and government and by "gross private investment," i.e., the acquisition of newly produced capital goods by private business and nonprofit institutions, including housing, change in inventories and change in net foreign investment.
4. "Capital Formation Under Free Enterprise," National Association of Manufacturers.
5. p. 143.
6. Among American economists, Dahlberg is the foremost exponent of the use of engineering models and flow systems to explain economic relationships. His "National Income Visualized" (Columbia University Press) and his "Money in Motion" (John de Graff, New York) are recommended to any reader who desires a simple explanation of how the economy works.
7. See, for example, *The Capitalist Manifesto,* Louis O. Kelso and Mortimer Adler (New York: Random House, 1958), pp. 210-212.

Chapter Seven

1. Gordon, Clinton S. and Harold J. Ruttenberg, *The Dynamics of Industrial Democracy,* p. 6.
2. This figure would be a trifle higher if the influence of rapid amortization were allowed for.
3. *The Economic Almanac,* 1959, p. 203.
4. *Progress in Productivity and Pay,* p. 12.
5. The difference between labor's share (forty per cent) of value added and the employee's share (eighty-four per cent) of the employee-profit dollar is, of course, due to the fact that value

added includes taxes and costs like insurance, research, advertising, etc., as well as wages and profits, thereby increasing the size of the base against which labor's share is compared.

6. "Changes in the Functional Distribution of Income," *Journal American Statistical Association,* June 1953.
7. "The Functional Distribution of Income in the United States, 1850-1952," *Review of Economics and Statistics,* May 1954.
8. "The Relative Importance of Labor Claims, Property Claims, Tax Claims," National Industrial Conference Board *Studies in Business Economics,* May 1959, No. 64.
9. "Argument for 'Creeping' Inflation," *New York Times,* March 8, 1959.
10. Under the Federal Reserve System the minimum reserves required are seven per cent to twenty per cent.
11. *Wall Street Journal,* March 30, 1959.
12. Speech before the Associated Press as reported in *The Wall Street Journal,* April 22, 1959.
13. *Handbook of Labor Statistics* (1947). *Monthly Labor Review.* Also see "The Sources of Union Gains," Gordon Tullock (Virginia: The Thomas Jefferson Center for Studies in Political Economy, University of Virginia) *Research Monograph 2.*
14. Brozen, Yale, "Manpower, Productivity and Costs," (Chicago: Industrial Relations Center, University of Chicago).
15. *America's Needs and Resources,* (1955 Edition), p. 40.
16. Fabricant, Solomon, "Basic Facts on Productivity Change," (*Occasional Paper #63,* National Bureau of Economic Research. Unweighted man-hour series).
17. Oliver, John W., *History of American Technology* (New York: Ronald Press, 1956). Gives a good account of the advance in technology.
18. Dewhurst, J. Frederic and Associates, *America's Needs and Resources* (New York: Twentieth Century Fund, 1955 edition), p. 908.
19. *Ibid.,* p. 903.
20. *Ibid.,* pp. 40 and 116.
21. Kuznets, Simon, *Capital Formation and Financing* (National Bureau of Economic Research).
22. "Capital and Output Trends in Manufacturing Industries, 1880-1948," *Occasional Paper #41,* National Bureau of Economic Research.

23. Capital in manufacturing averages about $15,000 per employee which is about double that shown in Chart 17 for the work force as a whole. Capital per job holder includes borrowed as well as invested capital.
24. "The Relative Importance of Labor Claims, Property Claims, Tax Claims," National Industrial Conference Board *Studies in Business Economics*, May 1959, No. 64.
25. The Bureau computes this series by dividing its index of total payrolls in all manufacturing by its index of the volume of manufacturing production.
26. See especially: Slichter, Sumner, "Union Policies and Industrial Management;" Daykin, Walter L., "Featherbedding," *The Labor Law Journal*, November 1956.
27. *Ibid.*, Slichter, p. 169.
28. *U.S. News & World Report*, November 9, 1959.
29. *The Impact of the Union*, pp. 222-3.
30. The late Sumner Slichter called it a system of "industrial jurisprudence."
31. *Chicago Daily News*, April 2, 1959.
32. *Congressional Record*, April 22, 1959.

Chapter Eight

1. *The Christian Century*, August 19, 1953.
2. William Bradford of Plymouth.
3. *Ibid.*, pp. 120-121.
4. Martin, James J., *Men Against the State*, p. 15.
5. See Bienstock, G., Schwarz, S., and Yugow, A., *Management in Russian Industry and Agriculture*. Also Gorden, Manya Strunsky, *Workers Before and After Lenin* (New York: Dutton, 1951).
6. *New York Times*, September 28, 1959.
7. For a very readable analysis of government intervention in agriculture, see *The Great Farm Problem*, by William H. Peterson (Chicago: H. Regnery Co., 1959).
8. *U.S. News & World Report*, October 1959. Also see Chart 15.
9. See von Mises, Ludwig, *Human Action* (New Haven: Yale University Press, 1949), Part 4. Also, Knight, Frank H., *Risk, Uncertainty and Profit* (Boston: Houghton Mifflin Co., 1921) for an elaboration of this point of view.

10. Many writers take issue with the idea that profit maximization is the primary motive of corporate officers. William Baumol, *Business Behavior, Value and Growth* (New York: Macmillan, 1959) thinks executives are more interested in sales volume than profitability. Richard Eells, *The Meaning of Modern Business,* (New York: Columbia University Press, 1960) says that corporate goals are the extension of the values of the flesh and blood people who manage companies, hence prestige, power, leadership and other values drive the corporation on, as well as desire for profit.
    Granting that there is no such thing as pure economic motivation, the concept of long term profit maximization is still the best explanatory principle for corporate behavior. Company heads are required to make decisions on a constant stream of alternate courses—should we make the part or sub-contract it; should we borrow money or sell preferred stock. The guiding principle for these decisions is and must be: which course will produce the most profit over the long run. Should company heads become more interested in prestige than profit, the income statement will sooner or later furnish them an ugly reminder of the economic facts of life. In the writer's experience, the command decisions in corporations that brook no interference are usually those that are closely geared to profitability.
11. "The Customer is Sometimes Right," *New York Times,* November 29, 1959.
12. Hayek, Friedrick, *The Road to Serfdom* (Chicago: University of Chicago Press, 1955), Chapter IV.
13. Orwell, George, *1984* (New York: New American Library of World Literature, Inc., 1954).

Chapter Nine

1. Smith also classified land as a monopoly on the ground that the supply was fixed.
2. Knight, Frank H., *Risk, Uncertainty and Profit* (Boston: Houghton Mifflin Co., 1921).
3. In the Dominican Republic, Trujillo, "The Benefactor," has provided a good case study of how a dictator can build a lucrative business monopoly by controlling the State. See "Tycoon Trujillo.

Boycotts and Kickbacks Help Dominican Ruler Build Business Empire," *Wall Street Journal,* March 9, 1960.
4. *American Capitalism* (Boston: Houghton Mifflin, 1952), p. 46.
5. *Economics*—Fourth Edition (New York: McGraw-Hill, 1958), p. 488.
6. Temporary National Economic Committee, Investigation of Concentration of Economic Power, Final Report and Recommendations; S. Doc. 35.77, Congress 1 Session, p. 11.
7. *Ibid.,* p. 9.
8. *Steel Labor,* November 1959, p. 11.
9. *The Public Opinion Index,* Opinion Research Corporation, April 1955.
10. p. 316.
11. Chamberlin, *Toward a More General Theory of Value* (New York: Oxford Press, 1957).
12. Kaplan, A. D. H., *Big Enterprise in a Competitive System* (Washington: Brookings Institution, 1954), p. 51.
13. "Industrial Prices and Their Inflexibility," Gardner Means, *Senate Document 13,* January 17, 1935, First Session, p. 12.
14. Part 1 (1939), p. 143.
15. "The Structure of Industry," *TNEC Monograph 27,* p. 404.
16. Galbraith, J. K. and H. S. Dennison, *Modern Competition and Business Policy* (New York, Oxford, 1938), Chapter 3.
17. Chamberlain, John, *The Roots of Capitalism* (Princeton: D. Van Nostrand Co., Inc., 1959), p. 157.
18. Kaplan, p. 45.
19. *Ibid.,* p. 142.
20. *Ibid.,* p. 99.

Chapter Ten

1. Addystone Pipe and Steel Co. v. United States—175 US 211 (1899).
2. United States v. Trenton Potteries—273 US 392 (1927).
   United States v. Socony—310 US 150 (1940).
   Agreements between competitors to fix prices are not always conclusively presumed to be illegal. In Board of Trade v. United States (246 US 231-1918) the Board's rule prohibiting purchases after the close of business at any price other than the closing bid

was held not to violate Section 1 of the Sherman Act, because the enforcement of the rule had no appreciable effect on general market prices. In Appalachian Coals, Inc. v. United States (288 US 344-1933) the agreement of the bituminous coal operators in the Appalachian district to sell their products through a common selling agent which fixed the price for all the producers in the area, was held lawful as not having an anticompetitive effect on the general market and as a justifiable device in a depressed market.

3. Klors, Inc. v. Broadway-Hale Stores,
   Fashion Originators Guild v. Federal Trade Commission,
   International Salt Co. v. United States, 332 US 392 (1947).
4. American Tobacco v. the United States—328 US 781 (1946).
   United States v. Griffith—334 US 100 (1948).
5. Standard Oil of California v. United States, 337 US 293, 299 (1949).
6. 201 F2nd 534 (1953) Cert. Denied 345 US 942.
7. 334 US 495 at 523 (1948).
8. Indiana Farmer's Guide Publishing Co. v. Prairie Farmer Publishing Co. 293 US 268 (1934).
9. United States v. Paramount Pictures 334 US 131 (1948).
10. United States v. duPont, 351 US 377 (1953).
11. United States v. U.S. Steel Corporation, 251 US 417 (1920).
12. U.S. v. Aluminum Co. 148 F 2d 416 (1945).
13. 334 US 108 (1948).
14. Federal Trade Commission v. Cement Institute 333 US 683 (1948). American Tobacco Co. v. US, 328 781 (1946).
15. Triangle Conduit and Cable Co. v. Federal Trade Commission, 168 F2d 175 (1948).
16. Theatre Enterprise v. Paramount Film, 346 US 537 (1948).
17. Thatcher Manufacturing Co. v. Federal Trade Commission, 272 US 554 (1926).
18. United States v. Columbia Steel, 334 US 495 (1948).
19. Pillsbury Mills, Inc., F.T.C. Docket No. 6000, Order and Remand, Dec. 21, 1953 50 FTC 555.
20. U.S. v. Bethlehem Steel Corporation and Youngstown Sheet and Tube Company, U.S. District Court, Southern New York Civil (No. 115-328).
21. U.S. v. Brown Shoe Co., G. R. Kinney Co., Inc., and G. R. Kinney Corporation 179 F Supp 721 Appeal filed April 1, 1960. See also Mergers and Markets, An Economic Analysis of Case Law, Na-

tional Industrial Conference Board, Studies in Business Economics No. 69, 1960.

22. Terborgh, George, *Price Control Devices in NRA Codes* (Washington: Brookings, 1934).
23. Schlesinger, Arthur M. Jr., *The Coming of the New Deal* (Boston: Houghton Mifflin Co., 1959), p. 122.
24. *Ibid.*, p. 135.
25. "A Marketing Appraisal of the Robinson-Patman Act," *Journal of Marketing,* July 1959.
26. Stocking, George W. and Myron W. Walker, *Monopoly and Free Enterprise* (New York: Twentieth Century Fund), p. 370.
27. "Effective Competition and the Antitrust Laws," Morris Adelman, *Harvard Law Review,* September 1948, pp. 1331-1332.
28. "The Robinson-Patman Act—Is It In The Public Interest?" *Proceedings of the American Bar Association,* Section of Antitrust Law for 1952, pp. 60-75.
29. *Journal of Marketing,* July 1959.
30. Samuel H. Moss, Inc. v. Federal Trade Commission, F2d 453 (1943).
31. Corn Products Refining Co. v. Federal Trade Commission. 324 US 726 (1945).
32. Federal Trade Commission v. Morton Salt Co. 334 US 37 (1948).
33. Federal Trade Commission Dockets 3977.5620.5624 (1953).
34. Federal Trade Commission Docket 5675 (1954).
35. Federal Trade Commission Docket 5897 (1955).
36. Federal Trade Commission Docket 6232 (1956).
37. Whitaker Cable Corporation v. Federal Trade Commission 239 F 2d 253,256 (7th Amend. 1956).
38. Rostow, Eugene, *Planning for Freedom: The Public Law of American Capitalism* (New Haven: Yale University Press, 1959).
39. Berle, A. A. Jr., *The 20th Century Capitalist Revolution* (New York: Harcourt, Brace and Co., Inc., 1954).
40. "Toward a Concept of Workable Competition," *American Economic Review,* Vol. 30, No. 2, Part 1, pp. 241-56.
41. Griffin, Clare E., *An Economic Approach to Anti-Trust Problems,* American Enterprise Association, 1951, p. 22.
42. Markham, Jesse W., "An Alternative Approach to the Concept of Workable Competition," *American Economic Review,* June 1950, pp. 349-61.
43. Machlup, Fritz, *The Political Economy of Monopoly* (Baltimore: Johns Hopkins Press, 1952), p. 182.

44. Von Mises, Ludwig, *Human Action* (New Haven: Yale University Press, 1949), p. 363.
45. Office of Price Administration, *General Standards for Setting Maximum Prices, OPA Manual,* Vol. 5, Chapter 5, Section 5-5303 (Washington: n.d).
46. Harris, Seymour E., *Price and Related Controls in the United States* (New York: McGraw-Hill, 1945).
47. "Price Control in a Defense Economy," National Industrial Conference Board, *Studies in Business Economics,* No. 26, December 1950, p. 57.
48. Nelson, James C., *Railroad Transportation and Public Policy* (Washington: Brookings Institution, 1959), p. 140.
49. Nelson, *op. cit.,* p. 10. *U.S. News and World Report,* April 3, 1961.
50. Walter S. Franklin, President of the Pennsylvania Railroad, testified before a Congressional Committee that Class I railroads would have had more than one billion dollars of additional gross revenue during 1946-1952 if rate increases ultimately allowed by the Interstate Commerce Commission had been effective within sixty days of the time petitions or amended petitions for increased rates were filed, Nelson, *op. cit.,* p. 126.

Chapter Eleven

1. Fabricant, Solomon, "Basic Facts on Productivity Change," *Occasional Paper No. 63,* National Industrial Conference Board.
2. A more detailed discussion of this point is given in Chapter 4.
3. Professor John W. Kendrick, the country's leading authority on productivity measurement, finds that during the 38 year period, 1919-1957, the output per unit of input in the national economy has increased at an average rate of two and one-tenths per cent per year. Since there was virtually no change in the rate of return on capital during this period, Kendrick concludes that "practically all of the productivity increment accrued to labor." *California Management Review,* Spring 1960, p. 44.
4. Readers who wish to explore recent writings will find a guide to the literature in "An Extensive, Indexed Bibliography of American Profit Sharing Between 1950-1958," by Bertram L. Metzger,

Profit Sharing Research Foundation, 1718 Sherman Avenue, Evanston, Illinois.
5. Thompson, Kenneth M., *Profit Sharing* (New York: Harper & Brothers, 1949), Chapter 3.
6. *Ibid.*, Chapter 3.
7. The maximum for the Revenue Act of 1942 was ninety per cent. In 1944 the maximum was ninety-five per cent. In the 1951 Revenue Act this maximum was set at eighty-two per cent.
8. *Management Record,* National Industrial Conference Board. May, 1960.
9. Brower, Beatrice F., *Sharing Profits with Employees,* National Industrial Conference Board, Studies in Personnel Policy No. 162, 1957.
10. Knowlton, P. A., *Profit Sharing Patterns,* Profit Sharing Research Foundation, Evanston, Illinois, 1954.
11. Flippo, Edwin, *Profit Sharing in American Business,* Bureau of Business Research, Ohio State, 1954.
12. Hearings Before the Subcommittee of the Committee on Finance. U. S. Senate, 1938, pp. 24-25.
13. Flippo, Edwin, *Profit Sharing in American Business,* Bureau of Business Research, Ohio State, 1954, p. 51.
14. *Ibid.*, p. 78.
15. *Ibid.*, p. 87.
16. Hearings Before the Subcommittee of the Committee on Finance, U. S. Senate, 1938, p. 190.
17. *Ibid.*, p. 106.
18. Brower, F. Beatrice, *Sharing Profits with Employees,* National Industrial Conference Board, Studies in Personnel Policy No. 162, 1957.

Chapter Twelve

1. McKee, C. W. and H. G. Moulton, *A Survey of Economic Education* (Washington: Brookings Institution, 1951).
2. Conant, James B., *The American High School Today* (New York: McGraw Hill, 1959).
3. "The Teaching of Undergraduate Economics," *American Economic Review,* Dec. 1950.
4. Epstein, Ralph C., *Industrial Profits in the United States* (New

York: National Bureau of Economic Research in cooperation with the Committee on Recent Economic Changes, 1934).

5. Six companies including earthmoving equipment, chemical, oil, electronics, gas utility, electric utility.
6. Drucker, Peter, *The New Society* (New York: Harper & Brothers, 1950).
7. Argyris, Chris, *Personality and Organization* (New York: Harper & Brothers, 1957).
8. For a scholarly discussion of varying points of view on the purpose of the corporation, see Richard Eells' *The Meaning of Modern Business* (New York: Columbia University Press, 1960).
9. *Fortune,* August 1960.
10. Mason, Edward S., *Journal of Business* (Chicago: University of Chicago, Vol. 31:1-1958).
11. "The Dangers of Social Responsibility," Theodore Levitt, *Harvard Business Review,* September-October 1958.
12. Mason, Edward S. (Editor), *The Corporation in Modern Society,* Chapter 3 in a symposium (Boston: Harvard University Press, 1959).
13. Page, Arthur W., *The Bell Telephone System* (New York & London: Harper & Brothers, 1941).
14. *Hearings Before the Subcommittee on Anti-trust and Monopoly,* Part 14, Eighty-Sixth Congress.
15. *Ibid.*, Part 14, p. 7855.
16. *Ibid.*, Part 14, p. 8311.
17. These and other data on public health and the drug industry are from the testimony of Dr. Austin Smith, President, Pharmaceutical Manufacturers Association, Part 19, pp. 10678 f.
18. *Ibid.*, Part 14, p. 8032.

Chapter Thirteen

1. Gray, Alexander, *The Socialist Tradition; Moses to Lenin* (New York & London: Longmans, Green & Co., Inc., 1946), Chapter 2.
2. Tawney, R. H., *Religion and the Rise of Capitalism* (New York: New American Library of World Literature, Inc.), p. 36.
3. Tawney, *op. cit.,* p. 35.

4. Tawney, *op. cit.*, p. 42.
5. "The Tradesman's Calling," pp. 1-4, as quoted in *Religion and the Rise of Capitalism,* R. H. Tawney, p. 240.
6. From the *Christian Directory,* Vol. 1, p. 378b, as quoted in *Religion and the Rise of Capitalism,* R. H. Tawney, p. 243.
7. From the "Tradesman's Calling" as quoted in *Religion and the Rise of Capitalism,* R. H. Tawney, p. 246.
8. Tawney, *op. cit.*, p. 36.
9. Gray, Alexander, *The Socialist Tradition* (New York & London: Longmans, Green & Co., Inc., 1946), Chapter 12.
10. Rauschenbusch, Walter, *Christianizing the Social Order* (New York: Macmillan, 1914), p. 152.
11. "Christian Principles and Assumptions for Economic Life"—statement adopted by the General Board of the National Council of Churches of Christ in the U.S.A., September 15, 1954.
12. From a statement issued by the Administrative Board of the National Catholic Welfare Conference on behalf of the Cardinals, Archbishops and Bishops of the United States.
13. Bennett, John C., and others, *Christian Values and Economic Life* (New York: Harper & Brothers, 1954), p. 199.
14. For discussions of the Protestant point of view on work, see: De Mille, George E. (Editor) *Men at Work in God's World* (New York & London: Longmans, Green & Co., Inc., 1956), "The Church and Work" by The Right Reverend Richard S. W. Emrich.

    Brunner, Emil, *Justice and the Social Order* (New York: Harper & Brothers).

    Bowen, Howard R., *The Social Responsibilities of the Businessman* (New York: Harper & Brothers, 1953).

    Hall, Cameron Parker, *The Christian at His Daily Work,* National Council of Churches.

    Report of the North American Lay Conference on the Christian and His Daily Work, National Council of Churches.
15. Hayek, Friedrick, *The Road to Serfdom* (Chicago: University of Chicago Press, 1955), Chapter 7.
16. Hazlitt, Henry, *The Freeman's Library* (Princeton: D. Van Nostrand Co., Inc., 1956), p. 3.
17. Rauschenbusch, Walter, *Christianizing the Social Order,* p. 256.

NOTES ON APPENDICES

The best way to understand profits is to work with profits data. Earnings statistics, of course, are available from many sources but it represents an economy of time and effort for the reader to find key data in a single source. Accordingly, tabular material is presented here that will provide a good over-all view of profit trends for industries and for leading companies.

For the reader who wishes more detailed statistical information on profits, the following sources are indicated:

Statistics of Income — Corporation Income Tax Returns, U.S. Treasury Department, Internal Revenue Service

U.S. Income and Output, Department of Commerce

Statistics of Electric Utilities in the United States, Federal Power Commission

Quarterly Financial Report for Manufacturing Corporations, Federal Trade Commission — Securities and Exchange Commission

Statistics of Communications — Common Carriers, Federal Communications Commission

Transport Statistics in the United States, Interstate Commerce Commission

First National City Bank *Monthly Letter on Business and Economic Conditions.*

The Economic Almanac — National Industrial Conference Board

Moody's

Standard & Poor's

The Fortune Directory

Annual Stockholder Reports by publicly held companies

Trade Association Publications —

Electric Utility Industry Statistics in the United States, Edison Electric Institute

Annual Statistical Report — American Iron & Steel Institute

Appendix A — Adjustments of Inventory Valuation and Depreciation. Manufacturing Corporations, 1929-1955, U.S. Department of Commerce.

Appendix B — Number of Corporations Reporting Loss — and Profit and Loss — 1916-1959, U.S. Treasury.

Appendix C-1 — Statistics of Income as reported by the U.S. Treasury for 36 industry categories, 1926 to 1958, for years where data are available.

Appendix

Definitions:

Sales are business receipts – gross sales and gross receipts from operations. Does not include interest on government and other obligations, rents, royalties, capital gains, net gains from sales other than capital assets or dividends from holdings in other corporations.

For the years 1926-1931 gross sales consist of "gross sales, less goods returned and any allowances or discounts from the sale price for trading or manufacturing." For 1932 and thereafter gross sales consist of "amounts received for goods less returns and allowances in transactions where inventories were an income determining factor."

Net Worth consists of common and preferred capital stock, surplus reserve and surplus reserve and surplus and undivided profit.

Net Profit is compiled net profit less total tax. Net profits reflect capital gains and losses, dividends received from domestic and foreign corporations. Depreciation and inventory accounting are in conformity with tax regulations.

Dividends are cash and assets other than the companies' own stock.

Balance Sheet Corporations. From 1931 and thereafter all data are from balance sheet corporations. Prior to 1931 returns of balance sheet corporations were available only to determine net worth. For these years returns from all corporations were used to determine profits, sales and dividends. The profit on net worth ratios are not strictly comparable for the periods 1926-1930 and 1931 and thereafter but variance is small, since balance sheet corporations represent most of the activity of all corporations.

Consolidated Returns. Before 1934 and after 1941 companies were allowed to elect whether or not they would file consolidated returns. For the years 1934-1941 the filing of consolidated returns was required. This meant that the profits of subsidiaries theretofore reported in various industrial classifications were now classified as profit for the principal line of business of the consolidated return. There is no adequate way to measure the effect of consolidation industry profit trends. See in this connection "Corporate Size and Earning Power," William L. Crum.

Industrial Groupings. The industry data represent the best comparisons that could be worked out to show profit trends over the years. The data are not always entirely comparable because certain industrial activities within minor industrial groups in one year were reported by the U.S. Treasury in different industrial groups in other years. These distortions are likely to be minor, but there is no way of evaluating the effects of these shifts in industrial categories. Availability of data varies by industry groupings during period 1926 to 1958.

Appendix C-2 – Profits on Sales and Book Net Assets for Leading Companies (i.e., those that publish income statements) as compiled by the First National City Bank of New York.

Definitions:

Book Net Assets at the beginning of each year are based upon the excess of total balance sheet assets over liabilities, and is equivalent to net worth as usually defined: i.e., the sum of book value of preferred and common stock and surplus accounts.

Net income in coal mining, metal mining and other mining, quarrying, is reported before depletion charges in some cases. For investment trends most cases exclude capital gains or losses on investments.

Appendix C-3 – Fortune Directory tabulations of Profit on Sales and on Investment for 500 largest industries and 50 largest banks, Merchandising, Transportation, Life Insurance and Utility Companies.

Definitions:

Sales include service and rental revenues for companies that derive at least 50% of their revenue from manufacturing or mining for fiscal years ending not later than January 2, 1957.

Net Worth consists of capital stock, surplus and retained earnings.

Annual data may be non-comparable for recently merged companies.

In examining the profits data from the various sources, the reader may wish to bear in mind differences such as the following:

All profit figures reported in Appendices C-1, C-2, and C-3 are profits after taxes. U.S. Treasury figures reflect accounting for tax purposes. First National City Bank and Fortune data are drawn from company annual reports that reflect book accounting for purposes of business control.

U.S. Treasury data include all balance sheet companies reporting income for tax purposes – large and small in every line of enterprise. The First National City Bank data include only the profit returns for corporations that publish their earnings, i.e., the enterprises that tend to be the largest and most successful.

The First National City Bank data represent sampling of corporations. In 1925 the number included was 232; in 1960 it was 3,433.

In concept, the definitions of net worth used by the three reporting sources, Internal Revenue Service, First National City Bank and *Fortune* are the same. Differences will arise, however, from the fact that the latter two use published financial statements while the former uses returns filed in conformity with tax regulations. These differences cannot be measured precisely because of the unavailability of individual company returns for tax purposes.

Appendix

ADJUSTMENTS FOR INVENTORY VALUATION AND DEPRECIATION
MANUFACTURING CORPORATIONS – 1929-1959.
U. S. DEPARTMENT OF COMMERCE

(Millions of Dollars)

Year	*Reported Profits After Taxes*	*Inventory Valuation Adjustment*	*Per cent Inventory Adjustment*	*Depreciation Adjustment*	*Per cent Depreciation Adjustment*	*Corrected Profits After Taxes*	*Per cent Over or Understated*
1929	4,230	301	7	−298	7	4,233	0
1930	1,263	2,215	175	−146	12	3,332	163
1931	−511	1,585	—	17	—	1,091	—
1932	−1,428	655	—	126	—	−647	
1933	563	+1,340	238	122	22	−655	
1934	1,020	−457	45	−26	2	537	47
1935	1,644	−161	10	−26	2	1,457	12
1936	2,834	−478	17	−52	2	2,304	19
1937	2,883	−11	4	−179	6	2,693	6
1938	1,110	619	56	−153	14	1,576	—
1939	2,896	−471	16	−130	4	2,295	20
1940	3,781	−135	4	−199	5	3,447	9
1941	5,576	−1,511	27	−359	6	3,706	33
1942	5,109	−726	14	−474	9	3,909	23
1943	5,564	−552	10	−530	9	4,482	19
1944	5,458	−206	4	−475	9	4,777	13
1945	4,030	−413	10	−493	12	3,124	22
1946	6,658	−3,041	46	−727	11	2,890	57
1947	10,055	−3,737	37	−1,270	13	5,048	50
1948	11,177	−1,442	13	−1,629	15	8,106	28
1949	8,490	1,107	13	−1,646	20	7,951	7
1950	12,666	−3,183	25	−1,679	13	7,804	38
1951	10,635	−601	6	−2,227	21	7,807	27
1952	8,846	654	7	−2,095	25	7,405	18
1953	9,721	−692	7	−2,045	21	6,984	28
1954	9,066	−315	3	2,196	25	6,555	28
1955	13,201	−1,348	10	2,248	17	9,605	27
1956	12,973	−1,645	12	−2,300	18	9,028	30
1957	12,215	−949	8	−2,800	22	8,466	30
1958	9,776	−189	2	−2,700	28	6,887	30
1959	12,681	−335	3	−2,200	22	9,546	25
1950–59	11,178	−860	8	−2,259	20	8,009	28

NUMBER OF CORPORATIONS REPORTING LOSS — AND AMOUNT OF PROFIT AND LOSS
SOURCE: U. S. TREASURY — STATISTICS OF INCOME

Year	*Total Corporations Reporting (000)*	*Total Reporting Loss*	*Per cent Reporting Loss*	*Profit Before Tax*	*Loss*	*$ Loss Per $100 gain*
				(*millions*)		
1916	341	134	39	8,765	656	7
1917	351	119	34	10,730	629	6
1918	317	115	36	8,361	689	8
1919	320	110	34	9,411	995	11
1920	345	142	41	7,902	2,029	26
1921	356	185	52	4,336	3,876	89
1922	382	170	45	6,963	2,193	31
1923	398	165	41	8,321	2,013	24
1924	417	181	43	7,586	2,223	29
1925	430	179	42	9,583	1,962	20
1926	455	197	43	9,673	2,168	22
1927*	426	165	39	8,981	2,471	28
1928	443	174	39	10,617	2,391	23
1929	456	186	41	11,653	2,914	25
1930	463	241	52	6,428	4,877	76
1931	516	283	55	3,683	6,970	189
1932	452	369	82	2,153	7,796	362
1933	504	337	67	2,985	5,533	185
1934	528	324	61	4,275	4,183	98
1935	533	312	59	5,164	3,468	67
1936	530	275	52	9,478	2,152	23
1937	529	337	64	9,634	2,280	24
1938	471	307	65	6,525	2,853	44
1939	469	270	58	8,826	2,092	24
1940	473	253	53	11,203	2,283	20
1941	468	204	44	18,111	1,778	10
1942	441	172	39	24,052	1,000	4
1943	419	136	32	28,717	898	3
1944	411	123	30	27,123	819	3
1945	421	118	28	22,165	1,026	5
1946	491	132	27	27,184	1,991	7
1947	551	169	31	33,381	1,958	6
1948	594	199	34	36,273	1,848	5
1949	614	230	37	30,576	2,381	8
1950	629	203	32	44,140	1,527	3
1951	652	213	33	45,333	1,787	4
1952	672	230	34	40,431	1,975	5
1953	697	257	37	41,819	2,334	6
1954	722	281	39	39,572	3,249	8
1955	807	294	36	50,329	2,850	6
1956	885	326	37	50,184	3,299	7
1957	940	367	39	48,664	4,187	9
1958	990	379	38	43,490	4,967	11

* Total Active Corporations from 1927

All Manufacturing (Millions of Dollars)

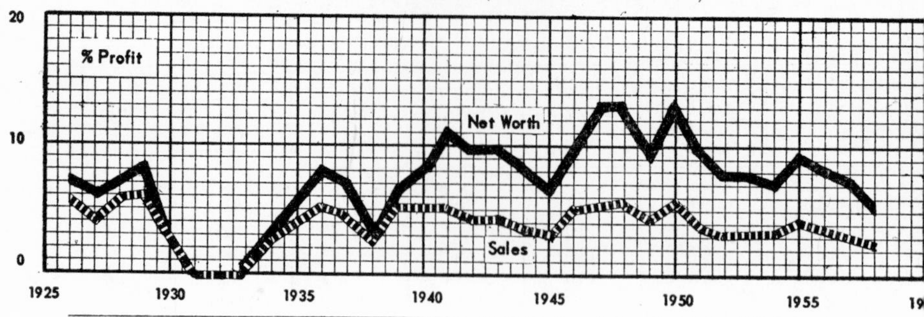

Year	Net Profit (After Taxes)	Sales	Net Worth	Dividends (Cash)	% Profit of		Div. as % Profit
					Sales	Net Worth	
1926	3,640.1	60,704.6	46,273.5	2,544.2	6.0	7.9	70.
1927	3,050.4	61,917.9	48,049.2	2,602.6	4.9	6.3	85.
1928	3,935.5	65,339.4	50,017.6	2,990.6	6.0	7.9	76.
1929	4,537.2	70,118.5	52,694.0	3,322.9	6.5	8.6	73.
1930	1,424.5	56,843.5	52,122.2	3,161.0	2.5	2.7	222.
1931	472.1	42,051.8	47,639.8	2,276.0	—	—	—
1932	1,567.9	30,703.3	43,976.1	1,324.1	—	—	—
1933	295.8	33,932.2	43,341.0	1,158.5	.9	.7	392.
1934	1,155.2	39,451.1	38,151.0	1,578.1	2.9	3.0	157.
1935	2,139.0	46,157.7	37,611.2	2,183.8	4.6	5.7	102.
1936	3,049.2	54,163.5	37,466.9	2,867.1	5.6	8.1	94.
1937	3,044.8	60,294.6	41,239.3	2,899.9	5.0	7.4	95.
1938	1,243.2	49,387.9	41,260.4	1,633.7	2.5	3.0	131.
1939	2,941.7	56,473.1	42,438.4	2,170.1	5.2	6.9	74.
1940	3,768.6	65,023.1	44,163.1	2,389.9	5.8	8.5	63.
1941	5,428.6	96,214.1	48,397.6	2,800.3	5.6	11.2	57.
1942	5,395.2	116,429.3	55,071.5	2,486.1	4.6	9.8	46.
1943	5,998.1	142,919.3	60,687.7	2,595.7	4.2	9.9	43.
1944	5,435.3	150,864.2	63,070.6	2,827.6	3.6	8.6	52.
1945	4,115.3	138,000.1	64,150.5	2,801.0	3.0	6.4	68.
1946	6,965.4	134,615.7	67,589.9	3,377.7	5.2	10.3	48.
1947	10,235.8	175,657.2	76,673.4	4,143.3	5.8	13.3	40.
1948	11,224.6	195,399.8	84,083.7	4,616.9	5.7	13.3	41.
1949	8,711.1	182,447.8	88,884.9	4,838.3	4.8	9.8	55.
1950	13,032.8	214,827.7	97,041.7	6,037.2	6.1	13.4	46.
1951	10,637.3	249,201.5	104,725.0	5,715.3	4.3	10.2	54.
1952	8,880.1	255.219.6	109,496.3	5,664.8	3.5	8.1	64.
1953	9,235.6	274,630.1	113,813.7	5,848.0	3.4	8.1	63.
1954	8,808.3	261,214.1	119,253.1	5,817.6	3.4	7.4	66.
1955	12,924.5	298,530.3	131,956.2	6,770.5	4.3	9.8	52.
1956	12,295.5	311,555.3	138,993.0	7,120.5	3.9	8.8	58.
1957	11,195.8	325,699.7	146,275.9	7,365.8	3.4	7.7	66.
1958	9,047.3	321,676.2	154,849.9	7,238.7	2.8	5.8	80.
1949–58	10,476.8	269,500.1	120,528.5	6,241.7	3.9	8.6	59.

Apparel and Products Made From Fabrics (Millions of Dollars)

Men's Clothing; Women's Clothing; Millinery; Fur Goods; Other Apparel and Accessories Like Gloves and Mittens; Other Fabricated Textile Products Like Awnings.

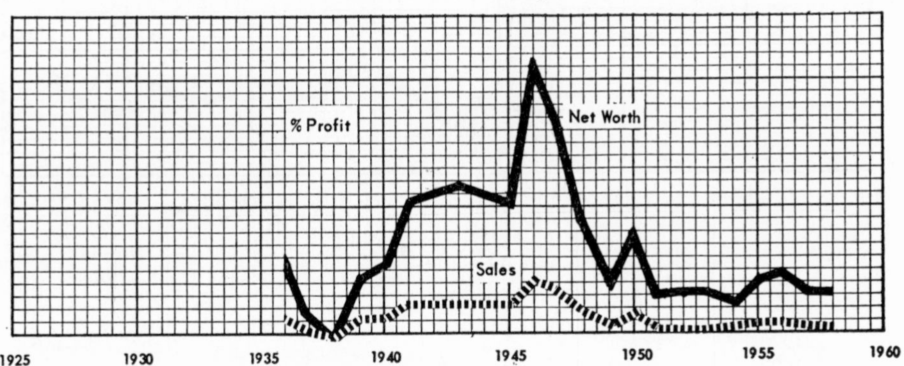

Year	*Net Profit (After Taxes)*	*Sales*	*Net Worth*	*Dividends (Cash)*	*% Profit of*		*Div. as % Profit*
					Sales	*Net Worth*	
1926							
1927							
1928							
1929							
1930							
1931							
1932							
1933							
1934							
1935							
1936	34.8	2,220.1	549.6	28.1	1.6	6.3	81.
1937	9.5	2,182.4	529.6	22.6	.4	1.8	238.
1938	−2.1	2,036.1	549.4	13.9	—	—	—
1939	27.0	2,294.8	556.1	19.5	1.2	4.9	72.
1940	32.7	2,457.3	589.1	20.3	1.3	5.6	62.
1941	76.8	3,273.5	704.6	23.7	2.3	10.9	31.
1942	87.8	3,791.8	768.4	21.8	2.3	11.4	25.
1943	97.3	3,934.2	815.1	27.8	2.5	11.9	29.
1944	95.5	3,856.0	856.2	26.1	2.5	11.2	27.
1945	101.9	3,912.6	935.0	25.7	2.6	10.9	25.
1946	289.4	6,521.6	1,325.6	52.3	4.4	21.8	18.
1947	265.2	7,549.7	1,603.1	51.6	3.5	16.5	20.
1948	156.1	8,213.3	1,724.1	59.3	1.9	9.1	38.
1949	73.7	9,616.0	1,736.6	45.2	1.0	4.2	61.
1950	155.8	8,159.3	1,832.1	44.4	1.9	8.5	29.
1951	59.8	8,772.0	1,868.7	37.7	.7	3.2	63.
1952	70.1	8,967.1	1,885.6	35.2	.8	3.7	50.
1953	59.8	8,777.3	1,839.6	33.6	.7	3.3	56.
1954	56.4	8,775.6	1,918.9	30.9	.6	2.9	55.
1955	96.4	9,950.6	2,053.4	31.9	1.0	4.7	33.
1956	98.9	9,469.6	1,932.0	32.1	1.0	5.1	33.
1957	70.7	9,159.6	1,874.3	28.5	.8	3.8	40.
1958	76.9	10,857.2	2,168.9	29.0	.7	3.5	38.
1949–58	81.9	9,250.4	1,911.0	34.9	.9	4.3	43.

Banks and Trust Companies (Millions of Dollars)

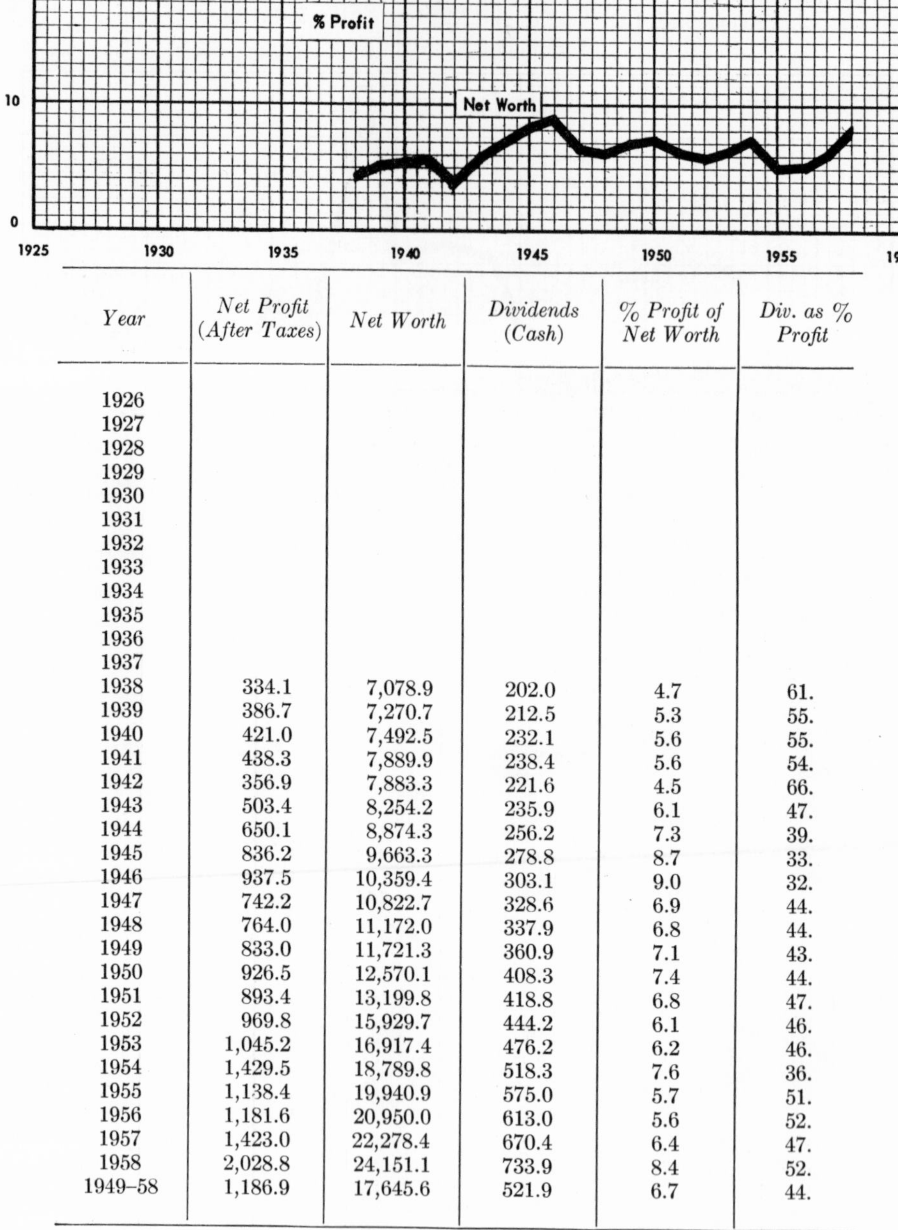

Year	*Net Profit (After Taxes)*	*Net Worth*	*Dividends (Cash)*	*% Profit of Net Worth*	*Div. as % Profit*
1926					
1927					
1928					
1929					
1930					
1931					
1932					
1933					
1934					
1935					
1936					
1937					
1938	334.1	7,078.9	202.0	4.7	61.
1939	386.7	7,270.7	212.5	5.3	55.
1940	421.0	7,492.5	232.1	5.6	55.
1941	438.3	7,889.9	238.4	5.6	54.
1942	356.9	7,883.3	221.6	4.5	66.
1943	503.4	8,254.2	235.9	6.1	47.
1944	650.1	8,874.3	256.2	7.3	39.
1945	836.2	9,663.3	278.8	8.7	33.
1946	937.5	10,359.4	303.1	9.0	32.
1947	742.2	10,822.7	328.6	6.9	44.
1948	764.0	11,172.0	337.9	6.8	44.
1949	833.0	11,721.3	360.9	7.1	43.
1950	926.5	12,570.1	408.3	7.4	44.
1951	893.4	13,199.8	418.8	6.8	47.
1952	969.8	15,929.7	444.2	6.1	46.
1953	1,045.2	16,917.4	476.2	6.2	46.
1954	1,429.5	18,789.8	518.3	7.6	36.
1955	1,138.4	19,940.9	575.0	5.7	51.
1956	1,181.6	20,950.0	613.0	5.6	52.
1957	1,423.0	22,278.4	670.4	6.4	47.
1958	2,028.8	24,151.1	733.9	8.4	52.
1949–58	1,186.9	17,645.6	521.9	6.7	44.

BEVERAGES (Millions of Dollars)

Nonalcoholic Beverages; Wines; Malt liquors and malt; Distilled, Rectified and Blended Liquors.

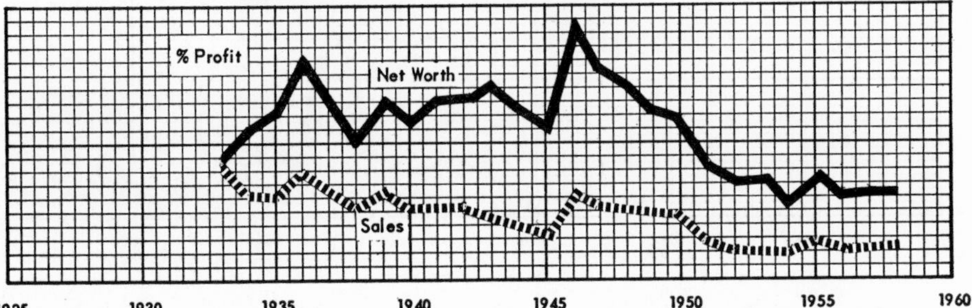

Year	*Net Profit (After Taxes)*	*Sales*	*Net Worth*	*Dividends (Cash)*	*% Profit of*		*Div. as % Profit*
					Sales	*Net Worth*	
1926							
1927							
1928							
1929							
1930							
1931							
1932							
1933	51.4	570.6	566.4	19.6	9.0	9.1	38.
1934	66.9	1,019.6	604.9	24.9	6.6	11.1	37.
1935	80.3	1,299.9	665.8	57.7	6.2	12.1	72.
1936	130.7	1,588.0	805.9	97.3	8.2	16.2	74.
1937	115.9	1,757.6	866.8	97.4	6.6	13.4	84.
1938	87.5	1,578.8	831.5	58.3	5.5	10.5	67.
1939	109.2	1,666.5	834.6	72.7	6.6	13.1	67.
1940	99.4	1,790.2	865.6	66.9	5.6	11.5	67.
1941	123.0	2,217.8	940.0	69.1	5.5	13.1	56.
1942	135.5	2,621.2	1,023.9	66.9	5.2	13.2	49.
1943	153.6	3,208.1	1,071.9	79.7	4.8	14.3	52.
1944	148.6	3,735.0	1,205.5	69.8	4.0	12.3	47.
1945	153.2	4,371.8	1,325.3	72.2	3.5	11.6	47.
1946	302.8	4,709.9	1,605.0	96.9	6.4	18.9	32.
1947	272.9	4,865.9	1,727.3	113.7	5.6	15.8	42.
1948	276.9	5,217.6	1,928.8	108.0	5.3	14.4	39.
1949	262.2	5,366.8	2,068.3	108.2	4.9	12.7	41.
1950	257.9	5,476.9	2,211.1	108.6	4.7	11.7	42.
1951	206.2	6,852.5	2,445.4	112.4	3.0	8.4	55.
1952	183.0	7,206.9	2,539.2	118.6	2.5	7.2	65.
1953	179.7	7,255.7	2,477.9	120.7	2.5	7.3	67.
1954	153.0	7,311.7	2,545.9	120.7	2.1	6.0	79.
1955	198.0	6,595.9	2,662.2	114.5	3.0	7.4	58.
1956	166.8	6,769.5	2,670.1	84.5	2.5	6.2	51.
1957	181.9	7,014.9	2,856.3	104.8	2.6	6.4	58.
1958	211.3	7,679.0	3,206.2	120.7	2.8	6.6	57.
1949–58	200.0	6,753.0	2,568.3	111.4	3.0	7.8	56.

BITUMINOUS COAL (Millions of Dollars)

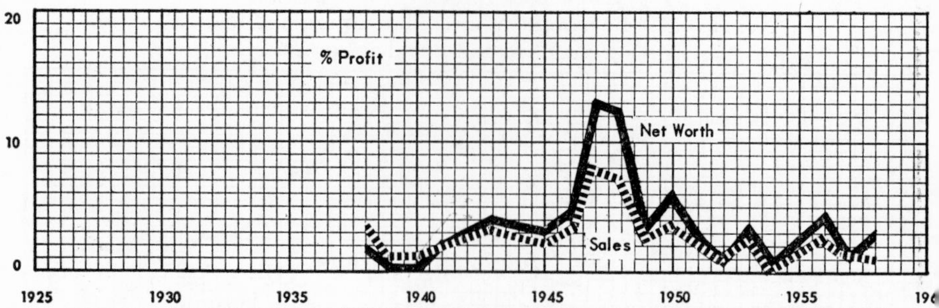

Year	Net Profit (After Taxes)	Sales	Net Worth	Dividends (Cash)	% Profit of Sales	% Profit of Net Worth	Div. as % Profit
1926							
1927							
1928							
1929							
1930							
1931							
1932							
1933							
1934							
1935							
1936							
1937							
1938	D 25.9	671.4	1,269.5	10.2	—	—	D 39.
1939	7.6	771.6	1,237.5	13.0	—	—	D171.
1940	9.0	900.7	1,232.1	18.2	1.0	.7	202.
1941	25.1	1,142.0	1,215.7	20.3	2.2	2.1	81.
1942	35.6	1,240.9	1,123.5	24.0	2.9	3.2	67.
1943	47.4	1,392.3	1,107.8	24.1	3.4	4.3	51.
1944	45.4	1,546.3	1,155.6	25.3	2.9	3.9	56.
1945	37.6	1,490.8	1,092.8	28.8	2.5	3.4	77.
1946	50.4	1,552.3	1,083.5	32.6	3.2	4.7	65.
1947	169.6	2,104.9	1,297.6	58.4	8.1	13.1	34.
1948	195.1	2,590.2	1,537.4	76.6	7.5	12.7	39.
1949	54.6	1,848.6	1,400.3	57.6	3.0	3.9	105.
1950	93.0	2,318.1	1,531.3	62.7	4.0	6.1	67.
1951	57.0	2,465.0	1,535.0	55.0	2.3	3.7	96.
1952	34.0	2,208.0	1,541.0	52.0	1.5	2.2	153.
1953	43.5	1,474.9	1,202.3	39.2	2.9	3.6	90.
1954	0.8	1,586.2	1,399.5	35.4	.1	.1	4,425.
1955	33.7	1,896.3	1,435.1	39.9	1.8	2.3	118.
1956	70.6	2,347.5	1,536.6	57.9	3.0	4.6	82.
1957	45.4	2,501.3	1,561.3	47.4	1.8	2.9	104.
1958 P	22.0	1,941.1	1,588.1	51.2	1.1	1.4	233.
1949–58	45.5	2,058.7	1,473.1	49.8	2.2	3.1	109.

Chemicals and Allied Products (Millions of Dollars)

Drugs and Medicines; Soaps and Glycerin Cleaning and Polishing Preparations; Paints, Varnishes, Lacquers; Perfumes, Cosmetics and Other Toilet Preparations; Fertilizers; Fats and Oils, Animal and Vegetable except Edible Cooking Oil. Industrial inorganic chemicals. Industrial organic chemicals including plastic materials, synthetic rubber and synthetic fibers.

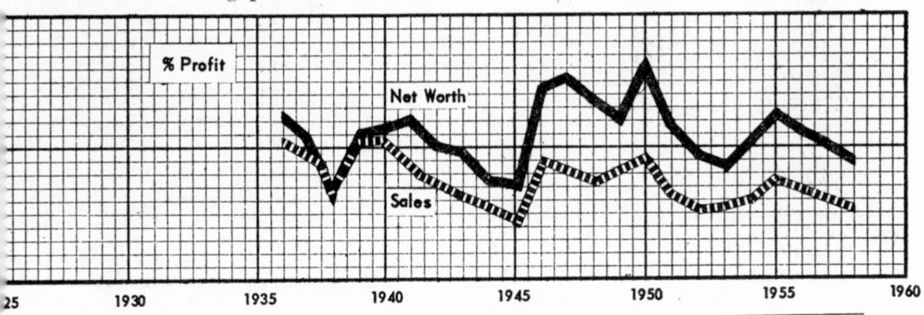

Year	*Net Profit (After Taxes)*	*Sales*	*Net Worth*	*Dividends (Cash)*	*% Profit of*		*Div. as % Profit*
					Sales	*Net Worth*	
1926							
1927							
1928							
1929							
1930							
1931							
1932							
1933							
1934							
1935							
1936	389.5	3,637.7	3,139.8	346.3	10.7	12.4	89.
1937	373.6	4,032.1	3,475.5	342.7	9.3	10.7	92.
1938	259.6	3,587.4	3,714.2	222.6	7.2	7.0	86.
1939	445.9	4,159.2	3,966.5	328.1	10.7	11.2	74.
1940	484.9	4,687.4	4,121.7	335.2	10.3	11.8	69.
1941	546.9	6,223.1	4,503.0	335.7	8.8	12.1	61.
1942	525.0	7,109.8	5,203.8	310.7	7.4	10.1	59.
1943	528.9	8,494.5	5,582.5	320.6	6.2	9.5	61.
1944	544.3	9,679.1	6,084.2	377.6	5.6	8.9	69.
1945	465.6	9,660.9	6,149.8	382.1	4.8	7.6	82.
1946	937.3	10,389.1	6,382.5	464.6	9.0	14.7	50.
1947	1,116.2	13,056.3	7,233.8	522.8	8.5	15.4	47.
1948	1,066.8	13,856.9	7,652.9	537.2	7.7	13.9	50.
1949	1,042.6	12,944.0	8,381.5	596.9	8.1	12.4	57.
1950	1,507.2	16,015.2	9,162.8	772.6	9.4	16.4	51.
1951	1,183.9	17,752.4	9,936.5	690.8	6.7	11.9	58.
1952	966.4	17,538.5	10,339.1	706.6	5.5	9.3	73.
1953	992.8	18,208.2	10,421.4	696.4	5.5	8.7	70.
1954	1,116.1	18,476.9	10,983.6	818.3	6.0	10.2	73.
1955	1,528.7	21,093.8	12,094.8	967.9	7.2	12.6	63.
1956	1,517.6	22,420.9	13,037.9	1,002.5	6.8	11.6	66.
1957	1,478.3	23,596.8	13,664.0	1,048.6	6.3	10.8	71.
1958	1,333.8	22,685.7	14,241.1	1,032.6	5.9	9.4	77.
1949–58	1,266.7	19,073.2	11,226.2	833.3	6.6	11.3	66.

CONSTRUCTION (Millions of Dollars)

General Building Contractors
General Contractors Other Than Building
Special Trade Contractors

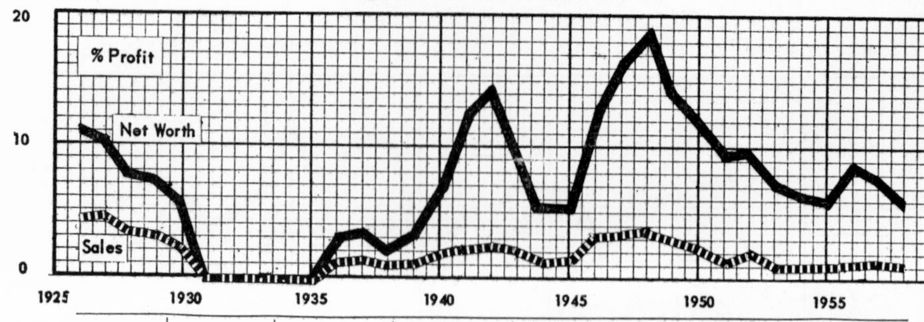

Year	Net Profit (After Taxes)	Sales	Net Worth	Dividends (Cash)	% Profit of Sales	% Profit of Net Worth	Div. as % Profit
1926	105.0	2,454.5	956.0	55.3	4.3	11.0	53.
1927	120.6	2,601.9	1,164.6	75.1	4.6	10.4	62.
1928	98.3	2,556.9	1,250.6	65.4	3.8	7.9	67.
1929	109.3	2,908.2	1,393.6	77.8	3.8	7.8	71.
1930	82.4	2,931.1	1,455.5	113.5	2.8	5.7	138.
1931	−11.1	2,042.5	1,259.0	62.5	—	—	—
1932	−87.2	1,305.9	1,123.8	40.2	—	—	—
1933	−53.8	979.3	996.9	27.7	—	—	—
1934	−27.5	1,178.0	905.0	23.3	—	—	—
1935	−1.9	1,385.3	825.5	29.5	—	—	—
1936	26.6	1,882.6	796.3	49.4	1.4	3.3	186.
1937	33.4	2,311.6	890.5	49.2	1.4	3.8	147.
1938	17.7	1,846.0	740.2	23.2	1.0	2.4	131.
1939	23.8	2,118.0	695.0	27.5	1.1	3.4	116.
1940	47.2	2,386.0	718.2	30.1	2.0	6.6	64.
1941	97.9	3,330.0	801.7	31.7	2.9	12.2	32.
1942	133.3	4,555.6	929.4	32.4	2.9	14.3	24.
1943	90.3	4,084.1	920.6	30.3	2.2	9.8	34.
1944	49.8	3,037.1	892.4	25.2	1.6	5.6	51.
1945	51.0	2,827.3	887.1	29.2	1.8	5.7	57.
1946	148.6	4,135.7	1,153.1	38.0	3.6	12.9	26.
1947	248.7	6,781.3	1,499.3	42.3	3.7	16.6	17.
1948	362.4	9,041.1	1,916.8	67.2	4.0	18.9	19.
1949	314.3	9,516.3	2,219.4	70.6	3.3	14.2	23.
1950	307.2	11,063.9	2,478.9	81.4	2.8	12.4	27.
1951	266.6	13,721.8	2,755.6	71.9	1.9	9.7	27.
1952	291.9	14,804.5	2,981.8	74.7	2.0	9.8	26.
1953	240.7	15,686.2	3,073.2	74.4	1.5	7.8	31.
1954	230.3	16,941.9	3,382.2	74.6	1.4	6.8	32.
1955	228.1	19,427.2	3,700.7	84.8	1.2	6.2	37.
1956	353.7	22,946.5	3,951.8	79.5	1.5	9.0	22.
1957	361.7	26,370.1	4,529.1	95.2	1.4	8.0	26.
1958	302.9	27,823.5	4,923.0	88.9	1.1	6.2	29.
1949–58	289.7	17,829.1	3,399.6	79.6	1.6	8.5	27.

COMMUNICATIONS (Millions of Dollars)

Telephone
Telegraph

Radio Broadcasting and Television
Other Communications

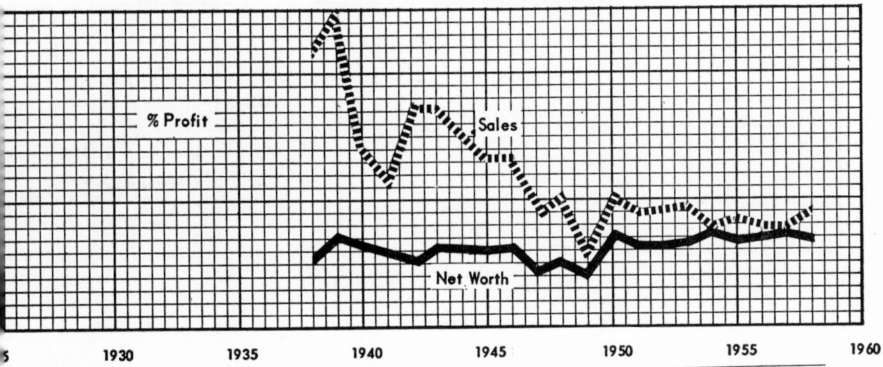

% Profit
Sales
Net Worth

1930 1935 1940 1945 1950 1955 1960

Year	Net Profit (After Taxes)	Sales	Net Worth	Dividends (Cash)	% Profit of Sales	% Profit of Net Worth	Div. as % Profit
1926							
1927							
1928							
1929							
1930							
1931							
1932							
1933							
1934							
1935							
1936							
1937							
1938	320.1	1,431.6	5,422.1	358.9	22.4	5.9	112.
1939	380.7	1,510.0	5,447.0	364.6	25.2	7.0	96.
1940	215.1	1,498.5	3,134.3	201.7	14.4	6.9	94.
1941	198.7	1,650.8	3,272.2	201.7	12.0	6.1	102.
1942	349.5	2,011.7	5,874.5	353.2	17.4	5.9	101.
1943	392.3	2,273.7	5,875.6	362.5	17.3	6.7	92.
1944	386.7	2,505.5	5,989.8	365.7	15.4	6.5	95.
1945	372.9	2,712.8	6,100.6	376.9	13.7	6.1	101.
1946	401.7	2,912.0	6,366.9	392.8	13.8	6.3	98.
1947	301.9	3,115.0	6,576.0	347.8	9.7	4.6	115.
1948	390.9	3,606.3	7,469.9	400.2	10.8	5.2	102.
1949	218.9	3,707.5	5,062.2	237.3	5.9	4.3	108.
1950	449.2	4,447.2	5,963.4	356.5	10.1	7.5	79.
1951	467.5	5,043.0	6,888.5	388.7	9.3	6.8	83.
1952	512.7	5,597.4	7,925.2	445.0	9.2	6.5	87.
1953	601.7	6,137.1	8,747.2	507.4	9.8	6.9	84.
1954	637.7	8,416.0	9,289.0	509.1	7.6	6.9	80.
1955	818.0	9,737.8	10,601.1	562.1	8.4	7.7	69.
1956	878.5	11,939.4	12,519.3	670.2	7.4	7.0	76.
1957	957.7	11,912.0	13,293.9	752.7	8.0	7.2	79.
1958	1,118.6	12,259.8	14,952.5	1,452.3	9.1	7.5	130.
1949–58	666.1	7,819.7	9,524.2	588.1	8.5	7.0	88.

Electric and Gas Utilities (Millions of Dollars)

Electric Light and Power; Gas Production and Distribution, Except Natural Gas Production

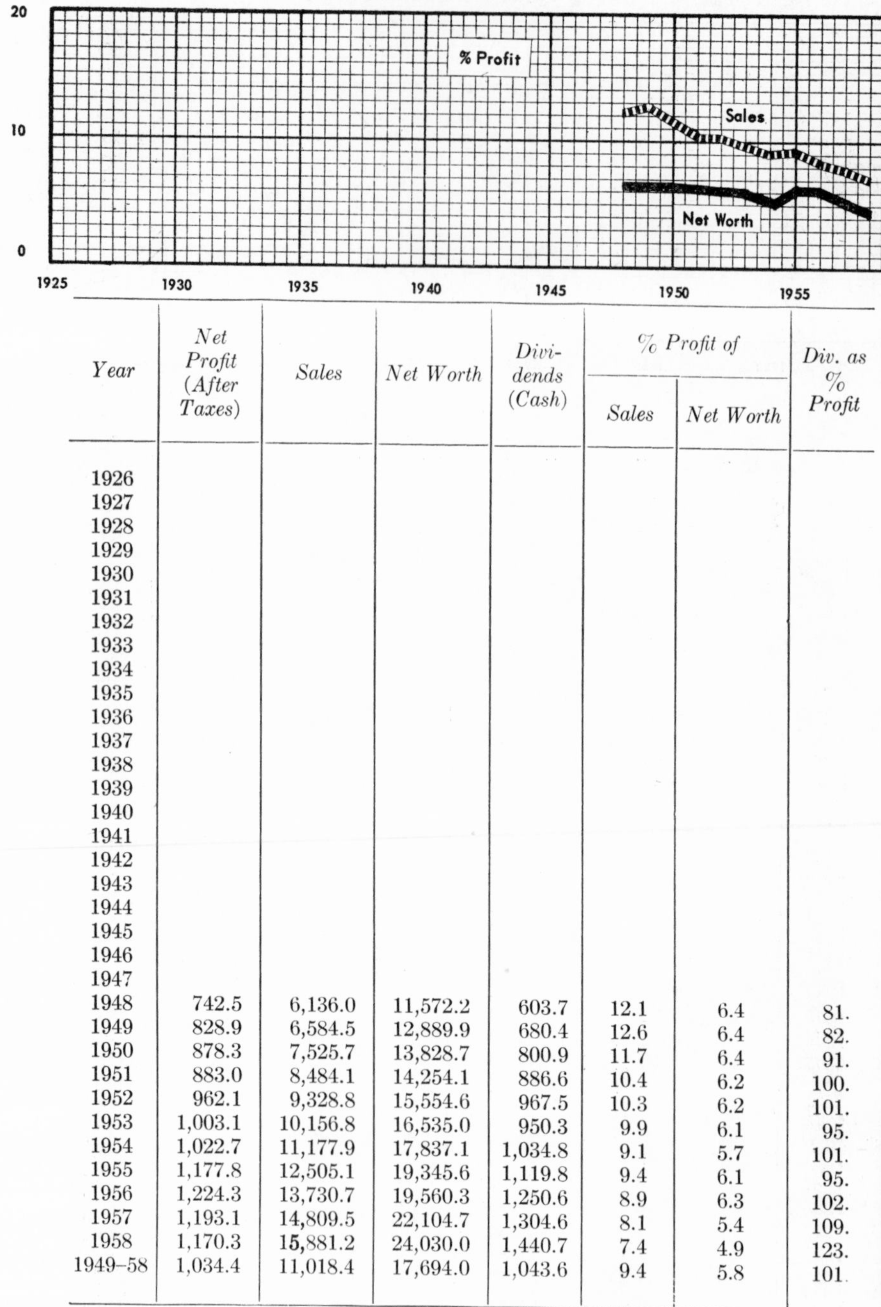

Year	*Net Profit (After Taxes)*	*Sales*	*Net Worth*	*Dividends (Cash)*	*% Profit of*		*Div. as % Profit*
					Sales	*Net Worth*	
1926							
1927							
1928							
1929							
1930							
1931							
1932							
1933							
1934							
1935							
1936							
1937							
1938							
1939							
1940							
1941							
1942							
1943							
1944							
1945							
1946							
1947							
1948	742.5	6,136.0	11,572.2	603.7	12.1	6.4	81.
1949	828.9	6,584.5	12,889.9	680.4	12.6	6.4	82.
1950	878.3	7,525.7	13,828.7	800.9	11.7	6.4	91.
1951	883.0	8,484.1	14,254.1	886.6	10.4	6.2	100.
1952	962.1	9,328.8	15,554.6	967.5	10.3	6.2	101.
1953	1,003.1	10,156.8	16,535.0	950.3	9.9	6.1	95.
1954	1,022.7	11,177.9	17,837.1	1,034.8	9.1	5.7	101.
1955	1,177.8	12,505.1	19,345.6	1,119.8	9.4	6.1	95.
1956	1,224.3	13,730.7	19,560.3	1,250.6	8.9	6.3	102.
1957	1,193.1	14,809.5	22,104.7	1,304.6	8.1	5.4	109.
1958	1,170.3	15,881.2	24,030.0	1,440.7	7.4	4.9	123.
1949–58	1,034.4	11,018.4	17,694.0	1,043.6	9.4	5.8	101.

FABRICATED METAL PRODUCTS (Millions of Dollars)

Fabricated Metal Products, Except Ordnance, Machinery and Transportation Equipment; Tin Cans and Other Tinware; Cutlery, Hand Tools and General Hardware; Heating Apparatus, Except Electrical and Plumbing Supplies; Metal Stamping, Coating and Engraving; Lighting Fixtures; Fabricated Wire Products

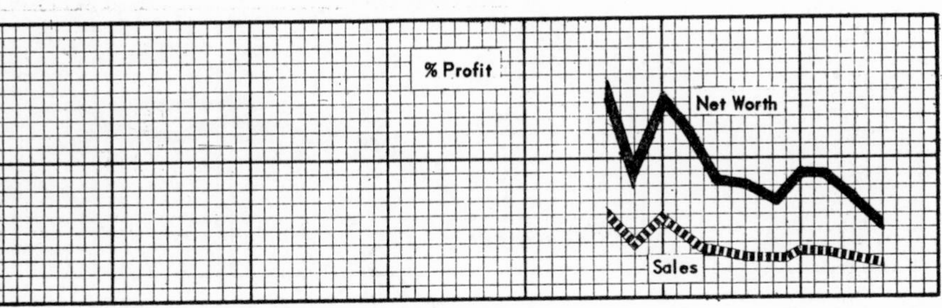

Year	*Net Profit (After Taxes)*	*Sales*	*Net Worth*	*Dividends (Cash)*	*% Profit of*		*Div. as % Profit*
					Sales	*Net Worth*	
1926							
1927							
1928							
1929							
1930							
1931							
1932							
1933							
1934							
1935							
1936							
1937							
1938							
1939							
1940							
1941							
1942							
1943							
1944							
1945							
1946							
1947							
1948	622.1	9,167.1	3,897.9	215.8	6.8	16.0	35.
1949	395.8	8,379.3	3,989.2	202.6	4.7	9.9	51.
1950	656.0	10,711.5	4,474.6	240.5	6.1	14.7	37.
1951	599.2	12,536.7	5,010.9	236.1	4.8	12.0	39.
1952	451.7	12,405.7	5,114.4	211.4	3.6	8.8	47.
1953	453.9	13,970.7	5,388.2	211.7	3.2	8.4	47.
1954	413.0	13,543.1	5,590.6	220.0	3.0	7.4	53.
1955	559.7	15,255.9	5,959.4	231.1	3.7	9.4	41.
1956	564.3	15,941.8	6,284.8	240.0	3.5	9.0	43.
1957	518.5	17,027.7	6,854.5	252.2	3.0	7.6	49.
1958	424.8	17,129.7	7,408.9	254.0	2.5	5.7	60.
1949–58	503.7	13,690.2	5,607.6	230.0	3.7	9.0	46.

Total Finance, Insurance, Real Estate and Lessors of Real Property

Savings and Loan, Building and Loan Associations; Personal Credit Agencies; Business Credit Agencies; Holding and Other Investment Companies; Security and Commodies – Exchange Brokers and Dealers; Insurance Carriers and Agents; Lessors of Real Property, Except Buildings; Real Estate Operators, Developers, Agents, Brokers, Managers, Title Abstract Companies

(Millions of Dollars)

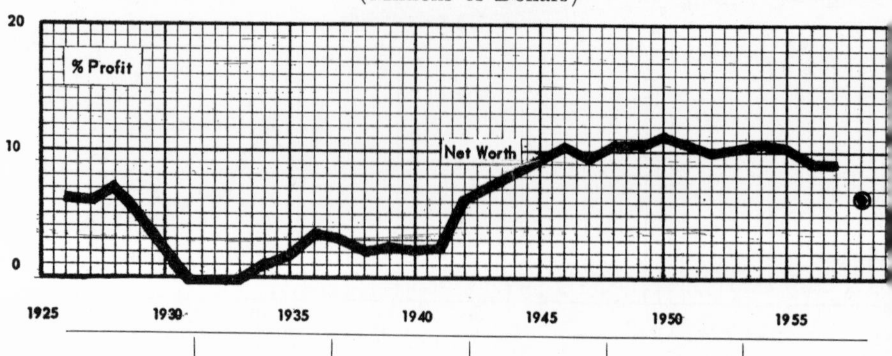

Year	*Net Profit (After Taxes)*	*Net Worth*	*Dividends (Cash)*	*% Profit of Net Worth*	*Div. as % Profit*
1926	1,459.8	21,168.4	978.6	6.9	67.
1927	1,687.3	25,119.7	1,069.0	6.7	63.
1928	2,244.8	30,050.4	1,313.9	7.5	59.
1929	2,324.3	43,390.9	1,762.9	5.4	76.
1930	858.4	40,533.3	1,646.8	2.1	192.
1931	−380.7	33,750.7	1,222.4	—	—
1932	−988.3	30,253.4	752.9	—	—
1933	−969.3	28,447.8	560.5	—	—
1934	662.0	46,812.9	1,256.0	1.4	190.
1935	904.3	47,242.6	1,534.6	1.9	170.
1936	1,698.0	42,651.8	1,738.1	4.0	102.
1937	1,623.0	44,122.1	1,736.4	3.7	107.
1938	1,146.2	45,269.3	1,325.7	2.5	116.
1939	1,258.6	43,846.8	1,420.5	2.9	113.
1940	1,177.8	45,658.8	1,621.6	2.6	138.
1941	1,184.4	44,247.3	1,631.0	2.7	138.
1942	1,997.3	30,710.0	1,004.1	6.5	50.
1943	2,230.8	30,167.5	965.4	7.4	43.
1944	2,579.7	30,818.3	1,003.8	8.4	39.
1945	3,025.3	32,019.7	1,076.0	9.4	36.
1946	3,432.4	33,700.6	1,260.6	10.2	37.
1947	3,353.6	33,994.9	1,264.8	9.9	38.
1948	3,819.5	35,478.2	1,427.7	10.8	37.
1949	4,418.7	40,739.7	1,655.5	10.8	38.
1950	4,620.5	40,067.9	1,748.5	11.5	38.
1951	4,572.3	42,556.7	1,700.3	10.7	37.
1952	4,917.6	48,775.6	1,711.5	10.1	35.
1953	5,288.2	52,064.5	1,816.9	10.2	34.
1954	6,239.7	57,317.7	2,026.8	10.9	33.
1955	6,512.8	62,949.7	2,238.5	10.3	34.
1956	6,661.1	70,518.0	2,491.5	9.4	37.
1957	6,939.4	73,665.3	2,698.0	9.4	39.
1958d	5,360.6	83,938.9	2,679.8	6.4	50.
1949–58	5,553.1	57,259.6	2,076.7	9.7	37.

a—Data for 1958 are non-comparable with previous years due to new definition of business receipts and business deductions.

Food and Kindred Products (Millions of Dollars)

Meat Products; Dairy Products; Canning Fruits, Vegetables and Sea Foods; Grain Mill Products; Bakery Products; Confectionery; Cereal Preparations

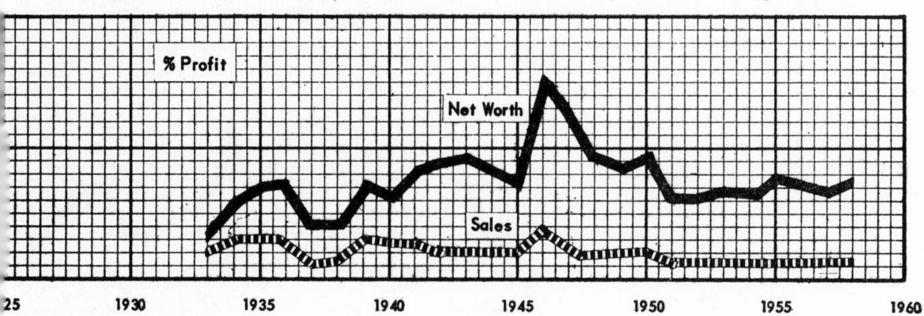

Year	Net Profit (After Taxes)	Sales	Net Worth	Dividends (Cash)	% Profit of Sales	% Profit of Net Worth	Div. as % Profit
1926							
1927							
1928							
1929							
1930							
1931							
1932							
1933	171.7	7,109.0	4,464.3	191.4	2.4	3.8	112.
1934	249.3	8,134.6	4,063.9	251.6	3.1	6.1	101.
1935	286.3	9,028.3	3,904.4	262.5	3.2	7.3	92.
1936	309.3	10,021.4	3,982.2	298.7	3.1	7.8	97.
1937	184.6	10,588.2	4,203.7	256.3	1.7	4.4	139.
1938	180.7	9,638.0	4,063.3	214.0	1.9	4.4	118.
1939	321.3	9,937.0	4,222.4	239.0	3.2	7.6	74.
1940	310.7	10,403.4	4,484.4	244.4	3.0	6.9	79.
1941	401.3	13,205.3	4,628.0	270.6	3.0	8.7	67.
1942	446.1	17,447.4	4,901.3	234.5	2.6	9.1	53.
1943	475.3	18,657.7	5,045.6	245.2	2.5	9.4	52.
1944	444.5	19,423.1	5,189.1	254.0	2.3	8.6	57.
1945	427.0	19,033.7	5,306.7	258.4	2.2	8.0	61.
1946	937.0	22,709.4	6,060.7	325.9	4.1	15.5	35.
1947	854.0	29,947.8	6,591.4	380.3	2.9	13.0	45.
1948	665.2	31,063.8	6,881.2	356.7	2.1	9.7	54.
1949	640.2	29,362.2	7,117.2	354.0	2.2	9.0	55.
1950	767.1	31,120.7	7,747.7	373.7	2.5	9.9	49.
1951	548.6	35,496.1	8,035.2	374.9	1.5	6.8	68.
1952	506.0	35,552.0	8,246.5	346.6	1.4	6.1	69.
1953	579.3	35,421.5	8,239.3	406.9	1.6	7.0	70.
1954	575.2	36,336.0	8,460.5	354.3	1.6	6.8	62.
1955	725.4	37,761.6	9,006.5	379.1	1.9	8.1	52.
1956	699.7	38,050.3	9,091.8	390.0	1.8	7.7	56.
1957	653.2	40,153.0	9,345.4	406.8	1.6	7.0	62.
1958	782.4	48,010.6	10,633.9	421.4	1.6	7.4	54.
1949–58	647.7	36,726.4	8,592.4	380.8	1.8	7.5	59.

Furniture and Fixtures (Millions of Dollars)

Furniture, Household, Office, Public Building and Professional; Partitions, Shelving, Lockers; and Office and Store Fixtures; Window and Door Screens, Shades and Venetian Blinds

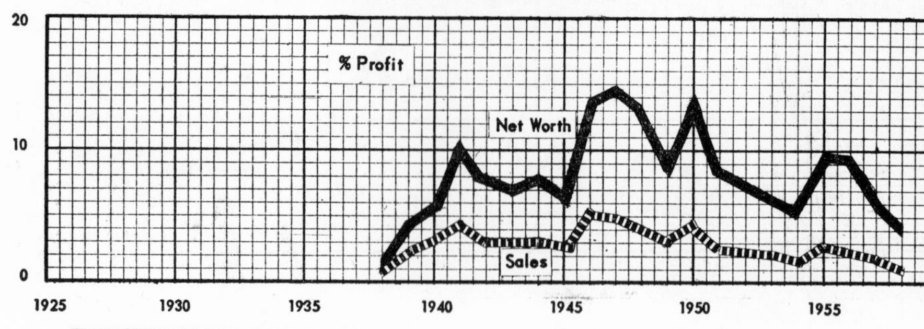

Year	*Net Profit (After Taxes)*	*Sales*	*Net Worth*	*Dividends (Cash)*	*% Profit of*		*Div. as % Profit*
					Sales	*Net Worth*	
1926							
1927							
1928							
1929							
1930							
1931							
1932							
1933							
1934							
1935							
1936							
1937							
1938	5.6	1,003.1	716.2	22.0	0.6	0.8	393.
1939	35.1	1,199.6	723.6	27.4	2.9	4.9	78.
1940	44.8	1,352.2	757.4	28.0	3.3	5.9	63.
1941	79.6	1,759.3	766.1	30.1	4.5	10.4	38.
1942	63.4	1,851.1	788.1	25.8	3.4	8.0	41.
1943	58.5	1,903.5	796.1	24.2	3.1	7.3	41.
1944	65.7	1,969.8	826.1	24.9	3.3	8.0	38.
1945	59.6	1,966.1	849.4	23.7	3.0	7.0	40.
1946	143.4	2,700.9	1,021.7	38.9	5.3	14.0	27.
1947	168.6	3,349.9	1,189.2	51.2	5.0	14.2	30.
1948	102.8	2,415.2	784.7	34.5	4.3	13.1	34.
1949	73.7	2,244.0	818.4	32.4	3.3	9.0	44.
1950	130.8	2,963.5	936.7	43.9	4.4	14.0	34.
1951	88.8	3,200.1	1,002.5	34.1	2.8	8.9	38.
1952	82.5	3,344.1	1,078.6	32.3	2.5	7.6	39.
1953	69.0	3,319.5	1,066.9	31.7	2.1	6.5	46.
1954	61.3	3,385.8	1,141.7	31.9	1.8	5.4	52.
1955	122.7	4,133.5	1,254.7	38.4	3.0	9.8	31.
1956	123.5	4,189.5	1,291.8	39.1	2.9	9.6	32.
1957	94.4	4,344.9	1,373.2	38.1	2.2	6.9	40.
1958	60.8	4,266.5	1,377.1	31.3	1.4	4.4	52.
1949–58	90.8	3,539.1	1,134.2	35.3	2.6	8.0	39.

Hotels and Lodging Places (Millions of Dollars)

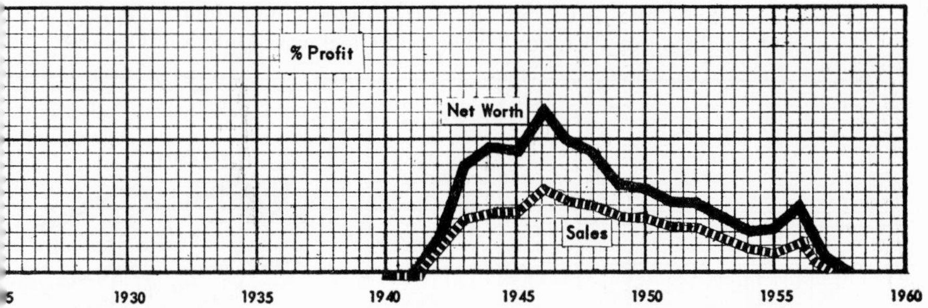

Year	Net Profit (After Taxes)	Sales	Net Worth	Dividends (Cash)	% Profit of		Div. as % Profit
					Sales	Net Worth	
1926							
1927							
1928							
1929							
1930							
1931							
1932							
1933							
1934							
1935							
1936							
1937							
1938							
1939							
1940	−15.1	589.2	433.0	6.1	—	—	—
1941	−6.5	643.4	420.9	7.5	—	—	—
1942	11.0	697.1	426.3	7.2	1.6	2.6	66.
1943	37.0	856.8	457.2	9.3	4.3	8.1	25.
1944	45.8	931.0	475.9	11.0	4.9	9.6	24.
1945	48.7	1,006.7	522.5	10.8	4.8	9.3	22.
1946	79.6	1,181.4	643.9	20.8	6.7	12.4	26.
1947	70.8	1,304.9	707.8	17.7	5.4	10.0	25.
1948	70.9	1,373.2	780.0	23.0	5.2	9.1	32.
1949	59.0	1,347.4	848.4	22.6	4.4	7.0	38.
1950	57.8	1,342.6	884.6	25.6	4.3	6.5	44.
1951	49.1	1,428.7	884.8	21.6	3.4	5.5	44.
1952	50.8	1,465.7	897.9	29.0	3.5	5.7	57.
1953	38.1	1,579.7	901.6	20.6	2.4	4.2	54.
1954	29.1	1,564.9	920.0	20.6	1.9	3.2	71.
1955	30.4	1,733.2	906.4	33.3	1.8	3.4	110.
1956	52.9	1,884.6	992.6	33.5	2.8	5.3	63.
1957	24.5	2,055.3	1,111.6	23.4	1.2	2.2	96.
1958	−1.1	1,966.8	1,140.2	21.8	—	—	—
1949–58	39.1	1,636.9	948.8	25.2	2.4	4.1	64.

Instruments (Millions of Dollars)

Professional, Scientific and Controlling Instruments including Photographic and Optical Goods; Watches, Clocks and Clockwork Operated Devices

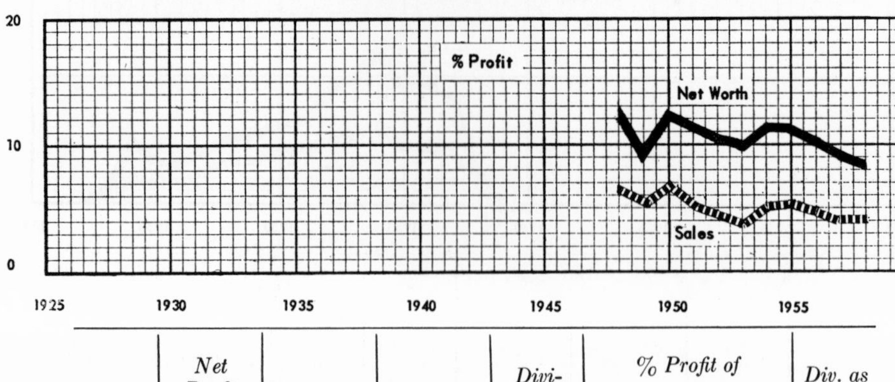

Year	*Net Profit (After Taxes)*	*Sales*	*Net Worth*	*Divi-dends (Cash)*	*% Profit of*		*Div. as % Profit*
					Sales	*Net Worth*	
1926							
1927							
1928							
1929							
1930							
1931							
1932							
1933							
1934							
1935							
1936							
1937							
1938							
1939							
1940							
1941							
1942							
1943							
1944							
1945							
1946							
1947							
1948	130.9	1,889.9	993.9	65.1	6.9	13.2	50.
1949	100.5	1,819.7	1,057.0	64.7	5.5	9.5	64.
1950	160.3	2,284.9	1,272.4	79.2	7.0	12.6	49.
1951	162.3	3,014.0	1,417.3	76.5	5.4	11.5	47.
1952	154.9	3,530.9	1,511.4	81.3	4.4	10.2	53.
1953	162.2	4,016.0	1,623.2	87.9	4.0	10.0	54.
1954	195.3	3,798.6	1,700.2	93.6	5.1	11.5	48.
1955	224.8	4,190.4	1,990.8	115.6	5.4	11.3	51.
1956	247.8	4,948.7	2,230.9	133.5	5.0	11.1	54.
1957	223.7	5,254.1	2,391.5	138.9	4.3	9.4	62.
1958	222.0	5,309.3	2,535.1	142.1	4.2	8.8	64.
1949–58	185.4	3,816.7	1,773.0	101.3	4.9	10.5	55.

Leather and Products (Millions of Dollars)

Leather, Tanned, Curried and Finished; Footwear, Except Rubber; Other Leather Products

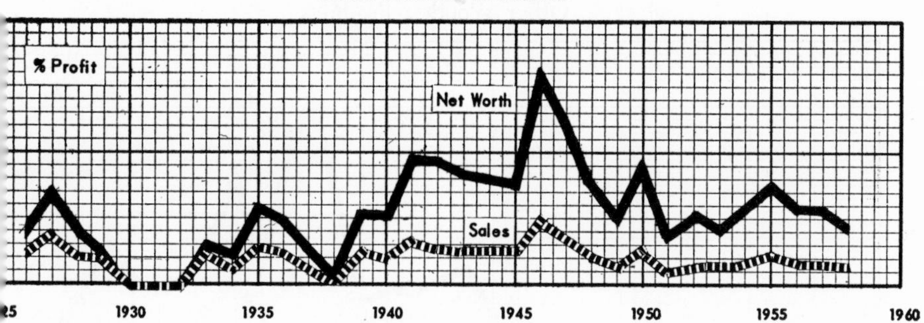

Year	Net Profit (After Taxes)	Sales	Net Worth	Dividends (Cash)	% Profit of		Div. as % Profit
					Sales	Net Worth	
1926	39.5	1,648.1	867.6	33.3	2.4	4.6	84.
1927	67.9	1,714.3	905.4	29.3	4.0	7.5	43.
1928	44.5	1,705.3	909.1	47.7	2.6	4.9	107.
1929	35.1	1,715.3	892.3	39.3	2.0	3.9	112.
1930	−26.8	1,368.2	827.9	40.0	—	—	—
1931	−35.3	1,061.8	712.7	28.4	—	—	—
1932	−41.8	821.7	636.1	20.5	—	—	—
1933	23.1	966.7	626.1	19.4	2.4	3.7	84.
1934	15.8	1,004.4	556.0	22.2	1.6	2.8	141.
1935	34.9	1,146.4	573.4	23.4	3.0	6.1	67.
1936	29.7	1,256.3	570.4	29.4	2.4	5.2	99.
1937	16.6	1,300.4	527.4	29.4	1.3	3.1	177.
1938	3.1	1,104.9	510.5	19.1	.3	.6	616.
1939	29.5	1,219.2	532.2	22.8	2.4	5.5	77.
1940	28.0	1,269.8	525.8	22.5	2.2	5.3	80.
1941	57.4	1,746.8	581.7	28.5	3.3	9.9	50.
1942	61.0	2,085.7	649.6	27.0	2.9	9.4	44.
1943	59.8	2,120.3	681.4	28.1	2.8	8.8	47.
1944	57.6	2,109.5	700.0	27.0	2.7	8.2	47.
1945	58.1	2,168.4	731.0	27.1	2.7	7.9	47.
1946	139.0	2,786.2	859.9	36.6	5.0	16.2	26.
1947	126.0	3,206.4	974.0	45.9	3.9	12.9	36.
1948	75.2	3,120.7	940.6	42.2	2.4	8.0	56.
1949	48.1	2,873.3	925.4	38.8	1.7	5.2	81.
1950	89.7	3,153.3	965.2	38.4	2.8	9.3	43.
1951	38.9	3,435.3	983.7	35.4	1.1	4.0	91.
1952	52.7	3,261.7	984.8	31.4	1.6	5.4	60.
1953	46.2	3,192.4	956.4	29.3	1.4	4.8	63.
1954	51.0	3,021.1	968.2	28.9	1.7	5.3	57.
1955	74.4	3,373.2	997.7	31.3	2.2	7.5	42.
1956	62.9	3,445.3	1,056.7	34.3	1.8	6.0	55.
1957	63.0	3,468.5	1,028.9	33.2	1.8	6.1	53.
1958	48.9	3,548.0	1,043.9	37.8	1.4	4.7	77.
1949–58	57.6	3,277.2	991.1	33.9	1.8	5.8	59.

Lumber and Wood Products Except Furniture (Millions of Dollars)

Logging Camps, Logging Contractors, Sawmills and Planing Mills; Millwork, Plywood and Prefabricated Structural Wood Products; Wooden containers; Other Wooden Products

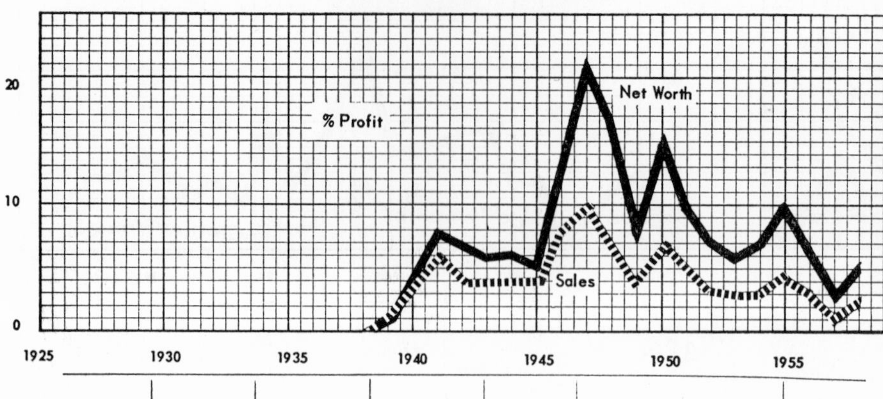

Year	Net Profit (After Taxes)	Sales	Net Worth	Dividends (Cash)	% Profit of		Div. as % Profit
					Sales	Net Worth	
1926							
1927							
1928							
1929							
1930							
1931							
1932							
1933							
1934							
1935							
1936							
1937							
1938	−10.9	717.8	1,026.8	16.8	—	—	—
1939	12.0	886.7	1,015.2	25.6	1.4	1.2	213.
1940	40.7	1,045.0	990.3	37.7	3.9	4.1	93.
1941	89.2	1,463.9	1,049.5	50.7	6.1	8.5	57.
1942	80.4	1,673.9	1,048.4	42.2	4.8	7.7	53.
1943	66.8	1,609.1	1,062.7	38.8	4.2	6.3	58.
1944	68.5	1,570.7	1,074.6	36.4	4.4	6.4	53.
1945	62.2	1,386.0	1,069.1	37.8	4.5	5.8	61.
1946	171.3	1,961.9	1,219.6	49.2	8.7	14.0	29.
1947	315.1	3,020.1	1,487.1	70.7	10.4	21.2	22.
1948	338.3	4,338.3	2,000.1	98.8	7.8	16.9	29.
1949	163.3	3,826.4	2,106.5	80.3	4.3	7.8	49.
1950	378.4	5,111.7	2,383.3	105.9	7.4	15.9	28.
1951	293.7	5,427.4	2,577.2	101.8	5.4	11.4	35.
1952	205.8	5,391.5	2,673.6	91.1	3.8	7.7	44.
1953	166.7	5,151.2	2,577.4	77.0	3.2	6.5	46.
1954	189.5	5,059.2	2,656.8	82.2	3.7	7.1	43.
1955	301.4	6,207.4	2,875.6	94.0	4.9	10.5	31.
1956	209.1	6,189.6	3,159.9	91.7	3.4	6.6	44.
1957	101.0	5,592.9	3,076.6	82.9	1.8	3.3	82.
1958	178.3	6,092.0	3,325.5	83.7	2.9	5.4	47.
1949–58	218.7	5,404.9	2,741.2	89.1	4.0	8.0	41.

Machinery-Electrical and Equipment (Millions of Dollars)

Electrical Generating, Transmission, Distribution and Industrial Apparatus; Electrical Appliances; Insulated Wire and Cable; Electrical Equipment for Motor Vehicles, Aircraft and Railway Locomotives and Cars; Electric Lamps; Radio, Radar and Television Equipment (Except Radio Tubes) and Phonographs; Other Communications Equipment and Related Products

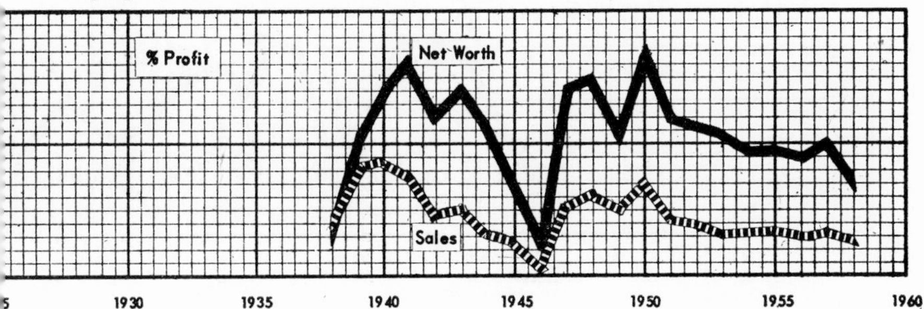

Year	Net Profit (After Taxes)	Sales	Net Worth	Dividends (Cash)	% Profit of Sales	% Profit of Net Worth	Div. as % Profit
1926							
1927							
1928							
1929							
1930							
1931							
1932							
1933							
1934							
1935							
1936							
1937							
1938	63.7	1,529.9	1,396.9	65.3	4.2	4.6	103.
1939	149.2	1,821.2	1,429.5	110.0	8.2	10.4	74.
1940	215.3	2,419.7	1,500.5	147.0	8.9	14.3	68.
1941	292.9	3,678.7	1,678.7	145.6	8.0	17.4	50.
1942	245.3	4,885.9	2,029.6	104.6	5.0	12.1	43.
1943	344.8	6,745.0	2,438.9	142.7	5.1	14.1	41.
1944	315.1	8,014.9	2,637.4	131.8	3.9	11.9	42.
1945	199.2	6,983.6	2,704.8	144.9	2.9	7.4	73.
1946	61.2	5,361.2	2,890.4	146.8	1.1	2.1	240.
1947	473.5	8,067.6	3,332.2	187.1	5.9	14.2	40.
1948	539.9	8,664.8	3,587.9	207.4	6.2	15.0	38.
1949	424.5	8,021.5	3,867.1	224.3	5.3	11.0	53.
1950	754.0	10,408.2	4,397.4	311.8	7.2	17.1	41.
1951	575.1	12,080.2	4,774.4	288.7	4.8	12.0	50.
1952	604.5	14,742.2	5,274.6	314.5	4.1	11.5	52.
1953	619.5	16,642.2	5,671.4	347.6	3.7	10.9	56.
1954	536.7	14,162.1	5,403.5	327.5	3.8	9.9	61.
1955	573.8	15,149.0	5,799.5	371.1	3.8	9.9	65.
1956	571.0	17,509.9	6,128.8	395.7	3.3	9.3	69.
1957	671.7	18,391.9	6,523.6	393.8	3.7	10.3	59.
1958	586.6	19,584.3	7,395.3	416.3	3.0	7.9	71.
1949–58	591.7	14,669.2	5,523.6	339.1	4.0	10.7	57.

Machinery-Nonelectrical (Millions of Dollars)

Engines and Turbines, Except Automotive, Aircraft and Railway; Agricultural Machinery and Tractors; Construction and Mining Machinery; Metalworking Machinery Including Machine Tools; Office and Store Machines

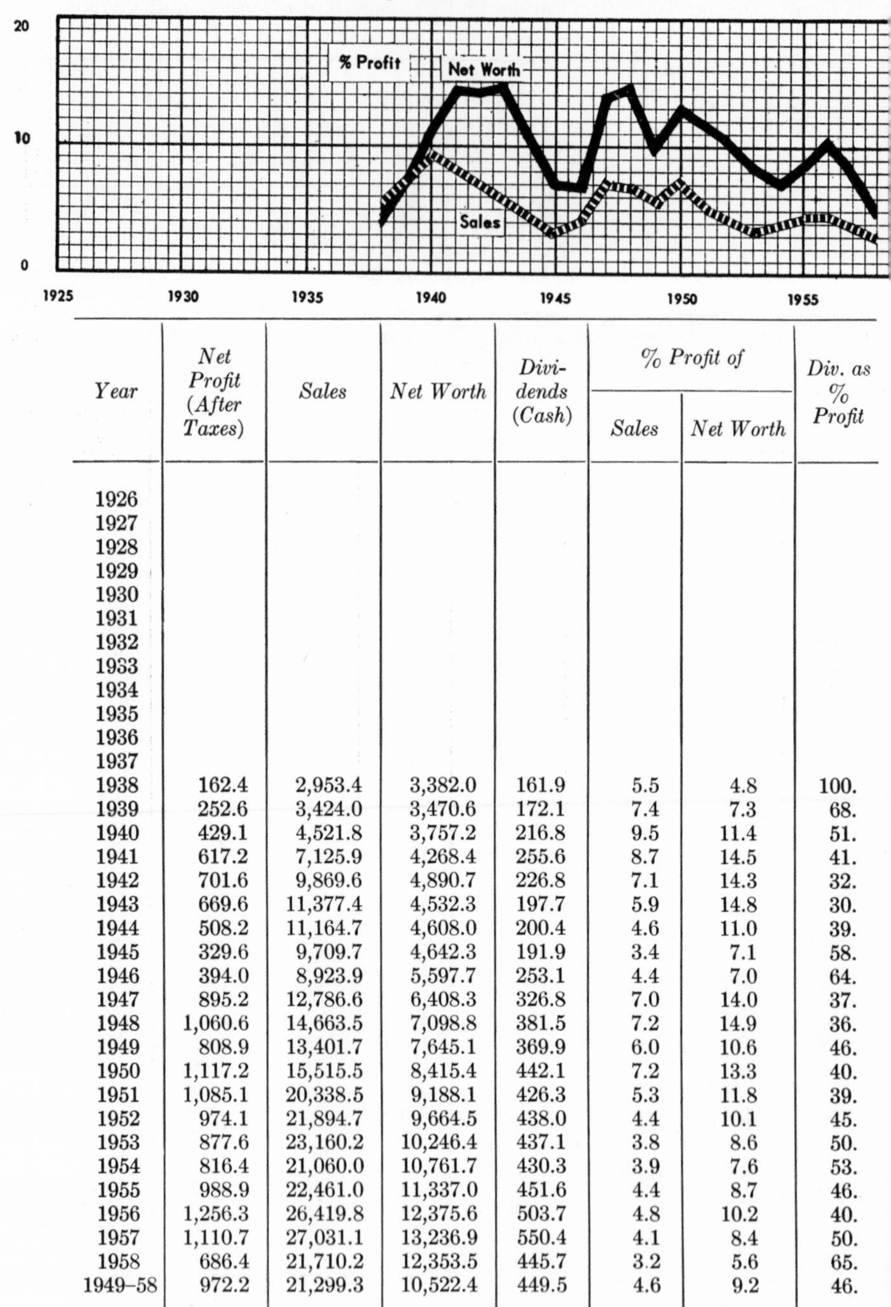

Year	Net Profit (After Taxes)	Sales	Net Worth	Dividends (Cash)	% Profit of		Div. as % Profit
					Sales	Net Worth	
1926							
1927							
1928							
1929							
1930							
1931							
1932							
1933							
1934							
1935							
1936							
1937							
1938	162.4	2,953.4	3,382.0	161.9	5.5	4.8	100.
1939	252.6	3,424.0	3,470.6	172.1	7.4	7.3	68.
1940	429.1	4,521.8	3,757.2	216.8	9.5	11.4	51.
1941	617.2	7,125.9	4,268.4	255.6	8.7	14.5	41.
1942	701.6	9,869.6	4,890.7	226.8	7.1	14.3	32.
1943	669.6	11,377.4	4,532.3	197.7	5.9	14.8	30.
1944	508.2	11,164.7	4,608.0	200.4	4.6	11.0	39.
1945	329.6	9,709.7	4,642.3	191.9	3.4	7.1	58.
1946	394.0	8,923.9	5,597.7	253.1	4.4	7.0	64.
1947	895.2	12,786.6	6,408.3	326.8	7.0	14.0	37.
1948	1,060.6	14,663.5	7,098.8	381.5	7.2	14.9	36.
1949	808.9	13,401.7	7,645.1	369.9	6.0	10.6	46.
1950	1,117.2	15,515.5	8,415.4	442.1	7.2	13.3	40.
1951	1,085.1	20,338.5	9,188.1	426.3	5.3	11.8	39.
1952	974.1	21,894.7	9,664.5	438.0	4.4	10.1	45.
1953	877.6	23,160.2	10,246.4	437.1	3.8	8.6	50.
1954	816.4	21,060.0	10,761.7	430.3	3.9	7.6	53.
1955	988.9	22,461.0	11,337.0	451.6	4.4	8.7	46.
1956	1,256.3	26,419.8	12,375.6	503.7	4.8	10.2	40.
1957	1,110.7	27,031.1	13,236.9	550.4	4.1	8.4	50.
1958	686.4	21,710.2	12,353.5	445.7	3.2	5.6	65.
1949–58	972.2	21,299.3	10,522.4	449.5	4.6	9.2	46.

Metal Mining (Millions of Dollars)

Iron; Copper; Lead; Zinc; Gold; Silver; Other Metal Mining

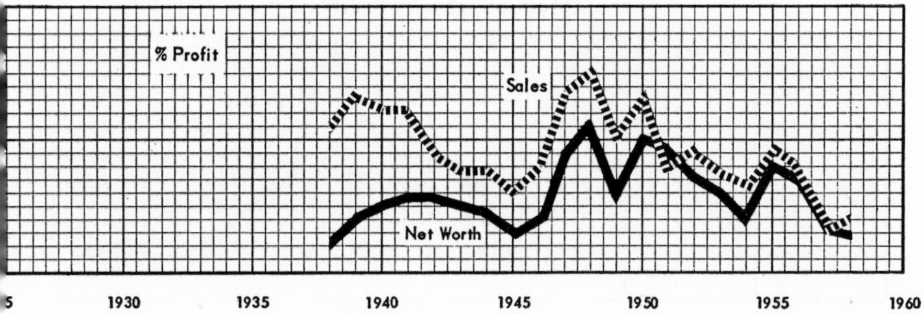

Year	*Net Profit (After Taxes)*	*Sales*	*Net Worth*	*Dividends (Cash)*	*% Profit of*		*Div. as % Profit*
					Sales	*Net Worth*	
1926							
1927							
1928							
1929							
1930							
1931							
1932							
1933							
1934							
1935							
1936							
1937							
1938	65.4	590.9	2,325.7	89.2	11.1	2.8	136.
1939	105.1	792.4	2,263.4	120.9	13.3	4.6	115.
1940	121.8	965.8	2,306.0	141.0	12.6	5.3	116.
1941	127.1	1,039.4	2,150.3	147.5	12.2	5.9	116.
1942	113.3	1,247.5	1,931.9	161.3	9.1	5.9	142.
1943	64.3	812.1	1,257.2	82.7	7.9	5.1	129.
1944	58.2	740.0	1,215.8	78.7	7.9	4.8	135.
1945	43.3	709.9	1,277.9	52.1	6.1	3.4	120.
1946	50.9	637.0	1,274.6	68.2	8.0	4.0	134.
1947	125.3	919.5	1,361.6	100.2	13.6	9.2	80.
1948	184.4	1,203.5	1,583.4	156.5	15.3	11.6	85.
1949	93.7	917.9	1,535.9	111.9	10.2	6.1	119.
1950	172.6	1,247.1	1,656.6	157.5	13.8	10.4	91.
1951	168.9	1,493.8	1,812.8	166.9	8.0	9.3	99.
1952	119.6	1,279.0	1,613.2	139.9	9.4	7.4	117.
1953	104.1	1,310.6	1,545.2	133.9	7.9	6.7	129.
1954	91.4	1,357.2	1,983.3	151.5	6.7	4.6	166.
1955	167.9	1,772.6	2,069.1	228.0	9.5	8.1	136.
1956	166.1	1,991.2	2,254.8	252.3	8.3	7.4	152.
1957	75.6	1,937.7	2,251.0	191.4	3.9	3.4	253.
1958	68.0	1,616.4	2,258.8	148.4	4.2	3.0	218.
1949–58	122.8	1,492.3	1,898.1	168.2	8.2	6.5	137.

Motion Pictures (Millions of Dollars)

Motion Picture Production
Motion Picture Theatres

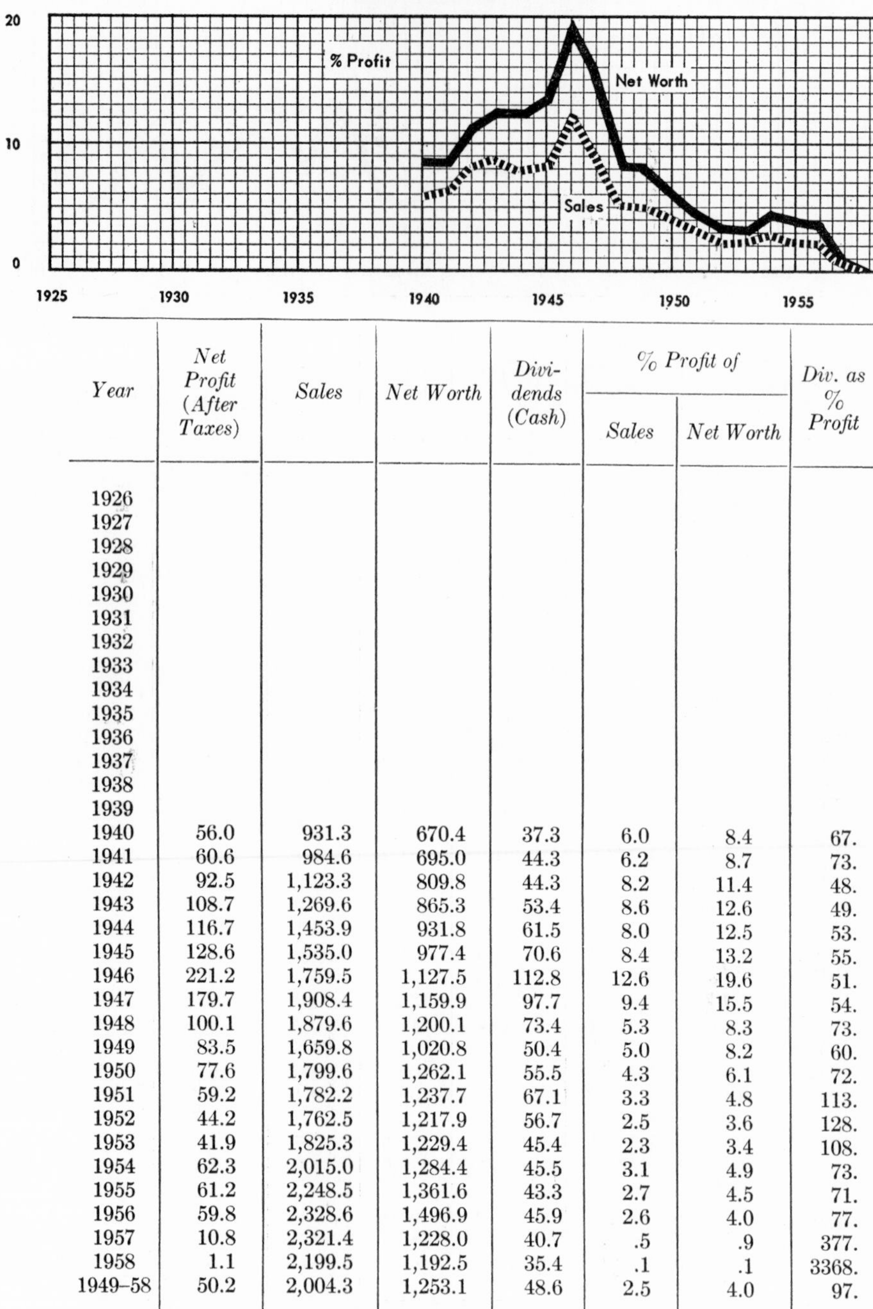

Year	*Net Profit (After Taxes)*	*Sales*	*Net Worth*	*Dividends (Cash)*	*% Profit of Sales*	*% Profit of Net Worth*	*Div. as % Profit*
1926							
1927							
1928							
1929							
1930							
1931							
1932							
1933							
1934							
1935							
1936							
1937							
1938							
1939							
1940	56.0	931.3	670.4	37.3	6.0	8.4	67.
1941	60.6	984.6	695.0	44.3	6.2	8.7	73.
1942	92.5	1,123.3	809.8	44.3	8.2	11.4	48.
1943	108.7	1,269.6	865.3	53.4	8.6	12.6	49.
1944	116.7	1,453.9	931.8	61.5	8.0	12.5	53.
1945	128.6	1,535.0	977.4	70.6	8.4	13.2	55.
1946	221.2	1,759.5	1,127.5	112.8	12.6	19.6	51.
1947	179.7	1,908.4	1,159.9	97.7	9.4	15.5	54.
1948	100.1	1,879.6	1,200.1	73.4	5.3	8.3	73.
1949	83.5	1,659.8	1,020.8	50.4	5.0	8.2	60.
1950	77.6	1,799.6	1,262.1	55.5	4.3	6.1	72.
1951	59.2	1,782.2	1,237.7	67.1	3.3	4.8	113.
1952	44.2	1,762.5	1,217.9	56.7	2.5	3.6	128.
1953	41.9	1,825.3	1,229.4	45.4	2.3	3.4	108.
1954	62.3	2,015.0	1,284.4	45.5	3.1	4.9	73.
1955	61.2	2,248.5	1,361.6	43.3	2.7	4.5	71.
1956	59.8	2,328.6	1,496.9	45.9	2.6	4.0	77.
1957	10.8	2,321.4	1,228.0	40.7	.5	.9	377.
1958	1.1	2,199.5	1,192.5	35.4	.1	.1	3368.
1949–58	50.2	2,004.3	1,253.1	48.6	2.5	4.0	97.

Motor Vehicles and Equipment, Except Electrical
(Millions of Dollars)

Motor Vehicles Including Bodies and Truck Trailers; Motor Vehicle Parts and Accessories, and Passenger Trailers

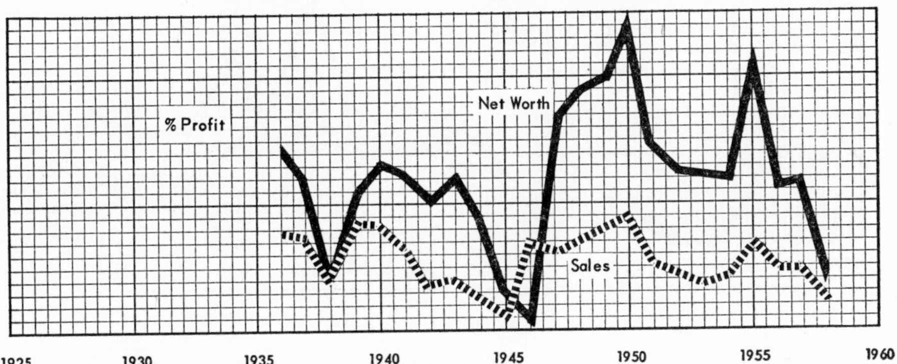

Year	Net Profit (After Taxes)	Sales	Net Worth	Dividends (Cash)	% Profit of Sales	% Profit of Net Worth	Div. as % Profit
1926							
1927							
1928							
1929							
1930							
1931							
1932							
1933							
1934							
1935							
1936	354.5	4,646.2	2,417.8	321.1	7.6	14.7	91.
1937	338.5	4,627.3	2,646.9	275.8	7.3	12.8	82.
1938	117.2	2,888.1	2,630.8	97.9	4.1	4.5	84.
1939	306.4	3,551.8	2,722.3	219.7	8.6	11.3	72.
1940	389.1	4,650.2	2,946.4	249.3	8.4	13.2	64.
1941	417.0	6,431.3	3,328.4	254.4	6.5	12.5	61.
1942	156.7	4,036.7	1,535.1	45.4	3.9	10.2	29.
1943	146.8	3,554.1	1,143.0	22.3	4.1	12.8	15.
1944	106.4	3,672.2	1,195.3	32.0	2.9	8.9	30.
1945	46.9	3,057.8	1,379.4	25.1	1.5	3.4	54.
1946	43.5	6,462.6	3,904.2	165.8	0.7	1.1	381.
1947	775.0	11,255.7	4,802.3	255.7	6.9	16.1	33.
1948	1,054.6	13,511.8	5,537.7	362.7	7.8	19.0	34.
1949	1,248.8	14,761.6	6,268.1	529.5	8.5	19.9	42.
1950	1,668.0	18,416.4	6,695.0	847.7	9.1	24.9	51.
1951	1,013.0	19,391.4	7,021.9	585.2	5.2	14.4	58.
1952	957.5	19,741.3	7,583.4	564.1	4.9	12.6	59.
1953	971.2	24,347.1	7,891.5	574.4	4.0	12.3	59.
1954	975.6	19,975.6	7,892.6	659.3	4.9	12.4	68.
1955	2,077.8	26,891.9	9,342.1	903.8	7.7	22.2	44.
1956	1,172.6	22,635.8	9,889.4	824.9	5.2	11.9	70.
1957	1,260.1	24,991.0	10,434.0	828.2	5.0	12.1	66.
1958	492.6	19,497.8	10,598.4	787.3	2.5	4.6	160.
1949–58	1,183.7	21,065.0	8,361.6	710.4	5.6	14.2	60.

Paper and Allied Products (Millions of Dollars)

Pulp Paper and Paperboard; Paper Bags and Paperboard Containers and Boxes; Pulp Goods and Other Converted Paper Products

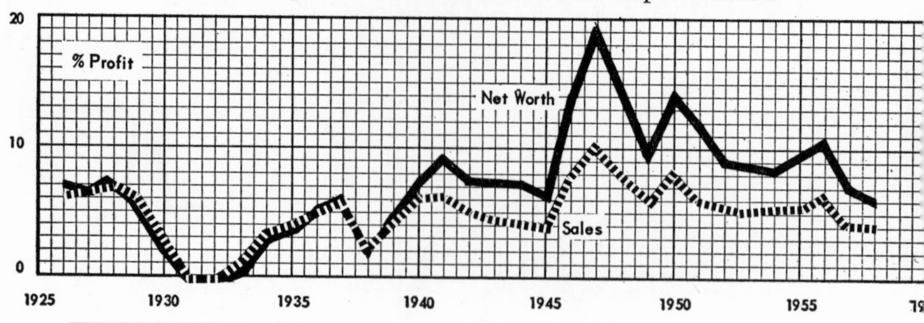

Year	Net Profit (After Taxes)	Sales	Net Worth	Dividends (Cash)	% Profit of Sales	% Profit of Net Worth	Div. as % Profit
1926	100.6	1,626.9	1,443.9	56.2	6.2	7.0	56.
1927	105.3	1,638.8	1,546.0	65.9	6.4	6.8	63.
1928	107.3	1,686.8	1,479.9	80.7	6.4	7.3	75.
1929	115.5	1,731.6	1,783.7	79.5	6.7	6.5	69.
1930	54.2	1,514.7	1,849.2	75.3	3.6	2.9	139.
1931	−8.8	1,203.8	1,778.1	45.6	—	—	—
1932	−58.4	956.4	1,717.4	25.6	—	—	—
1933	14.0	1,116.2	1,665.3	29.8	1.3	0.8	213.
1934	48.7	1,269.0	1,592.6	44.1	3.8	3.1	90.
1935	61.9	1,446.7	1,554.8	58.2	4.3	4.0	94.
1936	81.4	1,602.8	1,518.9	71.1	5.1	5.4	87.
1937	102.5	1,801.4	1,631.6	83.2	5.7	6.3	81.
1938	34.1	1,474.5	1,573.0	44.3	2.3	2.2	130.
1939	81.9	1,720.7	1,616.3	54.7	4.8	5.1	67.
1940	129.7	1,987.1	1,706.9	64.8	6.5	7.6	50.
1941	177.3	2,628.8	1,838.0	83.0	6.7	9.6	47.
1942	149.4	2,839.6	1,892.6	71.4	5.3	7.9	48.
1943	153.4	3,218.1	2,001.2	76.4	4.8	7.7	50.
1944	153.2	3,422.2	2,083.1	72.9	4.5	7.4	48.
1945	144.3	3,496.4	2,129.3	77.1	4.1	6.8	53.
1946	355.4	4,233.6	2,419.9	110.8	8.4	14.7	31.
1947	570.3	5,543.9	2,886.0	152.2	10.3	19.8	27.
1948	483.9	5,863.5	3,215.3	170.8	8.3	15.0	35.
1949	338.6	5,316.0	3,384.1	154.0	6.4	10.0	46.
1950	549.7	6,755.0	3,815.6	195.8	8.1	14.4	36.
1951	526.1	8,215.3	4,305.5	220.9	6.4	12.2	42.
1952	412.4	7,673.6	4,486.7	200.4	5.4	9.2	49.
1953	419.9	8,171.4	4,709.4	213.9	5.1	8.9	51.
1954	431.8	8,295.7	5,065.7	228.6	5.2	8.5	53.
1955	558.7	9,567.3	5,622.5	250.2	5.8	9.9	45.
1956	657.6	10,316.9	6,167.5	285.0	6.4	10.7	43.
1957	495.4	10,559.8	6,362.9	288.5	4.7	7.8	58.
1958	430.9	10,583.0	6,563.3	276.8	4.1	6.6	64.
1949–58	482.1	8,545.4	5,048.3	231.4	5.6	9.5	48.

Personal Services, Excluding Hotels (Millions of Dollars)

Laundries, Cleaners and Dyers; Photographic Studios, Including Commercial Photography and Other Personal Services

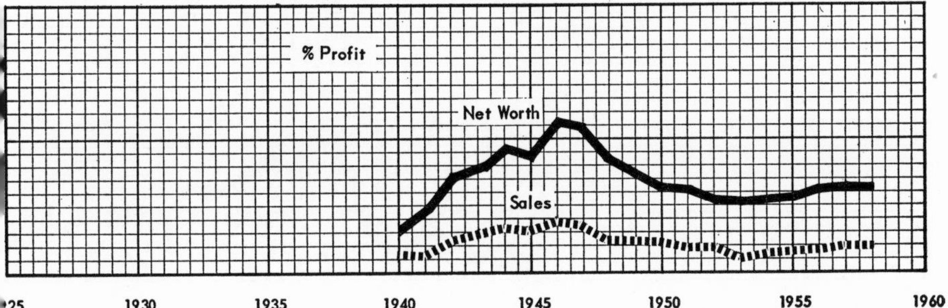

Year	Net Profit (After Taxes)	Sales	Net Worth	Dividends (Cash)	% Profit of Sales	% Profit of Net Worth	Div. as % Profit
1926							
1927							
1928							
1929							
1930							
1931							
1932							
1933							
1934							
1935							
1936							
1937							
1938							
1939							
1940	9.1	624.3	274.9	7.9	1.5	3.3	87.
1941	12.7	694.3	277.6	7.6	1.8	4.6	60.
1942	21.3	766.9	295.4	7.1	2.8	7.2	33.
1943	25.0	817.0	312.8	9.1	3.1	8.0	36.
1944	30.3	867.5	324.1	10.1	3.5	9.3	33.
1945	30.4	917.9	341.9	10.8	3.3	8.9	36.
1946	44.1	1,112.9	381.9	13.4	4.0	11.5	30.
1947	47.9	1,324.9	435.9	12.4	3.6	11.0	26.
1948	42.0	1,428.4	479.9	14.5	2.9	8.8	35.
1949	39.4	1,450.0	510.3	14.5	2.7	7.7	37.
1950	35.7	1,487.7	531.2	14.8	2.4	6.7	42.
1951	34.2	1,646.3	544.2	12.3	2.1	6.3	36.
1952	33.3	1,634.1	562.3	12.9	2.0	5.9	39.
1953	32.4	1,806.1	592.1	12.3	1.8	5.5	38.
1954	33.4	1,803.3	600.7	13.7	1.9	5.6	41.
1955	38.9	2,061.4	663.1	13.9	1.9	5.9	36.
1956	46.2	2,313.6	717.1	17.4	2.0	6.4	38.
1957	51.2	2,386.3	738.3	15.3	2.1	6.9	30.
1958	55.4	2,607.5	833.0	12.3	2.1	6.7	22.
1947–58	40.0	1,919.6	629.2	13.9	2.1	6.4	35.

Petroleum-Crude and Natural Gas Producers (Millions of Dollars)

Crude petroleum, natural gas and natural gasoline; oil and gas field contract services

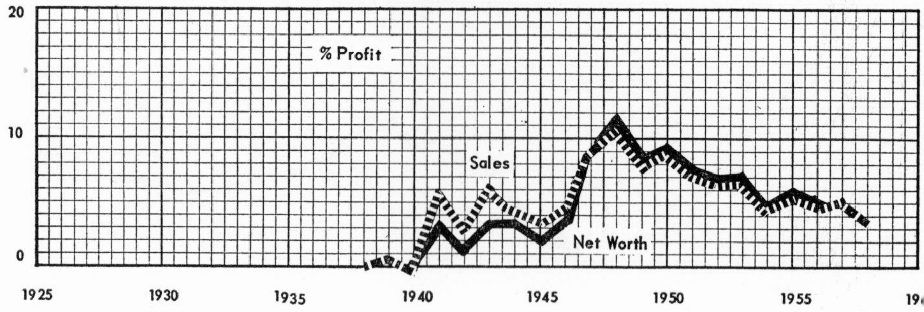

Year	Net Profit (After Taxes)	Sales	Net Worth	Dividends (Cash)	% Profit of Sales	% Profit of Net Worth	Div. as % Profit
1926							
1927							
1928							
1929							
1930							
1931							
1932							
1933							
1934							
1935							
1936							
1937							
1938	2.3	674.8	1,364.9	82.9	.3	.2	3,604.
1939	3.5	689.8	1,345.4	62.9	.5	.3	1,797.
1940	−4.3	707.8	1,340.3	97.3	—	—	—
1941	4.1	795.9	1,307.4	115.5	6.0	3.7	240.
1942	19.2	619.2	1,057.4	50.9	3.1	1.8	265.
1943	40.4	630.8	1,056.1	63.5	6.4	3.8	157.
1944	37.4	794.4	1,133.2	56.0	4.7	3.3	148.
1945	28.3	833.0	1,153.3	50.3	3.4	2.5	178.
1946	45.5	966.7	1,220.3	67.6	4.7	3.7	149.
1947	139.0	1,470.5	1,542.0	107.5	9.5	9.0	77.
1948	257.6	2,391.6	2,181.3	175.0	10.8	11.8	68.
1949	208.4	2,562.9	2,547.6	196.7	8.1	8.2	94.
1950	286.4	3,253.5	3,093.3	271.0	8.8	9.3	94.
1951	267.5	3,765.3	3,394.4	312.5	7.1	7.9	117.
1952	260.9	4,138.8	3,701.9	359.7	6.3	7.0	138.
1953	276.9	4,126.6	3,925.5	420.9	6.7	7.1	152.
1954	164.3	3,453.7	3,342.8	494.7	4.8	4.9	301.
1955	207.2	3,959.5	3,620.9	446.1	5.2	5.7	215.
1956	188.9	4,120.7	3,775.1	459.5	4.6	5.0	243.
1957	223.6	4,468.8	4,215.6	387.9	5.0	5.3	173.
1958	149.2	4,104.8	4,290.8	497.0	3.6	3.5	333.
1949–58	223.3	3,795.5	3,590.8	384.6	5.9	6.2	172.

Petroleum and Coal Products (Millions of Dollars)

Petroleum Refining; other petroleum and coal products like roofing and paving materials and fuel briquettes

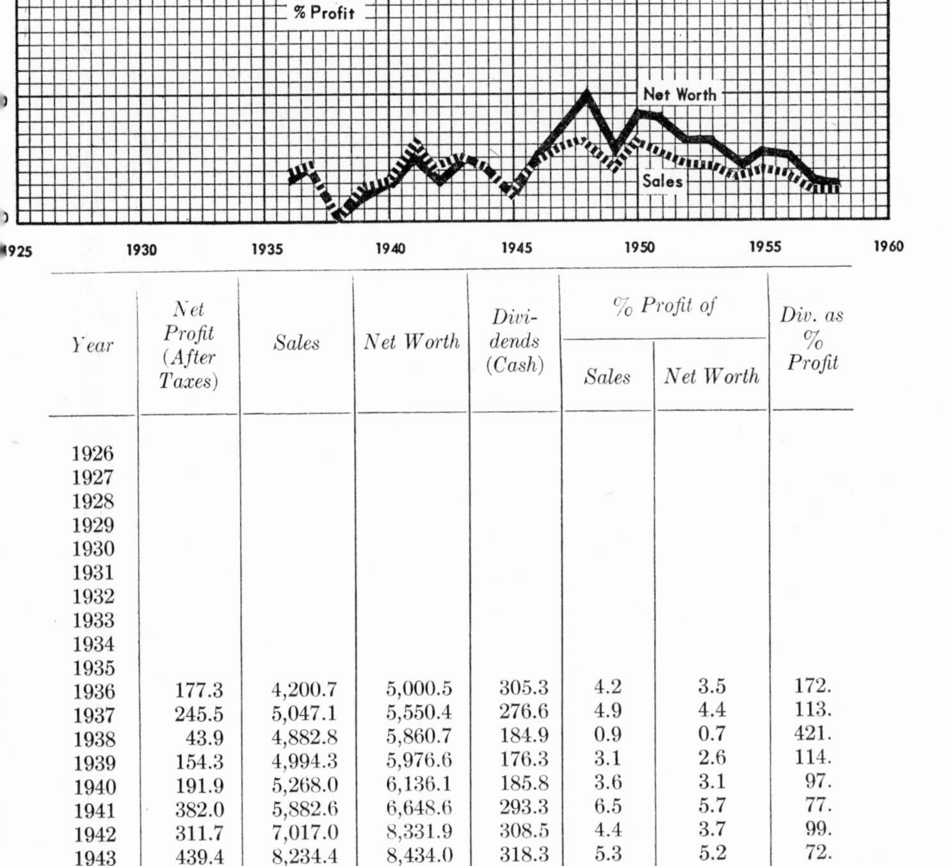

Year	Net Profit (After Taxes)	Sales	Net Worth	Dividends (Cash)	% Profit of Sales	% Profit of Net Worth	Div. as % Profit
1926							
1927							
1928							
1929							
1930							
1931							
1932							
1933							
1934							
1935							
1936	177.3	4,200.7	5,000.5	305.3	4.2	3.5	172.
1937	245.5	5,047.1	5,550.4	276.6	4.9	4.4	113.
1938	43.9	4,882.8	5,860.7	184.9	0.9	0.7	421.
1939	154.3	4,994.3	5,976.6	176.3	3.1	2.6	114.
1940	191.9	5,268.0	6,136.1	185.8	3.6	3.1	97.
1941	382.0	5,882.6	6,648.6	293.3	6.5	5.7	77.
1942	311.7	7,017.0	8,331.9	308.5	4.4	3.7	99.
1943	439.4	8,234.4	8,434.0	318.3	5.3	5.2	72.
1944	388.8	9,402.0	8,920.3	387.0	4.1	4.4	100.
1945	230.6	9,670.1	8,916.2	360.6	2.4	2.6	156.
1946	493.2	10,004.0	9,510.4	435.5	4.9	5.2	88.
1947	874.9	14,550.8	11,356.7	589.8	6.0	7.7	67.
1948	1,320.9	19,363.8	12,863.3	702.5	6.8	10.3	53.
1949	764.9	16,935.2	13,539.2	842.0	4.5	5.6	110.
1950	1,200.2	19,250.4	14,417.6	950.5	6.2	8.3	79.
1951	1,304.3	23,460.6	16,052.3	1,087.4	5.6	8.1	83.
1952	1,097.2	23,745.3	17,068.6	1,166.3	4.6	6.4	106.
1953	1,163.9	25,634.2	18,123.6	1,215.8	4.5	6.4	105.
1954	960.9	26,414.1	20,585.9	1,027.7	3.6	4.7	107.
1955	1,211.6	30,535.8	22,411.9	1,116.2	4.0	5.4	92.
1956	1,262.6	33,683.2	25,485.2	1,306.8	3.7	5.0	104.
1957	961.7	35,923.4	26,120.2	1,336.3	2.7	3.7	139.
1958	866.5	35,037.0	28,031.1	1,419.5	2.5	3.1	164.
1949–58	1,079.4	27,062.0	20,103.6	1,146.9	4.0	5.3	106.

PRIMARY METAL INDUSTRY (Millions of Dollars)

Blast Furnaces, Steel Works and Rolling Mills; Iron and Steel Foundries; Smelting, Refining, Rolling, Drawing and Alloying of Non-Ferrous Metals; Non-Ferrous Foundries; Other Primary Metal Industries

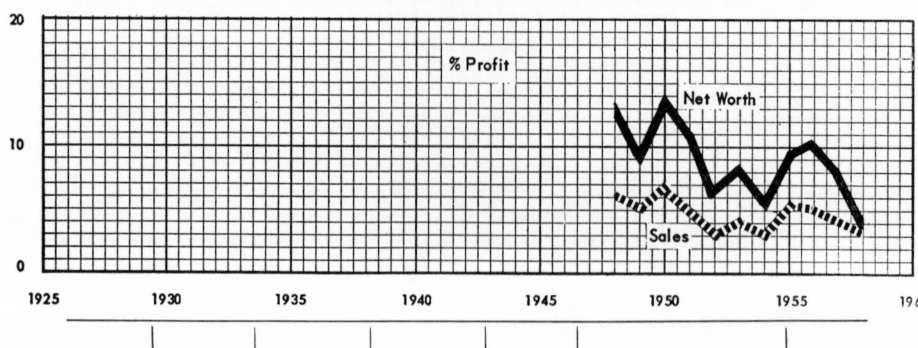

Year	*Net Profit (After Taxes)*	*Sales*	*Net Worth*	*Dividends (Cash)*	*% Profit of*		*Div. as % Profit*
					Sales	*Net Worth*	
1926							
1927							
1928							
1929							
1930							
1931							
1932							
1933							
1934							
1935							
1936							
1937							
1938							
1939							
1940							
1941							
1942							
1943							
1944							
1945							
1946							
1947							
1948	1,060.3	16,626.4	7,850.5	366.3	6.4	13.5	35.
1949	798.5	14,457.1	8,335.7	358.1	5.5	9.6	45.
1950	1,283.5	18,595.5	9,172.1	526.8	6.9	14.0	41.
1951	1,141.3	22,417.9	9,947.6	490.6	5.1	11.5	43.
1952	744.4	20,152.8	10,623.5	478.4	3.7	7.0	64.
1953	938.9	23,132.0	11,151.8	482.2	4.1	8.4	51.
1954	702.4	19,538.6	11,542.2	455.3	3.6	6.1	65.
1955	1,416.8	25,867.1	14,405.1	641.1	5.5	9.8	45.
1956	1,412.9	27,335.5	13,800.1	647.5	5.2	10.2	46.
1957	1,237.1	27,398.7	14,918.1	693.0	4.5	8.3	56.
1958	763.3	23,483.0	16,072.2	628.3	3.3	4.7	82.
1949–58	1,043.9	22,237.8	11,996.8	540.1	4.7	8.7	52.

Printing, Publishing and Allied Industries (Millions of Dollars)

Newspapers; periodicals; books; commercial printing, including lithographing; other printing and publishing

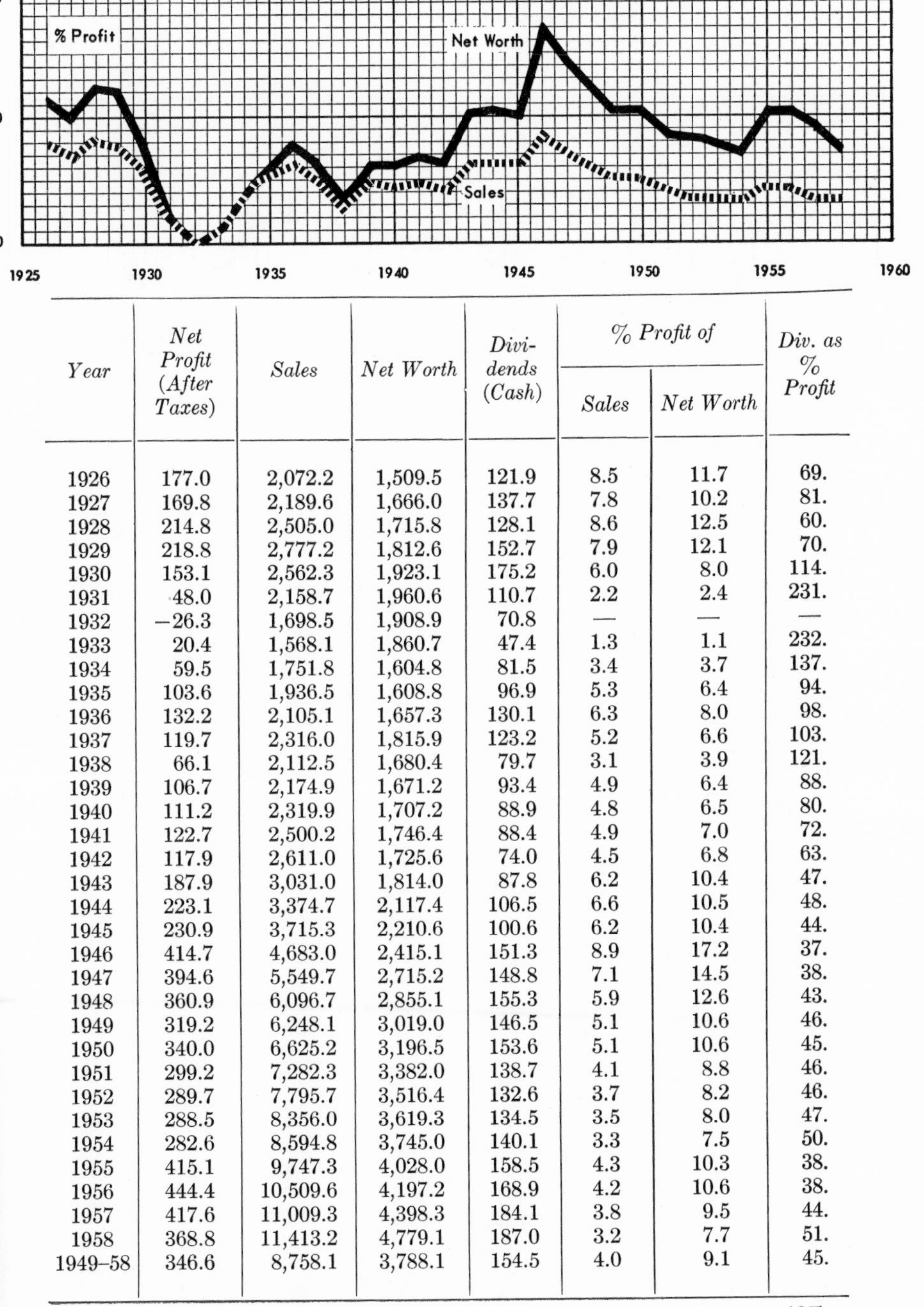

Year	Net Profit (After Taxes)	Sales	Net Worth	Dividends (Cash)	% Profit of Sales	% Profit of Net Worth	Div. as % Profit
1926	177.0	2,072.2	1,509.5	121.9	8.5	11.7	69.
1927	169.8	2,189.6	1,666.0	137.7	7.8	10.2	81.
1928	214.8	2,505.0	1,715.8	128.1	8.6	12.5	60.
1929	218.8	2,777.2	1,812.6	152.7	7.9	12.1	70.
1930	153.1	2,562.3	1,923.1	175.2	6.0	8.0	114.
1931	48.0	2,158.7	1,960.6	110.7	2.2	2.4	231.
1932	−26.3	1,698.5	1,908.9	70.8	—	—	—
1933	20.4	1,568.1	1,860.7	47.4	1.3	1.1	232.
1934	59.5	1,751.8	1,604.8	81.5	3.4	3.7	137.
1935	103.6	1,936.5	1,608.8	96.9	5.3	6.4	94.
1936	132.2	2,105.1	1,657.3	130.1	6.3	8.0	98.
1937	119.7	2,316.0	1,815.9	123.2	5.2	6.6	103.
1938	66.1	2,112.5	1,680.4	79.7	3.1	3.9	121.
1939	106.7	2,174.9	1,671.2	93.4	4.9	6.4	88.
1940	111.2	2,319.9	1,707.2	88.9	4.8	6.5	80.
1941	122.7	2,500.2	1,746.4	88.4	4.9	7.0	72.
1942	117.9	2,611.0	1,725.6	74.0	4.5	6.8	63.
1943	187.9	3,031.0	1,814.0	87.8	6.2	10.4	47.
1944	223.1	3,374.7	2,117.4	106.5	6.6	10.5	48.
1945	230.9	3,715.3	2,210.6	100.6	6.2	10.4	44.
1946	414.7	4,683.0	2,415.1	151.3	8.9	17.2	37.
1947	394.6	5,549.7	2,715.2	148.8	7.1	14.5	38.
1948	360.9	6,096.7	2,855.1	155.3	5.9	12.6	43.
1949	319.2	6,248.1	3,019.0	146.5	5.1	10.6	46.
1950	340.0	6,625.2	3,196.5	153.6	5.1	10.6	45.
1951	299.2	7,282.3	3,382.0	138.7	4.1	8.8	46.
1952	289.7	7,795.7	3,516.4	132.6	3.7	8.2	46.
1953	288.5	8,356.0	3,619.3	134.5	3.5	8.0	47.
1954	282.6	8,594.8	3,745.0	140.1	3.3	7.5	50.
1955	415.1	9,747.3	4,028.0	158.5	4.3	10.3	38.
1956	444.4	10,509.6	4,197.2	168.9	4.2	10.6	38.
1957	417.6	11,009.3	4,398.3	184.1	3.8	9.5	44.
1958	368.8	11,413.2	4,779.1	187.0	3.2	7.7	51.
1949–58	346.6	8,758.1	3,788.1	154.5	4.0	9.1	45.

Retail Total (Corporation – Millions of Dollars)

Food; Department Stores; Mail Order Houses; Variety Stores; Apparel and Accessories; Furniture and House Furnishings; Automobile and Truck Dealers; Parts, Accessories, Tires and Batteries; Filling Stations; Drug Stores; Eating and Drinking Places; Lumber and Building Materials; Hardware and Farm Equipment; Liquor Stores; Jewelry Stores; Other Retail Stores

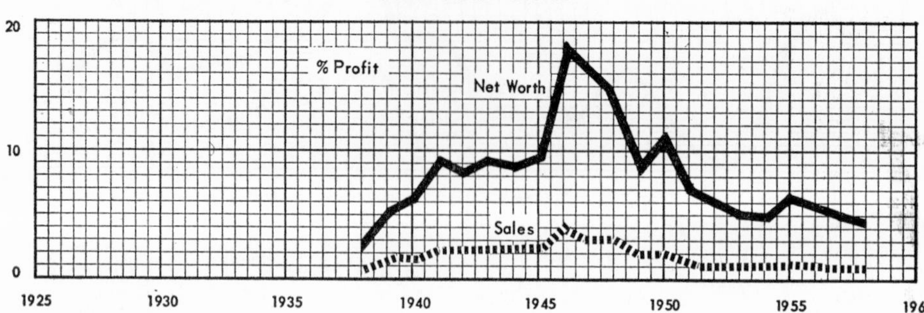

Year	*Net Profit (After Taxes)*	*Sales*	*Net Worth*	*Dividends (Cash)*	*% Profit of*		*Div. as % Profit*
					Sales	*Net Worth*	
1926							
1927							
1928							
1929							
1930							
1931							
1932							
1933							
1934							
1935							
1936							
1937							
1938	167.5	16,491.1	5,640.8	226.5	1.0	3.0	135.
1939	333.1	18,643.3	5,930.8	260.1	1.8	5.6	78.
1940	392.8	20,540.4	6,116.9	272.0	1.9	6.4	69.
1941	596.7	24,476.3	6,556.4	294.0	2.4	9.1	49.
1942	607.7	23,329.3	6,841.1	278.4	2.6	8.9	46.
1943	691.6	24,369.5	7,180.9	306.5	2.8	9.6	44.
1944	710.4	25,795.5	7,481.1	309.2	2.8	9.5	44.
1945	783.6	28,019.4	7,993.4	317.0	2.8	9.8	41.
1946	1,802.9	39,701.2	9,829.8	520.7	4.5	18.3	29.
1947	1,945.2	51,030.5	11,562.4	539.3	3.8	16.8	28.
1948	1,950.9	57,436.2	13,308.1	566.2	3.4	14.7	29.
1949	1,351.4	58,270.5	14,165.3	538.5	2.3	9.5	−40.
1950	1,884.7	67,039.2	15,948.9	614.6	2.8	11.8	33.
1951	1,304.6	70,712.5	16,751.4	575.7	1.8	7.8	44.
1952	1,129.3	73,368.4	17,011.8	559.2	1.5	6.6	50.
1953	964.2	77,610.2	17,468.4	529.3	1.2	5.5	55.
1954	904.0	78,559.2	17,868.6	518.2	1.2	5.1	57.
1955	1,295.7	95,152.4	19,659.8	577.6	1.4	6.6	45.
1956	1,235.9	98,379.9	20,510.0	581.2	1.3	6.0	47.
1957	1,073.9	103,843.7	21,009.0	598.3	1.0	5.1	56.
1958	1,041.3	104,013.7	21,592.0	591.9	1.0	4.8	57.
1949–58	1,218.5	82,694.8	18,198.8	568.5	1.5	6.7	47.

Rubber Products (Millions of Dollars)

Tires and Inner Tubes
Other Rubber Products, Including Rubberized Fabrics and Clothing

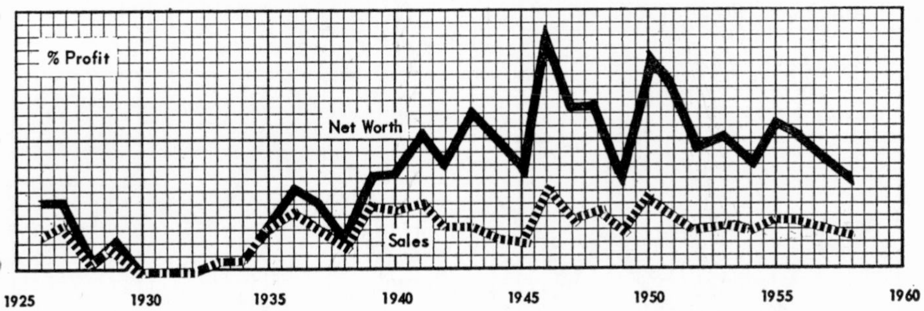

Year	Net Profit (After Taxes)	Sales	Net Worth	Dividends (Cash)	% Profit of		Div. as % Profit
					Sales	Net Worth	
1926	44.4	1,557.5	852.8	41.3	2.9	5.2	93.
1927	51.3	1,430.3	970.5	58.4	3.6	5.3	114.
1928	3.1	1,366.9	876.5	27.4	0.2	0.4	884.
1929	23.5	1,391.7	926.8	46.1	1.7	2.5	196.
1930	−40.2	1,063.0	895.7	44.1	—	—	—
1931	−20.2	786.0	822.2	26.9	—	—	—
1932	−31.2	608.6	739.4	19.3	—	—	—
1933	4.4	689.5	746.5	7.8	0.6	0.6	177.
1934	4.3	713.9	780.8	16.4	0.6	0.6	381.
1935	24.6	770.9	658.9	16.4	3.2	3.7	67.
1936	43.4	940.0	651.0	40.3	4.6	6.7	93.
1937	36.9	1,056.2	678.8	42.4	3.5	5.4	115.
1938	15.0	706.4	603.3	17.0	2.1	2.5	113.
1939	52.1	1,053.4	707.0	30.9	4.9	7.4	59.
1940	53.7	1,107.5	704.9	26.6	4.8	7.6	50.
1941	84.9	1,660.8	782.0	35.6	5.1	10.9	42.
1942	68.0	1,867.4	789.1	25.2	3.6	8.6	37.
1943	109.3	2,955.1	874.3	34.6	3.7	12.5	32.
1944	96.3	3,323.3	928.6	38.5	2.9	10.4	40.
1945	76.2	3,324.2	944.1	39.6	2.3	8.1	52.
1946	193.7	3,050.8	1,073.1	62.1	6.3	18.1	32.
1947	146.3	3,353.6	1,140.9	65.3	4.4	12.8	45.
1948	162.7	3,321.4	1,262.5	65.8	4.9	12.9	40.
1949	96.5	2,955.7	1,272.9	57.5	3.3	7.6	60.
1950	238.3	3,979.5	1,416.1	74.0	6.0	16.8	31.
1951	220.2	4,844.0	1,558.7	82.0	4.5	14.1	37.
1952	161.7	4,783.0	1,635.7	83.0	3.4	9.9	51.
1953	178.7	4,961.3	1,740.7	81.9	3.6	10.3	46.
1954	144.2	4,521.7	1,670.9	84.6	3.2	8.6	59.
1955	227.5	5,773.1	1,966.2	101.5	3.9	11.6	45.
1956	219.9	5,690.4	2,072.7	108.7	3.9	10.6	49.
1957	190.4	5,585.4	2,155.1	110.0	3.4	8.8	58.
1958	198.6	6,830.3	2,742.3	109.6	2.9	7.2	55.
1949–58	187.6	4,992.4	1,823.1	89.3	3.8	10.3	48.

Stone, Clay and Glass Products (Millions of Dollars)

Glass and Glass Products; Cement (Hydraulic); Structural Clay Products; Pottery and Related Products; Concrete, Gypsum and Plaster Products; Cut Stone and Stone Products; Abrasives, Asbestos and Other Non-Metallic Mineral Products

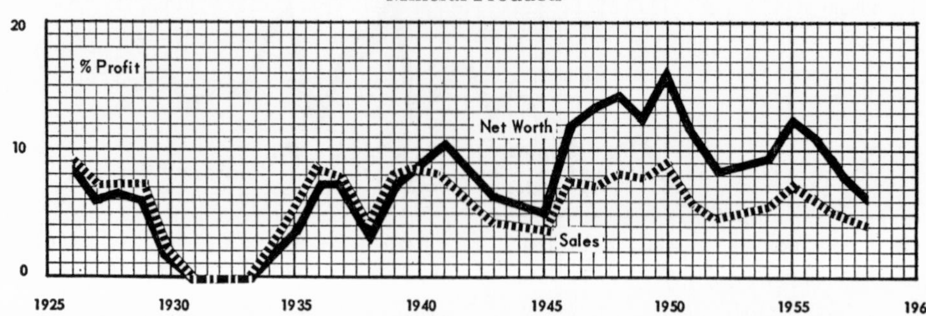

Year	*Net Profit (After Taxes)*	*Sales*	*Net Worth*	*Dividends (Cash)*	*% Profit of*		*Div. as % Profit*
					Sales	*Net Worth*	
1926	156.2	1,645.5	1,682.3	101.5	9.5	9.3	65.
1927	115.7	1,580.8	1,815.2	85.9	7.3	6.4	74.
1928	127.0	1,636.6	1,889.2	83.3	7.8	6.7	66.
1929	120.3	1,619.1	1,869.0	90.8	7.4	6.4	76.
1930	35.1	1,379.7	1,938.5	79.7	2.5	1.8	227.
1931	−33.1	995.2	1,674.2	58.7	—	—	—
1932	−91.8	643.9	1,516.3	29.4	—	—	—
1933	−20.6	696.7	1,452.4	24.6	—	—	—
1934	23.5	805.7	1,427.3	44.8	2.9	1.6	191.
1935	58.3	980.5	1,445.5	63.0	5.9	4.0	108.
1936	111.7	1,273.7	1,464.5	105.5	8.8	7.6	94.
1937	118.7	1,477.4	1,559.3	112.1	8.0	7.6	94.
1938	51.6	1,176.6	1,513.4	55.4	4.4	3.4	107.
1939	119.9	1,467.7	1,563.5	87.6	8.2	7.7	73.
1940	144.5	1,660.3	1,627.0	100.8	8.7	8.9	70.
1941	178.3	2,237.6	1,664.0	108.1	8.0	10.7	61.
1942	142.6	2,288.8	1,625.2	71.3	6.2	8.8	50.
1943	109.9	2,328.8	1,621.2	68.3	4.7	6.8	62.
1944	93.6	2,265.9	1,588.0	59.7	4.1	5.9	64.
1945	91.7	2,287.4	1,673.3	62.3	4.0	5.5	68.
1946	227.0	2,866.2	1,862.0	93.6	7.9	12.2	41.
1947	279.4	3,562.9	2,089.1	111.6	7.8	13.4	40.
1948	328.1	4,062.4	2,306.1	125.0	8.1	14.2	38.
1949	311.4	3,900.9	2,439.3	143.9	8.0	12.8	46.
1950	453.9	4,944.2	2,802.6	182.2	9.2	16.2	40.
1951	340.4	5,641.0	3,040.7	168.1	6.0	11.2	49.
1952	274.9	5,507.0	3,138.5	165.0	5.0	8.8	60.
1953	324.2	6,419.7	3,641.1	195.4	5.1	8.9	60.
1954	386.6	6,517.4	3,943.4	216.0	5.9	9.8	56.
1955	572.9	7,828.0	4,428.3	246.2	7.3	12.9	43.
1956	514.9	7,784.9	4,701.6	272.2	6.6	11.0	53.
1957	429.4	8,187.7	5,199.3	281.1	5.2	8.3	65.
1958	405.0	9,284.8	5,850.3	286.5	4.4	6.9	71.
1949–58	401.4	6,601.6	3,918.5	215.7	6.1	10.2	54.

TEXTILE-MILL PRODUCTS (Millions of Dollars)

Yarn and Thread (Cotton, Wool, Silk and Synthetic Fiber); Broadwoven Fabrics (Woolen and Worsted, Cotton); Narrow Fabrics and Other Small Wares; Knit Goods; Dyeing and Finishing Textiles, Except Knit Goods; Carpets and Other Floor Coverings; Hats, Except Cloth and Millinery

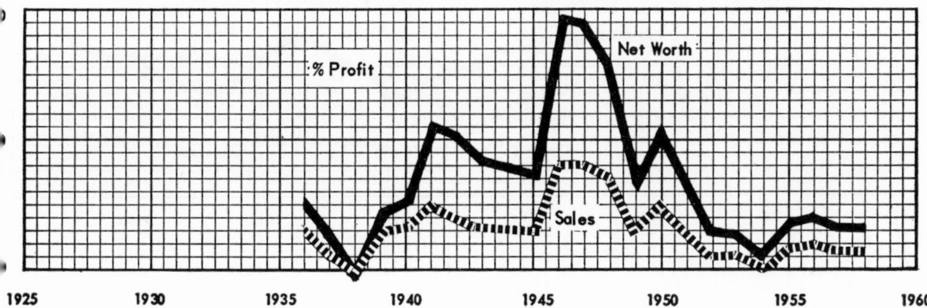

Year	Net Profit (After Taxes)	Sales	Net Worth	Dividends (Cash)	% Profit of Sales	% Profit of Net Worth	Div. as % Profit
1926							
1927							
1928							
1929							
1930							
1931							
1932							
1933							
1934							
1935							
1936	141.7	4,340.8	2,732.7	128.8	3.3	5.2	91.
1937	68.4	4,397.0	2,818.0	126.9	1.6	2.4	186.
1938	−31.9	3,133.9	2,443.2	48.4	—	—	—
1939	121.1	3,815.3	2,488.5	72.1	3.2	4.9	60.
1940	139.6	4,147.7	2,538.0	78.6	3.4	5.5	56.
1941	316.3	5,973.2	2,801.8	107.7	5.3	11.3	34.
1942	326.4	7,566.8	3,089.0	106.3	4.3	10.6	33.
1943	287.7	7,936.2	3,252.3	110.3	3.6	8.8	38.
1944	274.8	7,577.5	3,347.1	116.9	3.6	8.2	43.
1945	274.3	7,536.4	3,496.5	120.6	3.6	7.8	44.
1946	825.2	9,683.9	4,187.0	220.5	8.5	19.7	27.
1947	935.0	11,298.3	4,873.1	265.6	8.3	19.2	28.
1948	926.0	12,207.5	5,552.6	291.9	7.6	16.7	32.
1949	387.7	10,510.9	5,635.9	227.4	3.7	6.9	59.
1950	700.4	12,963.3	6,149.9	253.8	5.4	11.4	36.
1951	447.7	14,071.3	6,444.9	243.5	3.2	6.9	54.
1952	197.7	12,889.3	6,182.0	185.8	1.5	3.2	94.
1953	193.2	12,394.4	6,241.6	173.2	1.6	3.1	90.
1954	89.8	11,586.0	6,182.2	141.3	0.8	1.5	157.
1955	260.3	13,492.0	6,559.6	161.3	1.9	4.0	62.
1956	283.8	13,182.5	6,503.9	165.9	2.2	4.4	58.
1957	212.4	12,860.4	6,245.7	159.6	1.7	3.4	75.
1958	205.0	11,864.4	5,972.9	126.1	1.7	3.4	62.
1949–58	297.8	12,581.5	6,211.8	183.8	2.4	4.8	62.

Tobacco Manufacturers (Millions of Dollars)

Cigars; Cigarettes and Other Tobacco Products

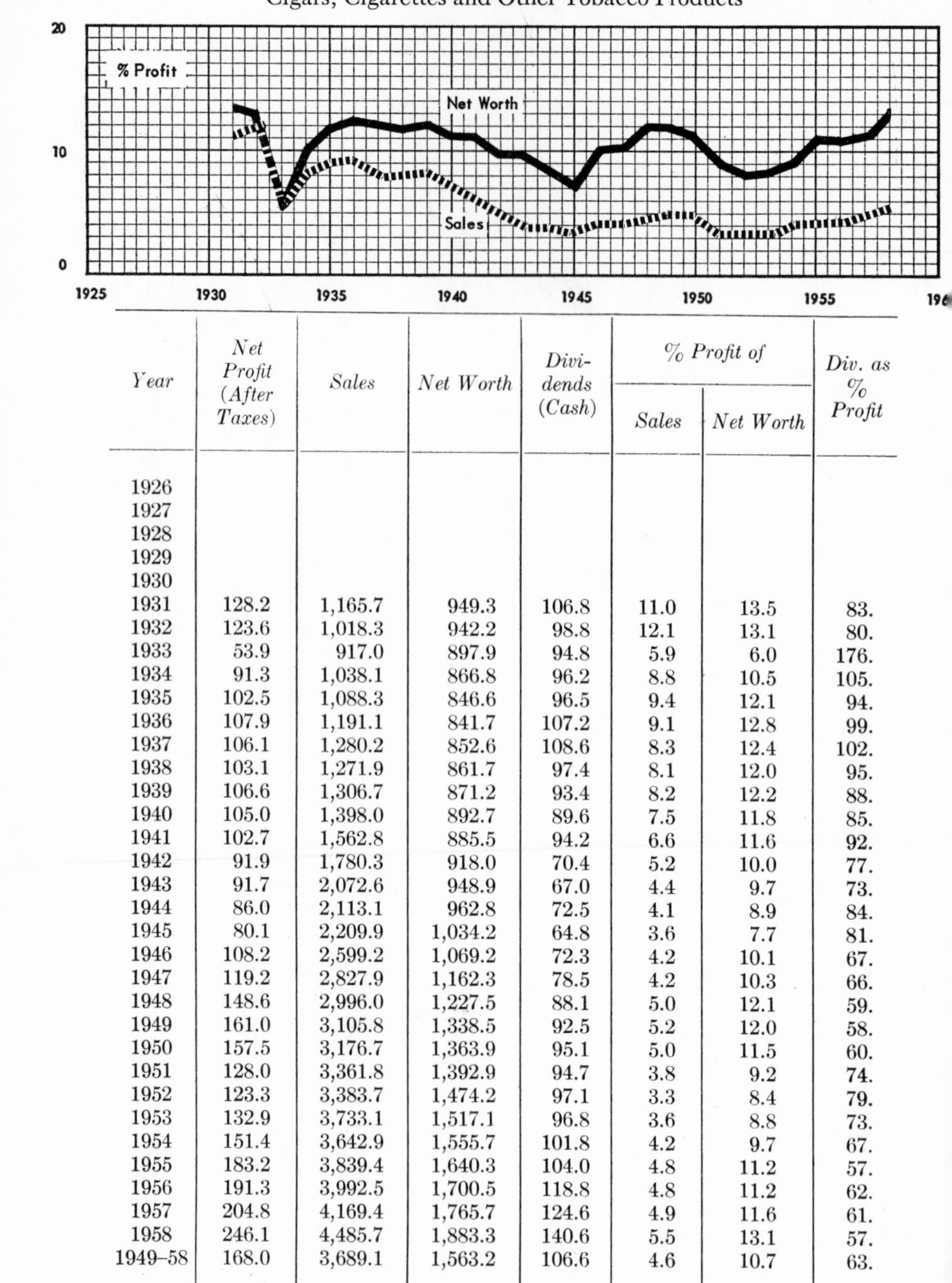

Year	Net Profit (After Taxes)	Sales	Net Worth	Dividends (Cash)	% Profit of Sales	% Profit of Net Worth	Div. as % Profit
1926							
1927							
1928							
1929							
1930							
1931	128.2	1,165.7	949.3	106.8	11.0	13.5	83.
1932	123.6	1,018.3	942.2	98.8	12.1	13.1	80.
1933	53.9	917.0	897.9	94.8	5.9	6.0	176.
1934	91.3	1,038.1	866.8	96.2	8.8	10.5	105.
1935	102.5	1,088.3	846.6	96.5	9.4	12.1	94.
1936	107.9	1,191.1	841.7	107.2	9.1	12.8	99.
1937	106.1	1,280.2	852.6	108.6	8.3	12.4	102.
1938	103.1	1,271.9	861.7	97.4	8.1	12.0	95.
1939	106.6	1,306.7	871.2	93.4	8.2	12.2	88.
1940	105.0	1,398.0	892.7	89.6	7.5	11.8	85.
1941	102.7	1,562.8	885.5	94.2	6.6	11.6	92.
1942	91.9	1,780.3	918.0	70.4	5.2	10.0	77.
1943	91.7	2,072.6	948.9	67.0	4.4	9.7	73.
1944	86.0	2,113.1	962.8	72.5	4.1	8.9	84.
1945	80.1	2,209.9	1,034.2	64.8	3.6	7.7	81.
1946	108.2	2,599.2	1,069.2	72.3	4.2	10.1	67.
1947	119.2	2,827.9	1,162.3	78.5	4.2	10.3	66.
1948	148.6	2,996.0	1,227.5	88.1	5.0	12.1	59.
1949	161.0	3,105.8	1,338.5	92.5	5.2	12.0	58.
1950	157.5	3,176.7	1,363.9	95.1	5.0	11.5	60.
1951	128.0	3,361.8	1,392.9	94.7	3.8	9.2	74.
1952	123.3	3,383.7	1,474.2	97.1	3.3	8.4	79.
1953	132.9	3,733.1	1,517.1	96.8	3.6	8.8	73.
1954	151.4	3,642.9	1,555.7	101.8	4.2	9.7	67.
1955	183.2	3,839.4	1,640.3	104.0	4.8	11.2	57.
1956	191.3	3,992.5	1,700.5	118.8	4.8	11.2	62.
1957	204.8	4,169.4	1,765.7	124.6	4.9	11.6	61.
1958	246.1	4,485.7	1,883.3	140.6	5.5	13.1	57.
1949–58	168.0	3,689.1	1,563.2	106.6	4.6	10.7	63.

Transport Equipment Except Motor Vehicles (Millions of Dollars)

Aircraft and Parts, including Aircraft Engines; Ship and Boat Building and Repairing; Railroad Equipment, including Locomotives and Streetcars; Motorcycles, Bicycles and Parts

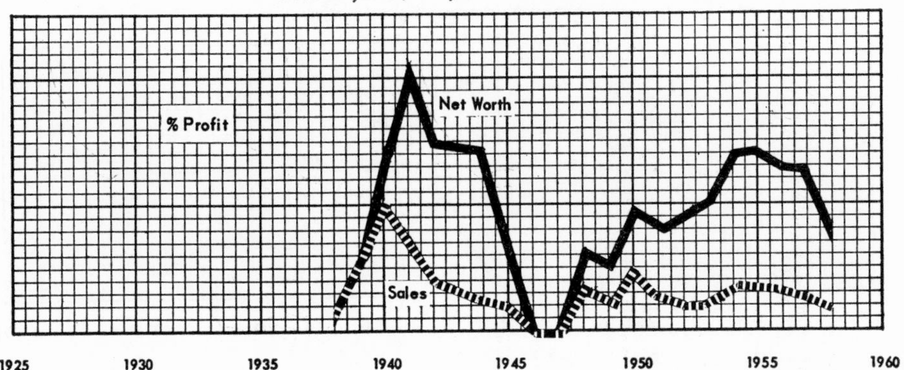

Year	Net Profit (After Taxes)	Sales	Net Worth	Dividends (Cash)	% Profit of Sales	% Profit of Net Worth	Div. as % Profit
1926							
1927							
1928							
1929							
1930							
1931							
1932							
1933							
1934							
1935							
1936							
1937							
1938	10.2	575.4	822.8	19.6	1.8	1.2	192.
1939	58.8	845.3	942.0	38.2	7.0	6.2	65.
1940	160.8	1,554.3	1,108.5	71.2	10.3	14.5	44.
1941	294.5	3,852.3	1,396.2	94.2	7.6	21.1	32.
1942	544.3	12,347.2	3,553.0	209.6	4.4	15.3	39.
1943	729.6	22,102.7	4,914.9	236.4	3.3	14.8	32.
1944	670.6	24,404.4	4,721.8	287.9	2.7	14.2	43.
1945	366.9	16,964.7	4,796.1	292.7	2.2	7.6	80.
1946	−74.2	2,685.8	1,928.5	92.9	—	—	—
1947	−64.6	2,948.9	1,827.7	78.8	—	—	—
1948	134.3	3,693.0	1,970.7	97.6	3.6	6.8	73.
1949	111.6	3,797.3	1,955.4	94.1	2.9	5.7	84.
1950	208.3	3,983.9	2,122.5	110.3	5.2	9.8	53.
1951	175.9	5,809.9	2,123.7	105.5	3.0	8.3	60.
1952	212.4	9,486.0	2,283.7	108.5	2.2	9.3	51.
1953	273.6	11,860.3	2,441.0	129.5	2.3	11.2	47.
1954	391.8	10,937.1	2,710.9	158.2	3.6	14.5	40.
1955	421.8	11,642.6	2,956.4	185.9	3.6	14.3	44.
1956	429.2	13,377.6	3,282.1	191.0	3.2	13.1	45.
1957	466.4	15,986.7	3,610.9	196.0	2.9	12.9	42.
1958	324.4	15,517.1	3,875.8	185.0	2.1	8.4	57.
1948–59	301.5	10,239.9	2,736.2	146.4	2.9	11.0	49.

Transportation (Millions of Dollars)

Railroads, Railway Express; Urban, Suburban and Interurban Railways and Bus Lines; Trucking and Warehousing; Other Vehicle Transportation, Including Taxicabs and Buses; Pipeline Transportation; Water Transportation; Air Transportation and Allied Services; Services Incidental to Transportation

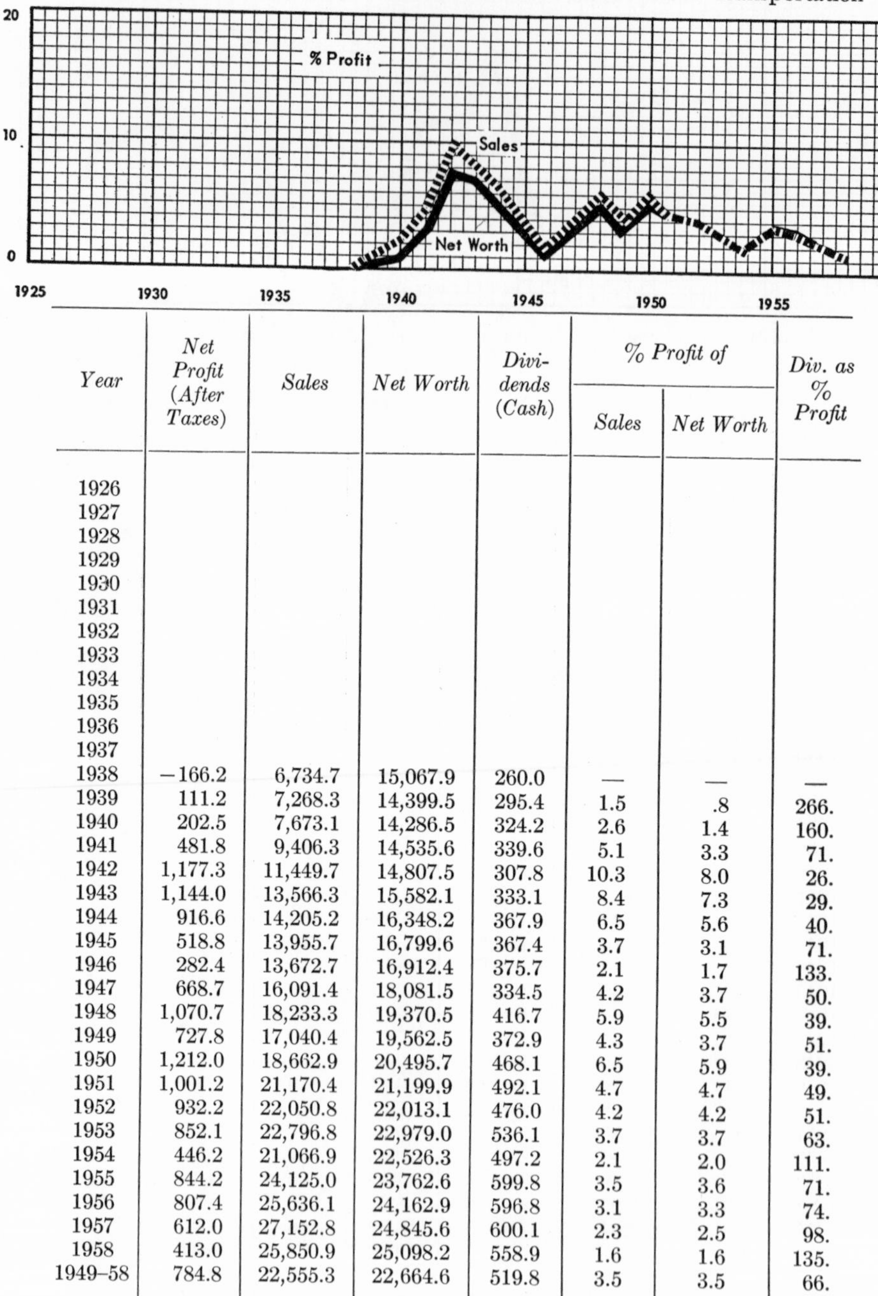

Year	Net Profit (After Taxes)	Sales	Net Worth	Dividends (Cash)	% Profit of Sales	% Profit of Net Worth	Div. as % Profit
1926							
1927							
1928							
1929							
1930							
1931							
1932							
1933							
1934							
1935							
1936							
1937							
1938	−166.2	6,734.7	15,067.9	260.0	—	—	—
1939	111.2	7,268.3	14,399.5	295.4	1.5	.8	266.
1940	202.5	7,673.1	14,286.5	324.2	2.6	1.4	160.
1941	481.8	9,406.3	14,535.6	339.6	5.1	3.3	71.
1942	1,177.3	11,449.7	14,807.5	307.8	10.3	8.0	26.
1943	1,144.0	13,566.3	15,582.1	333.1	8.4	7.3	29.
1944	916.6	14,205.2	16,348.2	367.9	6.5	5.6	40.
1945	518.8	13,955.7	16,799.6	367.4	3.7	3.1	71.
1946	282.4	13,672.7	16,912.4	375.7	2.1	1.7	133.
1947	668.7	16,091.4	18,081.5	334.5	4.2	3.7	50.
1948	1,070.7	18,233.3	19,370.5	416.7	5.9	5.5	39.
1949	727.8	17,040.4	19,562.5	372.9	4.3	3.7	51.
1950	1,212.0	18,662.9	20,495.7	468.1	6.5	5.9	39.
1951	1,001.2	21,170.4	21,199.9	492.1	4.7	4.7	49.
1952	932.2	22,050.8	22,013.1	476.0	4.2	4.2	51.
1953	852.1	22,796.8	22,979.0	536.1	3.7	3.7	63.
1954	446.2	21,066.9	22,526.3	497.2	2.1	2.0	111.
1955	844.2	24,125.0	23,762.6	599.8	3.5	3.6	71.
1956	807.4	25,636.1	24,162.9	596.8	3.1	3.3	74.
1957	612.0	27,152.8	24,845.6	600.1	2.3	2.5	98.
1958	413.0	25,850.9	25,098.2	558.9	1.6	1.6	135.
1949–58	784.8	22,555.3	22,664.6	519.8	3.5	3.5	66.

WHOLESALE, TOTAL (Millions of Dollars)

Commission Merchants; Wholesalers for Food; Alcoholic Beverages; Apparel and Dry Goods; Chemicals, Paints and Drugs; Hardware, Electrical Goods, Plumbing and Heating Equipment; Lumber, Millwork and Construction Materials, Machinery and Equipment; Farm Products (Raw Materials)

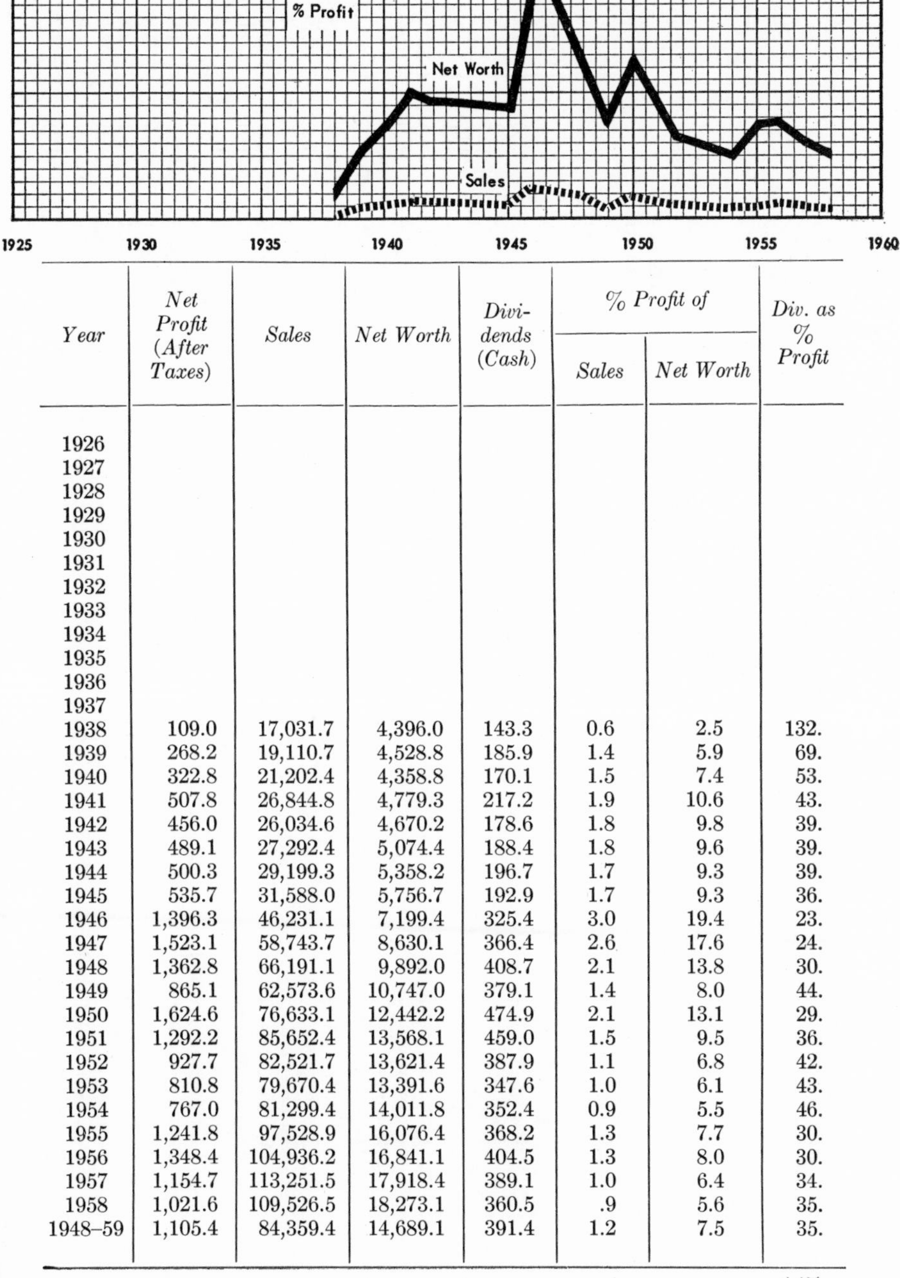

Year	Net Profit (After Taxes)	Sales	Net Worth	Dividends (Cash)	% Profit of Sales	% Profit of Net Worth	Div. as % Profit
1926							
1927							
1928							
1929							
1930							
1931							
1932							
1933							
1934							
1935							
1936							
1937							
1938	109.0	17,031.7	4,396.0	143.3	0.6	2.5	132.
1939	268.2	19,110.7	4,528.8	185.9	1.4	5.9	69.
1940	322.8	21,202.4	4,358.8	170.1	1.5	7.4	53.
1941	507.8	26,844.8	4,779.3	217.2	1.9	10.6	43.
1942	456.0	26,034.6	4,670.2	178.6	1.8	9.8	39.
1943	489.1	27,292.4	5,074.4	188.4	1.8	9.6	39.
1944	500.3	29,199.3	5,358.2	196.7	1.7	9.3	39.
1945	535.7	31,588.0	5,756.7	192.9	1.7	9.3	36.
1946	1,396.3	46,231.1	7,199.4	325.4	3.0	19.4	23.
1947	1,523.1	58,743.7	8,630.1	366.4	2.6	17.6	24.
1948	1,362.8	66,191.1	9,892.0	408.7	2.1	13.8	30.
1949	865.1	62,573.6	10,747.0	379.1	1.4	8.0	44.
1950	1,624.6	76,633.1	12,442.2	474.9	2.1	13.1	29.
1951	1,292.2	85,652.4	13,568.1	459.0	1.5	9.5	36.
1952	927.7	82,521.7	13,621.4	387.9	1.1	6.8	42.
1953	810.8	79,670.4	13,391.6	347.6	1.0	6.1	43.
1954	767.0	81,299.4	14,011.8	352.4	0.9	5.5	46.
1955	1,241.8	97,528.9	16,076.4	368.2	1.3	7.7	30.
1956	1,348.4	104,936.2	16,841.1	404.5	1.3	8.0	30.
1957	1,154.7	113,251.5	17,918.4	389.1	1.0	6.4	34.
1958	1,021.6	109,526.5	18,273.1	360.5	.9	5.6	35.
1948–59	1,105.4	84,359.4	14,689.1	391.4	1.2	7.5	35.

First National City Bank of New York
Profit on Investment for Leading Companies

(Net Income After Taxes as a Percent of Net Worth)

Industry Groups	*1925*	*1926*	*1927*	*1928*	*1929*	*1930*	*1931*	*1932*	*1933*	*1934*
Baking	15.4	13.6	14.7	14.7	15.5	13.5	11.0	7.6	7.1	5.9
Dairy products	16.5	19.9	16.3	20.0	21.5	17.8	12.2	6.2	4.2	4.8
Meat packing	5.7	5.2	2.0	5.9	5.5	4.1	−1.2	−0.3	3.6	3.8
Sugar	3.4	2.1	4.4	4.7	3.2	0.7	0.1	0.5	4.9	3.4
Other food products	13.9	14.4	14.6	16.7	16.5	11.9	8.4	5.6	9.4	11.9
Soft drinks	21.9	23.7	25.1	26.0	27.1	23.6	18.0	10.6	11.8	18.7
Brewing	*	*	*	*	*	*	*	*	*	7.6
Distilling	*	*	*	*	*	*	*	*	*	21.7
Tobacco products	13.4	14.0	14.4	13.2	14.2	14.5	14.4	13.4	8.3	10.7
Cotton goods	2.0	−0.3	5.9	3.7	4.0	−4.3	−5.0	−3.9	4.1	1.9
Silk and rayon	7.6	4.9	5.5	6.2	2.8	−1.4	−0.7	−1.4	10.7	3.6
Woolen goods	−0.4	−5.5	−1.7	−1.2	−3.7	−5.9	−3.1	−10.4	10.3	−7.2
Hosiery, knit. goods	12.9	11.0	9.9	11.8	12.6	2.3	−0.9	−2.9	3.2	2.3
Other textile products	10.5	6.9	9.0	8.9	8.8	1.3	0.1	−3.7	4.8	2.6
Clothing and apparel	9.9	11.1	12.4	13.0	11.8	3.8	−1.8	−4.9	2.7	3.7
Leather tanning	3.2	0.7	5.2	4.5	−5.6	−7.2	−5.5	−7.3	9.5	−3.0
Shoes, leather products	13.8	12.8	16.6	13.3	13.1	7.1	5.5	2.3	6.9	7.9
Rubber products	14.3	5.2	9.0	0.7	3.9	−3.1	−1.2	−2.8	2.4	2.4
Lumber	7.4	6.3	4.8	6.2	5.9	−2.5	−10.0	−8.5	−3.3	0.0
Furniture, wood products	10.1	6.1	4.9	6.6	5.2	−5.1	−7.8	−8.3	2.4	2.6
Pulp and paper products	6.1	5.5	6.2	8.0	12.0	3.0	−0.6	−2.2	0.0	2.6

Printing and publishing	15.5	15.0	15.9	20.4	21.5	15.1	9.6	5.0	2.9	7.7
Chemical products	8.6	10.5	10.3	17.2	18.0	11.4	8.0	4.9	8.0	9.6
Drugs, soap, etc.	19.7	20.5	21.3	20.9	23.7	19.2	15.6	8.8	12.3	15.1
Paint and varnish	9.9	11.5	7.9	12.4	13.4	2.4	3.4	0.0	6.4	6.7
Petroleum products	11.6	11.3	4.7	10.3	10.8	4.4	−1.5	0.9	1.4	2.6
Cement	17.1	12.5	8.8	9.1	6.7	5.4	−1.4	−4.7	−2.1	1.3
Glass products	11.9	11.8	7.9	7.9	10.9	5.1	2.5	1.5	9.4	8.9
Other stone, clay products	10.5	10.8	9.6	8.5	9.0	4.7	1.1	−3.6	−0.2	2.4
Iron and steel	5.8	7.3	5.3	7.0	11.2	4.5	−0.5	−4.0	−1.9	−0.4
Agricultural implements	8.3	10.4	10.0	12.0	13.4	8.8	−1.0	−5.2	−2.3	0.6
Bldg., heat., plb. equipment	15.0	13.9	10.7	12.1	14.2	4.8	−2.2	−5.3	−1.5	1.2
Electrical equipment	12.9	13.9	13.4	15.8	17.7	9.3	4.1	−2.5	−1.5	2.2
Hardware and tools	14.3	16.3	14.8	18.4	15.7	4.4	−5.6	−6.3	−0.2	3.5
Household equipment	15.6	16.1	14.0	14.5	14.7	7.7	1.8	1.3	6.1	7.2
Machinery	8.8	10.4	8.0	11.0	14.3	5.5	−1.6	−7.3	−4.0	1.1
Office equipment	12.4	13.2	14.7	17.4	21.1	12.0	4.7	−1.9	3.6	9.3
Nonferrous metals	7.7	7.6	6.3	10.9	15.6	3.6	0.1	−2.7	0.7	2.1
Other metal products	13.0	11.0	11.1	14.6	17.7	9.9	4.9	0.5	6.2	9.1
Autos and trucks	25.7	26.9	24.3	27.7	23.5	8.9	4.0	−2.9	7.4	7.9
Auto equipment	18.0	14.8	12.0	23.0	23.5	6.7	−0.1	−4.8	0.1	6.6
Railway equipment	6.1	9.8	8.2	5.9	8.3	6.3	0.1	−1.8	−1.4	0.1
Aircraft and parts	*	*	*	*	10.7	−5.2	−3.2	−7.8	0.7	−2.2
Shipbuilding	3.0	−5.0	0.4	3.5	6.1	0.4	−0.3	0.5	−1.0	0.2
Total Manufacturing	10.7	10.8	9.0	11.6	12.8	6.4	2.3	−0.5	2.5	4.3

— Deficit
* Not computed because of limited number of reports available for the group

First National City Bank of New York
Profit on Investment for Leading Companies

(Net Income After Taxes as a Percent of Net Worth)

Industry Groups	*1935*	*1936*	*1937*	*1938*	*1939*	*1940*	*1941*	*1942*	*1943*
Baking	5.5	8.2	7.6	8.8	8.7	7.6	7.4	9.3	9.9
Dairy products	5.9	9.8	7.8	8.4	9.9	9.1	10.2	10.1	10.0
Meat packing	4.5	5.5	3.2	−1.0	4.9	5.6	8.8	8.3	7.9
Sugar	5.2	7.0	6.6	0.4	4.1	4.8	5.7	10.4	6.2
Other food products	10.1	12.0	9.8	9.8	10.3	10.9	11.9	10.2	10.7
Soft drinks	20.1	25.7	38.5	36.6	37.5	33.9	35.5	26.5	23.0
Brewing	8.6	15.6	14.2	14.9	17.5	13.7	14.9	13.7	13.4
Distilling	21.5	18.1	17.0	11.8	10.0	11.0	13.5	13.0	14.8
Tobacco products	10.6	12.8	12.9	12.4	13.1	13.7	11.7	10.5	9.8
Cotton goods	−2.8	5.4	4.7	−2.2	3.6	5.4	12.1	10.4	8.4
Silk and rayon	6.1	8.7	11.1	4.5	11.5	11.5	9.7	8.6	7.5
Woolen goods	4.0	4.8	−0.9	−6.7	4.3	5.7	11.8	9.2	9.1
Hosiery, knit. goods	4.7	5.9	7.0	4.9	7.9	5.2	11.8	10.6	9.6
Other textile products	6.2	11.8	8.8	−0.1	8.9	11.6	13.3	10.3	9.2
Clothing and apparel	6.1	9.1	6.4	2.6	10.4	9.9	11.4	11.0	11.6
Leather tanning	5.7	4.4	3.4	09.5	7.7	4.6	10.8	11.0	10.3
Shoes, leather products	8.7	9.1	7.1	4.0	6.9	7.7	10.5	9.6	9.1
Rubber products	4.1	9.8	6.4	5.1	9.4	9.0	11.4	10.3	13.1
Lumber	0.9	3.9	6.8	0.5	4.1	7.6	16.3	11.8	8.4
Furniture, wood products	7.0	13.1	12.1	1.4	8.6	10.2	11.0	6.9	5.2

Pulp and paper products	3.3	4.0	7.5	3.0	6.4	9.6	10.5	7.6	7.2
Printing and publishing	9.1	13.3	8.2	4.6	7.2	8.8	8.5	8.0	11.6
Chemical products	11.8	15.2	14.7	7.9	12.9	13.1	13.6	10.8	10.4
Drugs, Soap, etc.	14.3	17.4	18.4	15.1	19.6	21.7	21.5	16.2	17.4
Paint and varnish	8.9	11.5	8.4	3.4	8.1	8.0	9.7	7.0	6.7
Petroleum products	4.8	7.8	10.0	5.0	5.4	5.4	9.9	7.0	7.9
Cement	0.7	7.0	5.5	3.7	7.1	6.7	8.6	7.1	4.0
Glass products	14.8	17.3	17.4	7.2	12.1	12.9	13.8	9.8	11.4
Other stone, clay products	5.3	8.7	8.7	3.7	8.3	9.2	10.8	8.6	7.2
Iron and steel	1.3	4.7	6.9	−0.2	4.5	8.5	9.6	6.5	5.6
Agricultural implements	7.7	12.2	13.1	6.6	5.1	8.5	10.6	9.1	8.5
Bldg., heat., plb. equipment	3.6	8.8	10.1	0.4	6.6	10.4	11.7	9.6	9.4
Electrical equipment	6.5	11.5	15.2	5.7	10.5	15.5	15.6	11.4	12.4
Hardware and tools	5.9	11.7	16.5	4.4	11.1	16.3	17.8	14.5	13.3
Household equipment	8.3	12.9	14.6	5.1	11.7	12.3	16.0	10.0	10.5
Machinery	5.4	11.7	14.5	5.2	8.6	14.6	19.7	15.9	14.5
Office equipment	12.5	16.3	20.2	10.2	10.4	12.4	17.1	13.8	11.2
Nonferrous metals	4.6	7.4	10.3	4.5	8.6	10.6	10.3	10.0	9.9
Other metal products	9.5	11.0	10.7	4.9	9.9	11.5	13.7	10.5	10.8
Autos and trucks	16.2	24.6	18.5	7.3	15.9	16.8	18.3	13.5	12.4
Auto equipment	16.3	16.6	17.9	1.1	12.8	17.2	19.9	16.7	17.6
Railway equipment	−0.1	3.7	7.6	−0.8	2.2	6.4	10.5	11.0	9.0
Aircraft and parts	4.1	7.8	7.2	15.5	21.0	33.2	48.8	45.0	36.8
Shipbuilding	−0.6	5.2	3.2	2.9	10.3	29.9	30.0	26.6	25.6
Total Manufacturing	6.7	10.4	10.8	4.8	8.5	10.3	12.4	10.1	9.9

First National City Bank of New York
Profit on Investment for Leading Companies

(Net Income After Taxes as a Percent of Net Worth)

Industry Groups	*1944*	*1945*	*1946*	*1947*	*1948*	*1949*	*1950*	*1951*	*1952*
Baking	9.2	10.0	21.8	20.2	21.4	17.8	16.1	12.2	12.2
Dairy products	11.0	11.7	18.9	15.4	14.0	15.2	13.9	10.8	10.5
Meat packing	7.6	5.4	10.8	12.0	7.2	3.8	6.4	5.5	3.8
Sugar	10.1	7.2	9.5	18.6	12.2	8.3	10.8	12.1	8.4
Other food products	11.1	11.0	18.1	20.9	17.4	14.4	15.5	11.6	10.0
Soft drinks	21.8	19.6	19.5	22.6	20.4	15.7	15.5	12.7	12.2
Brewing	14.3	13.5	23.4	25.6	22.8	18.8	14.7	11.8	10.4
Distilling	16.6	19.8	42.1	26.6	25.4	15.4	17.9	12.9	7.8
Tobacco products	9.3	9.2	11.4	12.8	14.3	14.4	12.6	9.8	9.2
Cotton goods	7.1	7.7	27.1	36.1	31.5	9.9	12.7	12.1	5.3
Silk and rayon	6.9	7.1	24.5	26.1	30.0	12.1	19.7	11.7	6.6
Woolen goods	8.3	10.3	25.2	21.2	20.9	5.0	8.1	8.3	−3.2
Hosiery, knit. goods	9.7	9.9	28.2	23.4	22.3	11.0	18.1	10.1	5.2
Other textile products	8.9	9.3	20.8	26.0	24.7	10.9	15.8	12.0	5.6
Carpets, floor coverings *							13.1	3.5	6.2
Clothing and apparel	9.5	9.5	23.3	20.1	13.8	7.8	10.7	7.5	6.2
Leather tanning **	8.7	8.0	10.8	21.2	13.6	3.3			
Shoes, leather products	8.0	8.2	12.7	16.2	14.7	10.2	12.1	9.6	8.0
Tires, rubber products	11.8	10.5	20.6	16.1	14.0	9.0	15.7	16.1	13.4
Lumber	9.2	9.0	14.1	31.9	29.3	11.3	16.2	15.8	11.5
Furniture, wood products	8.2	6.1	10.8	16.5	17.9	11.2	15.4	13.9	11.1
Pulp and paper products	7.3	6.8	14.4	22.6	20.4	12.4	16.9	16.1	12.2
Printing and publishing	10.2	9.3	17.9	21.3	17.4	11.1	15.1	12.3	11.1

Chemical products	10.6	10.2	14.7	17.2	17.7	16.5	21.3	16.3	13.7
Drugs and medicines ***							21.9	19.2	14.0
Soap, cosmetics, etc.	15.9	15.4	23.6	20.6	19.0	16.2	20.9	15.4	12.6
Paint and varnish	7.9	7.7	13.8	19.0	14.2	10.3	17.0	13.1	10.7
Petroleum products	9.7	8.4	10.7	15.8	22.1	13.2	15.2	16.7	14.5
Cement	1.8	2.5	9.7	12.2	16.6	18.1	18.2	14.1	14.1
Glass products	11.5	10.2	14.8	17.4	16.0	18.5	23.6	15.3	14.7
Other stone, clay products	6.9	6.2	13.4	17.7	18.9	13.7	18.5	14.7	12.4
Iron and steel	5.2	5.0	7.5	11.3	14.0	11.5	15.3	12.3	8.8
Agricultural implements	8.6	7.1	5.7	11.1	14.8	15.6	15.6	11.9	10.9
Bldg., Heat., plb. equipment	9.4	8.0	11.4	19.0	21.0	12.7	17.7	13.7	10.8
Electrical equipment	13.1	11.9	8.9	19.3	20.5	17.2	23.0	16.2	14.8
Hardware and tools	11.3	10.2	14.0	18.9	17.1	9.7	14.7	14.0	10.8
Household equipment	11.3	10.2	18.4	34.3	27.8	13.9	22.3	13.0	12.2
Machinery	11.8	9.8	11.3	16.8	19.3	12.7	14.1	14.9	14.1
Office equipment	11.8	9.6	18.9	27.1	25.6	18.5	19.0	16.9	14.3
Nonferrous metals	7.7	5.9	7.1	14.0	14.9	8.2	14.2	13.5	11.5
Other metal products	10.8	9.7	9.5	15.4	17.7	10.9	16.2	14.7	11.4
Autos and trucks	12.9	13.6	6.9	20.8	26.0	30.8	32.3	17.5	18.5
Auto equipment	15.5	14.6	8.9	23.5	23.5	18.7	22.7	15.6	13.2
Railway equipment	9.3	8.6	9.3	10.5	10.2	7.2	7.3	9.8	8.9
Aircraft and parts	23.6	18.4	0.9	−3.7	3.1	8.6	14.1	8.9	17.6
Shipbuilding	20.8	19.7	17.4	13.3	11.7	9.0	−1.8	9.6	10.8
Total manufacturing	9.8	9.1	12.1	17.0	18.9	13.8	17.1	14.4	12.3

* Combined with "Other textile products" prior to 1950
** Combined with "Shoes, leather products" after 1950
*** Combined with "Drugs and soap" prior to 1950

First National City Bank of New York
Profit on Investment for Leading Companies

(Net Income After Taxes as Percent of Sales Dollar)

Industry Groups	*1953*	*1954*	*1955*	*1956*	*1957*	*1958*	*1959*	*1960*	*No. of Companies 1960*
Baking	12.0	11.3	11.9	12.1	12.6	11.7	11.4	11.4	16
Dairy products	11.0	12.1	12.2	12.4	12.1	11.9	12.0	11.2	11
Meat packing	6.7	3.3	6.7	7.7	4.3	4.5	7.8	6.3	15
Sugar	4.0	4.9	5.5	6.7	8.9	6.1	5.8	5.6	18
Other food products	10.9	11.3	11.7	11.8	11.3	11.4	11.7	11.4	86
Soft drinks	12.0	12.5	14.1	13.9	14.2	14.4	15.7	15.6	13
Brewing	10.3	8.6	6.5	8.1	7.2	6.8	8.6	8.1	14
Distilling	7.3	6.3	6.4	6.3	7.3	7.3	7.9	7.3	13
Tobacco products	10.0	10.2	11.7	12.0	12.7	14.7	15.0	14.6	17
Cotton goods *	6.8	3.6							
Silk and rayon *	5.5	4.7							
Woolen goods *	−4.6	−5.1							
Hosiery, knit. goods *	6.5	4.2							
Carpets, floor coverings *	7.6	6.3							
Other textile products *	6.8	4.5							
Textiles			7.1	6.6	5.9	4.1	8.0	6.9	62
Clothing and apparel	6.8	5.1	7.0	7.7	6.6	6.2	9.7	10.0	53
Shoes, leather, etc.	10.1	10.1	11.5	10.3	10.8	9.2	11.1	8.9	24
Tires, rubber products	13.9	12.0	15.1	13.6	12.4	10.6	12.8	10.6	25
Lumber	10.3	9.7	14.2	13.2	9.1	9.2	11.6	8.0	26
Furniture, wood products	10.3	10.1	12.6	11.8	10.5	8.6	11.1	7.9	23
Paper and allied products	12.1	12.2	13.8	13.8	10.8	9.3	10.5	9.2	72

Printing and publishing	10.4	10.9	12.9	14.0	14.4	11.3	12.1	12.3	49
Chemical products	13.3	14.5	17.7	15.6	14.0	11.1	14.4	12.9	78
Drugs and medicines	13.7	15.8	18.3	22.4	24.0	21.9	21.9	20.0	29
Soap, cosmetics, etc.	12.4	14.6	16.0	16.2	17.8	15.8	16.8	17.0	26
Paint and varnish	12.6	13.0	16.4	17.5	15.9	12.8	14.8	10.0	21
Petroleum products & ref.	14.4	13.9	14.2	14.7	13.6	9.9	10.0	10.2	125
Cement	14.7	18.8	20.3	19.5	15.9	16.4	17.2	11.3	22
Glass products	14.9	16.3	20.5	16.6	15.3	11.9	16.7	13.3	19
Other stone, clay products	12.0	13.0	16.4	15.8	13.3	11.9	14.5	12.0	53
Iron and steel	11.6	9.4	15.2	13.9	13.2	8.2	8.4	7.8	48
Agricultural implements	8.1	6.9	8.8	8.3	6.9	7.3	10.8	4.2	11
Bldg., heat., plb. equipment	10.5	9.7	11.5	11.2	9.7	8.1	9.2	7.7	90
Electrical equipment	15.1	15.4	12.8	11.9	13.7	12.4	14.4	11.6	161
Hardware and tools	9.5	8.2	10.7	12.2	10.4	6.2	8.6	8.2	43
Household equipment	10.8	9.6	11.6	12.1	10.0	7.7	10.9	10.9	28
Machinery	13.6	11.6	11.6	14.9	13.4	7.9	9.9	8.8	160
Office equipment	12.8	15.1	16.9	17.3	17.5	13.7	14.0	14.2	29
Nonferrous metals	10.8	10.3	16.7	17.8	9.8	6.8	8.2	7.8	52
Instruments, photo goods, etc.	13.5	16.9	17.7	16.4	14.6	12.2	16.4	14.1	115
Other metal products	11.6	11.0	12.8	12.1	11.1	8.9	11.3	8.7	130
Autos and trucks	18.0	21.1	29.1	15.7	16.4	9.1	17.4	15.8	17
Automobile equipment	13.3	10.4	15.3	13.3	11.9	7.4	12.5	8.7	53
Railway equipment	9.0	7.3	9.0	9.9	10.2	6.1	7.9	6.8	19
Aircraft and parts	21.0	27.4	24.7	21.6	20.1	14.1	8.9	6.1	43
Miscellaneous manufacturing						9.2	12.5		
Total manufacturing	12.5	12.4	15.0	13.9	12.8	9.8	11.6	10.5	2,034

* Combined with "Textiles" after 1955

First National City Bank of New York
Profit on Investment for Leading Companies

(Net Income After Taxes as a Percent of Net Worth)

Industry Groups	*1928*	*1929*	*1930*	*1931*	*1932*	*1933*	*1934*	*1935*	*1936*
Coal mining*	1.8	1.6	1.3	1.1	−1.9	−1.5	1.6	−0.4	0.7
Metal mining*	13.3	14.9	3.9	0.3	−1.2	3.8	4.2	6.3	7.9
Oil and gas*	—	—	—	—	—	—	—	—	—
Other mining, quarrying*	—	—	—	—	—	—	—	—	—
Total mining, quarrying*	10.9	11.8	3.4	0.5	−1.4	1.9	3.6	4.9	6.5
Chain stores—food	22.9	18.9	10.3	11.6	9.5	10.7	9.2	8.2	9.0
Chain stores—variety, etc.	22.4	16.8	11.9	13.0	7.2	12.8	16.3	14.9	16.6
Department & specialty	10.9	8.9	4.8	0.7	−4.0	0.4	1.6	4.0	7.8
Mail order	20.0	14.5	2.1	−0.01	−2.4	4.9	8.6	11.4	15.2
Wholesale & miscellaneous	7.6	7.0	−1.1	−3.2	−5.7	2.6	4.1	4.7	8.0
Total trade	17.3	13.9	7.0	6.0	1.3	7.7	9.9	10.7	13.2
Class 1 railroads	5.5	6.1	3.5	0.9	−0.9	−0.0	−0.1	0.1	1.2
Traction and bus	—	—	—	2.0	0.1	0.2	0.4	−1.0	−0.4
Shipping	3.6	5.7	4.3	2.1	−0.01	2.3	0.1	1.8	4.3
Air transport	—	—	—	—	—	—	—	—	—
Misc. transportation	—	—	—	—	—	—	—	—	—
Total transportation	5.7	6.1	3.5	1.2	−1.1	−0.01	−0.1	0.02	1.5

Electric power, gas, etc.	10.9	11.0	9.5	8.3	6.0	5.5	5.0	5.7	6.0
Telephone & telegraph (AT&T)	11.6	11.2	9.7	6.8	4.8	4.1	4.4	5.2	7.2
Total public utilities	11.2	11.0	9.5	7.7	5.6	5.2	4.7	5.4	6.2
Amusements	10.9	17.0	14.0	3.9	−3.6	−0.01	4.8	5.8	9.7
Restaurant & hotel	10.8	12.5	6.7	6.5	1.8	−0.5	0.01	2.3	4.9
Other business services	—	10.7	7.1	2.1	1.4	−4.7	2.2	5.6	6.4
Construction	—	—	—	5.4	1.5	−3.3	−2.6	−0.4	3.4
Total amuse., serv., etc.	11.1	14.1	11.9	3.4	−0.5	−2.1	2.4	4.7	7.6
Commercial banks	—	14.2	6.7	−3.4	−1.6	−9.2	9.1	8.3	8.2
Fire & casualty insurance	—	8.4	−11.4	−17.6	−15.7	21.0	14.1	28.9	26.2
Investment companies	—	—	—	—	0.4	2.8	3.2	5.7	7.4
Sales finance companies	—	17.4	10.7	8.3	6.0	9.2	12.9	16.9	18.3
Real estate companies	11.6	9.4	7.4	2.5	−1.1	−1.6	0.2	−0.3	−0.6
Total finance	—	12.0	1.1	−5.4	−3.4	−0.8	8.0	11.1	11.7
Grand total (incl. mfg.)	10.0	10.6	5.7	2.4	0.2	2.1	3.6	5.1	7.4

− Deficit
* Before depletion charges in some cases

First National City Bank of New York
Profit on Investment for Leading Companies

(Net Income After Taxes as a Percent of Net Worth)

Industry Groups	*1937*	*1938*	*1939*	*1940*	*1941*	*1942*	*1943*	*1944*
Coal mining *	0.3	−1.4	−0.3	2.2	3.8	4.3	4.2	5.3
Metal mining *	10.3	5.5	7.7	8.8	9.8	8.8	7.1	6.1
Oil and gas *	9.2	6.5	4.8	4.3	8.3	9.0	10.8	12.5
Other mining, quarrying *	13.5	8.5	11.2	12.9	14.9	12.9	12.8	14.1
Total mining, quarrying *	8.7	4.6	6.3	5.5	7.8	7.5	6.9	7.6
Chain stores—food	5.8	6.9	10.4	9.1	9.8	8.4	8.4	8.8
Chain stores—variety, etc.	15.3	11.3	13.3	12.1	12.9	11.7	11.4	11.2
Department & specialty	4.4	3.2	5.7	7.9	8.4	9.0	9.4	9.2
Mail order	12.2	9.7	14.0	12.1	11.7	9.9	9.7	9.9
Wholesale and miscellaneous	6.9	2.8	5.5	6.9	9.5	8.2	9.5	10.3
Total trade	10.9	8.4	11.3	10.5	11.3	9.9	10.1	10.2
Class 1 railroads	0.7	−0.9	0.7	1.7	4.6	8.3	7.8	5.7
Traction and bus	−1.6	−4.4	−2.0	0.8	0.9	5.8	5.8	5.7
Shipping	2.2	−1.3	4.3	9.6	10.9	9.6	6.5	6.3
Air transport	—	—	10.3	15.8	8.2	22.4	20.4	22.6
Misc. transportation	2.3	1.8	5.5	5.1	5.5	5.5	6.2	6.9
Total transportation	0.7	−1.0	0.8	1.6	4.6	8.7	7.7	5.8

Electric power, gas, etc.	6.5	6.0	6.7	6.9	6.5	6.0	6.4	6.4
Telephone & telegraph (AT&T)	7.2	6.2	7.7	8.5	7.6	6.5	7.0	6.7
Total public utilities	6.6	5.9	6.9	7.2	6.7	6.0	6.5	6.5
Amusements	9.4	5.8	6.1	7.7	9.5	13.4	12.0	12.6
Restaurant & hotel	1.3	−1.3	0.01	−0.7	1.2	3.3	10.5	11.8
Other business services	7.2	3.7	10.5	6.7	11.5	11.5	11.2	11.2
Construction	2.7	4.5	8.5	16.9	11.2	18.9	13.1	4.5
Total amuse., serv., etc.	7.2	4.4	6.3	7.8	8.8	12.3	11.7	11.7
Commercial banks	8.4	7.7	8.5	8.2	8.0	7.2	8.9	9.4
Fire & casualty insurance	8.7	9.3	9.0	8.6	8.2	8.2	9.9	6.9
Investment companies	6.9	3.2	5.4	5.9	6.1	4.1	5.3	5.9
Sales finance companies	17.9	12.7	12.1	12.7	13.1	10.5	7.8	6.3
Real estate companies	−0.5	−0.5	−0.6	−0.5	0.1	−0.3	1.3	2.0
Total finance	8.6	7.0	7.9	7.9	7.9	6.5	7.9	7.7
Grand total (incl. mfg.)	7.2	3.8	6.2	7.4	9.2	8.7	8.6	8.2

− Deficit
* Before depletion charges in some cases

FIRST NATIONAL CITY BANK OF NEW YORK
PROFIT ON INVESTMENT FOR LEADING COMPANIES

(Net Income After Taxes as a Percent of Net Worth)

Industry Groups	*1945*	*1946*	*1947*	*1948*	*1949*	*1950*	*1951*	*1952*
Coal mining *	4.9	7.5	12.3	14.8	7.7	8.8	8.9	6.6
Metal mining *	5.7	6.6	11.5	12.1	8.3	15.6	15.2	10.3
Oil and gas *	13.2	12.6	19.9	35.9	21.7	18.3	**	**
Other mining, quarrying *	15.3	20.4	24.5	25.8	29.2	30.1	25.8	24.3
Total mining, quarrying *	7.6	9.5	15.1	20.5	13.5	15.0	13.3	10.1
Chain stores—food	9.1	18.6	17.6	16.5	17.8	17.9	11.7	10.7
Chain stores—variety, etc.	12.0	23.0	18.8	19.1	12.4	13.2	10.8	9.6
Department and specialty	11.1	20.8	14.7	14.1	13.2	13.4	9.8	9.0
Mail order	10.3	25.6	21.1	22.6	14.5	18.3	13.2	11.8
Wholesale and miscellaneous	10.5	20.2	19.0	16.1	10.2	12.5	13.0	9.5
Total trade	10.9	22.3	18.3	18.1	13.2	14.8	11.5	10.1
Class 1 railroads	3.6	2.3	3.6	5.4	3.2	5.6	4.8	5.5
Traction and bus	3.8	7.5	1.0	4.8	1.5	1.9	3.8	4.3
Shipping	7.3	15.3	12.9	7.6	4.9	7.4	9.4	10.1
Air transport	12.2	−0.9	−16.9	−0.2	6.6	12.1	15.7	15.6
Misc. transportation	6.7	4.5	9.5	9.3	8.4	9.9	7.9	8.5
Total transportation	3.8	2.6	3.7	5.4	3.3	5.7	5.2	5.9

Electric power, gas, etc.	6.8	8.9	9.0	9.0	9.6	9.9	9.0	9.3
Telephone and telegraph	6.5	6.9	5.8	7.3	6.9	9.5	8.9	8.4
Total public utilities	6.7	8.2	8.0	8.4	8.7	9.8	9.0	9.0
Amusements	12.5	22.4	15.9	6.1	6.1	6.9	6.2	6.2
Restaurant and hotel	9.9	15.4	15.5	11.0	8.5	8.5	7.1	7.4
Other business services	11.6	13.9	15.8	16.5	14.3	16.6	14.8	13.7
Construction	6.3	10.0	14.7	19.1	14.7	15.0	13.2	15.0
Total service and construction	11.6	19.4	15.8	10.5	9.4	10.5	9.8	9.6
Commercial banks	8.8	8.5	7.9	8.4	8.1	8.4	8.0	8.4
Fire and casualty insurance	6.6	1.6	3.1	9.1	13.3	8.0	5.7	7.3
Investment trusts	6.2	6.0	6.0	7.0	8.4	8.2	6.9	6.4
Sales finance companies	7.4	5.5	10.5	15.4	15.6	18.4	16.3	15.6
Real estate companies	4.7	9.0	10.6	10.6	9.0	11.7	9.1	13.1
Total finance	7.6	6.5	6.8	8.5	9.4	9.0	7.9	8.2
Grand total (incl. mfg.)	7.6	9.5	12.2	14.0	11.0	13.3	11.4	10.3

— Deficit
* Before depletion charges in some cases.
** Included in Petroleum Producing and Refining group under Manufacturing.

First National City Bank of New York
Profit on Investment for Leading Companies

(Net Income After Taxes as a Percent of Net Worth)

Industry Groups	*1953*	*1954*	*1955*	*1956*	*1957*	*958*	*1959*	*1960*	*No. of Companies 1960*
Coal mining *	3.6	1.8	5.6	10.0	9.3	6.3	7.3	6.5	22
Metal mining *	9.2	9.7	13.7	15.3	7.9	6.3	7.4	7.3	26
Oil and gas	—	—	—	—	—	—	—	—	—
Other mining, quarrying *	24.4	26.7	26.2	21.6	15.7	12.4	10.7	9.6	8
Total mining, quarrying *	8.1	7.9	11.9	13.8	9.7	7.3	8.0	7.3	65
Chain stores—food	12.7	13.9	13.4	15.5	15.8	14.6	13.9	13.0	47
Chain stores—variety, etc.	9.3	8.4	10.6	9.8	9.3	8.8	9.9	8.5	59
Department and specialty	9.2	9.3	10.6	10.4	10.1	9.3	10.4	9.4	47
Mail order	11.0	11.4	12.3	11.9	10.9	10.5	12.2	10.4	7
Wholesale and miscellaneous	8.3	8.8	8.5	11.0	10.1	9.7	11.0	10.6	104
Total trade	9.9	10.0	11.1	11.3	10.9	10.5	11.5	10.4	264
Class 1 railroads	5.7	4.1	5.7	5.3	4.4	3.5	3.4	2.6	108
Traction and bus	5.0	4.4	4.6	5.4	5.5	4.7	7.5	10.1	21
Shipping	9.3	4.8	9.5	13.5	12.1	7.9	5.5	5.1	13
Air transport	14.0	14.4	13.9	11.4	5.8	6.4	9.6	2.8	13
Misc. transportation	10.0	10.6	12.2	14.1	11.4	9.8	13.0	7.5	75
Total transportation	6.0	4.5	6.1	5.8	4.8	4.0	4.0	2.9	220

Electric power, gas, etc.	9.5	9.5	9.9	10.0	9.9	9.8	10.2	10.2	233
Telephone and telegraph	8.7	8.8	9.5	9.4	8.9	9.6	10.1	9.9	33
Total public utilities	9.2	9.3	9.7	9.8	9.6	9.7	10.1	10.0	266
Amusements	7.5	8.6	8.6	7.8	6.4	2.8	9.5	9.2	41
Restaurant and hotel	9.6	8.4	11.5	11.0	9.3	9.3	8.6	9.3	31
Other business services	14.6	15.7	16.1	20.4	19.5	10.0	10.9	9.6	58
Construction	13.2	11.9	12.6	14.3	16.4	12.6	11.8	11.2	31
Total service and construction	11.0	11.8	12.3	13.2	12.7	8.4	10.4	9.7	161
Commercial banks	9.4	9.5	9.7	9.9	10.1	9.7	7.9	10.0	
Fire and casualty insurance	7.0	7.0	5.5	2.2	1.8	5.6	6.8	5.8	64
Investment trusts	5.8	6.2	5.3	4.7	4.7	4.7	3.9	3.7	220
Sales finance companies	16.4	16.3	16.6	16.2	15.8	14.6	13.7	13.3	90
Real estate companies	9.5	14.0	10.1	10.1	8.4	8.3	11.2	5.6	58
Total finance	8.3	8.5	7.7	6.9	7.0	7.8	6.5	7.0	432
Grand total (incl. mfg.)	10.5	10.3	12.0	11.3	10.6	8.9	9.8	9.1	3,433

— Deficit
* Before depletion charges in some cases.

FIRST NATIONAL CITY BANK OF NEW YORK
PROFIT ON SALES FOR LEADING COMPANIES

(Net Income After Taxes as Percent of Sales Dollar)

Manufacturing	*1936*	*1937*	*1938*	*1939*	*1940*	*1941*	*1942*	*1943*
Baking	6.6	5.6	6.5	6.2	5.2	4.6	4.1	3.6
Dairy products	3.5	2.7	3.1	3.8	3.2	2.9	2.3	2.2
Meat packing	1.3	0.7	−0.3	1.2	1.3	1.2	1.2	1.1
Sugar	8.5	6.4	0.6	4.6	8.1	8.6	9.5	5.1
Other food products	6.8	5.4	7.8	8.3	7.5	7.0	6.0	4.3
Beverages	13.6	9.1	9.4	8.5	6.2	5.9	5.3	4.4
Tobacco products	9.6	8.7	9.0	9.1	8.9	7.0	5.4	4.5
Cotton goods	4.3	3.2	−2.9	2.8	3.7	5.8	4.0	3.2
Other textile products	5.8	2.9	−1.5	5.0	5.0	6.7	4.6	4.3
Leather and shoes	5.7	4.0	1.4	4.6	4.7	4.7	3.7	3.5
Rubber products	5.9	3.4	3.6	5.3	4.7	4.3	3.5	3.0
Lumber, furniture, etc.	7.6	8.2	2.2	5.7	6.5	7.1	4.8	3.3
Pulp, paper products	4.9	7.1	1.0	6.3	7.4	8.2	5.9	5.0
Chemical products	12.5	15.0	6.7	8.5	9.6	9.1	6.6	6.2
Drugs, soap, etc.	7.5	8.7	9.4	9.9	12.8	12.2	7.9	7.4

Paint and varnish	7.5	5.5	2.5	5.7	5.2	4.6	3.3	3.1
Petroleum products	9.6	11.4	5.6	7.4	7.8	10.1	7.4	6.8
Cement, glass, stone	12.4	9.9	6.0	10.0	8.8	7.4	5.7	5.1
Iron and steel	5.9	7.5	−0.6	5.3	8.1	6.2	3.4	2.8
Agricultural implements	13.2	11.0	6.1	6.1	8.9	8.2	6.2	4.5
Building equipment	7.4	8.3	1.4	5.9	7.6	5.8	4.4	3.9
Electrical eq. & radio	11.5	12.1	6.3	9.4	10.4	6.9	3.6	3.0
Machinery	11.2	9.1	4.1	6.8	9.8	8.8	4.9	3.9
Office equipment	11.6	13.9	8.8	8.6	10.1	10.1	7.1	5.3
Nonferrous metals	12.9	14.1	8.6	13.7	14.1	12.3	12.1	9.0
Other metal products	10.6	9.2	5.1	8.0	8.4	7.1	5.2	4.4
Autos & trucks	12.5	9.5	6.0	9.7	8.2	6.6	5.2	3.2
Automobile parts	6.5	6.3	−0.7	5.7	6.8	5.6	3.7	3.1
Railway equipment	7.1	10.4	−4.3	4.8	8.6	6.6	3.2	3.1
Aircraft and parts	7.7	7.6	8.5	11.3	13.1	7.4	3.2	1.8
Miscel. mfg.	9.0	7.9	4.5	6.4	7.2	9.8	4.5	4.7
Total manufacturing	7.6	7.4	4.0	6.5	7.5	6.5	4.3	3.6

− Deficit

First National City Bank of New York
Profit on Sales for Leading Companies

(Net Income After Taxes as Percent of Sales Dollar)

Industry Groups	*1944*	*1945*	*1946*	*1947*	*1948*	*1949*	*1950*	*1951*
Baking	3.1	3.3	6.5	5.0	5.2	5.2	5.0	3.5
Dairy products	2.1	2.1	3.2	2.5	2.4	3.2	3.0	2.2
Meat packing	0.9	0.9	1.7	1.4	0.7	0.5	0.8	0.6
Sugar	6.1	4.7	6.0	7.7	6.0	4.4	5.5	6.2
Other food products	4.3	3.2	5.1	5.8	4.6	4.8	5.1	3.6
Soft drinks				13.0	11.2	10.4	11.2	8.7
Brewing				9.5	8.0	8.2	6.6	4.7
Distilling				6.5	7.2	5.5	6.6	5.0
Beverages	4.1	3.6	7.1					
Tobacco products	4.2	4.1	4.4	4.5	5.2	5.5	5.2	3.9
Cotton goods	3.1	3.3	10.1	11.7	12.2	5.8	6.2	5.6
Silk and rayon				12.4	13.8	9.1	12.8	9.0
Woolen goods				7.5	7.1	2.6	3.9	3.0
Hosiery, knitted goods				9.1	9.2	5.1	8.2	5.1
Carpets, floor coverings }	2.8	4.5	9.3	9.1	8.7	5.3	6.1	1.9
Other textile products }							6.8	4.9
Clothing and apparel				5.5	4.5	3.1	4.2	3.0
Leather tanning }	3.1	3.0	4.2	6.1	3.9	1.0	4.0	3.0
Shoes, leather, etc. }				4.5	4.1	3.4		
Tires, rubber products	2.7	2.5	5.6	4.4	4.1	3.6	4.9	4.3
Lumber }	3.7	3.9	7.7	11.7	11.2	8.3	9.9	9.7
Furniture, wood products }				6.5	6.6	5.5	6.8	4.5
Paper and allied products	4.5	4.3	8.6	11.4	10.6	8.1	10.2	8.3

Printing and publishing				6.9	6.2	5.5	5.7	4.6
Chemical products	5.4	7.4	8.9	9.6	9.9	10.3	11.7	9.9
Drugs and medicines }	6.5	6.4	9.8	7.9	7.1	7.1	11.3	9.4
Soap, cosmetics, etc. }							8.5	5.5
Paint and varnish	3.4	3.2	5.5	6.0	4.4	4.5	6.4	4.7
Petroleum prod. & refining	7.0	7.0	9.4	11.1	12.9	9.9	11.2	11.5
Cement }				11.5	14.0	15.8	15.4	11.8
Glass products }	4.9	4.5	8.5	8.2	7.8	9.9	10.9	6.8
Other stone, clay products }				9.5	10.0	9.5	10.8	8.1
Iron and steel	2.6	3.0	5.6	6.2	6.7	7.2	8.1	5.8
Agricultural implements	3.7	3.6	4.5	5.9	6.2	7.6	8.3	5.4
Building, heat., plumb, equip.	4.0	3.6	6.2	7.5	7.9	6.3	7.8	5.5
Electrical equip., radio & tv.	2.9	2.9	4.0	5.9	6.0	6.1	7.3	5.2
Hardware and tools				8.7	8.0	5.8	8.2	6.1
Household appliances				8.3	7.6	5.3	7.7	4.9
Machinery	3.2	3.6	5.9	7.5	8.0	7.0	7.6	5.9
Office equipment	5.3	4.4	8.7	10.3	10.5	9.6	9.8	7.4
Nonferrous metals	8.6	6.4	10.2	12.4	11.7	8.2	9.8	8.8
Instruments, photo. gds., etc.	—	—	—	—	—	—	—	—
Other metal products	3.8	3.6	6.1	6.5	6.8	5.0	6.3	5.2
Autos and trucks	3.1	4.5	3.6	6.4	7.4	8.9	8.9	5.2
Automobile parts	2.8	2.8	3.4	7.1	7.1	6.3	7.4	4.5
Railway equipment	3.1	3.9	6.0	6.1	5.4	4.4	5.5	4.8
Aircraft and parts	1.2	1.2	0.5	4.0	1.4	3.3	4.5	2.2
Shipbuilding				3.2	5.1	5.0	1.4	4.0
Misc. manufacturing	4.7	5.9	7.8	8.5	8.9	7.6	9.0	6.3
Total manufacturing	3.3	3.9	6.0	7.1	7.5	6.8	7.7	6.2

— Deficit

FIRST NATIONAL CITY BANK OF NEW YORK
PROFIT ON SALES FOR LEADING COMPANIES

(Net Income After Taxes as Percent of Sales Dollar)

Industry Groups	*1952*	*1953*	*1954*	*1955*	*1956*	*1957*	*1958*	*1959*	*1960*	*No. of Companies 1960*
Baking	3.6	3.5	3.3	3.4	3.3	3.4	3.2	3.4	3.1	16
Dairy products	2.1	2.2	2.5	2.5	2.6	2.5	2.6	2.6	2.5	11
Meat packing	0.4	0.7	0.4	0.8	0.9	0.5	0.5	1.0	0.8	15
Sugar	4.4	2.3	2.9	3.2	3.7	4.9	3.5	3.0	2.8	18
Other food products	3.1	3.3	3.7	4.0	4.2	3.9	4.2	4.1	4.2	86
Soft drinks	7.7	7.8	5.2	8.6	8.6	#	7.9	8.3	7.2	13
Brewing	4.2	3.8	3.6	3.1	3.3	2.5	3.0	3.4	3.3	14
Distilling	3.6	3.3	3.1	3.5	3.0	3.6	3.6	3.8	3.7	13
Tobacco products	3.4	3.9	4.4	5.0	5.1	5.2	5.7	5.8	5.8	17
Textile products	—	—	—	4.1	3.6	3.1	2.7	4.2	3.5	62
Cotton goods	2.9	3.6	2.3							
Silk and rayon	6.7	5.4	5.2							
Woolen goods	−2.4	−3.8	−4.4							
Hosiery, knitted goods	3.0	3.4	2.1							
Carpets, floor coverings	3.4	4.1	3.6							
Other textile products	2.5	3.0	2.3							
Clothing and apparel	2.6	2.7	2.3	3.1	3.2	2.9	2.7	3.6	3.5	53
Shoes, leather, etc. / Leather tanning	2.6	3.2	3.2	3.5	3.3	3.4	3.0	3.3	2.7	24
Tires, rubber products	3.9	4.2	4.2	4.5	4.5	4.4	4.1	4.5	4.0	25
Lumber	8.0	7.0	6.9	9.1	8.6	6.9	6.7	7.5	5.9	26
Furniture, wood products	3.9	3.8	4.5	5.8	5.2	4.4	3.5	4.5	4.0	23
Paper and allied products	7.3	7.1	7.6	8.3	8.0	6.9	6.2	6.5	5.7	72
Printing and publishing	4.0	3.1	3.6	4.3	5.2	4.9	4.3	4.3	4.7	49

Chemical products	7.7	7.6	8.9	10.0	9.1	8.5	7.2	8.9	8.0	78
Drugs and medicines	8.4	8.1	9.2	10.5	11.9	11.7	11.4	11.6	11.1	29
Soap, cosmetics, etc.	4.8	4.8	5.0	5.3	5.1	5.5	5.4	5.9	6.1	26
Paint and varnish	4.3	4.9	5.8	6.7	6.9	7.0	6.4	7.0	4.9	21
Petroleum prod. and ref.	10.5	10.6	10.7	10.6	10.4	9.7	8.4	8.4	8.7	125
Cement	11.9	12.3	15.3	16.5	16.4	15.5	16.1	16.3	11.5	22
Glass products	7.1	6.8	7.9	9.0	8.3	8.1	7.1	8.9	7.7	19
Other stone, clay products	7.5	7.1	8.1	9.0	8.9	8.3	7.9	8.9	8.1	53
Iron and steel	5.0	5.7	6.0	7.8	7.2	7.4	6.3	6.0	5.8	48
Agricultural implements	5.3	4.2	4.4	5.2	4.8	4.1	4.6	5.8	2.4	11
Building, heat., plumb., eq.	4.4	4.0	4.2	4.9	4.6	3.9	3.4	4.0	3.6	90
Electrical eq., radio & tv.	4.6	4.3	5.0	4.4	3.7	4.2	4.2	4.8	4.1	161
Hardware and tools	5.1	4.5	4.8	5.7	6.3	5.9	4.0	4.7	4.9	43
Household appliances	4.5	3.6	3.7	4.6	4.7	4.0	3.9	5.8	4.5	28
Machinery	5.0	4.8	5.5	5.7	6.2	5.7	4.3	5.0	4.5	160
Office equipment	6.3	5.5	6.6	7.0	6.6	6.4	6.6	6.5	6.8	29
Nonferrous metals	7.7	6.9	7.3	9.5	10.5	7.9	6.4	6.7	6.7	52
Instruments, phto. gds., etc.	—	5.3	7.2	7.8	7.2	6.5	5.7	6.7	5.7	115
Other metal products	4.1	4.0	4.2	4.8	4.3	4.1	4.0	4.4	3.6	130
Autos and trucks	5.5	4.4	6.4	7.4	5.7	5.7	4.2	6.7	6.4	17
Automobile parts	4.0	3.8	4.2	5.3	5.0	4.9	3.6	4.2	3.9	53
Railway equipment	3.8	3.3	4.1	4.7	4.4	4.4	3.5	4.4	3.9	19
Aircraft and parts	2.4	2.4	3.8	3.9	3.4	3.0	2.6	1.8	1.2	43
Shipbuilding	2.9	—	—	—	—	—	—	—	—	
Misc. manufacturing	5.4	4.8	4.3	4.6	4.6	4.0	3.8	4.7	3.9	125
Total manufacturing	5.4	5.3	5.9	6.7	6.0	5.9	5.2	5.8	5.4	2,034

Not computed because of limited number of sales figures available for the group.
– Deficit

FIRST NATIONAL CITY BANK OF NEW YORK
PROFIT ON SALES FOR LEADING COMPANIES

(Net Income After Taxes as Percent of Sales Dollar)

Industry Groups	*1947*	*1948*	*1949*	*1950*	*1951*	*1952*	*1953*	*1954*
Coal Mining *	6.7	7.9	5.2	5.9	5.5	4.1	2.4	1.4
Metal mining *	12.7	11.6	9.2	12.2	13.2	10.5	8.6	9.3
Oil and gas *	28.9	33.1	26.9	**	**	**	**	**
Other mining, quarrying *	26.4	26.6	26.9	26.6	24.0	23.7	22.2	24.0
Total mining, quarrying *	13.1	14.5	12.3	10.3	9.7	7.8	6.3	7.2
Chain stores—food	1.4	1.3	1.6	1.7	1.1	1.0	1.1	1.2
Chain stores—variety, etc.	5.0	5.1	4.3	4.8	3.7	3.3	3.3	3.0
Department and specialty	3.5	3.5	3.5	3.6	2.7	2.5	2.5	2.6
Mail order	5.0	5.4	4.6	5.7	4.2	3.8	3.8	4.3
Wholesale & miscellaneous	3.5	3.3	2.5	2.9	2.5	2.1	1.8	2.1
Total trade	3.7	3.8	3.3	3.8	2.7	2.4	2.4	2.5
Class 1 railroads	5.5	7.2	5.1	8.3	6.7	7.8	8.2	7.2
Traction and bus	4.5	4.2	1.2	1.5	2.5	3.1	3.7	3.0
Shipping	8.7	3.1	3.3	6.9	7.5	7.8	6.6	5.2
Air transport	−3.0	−0.3	3.3	4.9	5.6	5.3	5.2	5.1
Misc. transportation	8.7	8.1	6.6	7.7	6.7	6.4	6.6	6.1
Total transportation	5.3	6.9	4.8	7.7	6.4	7.3	7.6	6.7

Electric power, gas, etc.	14.7	13.5	14.4	14.6	13.1	13.3	13.4	13.6
Telephone and telegraph	7.2	8.2	7.8	10.7	9.9	9.9	11.0	10.9
Total public utilities	11.9	11.4	11.9	13.1	11.9	12.1	12.5	12.6
Amusements	7.9	3.9	4.4	4.9	4.3	4.2	3.9	4.3
Restaurant and hotel	5.3	4.6	3.9	4.4	3.3	3.2	4.4	3.5
Other business services	7.6	7.1	7.1	8.5	6.6	5.9	6.2	6.9
Construction	4.0	3.7	3.7	4.1	2.3	3.9	2.7	2.7
Total amusement, services, etc.	6.7	4.7	4.8	5.7	4.5	4.5	4.3	4.7
Commercial banks								
Fire & casualty insurance								
Investment companies								
Sales finance companies								
Real estate companies								
Grand total (including mfg.)	6.8	7.3	6.6	7.7	6.2	5.6	5.6	6.1

– Deficit.
* Net income is reported before depletion charges in some cases
** Included in Petroleum Producing & Refining group under Manufacturing

FIRST NATIONAL CITY BANK OF NEW YORK
PROFIT ON SALES FOR LEADING COMPANIES

Industry Groups	*1955*	*1956*	*1957*	*1958*	*1959*	*1960*	*No. of Companies 1960*
Coal mining*	4.2	7.2	6.3	5.4	5.1	5.6	22
Metal mining*	13.4	10.8	6.1	6.2	6.1	7.5	26
Other mining, quarrying*	23.5	22.2	19.2	19.5	18.0	17.0	8
Total mining, quarrying*	10.2	10.3	7.6	6.9	6.5	7.5	56
Chain stores—food	1.2	1.4	1.4	1.4	1.4	1.3	47
Chain stores—variety, etc.	3.7	3.3	3.1	2.8	3.1	2.6	59
Department and specialty	2.9	2.9	2.8	2.5	2.7	2.4	47
Mail order	4.4	4.2	4.0	3.9	4.3	3.8	7
Wholesale & miscellaneous	1.8	2.0	1.9	2.0	2.2	2.1	104
Total trade	2.7	2.6	2.5	2.3	2.5	2.2	264
Class 1 railroads	9.2	8.3	7.0	6.3	5.9	4.7	108
Traction and bus	3.1	3.6	3.4	1.0	2.7	2.1	21
Shipping	8.2	9.3	7.9	9.2	4.7	5.7	13
Air transport	5.0	4.1	2.2	2.7	3.4	1.0	13
Misc. transportation	6.9	6.4	5.0	4.0	4.1	3.8	65
Total transportation	8.3	7.5	6.2	5.6	5.2	4.0	220

Electric power, gas, etc.	13.9	13.7	13.4	13.4	13.2	13.1	233
Telephone and telegraph	12.6	13.2	13.2	13.8	14.1	13.8	33
Total public utilities	13.4	13.5	13.3	13.5	13.6	13.4	266
Amusements	4.4	4.6	3.1	2.2	4.0	4.0	41
Restaurant and hotel	3.9	3.9	3.3	2.6	3.2	3.2	31
Other business services	7.4	7.5	7.5	6.0	6.3	6.8	58
Construction	3.7	4.0	3.4	3.7	4.4	3.9	31
Total amusement, services, etc.	5.1	5.4	4.6	3.9	4.7	4.8	161
Commercial banks	—	—	—	—	—	—	—
Fire & casualty insurance	—	—	—	—	—	—	64
Investment companies	—	—	—	—	—	—	220
Sales finance companies	—	—	—	—	—	—	90
Real estate companies	—	—	—	—	—	—	58
Total finance	—	—	—	—	—	—	432
Grand total (including mfg.)	6.8	6.3	6.1	5.5	6.0	5.7	3,433

* Net income is reported before depletion charges in some cases.

Appendix

Profit on Sales and Investment

600 Leading Companies Ranked by Sales Volume
as Compiled by the Annual *Fortune* Directory

Manufacturing

- Agricultural Machinery
- Aircraft - Missiles
- Aluminum
- Appliances
- Autos and Trucks
- Auto Accessories
- Beer
- Building Materials
- Business Machines
- Cement
- Chemicals
- Coal
- Communication Equipment
- Containers
- Copper - Brass - Lead
- Dairy Products
- Drugs
- Electrical
- Food
- Furniture - Floor Coverings
- Glass
- Instruments
- Liquor
- Lumber
- Machinery
- Meat Packing
- Miscellaneous Mfg.
- Paint
- Paper
- Petroleum
- Printing & Publishing
- Railroad Equipment
- Rubber
- Shipbuilding
- Shoes
- Soft Drinks
- Steel
- Soap and Cosmetics
- Sugar
- Textiles
- Tobacco

Commercial Banks

Trade

- Auto Supply
- Department and Variety Stores
- Drug Chains
- Grocery Chains
- Mail Order

Transportation

- Airlines
- Bus Lines
- Railroads
- Shipping

Utilities

Profit on Sales and Investment for Leading Companies

Source: *Fortune* Directory

	Percent Profit — Sales					*Percent Profit — Investment*				
	1956	*1957*	*1958*	*1959*	*1960*	*1956*	*1957*	*1958*	*1959*	*1960*
Agricultural Machinery										
International Harvester	4.0	3.9	3.9	5.6	3.2	6.5	5.9	5.5	9.3	5.3
Caterpillar Tractor	8.1	6.0	5.5	6.3	6.0	20.1	13.0	10.6	14.3	12.5
Deere	6.4	7.4	8.9	8.9	3.8	6.2	8.4	13.4	13.9	5.0
Case (J. I.)	D	1.1	2.5	3.2	D	D	1.2	3.9	5.3	D
Aircraft-Missiles, Defense										
General Dynamics	3.1	2.8	2.4	1.7	D	22.5	19.7	13.4	9.4	D
Boeing	3.2	2.4	1.7	0.8	1.6	21.6	21.3	14.6	6.0	10.3
Lockheed	1.9	1.9	1.9	0.7	D	13.0	14.4	13.6	5.9	D
United Aircraft	3.9	4.2	3.5	2.7	1.4	17.0	20.3	15.2	9.9	4.8
North American Aviation	3.2	2.7	3.0	2.9	2.4	18.9	19.9	14.5	14.9	11.0
Douglas	3.1	2.8	1.4	D	D	21.7	18.2	9.6	D	D
Martin	3.0	2.7	1.8	2.3	2.4	17.0	16.9	12.4	15.0	17.3
McDonnell	3.6	2.9	2.3	2.3	2.8	24.3	26.4	22.2	18.7	19.1
Curtiss Wright	7.6	6.7	6.4	4.3	3.7	23.5	19.8	12.1	7.1	4.9
Avco	D	4.1	4.1	3.1	3.1	D	14.2	11.8	9.0	9.0
Grumman	3.9	2.6	1.1	1.7	2.2	16.2	10.7	5.2	9.9	13.4
Republic Aviation	2.1	2.3	2.3	1.7	2.2	15.9	12.3	9.9	6.4	8.4
Northrop	1.5	2.0	2.7	2.8	3.3	17.6	17.6	19.3	16.4	15.6
Chance Vought	3.5	2.6	2.7	1.9	1.8	14.4	18.5	20.4	10.5	8.1
Garrett	3.5	2.8	2.4	2.5	2.6	16.9	15.7	12.2	13.1	14.5

Rohr Aircraft	3.5	3.2	2.7	1.4	D	25.4	25.0	22.6	9.8	D
Bell Intercontinental	2.7	2.2	2.6	2.7	2.6	14.7	10.3	10.6	7.2	4.5
Fairchild Engine & Airplane	1.3	0.3	D	1.3	D	5.3	1.3	D	7.0	D
Cessna Aircraft	2.5	2.1	2.2	1.2	7.1	26.9	21.0	27.6	24.1	19.0
Ling-Temco Electronics	2.5	2.1	2.2	1.2	2.1	19.8	19.9	18.0	8.0	10.7
Beech Aircraft	4.5	3.2	3.5	4.4	4.9	21.8	19.1	14.4	15.3	16.3
Ryan Aeronautical	—	2.4	3.1	3.3	2.4	—	14.3	15.6	11.8	10.9
Aluminum										
Alcoa	10.4	8.7	5.7	6.5	4.7	14.4	11.3	6.2	7.6	5.3
Reynolds Metals	10.2	8.5	8.6	9.2	5.9	18.2	12.9	11.9	10.8	6.0
Kaiser	12.3	6.9	6.2	5.1	5.6	18.0	9.8	9.0	7.4	7.5
Appliances										
Whirlpool	3.6	2.6	2.5	4.8	3.5	14.3	10.2	9.5	16.9	12.2
Maytag	7.5	6.7	9.4	10.5	9.7	20.3	15.1	22.2	28.0	21.2
Autos & Trucks										
General Motors	7.9	7.7	6.7	7.8	7.5	18.5	17.2	12.6	16.3	16.5
Ford Motor	5.1	4.9	2.3	8.4	8.2	11.9	13.2	4.5	17.3	14.9
Chrysler	0.8	3.4	D	D	1.1	3.1	16.4	D	D	4.6
American Motors	D	D	5.6	6.9	4.6	D	D	19.0	31.6	21.6
Studebaker Packard	D	D	D	7.4	0.2	D	D	D	31.9	0.7
White Motor	3.5	3.0	2.7	4.3	3.1	10.4	9.4	9.4	16.3	7.2
Mack Trucks	4.8	5.0	3.1	5.3	4.3	15.0	14.5	8.3	13.4	9.1
Fruehauf Trailer	2.5	0.7	D	5.2	4.5	5.6	1.6	D	11.4	8.2

Profit on Sales and Investment for Leading Companies

Source: *Fortune* Directory

	Percent Profit — Sales					*Percent Profit — Investment*				
	1956	*1957*	*1958*	*1959*	*1960*	*1956*	*1957*	*1958*	*1959*	*1960*
Auto Accessories										
Bendix	4.2	3.9	3.4	4.0	3.3	13.7	13.4	9.9	11.8	10.7
Borg Warner	6.0	5.6	4.0	6.1	4.6	12.5	11.2	6.9	11.9	8.0
Thompson-Ramo-Wooldridge	4.3	3.2	2.6	2.3	2.9	13.3	11.3	8.2	8.4	9.8
Budd	3.0	2.8	0.9	3.4	1.4	7.4	7.1	1.7	8.7	3.7
Eaton Manufacturing	5.7	5.0	4.0	6.0	4.2	15.6	12.4	7.6	14.6	8.9
A. O. Smith	3.0	3.7	2.8	4.1	2.4	9.5	11.7	8.2	12.2	6.7
Rockwell Standard	4.8	6.0	4.5	6.7	5.2	11.2	14.0	7.9	14.7	9.8
Dana	7.6	6.9	5.9	8.3	7.2	19.7	14.7	10.4	17.5	15.0
Electric Autolite	1.0	3.6	1.7	5.0	2.5	2.3	8.8	2.6	8.9	5.2
Kelsey-Hayes	4.6	4.2	2.1	3.5	2.3	13.0	14.0	5.5	9.9	5.4
Electric Storage Battery	3.8	4.0	3.2	4.3	4.1	5.9	7.6	5.2	7.7	7.3
Cummings Engine	5.4	4.6	.6	5.5	4.4	21.7	16.8	11.7	20.4	13.4
Continental Motors	1.3	2.6	2.7	1.9	1.0	3.6	7.5	7.2	5.3	2.9
Federal Mogul Bearings	8.8	8.4	7.1	9.7	8.2	17.9	17.3	15.4	19.8	14.9
Stewart Warner	5.5	5.4	5.6	6.9	5.8	14.1	12.0	10.0	14.1	10.7
Champion Spark Plug	—	—	16.5	15.6	16.6	—	—	26.6	25.3	23.7
Midland-Ross	3.9	5.1	4.0	4.5	3.3	8.5	13.8	7.7	9.8	9.4
Raybestos-Manhattan	4.9	4.2	2.6	4.4	3.6	9.9	8.0	4.4	8.8	6.4
Clevite	5.4	5.6	4.9	7.7	7.3	9.1	9.3	7.3	13.5	12.7

Beer										
Anheuser-Busch	4.5	4.3	4.2	4.4	5.0	8.2	7.9	8.4	9.6	10.6
Falstaff Brewing	4.8	4.2	4.2	4.8	5.1	16.4	12.6	12.5	14.5	14.5
Pabst Brewing	D	D	D	1.1	1.9	D	D	D	1.8	3.0
Building Materials										
American Radiator & Standard Sanitary	4.9	3.4	2.9	4.1	2.8	8.7	5.6	4.5	7.7	4.7
Johns-Manville	8.1	5.8	7.2	8.4	7.3	12.6	8.8	10.4	12.3	9.6
Crane	2.9	2.3	0.6	2.1	1.7	6.3	4.6	1.2	4.5	3.3
U. S. Gypsum	15.3	15.5	15.4	15.4	14.0	17.7	15.8	15.6	16.0	12.7
Carrier	4.9	2.8	3.0	3.1	2.0	11.0	6.1	6.2	6.4	3.9
Otis Elevator	8.5	8.2	8.9	10.6	11.6	17.1	16.3	17.9	21.8	20.0
National Gypsum	9.4	9.0	9.6	11.3	10.3	10.6	9.2	10.2	12.6	10.0
Flintkote	5.4	6.1	4.8	6.5	5.1	8.9	9.2	7.5	10.6	8.6
Grinnell	4.7	4.8	4.4	4.3	3.7	11.4	11.3	8.7	8.8	7.6
Yale & Towne	4.9	3.7	3.1	3.5	3.3	9.8	7.3	5.6	7.6	6.6
Ruberoid	5.6	5.9	5.5	5.2	3.9	8.2	8.9	7.8	9.7	6.7
Vulcan Materials	—	6.4	6.7	5.3	4.9	—	10.1	11.3	8.3	7.8
Certainteed Products	5.3	2.7	2.2	3.4	2.5	12.2	5.6	4.7	8.2	5.7
National Homes	3.5	3.7	4.7	2.0	1.8	8.8	9.8	13.9	6.4	4.3
Trane	7.7	7.7	7.4	6.0	6.6	19.6	15.5	13.5	10.5	12.8
Celotex	7.7	5.7	4.6	5.4	3.1	13.8	8.0	6.4	8.1	4.1

Profit on Sales and Investment for Leading Companies

Source: *Fortune* Directory

	Percent Profit — Sales					*Percent Profit — Investment*				
	1956	*1957*	*1958*	*1959*	*1960*	*1956*	*1957*	*1958*	*1959*	*1960*
Business Machines										
Internat'l Bus. Machines	9.4	8.9	10.8	11.1	11.7	20.7	14.3	17.5	17.3	17.3
Sperry Rand	5.8	5.7	3.2	2.8	3.2	14.5	14.7	8.1	8.0	10.3
National Cash Register	5.4	4.8	3.9	4.6	4.4	16.2	14.7	11.9	11.3	11.2
Burroughs	5.2	3.6	2.2	2.0	2.4	13.9	9.4	5.3	5.8	7.4
Addressograph-Multigraph	8.4	7.2	7.7	7.4	8.1	17.8	16.2	17.3	13.8	16.1
Royal-McBee	5.9	4.1	0.4	1.2	0.7	13.7	10.3	0.9	3.0	1.8
Smith-Corona-Marchant	—	—	2.6	0.6	D	—	—	6.5	1.5	D
Underwood	D	D	D	D	D	D	D	D	D	D
Cement										
Ideal	24.8	18.5	18.9	18.4	13.7	24.1	16.1	17.0	17.1	11.7
Lone Star	16.4	16.5	16.1	19.3	13.9	17.0	13.1	12.8	13.7	9.9
Lehigh-Portland	14.2	10.1	9.1	11.0	9.6	12.6	7.2	6.8	8.8	7.0
Chemicals										
Du Pont	13.7	13.5	11.5	13.5	11.6	11.3	11.0	8.2	10.5	8.5
Union Carbine	11.0	9.6	9.6	11.2	10.2	18.0	15.9	14.5	18.5	16.1
Eastman Kodak	12.4	12.3	11.9	13.6	13.5	17.4	16.7	15.7	18.2	17.4
Allied	7.0	7.5	5.4	7.0	6.7	11.0	11.5	7.6	10.6	10.4

Dow	10.6	8.5	7.2	8.9	10.6	15.9	12.4	9.9	12.2	14.1
Olin-Mathieson	7.5	6.1	1.6	5.3	5.0	12.4	9.5	2.7	10.0	8.7
Monsanto	7.1	6.6	6.3	8.0	7.6	10.6	9.6	8.6	11.0	11.3
American Cyanamid	11.1	9.6	8.4	9.0	8.1	15.1	13.2	11.0	12.4	10.7
Minnesota Mining & Mfgr.	11.7	10.7	11.7	12.7	12.9	20.7	18.9	19.1	23.1	21.3
Hercules Powder	7.5	7.4	7.4	8.3	8.1	15.5	14.3	12.8	15.4	14.4
Celanese	9.0	8.4	7.5	8.5	7.6	7.7	7.1	7.2	9.3	7.9
Koppers	4.0	2.9	2.6	2.3	2.5	8.5	6.4	4.4	3.6	4.9
American Viscose	6.2	3.7	3.2	6.4	3.3	6.3	3.6	3.0	6.3	2.4
Stauffer	8.6	8.4	9.1	9.7	9.0	13.9	12.4	12.7	13.8	11.7
Air Reduction	9.3	8.7	7.6	7.4	7.3	13.6	13.3	10.4	11.0	10.6
Thiokol	—	—	3.4	2.9	2.1	—	—	15.9	22.2	12.4
General Aniline & Film	3.8	3.9	4.0	4.4	4.5	4.6	4.6	4.7	5.4	5.2
Hooker	10.5	8.4	8.5	9.0	8.5	14.6	11.1	12.1	14.1	12.7
Diamond Aklaki	8.6	5.7	5.7	8.2	8.5	13.2	8.6	7.8	12.6	12.0
Chemetron	6.7	6.7	1.8	3.1	3.3	17.5	16.8	3.1	6.1	6.3
International Min & Chem.	5.6	7.2	5.1	5.5	6.0	6.5	8.8	6.0	8.8	7.9
American Enka	—	2.0	2.7	5.2	0.7	—	1.7	2.6	7.2	0.9
Wyandotte	6.3	8.1	3.5	4.8	5.0	7.1	9.2	3.9	5.8	7.1
Reichold	—	4.7	4.5	3.9	3.4	—	12.2	10.8	8.0	6.5
American Agric. Chemical	6.0	6.3	6.1	5.5	4.0	10.1	10.9	10.9	9.5	6.6
Pennsalt	5.0	3.8	4.7	5.2	5.4	7.0	5.6	6.5	7.7	8.0
Virginia-Carolina Chemical	2.0	1.3	2.5	1.4	3.8	2.7	1.9	3.4	2.3	6.1
Tennessee Corporation	13.4	11.2	10.0	12.7	13.3	20.1	15.1	12.4	16.9	17.1
Columbia Columbian Carbon	7.4	6.0	6.0	8.0	8.2	8.0	7.0	6.5	9.6	9.9

* Profit on operations.

PROFIT ON SALES AND INVESTMENT FOR LEADING COMPANIES

Source: *Fortune* Directory

	Percent Profit — Sales					*Percent Profit — Investment*				
	1956	*1957*	*1958*	*1959*	*1960*	*1956*	*1957*	*1958*	*1959*	*1960*
Coal										
Consolidation Coal	11.2	7.3	6.5	7.3	7.4	13.5	9.1	6.1	6.7	6.1
Eastern Gas & Fuel Assos.	6.1	7.1	4.8	3.2	4.7	10.1	11.7	6.2	4.5	5.9
Philadelphia & Reading	10.9	8.2	9.5	6.3	5.0	22.2	15.2	14.7	13.1	11.2
Peabody Coal	7.4	9.2	10.9	10.4	10.3	11.2	12.8	11.2	11.5	11.6
Island Creek Coal	7.5	7.7	5.2	3.5	3.8	14.2	13.8	6.9	5.1	5.0
Communication Equipment										
International Tel & Tel	5.2	3.5	3.9	3.8	4.7	7.7	6.0	6.0	7.0	9.3
Western Electric	3.4	3.4	4.0	4.4	4.7	12.2	10.9	9.7	11.0	11.4
Containers										
Continental Can	4.3	3.9	3.8	3.5	2.5	11.5	10.4	10.0	8.9	6.1
American Can	4.5	4.5	4.5	3.7	3.3	9.8	9.3	9.4	8.2	7.0
Container Corp. of Amer.	6.6	5.7	5.6	6.1	5.2	15.8	12.2	11.8	14.3	11.7
Anchor Hocking Glass	5.2	5.6	5.7	5.9	4.9	12.9	13.5	13.7	13.6	11.0
Crown Cork & Seal	0.3	2.1	1.9	2.2	2.8	0.8	4.7	4.7	5.8	5.7
National Can	2.7	1.6	0.9	0.3	1.0	10.1	6.0	3.5	1.3	4.4
Copper-Brass-Lead										
American Metal Climax	3.6	4.8	3.4	4.6	5.7	19.8	14.5	9.4	14.9	17.0
Anaconda	14.9	7.7	6.5	9.4	7.4	14.5	5.1	3.8	6.5	4.9
Kennecott	25.3	16.9	15.2	13.1	15.6	19.8	32.4	7.9	7.6	10.4

Amer. Smelting & Refining	6.7	5.0	4.1	7.4	6.1	12.2	7.5	5.1	8.0	7.7
Phelps-Dodge	20.8	15.4	13.5	11.7	12.6	24.3	11.9	9.7	8.8	9.3
Revere Copper & Brass	3.8	4.3	1.4	4.1	3.4	12.1	10.4	3.1	10.3	7.3
Bridgeport Brass	2.9	3.7	3.4	4.1	2.1	7.6	8.7	7.1	10.2	4.2
General Cable	6.4	6.4	4.9	5.1	5.0	17.4	14.5	8.5	10.1	9.4
Cerro Corporation	8.4	3.8	3.8	5.1	5.6	6.4	3.1	2.8	4.9	5.5
Scovill Mfgr.	2.9	1.8	D	2.6	1.6	5.9	3.1	D	5.2	2.9
Anaconda Wire & Cable	6.0	4.0	1.3	2.1	0.2	16.8	8.3	2.1	4.9	0.4
St. Joseph Lead	8.6	7.5	5.5	7.3	3.7	14.4	10.8	5.3	7.9	3.8
Dairy Products										
National Dairy Products	3.1	3.1	3.1	3.1	3.0	13.0	12.9	12.5	12.2	11.8
Borden	2.7	2.6	2.7	2.7	2.8	11.1	10.9	10.6	10.4	10.3
Foremost	2.0	2.1	2.2	2.4	1.7	9.5	10.3	10.1	15.3	10.1
Beatrice Foods	2.0	2.1	2.2	2.3	2.3	9.5	10.3	10.1	10.0	9.9
Fairmont Foods	1.2	1.2	1.3	1.6	1.7	4.9	4.8	5.6	5.8	6.2
Drugs										
American Home Products	10.6	11.1	11.3	11.1	10.9	32.2	34.3	33.5	32.2	29.8
Johnson & Johnson	5.3	5.1	4.8	5.2	5.2	11.3	10.6	9.4	10.3	9.8
Pfizer (Charles)	10.2	11.1	10.8	9.8	9.7	15.9	18.0	17.3	16.1	15.4
Merck	11.7	12.4	13.4	13.8	12.8	14.7	15.6	17.1	17.1	14.8
Rohm & Haas	9.8	9.0	8.2	10.7	9.8	16.7	14.2	11.9	16.4	13.4
Sterling Drug	9.5	9.5	9.7	10.0	10.2	20.0	20.5	22.7	22.7	22.0
Parke, Davis	13.2	17.2	16.3	16.2	15.2	17.2	23.9	21.6	22.1	20.3
Lilly (Eli)	16.6	16.2	13.1	12.5	10.5	19.7	18.9	13.2	12.9	10.2
Upjohn	—	—	13.7	14.8	14.3	—	—	18.0	18.5	16.5
Smith-Kline & French	18.1	17.8	16.8	18.5	16.6	42.5	37.6	33.1	33.5	29.4
Abbott Laboratories	11.2	11.4	11.0	10.6	9.8	14.2	15.6	14.6	13.7	12.4
Richardson-Merrell	8.4	8.3	9.4	10.6	10.9	13.8	14.1	16.3	13.9	14.9
Schering	—	19.0	16.6	14.7	11.9	—	31.1	21.8	18.5	14.4

Profit on Sales and Investment for Leading Companies

Source: *Fortune* Directory

	Percent Profit — Sales					*Percent Profit — Investment*				
	1956	*1957*	*1958*	*1959*	*1960*	*1956*	*1957*	*1958*	*1959*	*1960*
Electrical										
General Electric	5.2	5.7	5.9	6.4	4.8	18.7	20.1	18.5	19.2	13.2
Westinghouse	0.2	3.6	3.9	4.5	4.0	0.5	8.9	8.6	8.6	8.3
R.C.A.	3.6	3.3	2.6	2.9	2.4	14.6	13.4	10.5	12.4	8.1
Raytheon	0.7	2.6	2.5	2.7	2.1	3.0	13.8	15.7	16.8	12.5
Philco	0.1	1.2	0.8	1.9	0.6	0.4	4.3	2.8	6.6	2.1
Motorola	3.5	3.5	3.4	4.9	4.2	13.0	11.8	10.3	17.0	13.0
McGraw Edison	6.6	5.7	4.3	5.3	4.5	17.4	13.2	8.3	11.5	8.2
Zenith Radio	4.4	5.5	6.7	6.9	6.5	12.5	12.7	17.2	20.9	17.3
Admiral	0.6	0.6	0.9	2.2	D	1.8	1.7	2.3	6.4	D
Litton	—	—	4.5	4.8	4.0	—	—	13.2	17.3	14.7
I-T-E Circuit Breaker	4.9	5.1	3.5	2.3	D	13.2	14.2	8.3	5.9	D
Collins Radio	2.5	2.2	1.0	3.2	3.4	13.9	11.1	4.4	12.6	15.7
Cutler-Hammer	8.7	8.0	6.0	5.8	4.5	20.2	16.1	11.6	14.9	10.5
American Bosch Arma	4.0	3.8	4.1	3.0	0.8	20.6	19.2	16.5	11.7	3.5
Wagner Electric	6.2	6.3	4.9	5.9	4.0	13.4	11.4	7.6	11.2	7.0
Square D	11.4	8.7	6.4	9.5	10.1	23.3	16.7	10.6	17.3	17.7
Joslyn Mfg. & Supply	4.8	4.7	4.1	5.1	3.9	13.7	12.5	9.2	12.2	8.4
Emerson Electric	—	3.6	3.5	4.3	4.8	—	13.1	12.7	15.5	16.5
Sunbeam	9.5	9.5	9.0	9.5	9.3	20.1	19.9	14.9	13.0	13.1
Magnavox	4.4	4.3	3.2	3.7	5.2	15.2	16.6	11.1	13.3	20.2
Mallory (P.R.)	4.5	4.0	4.2	5.0	5.2	10.6	9.9	8.9	12.7	12.0
Reliance Elec. & Engineering	4.5	6.4	5.3	5.3	5.4	14.6	17.7	10.5	11.1	11.6
Daystrom	2.8	3.3	2.9	0.7	2.5	6.6	8.7	7.7	1.9	7.3

Food										
General Foods	4.2	4.4	4.8	5.1	5.6	16.6	16.5	16.9	17.2	17.6
Corn Products	7.7	6.8	6.9	4.9	5.5	13.3	11.8	15.6	12.8	14.0
General Mills	2.7	2.3	2.8	3.1	2.1	10.7	9.0	10.3	10.9	7.2
Ralston Purina	3.6	3.3	3.5	3.4	3.5	12.6	12.1	13.2	12.4	11.7
Campbell Soup	6.8	6.8	6.3	6.9	7.7	12.7	12.3	12.3	12.4	13.3
Standard Brands	2.6	2.7	2.8	3.7	4.0	8.9	9.7	9.9	10.2	11.0
National Biscuit	4.9	5.2	5.3	5.7	6.2	11.5	12.1	11.7	12.5	13.6
Carnation	2.5	2.6	2.6	2.5	2.7	11.0	11.0	10.9	10.1	10.0
Continental Baking	2.6	2.5	2.7	2.4	1.6	14.2	13.3	11.9	11.8	7.7
Pillsbury	1.3	1.2	1.6	2.2	1.8	6.5	5.9	8.0	9.7	7.8
California Packing	4.6	4.4	2.6	3.4	4.1	9.8	10.1	6.6	8.8	10.0
Quaker Oats	4.2	4.0	4.1	4.1	4.2	12.0	12.0	12.2	11.9	11.7
Heinz (H.J.)	4.0	3.8	3.2	3.5	3.6	9.5	9.0	7.6	8.5	8.9
Libby, McNeill & Libby	2.7	1.2	0.9	2.0	1.4	10.1	4.3	3.2	6.5	4.7
Central Soya	1.6	2.4	3.0	2.4	1.5	7.0	11.1	14.3	11.3	6.8
Kellogg	7.5	8.0	8.5	8.0	8.4	23.3	23.2	22.4	20.9	21.3
Archer-Daniels-Midland	2.8	2.4	1.8	2.3	1.5	6.3	5.6	4.1	5.5	4.0
Pet Milk	1.7	1.4	1.9	1.9	1.9	7.1	6.0	7.5	7.5	9.0
Sunshine Biscuits	4.6	4.4	4.5	4.2	4.2	12.5	12.2	12.2	11.1	10.9
Campbell Taggart	5.6	5.7	5.6	5.3	4.7	31.3	18.8	18.0	16.9	15.9
General Baking	1.7	1.7	1.7	1.2	0.5	7.1	7.6	7.6	5.7	2.4
Staley Manufacturing	2.7	3.4	3.7	3.4	2.9	8.3	8.5	9.1	8.4	6.5
Hershey Chocolate	8.7	9.5	7.8	9.1	10.9	17.9	19.2	17.4	19.0	20.6
American Bakeries	4.1	3.9	3.4	3.4	2.7	14.6	13.8	11.9	11.9	9.8
Stokely-Van Camp	2.8	2.0	1.8	2.9	2.1	8.8	6.1	5.3	8.2	5.7
Hunt Foods	3.9	3.8	3.9	4.2	2.4	7.3	7.4	6.8	7.4	5.6

Profit on Sales and Investment for Leading Companies

Source: *Fortune* Directory

	Percent Profit — Sales					*Percent Profit — Investment*				
	1956	*1957*	*1958*	*1959*	*1960*	*1956*	*1957*	*1958*	*1959*	*1960*
United Biscuit	2.7	2.9	1.6	1.4	1.9	8.1	8.4	4.5	3.8	6.1
Spencer Kellogg & Sons	1.3	1.0	1.0	1.3	0.9	2.6	2.7	2.7	3.4	2.2
Colorado Milling & Elevator	1.2	1.4	1.0	1.1	0.7	6.6	8.4	4.5	3.8	4.5
Gerber Products	6.0	7.2	6.4	5.7	5.4	18.8	21.1	18.3	16.3	14.8
Interstate Bakeries	3.3	3.6	3.1	3.4	2.7	16.6	17.1	14.2	14.8	12.3
Beech-Nut Life Savers	6.5	7.8	7.1	7.0	7.6	14.9	15.0	13.4	12.9	13.4
Allied Mills	3.1	2.6	3.1	2.7	2.3	8.2	6.8	8.3	7.6	6.1
Lipton (Thomas J.)	5.4	5.3	5.9	6.0	6.4	21.8	20.4	19.8	18.8	21.6
Ward Baking	1.3	1.4	1.1	0.9	0.7	6.2	6.7	5.5	4.2	3.9
United Fruit	8.8	9.2	7.0	3.9	0.7	—	8.8	6.4	3.4	0.7
Wrigley (Wm.) Jr.	12.4	11.8	11.2	10.9	10.2	15.3	14.8	13.4	13.1	13.0
Dole Corp.	3.7	1.7	4.1	4.6	2.9	6.3	3.1	7.3	8.3	5.0
Furniture — Floor Covering										
Armstrong Cork	5.4	4.5	5.5	6.6	5.6	9.7	7.8	9.2	12.0	9.7
Mohasco Industries	3.5	3.3	8.5	10.5	3.4	7.2	6.1	12.9	15.5	4.6
Simmons	4.7	4.0	4.4	4.5	3.1	11.3	9.7	7.8	9.9	6.1

Glass										
Pittsburgh Plate Glass	9.3	6.2	7.3	7.3	7.6	14.8	14.2	7.2	10.0	10.2
Owens-Illinois	7.1	7.0	7.4	7.4	5.9	14.0	13.4	13.3	13.2	10.2
Libbey-Owens-Ford	11.3	11.8	9.9	17.5	14.9	20.8	18.7	14.0	29.8	22.2
Corning Glass Works	11.3	10.4	10.8	11.9	9.2	19.3	16.1	15.6	19.5	14.9
Owens-Corning Fiberglas	6.0	5.5	6.2	7.7	6.7	13.9	9.4	10.8	14.3	12.0
Instruments										
Minneapolis-Honeywell	7.8	6.6	6.9	7.7	6.2	18.8	13.6	13.3	15.7	13.1
General Precision Equipment	1.6	2.3	0.2	2.0	2.2	4.6	6.9	0.5	6.3	7.7
Texas Instruments	—	5.6	6.5	7.3	6.7	—	19.2	23.4	24.9	21.4
Lear	—	—	2.5	2.8	4.0	—	—	11.8	13.7	17.2
Robertshaw-Fulton Controls	5.8	5.5	5.8	7.3	4.0	15.4	12.4	12.1	15.6	7.7
Liquor										
National Distillers & Chem.	8.8	9.6	8.6	9.4	7.8	7.6	8.0	6.8	8.1	7.5
Seagrams (Joseph E.) & Sons	5.4	5.1	5.8	5.3	5.5	4.4	4.8	5.1	4.7	5.1
Schenley Industries	5.3	5.5	8.4	9.3	4.8	3.6	4.6	6.6	6.7	3.1
Lumber										
Weyerhaeuser	15.9	12.7	12.1	13.2	10.4	13.2	11.0	9.9	11.4	8.9
U. S. Plywood	5.6	4.1	3.1	5.6	4.7	11.6	8.3	6.3	12.3	11.1
Georgia Pacific	6.1	5.8	6.6	7.4	6.9	15.5	15.8	13.9	14.9	12.4
Potlatch Forests	—	7.7	6.7	8.0	5.5	—	7.4	7.0	9.3	5.6
American Forest Products	3.3	1.9	2.4	3.2	0.6	8.6	4.7	5.4	8.7	1.2

PROFIT ON SALES AND INVESTMENT FOR LEADING COMPANIES

Source: *Fortune* Directory

	Percent Profit — Sales					*Percent Profit — Investment*				
	1956	*1957*	*1958*	*1959*	*1960*	*1956*	*1957*	*1958*	*1959*	*1960*
Machinery										
Allis Chalmers	3.7	3.3	3.7	4.2	2.0	6.9	6.0	6.4	6.6	3.1
FMC Corporation	5.3	5.1	5.1	6.0	5.8	11.2	9.9	9.8	11.2	10.7
Babcock & Wilcox	5.0	4.5	3.6	4.8	5.7	11.2	10.6	8.0	9.3	9.8
Combustion Engineering	3.9	2.7	2.4	2.1	2.2	9.3	9.8	10.2	7.7	6.3
American Machine & Foundry	4.5	4.5	4.8	6.7	6.7	13.3	13.4	11.5	16.3	17.7
Dresser Industries	7.5	7.5	4.4	4.0	3.7	18.0	18.1	8.2	7.4	7.3
H. K. Porter	5.4	4.1	2.6	3.0	1.8	17.1	13.1	6.1	8.7	5.2
Clark Equipment	6.5	5.8	4.5	6.0	3.4	17.5	14.2	10.4	18.1	9.6
Worthington	5.4	5.2	4.3	4.6	4.0	11.5	11.5	8.6	7.9	7.1
Foster Wheeler	1.1	D	1.5	3.6	1.7	3.4	D	8.2	15.4	6.9
Ingersoll Rand	19.1	17.7	15.5	15.3	13.4	26.6	24.6	17.6	16.4	16.5
Blaw-Knox	4.2	4.3	4.1	3.6	2.2	14.4	14.6	11.7	9.3	6.6
Link-Belt	6.8	6.2	4.7	4.5	4.1	13.8	11.9	7.6	7.7	6.7
Baldwin-Lima-Hamilton	1.9	3.5	3.4	3.6	1.1	3.5	5.7	4.0	4.3	1.2
Ex-Cell-O	9.4	8.3	8.7	7.1	6.0	23.3	19.4	13.0	9.9	9.8
Cincinnati Milling Machine	5.4	5.3	2.9	2.0	2.3	13.8	10.0	3.8	3.3	3.6
Joy Manufacturing	9.0	8.7	4.7	5.5	5.5	20.0	19.3	7.2	8.5	8.8
United Shoe Machinery	18.1	13.1	11.2	10.2	11.1	18.7	12.1	9.1	8.4	9.4
Briggs & Stratton	10.3	10.0	9.2	10.0	9.0	30.4	22.7	20.2	24.2	18.4
U. S. Industries	4.2	3.1	0.8	D	D	11.6	8.4	1.7	D	D
Harnischfeger	4.0	4.4	0.1	2.9	1.4	9.6	10.2	0.1	6.4	2.7
Chicago Pneumatic Tool	12.4	14.9	10.1	11.0	10.9	17.4	19.5	10.3	11.9	11.7
Sunstrand	5.1	4.6	4.1	4.6	2.7	16.3	13.6	11.7	12.4	6.5
Gardner-Denver	11.5	11.0	8.7	10.3	8.4	21.7	20.6	12.3	14.8	12.1

Meat Packing										
Swift & Company	0.6	0.5	0.4	0.8	0.8	3.7	3.6	2.7	4.9	4.7
Armour	0.7	0.2	0.3	0.8	0.9	7.2	1.6	2.7	7.9	8.6
Wilson	1.2	0.9	1.1	1.5	0.3	8.4	6.5	8.4	9.9	2.1
Morrell (John)	2.7	2.5	2.3	1.4	0.7	18.3	17.9	15.6	14.1	7.6
Hygrade Food Products	0.7	0.4	0.3	0.7	0.6	9.5	5.2	5.1	10.5	8.5
International Packers	—	1.5	2.0	2.2	1.1	—	8.3	13.0	13.8	6.5
Hormel	1.6	1.0	0.8	1.5	1.2	15.4	9.4	8.2	14.3	10.7
Cudahy	2.1	0.6	0.7	0.8	0.2	18.2	6.0	7.3	6.8	2.1
Rath Packing	1.4	0.4	0.4	0.6	0.5	13.0	4.5	3.8	6.0	4.7
Mayer (Oscar)	2.6	1.7	1.6	2.4	2.2	16.0	10.4	9.6	13.1	10.8
Tobin Packing	—	2.2	2.1	2.2	2.6	—	12.2	12.2	11.7	13.6
Miscellaneous Manufacturing										
Singer Manufacturing	5.3	5.1	3.0	4.3	4.0	8.2	7.5	4.5	7.0	6.7
Brunswick Corporation	—	5.6	7.4	9.8	10.6	—	19.8	24.1	26.6	26.8
Kaiser Industries	5.6	4.5	6.0	7.3	2.7	12.8	9.2	7.6	7.5	3.0
Gillette	15.7	13.3	13.2	14.9	16.5	43.0	34.6	32.4	35.6	39.3
Outboard Marine	9.9	8.7	5.7	8.0	7.3	25.5	18.6	12.4	16.9	13.5
Rheem Manufacturing	D	1.0	0.2	2.0	D	D	4.0	0.6	5.8	D
Rockwell Manufacturing	8.2	7.9	6.9	7.9	6.9	15.5	14.4	10.7	13.1	10.0
Interchemical	4.2	3.6	4.3	5.4	4.5	12.2	9.8	11.1	14.4	11.2
Eagle-Picher	5.1	3.6	2.1	3.9	4.0	15.2	10.4	5.1	10.8	10.6
Carborundum	6.0	5.6	4.0	6.2	5.3	10.3	9.6	5.8	9.9	8.5

Profit on Sales and Investment for Leading Companies

Source: *Fortune* Directory

	Percent Profit — Sales					*Percent Profit — Investment*				
	1956	*1957*	*1958*	*1959*	*1960*	*1956*	*1957*	*1958*	*1959*	*1960*
Stanley Works	5.1	3.5	3.8	4.6	3.2	8.2	5.4	5.5	7.5	4.6
Polaroid	—	—	11.1	12.0	8.9	—	—	21.0	24.3	16.7
American Optical	3.2	3.3	2.1	3.2	3.1	5.3	5.5	3.6	6.0	5.8
Harbison-Walker Refractories	11.7	12.9	11.0	10.4	10.6	16.5	17.8	11.1	11.1	11.8
Ceco Steel Products	4.2	3.9	2.7	3.1	2.3	11.9	11.1	7.3	8.5	6.0
Paint										
National Lead	11.0	10.5	9.8	9.9	9.6	24.2	20.3	15.7	17.4	16.0
American Marietta	8.0	7.3	7.0	7.4	6.6	19.8	14.8	11.6	12.4	10.5
Sherwin-Williams	—	5.9	6.0	6.4	5.7	—	11.9	11.3	12.1	10.6
Glidden	3.6	3.2	2.8	3.9	3.4	9.8	8.5	6.9	8.4	7.2
Paper										
International Paper	8.9	8.3	7.9	8.1	7.1	12.8	10.9	9.5	10.4	8.6
Crown Zellerbach	15.9	8.3	7.1	8.0	7.2	19.9	10.0	8.9	10.8	9.9
St. Regis Paper	6.8	5.9	5.6	6.0	9.3	11.0	8.5	7.9	9.1	12.1
Kimberly Clark	8.5	8.0	7.3	7.2	7.8	11.7	11.6	10.9	10.9	12.2
Mead	8.0	6.2	4.2	4.2	4.1	14.2	10.5	7.8	8.6	8.2
Scott Paper	8.3	7.8	7.8	8.3	8.9	13.7	12.8	12.7	13.4	13.6
West Virginia Pulp & Paper	8.7	6.3	4.6	10.1	4.4	10.6	7.6	5.9	13.1	6.0
Diamond National	6.7	4.8	4.4	4.5	5.4	11.4	8.0	7.1	8.3	9.6

Union Bag—Camp Paper	13.2	11.3	10.0	10.5	8.7	16.6	12.8	10.5	12.0	10.7
Champion Paper & Fibre	8.5	8.5	6.8	4.6	5.0	14.0	14.0	10.7	7.0	7.8
Bemis Bros. Bag	2.2	1.5	2.2	2.3	2.2	5.5	3.6	5.0	5.6	5.1
Rayonier	10.1	5.3	3.3	10.3	7.4	18.3	7.6	4.3	14.3	9.7
Fibreboard Paper Products	4.6	3.3	4.2	4.0	1.9	11.5	8.2	9.1	8.6	3.7
Lily Tulip Cup	8.5	8.4	7.3	7.4	7.1	16.1	15.7	13.3	13.6	12.3
Minnesota Ontario Paper	9.9	7.4	6.3	6.8	6.7	10.8	8.2	6.7	7.7	7.4
Cons. Water Power & Paper	10.4	8.8	7.8	8.5	9.0	12.4	10.1	9.2	10.4	10.9
Petroleum										
Standard Oil (N. J.)	11.3	10.3	7.5	8.0	8.6	15.8	14.0	8.7	9.4	10.1
Socony-Mobil	9.1	7.4	5.4	5.3	5.8	12.0	9.3	6.4	6.5	7.0
Gulf Oil	12.1	13.0	11.9	10.7	12.1	14.8	16.2	13.5	11.0	11.6
Texaco	14.8	14.2	13.3	13.2	13.1	16.5	16.2	13.6	14.1	14.3
Standard Oil (Indiana)	7.9	7.5	6.3	7.1	7.2	7.9	7.5	5.7	6.5	6.4
Shell Oil	8.3	7.7	7.0	8.1	7.9	15.0	13.8	9.4	11.1	10.3
Standard Oil (California)	18.4	17.5	16.5	16.2	16.0	15.8	15.5	13.0	12.0	11.8
Sinclair Oil	8.1	6.3	4.2	3.7	4.3	10.4	8.2	5.1	4.7	5.6
Phillips Petroleum	9.2	8.5	7.9	9.0	9.4	10.1	9.8	8.4	9.9	10.2
Cities Service	6.4	5.7	4.4	4.3	4.2	10.7	9.6	7.1	6.5	6.2
Sun Oil	7.7	6.2	4.4	5.8	6.6	11.4	9.0	5.8	7.4	8.0
Tidewater Oil	7.3	5.9	0.5	6.1	6.0	9.2	8.0	0.6	7.1	6.9
Atlantic Refining	8.7	6.3	6.3	5.6	8.3	10.1	6.4	6.8	5.8	8.6
Pure Oil	7.5	7.0	6.1	5.8	6.2	10.7	9.8	7.6	7.3	7.5
Sunray Mid-Continent Oil	13.6	16.0	10.9	9.7	8.9	11.6	13.5	9.3	9.5	8.7
Union Oil of California	8.6	8.8	6.1	6.5	7.8	8.8	9.3	5.9	6.1	7.3
Standard Oil (Ohio)	6.8	5.7	6.2	6.5	6.2	10.8	9.3	9.0	8.9	8.5
Ohio Oil	15.0	14.9	11.8	11.2	11.1	12.3	11.7	8.8	9.5	9.3
Ashland Oil & Refining	4.8	5.1	3.7	4.8	4.9	12.3	13.8	8.6	11.4	11.2

PROFIT ON SALES AND INVESTMENT FOR LEADING COMPANIES

Source: *Fortune* Directory

	Percent Profit — Sales					*Percent Profit — Investment*				
	1956	*1957*	*1958*	*1959*	*1960*	*1956*	*1957*	*1958*	*1959*	*1960*
Richfield Oil	10.5	11.1	7.8	10.4	9.9	12.7	12.6	8.7	11.4	11.0
Skelly Oil	13.6	14.0	10.9	10.9	9.6	11.4	11.3	8.1	7.8	6.9
Continental Oil	9.0	7.7	8.0	8.8	8.8	14.7	12.6	12.3	7.8	12.0
Signal Oil & Gas	—	18.5	13.7	9.7	6.3	—	13.6	10.1	8.6	8.3
Kerr-McGee Oil Industries	—	5.7	3.9	4.4	4.6	—	8.6	7.2	7.5	8.8
Superior Oil	5.7	17.4	15.1	14.9	16.7	4.6	14.6	11.4	11.8	11.9
Amerada Petroleum	24.6	25.7	21.9	23.5	26.9	20.6	20.4	14.4	14.3	15.0
Printing & Publishing										
Time Inc.	12.6	7.0	3.6	3.3	3.2	44.7	20.3	9.7	9.7	9.7
Hearst Consolidated Pub.	0.6	0.1	D	D	D	1.7	0.3	D	D	D
Curtis Publishing	3.3	3.1	1.6	2.2	0.6	17.1	16.1	5.7	8.6	2.3
Donnelley (R. R.) & Sons	6.9	6.7	6.8	7.1	6.8	10.7	10.5	10.0	10.3	10.5
McGraw-Hill	8.9	8.2	7.6	7.7	7.7	29.0	26.2	20.3	19.2	16.8
New York Times	—	3.5	1.5	2.9	1.5	—	8.2	3.5	7.4	4.0
Times-Mirror	4.4	3.0	3.6	5.0	4.2	10.5	7.0	7.8	10.9	9.2
Western Publishing	6.4	5.9	5.5	6.1	6.0	13.1	12.6	12.4	13.4	13.9
McCall	—	1.5	1.7	1.7	1.6	—	7.1	7.7	8.0	8.3
Railroad Equipment										
Pullman	3.5	3.5	2.2	3.4	2.9	7.6	8.6	4.5	7.5	6.6
Westinghouse Air Brake	5.6	5.1	4.3	5.4	4.1	12.0	11.3	8.0	10.1	6.6
General Amer. Transportation	7.0	7.1	7.5	8.5	7.7	11.7	12.7	10.9	10.3	10.9

ACF Industries	3.3	3.1	2.7	1.0	1.5	7.1	7.7	6.5	1.4	3.3
American Brake Shoe	4.8	4.9	3.5	4.6	3.5	11.5	11.0	5.7	8.7	6.3
Alco Products	2.3	1.8	3.1	2.9	0.1	5.8	4.3	6.5	5.0	0.1
American Steel Foundries	7.2	6.5	4.8	6.4	6.5	11.7	10.5	5.8	7.9	8.4
Pacific Car & Foundry	3.3	2.1	3.0	2.5	2.9	15.3	8.7	10.7	11.0	14.0
Rubber										
Goodyear	4.6	4.6	4.8	4.8	4.6	15.1	14.2	12.9	13.5	11.8
Firestone	5.4	5.3	5.1	5.4	5.4	14.8	13.4	11.0	12.1	11.4
U. S. Rubber	3.5	3.4	2.6	3.6	3.2	11.8	10.3	7.7	11.4	9.4
Goodrich (B. F.)	6.0	5.4	5.1	4.9	3.9	12.3	11.5	9.9	10.0	7.7
General Tire & Rubber	2.8	2.7	2.4	3.9	3.0	10.5	9.9	10.1	18.2	14.1
Dayco	3.4	1.9	1.6	2.4	D	12.0	6.7	5.4	9.1	D
Armstrong Rubber	3.9	3.9	4.0	5.1	4.3	11.6	11.6	12.0	16.4	11.9
Ship Building										
Merritt-Chapman & Scott	4.5	3.9	2.4	2.1	D	12.4	9.9	6.5	6.3	D
Newport News Shipbuilding	2.9	3.6	3.9	4.1	4.1	6.8	12.0	11.8	12.7	12.1
Todd Shipyards	2.7	5.0	3.1	3.7	D	4.6	11.0	6.5	6.6	D
Shoes										
International Shoe	4.4	3.6	3.1	3.3	3.0	11.5	9.3	7.3	8.5	8.0
Brown Shoe	3.9	3.9	3.5	4.2	3.7	15.0	14.5	12.6	15.3	13.3
Genesco	3.0	2.6	2.4	3.1	2.6	9.5	9.2	8.4	11.3	8.2
Endicott-Johnson	1.8	1.9	1.7	1.0	D	4.3	4.1	4.8	3.2	D
Soft Drinks	10.7	10.1	9.7	9.8	7.8	15.2	14.9	14.3	15.3	15.0
Pepsi-Cola	9.2	8.0	8.4	8.8	9.0	21.1	21.0	23.6	23.7	21.4
Canada Dry	4.8	4.9	4.6	4.7	4.1	10.1	11.1	8.9	9.8	8.9

Profit on Sales and Investment for Leading Companies

Source: *Fortune* Directory

	Percent Profit — Sales					*Percent Profit — Investment*				
	1956	*1957*	*1958*	*1959*	*1960*	*1956*	*1957*	*1958*	*1959*	*1960*
Steel										
U. S. Steel	8.2	9.5	8.7	7.0	8.2	12.6	14.0	9.7	8.0	9.2
Bethlehem Steel	6.9	7.3	6.9	5.7	5.6	12.1	12.0	8.5	7.1	7.4
Republic Steel	7.3	6.9	6.8	5.0	5.0	13.8	12.2	8.7	7.5	7.3
Armco	8.6	7.1	6.6	7.5	7.5	15.3	10.8	9.0	11.5	10.1
Jones & Laughlin	6.1	5.4	3.6	3.9	4.3	10.0	8.9	4.5	5.6	6.2
National Steel	7.9	7.1	6.6	7.5	6.0	12.4	10.4	7.9	11.2	8.2
Inland Steel	7.3	7.7	7.3	6.9	6.3	14.4	14.5	11.1	10.5	9.7
Youngstown Steel & Tube	6.4	6.3	4.3	5.1	4.5	10.8	9.7	4.9	6.8	5.5
Colorado Fuel & Iron	4.9	4.2	0.8	1.6	D	12.0	9.8	1.5	2.9	D
Timken Roller Bearing	10.2	10.1	7.2	11.4	7.8	18.8	14.4	7.6	18.3	11.3
Allegheny Ludlum Steel	5.3	4.4	2.9	4.9	3.7	15.1	10.9	5.6	10.3	7.9
Crucible Steel	4.8	2.8	2.3	2.8	0.6	11.3	5.6	3.6	4.6	1.0
Wheeling Steel	6.9	4.9	4.1	3.4	3.7	9.2	6.2	4.5	3.4	4.0
Kaiser Steel	11.7	10.3	3.0	D	D	18.7	14.9	3.3	D	D
McLouth Steel	5.4	5.2	5.8	5.7	6.5	13.2	11.5	11.5	10.9	14.6
Granite City Steel	11.0	8.1	7.5	9.8	8.1	19.4	12.3	10.8	16.6	10.9
Pittsburgh Steel	3.5	2.3	D	D	0.7	6.9	4.6	D	D	1.2
Copperweld Steel	3.4	2.3	2.2	4.3	2.1	10.8	6.4	4.7	12.5	5.1
Acme Steel	5.2	4.1	4.1	2.7	1.6	12.7	8.9	7.1	4.7	2.7
Keystone Steel & Wire	8.5	7.5	6.1	7.6	6.5	20.0	15.3	10.4	14.4	12.3
U. S. Pipe & Foundry	10.2	8.7	6.8	9.1	6.4	14.6	10.9	7.8	11.1	6.6
Sharon Steel	7.5	2.7	D	2.1	1.0	17.1	5.1	D	3.2	1.5
Interlake Iron	7.4	6.4	3.4	6.4	4.7	9.1	7.6	3.1	7.7	4.4
Cleveland-Cliffs Iron	11.6	11.6	12.7	8.6	11.6	12.6	11.2	7.6	6.0	8.4
Lukens Steel	7.1	7.8	4.2	5.0	4.8	21.6	24.7	9.7	9.0	9.9

Soaps and Cosmetics										
Procter & Gamble	5.7	5.9	5.7	6.0	6.8	14.5	14.7	13.9	14.4	15.8
Colgate Palmolive	3.6	3.9	4.0	4.3	3.7	8.1	10.7	10.6	11.3	9.6
Lever Bros.	—	1.7	2.7	3.7	2.9	—	6.6	10.7	14.9	10.6
Warner Lambert	8.7	9.5	8.9	9.0	8.7	21.0	22.8	20.1	20.6	19.8
Avon	9.4	9.3	8.9	10.1	10.2	32.7	30.6	28.9	31.7	31.8
Bristol-Myers	6.3	6.0	6.4	6.8	7.3	14.0	14.7	14.2	14.1	15.6
Revlon	9.8	9.5	8.8	10.7	8.3	39.4	31.6	29.3	30.9	21.6
Sugar										
American Sugar Refining Co.	2.9	3.2	3.6	3.2	3.0	7.5	7.3	8.2	7.0	7.1
National Sugar Refining Co.	1.5	1.2	1.3	0.6	0.4	6.9	5.8	6.3	2.8	1.9
Great Western Sugar	5.8	6.5	7.1	6.8	6.0	6.9	8.5	10.1	10.6	9.1
Textiles										
Burlington Industries	3.3	2.4	1.8	3.4	3.9	8.5	6.3	4.6	9.3	9.8
Stevens (J. P.)	2.8	2.3	1.5	4.1	3.0	5.1	4.4	2.7	8.4	6.6
United Merchants & Mfrs.	3.8	2.5	1.9	3.0	3.1	11.1	7.7	5.5	9.1	9.7
Textron	2.7	3.4	4.4	5.4	3.7	8.4	10.8	11.4	14.3	11.9
Lowenstein (M.) & Sons	2.0	1.1	0.6	1.9	2.0	6.8	3.7	2.0	5.8	6.0
Cannon Mills	5.1	6.6	5.6	4.9	6.4	8.9	10.2	8.3	7.6	9.3
Cone Mills	3.5	2.6	1.8	2.8	2.0	4.9	3.9	2.6	4.6	3.2
Springs Cotton Mills	—	8.3	6.1	7.4	10.0	—	9.6	7.2	9.2	11.4
Dan River Mills	4.4	3.5	3.6	4.8	4.5	6.1	6.3	6.2	8.9	7.6
West Point Manufacturing	4.2	3.5	2.8	4.1	5.2	8.1	6.5	4.7	8.2	10.5
Cluett, Peabody	4.5	4.2	2.8	3.4	4.4	9.8	8.8	5.4	7.2	9.1

Profit on Sales and Investment for Leading Companies

Source: *Fortune* Directory

	Percent Profit — Sales					*Percent Profit — Investment*				
	1956	*1957*	*1958*	*1959*	*1960*	*1956*	*1957*	*1958*	*1959*	*1960*
Kendall	3.9	3.8	3.7	4.7	4.6	8.6	8.0	7.4	9.5	9.0
Beaunit Mills	8.3	5.5	3.4	2.9	5.1	14.8	9.8	5.4	4.6	9.5
Riegel Textile	3.5	2.8	0.9	1.9	2.6	8.1	6.0	1.7	4.3	5.4
Pepperell Manufacturing	2.3	2.8	2.3	3.9	3.5	4.8	5.3	3.9	7.4	6.8
Hart Schaffner & Marx	3.1	2.3	2.4	3.4	2.5	8.2	6.1	5.7	8.3	6.5
Bibb Manufacturing	4.4	4.1	3.3	3.3	3.9	5.9	5.8	4.4	4.7	5.9
Tobacco										
Reynolds (R. J.)	11.9	11.0	12.2	12.5	13.2	15.4	15.0	17.0	10.6	19.6
American Tobacco Co.	8.9	9.2	9.2	9.3	8.6	11.8	12.3	12.2	12.3	11.6
Liggett & Myers	8.6	8.9	9.9	9.5	9.3	10.0	10.4	11.1	10.5	9.8
Philip Morris	7.0	6.1	6.2	6.0	6.4	8.6	9.9	10.4	10.2	10.7
Lorillard	3.9	6.7	10.0	10.1	9.8	5.6	12.5	21.4	20.2	18.0
Consolidated Cigar	4.3	4.5	5.0	5.2	5.1	10.1	10.2	11.4	11.6	11.9
							Profit as Percent Capital Funds			
Commercial Banks							*1957*	*1958*	*1959*	*1960*
Bank of America							12.5	12.8	13.8	14.2
Chase Manhattan Bank							9.3	8.8	9.9	10.8
First National City Bank							8.2	8.1	8.9	9.4
Chemical Bank New York Trust							8.6	9.2	9.8	9.9
Morgan Guaranty Trust							7.6	7.2	8.5	9.5
Security First National							8.6	9.5	10.9	11.4
Manufacturers Trust							9.7	9.3	10.2	10.6
Bankers Trust							8.8	8.2	9.9	11.1
Continental Illinois National Bank							9.3	9.0	9.4	10.5

Mellon National Bank & Trust	8.1	7.7	7.9	8.2
National Bank of Detroit	10.7	10.2	10.5	11.0
Irving Trust	10.7	9.8	10.7	12.1
Wells Fargo American Trust	8.8	9.5	10.1	10.3
First National Bank of Boston	11.0	10.4	11.0	11.3
Crocker-Anglo National	10.6	9.8	10.6	12.4
Cleveland Trust	12.0	10.0	10.4	11.2
California Bank	9.9	9.6	11.9	12.5
First Pennsylvania Banking & Trust	10.1	8.6	9.6	10.6
First Western Bank	5.8	7.1	8.3	8.4
Philadelphia National Bank	9.6	8.7	9.2	10.4
Republic National Bank of Dallas	8.4	8.4	9.0	9.2
Seattle-First National Bank	9.6	10.5	11.3	12.2
Detroit Bank & Trust	15.0	13.5	11.6	13.2
First National Bank of Oregon	8.7	8.5	9.7	9.7
U. S. National Bank of Portland	8.4	8.1	9.0	8.7
First National Bank in Dallas	8.6	10.2	8.8	9.9
Manufacturers National Bank of Detroit	10.7	10.1	11.7	12.3
National City Bank of Cleveland	11.4	10.8	11.8	12.9
Harris Trust & Savings Bank	13.9	12.1	13.7	14.9
Marine Trust of Western New York	10.6	10.4	11.7	11.7
First Wisconsin National Bank	—	6.7	8.7	9.9
Girard Trust Corn Exchange	9.7	9.3	9.9	11.2
First City National Bank of Houston	13.7	13.2	11.9	11.9
Marine Midland Trust of New York	8.9	9.3	10.8	10.8
Franklin National Bank of Long Island	18.8	20.8	21.1	17.7
Mercantile Trust	10.5	9.7	10.2	10.8
Wachovia Bank	12.6	10.9	13.3	12.0
Bank of California	8.9	9.4	9.8	9.4
Bank of New York	10.2	8.7	10.2	11.1
First National Bank of St. Louis	9.5	8.7	9.7	9.6
Valley National Bank	—	11.2	12.7	11.9

PROFIT ON SALES AND INVESTMENT FOR LEADING COMPANIES

Source: *Fortune* Directory

	Percent Profit — Sales				*Percent Profit — Investment*			
	1957	*1958*	*1959*	*1960*	*1957*	*1958*	*1959*	*1960*
Trade								
Auto Supply								
Western Auto Supply	3.1	3.1	3.4	3.3	11.2	11.0	13.3	12.1
Department & Variety Stores								
J. C. Penney	3.8	3.3	3.6	3.1	18.3	16.6	17.2	14.6
F. W. Woolworth	4.0	3.7	4.3	4.5	9.5	9.1	10.5	9.7
Federated Dept. Stores	3.9	4.3	4.5	4.2	13.8	14.4	14.1	12.9
May Department Stores	3.8	3.4	3.5	3.3	10.0	9.0	9.0	8.4
Allied Stores	2.0	1.9	2.2	1.6	7.0	6.7	7.9	5.8
W. T. Grant	2.4	2.3	2.6	1.8	9.0	8.7	9.2	6.7
R. H. Macy	1.6	1.4	1.6	1.8	7.0	6.5	7.3	7.7
S. S. Kresge	3.8	3.6	3.1	2.7	7.3	6.9	6.2	5.4
Gimbel Brothers	2.5	2.6	2.4	2.3	9.8	10.2	9.5	8.6
Associated Dry Goods	3.0	2.9	3.1	3.1	11.5	9.1	10.0	9.2
City Stores	0.1	.7	1.0	0.7	0.4	3.0	4.4	3.0
G. C. Murphy	4.2	3.6	3.9	3.0	11.7	9.6	11.6	8.7
J. J. Newberry	2.2	2.4	2.3	1.8	6.9	7.6	7.8	6.1
Marshall Field	3.5	3.4	3.9	3.8	7.5	7.5	9.3	8.7
Lerner Stores	1.5	1.1	1.8	1.6	8.1	5.9	9.4	8.3

Drug Chains								
Rexall Drug & Chemical	2.8	3.5	3.9	3.9	9.1	10.6	12.2	10.8
Walgreen	1.8	2.0	2.0	1.9	12.4	14.1	14.0	13.3
Grocery Chains								
Great Atlantic & Pacific	1.1	1.1	1.0	1.2	13.2	12.8	11.5	12.1
Safeway	1.5	1.5	1.5	1.4	15.1	15.2	14.7	13.4
Kroger	1.2	1.2	1.3	1.2	14.4	13.6	14.7	12.7
American	1.3	1.3	1.1	1.3	11.3	11.3	9.0	10.4
National Tea	1.2	1.1	1.1	1.0	13.0	12.8	11.4	10.5
Food Fair	1.6	1.6	1.4	1.5	17.2	17.2	15.6	15.8
Winn-Dixie	2.1	2.1	2.1	2.2	24.0	23.6	23.2	23.0
Grand Union	1.4	1.3	1.5	1.2	13.7	11.4	13.8	10.1
First National	1.7	1.6	1.6	1.5	12.1	11.2	10.1	9.2
Jewel Tea	1.7	1.7	1.8	1.9	14.2	14.4	13.8	13.7
Colonial	1.4	1.1	0.7	0.5	16.0	11.9	8.0	5.8
A. C. F. Wrigley	1.5	1.6	1.0	1.1	19.5	17.5	10.6	10.4
Arden Farms	—	1.0	1.0	1.0	—	7.4	7.4	7.1
Loblaw	1.4	1.4	1.2	1.2	17.0	17.0	14.1	13.4
Red Owl	1.1	1.1	1.0	0.9	14.5	13.4	12.9	12.6
Pacific Gamble Robinson	.7	0.8	0.8	0.6	7.0	7.8	7.3	6.0
Super Valu	.6	0.6	0.7	0.7	13.2	13.2	14.0	15.3
Mail Order								
Sears, Roebuck	4.5	4.5	4.9	4.6	13.3	12.9	14.4	13.0
Montgomery Ward	2.8	2.6	2.5	1.2	4.6	4.4	4.7	2.4

Profit on Sales and Investment for Leading Companies

Source: *Fortune* Directory

	Percent Profit — Sales				*Percent Profit — Investment*			
	1957	*1958*	*1959*	*1960*	*1957*	*1958*	*1959*	*1960*
Transportation								
Air Lines								
American	3.6	5.1	5.6	2.8	8.5	11.7	14.0	7.7
Pan American	2.6	1.6	2.1	1.7	6.6	3.8	5.4	5.1
Transworld	D	D	2.7	1.7	D	D	7.9	5.1
United	2.8	4.5	4.2	2.9	6.7	10.9	10.0	7.5
Eastern	3.6	2.9	3.8	D	9.2	6.6	9.7	D
Northwest	5.8	5.5	4.5	1.3	14.6	11.6	10.9	3.1
Delta	3.3	3.4	2.4	2.4	7.7	9.0	6.9	8.1
Braniff	—	4.3	3.4	0.8	—	8.2	6.8	0.2
Bus Lines								
Greyhound	5.1	5.1	7.5	7.5	12.0	11.9	17.2	16.2
Railroads								
Pennsylvania	3.0	1.4	1.9	0.1	1.7	0.6	0.9	0.1
Southern Pacific	7.3	8.2	8.9	8.6	3.8	4.2	4.8	4.4
New York Central	1.5	0.9	1.7	0.6	1.0	0.6	1.0	0.4
Atchison, Topeka & Santa Fe	10.1	11.3	10.4	8.4	5.1	5.4	5.2	4.0
Union Pacific	15.1	15.4	12.6	13.2	6.9	6.5	5.3	5.2

Baltimore & Ohio	5.2	4.2	3.7	0.7	3.4	2.3	2.1	0.4
Chesapeake & Ohio	15.6	14.5	13.1	12.2	11.6	8.6	7.4	6.7
Missouri Pacific	6.2	5.4	5.1	4.0	7.8	6.3	6.0	4.3
Southern	12.8	11.8	12.2	11.8	6.6	5.8	6.3	5.7
Illinois Central	5.4	6.8	5.5	5.1	3.7	4.1	3.3	2.4
Chicago Burlington & Quincy	6.7	7.6	6.7	5.0	3.1	3.5	3.1	2.2
Great Northern	9.7	11.0	10.4	8.4	4.3	4.4	4.1	3.2
Norfolk & Western	17.7	21.3	24.6	25.3	7.7	7.3	8.5	8.3
Chicago, Milwaukee	3.1	3.4	2.4	0.6	2.3	2.4	1.7	0.4
Louisville & Nashville	7.6	5.8	5.9	4.6	5.1	3.6	3.7	2.9
Chicago, Rock Island	D	3.9	3.8	2.8	D	2.8	2.8	2.0
Chicago & Northwestern	4.6	1.3	D	D	3.4	1.0	D	D
Northern Pacific	11.5	12.3	13.0	10.6	3.3	3.4	3.6	2.8
Seaboard Airline	11.3	9.7	10.6	9.5	8.8	6.9	7.6	6.5
Atlantic Coast Line	6.4	6.7	7.6	6.5	3.2	3.1	3.5	3.0
Erie	2.1	D	D	D	1.9	D	D	D
N. Y., Chicago & St. Louis	8.5	7.4	8.8	8.1	6.3	4.4	5.5	5.0
N. Y., New Haven & Hartford	D	D	D	D	D	D	D	D
St. Louis-San Francisco	4.1	5.1	5.0	4.8	3.5	4.1	4.1	3.8
Wabash	7.4	3.7	3.2	3.6	5.2	2.3	2.1	2.2
Reading	7.6	3.1	1.7	1.1	3.8	1.2	0.7	0.4
Gulf, Mobile & Ohio	4.1	3.8	3.4	2.0	4.4	4.3	4.0	2.3
Denver & Rio Grande	15.6	13.5	11.5	11.3	12.0	8.9	7.4	7.2
Texas Pacific	7.4	5.6	4.7	5.1	3.5	2.4	2.1	2.5
Kansas City Southern	13.9	13.9	14.0	13.1	6.2	5.6	5.8	5.0

Profit on Sales and Investment for Leading Companies

Source: *Fortune* Directory

	Percent Profit — Sales				*Percent Profit — Investment*			
	1957	*1958*	*1959*	*1960*	*1957*	*1958*	*1959*	*1960*
Shipping								
W. R. Grace	3.4	2.3	3.2	2.9	6.8	4.4	6.2	6.4
United States Lines	8.4	7.6	6.0	5.7	14.3	11.2	8.8	7.9
Matson Navigation	2.6	0.4	3.0	2.3	13.5	0.5	6.3	5.4
American President	6.3	8.7	7.9	5.2	12.2	12.2	10.0	6.4
Moore McCormack	7.7	13.6	3.3	2.1	6.7	10.4	2.4	1.6
Utilities								
American Tel & Tel	13.0	14.1	15.0	16.3	8.1	8.3	9.0	9.1
Pacific Gas & Electric	15.3	16.0	14.5	14.3	7.6	7.9	7.6	8.5
Consolidated Edison	10.3	11.3	11.2	10.9	6.8	7.2	7.4	7.0
Commonwealth Edison	14.0	15.7	16.0	16.9	8.3	9.5	10.3	10.5
El Paso Natural Gas	11.5	9.6	8.2	10.0	9.4	8.9	10.0	12.3
American Electric Power	17.0	17.1	16.6	17.2	9.8	9.7	8.8	9.0
General Telephone and Electronics *	13.5	9.2	6.7	6.2	8.3	9.5	8.4	7.2
Tennessee Gas Transmission	12.2	11.5	11.3	11.0	11.3	10.9	10.2	10.0
Public Service Electric & Gas	10.7	10.3	10.6	11.8	8.2	7.3	8.0	8.7
Southern Company	13.7	14.0	14.6	14.0	8.1	8.6	8.6	8.8
Southern California Edison	14.7	15.8	15.6	16.7	7.0	7.9	7.8	8.9
Columbia Gas System	8.1	9.1	8.7	8.8	9.2	10.2	9.3	9.6
Philadelphia Electric	15.7	15.8	16.3	15.5	8.9	9.5	9.6	9.2
American & Foreign Power	6.9	6.8	4.4	7.5	5.2	4.8	3.2	3.4
Niagara Mohawk Power	10.4	11.5	11.0	11.7	7.1	7.5	7.4	8.1
Detroit Edison	13.1	12.2	12.5	13.8	9.6	8.0	8.5	9.5
General Public Utilities	16.4	15.7	15.5	17.8	8.8	8.1	8.7	8.6
Consumers Power	14.8	13.8	14.5	13.0	8.9	8.4	9.4	8.6
Texas Eastern Transmission	10.9	9.6	8.3	8.0	11.0	9.9	8.7	9.1
American Natural Gas	9.9	10.6	11.8	12.1	9.4	10.2	10.7	11.0

Texas Utilities	20.2	20.4	20.0	19.4	9.6	9.2	10.1	10.3
Middle South Utilities	11.3	11.5	11.4	11.7	7.3	7.7	7.7	7.9
United Gas	10.8	9.8	8.3	7.5	12.6	11.5	10.4	10.0
Consolidated Natural Gas	9.9	8.5	8.3	7.9	8.7	7.8	7.4	7.4
Pacific Lighting	8.0	8.5	7.6	8.0	6.1	6.7	6.4	8.6
Central & South West	18.1	17.8	18.0	17.8	9.3	9.7	9.6	9.9
Ohio Edison	19.0	18.7	18.6	18.8	9.0	9.0	9.5	10.0
Virginia Electric Power	18.9	18.8	18.7	19.0	9.5	9.7	9.1	9.4
Peoples Gas Light & Coke	9.3	8.8	10.5	10.5	8.4	7.1	9.6	9.4
New England Electric System	8.7	9.5	9.9	9.8	8.0	6.9	6.9	6.9
Transcontinental Gas Pipe Line	15.7	14.8	12.7	11.2	11.6	10.5	10.5	9.8
Union Electric	17.2	15.6	15.8	16.9	10.5	9.4	9.1	10.4
West Penn Electric	14.1	14.2	13.9	—	8.8	8.7	9.5	—
Northern States Power	14.3	14.3	14.7	14.5	8.7	9.2	9.4	9.7
Pennsylvania Power & Light	17.7	17.4	18.3	17.8	9.9	9.5	10.4	10.1
Duke Power	15.3	15.8	15.8	15.4	9.9	10.4	9.7	9.8
Florida Power & Light	15.5	17.1	17.5	17.6	11.4	11.3	11.5	11.6
Long Island Lighting	11.5	12.0	13.7	14.0	6.7	7.0	8.6	8.4
Northern Natural Gas	11.8	11.2	11.5	11.8	9.6	8.6	9.0	10.3
Baltimore Gas & Electric	12.4	11.7	12.4	12.6	8.9	8.9	10.0	10.1
Cleveland Electric Illum.	15.9	15.8	16.2	15.7	9.8	9.2	10.0	9.3
Public Service of Indiana	19.1	20.1	18.6	16.7	8.7	8.1	8.0	7.6
Wisconsin Electric Power	11.8	11.1	12.9	12.7	8.0	7.0	9.0	8.3
Duquesne Light	19.4	21.2	21.2	21.4	10.5	11.0	11.0	11.1
Houston Lighting & Power	21.8	21.4	20.0	19.4	13.4	13.4	13.1	13.1
Potomac Electric Power	—	14.7	17.5	18.6	—	8.4	8.8	9.2
Illinois Power	16.8	17.0	18.6	19.0	8.9	9.3	11.1	11.6
Boston Edison	8.9	10.0	11.2	11.4	6.4	6.2	6.7	7.2
New York State Elec. & Gas	13.2	14.9	14.3	—	8.0	9.5	8.7	—
Pacific Power & Light	—	22.4	17.4	19.2	—	9.9	7.6	10.0

* Merged with Sylvania Electric Company.

INDEX

Index

Index

Index

Index

Index